THE SEMITIC
LANGUAGES

Other works in the series

The Romance Languages
The Celtic Languages
The Slavonic Languages
The Germanic Languages
The Dravidian Languages
The Uralic Languages
The Semitic Languages
The Bantu Languages
The Austronesian Languages of Asia and Madagascar
The Oceanic Languages
The Mongolic Languages
The Indo-Aryan Languages
The Sino-Tibetan Languages
The Indo-European Languages
The Turkic Languages

Forthcoming works in the series

The Tai-Kadai Languages
The Iranian Languages

THE SEMITIC LANGUAGES

EDITED BY
Robert Hetzron

Routledge
Taylor & Francis Group

LONDON AND NEW YORK

First published 1997
by Routledge
2 Park Square, Milton Park, Abingdon, Oxon, OX14 4RN
270 Madison Ave, New York NY 10016

Routledge is an imprint of the Taylor & Francis Group

Typeset in 10/12 Ecological Linguistics SemiticPhon by Peter T. Daniels

Every effort has been made to ensure that the advice and information in this book is true
and accurate at the time of going to press. However, neither the publisher nor the authors
can accept any legal responsibility or liability for any errors or omissions that may be
made. In the case of drug administration, any medical procedure or the use of technical
equipment mentioned within this book, you are strongly advised to consult the
manufacturer's guidelines.

British Library Cataloguing in Publication Data

A catalogue record for this book is available from the British Library

Library of Congress Cataloging-in-Publication Data

The Semitic languages / edited by Robert Hetzron.
    p.   cm.
  Includes bibliographical references and index.
  (alk. paper)
    1. Semitic languages—Grammar.   I. Hetzron, Robert.
PJ3021.S46 1998   96-45373
492—dc21   CIP

ISBN10: 0-415-41266-8
ISBN13: 978-0-415-41266-7

Contents

List of Maps   viii

List of Tables   ix

List of Contributors   xiii

Preface   xv

List of Abbreviations   xviii

Part I: Generalities
1	Genetic Subgrouping of the Semitic Languages Alice Faber	3
2	Scripts of Semitic Languages Peter T. Daniels	16
3	The Arabic Grammatical Tradition Jonathan Owens	46
4	The Hebrew Grammatical Tradition Arie Schippers	59

Part II: Old Semitic
5	Akkadian Giorgio Buccellati	69
6	Amorite and Eblaite Cyrus H. Gordon	100

7   Aramaic   114
    Stephen A. Kaufman

8   Ugaritic   131
    Dennis Pardee

9   Ancient Hebrew   145
    Richard C. Steiner

10 Phoenician and the Eastern Canaanite Languages   174
    Stanislav Segert

11 Classical Arabic   187
    Wolfdietrich Fischer

12 Sayhadic (Epigraphic South Arabian)   220
    Leonid E. Kogan and Andrey V. Korotayev

13 Ge'ez (Ethiopic)   242
    Gene Gragg

Part III: Modern Semitic
14 Arabic Dialects and Maltese   263
    Alan S. Kaye and Judith Rosenhouse

15 Modern Hebrew   312
    Ruth A. Berman

16 The Neo-Aramaic Languages   334
    Otto Jastrow

17 The Modern South Arabian Languages   378
    Marie-Claude Simeone-Senelle

18 Tigrinya   424
    Leonid E. Kogan

19 Tigré   446
    Shlomo Raz

20 Amharic and Argobba   457
    Grover Hudson

21 Harari   486
Ewald Wagner

22 The Silte Group (East Gurage)   509
Ernst-August Gutt

23 Outer South Ethiopic   535
Robert Hetzron

Index   550

List of Maps

1 The Semitic languages   xiv
2 The main dialect groups   264
3 The approximate distribution of the affricated variants of ك and ق   272
4 Location of the MSAL region   380
5 The Modern South Arabian Languages   381

List of Tables

2.1	Phonetic arrangement of Neo-Assyrian cuneiform syllabary	26
2.2	Scripts using the Northwest Semitic order	28
2.3	Script using modified Northwest Semitic order (Arabic)	29
2.4	Vocalization systems of the abjads	31
2.5	Scripts using South Semitic order	34
2.6	Letter names	35
2.7	Maltese	37
2.8	Soviet Assyrian	37
2.9	Turoyo of Sweden	37
2.10	Script using modified South Semitic order (Ethiopic/Amharic)	39
2.11	Numerals	40
5.1	Finite forms with affixes of external inflection	72
5.2	The normal state	77
5.3	The construct state in syntactical context with morphophonemic resolution of forms with Ø	80
5.4	The personal pronoun, set 1	84
5.5	The personal pronoun, set 2	84
8.1	G-stem of strong verbs	139
9.1	Roots with "weak" radical	156
9.2	Biblical Hebrew *binyanim*	159
11.1	Triptotic inflection	196
12.1	Attested forms of pronominal enclitics	225
12.2	Attested forms of relative particles	225
12.3	Nearer demonstratives	231
12.4	Remote demonstratives	231
13.1	Ge'ez deictics	250
13.2	Ge'ez numerals	251
13.3	Strong verb stem paradigms	254
13.4	Weak verb stem paradigms	254
14.1	Arabic consonant phonemes	268

14.2	Reflexes of Classical Arabic *q* in some dialects	268
14.3	Reflexes of Classical Arabic *k* in some dialects with CA correspondences	271
14.4	Independent pronouns in seven Arabic dialects	288
14.5	Bound pronouns in seven Arabic dialects	288
14.6	Demonstratives in seven Arabic dialects: near objects	289
14.7	Demonstratives in seven Arabic dialects: far objects	289
14.8	Interrogative pronouns in seven Arabic dialects	290
14.9	Perfect and imperfect affixes in Arabic dialects	292
14.10	Perfect conjugation in seven Arabic dialects	292
14.11	Imperfect conjugation in seven Arabic dialects	293
14.12	Comparison of glosses in Nigerian, Cairene, Damascene, Iraqi, Meccan, Maltese and Lebanese dialects	309
14.13	Comparison of glosses in Anatolian, Israeli, Mauritanian, Moroccan, Algerian, Tunisian and Libyan dialects	309
15.1	Personal pronouns	317
15.2	Verb inflections	318
16.1	Independent personal pronouns	337
16.2	Verb Derivation	341
16.3	Tense formation	342
16.4	Imperative	344
16.5	Weak verbs	345
16.6	Verb with object suffixes	346
16.7	Verb with dative pronominal suffixes	347
16.8	Independent personal pronouns, Mlaḥsô, Ṭuroyo, Hertevin and Hassana	354
16.9	Independent personal pronouns, Chr. Mangeš, Chr. Urmi, J. Azerbaijan and Neo-Mandaic	354
16.10	Demonstrative pronouns	355
16.11	Pronominal suffixes, Mlaḥsô, Ṭuroyo, Hertevin and Hassana	355
16.12	Pronominal suffixes, Chr. Urmi, J. Azerbaijan, Kerend and Neo-Mandaic	356
16.13	Numerals 1–10	358
16.14	Numerals 11–19	359
16.15	Predicative inflection, active	363
16.16	Predicative inflection, passive	363
16.17	Ergative inflection	363
16.18	Copulative inflection	364
16.19	The preterite	367
16.20	Weak verbs, present	369
16.21	Pronominal suffixes	371
16.22	Enclitic copula (allomorphs after a consonant)	373
16.23	Free copula	373
16.24	Negative copula	374

16.25	To have	374
16.26	To have not	375
17.1	Independent pronouns	387
17.2	Pronouns with singular and plural nouns, verbs and prepositions	388
17.3	Deictics referring to persons and things (demonstratives)	394
17.4	Deictics referring to space	394
17.5	Cardinal numbers	395
17.6	Ordinal numbers	397
17.7	Verbal themes (ō/ū in Mehri, é/í in JL and Soqoṭri)	398
17.8	Perfect suffixes	402
17.9	Imperfect affixes	402
17.10	Simple verb (type A): active voice, perfect	403
17.11	Simple verb (type A): active voice, imperfect	404
17.12	Subjunctive	405
17.13	Conditional	405
17.14	Simple verb (type B), perfect	406
17.15	Simple verb (type B), imperfect	406
17.16	Subjunctive conjugation in Jibbāli (JL)	406
18.1	Personal pronouns	429
18.2	Pronominal suffixes	430
18.3	Pronominal suffixes with verb	430
18.4	IA perfect	438
18.5	IA imperfect	438
18.6	IA gerund	439
18.7	Copula	444
20.1	Independent pronouns	462
20.2	Object suffix pronouns	462
20.3	Possessive suffix pronouns	462
20.4	Amharic verb stems	468
20.5	Amharic stems of verbs with initial a	469
20.6	Amharic stems of doubled verbs	469
20.7	Argobba verb stems	470
20.8	Past	470
20.9	Nonpast	471
20.10	Compound nonpast	472
20.11	Jussive	473
20.12	Conjunctive	473
20.13	Compound conjunctive	474
20.14	Affirmative copula	475
20.15	Negative copula	476
20.16	Verbs of presence	477
20.17	Amharic passive stems	479
21.1	Object suffixes: verbs ending in a vowel	490
21.2	Preposition and suffix	491

21.3	Conjugated forms	497
22.1	Active vs. passive stem forms	524
23.1	Independent pronouns	540
23.2	Possessive pronouns	540
23.3	Complement pronoun suffixes: O, L, B	541
23.4	Person marking	545

List of Contributors

Ruth A. Berman, Department of Linguistics, Tel-Aviv University, Tel Aviv, Israel.

Giorgio Buccellati, University of California, Los Angeles, California, USA.

Peter T. Daniels, New York, New York, USA.

Alice Faber, Haskins Laboratories, New Haven, Connecticut, USA.

Wolfdietrich Fischer, Orientalisches Seminar, University of Erlangen-Nürnberg, Erlangen, Germany.

Cyrus H. Gordon, Brookline, Massachusetts, USA.

Gene Gragg, The Oriental Institute, The University of Chicago, Chicago, Illinois, USA.

Ernst-August Gutt, Addis Ababa, Ethiopia.

Robert Hetzron, Professor Emeritus, University of California at Santa Barbara, Santa Barbara, California, USA.

Grover Hudson, Department of Linguistics and Germanic, Slavic, Asian and African Languages, Michigan State University, East Lansing, Michigan, USA.

Otto Jastrow, Orientalische Philologie, University of Erlangen-Nürnberg, Erlangen, Germany.

Stephen A. Kaufman, Hebrew Union College, Cincinnati, Ohio, USA.

Alan S. Kaye, Department of English and Comparative Literature, California State University, Fullerton, California, USA.

Leonid E. Kogan, St. Petersburg State University, St. Petersburg, Russia.

Andrey V. Korotayev, The Oriental Institute, Moscow, Russia.

Jonathan Owens, Bayreuth University, Germany.

Dennis Pardee, The Oriental Institute, The University of Chicago, Chicago, Illinois, USA.

Shlomo Raz, Department of Hebrew and Semitic Languages, Tel-Aviv University, Tel Aviv, Israel.

Judith Rosenhouse, Department of General Studies, Israel Institute of Technology, Haifa, Israel.

Arie Schippers, University of Amsterdam, The Netherlands.

Stanislav Segert, University of California, Los Angeles, California, USA.

Marie-Claude Simeone-Senelle, CNRS-LLACAN, Meudon, France.

Richard C. Steiner, Bernard Revel Graduate School, Yeshiva University, New York, New York, USA.

Ewald Wagner, Justus-Liebeg University, Giessen, Germany.

Map 1   The Semitic languages

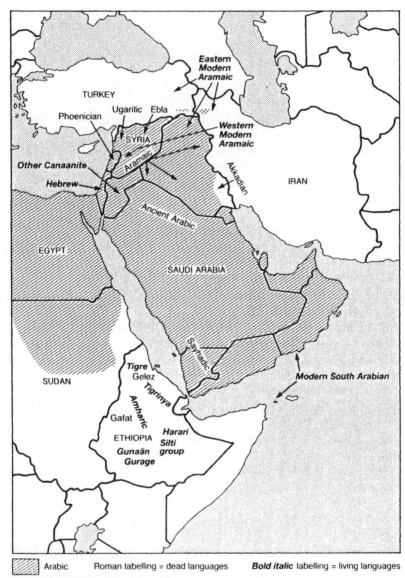

Arabic   Roman labelling = dead languages   **Bold italic** labelling = living languages

For Arabic dialects see Chapter 14
For Modern South Arabian see Chapter 17

Preface

This is the first general survey of Semitic that mentions all the languages of this family, doing justice to the modern tongues such as the Arabic and Aramaic dialects and various languages of Ethiopia. Even the least-known Semitic language, Zway, is occasionally referred to in the chapter on the Silte group, inserted by me on the basis of data from Professor W. Leslau.

For different reasons, every language could not be represented by a separate chapter. The chapters on the Phoenician and Eastern Canaanite, Sayhadic, Arabic and Modern Aramaic dialects, the varieties of Modern South Arabian, the Silte group, Amharic and Argobba all contain comparative material on closely related linguistic entities, and the one on Outer South Ethiopic presents descriptive samples of an even more diverse group. The chapter on Ancient Hebrew deals with two distinct periods of the language: Biblical (itself subject to subdivision) and Mishnaic.

We have tried to make the presentation as uniform as possible. Exactly the same pattern and terminology is, however, not realistic. First of all, several languages have a long linguistic tradition, including style of presentation and nomenclature. It seemed advisable to honor this. Secondly, in some cases the terms used reflect the author's theoretical approach and it would have been improper to impose another system on them.

In one instance modern linguistic terminology was imposed: "case" is used loosely, as a functional element. Thus, not only declensions are subsumed but also prefixes, prepositions and postpositions.

The most delicate case is the "tense vs. aspect" controversy: with which one of these categories do Semitic languages operate their verbal system, "tenses" like (a) "past," (b) "present–future" or "aspects" like (a) "completed" ~ "perfective" and (b) "noncompleted ~ imperfect(ive)" (where the two (a)'s and (b)'s are respectively equivalent)? I myself seem to be in a minority in being fully convinced that the relevant category is "tense." The majority of writers preferred aspectual terms. Yet this should not be taken at face value. For example, Professor Segert uses aspectual labels but calls the actual forms "tenses." Professor Steiner diplomatically speaks of "tense and/or aspect" without separating them. Dr. Gutt uses the term "aspect" for the basic stem forms of the verb (including a non-aspectual one), and the complete forms based on these are called "tenses." Professors Wagner and Hudson use plain "tense." What matters is that in each chapter the use of the author's preferred term is always clearly illustrated.

The wisest statement I know about this controversy was uttered by Professor Chaim Rabin in a lecture: "Semitic has either aspects that express tenses or tenses that express aspects." (In the printed version of this paper, Rabin n.d., this statement is not reproduced, only the term "tense" is used.)

Another terminological problem, though always clear in the context used, is how to name basic forms of the verb and the derived forms such as "passive." In the Arabic tradition, Roman numeral + "form" is used. Hebrew imported its own term *binyan* (lit. 'building') into English; others use "stem" or "theme" (the latter is a Gallicism). The term "stem" is used by others for the internally vocalized form of the verb to which affixes are added, in agreement with the general linguists' usage. "Derivational class" is quite adequate and is used by Professor Wagner.

Ethiopian Semitic has a special form for the verb of a nonfinal clause "coordinated" (at least this is the equivalent of a coordination) with a final clause. This has been traditionally called "gerund" (a Gallicism). More recently, "converb" was introduced.

As far as transcription is concerned, I have respected the authors' preferences as much as possible. For the so-called "emphatic" consonants, underdot is the generally accepted mark. For clarity *ṗ* receives an overdot instead. These consonants are velarized in Arabic and Modern Aramaic. In Modern South Arabian and Ethiopian they are glottalized/ejective (produced by closing the glottis, compressing the air in the mouth, then opening the dental, velar, etc., closure suddenly followed by the release of the glottal closure): glottalization is deemed to be the original articulation. The only disagreement concerns the alternate use of *ḳ* or *q* for the same sound.

Underline marks lenition in ancient Central Semitic, replaced by overline for *p̄* and *ḡ*. The traditional letter *ḫ* is used for dead languages, phonetically identical to *x* in the modern ones.

Semitic *a* has been raised in Ethio-Semitic, yielding what IPA would transcribe as [ɐ], but is rendered as *a* by Marcel Cohen, and as *ä* by most specialists, though, in my opinion quite incorrectly, *ə* is also used. This letter *ə* is the standard symbol for the shwa, the least significant and most easily reducible vowel. For those who use this character for [ɐ], the shwa is *ɨ*. In this volume, independently of one another, Professor Wagner and Dr. Gutt chose *a* for the same [ɐ] with the reasoning that their respective languages distinguish between long and short vowels, so that the correlation [aː/ɐ] is more clearly rendered by using *aa/a* respectively.

This brings us to the mark of length. In general linguistics a ":" symbol indicates length, but a number of linguists prefer reduplication, some the macron (for vowels only). Thus, there is equivalence in the following cases: *m:* = *mm*, *a:* = *aa* = *ā*.

Finally, let me thank all the contributors and consultants for their cooperation, and Ms. Denise Rea of Routledge for the energy she invested in this work.

Robert Hetzron
August 1996

Reference

Rabin, Chaim. n.d. *The Scope of Semitic* (Occasional papers series of the Institute of Semitic Studies 1). Princeton, New Jersey.

Publisher's Note

We are sorry to announce that the editor, Robert Hetzron, died in August 1997 just weeks prior to the publication of this volume – a sad loss to the field of linguistics.

List of Abbreviations

A	Ammonite	CPWG	Central Peripheral Western Gurage
abl.	ablative		
abs.	absolute	CWG	Central Western Gurage
acc.	accusative		
adj.	adjective	Cy.	Cyprus dialect
Akk.	Akkadian	Dam.	Damascene
Alg.	Algerian	dat.	dative
Anat.	Anatolia/Anatolian	def.	definite
Ar.	Arabic	dem.	demonstrative
Ara.	Arabian	det.	determiner
art.	article	detr.	detrimental
aux.	auxiliary	dim.	diminutive
B	Baṭḥari	DN	divine name
Ba.	Baxʻa	du.	dual
Bag.	Baghdad/Baghdadi	E	Edomite
bed.	bedouin	Eg.	Egypt/Egyptian
ben.	benefactive	ENA	Eastern Neo-Aramaic
By.	Byblian	ESA	Epigraphic South Arabian
CA	Classical Arabic		
Ca.	Cairene	G	Ǧubbʻadin
c/e	central or eastern	Gal.	Galilee/Galilean
Chad.	Chadian	gen.	genitive
Chr.	Christian	GG	Gunnän-Gurage
coll.	collective	GN	geographical name
conj.	conjunction	Gt	Grundstamm
conjunct.	conjunctive	Ḥ	Ḥarsūsi
const.	construct	Heb.	Hebrew
cop.	copula	Hadr.	Hadramitic
cps	complement person suffix	Hb.	Hobyōt
		IA	Imperial Aramaic

imp.	imperative	NENA	Northeastern
impf.	imperfect		Neo-Aramaic
ind.	indicative	Neo-Ar.	Neo-Aramaic
indef.	indefinite	NG	Northern Gurage
inf.	infinitive	Nig.	Nigeria/Nigerian
instr.	instrumental	NL	natural language
interr.	interrogative	nom.	nominative
intr.	intransitive	NP	noun phrase
Ir.	Iraq/Iraqi	NWS	Northwest Semitic
J	Jewish	O	object
Jib.	Jibbāli	OA	Old Aramaic
Jer.	Jerusalem	obl.	oblique
J (*ML*)	Jibbali from *Mehri*	OBy.	Old Byblian
	Lexicon	OSA	Old South Arabian
JPA	Jewish Palestinian	OSE	Outer South Ethiopic
	Aramaic	Pal.	Palestianian
juss.	jussive	Pal. Talm.	Palestinian Talmud
Ku.	Kuwaiti	part.	participle
LBH	Late Biblical Hebrew	pass.	passive
Leb.	Lebanon/Lebanese	PCA	Proto-Colloquial
lit.	literally		Arabic
loc.	locative	pf.	perfect
LPu.	Late Punic	Ph.	Phoenician
M	Mehri	PN	personal name
M.Ar.	Middle Aramaic	pol.	polite
Mag.	Maghreb/Maghrebine	pr.	present
Ma.	Maʻlūla	pre.	prefix
Mal.	Maltese	prep.	preposition
Maur.	Mauritania/	pro.	pronoun
	Mauritanian	PS	Proto-Semitic
Mes.	Mesopotamian	Pu.	Punic
MJb	Jādib	PWG	Peripheral Western
mmf	Muḥayfif		Gurage
Mo.	Moabite	Qat.	Qatabanian
Mor.	Morocco/Moroccan	quant.	quantifier
MH	Middle Hebrew	rel.	relative
Min.	Minean	S	subject
MSA	Modern Standard	So.	Soqoṭri
	Arabic	Sab.	Sabean
MSAL	Modern South Arabian	Sayh.	Sayhadic
	Languages	SBH	Standard Biblical
N	noun		Hebrew
NB	Neo-Babylonian	SE	South Ethiopic
neg.	negative	SJms	Soqoṭri from

	Johnstone's	Tna	Tigrinya
	manuscript notes	trans.	transitive
SLA	Standard Literary	Tun.	Tunisia/Tunisian
	Aramaic	Ug.	Ugaritic
S (ML)	Soqoṭri in *Mehri*	V	verb
	Lexicon	v.i.	verb intransitive
subj.	subject	v.t.	verb transitive
subjunct.	subjunctive	var.	variant
Sud.	Sudan/Sudanese	WG	Western Gurage
suf.	suffix	WNA	Western Neo-Aramaic
Sum.	Sumerian	Yem.	Yemen/Yemenite
Syr.	Syria/Syrian		

PART I

GENERALITIES

1 Genetic Subgrouping of the Semitic Languages

Alice Faber

Models of Language Relatedness

The question underlying, explicitly or implicitly, many discussions of the relationships among the Semitic languages is how appropriate for discovering such relationships are methods developed by Indo-Europeanists. That is, can the traditional methods of comparative linguistics lead to insights about the relationships among the Semitic languages? Or, is it more appropriate to view the obvious resemblances among the Semitic languages not as evidence of a shared linguistic heritage, but rather as resulting from the close cultural and geographic connections among communities speaking Semitic languages?

Even raising the question of the suitability of genetic models for the Semitic language family suggests in some way that genetic models are not applicable to the Semitic languages. Indeed, Garbini (1972) has attributed the resemblances among the Semitic languages to the linguistic influence of successive waves of Amorite migrants into Mediterranean, Red Sea, and Indian Ocean littoral regions and into Mesopotamia. For Garbini, the similarities among the Semitic languages simply reflect the efficacy of Amorite linguistic imperialism. This view of Semitic linguistic history begs the question of what (if any) the relationships among the Semitic languages were, prior to the Amorite invasions. If the autochthonous Canaanite vernacular was not genetically related to Amorite, to what was it related and why does no evidence of that relationship survive? And, if it was related to Amorite, how? The import of these questions is that influence of one Semitic language on another cannot be treated in isolation from the original relationship among the languages. Similarly, the question of genetic relationships among the Semitic languages cannot be treated in isolation from their subsequent patterns of contact. In other words, genetic models of linguistic relatedness and areal models of mutual linguistic influence are complementary rather than competitive. Some similarities serve as evidence of genetic relationship, while others serve as evidence for mutual influence.

In particular cases, it may be difficult – if not impossible – to determine whether a particular similarity between two Semitic languages results from their shared ancestry or from subsequent contact. Nonetheless, part of the task of comparative reconstruction – of any linguistic stock – is to distinguish similarities reflecting common ancestry from similarities reflecting influence of one language on another. That this distinction may be subtle does not mean that it is invalid. A further distinction is required between these two types of similarities, which both betoken linguistic relationship, and other similarities, which arise either by chance or are so "natural" that they recur in many, unrelated languages (see Hoenigswald (1960) on the comparative method and Greenberg (1957) for further discussion of methodology).

The establishment of a linguistic subgroup requires the identification of innovations that are shared among all and only the members of that subgroup. As already noted, random convergences and highly natural changes can prove misleading, and, hence, should be excluded. Areal features should also be excluded, since these reflect not an ancestral language state but rather post-split contact. Given these considerations, it has been suggested that morphological innovations will provide the best guide to subgrouping in a language family (Hetzron 1976, with references). Certainly, the Semitic languages have the kind of rich inflectional and derivational morphology that should, in principle, be valuable in the establishment of patterns of innovation. However, since many morphological innovations in the Semitic languages involve vowel alternations and many of the ancient Semitic languages are preserved in scripts which provide little or no indication of vowel quality, morphological comparisons are not always complete; it can be difficult, therefore, to provide a specification of the changes that have occurred precise enough to chart patterns of innovation. Nonetheless, the principle underlying reliance on shared morphological innovations in establishing subgroupings is sound. That is, more idiosyncratic innovations are less likely to have recurred independently. Morphological innovations are, by their nature, more likely to be idiosyncratic, but it is their idiosyncratic nature not their morphological nature that makes them valuable for subgrouping. While many phonological developments, like the change of *p to /f/ in Arabic and South Semitic, are so natural as to be useless for subgrouping, it does not follow that all phonological developments are natural and could have occurred independently many times in the history of a language family.

These considerations lead to a further distinction, between innovations that may lead to the establishment of a subgroup and those that may be attributed to the common stage of a subgroup that has already been established. Many phonological innovations fall into this second class. Thus, the change of *$\bar{a}$ to o, attested in all Canaanite languages (see p. 5), as a relatively natural change may not be sufficient basis for establishing Canaanite as a subgroup of Semitic. But given the other features defining Canaanite and the wide attestation of $o < *\bar{a}$, there is no reason not to treat the development of $o < *\bar{a}$ as a Proto-Canaanite innovation. Similarly, there is a sense in which loss of a form or distinction is as much an innovation as addition of a form or distinction. Nevertheless, subgroups are generally not posited only on the basis of a shared loss. However, as with phonologically natural innovations, a shared loss may be attributed to a subgroup established on the basis of other, more conventional criteria.

In the remainder of this chapter, I will outline two hypotheses regarding the internal structure of the Semitic language group. The first hypothesis is traditional, based in large measure on the geographical distribution and cultural importance of the various Semitic languages. It is included simply because it is presented in most reference works on the Semitic languages as if it were established fact. In fact, there is little evidence supporting it. The second hypothesis, first proposed by Hetzron (1976), is based on principles of the sort discussed above. The morphological and phonological innovations supporting Hetzron's proposal will be presented in some detail. I will not discuss lexicostatistical approaches to the structure of the Semitic language family (e.g., Rabin 1975), since lexicostatistics is based on assumptions about rate of lexical replacement that may not be applicable to the Semitic languages. Furthermore, it is in practice subject to pragmatic difficulties involving semantic shifts and the identification of loanwords, as is clear from the discussion following Rabin (1975: 99–102).

The Traditional Subgrouping of the Semitic Languages and its Cultural and Geographical Basis

The traditional subgrouping of the Semitic languages, as presented in handbooks (e.g., Bergsträsser 1983; Brockelmann 1961; Moscati 1969; Ullendorff 1970) is shown below:

```
East Semitic: Akkadian
West Semitic
        Northwest Semitic
                Canaanite: Hebrew, Phoenician, Moabite
                Aramaic
        South Semitic
                Arabic
                Southeast Semitic
                        Modern South Arabian: Jibbali, Mehri, Ḥarsūsi, Soqoṭri
                        Ethio-Sabean
                                OSA: Sabean, Qatabanian, Hadramauti, Minean
                                Ethiopian Semitic
```

This grouping is based on cultural and geographical principles (Moscati 1969: 4). That is, even though some of the divisions (e.g., West Semitic vs. East Semitic) are supported by patterns of innovation, the grouping itself was not formulated on an empirical basis. The group labels should be understood in terms of the geographical distribution of languages. There are two major omissions, both due to the discovery of "new" languages. The first omission is Ugaritic, whose position is left unclear (it could be either Canaanite, in parallel with Hebrew and Phoenician (Harris 1939), or a direct descendant of Northwest Semitic (Goetze 1941)).

The second omission is Eblaite, discovered in the mid-1970s. Here the question is whether the language is approximately equivalent to Proto-West Semitic (or even, Proto-Northwest Semitic or Proto-Canaanite), a variant of Akkadian (East Semitic), or a third branch of Proto-Semitic. Since these omissions are not defects of the traditional model *per se*, but rather general problems for Semitic subgrouping, they will be discussed further below.

A Model Based on Shared Innovations

Investigation of the internal structure of the Semitic language family was placed on an empirical footing by Hetzron (1972, 1973, 1975, 1976). Hetzron proposed, on the basis of shared morphological innovations, a grouping like that below; the grouping here incorporates modifications by Rodgers (1991) and Huehnergard (1992).

East Semitic
    Akkadian
    Eblaite
West Semitic
    Central Semitic
        Arabic
        Northwest Semitic
            Ugaritic
            Canaanite: Hebrew, Phoenician, Moabite, Ammonite, El-Amarna
            Aramaic
            Deir Alla
    South Semitic
        Eastern
            Soqoṭri
            Mehri, Ḥarsūsi, Jibbāli
        Western
            Old South Arabian
            Ethiopian Semitic
                North Ethiopic: Ge'ez, Tigré, Tigrinya
                Southern Ethiopic
                    Transverse SE
                        Amharic, Argobba
                        Harari, East Gurage (Silte, Wolane, Ulbarag, Inneqor, Zway)
                    Outer SE
                        n group: Gafat, Soddo, Goggot
                        tt group
                            Muher
                            West Gurage
                                Mäsqan
                                Central/Peripheral
                                    Central: Ezha, Chaha, Gura
                                    Peripheral: Gyeto, Ennemor, Endegen

Northwest Semitic in both models is identical and South Semitic in the second is equivalent to Southeast Semitic in the first. Thus, the primary difference between the groupings is Hetzron's suggestion that Arabic is more closely related to Canaanite and Aramaic than to Southeast Semitic; all three, Arabic, Canaanite, and Aramaic, constitute, for Hetzron, Central Semitic. Hetzron's (1972, 1975) methodology leads further to a division of Ethiopian Semitic into North Ethiopic (Ge'ez, Tigre, Tigrinya) and South Ethiopic. Hetzron subdivides Central Semitic into Canaanite and Arabic on the one hand and Aramaic on the other. This grouping is not shown in the second model, since the innovative form that he bases the Arabo-Canaanite group on, the verbal Pl. f. suffix -na/-nā, is, in fact, found in early Aramaic texts and, thus, may be a retention from Central Semitic (Voigt 1987: 10ff.) or Proto-Semitic (Goldenberg 1977: 477; Huehnergard 1990: 283). The subgrouping of Central Semitic in the second model follows, instead, proposals made by Huehnergard (1990, 1992, forthcoming), and that of South Semitic follows proposals made by Rodgers (1991); the subgrouping of Ethiopian Semitic follows that of Hetzron (1972, 1975).

The Major Divisions

East Semitic
Until the discovery of the Eblaite texts, there was no reason to focus inquiry on the structure of East Semitic, since the only language assigned to that group was Akkadian, and Akkadian/East Semitic was what was left out of West Semitic. Based on onomastic material, for the most part, Eblaite was first thought to be West Semitic, perhaps even Proto-Canaanite (Pettinato 1975). However, more detailed analysis of the language of the texts revealed (1) that the language does not manifest the innovations common to West Semitic, let alone those defining Central Semitic and Canaanite, and (2) that the language shares several innovations with Akkadian. These latter innovations, noted by Huehnergard (1992), are the development of pl. m. adjectives in -ūt and the development of distinct sg. 2/3 dative suffixes -kum and -šum. These features, not found in West Semitic, justify classifying Eblaite and Akkadian together as East Semitic. Huehnergard further notes that Eblaite is not a dialect of Akkadian, since there are several innovations found in all Akkadian dialects, but not in Eblaite. Among these is the dissimilatory change of word-initial m to n in words containing another labial (von Soden 1984). This treatment of Eblaite as an East Semitic sibling of Akkadian is compatible with that of Caplice (1981), who suggests that Eblaite is neither Akkadian nor West Semitic, and that of Gelb, who suggests that the closest relative of Eblaite is Old Akkadian, without treating it as a dialect of Akkadian (1977: 25ff.; 1981: 52).

West Semitic

Suffix Conjugation as Past Tense

The primary innovation that Hetzron (1976) identifies as characterizing West Semitic is the development of a suffix conjugation *qatala* (Hebrew *lɔmaδ*, Arabic *kataba*) denoting past tense actions. Akkadian has superficially similar stative constructions using similar suffixes, but both the meaning of the forms and the structure of the verb stem differ in crucial respects from the West Semitic.

Prohibitive Marker *ʾal(a)* 'Don't'

A further innovation that can be traced to the West Semitic period is the prohibitive negative marker *ʾal* 'don't' (Faber 1991), probably compounded from the inherited negative *ʾayy* and asseverative *la* (for *la*, see Huehnergard 1983). This negative particle is attested throughout West Semitic, with the exception of Arabic, as a prohibitive or as a marker of main clause negation. The latter function appears to be a South Semitic innovation (see p. 11). While *ʾal* is superficially similar to Akkadian *ul*, the older variant *ula* suggests that the Akkadian particle, is to be associated with the ancestor of Arabic *wala* instead (Faber 1991).

Central Semitic

Pharyngealization as a Secondary Articulation

One of the major innovations defining the Central Semitic group is the development of a series of pharyngealized consonants. All of the Semitic languages have a third, emphatic series of consonants /tṣ ṭ θ ṭ ḳ/, generally reconstructed as glottalic pressure consonants (Dolgopolsky 1977; Faber 1980, 1985, 1990). In Ethiopian Semitic and in Modern South Arabian, they are glottalic pressure stops /sʔ tʔ kʔ/, while in Arabic and Neo-Aramaic, they are pharyngealized /sˤ tˤ dˤ θˤ/ and uvular /q/. The Semitic languages known only from written records also had this third consonant series, but it is not always clear which realization – ejective or pharyngealized – they had. The dissimilatory change of one emphatic consonant to its non-emphatic counterpart in Akkadian roots containing two emphatics (Geers 1945) suggests that Akkadian emphatics were ejectives (Knudson 1961, Faber 1980, 1990), and the assimilation of /t/ to /ṭ/ adjacent to /ṣ/ in Hebrew *hitqattel* verbs suggests that Hebrew had pharyngealized emphatics (Faber 1980, 1990). Thus, it is only in Central Semitic that pharyngealized emphatics are observed.

Non-Geminate Prefix Conjugation for Non-Past

Central Semitic is characterized, according to Hetzron (1976), by several innovations in the verbal system. The most striking of these is the development of a new prefix conjugation for representation of nonpast events in main clauses. This *yaqtulu* form is superficially similar to the inherited jussive *yaqtul*, and replaced the inherited *yaqattal* nonpast, a form that is preserved in Ethiopian Semitic,

South Arabian, and Akkadian (Goldenberg 1977: 476–477; cf. Blau 1978: 27ff., Voigt 1987, Cohen 1984: 73–75, Zaborski 1991: 367).

Within-Paradigm Generalization of Vowels in Prefix Conjugation

No doubt related to the innovation of a new prefix conjugation is the leveling of prefix vowels in all prefix conjugations, new and old. In Akkadian, the four prefixes that occur in active, non-derived prefix conjugation verbs are ʾa, ta, ni, and yi, and Hetzron (1973) plausibly suggests that this a–i alternation in Akkadian reflects the Proto-Semitic state of affairs (cf. Blau 1978: 31–32). In Centrál Semitic, however, all of the prefixes for a particular verb stem have the same vowel, a or i, depending on such factors as verb voice and, for Hebrew, the phonological shape of the verb stem. Hetzron's proposal is that the a–i alternation depending on prefix was reanalyzed as an a–i alternation depending on verb stem in Central Semitic. The vowel a was later generalized in Arabic, while the a–i alternation in prefixes (yilmaδ vs. yɔqum [< yaqumu]) was preserved in Hebrew, and, apparently, in Ugaritic (Segert 1984: 60ff.); the Aramaic situation is less clear, due to the reduction of unstressed vowels in open syllables (yilmaδ vs. yɔqūm). While it is clear that in the Central Semitic languages all prefixes for a particular verb stem have the same vowel, it is less clear that Arabic ever had a stage in which any active non-derived verbs had i prefixes.

Generalization of -t- in Suffix Conjugation Verbs

As noted above, the innovation of the qatala suffix conjugation past tense form characterized West Semitic. The general shape of the suffixes for this conjugation was -(C)v(C). The initial consonant for the 1st person singular suffix was k and for all 2nd person suffixes it was t, as in the Akkadian stative as well. However, in Central Semitic, t was generalized throughout the paradigm. Thus, Arabic has katabtu 'sg. 1' and katabta 'sg. 2m.'.

Development of Compound Negative Marker *bal

The survey of Semitic negative markers in Faber (1991) reveals a set of negative adverbs, conjunctions, and prepositions found only in Central Semitic. These forms, like Hebrew bli 'without', Ugaritic/Phoenician bl 'not', and Arabic bal 'on the contrary', are of uncertain etymology, although they appear to involve rein-forcement of an inherited Afroasiatic negative marker *b with either the Proto-Semitic negative *la or the asseverative *la that was its source (Faber 1991).

Northwest Semitic

Huehnergard (1990, 1992, forthcoming) suggests that the major split in Central Semitic was between Arabic and Northwest Semitic, noting that this view entails no change in the composition of Northwest Semitic, only a change in which languages are seen as its closest neighbors. The two major innovations characterizing Northwest Semitic are the change of word-initial *w to /y/ (with the exception of the letter name waw and the conjunction w-), and the double plural marking of *qVtl* nouns with both *a* between the final two consonants and a suffixed plural marker (Harris 1939: 8–9; Huehnergard forthcoming). While doubly marked plural forms like Hebrew *dəyɔlim* 'flags' (sg. *dɛyɛl* < **digl*) and, possibly, Ugaritic *rašm* 'heads' (sg. *riš*) are superficially similar to Arabic broken plurals, a structure that is arguably a retention from Proto-(West) Semitic (see below), the obligatory double plural marking of these nouns represents an innovative combination of inherited morphological material. Also peculiar to Northwest Semitic is the assimilation of *l* to *q* in forms of the verb **lqḥ* 'take' in which the two would be adjacent, e.g., Hebrew *yiqqaḥ* < **yilqaḥ*) 'he will take' (Harris 1939: 9). Finally, Huehnergard (in press) notes the metathesis of *t* in the reflexive verb prefix *(h)it-* with a root-initial sibilant in such verbs as Hebrew *hištammer* (< **hit-šammer*) as a possible Northwest Semitic innovation.

Canaanite

Huehnergard identifies three innovations shared in Canaanite (Hebrew, Phoenician, Moabite, Ammonite, and the substratum for El-Amarna Akkadian). The first of these is the change of *a* to *i* in the first syllable of the derived D and C stems *limmid* and *hilmid*. The Canaanite languages also show the change of the sg. 1 verb agreement suffix from -*tu* to -*ti* (Harris 1939: 10). Finally, in Canaanite, the pl. 1 suffix -*nu* was generalized to genitive and accusative pronominal forms from the independent pronoun *'anu/'anaḥnu* 'we' and suffix conjugation verbs. The change of **ā* to *o*, noted throughout Canaanite, may also represent a Proto-Canaanite innovation, although Harris (1939: 44–45) suggests rather post-split diffusion.

Aramaic

As Huehnergard notes, most of the innovations generally considered Aramaic are not observed in the oldest Aramaic inscriptional material. It is therefore difficult to find innovations that can be said to characterize all and only Aramaic languages. One candidate, suggested by Huehnergard, is generalization of the pl. 1 suffix -*na* to the independent pronoun and to the suffix conjugation from the genitive and accusative pronominal forms. That is, given two inherited pl. 1 suffixes, -*nu* and -*na*, Canaanite generalized one and Aramaic the other. Aramaic is also characterized according to Huehnergard (forthcoming) by loss of the passive N stem (Hebrew *nilmaδ*) and the development of a new causative reflexive *hittagmar* replacing earlier *'istagmar* (Arabic *istaktaba*).

Ugaritic

In 1941 Albrecht Goetze published a paper asking the question "Is Ugaritic a Canaanite dialect?" Despite Goetze's impressive list of Canaanite features that are absent in Ugaritic, this question is today most often given an affirmative answer (e.g., "Zum Kanaanäischen rechnen die meisten auch das Ugaritische." (von Soden 1984: 16)). The alternative, of course, is that it was a Northwest Semitic sibling of Canaanite, partaking in the Northwest Semitic innovations, but not the

Canaanite ones. Now, Ugaritic did participate in the Central Semitic and Northwest Semitic innovations outlined above. But with the Canaanite innovations, the situation is murkier, since all concern vowel shifts in specific morphemes and the Ugaritic consonantal orthography will only in case of a vowel abutting ' indicate vowel quality. Thus, it is not clear whether the sg. 1 verb suffix in Ugaritic was -*tu* or -*ti* (Goetze 1941: 132); and it is not clear whether *any* 1st person plural pronominal form ended in -*u* or -*a*, although Goetze (1941: 132n.) suggests on the basis of onomastic evidence that the 1st person plural genitive marker was -*na*, not -*nu* as in Canaanite. It is clear, however, from cuneiform forms like *a-na-ku* that Ugaritic did not participate in the **ā* to *o* change, and, according to Huehnergard (1990: 285n.), it is clear from cuneiform forms like *ša-li-ma* 'has paid' that Ugaritic did not have *i* in the first syllable of D stem verbs either. Thus, Ugaritic was probably not Canaanite, but rather a Northwest Semitic sibling of Canaanite.

South Semitic

Generalization of -*k*- in Suffix Conjugation Verbs
As noted earlier, the West Semitic suffix conjugation had some suffixes beginning with *k* and some with *t*. While the *t* was generalized in Central Semitic, in South Semitic it was the *k* that was generalized throughout the suffix conjugation paradigm. So Ethiopian languages have suffixes based on -*ku* 'sg. 1' and -*ka* 'sg. 2m.'.

Generalization of **(')al* as Verbal Negative
One of the innovations listed above as characterizing West Semitic was the development of prohibitive **'al*. This marker was generally retained in Central Semitic as a prohibitive, but in South Semitic it was generalized as an indicative marker of negation. It is attested in Epigraphic South Arabian texts meaning 'not' and as a pre-verbal negative particle in Modern South Arabian and in Ethiopian Semitic; in Ethiopian Semitic, it cooccurs with a post-verbal -*m* in negative main clauses. Thus, the change of **'al* from a prohibitive to a marker of sentential negation is characteristic of South Semitic.

Eastern (Modern South Arabian)
The primary innovation separating Modern South Arabian from the rest of South Semitic (Ethiopian Semitic and Old South Arabian) is the prefixed definite article of the form C(*a*) where C is one of { ' ḥ h} (Rodgers 1991).

Western
The Western South Semitic group, consisting of Ethiopian Semitic and Old South Arabian, is characterized, according to Rodgers (1991), by the development of finite uses for non-finite verb forms; that is infinitives and/or gerundives are used in serial constructions in which the first verb is finite but the others are not. Hetzron (1975: 113) notes the widespread distribution of these 'converbal' constructions in Ethiopian Semitic, but not the Old South Arabian parallels.

Ethiopian Semitic

Although virtually all discussions of Semitic subgrouping assume a single Ethiopian Semitic branch which later split into North Ethiopic and South Ethiopic, there is virtually no linguistic evidence for such a Common Ethiopian stage. Yet as Hetzron (1972: 17, 122) notes, neither is there any evidence that the diverse forms attested in North and South Ethiopic do not reflect a stage of shared descent from South Semitic that is independent of Old and Modern South Arabian. Hetzron (1972: 18; 1975: 113) suggests that the pan-Ethiopian compounds of the form 'X+ say' (e.g., Amharic *əmbi alä* 'refuse') represent a Proto-Ethiopian calque of a Cushitic structure. Also probably Proto-Ethiopian is the existential verb **hlw* (Amharic *allä*), which is morphologically perfect but semantically present tense, and which cooccurs with temporal prefixes (Amharic *s-*) that otherwise only occur with imperfects (Hetzron 1972: 18; 1975: 113).

The internal structure of Ethiopian Semitic presented here follows Hetzron (1972, 1975). Ethiopian Semitic is divided into two branches, North Ethiopic and South Ethiopic. Hetzron provides no evidence supporting grouping Ge'ez, Tigre, and Tigrinya together as North Ethiopic. However, all three of these languages have replaced the inherited South Semitic verbal negative *'al* with *'iʔay*, attested elsewhere in Semitic but with more restricted uses (e.g. Hebrew *'i*-X 'un-X'). Hetzron treats the North Ethiopic *'i* as a phonological variant of *'al*, but without mentioning the extra-Ethiopian parallels for it (Faber 1991). The unity of South Ethiopic is more secure, resting on several analogical changes in verb stems. For type A verbs, the linked changes of perfect *säbärä*/imperfect *yəsäbbər* (preserved in Ge'ez) to *säbbärä*/*yəsäbər* can be attributed to a common SE period. Likewise the analogical extension of the stem vowel *e* in the imperfect of type B *yəfeṭṭəm* to the perfect *feṭṭama* (cf. Ge'ez *fäṣṣämä*) is common SE.

The Position of Arabic

The primary difference between the two proposals for Semitic subgrouping outlined in this chapter is the affiliation of Arabic. Is it a sibling of South(east) Semitic, or is it a Central Semitic sibling of Northwest Semitic? The issues regarding the classification of Arabic have been explicitly and clearly laid out by Diem (1980). Arabic shares features with both Northwest and Southeast Semitic, and if one set of features is to be treated as shared innovations, the other must be treated as the result of chance factors or of structural influence of another language on Arabic. Discussion of the affiliation of Arabic generally concedes the similarities between Arabic and Northwest Semitic, and focuses on the appropriate analysis of features that occur in Arabic and Southeast Semitic. These features include: (1) the unconditioned change of **p* to /f/; (2) the existence of verb stems with a long first vowel (*kātaba, takātaba*); (3) broken plurals, that is, plurals formed by prefixation and/or internal change rather than by suffixation (e.g., Tigré *qabər/ʔaqbər(t)* 'tomb'). Advocates of grouping Arabic with Southeast Semitic (Blau 1978; Diem 1980) treat these features, especially the second and third, as shared innovations; the features that Arabic and Northwest Semitic share are then attributed to convergence or diffusion. Advocates of grouping Arabic with Northwest Semitic (Hetzron 1973, 1976; Goldenberg 1977; Huehnergard 1990, 1992, forthcoming), on the other hand, treat the five similarities between Arabic and Northwest Semitic (see pp. 8–9) as common inheritance; the similarities between Arabic and Southeast Semitic are treated then as retentions of constructions that have been replaced in Akkadian and Northwest Semitic.

Advocates of the former point of view stress the agreement between Geʻez and Arabic in plurals of specific nouns; however, when Tigre, Tigrinya, and the South Arabian languages, both Old and Modern, are included in the picture, much less agreement is evident. For example, forty-nine Sabean nouns in Beeston, *et al.* (1982) form the plural with prefixed ʼ, presumably reflecting a *ʼvCCvC* template. Seven of them have apparent Jibbāli cognates (Johnstone 1981); only one of these (*ḳɔ̄r* 'tomb' < √ḳbr) has a sound plural (*ḳabrín*), but the other six, in contrast with their Sabean cognates, pluralize by internal modification alone, with no prefixation. Advocates of the latter point of view rely instead on relic broken plural forms in Hebrew and Syriac (e.g., Heb. *rɛxɛv* 'riders', sg. *roxev*) that suggest an earlier language stage in which internal pluralization strategies were more widespread than they are in attested stages of Northwest Semitic languages. Similarly, Hebrew *domem* verbs, generally treated as a variant of *limmeδ* restricted to verbs with identical second and third consonants, are formally equivalent to Arabic *kātaba*. Advocates of a Central Semitic Arabic suppose that the complementarity of *domem* and *limmeδ* is a later development, while advocates of a South Semitic Arabic treat the formal similarity of *domem* and *kātaba* as coincidental (see further Fleisch 1944: 18).

Acknowledgments

My thoughts on the questions addressed in this chapter have been influenced over the years by many individuals. At the risk of offending those not mentioned, I would like to acknowledge the influence of Robert Hetzron, John Huehnergard, Robert King, and the participants in the 1987 Workshop on the Comparative Method and Reconstruction Methodology, organized by Philip Baldi as part of the LSA Summer Institute at Stanford University. Any errors of omission or commission are, of course, my responsibility alone.

References

Beeston, A. F. L., M. A. Ghul, W. W. Müller, and J. Ryckman. 1982. *Sabaic Dictionary.* Leuven: Éditions Peeters.

Bergsträsser, Gotthelf. 1983 [1923]. *Introduction to the Semitic Languages,* trans. Peter T. Daniels. Winona Lake, Ind.: Eisenbrauns.

Blau, Joshua. 1978. "Hebrew and Northwest Semitic: Reflections on the Classification of the Semitic Languages." *Hebrew Annual Review* 2: 21–44.

Brockelmann, Carl. 1961 [1926]. *Grundriss der vergleichenden Grammatik der semitis-*

chen Sprache. Hildesheim: Georg Olms.

Caplice, Richard. 1981. "Eblaite and Akkadian." *La lingua di Ebla,* ed. L. Cagni. Naples: Istituto Universitario Orientale. 161–164.

Cohen, David. 1984. *La Phrase nominale et l'évolution du système verbal en sémitique.* Leuven: Éditions Peeters.

Diem, Werner. 1980. "Die genealogische Stellung des Arabischen in den semitischen Sprachen: Ein eingelöstes Problem der Semitistik." In *Studien aus Arabistik und Semitistik, A. Spitaler zum 70. Geburtstag,* ed. W. Diem and S. Wild. Wiesbaden: Harrassowitz. 65–85.

Dolgopolsky, Aaron. 1977. "Emphatic Consonants in Semitic." *Israel Oriental Studies* 7: 1–13.

Faber, Alice. 1980. "Genetic Subgrouping of the Semitic Languages." Ph.D. dissertation, University of Texas.

—— 1985. "Akkadian Evidence for Proto-Semitic Affricates." *Journal of Cuneiform Studies* 37: 101–107.

—— 1990. "Interpretation of Orthographic Form." *Linguistic Change and Reconstruction Methodology,* ed. P. Baldi. Berlin: Walter de Gruyter. 619–637.

—— 1991. "The Diachronic Relationship Between Negative and Interrogative Markers in Semitic." In *Semitic Studies in Honor of Wolf Leslau,* volume 1, ed. A. S. Kaye. Wiesbaden: Harrassowitz. 411–329.

Fleisch, Henri. 1944. *Les Verbes à allongement vocalique interne en sémitique.* Paris: Institut d'ethnologie.

Garbini, Giovanni. 1972. *Le lingue semitiche.* Naples: Istituto Orientale di Napoli.

Geers, F. W. 1945. "The Treatment of Emphatics in Akkadian." *Journal of Near Eastern Studies* 4: 65–67.

Gelb, I. J. 1977. "Thoughts about Ibla." *Syro-Mesopotamian Studies* 1: 3–28.

—— 1981. "Ebla and the Kish Civilization." In *La lingua di Ebla,* ed. L Cagni. Naples: Istituto Universitario Orientale. 9–73.

Goetze, Albrecht. 1941. "Is Ugaritic a Canaanite Dialect?" *Language* 17: 127–138.

Goldenberg, Gideon. 1977. "The Semitic Languages of Ethiopia and Their Classification." *Bulletin of the School of Oriental and African Studies* 40: 461–507.

Greenberg, Joseph. H. 1957. "The Problem of Linguistic Subgroupings." *Essays in Linguistics.* Chicago: University of Chicago Press. 46–55.

Harris, Zellig S. 1939. *Development of the Canaanite Dialects.* New Haven: American Oriental Society.

Hetzron, Robert. 1972. *Ethiopian Semitic: Studies in Classification (Journal of Semitic Studies* Monograph 2). Manchester: Manchester University Press.

—— 1973. "The Vocalization of Prefixes in Semitic Active and Passive Verbs." *Mélanges de l'Université Saint Joseph* 48: 35–48.

—— 1975. "Genetic Classification and Ethiopian Semitic." In *Hamito-Semitica,* ed. J. and T. Bynon. The Hague: Mouton. 103–127.

—— 1976. "Two Principles of Genetic Reconstruction." *Lingua* 38: 89–104.

Hoenigswald, Henry M. 1960. *Language Change and Linguistic Reconstruction.* Chicago: University of Chicago Press.

Huehnergard, John. 1983. "Asseverative *la and Hypothetical *lu/law in Semitic." *Journal of the American Oriental Society* 103: 569–593.

—— 1990. "Remarks on the Classification of the Northwest Semitic Languages." In *Deir 'Alla Symposium,* ed. J. Hoftijzer. Leiden: Brill. 282–293.

—— 1992. "Languages of the Ancient Near East." *The Anchor Bible Dictionary,* volume 4. 155–170.

—— forthcoming. "Recent Research in Early Northwest Semitic Grammar." In *The Bible and the Ancient Near East Revisited,* ed. J. Hackett, *et al.* Atlanta: Scholars Press.

Johnstone, T. M. 1981. *Jibbali Lexicon.* Oxford: Oxford University Press.

Knudson, E. E. 1961. "Cases of Free Variants in the Akkadian q Phoneme." *Journal of Cuneiform Studies* 15: 84–90.

Moscati, Sabatino. 1969. *An Introduction to the Comparative Grammar of the Semitic Languages.* Wiesbaden: Harrassowitz.

Pettinato, Giovanni. 1975. "Testi Cuneiformi del 3. millennio in paleo-cananeo rinvenuti nella campagna 1974 a Tell Mardikh=Ebla." *Orientalia* 44: 361–374.

Rabin, Chaim. 1975. "Lexicostatistics and the Internal Divisions of Semitic." In *Hamito-Semitica,* ed. J. and T. Bynon. The Hague: Mouton. 85–102.

Rodgers, Jonathan. 1991. "The Subgrouping of the South Semitic Languages." In *Semitic Studies in Honor of Wolf Leslau,* volume 2, ed. A. S. Kaye. Wiesbaden: Harrassowitz. 1323–1336.

Segert, Stanislav. 1984. *A Basic Grammar of the Ugaritic Language.* Berkeley: University of California Press.

Soden, Wolfram von. 1984. "Sprachfamilien und Einzelsprachen im Altsemitischen: Akkadisch und Eblaitisch." In *Studies in the Language of Ebla,* ed. P. Fronzaroli. Florence: Università di Firenze. 11–24.

Ullendorff, Edward. 1970. "Comparative Semitics." In *Current Trends in Linguistlcs,* volume 6: *Linguistics in South West Asia and North Africa,* ed. T. Sebeok. The Hague: Mouton. 261–273.

Voigt, Rainer M. 1987. "The Classification of Central Semitic." *Journal of Semitic Studies* 32: 1–19.

Zaborski, A. 1991. "The Position of Arabic within the Semitic Dialect Continuum." In *Proceedings of the Colloquium on Arabic Grammar,* ed. K. Dévényi and T. Iványi. Budapest: Eötvös Loránd University. 365–375.

2 Scripts of Semitic Languages

Peter T. Daniels

Most Semitic languages are known to us only because they were written down. Without writing, we would have only Arabic, South Arabian, Aramaic, and Ethiopic dialects; were it not for ancient literacy, we would have no Bible, no Qur'an, no hint even of Mesopotamian civilization.

Scripts have customarily been classified according to the schema set forth by Isaac Taylor (1883, vol. 1: 6), distinguishing logographic, syllabic, and alphabetic writing. But this is not adequate; it has resulted in much fruitless wrangling in past decades over what to call, for instance, the Phoenician script. For the scripts of the Semitic languages, five categories are needed: logography, syllabary, abjad, alphabet, and abugida. A sixth, featural script, appears when Arabic script is adapted to non-Semitic languages.

Writing is a system of more or less permanent marks representing an utterance in such a way that it can be recovered more or less exactly without the intervention of the utterer. **Logographic** writing uses one character to represent one morpheme. Such are Chinese script and Sumerian script (where each root or affix is represented by one character). In a **syllabary,** each character represents a syllable, ordinarily a simple open syllable with one consonant followed by one vowel (CV). The characters for syllables containing the same consonant or the same vowel generally bear no resemblance among themselves. An **abjad** (also known as a consonantary), in its pristine form, is a script wherein each character denotes a consonant and wherein vowels are not represented at all. Such a script has arisen once, to write some early Semitic tongue, and its organizing principle has undergone a considerable variety of developments across the times and places of its use. (The English word "abjad" is borrowed from the Arabic term for the letters of the script when taken in their ancestral order, as when they are used with their numerical values; it is a simple vocalization of the first four letters in that order.) An **alphabet,** ideally, includes a character for each segmental phoneme of the language it represents. Only one has ever been independently invented, the Greek alphabet, and from this have developed all the alphabets of Europe, which in turn have become the dominant script type of the modern world. (The English word "alpha-

16

bet" combines the names of the first two letters of the Greek ancestor.) An **abugida** is a script that uses characters for CV syllables wherein the several characters for some consonant plus the language's array of vowels are modifications of the character for that consonant followed by the unmarked vowel (phonemically /a/). (The English word "abugida" is borrowed from the Amharic term for the letters of the script when taken in the order known from the Ge'ez transliterations of the Hebrew letter names found in the superscriptions of the sections of Psalm 119, as used in liturgy; it takes the first four consonants and the first four vowels in their traditional order of presentation.) In a **featural** script, features (characteristics) of the written characters represent distinctive features within the phonology of the language.

History of Scripts of Semitic Languages

This chapter is called "Scripts of Semitic Languages" rather than "Semitic Scripts" or "Semitic Writing" because Semitic scripts underlie virtually every script in use outside East Asia today. Similarly at the other end of the story, at the beginning of history, the script of the early Semitic languages was not Semitic writing. Those first languages – Akkadian, Eblaite, Amorite, and doubtless others that have not been excavated – used a script borrowed from a language whose speakers seem to have been present in Mesopotamia before speakers of Semitic. That language is Sumerian; that script is logosyllabic cuneiform.

Logosyllabary

Sumerian is a largely monosyllabic, agglutinative language. This kind of structure seems to have been a necessary ingredient for the independent invention of writing: it is characteristic of the languages hosting the two other certain cases of independent invention, Archaic Chinese and Mayan, as well. When a civilization begins to write things down, what it writes down generally seems to be things that would not be spoken, and the resulting records are, in the Near East, economic documents: inventories of livestock and goods, lists of laborers, soon lists of everything within the writers' ken.

Some time perhaps in the second half of the fourth millennium BCE, accountants began pressing into lumps of clay marks – originally pictorial, but soon conventionalized; they are called **signs** – that represented livestock and commodities and quantities. Owners' names also needed to be written: because the objects depicted had names composed of single syllables, the marks inherently represented those syllables as well; so the syllables composing the names could be recorded with the marks that also designated the objects. (The syllables represented could be CV, VC, or CVC in shape.) The names were preceded by a mark indicating that the group of marks represented a name. At a later stage in recording Sumerian prose, some verbs and abstractions could be indicated by signs for related objects ("go" with "leg," "light" with "sun"); then additional words and affixes that could not be represented by pictures could also be written using only the sounds associated with signs. As help in interpretation, a series of **determinatives,** like the name sign mentioned earlier, could mark words falling into categories like "city," "bird," "wooden object," and so on.

The earliest Akkadian was written very like Sumerian: at first grammatical elements were not included, and only word order can suggest whether a particular passage was intended for Sumerian or Akkadian; but soon the full panoply of resources was in use: phonetic, logographic, and determinative signs. The range of consonants in Semitic, however, is richer than that in Sumerian, and certain phonetic signs did double or multiple duty in a principled way: the consonant in any VC sign represented the voiceless, voiced, and emphatic members of the set at one point of articulation (e.g. $t/d/t$); initial consonants, too, only gradually received fully specified representations. Signs with semivowels represented them with any of the vowels. Moreover, when logograms took on Akkadian as well as Sumerian readings, the phonetic values of the signs could reflect either the Sumerian or the Akkadian reading (e.g. ⸗⫟⊨ *sag, riš*; cf. Sum. SAG, Akk. *rēšu* 'head'). All told, around six hundred signs were used across the history of the language, but no more than about two hundred were of common occurrence at any particular time and place.

In their pictorial stage, the signs were incised by drawing fine lines in the clay with a pointed object. They were conventionalized by replacing the drawn lines with impressed **wedges,** made by touching the corner of a triangular prism, probably a reed, to the clay, at various orientations, so the script is called **cuneiform** (cf. Latin *cuneus* 'wedge').

Signs became gradually simpler, requiring fewer strokes of the stylus to complete, and there are characteristic treatments of recurring patterns of strokes, but the system retained its integrity for well over 2,500 years, into the first century CE (the latest known dated text is from the year 75). One can tell at a glance whether a particular inscription is Babylonian or Assyrian, early or late, and once one is accustomed to the handwriting of a certain period, the identification of the signs is not difficult.

Abjad

Origin

In the absence of any evidence whatsoever regarding the origin of the abjad, speculation has centered on the morphological structure of Semitic: according to the traditional view, Semitic words are composed of interdigitated consonantal "roots" and vocalic "patterns." Recognition has been growing, though, that Semitic word formation is not thus unique among the languages of the world, but can be efficiently described according to familiar patterns of bases, ablauts, and affixes; note that Semitic word structure did not result in a restructuring of Sumerian cuneiform into vowellessness when it came to be used for Akkadian.

The invention of the abjad resulted from a rather subtle observation. It has repeatedly been shown that it is not "segments" of the speech stream or phonemes of a language that are accessible to the consciousness of a speaker; unless people can read an alphabetic script, they cannot isolate stretches of speech smaller than a syllable. (Hence the primacy of syllabic writing.) Phonetically similar syllables were apparently not at first recognized to share any similarity, so that e.g. cuneiform signs ⟨𒋫⟩ *ta*, ⟨𒋾⟩ *ti*, and ⟨𒌅⟩ *tu* show no graphic similarity. There does, however, exist a Mesopotamian signlist that brings together phonetically similar syllables: it groups *ta*, *ti*, and *tu*; it also groups ⟨𒀜⟩ *at*, ⟨𒀉⟩ *it*, and ⟨𒌓⟩ *ut* – but it does *not* group these two triplets together. (Significantly, a copy of this list from Ugarit, where an abjad was in use, does give evidence that the sets were recognized as related.) Thus a segmental consciousness was emerging.

Further stimulus toward recognition of segments may have come from certain orthographic practices used for Hurrian, an unaffiliated language written with Mesopotamian cuneiform. A CV syllable (regardless of vowel length) was often written CV_i-V_i, with the vowel inherent in the CV sign repeated by an independent vowel sign – so that the CV sign in effect denoted only its inherent consonant. A second possibly relevant practice is found at the Hittite capital, Boğazköy. The sign ⟨𒉿⟩ PI represents *wa*, *we*, *wi*, and *wu* in cuneiform. When Hittite scribes wrote foreign languages (including Hurrian), they would add a subscript ⟨𒀀⟩ *a*, ⟨𒂊⟩ *e*, ⟨𒄿⟩ *i*, or ⟨𒌑⟩ *ú* to the ⟨𒉿⟩. This would seem to represent another sort of segmental consciousness.

Development
Often placed at the head of the stream of Semitic texts are the few "Proto-Sinaitic" inscriptions, found on votive objects from a mining settlement in the Sinai dating to the mid or even early second millennium BCE, but there is little evidence to support the language identification. More secure is the place of the handful of "Proto-Canaanite" characters at or near the wellspring: they are dated as far back as the early seventeenth century BCE, but the oldest that can be securely interpreted are the al-Khadr arrowheads, probably from the twelfth to the eleventh centuries. Not long afterward, probably, the earliest surviving recognizably Phoenician inscriptions were written. Another descendant of the ancestor of Phoenician is the South Semitic branch, in turn ancestral to the Epigraphic South Arabian and the Old North Arabic scripts. Materials have not been found that might clarify the early history of the southern branch, but some examples of cursive South Arabian have only recently been discovered.

Ugaritic
Earlier than the earliest Phoenician, though, is the first sizable abjad-written corpus: the tablets from Ugarit and environs composed in a variety of the Semitic abjad written on clay, beginning probably before 1300 BCE. Here, perhaps because of the need to write the Hurrian language, in which syllables could begin with vowels as well as consonants, the letter which elsewhere represented ʾ was used only before *a*; additional letters represented ʾ before *i* and ʾ before *u* (they are transliterated *ȧ*, *i*, and *ů* as a reminder that the letters do *not* represent vowels or

syllables). There are two varieties: a longer one, written left to right, used in the city of Ugarit itself; and a shorter one, containing the twenty-two letters still found in Hebrew, usually written right to left. The few texts using this form are nearly all from outside Ugarit.

Phoenician

Sufficient materials survive from the first millennium BCE (more plentifully from the later periods, of course) to follow the development of the abjad from its early Phoenician form to the considerable diversity of scripts that were in use as long as the diversity of Semitic languages persisted. While most communities allowed the abjad to change gradually over the generations, the tradition represented initially by the Hebrews and to this day by the Samaritans was very conservative, and has preserved a set of letter forms that is close to the ancestral shapes of 3,000 years ago. When the Dead Sea Scrolls were written, this script was still recognized as (ancient and thus?) holy. A few of the Scrolls are entirely in a revival of it called Paleo-Hebrew script, and in others, the Tetragrammaton appears in it, embedded in text using the Square Hebrew which is current to this day.

Aramaic

Square Hebrew is a form of the Aramaic branch of the abjad, apparently adopted by the Jewish community during the Babylonian Exile. Soon after the epigraphic record begins, about the turn of the first millennium BCE, a trend to two different styles of writing appears. The script of Phoenician proper is more angular, while that associated primarily with Aramaic languages becomes more curvaceous. (Canaanite languages, such as Ammonite, could also be written with Aramaic script, well before its adoption for Hebrew.) A possible explanation for this trend is that – as the (Imperial) Aramaic language became the lingua franca of successive Near Eastern empires – Aramaic script was widely used throughout the Fertile Crescent, so a tendency to cursiveness was tolerated, then encouraged, as writing became increasingly part of everyday life and speed in producing documents became desirable. In contrast, (allowing for accidents of preservation) Phoenician seems to have been written in fewer different circumstances, affording the script less opportunity to "evolve" through the centuries. The more cursive aspect of its later offshoot, Punic, suggests that Punic in turn came to be written more often in more contexts. The cursivity of the script of the Aramaic-writing community led at first to distinctive forms for some letters at the ends of words (the trend is already noticeable in the Aramaic papyri from Elephantine, fifth century BCE), and – by the turn of the era – in many areas to the writing of groups of letters, up to entire words, without lifting the pen.

Several corpora written with cursive versions of the Aramaic abjad have survived from the early first millennium CE (Klugkist 1982), but insufficient materials for working out the interrelations among them are available. They include: Nabatean, the ancestor of Arabic script, used (by an Arab tribe to write a form of Aramaic) around the rock-hewn city of Petra in modern Jordan and subsequently throughout the Sinai (the latter graffiti are known as "Sinaitic"); Palmyrene, from the majestic city-state of Palmyra; Hatran, used in the northern part of the Aramaophone region; Edessan, which developed into Syriac script; Mandaic, still in use by practitioners of a Gnostic religion; and the little-known Elymaic, from Elam in modern Iran, which seems to have been the main starting point for the scripts of the Iranian and Altaic languages that eventually spread all across Inner Asia. Some form of Imperial Aramaic script also underlay the Kharoshthi script used for Indic languages in northwest India in the fifth century BCE, and recent studies of the origin of Brahmi, the main ancestral script of India, attested only since the fourth century BCE, suggest that it was at least influenced by Kharoshthi (rather than based directly on an Aramaic script, as has generally been held).

Contemporary Reflections of Aramaic
The abjads that are still in use are the Mandaic, the Arabic, the Syriac, and the Hebrew. Each of the four has survived because it was the vehicle of sacred scripture, and for "Peoples of the Book," the physical instantiation of scripture is itself sacred: it is more or less sacrilegious to transfer the sacred text to some other written medium (even to translate it is more or less inappropriate).

Only a handful of pre-Islamic Arabic inscriptions are known, and it is clear the script was in crisis: different letters were nearly indistinguishable, and the larger consonantal inventory of Arabic was not well served by the abjad that was adequate for Canaanite and Aramaic. The scribal solution was to merge the letter shapes into just over a dozen forms, and to distinguish them with obligatory patterns of dots; the dots reflect letter history (distinguishing those whose basic shapes had converged) and, for the newly accommodated consonants, phonetic similarity. As Islam was brought to preliterate populations, the Arabic script was adapted on the same principles to the writing of the native languages. The ensuing cultural diversity, coupled with a prohibition of depictions of the human form, has led to a glorious variety of calligraphic styles and elaboration employed in Muslim art and architecture throughout the world.

Syriac Christianity, divided both between Roman and Persian imperial control and by Christological schism, developed two distinctive versions of the script from the earlier Estrangelo (either "round" or "gospel writing"): Jacobite or Serto ("[simple] stroke") in the west, which is usually found in European printing; and Nestorian in the east, which is now called East Syriac because it is the form generally used by speakers of Modern Aramaic, whichever church they adhere to. "Assyrian" orthography dates from the work of American missionaries in Kurdistan in the 1820s and is deliberately archaizing and not language specific. Some Jewish Modern Aramaic documents are known from a few centuries earlier, and they are written phonetically using Hebrew characters.

With the Jewish Diaspora, regional varieties of Hebrew script emerged everywhere. Square Hebrew remained the script of the sacred books, and is the standard form used in modern Israel. Of the many varieties, the broad designations "Sephardic" and "Ashkenazi" remain relevant: the script known (ahistorically) as

"Rashi," used for rabbinic commentaries, represents the former, and Modern Hebrew cursive handwriting perpetuates the latter. Hebrew script could be used for local languages wherever there were Jews, and one criterion for identifying a "Jewish language" such as Yiddish is that such orthography exists.

Alphabet

The aforementioned transfer of abjadic writing from Semitic-speakers to Greek-speakers was probably inevitable, but the emergence of alphabetic writing was an accident. It took no great Greek genius to deliberately devise letters for vowels; they were a virtually automatic result of the fact that the Greek language uses fewer consonantal phonemes than Northwest Semitic. Syllables beginning with laryngeal consonants and with semivowels in Semitic were heard by Greeks as beginning with vowels, so naturally, when, say, a Phoenician (or Aramaic?) scribe was explaining the script to an inquisitive Greek would-be scribe, perhaps by saying the names of the letters, the Greek would hear ['alp] as /alp/, [ḥet] as /et/, [jo:d] as /iot/, and so on. This would seem to be an ordinary sort of marketplace transaction, and hardly needs to be explained as a yearning to notate Greek oral epics, still less as a manifestation of Aryan genius.

Vowel Letters

It is, moreover, not correct to claim that the abjad could notate only consonants. In even the oldest Aramaic inscription yet known, there are what are called *matres lectionis* ('mothers of reading'). These are certain letters – some occurrences of ', *h*, *w*, *y*, and occasionally ' – that indicate not their consonantal value, but the presence of a phonetically similar vowel. Their origin is historical: consonants continued to be written after they had been lost from the spoken languages in some positions, and came to be interpreted as standing for the vowels that remained. Earliest, apparently, were final vowels no longer followed by ' or *h*; word-internally, diphthongs *ay* and *aw* contracted to *ê* and *ô* respectively; and *y* or *w* came to represent *ī* and *ū* in addition. The process was carried through most consistently in Aramaic; in its orthographic descendant Arabic, every *ā* is represented by ' as well. Mandaic is so thorough in its use of vowel letters as to have almost devised an alphabet.

Vowel Points

The Semitic abjad first became a full alphabet at the hands of Syriac grammarians. Perhaps because they were familiar with Greek, they recognized that it was possible and useful to explicitly notate all the vowels. Perhaps the large number of Greek and Iranian loanwords in Syriac – where vowel indication was perhaps less dispensible – provided the impetus toward devising such notation. But the Greek model, which would involve inserting vowel letters within the spellings of words, was not followed, for two reasons: the text of scripture was sacred as it had been transmitted through the generations, and could not be disfigured by insertions (this argument holds for Hebrew and Arabic as well); and if a new way of writing

Syriac came into fashion, all older manuscripts would become unreadable by the next generation of students. So ways were found to optionally notate vowels without infringing on the consonantal text. The resulting vocalization schemes, involving marks added above or below the line of letters, are known as **vowel pointing** (or **punctuation**), and not, contrary to several popular accounts of Semitic writing, *matres lectionis*.

Syriac

The earliest manuscripts in Syriac Estrangelo already employ several diacritic points. A pair of dots over a word indicates a plural. Where distinct words share a consonantal spelling, a dot above a letter indicates a "fuller" syllable (typically with *a*), and a dot under indicates a syllable with a lesser vowel or vowellessness: ܟ݁ܒ݂ܕ݁ܐ '*bādā* 'a work', ܥܒܕܐ '*abdā* 'a servant'. Since such dots could distinguish perfect forms from participial forms (ܩܛܠ *qtal* ~ ܩܛܠ *qātel* respectively), they came to mark such grammatical distinctions even when they contradicted the phonetic indications of the dots (ܣܡ *sām* 'he placed [pf.]').

Gradually, combinations of dots came into use in the East Syriac region to indicate shades of vowel color, with the full system distinguishing seven vowels by the ninth century CE. In the west, where Greek influence was strong, vowels could be specified with small Greek letters placed above or below the consonant which was followed by the vowel. Either system of vowel notation remained optional. Only in Modern Aramaic texts are vowel points – always the dot system – obligatory.

Hebrew

For Hebrew, a sequence of manuscripts illustrating the development of vowel pointing does not exist. As Hebrew ceased to be a spoken language, scholars – Masoretes – in several parts of the Jewish world devised schemes for notating vowels (and also the liturgical chants, which related in ways not well understood to the syntactic structure of the text). The Babylonian and Palestinian pointings eventually gave way to the Tiberian, which is the style found in today's Bible editions and is occasionally used for clarification of Modern Hebrew texts, such as poetry and elementary schoolbooks.

Arabic

Arabic, with its full complement of *matres lectionis* and its limited set of three vowels (short and long), quickly settled on a simple set of vowel diacritics. The full Arabic writing system, however, is morphophonemically quite complicated, allegedly because the consonantal text of the Qur'an was established by speakers of one dialect, and the vowel and other diacritics were added according to a different dialect.

Abugida

A scattering of Sabean inscriptions is found in Eritrea. Early in the history of the

Aksumite kingdom, shortly after 300 CE, missionaries succeeded in converting the king and the kingdom to Christianity, and simultaneously, vowel notation appears in the inscriptions beginning with the middle of the reign of King Ezana. The Ethiopic script was thus the first Semitic script to notate vowels consistently, and it does so in a way unique within the Semitic sphere: it uses the technique followed in India, of taking a basic consonantal shape to represent the consonant followed by *a* and modifiying that shape to represent the consonant followed by the other vowels (or no vowel). This technique may have been introduced by Christian missionaries from India; it seems unlikely that it was introduced by Greek or Coptic missionaries, whose alphabets provided separate letters for the vowels. The earliest surviving Ge'ez manuscripts date only from the fourteenth century, but the script changed little between its development and then, or between then and now.

Script Direction

Fairly early in the development of cuneiform, a 90 degree rotation in the direction of writing became established, so that the ancestral pictograms face upward and the lines of text are horizontal, reading left to right.

Right-to-left writing has been the rule throughout the history of the abjad. The principal exception is the Ugaritic tablets (in the long version of the script), where left-to-right practice seems to have been taken over from Mesopotamian cuneiform along with the medium and technique. Epigraphic South Arabian texts – which could be inscribed on very long walls – tend to be written **boustrophedon** ('as the ox plows'), with alternate lines beginning at opposite ends of the surface. This facilitates reading such a long-lined inscription. The first scribe to lay down the principles of writing with the abjad was probably left-handed: right-to-left writing with the right hand is more conducive to smearing of freshly deposited ink than left-to-right; since most of humankind is right-handed, said inventor must have been possessed of great prestige, so that he or she was imitated forever after. The persistence of right-to-left writing shows the force of tradition; Syriac scribes adopted the expedient of turning their pages 90 degrees counterclockwise to write downward in columns from left to right (this accounts for the unusual orientation of the Western vowel signs taken from Greek letters) while still reading horizontally right to left.

It seems that only when a script undergoes a catastrophic transformation can the tradition be breached. It happened with the transfer of the abjad to the Greeks, where the resulting alphabet made the transition via boustrophedony; and it happened in the development of the Ethiopic abugida: the ancestral Sabean inscriptions from Aksum are written from right to left, but both the unvocalized and then the vocalized Ethiopic inscriptions are written from left to right from the first.

Word and Clause Division

Word boundaries are treated in four different ways in the scripts of Semitic languages: they are ignored, they are marked by divider characters, they coincide with horizontal space in the line of writing, or they are indicated by distinctive shapes of letters at the ends of words.

No word-breaks appear on cuneiform tablets, but a gap may be left before the last sign of a line to achieve an even right margin; words are not split between lines. Such Proto-Canaanite texts as are interpretable generally comprise only single words, usually owners' names. In Ugaritic, a single vertical wedge (looking different from the wedges used in the letters) usually stands between words. The Aḥiram sarcophagus inscription uses short vertical strokes, other Phoenician and some Old Aramaic texts give no indication of word division. Most Archaic Hebrew inscriptions use a dot between words, and eventually it became normal to leave a bit of blank space between words. The slight pause thus engendered seems to induce the scribe's fingers to prolong a word-final stroke a bit, resulting in the special final forms of letters. In Arabic, where certain letters are not connected to the next even within a word, the tendency to extend a word-final stroke, but not a word-internal unconnected stroke, means that words can be distinguished even without leaving extra space between them. Epigraphic South Arabian texts generally follow each word with a short vertical stroke, and its Ethiopic descendant until very recently always used a vertical pair of dots (with two such pairs as "sentence" punctuation). The other scripts used for modern languages – Hebrew, Arabic, Syriac – have adopted the European punctuation marks.

Description of Scripts of Semitic Languages

Logosyllabary

The Akkadian cuneiform script comprises something more than 600 signs, nearly all of which have one or several phonetic readings, most of which have a logographic value, and a number of which are also used as determinatives. The number 600, though, can be misleading; fewer than 200 signs were in common use at any one stage of the language.

Signs are identified in modern study in two ways: by their reading, and by their designation. The reading of a sign (in a particular context) is given in lower case italic. The various signs with the same pronunciation are differentiated in **transliterations** via numerical subscripts, arranged in putative order of frequency of appearance; except that $_1$ is not marked, and $_2$ and $_3$ are usually replaced by acute and grave accents respectively. So some of the signs read [ʃu] are transliterated $šu$, $šú$, $šù$, $šu_4$, $šu_5$. The designation of a sign is usually its most common reading; it is a transliteration into capital letters – in careful typography, small capitals – of one of its pronunciations, and this is how logographic signs are represented. Determinatives are transliterated like logograms, or with a conventional series of superscripts. Phonetic complements (sometimes used to clarify a rare logogram or an unusual phonetic reading of a sign) are transliterated with italic superscripts. When passages of Akkadian are **transcribed,** the identities of the signs are ignored and vowel length is marked with a macron for a historically long vowel or a circumflex for a long vowel resulting from contraction or consonant loss.

Table 2.1 Phonetic arrangement of Neo-Assyrian cuneiform syllabary[†]

Ca	Ce	Ci	Cu			aC	eC	iC	uC
𒀸	𒀸 𒀸	𒀸	𒀸 𒀸 𒀸	—					
𒀸	𒀸	𒀸	𒀸	m		𒀸	𒀸		𒀸
𒀸	𒀸	𒀸	𒀸	b		𒀸	𒀸		𒀸
𒀸			𒀸	p					
				w					
	𒀸			y			𒀸		
𒀸									
𒀸	𒀸		𒀸	d					
𒀸			𒀸	ṭ		𒀸	𒀸		𒀸
𒀸	𒀸	𒀸	𒀸 𒀸	t					
𒀸	𒀸		𒀸	z		𒀸			𒀸
	𒀸	𒀸		ṣ			𒀸		𒀸
𒀸	𒀸	𒀸		s					
𒀸 𒀸	𒀸	𒀸	𒀸 𒀸	š		𒀸 𒀸	𒀸	𒀸	𒀸
𒀸	𒀸	𒀸	𒀸	n		𒀸	𒀸	𒀸	𒀸
𒀸	𒀸	𒀸	l	l		𒀸	𒀸	𒀸	𒀸
𒀸	𒀸 𒀸	𒀸	r	r		𒀸	𒀸		𒀸
𒀸	𒀸	𒀸	g	g					
𒀸	𒀸	𒀸	q	q		𒀸	𒀸		𒀸
𒀸	𒀸	𒀸	k	k					
𒀸	𒀸	𒀸	ḫ	ḫ		𒀸		𒀸	
	𒀸		'	'			𒀸		

† The table gives the most common monoconsonantal signs. The intersections of vowel columns and consonant rows are sometimes subdivided to include more than one homophonous sign. The "q row" thus reads qa qá qe/i qé/í qu qú aq e/iq uq (where qá is GA, qé/í is KI, and qú is KU) (after Daniels 1983: 253).

Uniquely among the world's syllabaries, which otherwise have characters only for Consonant + Vowel (CV) syllables, (Sumero-)Akkadian signs may have CV readings, VC readings, and CVC readings. The CV signs distinguish the full complement of consonants of the Akkadian language accompanied by the four vowels, but the VC signs collapse the triplets of voiced, voiceless, and emphatic consonants (Table 2.1, p. 26). Vocalic nuclei of syllables can be written with CV_i, with CV_i-V_iC, or with CV_iC; long vowels can be written with CV_i-V_i(-V_iC). Long consonants can be written with -C_iv or with -VC_i-C_iV; a writing -VC_i-V can only represent a sequence C_i'.

Abjads

Consonants

The oldest West Semitic language with a sizable literature is Ugaritic. The Ugaritic abjad comprises twenty-seven consonant letters (including a sibilant that seems to be used only in non-Semitic words) and three characters that represent ' followed (and possibly preceded) by the three vowels. The other Northwest Semitic languages are written with just the twenty-two letters that sufficed for the consonants of Phoenician (Table 2.2, p. 28) – even though in some languages some letters were used for more than one phoneme, as with the Hebrew distinction later marked with שׂ *ś* vs. שׁ *š*, or with the Aramaic interdentals *θ* and *δ* which early on were written with שׁ *š* and ז *z* and only later merged with and were written with ת *t* and ד *d*.

Many of the letters in the scripts developed from the ligatured Aramaic cursives scripts take on different shapes at the beginnings, middles, and ends of words; some of the letters do not connect to those that follow within a word.

Classical Arabic introduces some complications beyond the expanded roster of letters (Table 2.3, p. 29). When not word initial, the letter ' is always the *mater* for *ā*, and an additional sign ء (hamza) represents ['']. It is placed on one of the *matres* or alone within the line of writing, depending on the preceding and following vowels. Pausal morphophonemics are captured in the consonantal script by combining the final/independent forms ه ـه of *h* with the dots of ت *t*: ة ـة, used to end feminine nouns. Consonant length can be marked – even in otherwise unpointed texts – with ّ.

In both Hebrew and Syriac, the stop consonants can optionally be marked for plosive versus fricative pronunciation. Hebrew uses a dot within the letter for the stop and (very rarely) a dash above it for the fricative; Syriac uses a small dot respectively above or below the letter. Other marks in the text belong in the realm of specialists.

Table 2.2   Scripts using the Northwest Semitic order[†]

Value[§]	Ugaritic	Samaritan	Hebrew	Rashi	Mandaic	Estrangelo	Serto	Nestorian	Num. Val.
ʼ (å)			א						1
b			ב						2
g			ג						3
(ḫ)									
d			ד						4
h {-ī}			ה						5
w			ו						6
z			ז						7
ḥ {h}			ח						8
ṭ			ט						9
y			י						10
k			כ ך	כ ך					20
(š)									
l			ל						30
m			מ ם	מ ם					40
(δ)									
n			נ ן	נ ן					50
ẓ									
s			ס						60
ʿ			ע						70
p			פ ף	פ ף					80
ṣ			צ ץ	צ ץ					90
q			ק						100
r			ר						200
ś			ש						
š (θ)			ש						300
(γ)									
t			ת						400
(ì)									
(ù)									
(ŝ)									
{dī}									

† Where two forms are shown, that on the right occurs at the end of a word.

§ (Ugaritic values); {Mandaic values}.

Table 2.3 Script using modified Northwest Semitic order (Arabic)

Value	Alone	Final	Medial	Initial	Numerical Value
a	ا	ـا			1
b	ب	ـب	ـبـ	بـ	2
t	ت	ـت	ـتـ	تـ	400
θ	ث	ـث	ـثـ	ثـ	500
ǰ	ج	ـج	ـجـ	جـ	3
ḥ	ح	ـح	ـحـ	حـ	8
ḫ = x	خ	ـخ	ـخـ	خـ	600
d	د	ـد			4
δ	ذ	ـذ			700
r	ر	ـر			200
z	ز	ـز			7
s	س	ـس	ـسـ	سـ	60
š	ش	ـش	ـشـ	شـ	300
ṣ	ص	ـص	ـصـ	صـ	90
ḍ	ض	ـض	ـضـ	ضـ	800
ṭ	ط	ـط	ـطـ	طـ	9
ẓ	ظ	ـظ	ـظـ	ظـ	900
ʿ	ع	ـع	ـعـ	عـ	70
γ	غ	ـغ	ـغـ	غـ	1000
f	ف	ـف	ـفـ	فـ	80
q	ق	ـق	ـقـ	قـ	100
k	ك	ـك	ـكـ	كـ	20
l	ل	ـل	ـلـ	لـ	30
m	م	ـم	ـمـ	مـ	40
n	ن	ـن	ـنـ	نـ	50
h	ه	ـه	ـهـ	هـ	5
w	و	ـو			6
y	ي	ـي	ـيـ	يـ	10
lā	لا	ـلا			

Vowels
Vowels are inherent in the logosyllabary, the abugida, and the alphabets; most of
the abjads have devised ways of denoting vowels. In each case, the vowel point
accompanies the letter for the consonant which it follows (Table 2.4, p. 31).

The Classical Arabic scheme is straightforward, with three marks for the three
vowels; when they appear with the three possible *matres* (', *w*, *y*), they reinforce
their designations of the long vowels. In the consonantal spelling of some common words, the letter ' does not appear for *ā*; in carefully pointed texts, a small '
marks such *ā*'s. There are additionally indications for final nunation, eliding initial
['], and the sequence '*ā*.

For both Hebrew and Syriac, the conventional transliterations suggest that it is
vowel length that is encoded with the fairly large number of vowel points, but it
is clear that within each system, it is vowel *quality* that is distinguished, with
quantity to be deduced from the phonological context and the morphological
structure of the words.

Accents
Elaborately pointed Syriac documents include "accents" that can provide syntactic, pragmatic, and liturgical information. They were not extensively used, and different grammarians codify their use differently. They do not involve an additional
group of marks, but are composed of the same sorts of dots that also serve in several other functions.

In Hebrew, by contrast, every Hebrew Bible text that bears the Masoretic pointing includes on every (phonological) word an **accent** or **cantillation mark.** These
accents simultaneously mark the (syntactic) immediate constituents of the text –
the largest such constitutent corresponds to the verse of the English Bible – and
presumably the musical patterns to be employed during liturgical chant. The musical significance of the marks, however, has not been transmitted to the present.
A system of marks different from that which prevails in the rest of the Bible is
used in the three "poetical" books, Psalms, Proverbs, and Job.

Letter Order
An alphabetical order organizes the elements of a set of signs (an abjad, alphabet,
or abugida) in a specific sequence for mnemonic purposes. Only in fairly modern
times has alphabetization become a common way of organizing lists of information (in medieval Europe, only the first letter or two or three were taken into account in compiling such lists).

Two different orders, both with variations, are known for the letters of the
scripts used for Semitic; both seem to be completely arbitrary, despite numerous
attempts at uncovering a logical organizing principle, whether it be phonetic similarity, graphic similarity, or relationship of the meaning of the names. The parallels of known script inventions show that alphabetical order is simply the order in
which the characters were devised.

Table 2.4 Vocalization systems of the abjads†

Value	East Syriac		West Syriac		Hebrew		Arabic	
i	◌	ḥḇāṣā	◌	ḥḇāṣā	◌	ḥíreq	—ٍ (-̣-in)	kasra
e	◌	rḇāṣā karyā			◌	ṣērē		
ɛ	◌	rḇāṣā arrīḵā	◌	rḇāṣā	◌	səḡōl	—ً (-́-an)	fatḥa
a	◌	pṯāḥā	◌	pṯāḥā	◌	páṯaḥ		
ɔ	◌ (ā)	zqāp̄ā	◌	ṣāṣā	◌	qāmeṣ	آ (ʾā)	alif madda
o	◌	ʿṣāṣā rwīḥā	◌	zqāp̄ā	◌	ḥólem		
u	◌	ʿṣāṣā allīṣā	◌	ṣāṣā	◌	qibbūṣ	—ٌ (-́-un)	ḍamma
Ø					◌	šəwā	—ْ	sukūn
ə					◌	šəwā		
ě					◌	ḥāṭēp̄ səḡōl		
ă					◌	ḥāṭēp̄ páṯaḥ		
ŏ					◌	ḥāṭēp̄ qāmeṣ		

† Each symbol is shown alone and following *b*.

Northwest Semitic Order
The order with the earliest attestation is found at Ugarit. Several abecedaries have been recovered, and the order prevailing in them is:

ảbgḫdhwzḥṭykšlmδnẓsʿpṣqrθγtiủš

The three letters peculiar to Ugaritic are found at the end of the basic sequence (presumably added on to an earlier version, as has been the practice throughout history: compare upsilon through omega, Greek additions to the Semitic base, and U through Z, Roman additions to the Greek base). The twenty-two-letter Phoenician–Hebrew–Aramaic abjad uses the same order (attested earliest in a number of acrostic poems in the Bible, wherein successive verses begin with successive letters of the alphabet, e.g. Psalm 145), with the five superfluous letters ḫ š δ ẓ γ omitted. (The Canaanite š from whatever source is spelled with the letter used for *θ > /š/):

ʾbgdhwzḥṭyklmnsʿpṣqršt

A shakily written ostracon from ʿIzbet Ṣarṭah dating to the twelfth or early eleventh century BCE includes an approximation of the standard abecedary, but from left to right:

ʾbgdhwḥzṭyklnspʿṣqqšt

(Part of a sign is written between *l* and *n*; the two *q*'s are not the same, and *r* would have been quite similar to *q* about the time of writing.)

The suggestion that the twenty-two-letter signary is the original, with additional characters devised for Ugaritic, is most unlikely because, again, there is no pattern in either the shape or the "insertion" points of the five letters. Yet unexplained is the variant in some exemplars – including some of the biblical acrostics – which switch the order of ʿ and *p*.

The order of the Greek alphabet was taken over with the signary from the Phoenician (or Aramaic) model; the order of the Roman alphabet was taken over from the Greek via Etruscan (and so on through the history of European alphabets). In each case, local conditions brought additions at the end and alterations within the sequence.

Arabic order　The standard order of the letters in Classical Arabic is derived from the inherited Semitic pattern: the letters whose shapes have merged, to be distinguished only by diacritical dots, are listed together:

ʾbtθjḥḫ(=x)dδrzsšṣḍṭẓʿγfqklmnhwy

There is some regional variation regarding the last few letters; the ligature for *lā* can be added at the end.

Numerical order   The twenty-two letters of the Northwest Semitic signaries can be used as numbers (digits), in order with ' = 1 and *ṭ* = 9; the second decade of letters gives the tens, *y* = 10 through *ṣ* = 90; the last four represent 100 through 400. Numbers are built up by juxtaposing these elements, largest first (at the right). Any word can be "counted" – by summing or otherwise manipulating the values of its letters – and the resulting numbers enter into **gematria,** or mystical speculations.

The letters retain these numerical values in Arabic, despite the rearrangement; the letters taken in numerical order comprise the *abjad*. The six additional letters, *θ x δ ḍ ẓ γ*, appear at the end and represent 500 through 1,000 respectively.

Southwest Semitic Order

The Ethiopic abugida is learned in an order puzzlingly alien to that of the other Semitic signaries:

h l ḥ m š r s q b t ḫ n ' k w ʿ z y d g ṭ ṗ ṣ ḍ f p

In liturgical contexts, the Northwest Semitic order is used instead, apparently learned from the headings in Psalm 119. The order is called the *abugida*; the vowels in this name are taken from the first four orders of the traditional syllabary grid.

In recent years, evidence has been discovered of the conventional order of the Epigraphic South Arabian script (Table 2.5, p. 34): first in a sequence of paving stones, each marked with a different letter, then in some long-known but hitherto uninterpretable graffiti. The order is as follows:

h l ḥ m q w s² r b t s¹ k n ḫ ṣ s³ f ' ʿ ḍ g d γ ṭ z δ y θ ẓ

An abecedary excavated at Ras Shamra (Ugarit) in 1988 (Bordreuil and Pardee 1995) can be interpreted as giving the cuneiform abjad in the following order, in substantial agreement with one from Beth Shemesh that dates to about 1200 BCE:

h l ḥ m q w θ r b t š k n ḫ ṣ s p ' ʿ ẓ g d γ ṭ z δ y

The similarities and differences of the "southern" order with the Ethiopic are striking, and unexplained.

Letter Names

Contrary to received opinion, there is no evidence that the names of the letters of the Semitic signaries go back to the creation of the scripts. The earliest attestation is the headings over the twenty-two sections of the long acrostic Psalm 119 as transcribed into Greek in the Septuagint translation of the Hebrew Bible, from about the second century BCE. They thus cannot be used for deciphering the Proto-

Table 2.5   Scripts using South Semitic order

Value[†]	Ugaritic	South Arabian	(cf. Ethiopic)
h			
l			
ḥ			
m			
q			
w			
s^2 (θ)			
r			
b			
t			
s^1 (š)			
k			
n			
ḫ			
ṣ			
s^3 (s)			
f (p)			
ʾ			
ʿ			
ḍ (ẓ)			
g			
d			
ɣ			
ṭ			
z			
δ			
y			
θ			
ẓ			

† (Ugaritic value)

Table 2.6   Letter names

Hebrew	Greek	Syriac	Arabic	Ethiopic
ʾā́lep̄	alpha	ʾālap̄	ʾalif	älf
bḗt	bēta	bēt	bāʾ	bet
gī́mel	gamma	gāmal	ǰīm	gäml
dā́let	delta	dālat/d	dāl	dänt
hē	e psilon	hē	hāʾ	hoi
wāw	u psilon	waw	wāw	wäwe
záyin	zēta	zay(n)	zāy	zäi
ḥḗt	ēta	ḥēt	ḥāʾ	ḥaut
ṭēt	thēta	ṭēt	ṭāʾ	ṭäit
yṓd	iota	yō/ūd	yāʾ	yämän
kāp̄	kappa	kāp̄	kāf	kaf
lā́med	la(m)bda	lāmad	lām	läwə
mēm	mu	mīm	mīm	mai
nūn	nu	nūn	nūn	nähas
sā́mek	sigma	semkat	sīn	sat
ʿáyin	o micron	ʿē	ʿayn	ʿäin
pē	pi	pē	fāʾ	äf
ṣādē		ṣādē	ṣād	ṣädäi
qōp̄	(qoppa)	qōp̄	qāf	qaf
rēš	rhō	rēš	rāʾ	rəʾəs
šīn/śīn	(san)	šīn	šīn	šäut
tāw	tau	taw	tāʾ	täwə
			θāʾ	
			ḫāʾ	ḫärm
			ðāl	
			ḍād	ḍäppa
			ẓāʾ	
			ɣayn	
				p̣äit
				psa

Sinaitic inscriptions or as evidence of the alleged acrophonic origin of the values or conversely of the shapes of the Semitic signary. In particular, the divergences of the Ethiopic letter names from those in Hebrew and Syriac cannot be shown to pre-date the (European) Renaissance; these names seem to have been devised by or for Ethiopian clerics at the suggestion of European scholars on the basis of the Hebrew lexicon. (Thus the name of ፻ n, *nähas*, cannot be explained from Ethiopic, but represents a Hebrew word for 'snake'. And this is the only basis for supposing that a picture of a snake in the Proto-Sinaitic inscriptions represents /n/.)

The same names, with slight variations, are used in the Hebrew and Aramaic traditions. Most of the Ethiopic names agree, though less closely. Most of the Arabic letters are named simply for their sounds, but some preserve an echo of the Northwest Semitic originals (Table 2.6 above).

The final -*a* of the meaningless, Semitic-derived Greek letter names has been taken as evidence of an Aramaic rather than a Phoenician source of the alphabet (reflecting the Aramaic "emphatic state" marker), but the suffix can be explained equally well as an intrusion to make the final cluster pronounceable in Greek.

Alphabets

Mandaic

Mandaic orthography has usually been regarded as alphabetic, the only Semitic script that fully expresses the vowels without the addition of a separate, optional system of vocalization. It employs the familiar twenty-two letters, plus a digraph for the relative particle *di*. It has extended the use of *matres lectionis* nearly as far as possible, but does not quite explicitly and exhaustively record all vowels. The language has lost the glottal stop and the pharyngeals, so the letters ⟍ *ʾ and ⟍ *ʿ are available for other functions ([h] is spelled with ⟍ *ḥ, and ⟍ *h is used exclusively for the third person singular suffix). All [a]'s are represented by ⟍ *a*, all [i]'s by ⟍ *i* (final [i(:)] is ⟍), and all [u]'s by ⟍ *u*. But [o] is also written with ⟍ *u*, and the use of ⟍ and the representation of [e] are complicated. ⟍ appears at the start of any word that begins with a vowel other than [a]: alone for [e] (but initial [e] seems only to be a prothetic vowel before the *t*-prefix in the passive verbs or before a monoconsonantal word), or before ⟍ or ⟍ for initial [i] or [u] respectively. Within a word, [e], like [i], is spelled with ⟍ – except that when two adjacent ⟍'s would result, they are replaced by ⟍; and ⟍ is preferred to ⟍ after the consonants that have a point below the line (⟍ *k*, ⟍ *n*, ⟍ *p*, ⟍ *ṣ*; these enter into ligatures when they precede letters with a vertical right edge, e.g. ⟍ *kl*, ⟍ *nm*); and ⟍ can be used in place of ⟍ when it represents word-final [i:] (and not [ja]).

Roman

Two Semitic languages have regularly used as a script an expanded Roman alphabet, Maltese and Modern Aramaic.

Maltese

Since Malta, a small group of islands in the Mediterranean Sea between Italy and Tunisia, falls within the Italian culture area and is a Christian land, it is not surprising that the Roman alphabet came to be used for its Arabic language, beginning in at least the eighteenth century (Table 2.7, p. 37). (Before the expulsion of the Jews from Malta in 1492, Maltese was occasionally written in Hebrew characters.)

Modern Aramaic

Assyrian of the Soviet Union   Language policy in the Soviet Union required that all recognized literary languages be provided with an alphabetic orthography – first Roman, then Cyrillic. The Modern Aramaic ("Assyrian") language of the Caucasus region (adjacent to parts of Iran and Turkey where Aramaic-speakers also lived) underwent the first stage of literacization, but not the second. A Roman-based alphabet was in use for a few years in the mid 1930s; it is now known that some two hundred books in this orthography are housed in the Lenin Library in Moscow, but scientific knowledge is practically confined to a handful of literary works made available to Johannes Friedrich in 1942 and described by him in

Table 2.7	Maltese		Table 2.8	Soviet Assyrian		Table 2.9	Turoyo of Sweden	
Letter		Semitists' equivalent	Letter		Semitists' equivalent	Letter		Semitists' equivalent
A	a	a	A	a	a	A	a	a
B	b	b	B	в	b	B	b	b
Ċ	ċ	č	C	c	č	C	c	ʿ
D	d	d	Ç	ç	ǰ	Ĉ	ĉ	č
E	e	e	D	d	d	D	d	δ
F	f	f	E	e	e	Ḍ	ḍ	δ̣
Ġ	ġ	ǰ	Ə	ə	ä	Ḍ	ḍ	δ̣
G	g	g	F	f	f	E	e	e
H	h	†	G	g	g	Ë	ë	ı
Ħ	ħ	ḥ	H	h	h	F	f	f
I	i	i	I	i	i	G	g	g
J	j	y	J	j	y	Ĝ	ĝ	γ
K	k	k	K	k	k(ʰ)	H	h	h
L	l	l	L	l	l	Ḥ	ḥ	ḥ
M	m	m	M	m	m	I	i	i
N	n	n	N	n	n	J	j	ǰ
Għ	għ	§	O	o	o	K	k	k
O	o	o	P	p	p	L	l	l
P	p	p	Q	q	q	M	m	m
Q	q	ʾ	R	r	r	N	n	n
R	r	r	S	s	s	O	o	o
S	s	s	Ş	ş	š	P	p	p
T	t	t	T	t	t(ʰ)	Q	q	q
U	u	u	Ţ	ţ	ṭ	R	r	r
V	v	v	U	u	u	S	s	s
W	w	w	V	v	w	Ṣ	ṣ	ṣ
X	x	š	X	x	ḥ (ḫ)	Ŝ	ŝ	š
Ż	ż	z	Z	z	z	T	t	t
Z	z	ts	Ẓ	ẓ	ž	Ṭ	ṭ	ṭ
			ʙ	ь	ı	T	ţ	θ
						U	u	u
						W	w	u
						X	x	ḫ
						Y	y	i
						Z	z	z
						Ẑ	ẑ	ž

† Silent except finally = *h* and in the digraphs *għh* and *ħh* = *ḥ*.

§ Silent, representing CA ʿ; replaced by ' finally and after *a*.

1959. A grammar using this orthography was recently translated into French, but the Assyrian text is not given in that edition.

The alphabet comprises thirty letters (Table 2.8, p. 37). The divergences from the Roman norm coincide with those used in the Azerbaijani Roman script. Capital letters appear in Friedrich's edition where they would in French (sentence initially and beginning proper nouns), and punctuation is as in German.

Orthography is largely surface phonetic; unlike the Syriac-based orthography of Modern Aramaic, it permits the recognition of vowel harmony on the page (*ə* and *i* are the "clear" vowels, *a* and *ʙ* the "dark," with *e*, *o*, and *u* intermediate). The only vowel for which length is notated is *i* (*ij/ʙj*). *ʾ* (and *ʾ* < *ʿ*) is not marked.

Turoyo of Sweden   During the 1970s a sizable community of Turoyo-speaking gastarbeiters and refugees came to Sweden, and the Swedish government set to providing for the education of their children. In 1981 Dr. Yusuf Ishaq was commissioned to create a Roman orthography for the language, and his scheme (Table 2.9, p. 37) has been used in readers and a dictionary (see Ishaq 1990); Otto Jastrow (1996) reports, however, that it has not found acceptance in the Turoyo community of Sweden.

Abugida

The Geʿez script encodes twenty-six consonants and seven vowels (Table 2.10, p. 39). The basic shape of each consonant represents *Cä*; this shape is altered in a largely consistent fashion to change the vowel of the syllable to *u*, *i*, *a*, *e*, *ə*, and *o* respectively. There is, however, no unambiguous means of indicating that a consonant is followed by no vowel (either introducing a consonant cluster or syllable-finally) or that it is lengthened ("doubled").

In addition to the inherited and innovated simple consonants, Geʿez also employs a diacritic to mark the labiovelar consonants. The labiovelar feature is neutralized before rounded vowels, so there are only five forms for each of the four labiovelar consonants.

The Amharic script adds to the Geʿez script a series denoting the palatalized consonants, again by means of a consistent diacritic.

Geʿez manuscripts do not consistently distinguish the sibilants, laryngeals, etc., which merged in the language, using the *ʾ* and *ʿ* characters, the *ṣ* and *ḍ* characters, and so on, interchangeably; lexica by modern scholars assign letters consistently according to etymology. Amharic orthography is to some extent historical, writing etymological full spellings of some words that have cliticized into grammatical particles.

Numerals

Mesopotamian mathematics was highly developed, and cuneiform numeral notation combines decimal and sexagesimal elements. Place notation enabled the efficient recording of very large numbers, but there was no explicit zero.

Table 2.10   Script using modified South Semitic order (Ethiopic/Amharic)

| | *Classical Ethiopic* | | | | | | | | *Additional letters for Amharic* | | | | | | | | |
	ä	u	i	a	e	ə	o	ʷa		ä	u	i	a	e	ə	o	ʷa
h	ሀ	ሁ	ሂ	ሃ	ሄ	ህ	ሆ										
l	ለ	ሉ	ሊ	ላ	ሌ	ል	ሎ	ሏ									
ḥ	ሐ	ሑ	ሒ	ሓ	ሔ	ሕ	ሖ										
m	መ	ሙ	ሚ	ማ	ሜ	ም	ሞ	ሟ									
š	ሠ	ሡ	ሢ	ሣ	ሤ	ሥ	ሦ										
r	ረ	ሩ	ሪ	ራ	ሬ	ር	ሮ	ሯ									ⶌ riyä
s	ሰ	ሱ	ሲ	ሳ	ሴ	ስ	ሶ	ሷ	š	ሸ	ሹ	ሺ	ሻ	ሼ	ሽ	ሾ	
q	ቀ	ቁ	ቂ	ቃ	ቄ	ቅ	ቆ										
qʷ	ቈ		ቊ	ቋ	ቌ	ቍ											
b	በ	ቡ	ቢ	ባ	ቤ	ብ	ቦ	ቧ									
t	ተ	ቱ	ቲ	ታ	ቴ	ት	ቶ	ቷ	č	ቸ	ቹ	ቺ	ቻ	ቼ	ች	ቾ	ቿ
ḫ	ኀ	ኁ	ኂ	ኃ	ኄ	ኅ	ኆ										
ḫʷ	ኈ		ኊ	ኋ	ኌ	ኍ											
n	ነ	ኑ	ኒ	ና	ኔ	ን	ኖ	ኗ	ñ	ኘ	ኙ	ኚ	ኛ	ኜ	ኝ	ኞ	ኟ
ʾ	አ	ኡ	ኢ	ኣ	ኤ	እ	ኦ										ኧ ä
k	ከ	ኩ	ኪ	ካ	ኬ	ክ	ኮ		ḫ	ኸ	ኹ	ኺ	ኻ	ኼ	ኽ	ኾ	ዀ
kʷ	ኰ		ኲ	ኳ	ኴ	ኵ											
w	ወ	ዉ	ዊ	ዋ	ዌ	ው	ዎ										
ʿ	ዐ	ዑ	ዒ	ዓ	ዔ	ዕ	ዖ										
z	ዘ	ዙ	ዚ	ዛ	ዜ	ዝ	ዞ	ዟ	ž	ዠ	ዡ	ዢ	ዣ	ዤ	ዥ	ዦ	ዧ
y	የ	ዩ	ዪ	ያ	ዬ	ይ	ዮ										
d	ደ	ዱ	ዲ	ዳ	ዴ	ድ	ዶ	ዷ	ǰ	ጀ	ጁ	ጂ	ጃ	ጄ	ጅ	ጆ	ጇ
g	ገ	ጉ	ጊ	ጋ	ጌ	ግ	ጎ										
gʷ	ጐ		ጒ	ጓ	ጔ	ጕ											
ṭ	ጠ	ጡ	ጢ	ጣ	ጤ	ጥ	ጦ	ጧ	č̣	ጨ	ጩ	ጪ	ጫ	ጬ	ጭ	ጮ	ጯ
p̣	ጰ	ጱ	ጲ	ጳ	ጴ	ጵ	ጶ										
ṣ	ጸ	ጹ	ጺ	ጻ	ጼ	ጽ	ጾ	ጿ									
ḍ	ፀ	ፁ	ፂ	ፃ	ፄ	ፅ	ፆ										
f	ፈ	ፉ	ፊ	ፋ	ፌ	ፍ	ፎ	ፏ									
p	ፐ	ፑ	ፒ	ፓ	ፔ	ፕ	ፖ										

Table 2.11   Numerals

	Greek	Ethiopic	Arabic
0			٠
1	A	፩	١
2	B	፪	٢
3	Γ	፫	٣
4	Δ	፬	٤
5	E	፭	٥
6	Ϛ	፮	٦
7	Z	፯	٧
8	H	፰	٨
9	Θ	፱	٩
10	I	፲	١٠
20	K	፳	٢٠
30	Λ	፴	٣٠
40	M	፵	٤٠
50	N	፶	٥٠
60	Ξ	፷	٦٠
70	O	፸	٧٠
80	Π	፹	٨٠
90	Ϙ	፺	٩٠
100	P	፻	١٠٠
10,000	PP	፼	١٠٠٠٠

The numerals occasionally found in ancient West Semitic texts reflect Demotic Egyptian practice, with vertical strokes for units, horizontal strokes for tens, and some other symbols. The Hebrew, Syriac, and Arabic scripts can still (in non-scientific contexts) use the letters for the numerical values derived from their traditional order. The Ethiopic script likewise uses a set of numerals taken from an alphabet – but in this case it is the Greek alphabet, reshaped to conform to the Ethiopian esthetic (Table 2.11 above).

With the development of mathematics in the Muslim world, on an Indian foundation, in the late eighth century CE, the *hindi* numerals were adopted in forms quite similar to our "Arabic" (or "Hindu–Arabic") numerals, which are directly derived from them. Numbers are built up decimally, with the larger place values at the left (as with European numerals); so also when European-style numerals are used in Hebrew and Aramaic texts.

Writing Materials and Techniques

Mesopotamia and Ugarit

The earliest known writing material used for Semitic languages is clay. Surprisingly little is known about the collection and preparation of the clay used in tablets. The writing implement was a stylus with at least one sharp corner. The wedges that make up cuneiform characters are created by lightly touching it to the clay; the different orientations of wedges (only a few enter into signs) are achieved by rotating both the hand holding the stylus and the hand holding the tablet. Lines could be ruled on the tablet before writing by touching the surface with a taut string of some sort.

Short texts were written on small tablets. When the front (obverse) was filled, the tablet was rotated on the horizontal axis so the first line of the reverse adjoins the last line of the obverse. Longer texts could be written in several columns. The columns read from left to right on the obverse of the tablet; when the obverse was filled, the tablet was rotated similarly and the columns on the reverse written right to left (so the first column on the back adjoins the last column on the front). Short dedications could be mass-produced by impressing them into the bricks for a palace or temple with a wooden or ceramic stamp containing a full text.

Clay hardens, making the document relatively permanent. Wooden boards coated with wax (which took the stylus impressions equally well and was reusable) were apparently widely used for interim record keeping, though only one specimen has survived sufficiently intact to preserve a text. Cuneiform could be imitated by carving into the stone of building materials. Sometimes triangular outlines were incised on bronze; a few commemorative tablets have been found made of gold, which is soft enough to take a stylus impression.

Syro-Palestine and Arabia

The principal medium for writing the abjad was ink, used on papyrus, skin (prepared as leather by tanning or as parchment by liming and scraping) and potsherds. The organic materials can only survive in exceptionally dessicated climates such as prevail in Egypt and the Judean Desert; potsherds (which when inscribed are called ostraca) are not subject to decay, but are fragile, and not many have survived.

Specimens of the ink that have been analyzed always prove to be inorganic: soot, presumably lampblack, was mixed with water and a bit of binder, such as gum arabic, for ordinary black ink; red was made with a mineral, red ocher. The pen was cut from a round, hollow reed with a technique that has varied little through the ages, even as birds' flight feathers began to supplement and in some regions supplant reeds.

Papyrus paper, imported from Egypt, was made from the pith of a tall sedge. This was shaved or sliced into long strips, which were laid edge to edge, then covered with a second layer of strips laid perpendicular to the first, the whole pressed together so the material was bonded with the sap of the plant. When it dried, it provided a very white, flexible surface. Typically, twenty sheets were glued into a scroll, and it could be written upon on both sides. The codex (book with pages) was in use by the second century CE, associated particularly with Christian (as opposed to pagan or secular) writings.

It is not known how early leather and/or parchment came into use. One group of Aramaic documents from the fifth century BCE is leather (most are papyrus). By the fourth century CE, parchment was widespread (though papyrus remained in use beyond the end of the millennium).

When the Islamic conquest reached Inner Asia, in the middle of the eighth century CE, the craft of papermaking came from China to the West. Paper was made only from textile fibers until the nineteenth century, when wood pulp paper was introduced (to the despair of contemporary archivists, as the acids involved in its manufacture eventually embrittle the paper itself). It was paper that ultimately filled the need created by the diminution of the papyrus supply as the marshes where it grew were replaced by cultivated fields.

Printing

Printing from movable type, too, may reflect a Chinese stimulus to European culture. The first Latin books were produced in the mid-fifteenth century; vernacular printing soon followed, and then various Semitic languages. The earliest reported dates for printing are: Hebrew (first Rashi style, and a few months later Square Hebrew) 1475, Arabic 1514 (first Qur'an 1518, earliest known Qur'an 1537, but not until centuries later in any Muslim land), Ethiopic 1513, Syriac 1555 and Samaritan 1632 (Hessels 1911: 540).

During the nineteenth century, typefonts were cut for various epigraphic versions of the abjad (and for cuneiform), but they have been little used because the limited array of lettershapes cannot be faithful to the variations found in the texts. Transliteration into Hebrew or Roman characters is preferred. Mandaic type was available by 1900, but editions almost always used Hebrew letters, or reproduced manuscripts photolithographically.

Modifying typewriters to print Hebrew and Arabic from right to left was not a challenge, but reducing the inventory of contextual forms required for adequately representing Arabic (and Syriac) was. Even Amharic could be typed, using two or three strokes per letter. Hebrew and Arabic could be typed on personal computers (or their forerunners) – though not yet with vowel pointing – in the 1970s; Ethiopic in the late 1980s; and in the 1990s, Syriac (three varieties, with pointing), Mandaic, and even Neo-Assyrian cuneiform.

Study of Scripts of Semitic Languages

Decipherment

The classical Semitic languages that are the vehicles of scripture in many religions remained in use across the centuries, and manuscripts in them, each language in its proper script, were known to Europe all along, or were brought there along with scholarly instruction in how to read them: Hebrew, Syriac, Arabic, and also Mandaic and Ge'ez. All the other scripts, though, were recovered by archeology and needed to be deciphered.

The most important prerequisite for the decipherment of any unknown script is **accurate copies** of the enigmatic inscriptions; work begins with identification of a bilingual or virtual bilingual to provide the key. A **bilingual** is a document bearing what can be presumed to be the same inscription in both the unknown language and a familiar one; a **virtual bilingual** is a correspondence that can reliably be assumed between some passage in the unknown text and some phenomenon that is familiar. Choice of an appropriate virtual bilingual is often the key test of the spark of genius required of a decipherer. An unknown script can also be read by "triangulating" from known related scripts; in this case, it is important to have a good idea of the identity and nature of the hidden language.

Many methods of decipherment have come into play with respect to Semitic languages. The first task is to compile a catalog of all the characters in the unknown script. A short list suggests an abjad or alphabet, as in the case of Palmyrene, which was the very first script ever to be deciphered. This was done in 1754 by the French classicist Jean-Jacques Barthélemy – he was the first to read Phoenician, too. If one is fortunate enough to be faced with a bilingual, one hopes it includes proper names and that they can be identified in the unknown script. This was true of the first accurately reproduced Palmyrene/Greek inscriptions. Proper names also constituted the virtual bilingual used by the German schoolteacher Georg Friedrich Grotefend in his interpretation of Old Persian cuneiform, which in turn became the key to Akkadian because Achaemenid imperial inscriptions were erected in three languages (including Elamite). It was an Irish cleric, Edward Hincks, who between 1846 and 1852 made most of the advances in deciphering Mesopotamian cuneiform. He determined that several quite different-looking varieties were equivalent, that signs represented syllables but could have both phonetic and semantic readings – and several of each (and he explained why this was the case), and that Semitic morphological patterns could be used in assigning phonetic values to signs. (The pervasive assignment of credit to Henry Creswicke Rawlinson is due to the obscurity both of Hincks and of the venues in which he published his progress reports, and to Rawlinson's own celebrity.) The distribution of letters at the beginnings and ends of words compared with Hebrew prefixes and suffixes, as well as grammatical patterning, were the techniques used by Hans Bauer, Édouard Dhorme, Charles Virolleaud, and Johannes Friedrich from 1929 to 1933 in deciphering Ugaritic. Alphabets preserved in manuscripts by Muslim antiquarians, as well as information on a Modern South Arabian language, were used by Emil Rödiger and Wilhelm Gesenius in the initial work on Himyaritic (Epigraphic South Arabian) in 1837–1842. As new inscriptions are discovered, such comparison with known scripts and known linguistic varieties is generally how they can be interpreted – the field of epigraphy.

Epigraphy

Semitic epigraphy began in a small way with Barthélemy's decipherment of the principal scripts found on rock inscriptions. An influential synthesis, now very rare and never reprinted, was prepared in the early nineteenth century by Ulrich Friedrich Kopp; Wilhelm Gesenius in 1837 gathered and reproduced what was known of Phoenician and Aramaic inscriptions. Much new material was gathered by nineteenth-century explorers like le Comte de Vogüé; Mark Lidzbarski's *Handbuch der nordsemitischen Epigraphik* remains an invaluable synthesis. The *Corpus Inscriptionum Semiticarum* is nominally still in the course of publication, by the French Académie des Inscriptions et Belles Lettres.

The main current collections of texts useful for individual study, but restricted to Northwest Semitic, are *Kanaanäische und aramäische Inschriften*, edited by H. Donner and W. Röllig, and *Syrian Semitic Inscriptions*, edited by J. C. L. Gibson.

Paleography

Within Semitic studies, little differentiation is made to parallel that within classical studies between epigraphy, the study of inscriptions, and paleography, the study of manuscripts. Only Arabic and Hebrew paleography can be said to be well developed. For Arabic, the pioneer was Silvestre de Sacy at the end of the eighteenth century; great names from the modern period include B. Moritz, A. Grohmann, and N. Abbott. Nabia Abbott specialized in the study of Arabic papyri preserved in the Cairo Geniza.

Hebrew paleography has centered on two topics: medieval manuscripts (an elaborate corpus was published by S. R. Birnbaum) and the Dead Sea Scrolls (where the leading systematizer has been F. M. Cross). The sizable corpus of Aramaic papyri (and leather scrolls) from Egypt, many of which bear explicit dates, provides a solid foundation for these investigations.

Microfilm archives that could prove valuable in investigating the paleography of Syriac and Ethiopic manuscripts respectively have been assembled at the Lutheran School of Theology in Chicago (by the late Arthur Vööbus) and at the Hill Monastic Library, St. John's University, Collegeville, Minnesota, under the care of Getatchew Haile. Mandaic manuscripts have been preserved by Mandean clergy in Iraq, and the Swedish-American scholar Jorunn Buckley has focused her studies on them.

References

Abbott, Nabia. 1939. *The Rise of the North Arabic Script and Its Ḳurʾānic Development* (Oriental Institute Publications 50). Chicago: University of Chicago Press.
—— 1941. "Arabic Paleography." *Ars Islamica* 8: 65–104.
Birnbaum, Solomon R. 1957–1971. *The Hebrew Scripts*, 2 vols. London: Palaeographica; Leiden: Brill.
Bordreuil, Pierre, and Dennis Pardee. 1995 [pub. 1997]. "Un Abécédaire du type sud-sémitique découvert en 1988 dans les fouilles archéologiques françaises de Ras Shamra–Ougarit." Académie des Inscriptions et Belles Lettres (Paris), *Comptes Rendus.* 855–860.

Cross, Frank M., Jr. 1961. "The Development of the Jewish Scripts." In *The Bible and the Ancient Near East: Essays in Honor of William Foxwell Albright*, ed. G. Ernest Wright. Garden City, N.Y.: Doubleday. 133–202.

Daniels, Peter T. 1983. "Semitic Scripts." In *Introduction to the Semitic Languages: Text Specimens and Grammatical Sketches*, by Gotthelf Bergsträsser, trans. Peter T. Daniels. Winona Lake, Ind.: Eisenbrauns. 236–260.

Donner, Herbert and Wolfgang Röllig. 1968–1971. *Kanaanäische und aramäische Inschriften*, 2nd–3rd edn, 3 vols. Wiesbaden: Harrassowitz.

Friedrich, Johannes. 1959. "Neusyrisches in Lateinschrift aus der Sowjetunion." *Zeitschrift der Deutschen Morgenländischen Gesellschaft* 109: 50–81.

Gesenius, Wilhelm. 1837. *Scripturae linguaeque phoeniciae monumenta quotquot supersunt*. Leipzig: Vogel.

Gibson, John C. L. 1971–1982. *Textbook of Syrian Semitic Inscriptions*, 3 vols. Oxford: Clarendon Press.

Grohmann, Adolf. 1967–1971. *Arabische Paläographie*, 2 vols. Vienna: Österreichische Akademie der Wissenschaften.

Hessels, John Henry. 1911. "Typography: History." *Encyclopædia Britannica*, 11th edn. 27: 509–542.

Ishaq, Yusuf. 1990. "Turoyo: From Spoken to Written Language." In *Studies in Neo-Aramaic* (Harvard Semitic Studies 36), ed. Wolfhart Heinrichs. Atlanta: Scholars Press.

Jastrow, Otto. 1996. "The Project of a Comprehensive Turoyo Dictionary." Paper presented at the 24th North American Conference on Afroasiatic Linguistics, Philadelphia.

Klugkist, Alexander C. 1982. "Midden-aramese schriften in Syrië, Mesopotamië, Persië en aangrenzende gebieden." Doctoral dissertation, University of Groningen.

Kopp, Ulrich Friedrich. 1821. *Bilder und Schriften der Vorzeit*, 2 vols. Mannheim.

Lidzbarski, Mark. 1898. *Handbuch der nordsemitischen Epigraphik*, 2 vols. Weimar: Felber.

Moritz, B. 1905. *Arabische Paläographie*. Cairo: Bibliothèque khédiviale.

Silvestre de Sacy, Antoine Isaac. 1825. "Mémoires sur quelques papyrus écrits en arabe et récemment découverts en Égypte." *Journal des Savants*, 462–473.

Taylor, Isaac. 1883. *The Alphabet: An Account of the Origin and Development of Letters*, 2 vols. London: Kegan Paul, Trench.

Further Reading

For fuller bibliographies, see the relevant sections in Parts 2, 3, and 8 of Daniels and Bright (1996).

Daniels, Peter T. 1995. "The Decipherment of Ancient Near Eastern Scripts." In *Civilizations of the Ancient Near East*, ed. Jack M. Sasson. New York: Scribners. 81–93.

Daniels, Peter T., and William Bright, eds. 1996. *The World's Writing Systems*. New York: Oxford University Press.

Diringer, David. 1968. *The Alphabet: A Key to the History of Mankind*, 3rd edn., 2 vols. New York: Funk and Wagnalls.

Driver, G. R. 1976. *Semitic Writing*, 3rd edn, ed. S. A. Hopkins. London: Oxford University Press.

Gordon, Cyrus H. 1982. *Forgotten Scripts: Their Ongoing Discovery and Decipherment*, rev. edn, New York: Basic Books.

Jensen, Hans. 1969. *Sign, Symbol and Script*, 3rd edn, trans. George Unwin. London: George Allen and Unwin.

Naveh, Joseph. 1987. *Early History of the Alphabet*, 2nd edn. Jerusalem: Magnes.

Pope, Maurice. 1975. *The Story of Archaeological Decipherment: From Egyptian Hieroglyphs to Linear B*. New York: Scribners.

3 The Arabic Grammatical Tradition

Jonathan Owens

The Arabic grammatical tradition, over 1,000 years old, continues to serve as the basis of Arabic grammatical practice in the Arabic world, and through translations such as Howell's of Ibn Ya'ish and Caspari/Wright's reliance on Arabic grammars, has had a fundmental influence on the Western study of Arabic grammar as well. Though old, the Arabic tradition is not anachronistic, as I will attempt to show. I divide this chapter into four parts. The first discusses the development of Arabic grammatical thinking, the second sketches grammatical theory and methodology, the third Arabic lexicography, and the final briefly looks at it in relation to Semitic studies. I would note that the dates of death of the Arabic grammarians are given in the Islamic/Christian calendars. Literal translations of Arabic linguistic terminology are provided in quotes.

Historical Overview

The study of Arabic grammar developed under two driving impulses, one religious, one practical. The religious motivation was the need to render a correct interpretation of the Qur'an both in its formal and semantic dimensions. The original muṣḥaf, Qur'anic text, unvoweled and lacking diacritic marks, was subject to ambiguous interpretation in numerous places and for various reasons (lexical form, *xufyatan* vs. *xifyatan* 'secretly', morphosyntactic form, *li-tastabiyna/li-ya-stabiyna* 'to become clear', etc.). These problematic cases were never completely "solved," but they were eventually resolved by standardizing them in various Qur'anic readings (*al-qiraa'aat*), which gave list-like descriptions of the different versions of each variant case. The most widely institutionalized, though not the only variants, are the seven readings described by Ibn Mujahid (324/935) in his *Kitaab al-sabʿa fiy l-qiraa'aat* 'The seven variant readings'. These confirmed the readings of the late eighth-century Qur'anic readers Nafi', Ibn Kathir, 'Asim, Hamza, Kisa'i, 'Ala', and 'Amir, all of whom have a lineage (*nasab*) traceable to a companion of the prophet.

For purposes of linguistic theory, however, the *qiraa'aat* are of relatively minor interest since they did little more than list variants. Much more important in the religious domain were works which gave grammatical and semantic analyses of problematic Qur'anic passages, the *maʿaaniy* ('meanings') literature. In this genre problems of all sorts were addressed and various solutions offered, including questions of pronunciation, morphological and grammatical structure, and semantics. One of the earliest and most important works in this class, *Maʿaaniy al-qurʾaan* 'The meanings of the Qur'an', by Farra' (207/822) takes as its second topic, for example, the different pronunciations of the words *al-ḥamdu lillaahi* in the opening verse of the Qur'an. In all there are four different versions, the one cited, plus *al-ḥamda lillaahi*, *al-ḥamdi lillaahi*, and *al-ḥamdu lullaahi*. Most importantly, Farra' explains the linguistic cause for these variants, e.g. vocalic assimilation, cites parallel cases from other areas of the language (both the spoken language, particularly that of the bedouin, and poetry), and touches on questions of morphological analysis, in particular, word division. The *maʿaaniy* literature is a rich source for our understanding of linguistic thinking, with Farra' in particular playing a central role.

The second driving force in the development of an Arabic linguistic tradition was the pedagogical. One tradition has it, in fact, that Arabic grammar was born in response to this need. Grammar was founded when the linguist Abu Aswad al-Du'ali (68/668) heard his daughter say *maa ʾaḥsanu* 'what is more beautiful?' when she intended to say *maa ʾaḥsana* 'how beautiful is ...'. Horrified at her bad grammar, he established a grammatical system based upon the three inflectional endings of Arabic, so that such mistakes would not be repeated. Whatever the truth of this story, it was clear that pedagogical material for the teaching of Arabic was needed, not least for the Arabs themselves, most of whom were illiterate and hence unready for the administrative tasks which their new conquests had thrust upon them, as well as for the many non-Arabs who formed the backbone of the early civil service. Though languages other than Arabic were used in the earliest periods of Arab rule, the use of Arabic increased steadily over time.

The first extant grammar of Arabic is *al-Kitaab* 'The book' by Sibawayhi (177/793), himself a Persian. It is a prodigious work of nearly 1,000 densely written pages. While this book is itself unsuitable as pedagogical material (Carter 1972), it does have a strongly normative character (Ditters 1992: 17) and is so detailed that in it virtually every major aspect of classical Arabic grammar is defined. All later grammars effectively rely on the *Kitaab* both for their content as well as their theoretical orientation (see next section).

The question of the origins of the Arabic grammatical tradition is one which has been an issue for Western arabicists for over 100 years, and after a mid-century hiatus in the debate, it has again come to the fore in the last 25 years. It is far from being resolved. There are two main issues. First, to what extent did the Arabic grammatical tradition develop on its own or, alternatively, under the influence of other traditions? Second, when did Arabic grammatical theory come into being at all?

The prime issue in the first part of the question concerns the extent to which the

Arabic grammarians were dependent upon earlier Middle Eastern grammatical traditions in the development of their linguistic thinking. Particularly important is the role of the Greek tradition. Carter (1972) asserted that the influence of the Greek tradition was limited, arguing that the considerable Greek intellectual influence in Arabic culture came via translations of Greek works, and that these translations became available *en masse* after the end of the eighth century, by which time the Arabic grammatical tradition had already taken on a more or less fixed structure. Instead, the Arabic tradition developed largely under an internal impetus, in which, in particular, Islamic legal terminology and concepts provided a rich source of analogy for the linguistic (see also Fleisch 1994).

Against this, Versteegh (1977) sees the Greek tradition as having a key role, even in the formative stages of Arabic linguistic thinking. The influence, however, came not from the officially supported translations, but rather from a living Greek pedagogical tradition which the Arabs encountered in the conquered Greek territories. Furthermore, Versteegh suggests that the Arabic grammarians may have taken over certain methodological practices from the tradition of Greek empirical medicine. Moreover, Rundgren (1976: 140) has observed that Greek translations may have been available in Syriac or Persian in the conquered Persian territories before the later large-scale Greek translations into Arabic.

It is not a contradiction to say that both viewpoints have cogency. The Arabic grammatical tradition, as early as 200/800, had a depth and detail hardly to be accounted for in terms of borrowing. At the same time, certain similarities exist between aspects of Greek pedagogical grammar and Arabic practice which make independent development an implausible explanation. Progress is unfortunately hampered in answering the question of extent of outside influence by the relative dearth of original Greek sources.

The second question, period of origin, is one which had already been documented in considerable detail by the Arabic grammarians themselves. One example of this documentation, concerning Abu Aswad Al-Du'ali, was cited above. The most important constructs postulated by the Arabic grammarians for explaining the origins of the Arabic grammatical tradition were the existence of two linguistic schools, the Kufan and the Basran. According to this, the earliest Arabic grammarians were aligned in two opposing schools, one centered in Basra, the other in Kufa (near modern Najaf in Iraq). The chief protagonists were Xalil and Sibawayhi for the Basrans and Kisa'i and Farra' for the Kufans, though virtually all of the early grammarians were categorized as belonging to one school or the other. According to one popular view, a major methodological difference separating the two was that the Basrans tended to favor the use of analogy in solving linguistic problems, while the Kufans put greater emphasis on the existence of exceptions to general rules.

The historical existence of the two schools, as described in the Arabic tradition, was challenged in the early part of this century by Weil (1913), who argued that the two schools were the creation of fourth/tenth-century grammarians such as Mubarrad and Sarraj. In the need to systematize Arabic grammar, they were confronted by the fact that in the earlier period, particularly in the main works of Sibawayhi and Farra', differences of terminology and concept were found. The general labels of Basran and Kufan were then applied to these ideas *post hoc*, and grammatical thinking became orientated around these two poles. Generally speaking it was the Basran (Sibawayhian) version of grammar which became the standard one (see Ibn al-Anbari's *al-'Inṣaaf* 'Equitable treatment').

Weil's ideas receive some support from Baalbaki's (1981) observation that in the works of Sibawayhi and Farra' themselves there is no mention of schools of grammar, while Owens (1990) argues that the earlier period of grammar, up to the end of the third/ninth century, was characterized by a relative conceptual and terminological heterogeneity in regards to linguistic thinking, that was subsequently replaced by the *post hoc* Basran/Kufan dichotomy. Talmon (1992: 818), on the other hand, would see a linguistic reality in the two schools even in the earlier period, though to date his ideas have yet to be presented in detail.

How old the Arabic grammatical tradition is, remains an unanswered question. It appears quite suddenly, fully developed, around 200/800, in the works of Sibawayhi and Farra', and the lexicographic work of Xalil (*Kitaab al ʿayn* 'Book of the letter ʿayn'). To what extent and in what way these scholars were dependent on their predecessors is difficult to answer directly for the same reason that the potential Greek predecessors of Arabic linguistic thinking are problematic: lack of original texts prevents an easy overview of pre-second/eighth-century grammatical commentary. Versteegh (1993), showing that there are relatively few hints about the origin of Arabic grammatical theory in early (i.e. pre-800) exegetical texts, tends only to deepen the mystery. The study of indirect sources such as the extant grammars themselves and the bio-bibliographical literature, will hopefully shed more light on this question.

If the earliest period of Arabic grammar is still rather shrouded in darkness, the same is fortunately not true of the post-Sibawayhi period, in particular the period beginning with Mubarrad (285/898) and running up to the present day. While there remains a great deal to be studied in the medieval Arabic linguistic tradition, its important developmental stages are readily discernible. In the rest of this section I will very briefly outline what these were, and in the next will summarize the theoretical and methodological basis on which they were built.

Aside from the Qur'anic exegetical tradition (Farra', Naḥḥas, etc.), in which linguistic disputes are set out, but only in so far as they illuminate particular textual problems, the two bases of the linguistic tradition are grammar in the broad sense (*naḥw* 'way', including phonetics, phonology, morphology and syntax) and lexicography. Prototypical works are Sibawayhi's *Kitaab* for the former and Xalil's *Kitaab al ʿayn* for the latter. These two works represent the first compendia in these two genres, and one finds like-spirited works appearing at regular intervals from that time onwards.

The lexicographic tradition was by its nature the less variegated. The form of dictionaries remained much the same (see pp. 55–56), the main variation from the large reference dictionaries being the production of short lexica describing specialized subjects, such as vocabulary related to horses, Hadith (stories about the Prophet), the Qur'an, dialectal variants (*luɣaat*) and others.

The grammatical, on the other hand, underwent a slow but steady differentiation. Sibawayhi's grammar was basically about core grammar, even if it touched on related fields like pragmatics and markedness theory (see p. 000). It has, however, the nature of a reference grammar, and to fulfill more practical pedagogical needs two developments occurred. On the one hand, short summaries of a limited subject matter, like the category of gender in nouns (cf. Farra''s *al-Muðakkar wa l-mu'annaθ* 'Masculine and feminine gender') were written, or, simply, lists of examples contrasting certain morphological forms (the verb form *faʕala* vs. *'afʕala* for example) were drawn up. On the other, the reference grammars themselves were made more transparent in their organization, and short summaries of the reference grammars were written (e.g. Ibn al-Sarraj's *al-Muwjaz fiy al-naḥw* 'Summary of grammar', *c.* 100 pages, based on his *al-'Uṣuwl fiy al-naḥw* 'The foundations of grammar' *c.* 1,200).

As the organization of grammar was systematized, a greater interest developed in organizational principles. The notions of basic and secondary or marked and unmarked, *'aṣl/farʕ* 'root/branch' playing a decisive role here. These were especially prominent in the fourth/tenth century. Ibn Jinni's *al-Xaṣaa'iṣ* 'Characteristica' being the *tour de force* in this genre.

In the context of controversy surrounding the inimitability of the Qur'an (Bohas, Guillaume, Kouloughli 1990: 116), there developed a greater interest in the contextual, both textual and situational, and pragmatic aspects of language structure. Jurjani (471/1078) in his *Dalaa'il al-'iʕjaaz* 'The proofs of inimitability' paid particular attention to the information structure of language, and later al-Astarabadhi (686/1286) and Sakkaki (626/1228), among others, gave prominence to speech act theory. Still later (*c.* 1400) scholars working within the *ʕilm al-waḍʕ* (Weiss 1966) addressed the structure of semantic relations. In addition, works of bio-bibliographical summary, the *ṭabaqaat*, were produced at various periods, and there were linguistic analyses of Arabic poetry, particularly those important for linguistic analysis.

It is important to note that Arabic linguistic thinking developed in an accretionary rather than substitution-like fashion. If Jurjani developed a theory of sentential information structure, he saw it as complementing, not replacing, the grammatical analysis of the sentence that he inherited from his predecessors. While his *Dalaa'il* lays the foundation for a sub-discipline known as rhetoric (*balaaɣa*), his *Muqtaṣid* 'The mediating' is a wholly orthodox compendium of Arabic grammar.

The Form of Arabic Grammatical Theory

As I have emphasized in the previous section, Arabic grammar developed continually over a period of time. Nonetheless, discrete stages are discernible where the grammatical tradition took on a fixed form (see Owens 1991: 233), and one can use these as reference points in summarizing the theory and methodology behind the grammatical thinking.

As far as the core grammar goes – phonology, morphology and syntax – a key grammarian is the Baghdadian Ibn al-Sarraj (316/928). His *al-ʾUṣuwl fiy al-naḥw* effectively established the form of grammatical treatises which is in use in the Arabic world up to today. While I therefore make reference especially to Sarraj here, it should be noted that, by and large, his methodology and theoretical orientation follows that of his predecessor Sibawayhi.

Arabic grammars (including Sibawayhi's) treat syntax before morphology, giving equal weight to the two, phonology as part of morphology (i.e. morphophonology), and phonetics as part of phonology. There are three axiomatic elements in Arabic syntactic analysis. Items substitute for each other, forming classes. The places of substitution are identified as grammatical functions. The functions are linked to each other by means of dependency relations which determine case form. If this pithy summary makes Arabic syntactic practice sound like "prescient" structuralism it is because modern grammatical theory does indeed rest on the same foundation as that supporting Arabic theory (Carter 1973, Owens 1988). The following example, using the simplified, didactic style of the grammarians, serves as an illustration.

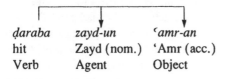

ḍaraba	zayd-un	ʿamr-an
hit	Zayd (nom.)	ʿAmr (acc.)
Verb	Agent	Object

'Zayd hit 'Amr'.

This sentence consists of three functions, a verb (*ḍaraba = fiʿl* lit. 'doing'), an agent (*zaydun = faaʿil* 'doer') and an object (*ʿamran = mafʿuwl bihi* 'done to it'). The verb governs both agent and object, the former in the nominative, the latter in the accusative. At each position other items could occur. In subject position, for example, one could have *muwsaa* 'Musa', for example:

ḍaraba muwsaa ʿamr-an

It happens that *muwsaa* has one invariable form, and the characteristic *-u* nominative suffix does not appear on it. By virtue of its substituting at the agent position, however, *muwsaa* is equally an agent, and it is equally governed by the verb, its form being implicitly (*muqaddar* 'implied') nominative. It is by the use of substitution techniques that a whole range of morphologically irregular forms, pronouns, demonstratives, compound and diptotic nouns, etc. are accommodated within a simple grammatical framework. An Arabic syntax is by and large an explication of what can occur and cooccur at each of the thirty or so syntactic positions which are customarily distinguished. Among the most important are topic (*mubtadaʾ* 'beginning') and comment (*xabar* 'news') in a nominal sentence, verb (*fiᶜl*), agent (*faaᶜil*) and the various types of objects in the verbal sentence (direct object, *mafᶜuwl bihi*, absolute object *mafᶜuwl muṭlaq* 'what is done unrestricted', locative (termed either *mafᶜuwl fiyhi* 'done in it' or *ẓarf* 'container'), as well as the various nominal elements, adjective (variously, *naᶜt* 'description', *ṣifa* 'quality' or *waṣf* 'description'), substitute (*badal* 'replacement') and conjunct (*ᶜatf* 'bending'), to name but a few. Within each of these categories various subclasses were distinguished.

The largest functional unit in Arabic is the sentence (*kalaam* 'speaking, talk, statement' or *jumla* 'sum'), though a function of special type since its existence is not established by a single substitution class. Nor are the functions which are in a sentence, *jumla*, said to be functions of the sentence. One never finds in Arabic grammars phrases such as 'agent of the sentence' (*faaᶜil al-jumla* or *faaᶜil al-kalaam*). Instead, the concept integrating the sub-parts of the sentence, verb, agent, object etc. is dependency. One item, a verb, for example, as in *ḍaraba zayd-un ᶜamr-an*, governs (*yaᶜmilu*) another in a particular form, nominative in the case of agent, accusative in the case of object. In general the Arabic notion of dependency and that defined in certain modern versions (e.g. Tesnière 1959) rest on common principles.

Arabic morphology, or *ṣarf* 'turning away', has as its basis a formal and a distributional component. The distributional consisted in the division of Arabic words into three major classes: noun (*ism* 'name'), verb (*fiᶜl*) and particle (*harf* 'edge'). Each of these in turn contained numerous subclasses. Under noun, for example, was understood common and proper nouns, adjectives, pronouns, demonstratives and relative pronouns. The rationale for the subclassification was partly formal – nouns have case endings but particles do not, for instance – but ultimately, distributional properties were decisive, each class being defined by its mutual commutational possibilities (see Owens 1989). The ability of an item to be substituted at a syntactic position defined the basic unit of morphology, the word (*kalima*): whatever can be commuted is a word, for instance the subject *muwsaa* in *ḍaraba muwsaa ᶜamr-an*. The *m* or *muw* of *muwsaa*, however, cannot alone be substituted with other items, are not therefore words, and hence are not units susceptible to analysis at the level of *ṣarf*.

While the word is the morphological element which is distributed in larger constructions, the basic unit of morphological analysis is the root (*ʾaṣl* 'root'), a consonantal skeleton. This skeleton was represented conventionally by the template *fᶜl* (the root for 'doing'), which stands for the three consonantal positions, initial, medial and final, that most roots have. Roots of more than three consonants were represented by adding an *l* for each basic consonant; *tarjama* 'translate', would have the structure *fᶜll*. The combination of root + vowel pattern, forming a stem, is designated *wazn* 'weight' or *binaaʾ* 'building'. It is the stems, of course, which make up the word classes. Short vowels generally had no special status in Arabic morphological theory, though their discrete morphological status was hinted at (Owens 1988: 110 on the thirteenth-century grammarian Astarabadhi). The stem *kataba* = the *wazn* "*faᶜala*" is simply an instance of a 3rd person perfect verb.

Of course, stems in Arabic can consist of more than basic root consonants + vowel patterns. They may contain, singly or in various combinations, prefixes (*ma-ktab* 'office'), infixes (*'in-t-aqala* 'move') and suffixes (*ḥamr-aa'* 'red (f.)'). It was well recognized that these elements often represented, relative to the consonantal root, extra-lexical semantic elements, and they were given a distinct status and representation in morphological theory. A basic distinction was drawn between the root (*'aṣl*) and non-root (*zaa'ida* 'increasing') consonants, the latter by and large comprising the affixes. Whereas the root consonants are represented in the standard template as *fˤl*, the added consonants were represented by themselves, so that the morphological structure of the three examples given above in this paragraph would be *ma-fˤal*, *'i-f-tˤala* and *faˤl-aa'*. Usually a consonantal root appears in a number of morphological guises, and identifying all of them was the domain of *taṣriyf* 'alteration, drainage', effectively the identification of all basic and derived forms applicable to a given root.

In most cases the added consonants are readily distinguishable from the root. In the relatively few cases where they are not, various criteria (semantic, morphotactic, derivational, see Owens 1988: 115) were developed for deciding what belonged to the root, what not.

A more fundamental problem to the representation of root/non-root structure was presented by the various phonological changes which root consonants could undergo. *Miyzaan* 'weight', for instance, is based on the root *wzn*, though no *w* is discernible in it. The greater part of Arabic morphology concerned itself with explaining the various phonological changes which roots could undergo.

The changes were phrased in terms of general phonological processes, deletion (*ḥaδf* 'deleting'), assimilation (*idɣaam* 'insertion'), substitution of one sound for another (*badal* metathesis) (*taḥwiyl* 'transformation'), and rules which affected the 'weak' consonants *w* and *y* (*qalb* 'heart, center'). The rules applied to ideal underlying morphological forms which served as the input. *Miyzaan* 'scales', for instance, is based on the underlying form *mi-fˤaal* (cf. *mi-qdaar* 'measure') = *mi-wzaan*. A general phonological rule changes the sequence *iw* to *iy* (cf. e.g. *duˤiya* 'be invited' < *duˤiwa*). The rules apply in succession, and a given underlying form may undergo four or five different rules before the final surface form is reached, as is the case, for instance, with *qul-tu* 'I said', from underlying **qawal-tu*.

The rules defining the changes are not strictly phonological, but rather morphophonological. That is, potentially every rule with phonological effect has its domain restricted by morphological domain: a rule may apply to nouns, but not to verbs, or vice versa; a rule that holds for a basic consonantal root may not apply to a non-basic (*zaa'id*) one; rules applying stem initially (at '*f*') may not apply stem finally (at '*l*').

Arabic morphophonological theory is entirely orientated toward explaining formal deviation from an underlying stem. It is thus not surprising that phonetics is not introduced as an independent component of grammar parallel to syntax and morphology, but rather in conjunction with one aspect of morphophonology, namely assimilation. Most assimilation rules, like the voicing of *t* in *iḍḍaraba* 'be

confused' (< *iḍtaraba*), or the emphatization of *t* in the same example, are speci-
fiable only with a precise phonetic description of the sounds involved, for assimilation can be due to various phonetic factors: in the example just cited two
independent assimilation processes are attested, one in terms of voicing, the other
in terms of manner (emphasis).

While phonetics is, within the Arabic model, conceptually a part of morphology, the classificatory categories used are largely articulatory and were sub-
categorized as to place (some fifteen points in all distinguished, starting from the
glottis, the classification being hampered by the fact that no theoretical distinction
was drawn between an active and passive articulator); manner (including stops
šadiyd 'strong', fricatives *rixw* 'loose, flabby' etc., eight in all) and voicing (or
tenseness, various interpretations have been given the terms *majhuwr/mahmuws*
'made loud/whispered'). A sound like *t* was thus given a multiple characteriza-
tion: voiceless (*mahmuws*), stop (*šadiyd*), pronounced at the tongue tip and inci-
sor tip, and implicitly, non-emphatic (not *muṭbaq* 'covered'). Assimilation could
affect a sound along one or more of these classificatory parameters.

The core grammar thus contained detailed treatment of syntax, morphology
(and morphophonology) and phonetics. As already mentioned, the data, and for
the most part, theoretical descriptive apparatus pertaining to this grammar are to
be found in Sibawayhi, and were organized in a coherent way by Ibn al-Sarraj.
Around Ibn al-Sarraj's time a further interest gained prominence, one touched on,
but not developed as an independent linguistic endeavor, in the pre-tenth-century
grammar. This was an interest in the relation between items fulfilling the ideal
grammatical/morphological structure (*ʾaṣl*) of the language and those deviating
from this ideal (*farʿ* 'branch, twig'). The ideal pertained both to structures and to
items realizing these structures. The ideal was in some sense the most basic, sim-
plest, or, the metaphor I prefer, unmarked to be found. For instance, in morphology the ideal root was one containing three consonants (not four or five, which are
statistically marked), none of which are "weak," i.e. *y* or *w*, since these consonants
tended to undergo various sorts of phonological changes. In syntax the most unmarked parts of the sentence were topic and comment of a nominal sentence and
verb and agent of the verbal sentence, whereas direct objects and locative objects
are marked (*farʿ*). The "proof" that topic/comment and verb/agent are unmarked
is that they, in opposition to objects, are obligatory. Virtually any grammatical category could be given a markedness status relative to another one, and in some
cases markedness hierarchies were postulated, one item being closer to the basic
(*ʾaṣl*) category than one (*farʿ*), but less close than another. For instance, Bohas
and Guillaume (1984: 68) point out that Sibawayhi draws up a three-way
hierarchy defining the sounds *ʾ–y–w* (going from least to most marked), whereby
the 'heaviest' (*ʾaθqal* 'heavier', most marked) may undergo certain changes
which the others do not. Thus, the initial *w* of *waqaʿa* 'he fell' is deleted in the
imperfect, *yaqaʿu*, whereas the *y* will usually be kept, *yayminu* 'go right'. The explanation for this is that *y* is lighter (*ʾaxaff*) 'lighter' or less marked than *w*.

Implicitly, the entire organization of Ibn al-Sarraj's grammar is built around the notion of markedness, always beginning with unmarked categories then moving to marked. In summarizing the various grammatical functions, for instance, he begins with a summary of the functions which the nominative case could assume (topic, comment, agent), since the nominative was assumed to be the basic case. He moves next to accusative functions (absolute, direct, locative object, etc.), and ends with the genitive (possessive, object of preposition), the least basic. Markedness considerations further informed the treatment within these categories. Among the nominative functions, for example, the nominal sentence is treated before the verbal, based on the assumption that nouns are unmarked relative to verbs.

Interest in pragmatic matters led to a further layer of grammatical analysis. Jurjani (471/1078) sought to explain the meaning difference between (a) and (b)

(a)   *δahaba zayd-un* '(What happened is that) Zayd left'
(b)   *zayd-un δahaba* '(It is) Zayd (who) left'

on the basis of new and old information. (a) would be appropriate if one were concentrating on the action itself, whereas (b) would be appropriate if the actor Zayd were the most important aspect of the discourse. The new information was placed first, the presupposed afterwards. It is important to note here that Jurjani essentially formalized a multi-systemic analysis of sentence structure: at the grammatical level (a) is a verbal sentence and (b) nominal, two fundamentally distinct sentence types. At the informational level both sentences share a common dichotomization into new/given information.

Pragmatics continued to interest linguists. A basic distinction was drawn between performative (*inšaaʾiy* 'creative') and enunciative (*xabariy* 'reportive') utterances (Larcher 1991), and detailed analyses were made of individual structures. The seventh/thirteenth-century grammarian al-Astarabadhi, for example, analyzed *laakinna* 'but' in terms of the predicate *ʾastadraktu* 'I have corrected', an abstract semantic element whose 1st person subject reflects al-Astarabadhi's assumption that each utterance presupposes a speaker (Larcher 1992).

Lexicons

Arab scholars were equally active in the field of lexicography. Ibn Manẓur's (711/1311) *Lisaan al-ʿarab* 'The Arabic tongue', for instance, runs to fifteen volumes, each volume about 400 pages long, approximately 80,000 entries in all. While the dictionaries were comprehensive to a fault, it is notable that they never attained the structured order found in the study of grammar (see Langhade 1994, Haywood 1959: 82, Wild 1965: 56). I will briefly illustrate this here with a summary of the entry for *kfr* (Vol. 5: 144–151) from the *Lisaan*.

The main organizing principle within the lemmas was semantic and pragmatic, a given stem form being repeated as often as distinct meanings were associated with it. The lemma for *kfr* begins with the verbal noun *kufr* with the (1) meaning 'disbelief' (*naqiyḍ al-ʾiymaan*); in the next short paragraph *kufr* is given with the (2) sense of 'disavowal of grace', and in the long third paragraph *kufr* in the (3) sense of 'denial (*juḥuwd*) of grace'. There is no explicit intimation that the meanings are related. Sometimes other derivationally related forms are listed with the different senses of *kufr*, sometimes not. With the first sense four related verb forms are given (*yakfuru, kafarnaa, kafaruw* twice), three in examples, one to illustrate verbal nouns. No definition of a verb *kafara* is offered. Three verbal noun forms in the function of absolute object are listed with the first meaning, *kufran, kufuwran* and *kufraanan*. There is no discussion of their respective meanings. With the second sense of *kufr* no other related forms are listed. With the third a large number are, including again the verbal nouns *kufuwran, kufraanan*, as well as other forms, *kaafir* (with its three plurals, *kuffaarun, kafaratun* and *kifaarun*), *mukaffar* 'denied grace and its goodness', and others (twelve in all). Again, there is usually no explicit definition of the meanings of these related forms. One would assume presumably that they are to be accommodated under meaning three. There is further discussion of various connotations of *kufr*, though under which of the first three senses they are subsumed is not made clear. *Kufr* in the sense of 'innocence' is discussed on p. 145. It is noteworthy that at the end of p. 145 the basic (*ʾaṣl*) meaning of *kfr* is said to relate to 'covering'. The basic meaning, however, is introduced only after lengthy discussion of the pragmatically more prominent religious connotations of the root. On p. 147 a new sub-entry, *kafr* 'covering' is introduced and on p. 148 *kufr* returns again, though with the meaning 'pitch for sealing ships'. The lemma for *kfr* ends with further morphological forms based on *kfr*.

Throughout the lemmas are found references from the Qur'an, Hadith, and poetry, and various grammatical points, mainly morphological are mentioned, such as whether a noun is diptotic or not. The interpretations of previous lexicographers are cited quite often.

In strong contrast to formally based grammar, meaning has a more central role than form. There is no single form *kufr*; rather there is *kufr*$_1$ with meaning 1, *kufr*$_2$ with meaning 2, *kufr*$_3$, etc. The derivationally related forms, the *taṣriyf* of *kfr*, are consequently listed only when they happen to have some special semantic relation to the sense of *kfr* under discussion. The basic passive participle form *makfuwr*, for example is mentioned only once and that in the sub-lemma *kafr* meaning 'dust' (*turaab*): *ramaad makfuwr* means 'dust-covered ashes'.

In terms of the structure of its lemmas, the *Lisaan* is more or less typical of earlier works (e.g. Ibn Sida's (458/1066) *Muḥkam* 'The precisely planned' and later lexicons like al-Zabiydi's (1205/1791) *Taaj al-ʿaruws* 'The crown of the bride' had relatively little organizational improvement. It was only in the nineteenth century that dictionaries took on the form common today.

The Arabic Grammatical Tradition and Comparative Semitics

As far as the theoretical and methodological underpinnings of the Arabic tradition go, there is little of special interest to comparative semitics, aside from what they have to say about the overall cultural history of the regions where Semitic languages are spoken. Such basic notions of linguistic analysis as substitution and dependency are, presumably, of universal application. The Arabic tradition has had a fundamental influence on other Middle Eastern grammatical traditions, like the Hebraic and Coptic, and it would be of interest to know to what extent the similar structure of the languages facilitated their adoption of the Arabic grammatical model. Such an investigation, however, is probably of more interest to general linguistic theory than to Semitic studies.

There is, however, an invaluable, if inadvertant, contribution in the Arabic grammatical tradition to general Semitics. This lies in the great compendia of facts recorded by the grammarians and lexicographers, dialectal forms, socially marked forms and outright mistakes (*laḥn*) for example. This material was used extensively by Rabin (1951), though it is far from being exhausted, and its judicious evaluation will be of fundamental interest to Arabic studies in particular and Semitics in general.

References

Arabic Sources
al-Astarabadhi, Raḍi l-Din. n.d. *Šarḥ kitaab al-kaafiya*. Beirut: Dar al-Kutub al-'Ilmiyya.
al-Farra', Abu Zakariya. 1975. *al-Muðakkar wa l-mu'annaθ*, ed. R. al-Tawwab. Cairo: Dar al-Turath.
—— 1983. *Ma'aaniy al-qur'aan*, ed. M. 'Ali l-Najjar and A. Yusuf Najati. Beirut: 'Alam al-Kutub.
Ibn al-Anbari, Abu Barakat. n.d. *al-'Inṣaaf fiy masaa'il al-xilaaf bayna l-naḥwiyyiyna l-baṣriyyiyna wa l-kuwfiyyiyna*, ed. M. 'Abd al-Hamid. Beirut: Dar al-Fikr.
Ibn Jinni, Abu l-Fatḥ. 1952–1956. *al-Xaṣaa'iṣ*, ed. M. 'Ali l-Najjar. Cairo: n.p. Reprint, n.d., Beirut: Dar al-Kitaab al-'Arabi.
Ibn Manẓur, Ibn Mukarram. n.d. *Lisaan al 'arab*. Beirut: Dar Saadir.
Ibn Mujahid, Abu Bakr. 1979. *Kitaab al-sab'a fiy l-qiraa'aat*, ed. Shawqi l-Ḍayf. Cairo: Dar al-Ma'arif.
Ibn al-Sarraj, Abu Bakr.1965. *al-Muwjaz fiy l-Naḥw*, ed. M. el-Chouémi and S. Damerdji. Beirut: Mu'assasat Badran.
—— 1985. *al-'Uṣuwl fiy al-nahw*, ed. A. al-Fatli. Beirut: Mu'assasat al-Risaala.
Jurjani, 'Abd al-Qahir. 1978. *Dalaa'il al-'i'jaaz*, ed. M. Rida. Beirut: Dar al-Ma'rifa.
—— 1982. *al-Muqtaṣid fiy šarḥ al-'iyḍaah*, ed. K. B. al-Murjan. Baghdad: Ministry of Culture and Information.
Mubarrad, Ibn Yazid. n.d. *al-Muqtaḍab*, ed. M. al-Xaliq 'Uḍayma. Beirut: 'Alam al-Kutub.
Sakkaki, Moḥammad. 1984. *Miftaaḥ al-'uluwm*, ed. N. Zarzur. Beirut: Dar al-Kutub al-'Alamiyya.
Sibawayhi, Ibn 'Uthman. 1970. al-Kitaab, ed. H. Derenbourg. Hildesheim: Georg Olms.
al-Zabiydi, M. 1986. *Taaj al-'aruws*, ed. A. Faraj. Kuwait: Government of Kuwait.

Secondary Sources
Baalbaki, R. 1981. "Arab Grammatical Controversies and the Extant Sources of the Second and Third Centuries A. H." In *Studia Arabica et Islamica: Festschrift for Ihsan 'Abbas*, ed. W. al-Qaḍi. Beirut: American University. 1–26.
Bohas, G. and J-P. Guillaume. 1984. *Études des théories des grammariens arabes*.

Damascus: Institut Français de Damas.
Bohas, G., J-P. Guillaume and D. Kouloughli. 1990. *The Arabic Linguistic Tradition.* London: Routledge.
Carter, Michael. 1972. "Les Origines de la grammaire arabe." *Revue des Études Islamiques* 40: 69–97.
—— 1973. "An Arabic Grammarian of the Eighth Century A.D." *Journal of the American Oriental Society* 93: 146–157.
Ditters, E. 1992. *A Formal Approach to Arabic Syntax.* Luxor: Nijmegen.
Fleisch, Henri. 1994. "Arabic Linguistics." In *History of Linguistics*, volume 1, ed. G. Lepschy. London: Longman. 164–184.
Haywood, J. 1959 (1965²). *Arabic Lexicography.* Leiden: Brill.
Howell, M. 1882–1903. *A Grammar of the Classical Arabic Language.* Delhi: Gian Publishing House.
Larcher, P. 1992. "La Particule *lakinna* vue par un grammarien arabe du XIIIe siècle." *Historiographia Linguistica* 19: 1–24.
Langhade, J. 1994. "Etudes linguistiques au Moyen-Âge, un regard interculturel: Le Silence des sources sur la science lexicographique arabe." *Bulletin d'Études Orientales* 46: 99–110.
Owens, Jonathan. 1988. *The Foundations of Grammar: An Introduction to Medieval Arabic Grammatical Theory.* Amsterdam: Benjamins.
—— 1990. *Early Arabic Grammatical Theory: Heterogeneity and Standardization.* Amsterdam: Benjamins.
—— 1991. "Models for the Interpretation of the Development of Medieval Arabic Grammatical Theory." *Journal of the American Oriental Society* 111: 225–238.
Rabin, Chaim. 1951. *Ancient Westarabian.* London: Taylor's University Press.
Rundgren, Frithiof. 1976. "Über den griechischen Einfluss auf die arabische Nationalgrammatik." Uppsala: Acta Universitatis Upsalensis.
Talmon, R. 1992. Review of Owens 1990, *Early Arabic Grammatical Theory. Linguistics* 30: 816–820.
Tesnière, L. 1959. *Éléments de syntaxe structurale.* Paris: Klincksieck.
Versteegh, C. 1977. *Greek Elements in Arabic Linguistic Thinking.* Leiden: Brill.
—— 1993. *Arabic Grammar and Qur'aanic Exegesis.* Leiden: Brill.
Weil, G. 1913. *Die grammatischen Streitfragen der Basrer und Kufer.* Leiden: Brill.
Weiss, B. 1966. "Language in Orthodox Muslim Thought: A Study of Wad' al-Luġa and its Development." Ph.D. dissertation, Princeton University.
Wild, S. 1965. *Das Kitaab al-'ain und die arabische Lexicographie.* Wiesbaden: Harrassowitz.

Further Reading

Arabic

Ibn Jinni, Abu l-Fatḥ. 1954. *al-Munṣif*, ed. I. Muṣtafa and A. Amin. Cairo: Idarat Iḥya' al-Turath al-Qadim.
Naḥḥas, Abu Ja'far. 1977. *'I'raab al-qur'aan*, ed. Z. Zahid. Baghdad: Wizarat al-Awqaf.

Secondary

Larcher, P. 1991. "Quand, en Arabe, on parlait de l'Arabe ... (II): Essai sur la catégorie de *'Insha'* (vs. *xabar*)." *Arabica* 38: 246–273.
Owens, Jonathan. 1989. "The Syntactic Basis of Arabic Word Classification." *Arabica* 36: 211–234.
Wright, W. 1859 (1977). *A Grammar of the Arabic Language.* Cambridge: Cambridge University Press.

4 The Hebrew Grammatical Tradition

Arie Schippers

Grammatical activities in the field of Hebrew appeared relatively late, in a period when Hebrew was no longer spoken. Even the most colloquial Hebrew variant, rabbinical Hebrew, had died out in the second century. Hebrew had for centuries been limited to synagogical and literary use. The Bible was transmitted by the Jews from generation to generation, but the vocalization and accentuation notes had to be added as "punctuation" to the consonantal text, probably only from the beginning of the seventh century. This was at least the opinion of the Rabbanites (the mainstream of Judaism) who recognized later traditions such as the orally revealed Mishnah and the Talmud as a completion of the Written Law of the Bible.

The Qara'ites, however, were of the opinion that the Bible was self-explanatory and required no completion by Oral Law such as the Mishnah and Talmud, which were considered by the Rabbanites as writings with great authority. The Qara'ites claimed that the Bible had been revealed in its entirety, "graven upon the tablets," i.e. "full with vowel and accent signs and not lacking in vowel and accent signs" *Eškol ha-kofer* (see p. 61). Consequently, they were very active in adding diacritics. This activity was called the Masorah, i.e. 'transmission' or 'numbering of the verses' (Arabic *al-ma:sirah*). The first Masoretes were the Ben Ašer family of whom Abu Sa'id Aharon ben Mošeh was the most conspicuous member (first half of the seventh century).

One of the systems of vocalizing, the so-called Tiberian system, acquired priority in the Jewish world. That may be the reason that a ninth-century author even pretended that he had heard common people in the streets of Tiberias speaking Hebrew, suggesting that there was still a living tradition.

The development of philology led to the addition of diacritics and served as a foundation for the grammatical work starting in the tenth century. In the beginning writing about grammar was considered by many to be a vain activity. Grammarians tried to prove that language studies were necessary for the proper understanding of the written Word. Qara'ites and Rabbanites disagreed in their interpretations of Biblical Hebrew. Another factor which stimulated grammar studies was the activity in the field of Arabic grammar by Muslim scholars. The

59

abundance of Arabic philological and grammatical literature was no doubt a stimulus for the Jews who occupied themselves with Hebrew. This phenomenon of the sudden renaissance of Hebrew studies in the tenth and eleventh centuries may also have been the reaction of the *šuʿu:biyyah* against the dominant position of the Arabic language. This movement, supported mainly by officials of Persian origin, stressed the particular values of the non-Arab peoples (*šuʿu:b*) within Islam.The Jews became more aware of the value of their own culture and their holy language as well.

The Golden Age of Hebrew Grammar: The Creative Period

The first among the philologists of the Hebrew language was Saʿadyah Gaʾon or Saʿadiyyah ibn Yu:suf (892–942), born in Fayyu:m (Egypt), the head of the Jewish community in Babylonia (Iraq) and the foremost personality in Rabbanite Judaism during the first half of the tenth century. He wrote the *Kita:b al-sabʿi:n lafẓah al-mufradah* 'Book of the seventy unique words', the first to explain *hapax legomena* (words or roots found only once in the text) of the Bible according to their use in rabbinical literature. He also compiled the *Kita:b uṣu:l al-šiʿr al-ʿibra:ni:* 'Book of the Roots of Hebrew Poetry', usually referred to by its Hebrew title *Agron* 'Compendium', the first Hebrew dictionary with glosses in Arabic. It consists of two alphabetic listings, according to the first and the last letters. Saʿadyah Gaʾon wanted poets to use a better Hebrew. He pointed out the difference between letters that stand for the basic meaning of the word, and added letters that represent affixes. Equally important was his *Kita:b faṣi:ḥ luɣat al-ʿibra:niyyah* 'Book of the pure Hebrew language', in which morphological questions of the Hebrew language were dealt with for the first time.

The interest in linguistic problems spread quickly through North Africa. In Tahort, a town in what is now Algeria, lived Yehudah ibn Quraysh (tenth century), who dedicated his *Risa:lah* 'Treatise, Epistle' to the Jewish community of Fez. He compared Biblical Hebrew with Aramaic, Mishnaic Hebrew, Arabic and other languages such as Berber.

In the East we have the work by the Qaraʾite Abu:-l-Faraǧ Haru:n ibn al-Faraǧ from Jerusalem, the *Kita:b al-ka:fi: fi-l-luɣah al-ʿibra:niyyah* 'The adequate book on the Hebrew language' and the 579-page manuscript, written in Jerusalem about 1000, *Muštamil ʿala:-l-uṣu:l wa-l-fuṣu:l fi:-l-luɣah al-ʿibra:niyyah* 'Comprehensive Book on the Roots and Branches of the Hebrew Language'. Part 1 of the latter is devoted to the ten principles (*uṣu:l*) used to determine a form in language; part 2 deals with infinitives; part 3 with the letters of the alphabet and their division into essential (*ǧawhariyyah*) and servant letters (*xawa:dim*; roughly the same distinction between basic letters and added ones as made by Saʿadyah, see p. 60). Part 4 deals with particles while part 5 considers many kinds of grammatical questions: gender, number, pronouns, transitivity and lexicology. Part 6 is concerned with the conjugation of the verb *ḥalēq*; part 7 with a lexicography and triliteral verbs according to the anagram system; part 8 is a comparison of Hebrew with biblical Aramaic.

Abu:-l-Farağ's anagram method looks very much like that of the Arabic grammarian al-Xali:l ibn Aḥmad (710–786) in his dictionary *Kita:b al-ʿayn*. This dictionary is not arranged alphabetically, but by groups of sounds, probably under Indian influence, starting with the consonant combinations with the Arabic letter 'ayn. Abu:-l-Farağ started by explaining all the root combinations containing the Hebrew consonant letter 'ayn, subsequently dealing with other consonant combinations. The following roots are found in the extant remnant of *al-Muštamil*'s letter 'ayn: ʿBR, ʿRF, ʿMR, ʿŠB, ʿFL, ʿṢB. Under ʿBR all the permutations of the three consonant letters are listed, namely: ʿBR, ʿRB, BʿR, BRʿ, RBʿ, RʿB.

Among other Qara'ite works are David ben Abraham al-Fa:si:'s extensive dictionary of Biblical Hebrew in Arabic, called *Kita:b ja:miʿ al-alfa:ẓ* 'Comprehensive book of sounds' and two grammatical texts: the anonymous book *Meʾor ʿayin* 'Eye Light' or 'Enlightenment of the Eye', composed at the end of the eleventh century and the *Eškol ha-kofer* 'The cluster of camphire' (cf. Song of Solomon 1:14)/'The grape of henna' by the twelfth-century author Yᵊhudah Hadassi. The former work does not seem to have been influenced by the Andalusian Rabbanites and has a completely different grammatical system, whereas the latter is heavily influenced by the Andalusian grammarians Ḥayyu:ğ and Ibn Ğana:ḥ (see pp. 62–63).

The renaissance of Hebrew which manifested itself in the study of Hebrew grammar and the new school of Hebrew secular poetry, took place in tenth- and eleventh-century Muslim Spain. Jewish patrons emulated the courtly habits of their Muslim colleagues. Mošeh ibn 'Ezra (1055–1138), himself a poet, tells us in his *Kita:b al-muḥa:ḍarah wa-l-muδa:karah* 'Book of discussion and commemoration' about the learned men who made the revival of Hebrew possible. In the fifth chapter of his *Kita:b*, devoted to a survey of Hebrew literature in Muslim Spain, Mošeh ibn 'Ezra begins (28b) by stating that the reason for the Spanish Jews' mastery of the Hebrew language was the fact that they originated from Jews in Jerusalem, where the purest Hebrew was acquired and from where God's Law and Word had come. After the arrival of the Arabs in Andalusia (711 CE), the Jews delved deeply into Arabic science, linguistics and poetry (29b). Thereupon God revealed to them the secret of their own holy language: phenomena such as weak and additional letters were recognized. The first grammarians lived at the Cordoban court of the Jewish patron Abu: Yu:suf Ḥasday ibn Isḥaq ibn Shapru:ṭ (915–970). About this maecenas, whose activities initiated the flowering of Hebrew Andalusian poetry, Mošeh ibn 'Ezra says in his *Kita:b* (30ab): "He firmly established the pillars of science by surrounding himself with wise men from Syria and al-'Iraq. The authors of his time ... wrote admirable works. They praised him in their beautiful poems and writings in the Arabic language. In exchange, therefore, he distinguished them with his graceful gifts, while he provided all the necessary means to satisfy their wishes."

One can conclude from Mošeh ibn 'Ezra's sketch that the new poetical school arose at a time when there were also many linguistic activities. Linguistic and poetic activities stimulated and influenced each other. Hebrew poets rivaled the Arabs in their poetry and adopted the ideal of distilling the purest poetic language from the Hebrew of Holy Scripture.

Mᵊnaḥem ibn Saruq (born c. 915, Tortosa) lived at the court of Ḥasday ibn Shapru:ṭ. His lexicon of the Hebrew language, the *Maḥbèrèt* 'Book, Compendium', was believed to be a step forward compared with Saʿadyah Gaʾon's dictionary. Menaḥem differentiated between roots (*yᵊsod*, *ʿiqqar*, *šòrèš*) and the paragogic or added element (*tosèfèt* 'addition', *mᵊšarᵊtim*, 'servants') within the Hebrew word (see p. 60).

This differentiation, however, already appears in the writings of the Tiberian Masorete Aharon ben Ašer (see p. 59) and of Saʿadya ha-Gaʾon (p. 60). But Mᵊnaḥem did not possess the theoretical foundations to discover the weak consonants. For him any consonant that could disappear during the flexion of a root does not belong to its basis, but is an added consonant. By means of this empirical process, he admits a large number of monoconsonantal and biconsonantal roots. Contrary to the widespread custom of writing scientific works in Arabic, his dictionary was written in Hebrew. It was therefore widely disseminated in Europe.

Mᵊnaḥem's critic, Dunaš ibn Labraṭ (a name of Berber origin; born c. 925 in Morocco; educated in Baghdad by Saʿadyah), established himself in Cordoba, at the court of Ḥasday ibn Shapru:ṭ. Dunaš ibn Labraṭ's criticisms were directed mainly against the identification of roots by Mᵊnaḥem and against the meanings he attributed to words, which often entailed theological consequences. Dunaš's criticisms of Mᵊnaḥem unleashed a polemic between the pupils of Mᵊnaḥem and of Dunaš. The pupils of Mᵊnaḥem also criticized the new metrics introduced by Dunaš in the poetry of the new Hebrew Andalusian school. This criticism of the inadequacy of the Arabic meters for Hebrew poetry was to be repeated later by Yᵊhudah ha-Le:wi (p. 63).

The discovery of the triradicalism of the Hebrew words and verbs by Yehudah (Abu: Zakariyya Yahya:) ben David al-Fa:si: Ḥayyu:ǧ (c. 930–c. 1000; born at Fez, lived in Cordoba) was revolutionary for Hebrew grammar. He hoped that, by the correct philological knowledge of Biblical forms, the holy language would be used again by scholars and poets just as in antiquity. Ḥayyu:ǧ wrote two monographs. He came to the conclusion that every Hebrew verbal root consisted of at least three letters (consonants). He called *alef*, *yod*, *waw* and *he:* "weak" or "soft," because these letters are not written phonetically, but visible in the text. He recognized that the *primae yod* verb *yašav* has three radicals, and not two, as earlier grammarians would say on the basis of the sometimes invisible *yod*. He also discovered the concept of compensatory lengthening (Arabic *madd* 'lengthening') from the basic forms (Arabic *aṣliyyah*) of the sound verbs (e.g. *paʿal*, or *šamar*). To represent the verbal forms he uses the root *p-ʿ-l* (inspired by the similar use of *f-ʿ-l* in Arabic). In his *Kita:b al-afʿa:l ðawa:t ḥuru:f al-li:n* 'Book of the verbs with weak letters' he recognizes the following four categories of weak verbs: (1) the *verba primae alef*; (2) the *verba primae yod*; (3) the *verba mediae infirmae* (with a medial weak radical: *yod* or *waw*); (4) the *verba tertiae infirmae* (whose final radical is weak *alef* or *he:* = *yod* or *waw*). These are weak because they may be omitted in part of the paradigms. In his *Kita:b al-afʿa:l ðawa:t al-miθlayn* 'Book of the geminate verbs' Ḥayyu:ǧ dealt with defective forms of verbs that have identical second and third radicals (*verba mediae geminatae*).

Yonah ibn Ǧana:ḥ (born in Cordoba *c*. 990) wanted to write a comprehensive and systematic grammar of Biblical Hebrew in the tradition of Ḥayyu:ǧ. In his old age, after 1039, he composed the work which he had been preparing for a long time, namely the *Kita:b al-tanqi:ḥ* 'Book of detailed investigation'. The first part of this book, the *Kita:b al-lumaʿ* 'Book of variegated flower beds' was a most comprehensive grammar in the tradition of Ḥayyu:ǧ. The second part, the *Kita:b al-uṣu:l* 'Book of the roots', contains a complete vocabulary of Biblical Hebrew, without personal or place names. The letters are listed under their Arabic equivalents, following the order of the Arabic alphabet (according to roots, geminates coming before *tertiae alef* words). Each derived word is translated into Arabic.

The poets Šᵊmu'el han-Nagid (993–1055), Šᵊlomo ibn Gabirol (1021–1058), and Yehudah ha-Le:wi (1075–1141) were also interested in grammar. Šᵊlomo wrote a didactic poem in Hebrew on grammar called *Se:fer ha-ʿanaq* 'Book of the necklace'; 98 lines from the original 400 are still extant. Šᵊmu'el han-Nagid is reported to have written some comments on grammatical works and a dictionary of Biblical Hebrew. Yehudah ha-Le:wi wrote his *Maqa:lat al-ʿaru:ḍ* 'Treatise on metrics' – metrics were considered to belong to linguistics – and his *Kita:b al-xazari:* 'Book of the Khazar king', in which he made important remarks on the contemporary situation of the Hebrew language.

Mošeh ibn Chiquitilla or Chicatella lived in the eleventh century. Mošeh ibn 'Ezra considered him "one of the principal learned men and linguists" (36b). He published a volume entitled *Kita:b al-taðki:r wa-l-taʾni:θ* 'The Book of masculine and feminine genders'.

Yᵊhudah ibn Bal'am or Bil'am also lived in the eleventh century. Apparently he was born in Toledo, but settled down in Seville after the Christian conquest of Toledo. He was gifted with a polemical spirit and criticized Sa'adyah Ga'on, Yonah ibn Ǧana:ḥ and Šᵊmu'el han-Nagid. He even accused Mošeh ibn Chiquitilla of being an atheist, and attacked his rationalism, he himself being a traditionalist. His writings include the *Kita:b al-tagni:s* 'Book of Homonyms' and the *Kita:b al-afʿa:l al-muštaqqah min al-asma:ʾ* 'Book on the denominative verbs'.

Ibn Baru:n (*c*. 1100, Saragossa) was the author of the *Kita:b al-muwa:zanah bayn al-luɣah al-ʿibra:niyyah wa-l-ʿarabiyyah* 'Book of comparison between the Hebrew and the Arabic language'. In this work he mentions nearly all the preceding linguists and also Arab grammarians. It contains a section on the comparative grammar of Arabic and Hebrew, and a lexicographical section. In the latter he presents the biblical roots which have an equivalent in Arabic in pronunciation and meaning.

The Second Period of the Grammarians of Hebrew: The Period of Dissemination

In this period the grammarians of Hebrew were less original than their predecessors. But philosophical linguistic questions still troubled them: they developed ideas about the essence of language and its epistemological nature, thoughts about the origin of language and the reason for the multiplicity of the languages, the links between language and climate, the question whether language was natural or conventional, and of whether it was created or pre-existent (Zwiep 1995).

After the Christian reconquest of some territories and the expulsion of the Jews from Muslim Spain by the Almoravids and Almohades, most Jewish intellectuals lived in Christian Spain and Provence, where the knowledge of Arabic was declining. They therefore translated most of the grammatical works from Arabic into Hebrew. The Hebrew versions were disseminated all over Europe. The translators tried to express in concise Hebrew the findings of Ḥayyu:ǧ and Ibn Ǧana:ḥ. Adaptations for Western Europe were made by Abraham ibn 'Ezra (1089–1164), Ibn Parḥon (twelfth century), Yᵊhudah ibn Tibbon (c. 1120–c.1190), Jose:f Qimḥi: (c. 1105–1235) and his sons Dawid Qimḥi: (c. 1160–1235) and Mošeh Qimḥi: (died c. 1190, and Yiṣḥaq ben Mošeh ha-Le:wi, called Profiat Duran (died c. 1414). Jose:f Qimḥi: is specially worth mentioning because of his vowel theory. Instead of the traditional seven 'kings' (vowels), he opted for five contrasting pairs of long and short vowels [a:-a; e:-è; u:-u; o:-o; i:-i]. In connection with David Qimḥi: we have to mention his *Miḳlol* 'Magnificence', the most widely disseminated grammar and dictionary of Hebrew in the Middle Ages.

Further Reading

For more detailed lists of recent and older editions of the Arabic and Hebrew versions of grammatical works, see Sáenz Badillos (1988a), Loewe (1994), Téné (1970), Del Valle Rodriguez (1988), and Zwiep (1997).

Bacher, W. 1894a. "Die hebräische Sprachwissenschaft." In *Geschichte des rabbinischen Litteratur während des Mittelalters und ihre Nachblüte in der neueren Zeit*, ed. J. Winter and A. Wünsche. Trier: Siegmund Meyer. 133–235.

—— 1894b. "Die Massora." In *Geschichte des rabbinischen Litteratur während des Mittelalters und ihre Nachblüte der neueren Zeit*, ed. J. Winter and A. Wünsche. Trier: Siegmund Mayer. 121–132.

Bekkum, W. J. van. 1982. "The 'Risāla' of Yᵊhuda ibn Quraysh and its Place in Hebrew Linguistics." In *The History of Linguistics in the Near East*, ed. C. H. M. Versteegh et al. Amsterdam: Benjamins. 71–91.

—— 1997. "Semantics in the Hebrew Tradition." In *Semantics in Four Traditions: Greek, Hebrew, Arabic, Sanskrit*, ed. C. H. M. Versteegh. Amsterdam: Benjamins.

Benavente, S., ed. 1986. *Tešubot talmide Menaḥem*. Granada: Universidad de Granada.

Drory, R. 1988. *Re:šit ha-maggaᶜim šel sifrut ha-yhudit ᶜim ha-sifrut ha-ᶜarbit ba-meᵓah ha-ᵓasirit* [The emergence of Jewish–Arabic contacts at the beginning of the tenth century]. Tel Aviv: ha-Qibbuṣ ha-me'uḥad.

Ibn 'Ezra, Mošeh. 1975. *Kita:b al-muḥa:ḍarah wa-l-muθa:karah*, ed. A. S. Halkin. Jerusalem: Nezike Nirdanim.

—— 1985–1986. *Kita:b al-muḥa:ḍarah wa-l-muθa:karah*, ed. M. Abumalhan Mas, 2 vols. (Volume 2, translation into Spanish.) Madrid: Consejo Superior de Investigaciones Cientificias.

Kutscher, E. Y. 1982. *The History of the Hebrew Language*. Jerusalem/Leiden: Magnes/Brill.

Loewe, Raphael. 1994. "Hebrew Linguistics." In *History of Linguistics*, volume 1: *The Eastern Traditions of Linguistics*, ed. Giulio Lepschy. London/New York: Longman. 97–163.

Sáenz Badillos, A. 1993. *A History of the Hebrew Language*, trans. John Elwolde. Cambridge: Cambridge University Press.

Sáenz Badillos, A., ed. 1980. *Tešubot de Dunaš ben Labraṭ*. Granada: Universidad de Granada.

Sáenz Badillos, A. and J. Targarona Borrás. 1988a. *Diccionario de autores judíos (Sefarad. Siglos X–XV)*. Cordoba: El Almendro.

—— 1988b. *Gramáticos hebreos de al-Andalus (siglos X–XII)* (Filología y Biblia). Cordoba: El Almendro.

Steinschneider, M. 1902/1964. *Die arabische Literatur der Juden*. Frankfurt: Kauffmann, repr. Hildesheim: Georg Olms.

Téné, David. 1970, "Linguistic Literature, Hebrew." In *Encyclopaedia Judaica*, volume 16. Jerusalem: Keter. 1352–1400.

Valle Rodriguez, C. del. 1982a. "Die Anfänge der hebräischen Grammatik in Spanien." In *The History of Linguistics in the Near East*, ed. C. H. M. Versteegh *et al.* Amsterdam: Benjamins. 153–166.

—— 1982b. *Die grammatikalische Terminologie der frühen Hebräischen Grammatikern*. Madrid: CISC, Inst. Francisco Suarez.

—— 1988. *El Divan poético de Dunash ben Labraṭ*. Madrid: Consejo Superior de Investigaciones Cientificias.

Valle Rodriguez, C. del, ed. 1977. *Sefer ṣaḥot de Abraham Ibn Ezra*. Salamanca: Universidad Pontificia.

Varela Moreno, M. E., ed. 1981. *Tešubot de Yehudi ben Šešet*. Granada: Universidad de Granada.

Versteegh, C. H. M., Konrad Koerner and Hans-J. Niederehe, eds. 1983. *The History of Linguistics in the Near East* (Studies in the History of Linguistics 28 = *Historiographia Linguistica* 8,2/3, 1981). Amsterdam: Benjamins.

Zeslin, M., ed. 1990. *Me'or ʿayin*. Moscow: USSR Academy of Sciences.

Zwiep, Irene E. 1995. "Aristotle, Galen, God: A Short History of Medieval Jewish Linguistic Thought." Ph.D. dissertation, University of Amsterdam.

—— 1997. *The Mother of Reason and Revelation: A Short History of Medieval Jewish Linguistic Thought*. Amsterdam: Gieben.

PART II

OLD SEMITIC

5 *Akkadian*

Giorgio Buccellati

Akkadian is the oldest attested Semitic language (with Eblaite, which several Assyriologists consider a branch of Akkadian, though it is treated separately in this volume). The earliest period, known as Old Akkadian, dates to between 2350 and 2200: the major textual evidence consists of royal inscriptions. After a Sumerian resurgence, from which fewer Akkadian texts are found, the documentation resumes shortly after 2000 BCE and continues unbroken until about the time of Christ, with all major types of texts attested for most periods. It is also from that date that begins the distinction between Babylonian in the South and Assyrian in the northeast. Four periods may be distinguished, corresponding roughly to cycles lasting about five centuries each: Old Babylonian and Old Assyrian in the first half, Middle Babylonian and Middle Assyrian in the second half of the second millennium; Neo-Babylonian and Neo-Assyrian in the first half and Late Babylonian in the second half of the first millennium. It is generally assumed that Akkadian came to be no longer spoken sometime in the first half of the first millennium, when it was effectively replaced by Aramaic. In addition, Assyriologists speak at times of Classic Babylonian, referring to the Old Babylonian dialect and its survivals. The most important such survival is also known as Standard Babylonian, which describes the language used in the literary texts copied and in some cases written in the first half of the first millennium.

The best-known literary texts, such as Gilgamesh or the Creation Epic, are preserved in their most complete textual versions in tablets from the late periods written precisely in Standard Babylonian, but there are significant literary texts from all periods, including especially political texts (royal inscriptions). The Code of Hammurapi is in part a legal text and in part a document of political literature, thus providing the best example of Classic Babylonian. We are also fortunate in having several thousand letters from all periods, which give us the best evidence for spoken language.

Phonemics

Akkadian phonemes show a considerable reduction of the inventory from an earlier/archaic stage. In particular, all pharyngeals and laryngeals came to be realized (at least by the beginning of the second millennium) as glottal stop, and all interdentals as sibilants. The only innovative element is the introduction of a vowel *e*, which in part was conditioned by the loss of pharyngeals and laryngeals (e.g., *ʿabār-* > *ʾebēr-* 'to cross'). The full inventory is as follows:

Consonants

p	t				k	ʾ
b	d				g	
	ṭ				q	
			s	š	ḫ	
			z			
			ṣ			
m	n					
		l				
		r				
w			y			

Vowels

i	u
e	a

All vowels and consonants may occur either long or short; notation of length in cuneiform writing is for the most part irregular. Assyriological practice distinguishes two degrees of lengths, marked respectively by a macron and a circumflex, e.g., *bānû* 'builder'. There is however no indication that such a distinction obtained in actual phonemic reality, and it is generally applied according to historical criteria: contraction length is rendered by a circumflex, and morphological length by a macron. It seems best to avoid Assyriological use and retain a single length indicated by a macron.

Very little is known about stress, but it, too, appears to be non-phonemic.

Internal Inflection

The Root

Internal inflection is a system comprising two interdigitating sets of discontinuous morphemes, roots and patterns.

Structurally, a root can be isolated only when it interdigitates with at least two patterns. For example, the three nouns, *dunn-* 'power', *ʾumm-* 'mother', and *ṭupp-* 'tablet', seem to be derived from the same pattern *purr-*. But while *dunn-* is part of a distributional array which includes *dann-* 'powerful', *dunnun-* 'to strengthen', there are no such forms as **ʾamm-*, **ʾummum-*, **ṭapp-*, **ṭuppup-* – hence we cannot isolate any such root as **ʾmm* or **ṭpp*.

Properly, the term "nominal root" should be used for such roots from which multiple noun formations (and no verb formations) may be derived. In Akkadian, this obtains only with numerals. Otherwise, all roots are verbal-nominal, in that both verbal and nominal patterns may be derived from them. This means that all verbs imply a root, while nouns may or may not imply it. There are no roots from which only verbs can be derived.

Also lexical in nature is the "root vowel." The term implies that this vowel is an element of the root, on the same level as the consonants and therefore a morphological element – but that is not so. The root vowel is a lexical determinant for appropriate patterns from finite verbal forms from any root, and will be treated below with patterns.

All Akkadian roots consist of three or four elements, called "radicals." Each radical can be either (1) a simple consonant, or (2) a set of possible realizations, including length and Ø next to regular consonants. Only one realization occurs for the radical at any given time, and it is conditioned morphophonemically. The roots of the first type are called "strong" roots, those of the second "weak" roots.

There are limits to the combinations of consonants which can occur together to form a root. For example, two emphatics do not cooccur in the same root, and when comparative considerations would require them, one of them is realized as voiceless (e.g., Akkadian ṣbt for Semitic ṣbṭ).

Patterns

Formal Aspects

There is a difference in pattern formation between nouns and verbs. They fall in different groups characterized by special sets of markers. While the nominal patterns may be arranged in a unilineal sequence, with each pattern becoming progressively more complex, the verbal patterns are bidimensional, defined by a system of two coordinates.

The system of verbal and nominal patterns overlap with regard to their internal inflection in three instances: the infinitive, verbal adjective and participle. From the point of view of external inflection, all three behave like nouns, receiving endings for number, gender, case, but not person, tense or mood. These three patterns however, are fully integrated from the viewpoint of internal inflection, into the coordinate system of verbal patterns. In addition, these three types of nouns, alone among all nouns, can govern both the genitive case (like other nouns) and the accusative case (like the verbs). Because of this special relationship with the verb, these nouns will be considered throughout as part of the system of verbal patterns and called "verbal nouns." The other nouns which are also derived from a verbal root, but do not fit into the coordinate system or govern the accusative, will be called "deverbal nouns." The verbal patterns proper (aside from verbal nouns) will be called the "finite forms."

The traditional paradigm is followed here (Table 5.1, p. 72), with some modification. Apart from minor points of nomenclature (e.g., B for the basic stem rath-

Table 5.1 Finite forms with affixes of external inflection

		Imperative	Preterite	Perfect	Present
B Sg.	3c.		ʾ-iprus	ʾ-iptaras	ʾ-iparras
	2m.	purus	t-aprus	t-aptaras	t-aparras
	f.	pur[u]s-ī	t-aprus-ī	t-aptar[a]s-ī	t-aparras-ī
	1c.		ʾ-aprus	ʾ-aptaras	ʾ-aparras
Pl.	3m.		ʾ-iprus-ū	ʾ-iptar[a]s-ū	ʾ-iparras-ū
	f.		ʾ-iprus-ā	ʾ-iptar[a]s-ā	ʾ-iparras-ā
	2c.	pur[u]s-ā	t-aprus-ā	t-aptar[a]s-ā	t-aparras-ā
	1c.		n-iprus	n-iptaras	n-iparras
N Sg.	3c.		ʾ-ipparis	ʾ-ittapras	ʾ-ipparras
	2m.	napris	t-apparis	t-attapras	t-apparras
	f.	napris-ī	t-appar[i]s-ī	t-attapras-ī	t-apparras-ī
	1c.		ʾ-apparis	ʾ-attapras	ʾ-apparras
Pl.	3m.		ʾ-ippar[i]s-ū	ʾ-ittapras-ū	ʾ-ipparras-ū
	f.		ʾ-ippar[i]s-ā	ʾ-ittapras-ā	ʾ-ipparras-ā
	2c.	napris-ā	t-appar[i]s-ā	t-attapras-ā	t-apparras-ā
	1c.		n-ipparis	n-ittapras	n-ipparras
D Sg.	3c.		ʾ-uparris	ʾ-uptarris	ʾ-uparras
	2m.	purris	t-uparris	t-uptarris	t-uparras
	f.	purris-ī	t-uparris-ī	t-uptarris-ī	t-uparras-ī
	1c.		ʾ-uparris	ʾ-uptarris	ʾ-uparras
Pl.	3m.		ʾ-uparris-ū	ʾ-uptarris-ū	ʾ-uparras-ū
	f.		ʾ-uparris-ā	ʾ-uptarris-ā	ʾ-uparras-ā
	2c.	purris-ā	t-uparris-ā	t-uptarris-ā	t-uparras-ā
	1c.		n-uparris	n-uptarris	n-uparras
Š Sg.	3c.		ʾ-ušapris	ʾ-uštapris	ʾ-ušapras
	2m.	šupris	t-ušapris	t-uštapris	t-ušapras
	f.	šupris-ī	t-ušapris-ī	t-uštapris-ī	t-ušapras-ī
	1c.		ʾ-ušapris	ʾ-uštapris	ʾ-ušapras
Pl.	3m.		ʾ-ušapris-ū	ʾ-uštapris-ū	ʾ-ušapras-ū
	f.		ʾ-ušapris-ā	ʾ-uštapris-ā	ʾ-ušapras-ā
	2c.	šupris-ā	t-ušapris-ā	t-uštapris-ā	t-ušapras-ā
	1c.		n-ušapris	n-uštapris	n-ušapras

er than *G* for the German "Grundstamm"), and of sequence (*BNDŠ* instead of *BDNŠ*), the main difference is that the permansive is not considered here a "tense" of the verb, but rather a special form of nominal sentence (see p. 81–82, 87).

In contrast to the verbal patterns, the nominal patterns do not exhibit such a correlation of markers, and can only be listed in a unilinear fashion. When a pattern is closely correlated with a given stem, it is formally limited to just that particular stem, i.e., the characteristic marker is not carried over into other stems. For example, the pattern *taprīs-* is characteristic of the *D* stem (it occurs frequently with roots which are attested only in the *D* stem, e.g., *teslīt-* 'prayer'). But, the characteristic *t* in front of the first radical does not occur with this meaning for patterns connected with other stems.

Even though the system of nominal patterns is unilinear, it is nevertheless a true system because each pattern does have a specific meaning which is then integrated with the semantic value of the root to form the word proper. In this the deverbal nouns are markedly different from non-interdigitating nouns (primary nouns and loanwords) which may be of the same shape but do not carry the meaning of the pattern. For example, all nouns of the pattern *mapras-* from verbal roots normally carry a meaning which can be placed under the category of noun of instrument (or place); but the word *mašmaš-* 'incantation priest', though outwardly of the same shape, does not have anything in common with that category, because it is a loanword from Sumerian.

Notional Categories

The formal system of coordinates outlined above has a close correlation with semantic categories and syntactic values. One set of forms include the infinite and finite forms, i.e., verbal nouns, moods and tenses. The two moods are the imperative to express positive command, and the indicative to express a statement. The indicative mood is divided into three tenses, i.e., forms which denote the temporal position of the action *vis-à-vis* the speaker: preterite for past action and present for present or future action. Traditional Akkadian grammar recognizes a third tense, the perfect, but a separate morphological status for this tense is doubtful, and it seems more likely that forms so understood should be treated as preterites of the *t*-stem. In this presentation, however, the perfect is retained as a separate tense.

The most important stems are the following:

B stem   for the basic meaning of the root
D stem   as factitive, intensive, pluralitive of *B* (lengthening of the middle radical)
Š stem   as causative or elative of *B* (prefix *Š*)
N stem   as passive or ingressive of *B* (prefix *N* or length)
t   as reciprocal or separative of *B* and passive of *D* and *Š*
tn   as iterative of *B, N, D, Š*

Here are some examples. For one set of forms, no relationship is involved: the infinitive (*'alākum* 'to go'), the stative participle (*damqum* 'good'), the active participle (*ṣābitum* 'the one who seizes'). Another set of forms does involve the relationship of time: the present–future refers to an action which is either contemporary or posterior (*iqabbī* 'he speaks' or 'he will speak'), the preterite refers to a past action (*iqbī* 'he spoke'), the imperative refers to an action contemporary with the speaker – command (*qibī* 'speak!'). If retained as a distinct verbal form, the perfect refers (in some periods of Akkadian) to an action which is following an earlier point in time, or which came before the speaker's utterance (*iqtabī* 'he then spoke', 'he will have spoken').

We have roots of condition (for which the term "stative" can be used), and of action ("fientive"). The infinitive is indifferent to aspect (*damāqum* is either stative 'to be good', or fientive 'to become good'), the first participle is stative (*dam[i]qum* 'good, endowed with the condition of goodness'), while the second participle is fientive (*ṣābitum* 'the one who seizes at a given point in time'). However, all finite forms are punctual.

, The attitude of the speaker refers to the stance taken *vis-à-vis* the process, depending on whether process is described in a statement, or solicited through a summons. The traditional terms used for this are 'indicative' in the first case, and 'imperative' in the second. Both are called moods. Note that this notional category is represented by two different types of formal categories, that is, the moods derived through internal inflection (described here) and those derived through external inflection (for which see below).

As indicated earlier, nominal patterns, or deverbal nouns, do not exhibit as complex a paradigm as the verbal patterns, because instead of a matrix, they have a more linear pattern. One major distinction obtains, on the notional level, depending on whether or not a reference is implied to the subject of the verbal process. In the first case we have subject nouns (*ṣabbātum* 'robber') and in the other description nouns (i.e., nouns which describe the process as such, without reference to a subject), for example, *ṣibtum* 'seizing'. In terms of the verbal nouns, the first category is parallel to the participles, and the second to the infinitive.

Patterns from Strong Triradical Roots

All verbal patterns (see Table 5.1, p. 72) include two to four vowels (except for the affixes which are elements of external, not internal, inflection). The vowels are always short except in two cases, the *B* infinitive and the *B* participle. Only the first and last vowels, however, are distinctive; the middle vowel(s), when present, is/are always, indistinctively, the same, namely *a* (which may have been realized as *ə*).

The function of the first vowel is to serve as auxiliary stem marker. It may be noted that a vocalic differentiation of the stems is often necessary, because consonantism by itself is not always distinctive – for example, in the *B* present (*pr:s*) and *D* present (also *pr:s*). The first vowel of the *B* and *N* stems is either *a* or *i*, with the exception of the *Bt(n)*, *N*, *Ntn* participle and the *B* imperative. The first vowel of the *D* and *Š* stems is *u* throughout.

The last vowel serves as the main noun/tense marker. A differentiation of the nouns and tenses by vowel is generally necessary, because consonantism by itself is usually not distinctive, as in the *D* preterite (*pr:s*) and present (also *pr:s*). In the derived stems, the final vowel is as follows: *u* for infinitive and durative participle, *i* for punctual participle, imperative preterite and perfect and *a* for present.

The root vowel is determined lexically, and one will derive notations as to vocalism (*a*, *i*, *u*, and *u/a*) from the lexicon. The vocalism of the last syllable is, in the patterns of the *B* and *N* stems, dependent upon this lexical item for each finite form and most imperatives.

The root vowel is either a single phoneme (*a*, *i*, *u*) or a set of two alternating phonemes (*u/a*). When the root is single, the same vowel is found in all finite forms of *B(tn)* or *N(tn)*. When the root vowel is alternating, *a* is found in all the same finite forms except for the imperative and preterite *B*, where *u* is found. In the case of some verbs, the imperative and preterite *N* (but not the perfect) show *i* as the last vowel, under partial influence of the vocalism of *D* and *Š*.

Patterns from Strong Quadriradical Roots

The patterns from quadriconsonantal roots are symbolized by *pršd* as equivalent of *prs*. The vocalism is identical to that of triconsonantal pattern, except that an extra vowel *a* is added whenever there would otherwise be three consonants in cluster.

No quadriradical occurs in the *B* stem, except for the verbal and deverbal nouns listed in the paradigm above. A few roots occur only in the *D* stem, while all others occur only in the *N(tn)* and *Š(tn)* stems. Some common roots are *šqll* 'to hang', *blkt* 'to cross, go over', *pršd* 'to flee'.

External Inflection

The Noun

General Concepts and Notional Categories

There are two basic types of nominal external inflection. The first consists of afformatives which are added immediately to the core of an interdigitating noun, or to the base of any other noun (primary, loanword, or even proper name). These afformatives serve to derive nouns from other nouns, hence they are here called denominal afformatives. The second type consists of markers for number, gender and case of which there are four different sets, traditionally called "states." Each noun can occur in any one of these states.

Denominal afformatives and markers for number and gender have a specific semantic value which is context free. Afformatives are an aspect of lexical derivation, and have traditionally been associated with internal inflection; however, this correlation is valid on the notional level only, while on the formal level afformative derivation and internal inflection are irreducible. Thus *Aššur-ī-um* 'Assyrian' on the one hand and *damq-um* 'good' on the other are identical in terms of derivational value (as adjectives), but presuppose completely different morphological processes.

There are cases where morphological marking does not correspond to the pertinent physical features, e.g., when a singular marker is used for items which are plural in count ("collective"), or when an item which is feminine in sex is not marked as feminine in gender. There are also cases where no sex differentiation is present in the pertinent items, e.g., with inanimates or abstracts, though they still have a grammatical gender.

The markers for state and case serve as overt signals of certain syntactical correlations, and as such they are intrinsically context bound. A syntactical description, however, will sort the data from the viewpoint of syntactical categories, which do not correspond on a one-to-one basis with morphological markers.

Hence it is useful here to index, as it were, the pertinent markers for their value, leaving for the syntax a structural explanation of what this value really is. The states of the noun serve as markers for predication and annexation (a special type of nominalization). The cases serve as markers for major and minor constituents within sentences or noun phrases.

The first or "normal" state (e.g., *sinništum* 'a woman') exhibits the fullest range of variations, with a basic distinction in three cases, two numbers and two genders.

The second or "construct" state (e.g., *sinništi* 'the woman of') differs from the normal state in the case inflection, in that the basic distinction is only between two cases, and also because of some difference in the case endings themselves.

The third or "absolute" state (e.g., *sinniš* 'woman') exhibits only a distinction for gender and number, and none for case.

The fourth or "predicative" state (e.g., *sinnišat* 'she is a woman') is completely undifferentiated, i.e., it exhibits no inflectional variation at all when bound with suffix. It differentiates for gender and number only when the suffix is zero.

Denominal Afformatives

The main denominal, or derivational, afformatives, are only three, but they are common in usage and structurally important. They all serve to form nouns out of other nouns. The first of these is used for description of condition, the others for the subject of action or condition.

1 *-ūt-* is used to form abstracts, e.g., from the core *šarr-* 'king' one derives *šarr-ūt-* 'kingship'; the afformative can be added to loanwords (e.g., *ṭupšarr-ūt-* 'scribal art') and even proper names (e.g., *Ḫanigalbat-ūt-* 'Ḫanigalbat citizenship').

2 *-ān-* is used to form an adjective from another noun, e.g., *ḫurāṣ-ān-* 'golden', or to emphasize the subject aspect when it is derived from a subject noun, e.g., *šarrāq-ān-* 'a particular thief'. In the latter usage the afformative *-ān-* is especially frequent before plural markers of the masculine, e.g., *il-ān-u* 'particular gods' (as different from *il-ū* 'the gods, the pantheon'). (Note that traditionally *-ānu* is considered as a single plural marker next to *-ū*; the reasons why I prefer to split the ending in two are: the "plural" *-ānū* does have a particularizing meaning which fits well with value of the denominal afformative, and the "plural" *-ānu* on the one hand and the denominal afformative *-ān-* on the other are in complementary distribution – in other words, there is no plural *-ān–ānu*.)

3 *-ī-* (known as *nisbe*) is used to form an adjective from another noun or pronoun, or from a proper name, e.g., *maḫr-ī-* 'first' (from *maḫr-* 'front'); *mimm-ī-* 'all any' (from *mimma* 'whatever'); *Uruk-ī-* 'Urukean'.

It should be noted that the afformatives are the only productive denominative devices in Akkadian when primary nouns, loanwords, or proper names are at stake. For, without the possibility of deriving verbs out of these nouns (as remarked already above), no adjective can be derived from them through internal inflection.

The Normal State

The normal state is characterized by the fullest range of inflectional variations. Gender and number on the one hand, and case and number on the other are closely intertwined, so that structurally it seems best to present the system as comprised of two subsystems, one for the singular and one for the plural.

Table 5.2 The normal state

Number	Gender Masculine Substantive	Adjective	Feminine After pars-, parr-	After other shapes	Case
Sg.	šarr-Ø-um	ṣeḫḫer-Ø-um	šarr-at-um	'il-t-um	nom.
	šarr-Ø-am	ṣeḫḫer-Ø-am	šarr-at-am	'il-t-am	acc.
	šarr-Ø-im	ṣeḫḫer-Ø-im	šarr-at-im	'il-t-im	gen.
Pl.	šarr-Ø-ū	ṣeḫḫer-ūt-um	šarr-āt-um	'il-āt-um	nom.
	šarr-Ø-ī	ṣeḫḫer-ūt-im	šarr-āt-im	'il-āt-im	acc./gen.

Glosses: *šarrum* 'king'; *ṣeḫḫerum* 'small'; *šarratum* 'queen'; *'iltum* 'goddess'

In the singular, the masculine is unmarked, the feminine is characterized by an infix *-at* after the pattern *pars-* and after patterns ending in a long consonant, and by an infix *-t-* in all other cases, e.g:

kalb-at- 'bitch'
šarr-at- 'queen'
damiq-t- 'good (f.)'

The set of case endings in the singular is triptotic, with *-um* for the nominative, *-am* for the accusative, and *-im* for the genitive.

In the plural, the masculine is marked only indirectly, by the fact that it has a special (diptotic) set of case markers, namely *-ū* for the nominative, and *-ī* for the oblique. Note the lack of mimation (final *m*) and the presence of length which is generally a marker of plural number. A masculine plural ending *-ānu* is generally recognized in Akkadian grammar, but it seems best to interpret forms of this type as a regular plural in *-ū* added to the afformative *-ān-*, e.g., *šarr-ān-ū* 'the particular kings' (see above).

The feminine plural is marked by a single infix *-āt-*, followed by a diptotic set of case endings, *-um* for the nominative, and *-im* for the oblique. In addition, there is a special marker for the plural masculine of adjectives, namely *-ūt-*, which is also followed by a diptotic set *-um* for the nominative and *-am* for the oblique.

The basic system just outlined applies regularly only to Old Babylonian. Beginning with Middle Babylonian and then especially in Neo-Babylonian and Standard Babylonian, mimation and case endings in the singular are not used regularly (perhaps because the final short vowel was dropped as a result of phonological change), while in the plural the ending -*ī* (often changed phonologically to -*ē*) is used for all cases. As a result, the basic case declension may be considered monoptotic in the later periods, with uniform endings Ø for the singular and -*ī*/-*ē* for the plural.

The -*m* found at the end of the singular and of the feminine plural is considered here an integral part of the case markers, but this requires some qualifications. This final -*m* is often dropped in Old Babylonian, and then regularly in later dialects: since no particular contrast is apparent between forms with and without final -*m*, this feature is generally considered a free variant, called "mimation."

A dual marker is used, already in Old Babylonian, only for words implying duality, e.g., *kilallān* 'both', and especially for parts of the body which occur in pairs, e.g., *šepān* 'the two feet', *ubān-ān* 'the fingers (of the two hands)', *šap-t-ān* 'the two lips', *šinn-ān* 'the two (rows) of teeth'. The dual case is not productive in the specific sense that it is not used to express dual number as such, but only a semantic category, i.e., parts of the body occuring in pairs. Thus "two kings" is not expressed by **šarr-ān*, but rather by a noun phrase with the numeral for "two": *šarrū šenā* 'two kings'.

Three additional postfixes belong in some respects to the same distributional class as the case markers, although they are different in other respects. They are:

locative	-*ūm*	*warḫ-ūm*	'on a given month'
modal	-*ī*	*šalš-ūm-ī*	'being the third day, the day before yesterday'
terminative	-*iš*	*il-iš*	'to god'

Traditionally, only the locative and terminative are recognized as being related to the case system, while the modal is considered separately under a variety of headings; it does, however, belong to the same distributional, and notional, class as the locative and terminative.

The main difference with respect to the other case markers is that -*īš* may also occur in conjunction with other case endings, specifically -*ūm* and -*am*, e.g., *ūm-iš-am* 'daily', *kir-īš-ūm* 'into the orchard'. Also, they are attested only in the singular, both in the masculine and the feminine, e.g., *šall-at-iš* 'as booty'. Another important difference is that the terminative can also be added to a proper name which is otherwise undeclinable (e.g., *Idiglat-iš* 'to the Tigris') – another indication that it is not fully aligned with the other case markers, and behaves more like a postposition. The terminative (and possibly also the locative, though this is disputed) serve also to express the comparative, e.g., *šall-at-iš* just quoted; often the ending *iš* in this function is preceded by the afformative -*ān*-, e.g., *rīm-ān-iš* 'like a bull'.

The Construct State

A noun in the construct state is bound with another element which can be either a noun or a pronominal suffix in the genitive, or a clause with the verb in the subjunctive. The term "construct" refers to the noun in the construct state, "construent" to the element bound with the construct, and "constructive" to the pair of both elements, e.g., *bēl bītim* 'master of the house' is a constructive in which *bēl* is the construct and *bītim* the construent.

Two types of constructs may be distinguished. Construct I occurs when the construent is a noun or a clause; Construct II when the construent is a pronominal suffix, e.g.:

Construct I:	*bēl bītim*	'the master of the house'
	bēl illiku	'the lord who went'
Construct II:	*bēl-šu*	'his lord'

This inflection for gender and number is identical to that of the normal state.

The inflection for case is more reduced. We must distinguish different sets of case endings, and while all together three cases may be isolated, no single set is in fact triptotic. (There are a few exceptions such as *ab-* 'father' or *aḫ-* 'brother' which exhibit the set *-ū, -ā, -ī* in Construct II.) A first set shows zero for all three cases; a second, zero for nominative and accusative, and *-ī* for genitive; and a third, *-ū* for the nominative and *-ī* for accusative and genitive:

	Set 1	Set 2	Set 3
Nominative	Ø	Ø	*ū*
Accusative	Ø	Ø	*ī*
Genitive	Ø	*ī*	*ī*

Set 1 is used in the singular of Construct I and in the plural of Construct I with preceding infixes; set 2 is used in the singular of Construct II; set 3 is used in the plural of Construct I without infixes and in the plural of Construct II. See Table 5.3, p. 80.

The dual is identical to the normal state, without final *n*, e.g., *šēp-ā* 'the two feet of'.'

The postfixes *-ūm, -ī* and *-iš* are the same in the construct as in the normal state. The locative is attested for all genders and numbers, the modal is attested only in the singular masculine, and the terminative is not attested in the masculine plural.

A special ending *-am* or *-a* is used in poetry, proper names and lexical lists. It is attested only for the singular masculine of Construct I, almost exclusively for the nominative, though occasionally also for vocative and accusative. It is never attested for the dual or the plural, nor for the genitive, nor for Construct II. In most cases it is used with adjectives, e.g., *rapšam uzni* 'broad of ear', 'broad of understanding', instead of expected *rapaš-Ø uzni*.

Table 5.3   The construct state in syntactical context with morphophonemic resolution of forms with Ø

Pattern with gender infixes	Word	Construct I		Construct II
Ends in simple consonant	bēl-um	*bēl* bītim ṭāb *bēl* bītim āmur ana *bēl* bītim the master of the house		*bēl*-šu ṭāb *bēl*-šu āmur (ana *bēlī*-šu) his master
Ends in vowel	kala-um	*kala* ilī ṭābū *kala* ilī āmur ana *kala* ilī all of the gods		*kalū*-šunū ṭābū *kalā*-šunū āmur (ana *kalī*-šunū) all of them
Polysyllabic, ends in long consonant	kunukk-um	*kunuk* šarrim ṭāb *kunuk* šarrim āmur ana *kunuk* šarrim the seal of the king		*kunukka*-šu ṭāb *kunukka*-šu āmur (ana *kunukkī*-šu) his seal
Monosyllabic, ends in long consonant	libb-um	*libbi* ālim ṭāb *libbi* ālim āmur ana *libbi* ālim the heart of the city		*libba*-šu ṭāb *libba*-šu āmur (ana *libbī*-šu) his heart
Polysyllabic, ends in cluster	nidint-um	*nidinti* šarrim ṭāb *nidinti* šarrim āmur ana *nidinti* šarrim the gift of the king		*nidinta*-šu ṭāb *nidinta*-šu āmur (ana *nidintī*-šu) his gift
Monosyllabic, ends in cluster	kalb-um	*kalab* awīlim ṭāb *kalab* awīlim āmur ana *kalab* awīlim the dog of the man		*kalab*-šu ṭāb *kalab*-šu āmur (ana *kalbī*-šu) his dog

Glosses: *ṭāb* 'is good'; *āmur* 'I saw'; *ana* 'to'
Note: Forms in parentheses do not have a case ending in Ø.

The Absolute State

The noun in the absolute state (used rarely, and mostly in an adverbial sense) inflects only for number and gender. In the singular, the masculine is unmarked, the feminine has a marker *-at*; in the plural, only the feminine marker *-ā* is attested. The feminine singular is unmarked with nouns which have no feminine singular marker in the normal state, whether they are feminine by agreement or have a feminine plural marker (e.g., *ubān-Ø-um/ubān-āt-um* 'finger' – absolute state *ubān-Ø/ubān-ā*). Primary nouns with a feminine singular marker in the normal state, and with no masculine counterpart may occur in the absolute state either unmarked (e.g., *sinniš-t-um* 'woman' – *sinniš-Ø*) or with *-at* (e.g., *bām-t-um* 'half' – *bām-at*; *kall-at-um* 'daughter-in-law' – *kall-at*). There is no inflection for case. The complete inflectional scheme therefore is quite simple:

		Masculine	Feminine		
Normal state		(*mār-Ø-um*)	(*mār-t-um*	*sinniš-t-um*	*ubān-Ø-um*)
Absolute state	Sing.	*mār-Ø*	*mār-at*	*sinniš-Ø*	*ubān-Ø*
	Pl.	?	*mār-ā*	*sinniš-ā*	*ubān-ā*

The Predicative State

A noun in the predicative state is bound with pronominal suffixes in the nominative. The pronominal suffixes of the third person are marked (suffix Ø, and in this case the predicative state inflects for number and gender); with the other suffixes instead the predicative state is completely undifferentiated. It must be stressed that the predicative state of the feminine is unmarked even with primary nouns which are only feminine and which have the feminine marker *(a)t-* in all other states, e.g., *kall-at-um* 'daughter-in-law' occurs in the predicative state as *kall+(āku)* 'I am the daughter-in-law'. A complete inflectional differentiation may thus be noted among all states of the noun:

Normal	*nidin-t-um*
Construct I	*nidin-t-i*
Construct II	*nidin-t-a+(šu)*
Absolute	*nid[i]n-at-Ø*
Predicative + Ø	*nid[i]n-at-Ø+(Ø)*
Predicative + suffix	*nid[i]n-Ø+(āku)*

The distinction of two sets of postfixes, one marked before unmarked suffix, the other unmarked before marked suffix may seem arbitrary because the two sets are obviously in complementary distribution. This situation may best be illustrated by listing all possible combinations with pronominal suffixes:

šarr-Ø + āku	'I am a/the king/queen'
šarr-Ø + āta	'you are a/the king'
šarr-Ø + āti	'you are a/the queen'
šarr-Ø + ānū	'we are (the) kings/queens'
šarr-Ø + ātunū	'you are (the) kings'
šarr-Ø + ātinā	'you are (the) queens'
šarr-Ø + Ø	'he is (the) king'
šarr-at + Ø	'she is (the) queen'
šarr-ū + Ø	'they are (the) kings'
šarr-ā + Ø	'they are (the) queens'

Traditionally, the predicative state of the verbal adjective, in its bound form with the pronominal suffixes in the subject case, is considered a tense of the verb, and included in the verbal paradigms. This interpretation is uneconomical (because it accounts twice for the same phenomenon), and it is erroneous (because the predicative state is not restricted to the verbal adjective). The predicative state must be considered uniformly as a special morphological realization of the predicate of a nominal sentence. Hence the terms "permansive" or "stative" may be retained to refer to a special type of nominal sentence, i.e., the bound form resulting from the combination of (any) noun in the predicative state plus the pronominal suffix of the subject.

Any noun may be inflected for the predicative state, e.g.:

Unmotivated	primary	*šarr-āku*	'I am a king/queen'
	loanword	*ṭupsarr-āku*	'I am a scribe'
Deverbal		*šarrāq-āku*	'I am a thief'
Verbal		*dam(i)q-āku*	'I am good'

In the vast majority of cases, when a verbal noun is inflected for the predicative state, it is the verbal adjective; in fact, this is so prevalent that grammars and dictionaries consider traditionally a form like *dam(i)q-āku* to be the "permansive" of the verb *damāqum*. In point of fact, the form *dam(i)q-āku* is specifically the "permansive" of the verbal adjective *dam(i)q-um*, and not generically of the verb as such.

The Verb

Person, Number and Gender
In the indicative, a set of prefixes serves as person markers, and a set of postfixes as gender and number markers (for the first person, the prefix already includes an indication of number). Traditionally, the prefixes include the first vowel of the verbal form; it seems best, however, to consider the prefix as being exclusively consonantal, because the vowel serves a stem determinant function. The imperative occurs only in the second person, hence the marker for person (prefixes) are omitted; the gender and number markers are the same postfixes as in the indicative. See Table 5.1, p. 72.

Mood
Traditionally, the term is used to refer to two quite distinct types. The first pertains to context-free categories, not conditioned by the presence or absence of other syntactic constituents in the sentence. This includes the imperative and indicative (see above),and the desiderative (see below).

Two other moods are instead context bound inasmuch as they must cooccur with, i.e., are conditioned by, other constituents. The subjunctive (as it is generally called) is the correlative of subordination, i.e., it occurs whenever a verb is introduced by a conjunction or a relative pronoun: it thus corresponds to the state and case of the noun. The allative (or ventive) is the correlative of an adjunct of motion toward a given point: it thus corresponds semantically to the separative.

The subjunctive is marked by a postfix *-u* after forms of the indicative which end in a consonant. It is the regular mood of subordinate (except conditional) and relative clauses, e.g., *ša iprusu* 'who divided'.

The ventive or allative is characterized by a set of postfixes added to the indicative or the imperative, namely: *-am* after a radical, *-m* after +*ī*, *-nim* after +*ū* or +*ā*. The meaning is often that of direction toward the speaker, but in many cases it seems undistinguishable from the indicative. Examples: *taprus-am* 'you went toward me = you came', *taprusī-m, iprusū-nim.*

The desiderative expresses positive or negative wish on the part of the speaker, and is normally rendered in English simply by the auxiliary "may" or "let" in front of the main verb, e.g., "I wish that he may (not) go" = "may he (not) go," "let him (not) go." When the subject of the main action is of the third person, and the action is positive, the desiderative is traditionally called precative (or optative or jussive); with a first person subject and positive action, the traditional term is cohortative; with negative action and any person as subject, the traditional term is vetitive. Since precative, cohortative and vetitive are in complementary distribution, they should all be subsumed under the same category, which is here called "desiderative."

The desiderative is formed by prefixes added to the pattern of the preterite. Note that the first vowel of the pattern is omitted when the prefix ends in a vowel. This causes some differences between the desiderative and the indicative preterite, which it may be well to point out:

	B stem		D stem	
Singular	3rd	1st	3rd	1st
Indicative	*ʾiprus*	*ʾaprus*	*ʾuparris*	*ʾuparris*
Desiderative	*liprus*	*luprus*	*līparris*	*lūparris*

Positive wish for the 2nd person is not normally expressed by the desiderative. In its place one finds (with different nuances in meaning) either (1) the imperative, or (2) the independent particle *lū* followed by the present or the noun in the predicative state, e.g., *lū taḫassas* 'you should think', *lū balṭ-āta* 'may you be in good health'.

The Pronoun

While inflection proper occurs only for gender, number and case (see Tables 5.4 and 5.5, p. 84), the alternation of forms for the different persons is not inflectional; rather different word bases are used to refer to the different subjects.

The two sets of pronouns (for subject and oblique case respectively) are characterized by the following consonants:

	Set I		Set II	
Sg. 1	*k*	'I'	*y, n, ʾ*	'me'
Pl. 1	*n*	'we'	*n*	'us'
Sg./Pl. 2	*t*	'you'	*k*	'you'
Sg./Pl. 3	Ø	'he, she, they'	*š*	'him, her, them'

Table 5.4   The personal pronoun, set 1

		Nominative Independent	Suffix
Sg.	1c.	anāku	-āku
	2m.	ʾatta	-āta
	f.	ʾatti	-āti
	3m.	šū	Ø
	f.	šī	Ø
Pl.	1c.	nīnū	-ānū
	2m.	ʾattunū	-ātunū
	f.	ʾattinā	-ātinā
	3m.	šunū	Ø
	f.	šinā	Ø

Table 5.5   The personal pronoun, set 2

		Possessive and genitive Independent	Suffix	Accusative and after preposition Independent	Suffix
Sg.	1c.	yūm	-ma/-ya/-ī	yāti	-ni
	2m.	kūm	-ka	k(u)āti	-ka
	f.		-ki	kāti	-ki
	3m.	šūm	-šu	š(u)āti	-šu
	f.		-ša	š(i)āti	-ši
Pl.	1c.	nūm	-ni	niāti	-niāti
	2m.	?	-kunū	kunūti	-kunūti
	f.		-kinā	kināti	-kināti
	3m.	šunūm	-šunū	šunūti	-šunūti
	f.		-šinā	šināti	-šināti

Other pronouns include the following:

Interrogative   *mannum* 'who'; *mīnum* 'what'
Relative   *ša* 'who, which'; *mala* 'which'
Determinative   *ša* 'the one of'
Demonstrative   *ann-ī-um* 'this'; *ull-ī-um* 'that'
Possessive   *yūm* 'mine'; *kūm* 'yours'; *šūm* 'his'; *nūm* 'ours'

The latter two types of pronouns show occasionally /n/ as final consonant (nunation) instead of *m*.

Morphophonemics

Alternations Conditioned by Internal Inflection

Alternations Affecting Patterns
Only two alternations, particularly characteristic of Akkadian, are desribed here.
1   The conditioning factor is a root with *r* as one radical and *i* as root vowel, e.g.,
qrib as in *qerēbum* 'to approach', or *ṣḫir* as in *ṣeḫērum* 'to be small'. The alternation affects all patterns containing one or more vowels *a*, which are realized with vowel *e* instead:

{qarāb}	= *qerēb*	'approaching of'
{ṣaḫir}	= *ṣeḫir*	'he is small'
{ṣaḫir+am}	= *ṣeḫram*	'small'

Note that the morphophonemic alternation is limited to the pattern (resulting from internal inflection) and does not extend to the accusative postfix *-am* (resulting from external inflection), though exceptions are known, e.g.,

{ṣaḫir+āta}	= *ṣeḫrēta*	'you are small'

The existence of words such as *maḫārum* 'to receive' and *gamir* 'it is complete' (both with root vowel *u/a*) clearly shows that the alternation {a} = /e/ is truly morphophonemic; the simple presence of *r* as a radical, and even *i* as a vowel other than root vowel (i.e. as a pattern vowel), are not sufficient to cause the alternation automatically.
2   The conditioning factor is a root with a labial as a radical (in any position), e.g., *pḫr* (labial in first position) as *paḫārum* 'to gather', *špr* (labial second) as in *šapārum* 'to send', *rkb* (labial third) as in *rakābum* 'to ride'. The alternation affects the pattern *mapras*, which, when derived from these roots, is realized as *napras*, with alternation of the first consonant:

{mapḫar+um}	= *napḫarum*	'gathering'
{mašpar+t+um}	= *našpartum*	'letter'
{markab+t+um}	= *narkabtum*	'chariot'

The purely morphophonemic nature of the alternation is substantiated by the existence of words with initial *ma* which retain a labial in the remainder of the base because they are not subject to the terms of the morphophonemic alternation as stated, e.g., *mamītum* 'oath' (labial as first consonant after *ma*), or *madbarum* 'desert' (labial as second consonant after *ma*).

Alternations Affecting Roots and Patterns: Weak Roots
What are traditionally treated as weak roots (generally one speaks of weak verbs,

but the alternations affect nominal derivation as well) can be analyzed as morpho-phonemic alternations conditioned by internal inflection and affecting the realization of both the root and the pattern.

Weak roots may be described as having unstable radicals. Such instability affects the quality and occasionally the quantity, though never the order. For example, the first radical of the root meaning 'to bring' may occur as *w*, ' or length (variation as to quality) or it may not appear at all (variation as to quantity – only two radicals are left). The complete notation of the weak radical would be *w*/:*ʾ*/ *Ø*, and the notation of the root *(w/:ʾ/Ø)bl*, with the pertinent variations exemplified in the infinitive B *wabālum*, the perfect B *it:abal*, the infinitive Bt *ʾitbulu*, and the imperative B *(Ø)bil*.

From the fact that the first radical may be realized as length or zero it is clear that this root may not be considered as purely triconsonantal, precisely because the first radical is not consistently consonantal in nature. It is for this reason that such roots are traditionally known as "weak": they are conceived as having one radical which does not succeed, as it were, in maintaining its consonantal integrity, in contrast with the strong roots which remain triconsonantal throughout. The specific meaning which is given here to the notion of "weak radical" may be stated as "a set of alternating realizations." To indicate such sets capital letters will be used, e.g., *W* for *w*/:*ʾ*/*Ø* (hence *Wbl*).

The possible realizations of the weak radical are only six: length, ', *n*, *w*, *y*, and zero. Starting from the notion of weak radical as a set of alternating realizations, statements will be necessary to predict the manner of alternation for any given set. These statements are based on the morphophonemic environment, which may be reduced to two main types, with two subtypes each, as follows:

1 cluster   (a) radical as first element of cluster
               (b) radical as second element of cluster
2 non-cluster (a) radical intervocalic
               (b) radical initial or final

Occasionally it will be necessary to differentiate between verbal and nominal patterns, though normally the same statements apply to both categories.

We cannot review here the details of conjugation of each class of weak verb. Suffice it to say that there is a high degree of regularity in such conjugations: even so-called "irregular" verbs such as *ʾizuzzu* and *ʾitūlu* can be considered as regular, since they can be analyzed as weak quadriradicals.

Alternations Conditioned by External Inflection

Various types of assimilation occur only at the morphemic boundary between elements of external inflection, for instance {īpuš+am+šum} = *īpušaššum* 'he did to him' but *šamš+um* 'sun' (no morphemic boundary between *m* and *š*, hence no assimilation).

A distinctive Akkadian phonotactic rule states that when, through the addition of inflectional postfixes, a sequence of three syllables results, of which the first two are short, the sequence is realized as bisyllabic without the middle vowel (alternatively, the middle vowel is syncopated). See, e.g., {damiq+um} = *damqum* 'good'; {iktašad+ūm} = *iktašdūm* 'they reached'. The rule does not apply with suffixes and enclitics, in which case the morpheme boundary is obviously of a different nature than the boundary occurring before postfixes, e.g., *šarra+kunū* 'your king' (not *šarkunū*).

Alternations affecting syllabic structure at morphemic boundary with zero occur only in the construct state. Problems arise only when a long consonant or a consonantal cluster result in word-final position. In such cases, a vowel is generally added, the quality of which is governed by rules which consider the phonological structure of the base, for instance {ṭupp + Ø šarrim} = *ṭuppi šarrim* 'the tablet of the king'. In other cases, a long consonant is shortened, e.g., {kunukk + Ø šarrim} = *kunuk šarrim* 'the seal of the king'. See Table 5.3, p. 80.

Syntax

Government

Verbal and Nominal Predicate: The "Permansive"
The predicate of a sentence may consist of either a verb phrase or a noun phrase. The difference between the two is primarily that the verbal predicate refers to an action, and is temporally determined according to tense inflection, whereas the nominal predicate refers to a state or condition, and can be determined temporally only by means of adverbs.

Traditionally, the predicative state of the noun is considered separately from the other nominal predicates. In fact, most Akkadian grammars today do not even recognize the existence of a predicative state as part of nominal inflection; rather they consider predicative state and subject pronominal suffixes as one unit, which is called "permansive" (also "stative") and subsumed under the forms of the verb. As a result, *šarrāta* 'you are king' is completely separated from *atta šarrum dannum* 'you are a powerful king'. Syntactically, however, they serve the same function and should be considered together.

Predicate and Complements
Complements are all adverbial, i.e., they occur regularly in a verb phrase, in that they serve to "complete" the process described by the verb. In the terminology adopted here, a complement differs from an adjunct in that it is an essential, or nuclear, part of phrase, in contradistinction from an adjunct, which is non-essential. Complements consist of either noun phrases or subordinate clauses.

The direct object occurs regularly in the accusative, unless it is invariable. Of the transitive verbal nouns, participle and infinitive do not as a rule occur as predicates; hence their occurrence is treated below in connection with the nominalizing transformation.

The verbal adjective of transitive roots, on the other hand, occurs regularly as the predicate, and in that case it often governs the direct object, although it occurs even more frequently without direct object and then normally with a passive function. The direct object is always in the accusative, e.g., *tertam ṣabit* 'he holds office'.

When the context does not allow the use of a substantive or a pronoun as single complement, the latter is expressed by means of a noun of description derived from the same root of the verb. This is normally expressed in English by an indefinite pronoun, which serves the same purpose of what has been called a "dummy object." See for example *ḫubtam aḫbut* 'I stole something' (lit. 'a stealing'). Since the same root of the predicate is used for the object, this is traditionally called the paronomastic, cognate or internal accusative.

The complement of a transitive verb may be expressed twice, the second time in the form of a personal pronominal suffix appended to the verb. The use of the resumptive pronoun seems to be a matter of free variation, conditioned at most by stylistic emphasis or the need for better clarification of the relationships among the constituents. See, for example, *dayyānam šuāti ina dīn idīnu enēm ukannūšu* 'that judge they will convict him for having changed the verdict he had given'.

The place of the direct object may be taken by a clause, called the "objective clause." Such clauses are introduced by the conjunction *kīma* 'that' in Old Babylonian, and *kī* 'that' in Middle and Neo-Babylonian. Negation is regularly *lā* and the verb in the subjunctive. See for example *Nidnat-Sīn … kīma puḫādi nēmettaka ana ekallim lā tublam iqbīam* 'Nidnat-Sīn … said to me that you have not yet brought to the palace the lambs which represent your tax'.

Predicate and Adjuncts

From a formal point of view, or in terms of surface structure, three categories may be distinguished. The first two may be called analytic, and consist of either prepositional phrases (i.e., a preposition plus a noun in the genitive) or subordinate clauses (i.e., a conjunction plus a sentence). The third category may be called synthetic, in that the adverbial nature of the construction is expressed purely by inflectional means, without prepositions. The relevant markers of the synthetic adjuncts are:

1   the accusative singular (*-am*), as in *ūmam* 'today';
2   the locative (*-ūm*) as in *warkānūm* 'afterwards' or in the "absolute infinitive";
3   the terminative (*-iš*), occasionally combined with the accusative (*-iš-am*), as in *šapliš* 'below' or *šattišam* 'yearly';
4   the modal (*-ī*), as in *amšalī* 'yesterday';
5   the absolute state, as in *kayyān* 'constantly'.

More than one adjunct may occur in any sentence, and an adjunct in the accusative may occur in the same sentence next to the direct object complement, also in the accusative. This gives rise to the so-called double accusative, where it must be noted, however, that similarity in the inflection is only one of surface, and does not reflect identity of structure at a deeper level. Thus in the sentence *ṣubāta qaqqad-ka kuttim* 'cover your head by means of a cloth' only the second accusative (*qaqqad* 'head') is a complement, while the first one (*ṣubāta* 'cloth') is a non-essential adjunct.

While it seems possible that adjuncts of all notional categories could have been expressed both analytically (prepositional phrases) and synthetically (noun phrases), in fact the first type is the most common, and the only one of the two attested for all notional categories.

The place of an adjunct may also be taken by a subordinate clause, which is regularly introduced by a conjunction, and is further characterized by the predicate in the subjunctive and the negative particle *lā* (rather than *ul*). The notional content of the clause is partly determined by the conjunction, though some of them are ambiguous as to their meaning.

Word Order

Absolute Positions
The only instances where contact sequences between constituents may clearly be established are when either the subject or the complement or, more rarely, the adjunct consist of suffixes: then they always follow the predicate, and are in close juncture with it. Examples:

Subject	*šarr-āku*	'I am king'
Direct object	*āmur-šu*	'I saw him'
Indirect object	*addin-šum*	'I gave to him'
Adjunct	*ēkim-šu*	'I took away from him'

Two complements may both occur together as suffixes, in which case the indirect object precedes the direct object, e.g.

addin-šuš-šu   'I gave it to him'

The only other instance, outside of suffixation, in which a contact sequence seems to obtain is between subject and predicate when the subject is an interrogative pronoun and the predicate a nominal predicate. See for instance:

Ina Bābilim ana dummuqīkunū mīnu ḫištakunū?
'What is your reward in Babylon for your good behavior?'

In discontinuous sequences, i.e., sequences in which no contact is required between constituents, rules can be established only for sentence- and clause-final and initial position. These position rules apply whether the sequence is a sentence or a clause.

Two elements only are normally found in sentence- or clause-final position.

1   The subject is sentence final when it is an independent personal pronoun and the predicate is nominal. (Note the close parallelism with the contact sequence found in the stative.) Examples are:

Ina Bābilim warad ekallim anāku
'In Babylon I was a servant of the palace.'

kī yatīma atta
'You are like me.'

Note that *-ma* in the latter example indicates clearly that *kī yati* is the predicate. Clear exceptions (identifiable because of the *-ma* after the predicate) are not frequent, e.g.

anāku wēdišīyāma 'I am all alone.'

2   In all other cases, and that means in the vast majority of the cases, sentence-final position is normally occupied by the predicate, be it verbal, be it nominal, e.g.:

Verbal predicate	*šarrum illik*	'The king went.'
Nominal predicate	*bītum annūm bīt-ka*	'This house is your house.'

Exceptions are not infrequent, especially in poetry and political literature (royal inscriptions). They seem to occur mostly for euphonic and stylistic reasons, and may be divided in two groups accordingly:
(a)   The predicate occurs in penultimate rather than final position in order for the sentence to end with a syllabic sequence consisting of long and short syllables "trochaic clause"), which is a preferred prosodic feature for sentence-final position, e.g.: *išpura rakbūšu* 'he sent his messengers'.

With the predicate in final position, the sentence would end with a dactyl rather than a trochee: *rakbūšu išpura*.

Often, however, the inversion occurs even without any effect on prosody, and one may perhaps conclude that, especially in political literature, a new sentence-final position had become acceptable, namely the sequence predicate–direct object, at least when the direct object consists of a single word ending in a trochee, e.g. *uṣaḫḫir massu* 'I reduced his country.'
(b)   Another common exception to the rule which places the predicate in sentence-final position is to emphasize the predicate by inverting the order of constituents, especially by placing the predicate in initial position. This occurs in initial position, e.g.:

ana nawēm ša Ḫana ... šulmum
'There is peace in the encampment of the Ḫaneans,'
'As for the encampment of the Ḫaneans, it's at peace.'

Two elements can occur only in clause-initial position, namely conjunctions and relative pronouns; they are also mutually exclusive, as they can never occur together in the same clause.

Similarly, the subject, object or adjunct of a non-pronominal attributive clause can only occur in clause-initial position when they are the same as the head from which the attributive clause depends (see p. 93).

Exceptions are rare, e.g.:

PN *išti* PN$_2$ *šumma ittāmar*
'If PN is seen with PN$_2$'

Relative Positions
No clear role may be formulated for relative sequence of constituents, i.e., no rank may be assigned the constituents of a sentence (unlike the case with the constituents of a phrase resulting from the nominalizing transformation, see p. 93). Certain trends, however, may be pointed out, the validity of which still needs to be tested statistically on a representative body of texts. The trends may be stated as follows:

1 the subject tends to occur before the direct object, e.g.:
    šumma dayyānum dīnam idīn 'if the judge has issued a verdict';
2 the direct object tends to occur before the indirect object:
    ūmam ana mūšim lītēr 'may he turn day into night';
3 the major emphasis tends to fall on the element which is farther away from the predicate toward the beginning of the clause, e.g.:

    ana warkat ūmī, ana matīma (adjuncts of time)
    šarrum, ša ina mātim ibbaššū (subject + attributive clause)
    awāt mīšarim, ša ina nāriya ašṭuru (object + attributive clause)
    liṣṣur (predicate)
    'In the future, forever,
    the king who will be in the land
    the words of justice, which I wrote on my stela,
    let him keep.'

Feature Analysis
Of particular interest are two lexical features pertaining to the verb. They are:

⟨action⟩ $\begin{cases} + & \text{\textit{alāku} 'to go', \textit{ṣabātu} 'to seize'} \\ - \text{⟨condition⟩} & \text{\textit{damāqu} 'to be good' = ⟨intransitivity⟩} \end{cases}$

⟨transitivity⟩ $\begin{cases} + & \text{\textit{ṣabātu} = ⟨action⟩} \\ - \text{⟨intransitivity⟩} & \text{\textit{damāqu, alāku}} \end{cases}$

The adjective which is commonly used in Akkadian grammar to refer to ⟨+action⟩ is "fientive," while the adjective referring to ⟨–action⟩ is "stative" (not to be confused with the "stative" or "permansive" as a special type of nominal sentence).

The distinction between verbs of action and verbs of condition, which is essential for Akkadian, is borne out especially by the following considerations:

1   Verbs of condition do not occur as imperatives. See for example the following contrasting pair:
⟨+action⟩ : *ilik* 'go'
⟨–action⟩ : **dimiq*.
2   Verbs of condition occur in finite forms with an ingressive aspect only:
⟨+action⟩ : *illak* 'he goes'
⟨–action⟩ : *idammiq* 'he becomes good' vs. *damiq* 'he is good'.
3   The causative transformation operates differently with verbs of action and verbs of condition.

Nominalization

Relative Clauses
Relativization is the more common type of nominalization with finite verb. A relative clause is introduced by the pronoun *ša*, which may be resumed by a personal pronoun when the relative pronoun corresponds to the object, and must be so resumed when it corresponds to a genitive or dative:

ša (nom.)	*ṭuppam išpuru* '(the man) who sent a tablet'
ša (acc.)	*šarrum išpuru-(šu)* 'whom the king sent'
ša (dat.)	*šarrum bītam iddinušum* 'to whom the king gave a house'
ša (gen.)	*mārūšu ṭuppam išpurū* 'whose sons sent the tablet'
ša (gen.)	*ina bītišu uššabu* 'in whose house I dwell'

In all cases the predicate is placed in the subjunctive. With the desiderative, which morphologically does not allow a subjunctive, a construction with *ša* and the genitive of the infinitive is used instead:

lišpur	'he ought to send'
ša šapārim	'which he ought to send' (**lišpuru* is impossible)

When the relative clause is restrictive, the relative pronoun is normally deleted and the noun to which the relative pronoun refers is placed in the construct state. Deletion of the pronoun is only possible when the predicate is verbal, but (unlike English) it may occur with all cases:

awīl ṭuppam išpuru	'the man who sent the tablet'
awīl šarrum išpuru	'the man the king sent'
awīl šarrum bītam iddinušum	'the man to whom the king gave a house'

Subjective and Objective Genitive

Any verbal predicate (whether stative, transitive or intransitive) and its relative subject may be nominalized by transforming the predicate or the complement into a corresponding noun of description, in the construct state, and the subject into a dependent genitive.

Stative verb	*šū dan* 'he is powerful' ~ *dunnašu* 'his strength'
Intransitive verb	*šū illik* 'he went' ~ *alakšu* 'his going'
Transitive verb	*šū inaṣṣar* 'he watches' ~ *maṣṣartašu* 'his watch'
Complement	*šarrum qištam (iddin)* 'the king (gave) a gift' ~
	qišti šarrim 'the gift of the king'

A transitive predicate may occur nominalized in the construct state followed by the genitive of the complement:

qištam iddin	'he gave a gift'	~ *nādin qištim* 'the giver of the gift' or
		~ *nidinti qištim* 'the giving of the gift'

Attribute and "Attributive" Genitive

A predicate consisting of a verb of condition is nominalized by transforming the finite predicate into a verbal adjective, which is then in concord with the subject of the kernel sentence and functions as an attribute proper:

šarrum dan 'the king is powerful' ~ *šarrum dannum* 'the powerful king'

A very frequent expression in Akkadian, as in other Semitic languages, is the so-called "attributive genitive", e.g.: *āl dannūti* 'city of strength' or 'strong city'. The attributive value, however, is inferred intuitively from the translation into modern languages and cannot properly be derived from linguistic analysis. In the specific example quoted, the verb *danānu* cannot be predicated of the subject *ālu*, since the correlative lexical feature for the subject is ⟨+animate⟩. In such constructions, then, the noun in the construct does not correspond to the subject of an underlying sentence such as "the city is strong," but rather to the adjunct of a sentence with a deleted subject, such as "in the city (people) are strong."

The so-called "attributive" genitive is especially frequent with abstracts derived from primary nouns, e.g.: *šubat ilūti* 'the dwelling of divinity', i.e., 'divine dwelling'. Here too the construct is not equated with the quality of the genitive (it is not that 'the dwelling is god' or even 'godlike'), but rather it is the adjunct of a sentence of which one may understand "gods" to be the subject: 'dwelling in which the gods (may dwell)'. This construction appears at first to be especially suited for a qualification as "attributive" because adjectives from primary nouns are not productive (for example, there is no adjective *il-ī-u, and il-ān-ī-u has the special meaning 'blessed by god, prosperous'); in fact, however, it has a potential value: 'the city in which one may feel secure', 'dwelling where the gods may reside'.

Limitative, Partitive, Superlative

A transformational analysis of the nominalized construction ṣalmāt qaqqadim 'the black (ones) of head' presupposes an underlying sentence such as "the people are black as to the head." This is generally called a "genitive of relation," but it seems more appropriate to call it a genitive of limitation, since it limits the range of effectiveness of the predicate. Other examples are:

> damqam īnim 'good of eyes' (with the unusual construct state in -am)
> kabit kaspim 'heavy in silver'

A special type corresponds to the use of a paronomastic infinitive in the kernel sentence, e.g., le'ū le'ūti 'strong of strength' (corresponding to le'ūm le'ī 'in being strong he is strong').

Conjunction

Reversible Sequences

Only two types of conjoined sentences may be recognized as reversible in terms of surface structure, i.e., by means of specific markers. The first type includes the disjunctive sentences, i.e., sentences which are notionally mutually exclusive. They are characterized formally either by the particle ū 'or' occurring between the two sentences, or by the particles lū ... lū, šumma ... šumma 'whether ... or', either ... or', with one particle occurring in front of either sentence. Sentences of this type, namely īkul ū išti 'he ate or drank' = ištī ū īkul 'he drank or ate' are always reversible. Examples are:

ū	šumma sābitum ana šīm šikarim še'am lā imtaḫar,
	ina abnim rabītim kaspam imtaḫar,
	ū maḫīr šikarim ana maḫīr še'im umtaṭī ...
	'If an innkeeper has not received barley in payment for beer and has received instead silver by the heavy weight, or if she has reduced the value of beer in relation to the value of barley ...'.
ū lū	šumma ... eqlam Adad irtaḫiṣ
	ū lū bibbulum itbal
	'If either Adad has flooded the field or a flood has carried it away ...'.

šumma   *šumma kisām ilqī-ma ittalak,*
            šumma maḫrīkum ...
            'Whether he took the purse and went away, or whether he is still with you ...'.

Direct speech and the sentence introducing it may be considered as conjoined sentences. They are normally reversible, and characterized by special markers which occur with the first sentence. The markers vary depending on whether the sentence introducing direct speech or the direct speech itself comes first. If direct speech is first, then the suffix -*mi* is added, optionally, to one of the constituents of direct speech (occasionally more than once if direct speech includes in turn several sentences):

nādinānum-mi iddinam, maḫar šībī-mi ašām iqtabī
'"A seller gave to me, I bought (it) in front of a witness" he has said.'

If the introductory sentence comes first, then the particle *umma* begins the sentence, and the suffix -*ma* is added to the subject of the introductory sentence:

umma Ḥammurapī-ma rabiān Medēm aššum ḫibiltīšu ulammidanni
'Thus (said) Ḥammurapi: the mayor of Medūm has informed me about his loss.'

This is the standard form in letters (as in the previous example), in which case the entire letter may be considered as a single direct speech.

Irreversible Sequences
Of the two sentences constituting an irreversible sequence, only one may be introduced by a conjunctive particle. The two possible subtypes are thus characterized according to whether the particle precedes the first or the second sentence.
1   A sentence introduced by *šumma* 'if' occurs regularly first in a conjoined transform. This first sentence is known as protasis, while the second is known as apodosis, e.g.:

protasis: *šumma awīlum šinni awīlim meḫrīšu ittadī*
apodosis: *šinnašu inaddū*
'If a man knocks out the tooth of a man who is his peer,
they will knock out his tooth.'

The protasis and apodosis are properly two conjoined sentences rather than a subordinate and main sentence: the protasis, in fact, does not correspond to any other constituent of the sentence, such as complement and adjunct, or of the phrase, such as attribute. It is rather an irreducible sentence which may only be analyzed as the result of a conjoining transformation, which combines two separate sentences.

Negation in the protasis occurs with the particle *lā* as with subordinate clauses, rather than *ul* as with main sentences:

šumma nukaribbum eqlam ina zāqāpim lā igmur
'If a gardener has not finished planting a field'

Only seldom is the negation *ul* employed, and then in a potential sense, apparently to reduce the strength of negation when the speaker hopes that the negative hypothesis may not come true:

šumma GN ul ikšudū ṭuppam lišakšidū-šu
'Should they not (be able to) reach GN (as I hope they will) one should have (at least) the letter reach him.'

2   A typical Akkadian construction (generally called "virtual subordination") uses the particle *-ma* suffixed to the predicate of the first sentence. Many notional ranges may be expressed by this construction.

Deletion

Subject
The subject is often deleted when it can easily be resupplied on the basis of the context. It must be noted, however, that the subject is always implicitly present in a verbal predicate, since indication of the subject is included in the inflection markers for person (historically connected with pronominal subject markers). With a nominal predicate the subject may only be deleted if it is of the third person (and then again, the subject must be known from the context). See for instance:

nukurtum-ma   '(it) is a case of hostility'
ana bēlīšu-ma   '(the loss) is of its owner'

The subject is normally deleted with the imperative, since a command is as a rule addressed to a person immediately present to the speaker; if the subject is retained for emphasis, it may be considered in the vocative:

attunū ... ana Bābilim alkā 'You, leave for Babylon!'

For examples of subject deletion with the indicative one may quote instances in which the topic of discussion is known from previous sentences within the same discourse and is not repeated, not even in pronominal form (square brackets indicate deletion):

Anumma Sīn-ayyabāš, ištēn guzalām u šatammī ... uwa''eram ...
Inūma [Sīn-ayyabāš, guzalūm u šatammū] issanqūnikkum,
ittišunū alik.

'Now I have sent S., one servant and the managers.
When [S., one servant and the managers] come to you,
go with them.'

Similarly the subject may be deleted when an adjunct clause has the same subject as the main clause in which it is embedded, in which case deletion affects normally the subject not of the first, but of the subsequent sentence:

deletion:	*inūma aḫḫū izuzzū*
	ina makkūr bīt abim ana aḫišunū ṣeḫrim ...
	kasap terḫatim [aḫḫū] išakkanūšum
	'When the brothers divide (the inheritance),
	they will set aside the bride price from the
	family estate for their younger brother."
no deletion:	*ištu bēlī ... lā iddinam*
	bēlī ... liddinam
	'Since my lord did not give (before),
	let my lord give (now).'

A special case of subject deletion is found with the "impersonal" predicate, i.e., a predicate in the third plural with generic subject, normally translated in English with "one" and the third singular, e.g.

iqabbū ... 'on says (that) ...'

Complement
Deletion of single complement is less frequent than subject deletion, but is similarly conditioned by contextual environment; if not repeated literally, the object is normally present at least in the form of a pronominal suffix. (Object deletion is more frequent on the level of the nominalizing and conjoining transforms, for which see p. 98.)

A special case of object deletion is what is known as "lexical" deletion, i.e., a deletion which occurs regardless of context and only with reference to a specific object which is assumed to be generally known. Thus for example *šaqālum* 'to weigh' has become lexicalized with meaning 'to pay' whether or not it governs an object such as *kaspam* 'silver'.

Predicate
Deletion of predicate is very rare, and is always conditioned by a clear contextual situation. See for instance how in the following sentence the predicate is to be supplied from the previous sentence:

... mimmāšu ḫalqam irīabbū-šum.
Šumma napištum [ḫalqat]
ālum u rabiānum 1 mana kaspam ... išaqqalū
'Whatever was lost they will return to him.
If a life (was lost),
the city and the mayor will pay one mina of silver.'

Only in one instance is the deletion of the predicate regular, namely in the introductory sentence in front of direct speech, where the standard formula calls only for the name of the speaker, with regular deletion of a verb for saying or speaking:

umma Ḫammurapī-ma [iqbī]
'Thus Ḫammurapi spoke, said.'

Noun Phrase
One of the three major constituents is always deleted as the result of nominalization, since only two constituents may appear in any given transform.

In some cases more than one constituent may be deleted, sometimes as the result of a lexical deletion, e.g., *nādinānum* 'seller' (without specific reference to what is being sold).

While all other deletions do not entail any other transformation in the sentence besides deletion itseif, pronoun deletion with attributive clauses also transforms the head of the attributive clause from the normal into the construct state, e.g.:

awātum ša iqbū ul uktīn
'The word which he spoke he did not confirm.'
awāt iqbū ul uktīn
'The word he spoke he did not confirm.'

Further Reading

Aro, Jussi. 1957. *Studien zur mittelbabylonischen Grammatik* (Studia Orientalia 22). Helsinki: Societas Orientalis Fennica.
Buccellati, Giorgio. 1988. "The State of the 'Stative'." In *Fucus: A Semitic/Afrasian Gathering in Remembrance of Albert Ehrman* (Current Issues in Linguistic Theory 58). Amsterdam: John Benjamins. 153–189.
—— 1996. *A Structural Grammar of Babylonian.* Wiesbaden: Harrassowitz.
De Meyer, Léon. 1962. *L'Accadien des contrats de Suse* (Suppléments Iranica Antiqua 1). Leiden: Brill.
Finet, André. 1956. *L'accadien des lettres de Mari* (Academie Royale de Belgique, Classe des Lettres et des Sciences Morales et Politiques, Memoires 51, 1). Brussels: Palais des Academies.
Gelb, I. J. 1961. *Old Akkadian Writing and Grammar,* 2nd edn. (Materials for the Assyrian Dictionary 2). Chicago: University of Chicago Press.
—— 1969. *Sequential Reconstruction of Proto-Akkadian* (Assyriological Studies 18). Chi-

cago: University of Chicago Press.

Hecker, Karl. 1968. *Grammatik der Kültepe-Texte* (Analecta Orientalia 44). Rome: Pontificium Institutum Biblicum.

Huehnergard, John. 1987. " 'Stative,' Predicative Form, Pseudo-Verb." *Journal of Near Eastern Studies* 47: 215–232.

—— 1988. *The Akkadian of Ugarit* (Harvard Semitic Studies 34). Atlanta, Ga.: Scholars Press.

Kraus, F. R. 1987. *Sonderformen Akkadischer Parataxe: Die Koppelungen* (Mededelingen der Koninklijke Nederlandse Akademie van Wetenschapen, Afd. Letterkunde 50, 1). Amsterdam: Noord-Hollandische Uitgevers Maatschappij.

Mayer, Werner. 1971. *Untersuchungen zur Grammatik des Mittelassyrischen* (Alter Orient und Altes Testament – Sonderreihe 2). Neukirchen: Neukirchener Verlag.

Reiner, Erica. 1964. "The Phonological Interpretation of a Subsystem in the Akkadian Syllabary." In *Studies Presented to A. Leo Oppenheim.* Chicago: The Oriental Institute of the University of Chicago. 167–180.

—— 1966. *A Linguistic Analysis of Akkadian* (Janua Linguarum, Series Practica 21). The Hague: Mouton.

Salonen, Erkki. 1962 *Untersuchungen zur Schrift und Sprache des altbabylonischen von Susa, mit Berücksichtigung der Mālamir-Texte* (Studia Orientalia 27, 1). Helsinki: Societas Orientalis Fennica.

Soden, Wolfram von. 1932–1933. "Der hymnisch-epische Dialekt des Akkadischen." *Zeitschrift für Assyriologie* 40: 163–227; 41: 90–183, 236.

—— 1952. *Grundriss der akkadischen Grammatik* (Analecta Orientalia 33). 2nd edn. 1969, Analecta Orientalia 47. Rome: Pontificium Institutum Biblicum.

Ungnad, Arthur. 1903–1904. "Zur Syntax der Gesetze Hammurabis." *Zeitschrift für Assyriologie* 17: 353–378; 18: 1–67.

—— 1964. *Grammatik des Akkadischen,* 4th edn., revised L. Matouš. (1906^1, 1926^2, 1949^3.) Munich: C. H. Beck.

—— 1992. *Akkadian Grammar,* revised by Lubor Matouš, translated by Harry A. Hoffner, Jr. Atlanta, Ga.: Scholars Press.

6 Amorite and Eblaite

Cyrus H. Gordon

Amorite is (literally) the language of Amurru, which in Akkadian means 'the west'. The infiltration of Amorites into Babylonia and other parts of Mesopotamia started before 2000 BCE. During the early centuries of the second millennium, Amorite dynasties were entrenched all through the land, from Babylonia in the south to Assyria in the north, and in between, notably at Mari on the Middle Euphrates.

The classical stage of Akkadian is the Old Babylonian written during the First Dynasty of Babylon, which is the Amorite dynasty whose most famous monarch was Ḥammurapī. His Law Code is carefully couched in the most regular, consistent and precise morphology and syntax known to us in the three millennia of Akkadian scribalism. The language and especially the proper names in the tablets written during the First Dynasty of Babylon, reflect Amorite innovations. It is from those new factors that we reconstruct what we can of the Amorite language, for there are no texts written in Amorite. That something substantial can be reconstructed is due mainly to the nature of Amorite personal names, which are often in the form of whole sentences. The main source of Amorite personal names is from Mari and has been collected by Huffmon (1965). Additional primary evidence has been published by Gelb (1980) and Zadok (1993), but much of it has been dubiously classified as Amorite.

The most confusing part of Amorite studies is the wide range of applications of the terms Amurru and Amorite in the ancient sources. For example, in the Ugaritic and Amarna tablets of the fourteenth century BCE, there is mentioned a small but active kingdom in Lebanon called Amurru. The names of its leaders are quite different from those in Mesopotamia during the First Dynasty of Babylon. The Old Testament refers to Canaan as the Land of the Amorites; and Abraham (in Genesis 14) forms a military coalition with three Amorite brothers named Mamre, Eshkol and Aner. No ethnic or linguistic connection has been established between the Mesopotamian Amorites in the first half of the second millennium and the Amorites in Canaan during the second half of the second millennium. The different locations and identities of "Amurru" and "Amorite" in the ancient sources are treated fully in Haldar (1971).

Eblaite designates the language of the largest archives known from anywhere in the world during the Early Bronze Age (3000–2000 BCE). The inscriptions of the Ebla Archives already unearthed number about 15,000; many on large well-preserved clay tablets. They have been excavated by an Italian expedition at the ancient site of Ebla, a little over thirty miles south of Aleppo, Syria. The Archives were written during a period of only half a century, from around 2300 to 2250 BCE.

Eblaite is a Semitic language embodying East and West Semitic features. Texts in the same language have been found at Mesopotamian sites such as Mari, Tell Abu-Ṣalābīḫ and Kish. Eblaite is essentially a written lingua franca used by scribes, merchants and diplomats. It was not limited to Ebla, nor was it the spoken language of Ebla. Scribes, and some of their employers, could probably converse in it, but it is most unlikely that the scribes, merchants, diplomats or anyone else spoke Eblaite at home.

The Eblaite texts are written in the cuneiform system of Mesopotamia, developed by the Sumerians and adopted by the Semitic Akkadians. The system has ideograms in addition to syllabic signs. It also employs determinatives to fix the semantic category of a word. So many Sumerograms are used that it is often possible for an Assyriologist to sense the meaning of a passage, or even of an entire tablet, without knowing how to pronounce it in Eblaite. The ends of words are sometimes added syllabically to the Sumerograms so that we can deduce the case endings of nouns and the modal suffixes of verbs, as well as the suffixed personal pronouns and conjugational suffixes. Particles (conjunctions, prepositions and the like) are often spelled out phonetically. There are also extensive bilingual school-texts (Pettinato 1982) giving us the Eblaite translations of Sumerograms. However, much of that vocabulary is highly specialized and not as applicable as we might wish to the other tablets found by the excavators.

In the Ebla Archives, the Sumerograms do not follow Sumerian word order, but instead are placed in accordance with the rules of Eblaite syntax. We can thus learn much about Eblaite phrase and sentence structure even when we cannot pronounce the Eblaite words for which the Sumerograms stand.

The reconstruction of Eblaite does not involve the decipherment of a script, nor essentially the interpretation of the texts. It is rather the extracting, analyzing, classifying and assembling of seemingly endless linguistic details with the aim of enabling us to compose a grammar and glossary of the Eblaite language. For the ongoing process, see Archi 1987; Cagni 1981; Diakonoff 1990; and Gordon 1987, 1990, 1992.

Both Amorite and Eblaite are written in the Mesopotamian cuneiform system, which was not designed for, and hence is not well suited for, recording Semitic languages. In spite of nearly a century and a half of linguistic scholarship devoted to Akkadian, many details of the phonology remain controversial. The script is characterized by the two opposing (and confusing) principles of polyphony and homophony. Polyphony means that a sign may have several (often many) different phonetic values; e.g., there is a common sign that is to be pronounced *ur*, or *taš*, or *lik* (along with several other values) depending on context. Homophony means that the same sound may be represented by several (often many) entirely different signs.

When whole phonetically spelled Amorite and Eblaite texts do come to light, no seasoned Semitist should experience insuperable trouble in reading, translating and describing them linguistically in detail. This will be the case no matter whether the script is syllabic or alphabetic. Our present obstacles are simply that there are neither any Amorite texts at all, nor any Eblaite prose or poetic literature spelled out phonetically, without a plethora of Sumerograms and proper names. Names are often unconnected with the language of the people who bear them. My name (Cyrus) is Persian and my wife's name (Constance) is Latin (Constantia). Neither of us is Iranian or Italic and our language is English.

Amorite

Phonology

Consonants

The Semitic repertoire of consonants is almost covered by the Arabic alphabet of twenty-eight consonantal letters. The only additional one is $\acute{s}$ which is preserved in Masoretic Hebrew and South Arabian. The trend is for certain consonants to merge, like ʿayin and ɣayin (which fall together as ʿayin in Hebrew and Aramaic) or ḥ and ḫ (which fall together as ḥ in those languages. The problem in Amorite is that consonants which did not merge phonetically (such as h, ḥ and ʿ), can fall together orthographically because of polyphony in the Mesopotamian syllabary; e.g., the personal name (PN) Na-aḫ-ma-nu can stand for either Naʿman ('Naaman') or Naḥman. The word for "sun" is šams-u in Arabic, šemeš in Hebrew (= šamš-u in Akkadian) but it is spelled sa-am-su (as in the PN Sa-am-su-i-lu-na, meaning 'The Sun is Our God'). Since the syllabary differentiates sa from ša and su from šu, we conclude that the Amorite word for "sun" is samsu.

Amorite has the Northwest Semitic shift of initial w- to y-. The divine name (DN) Yaddu/Yandu may be derived from *wdd > ydd 'love'. It appears in the PN Ḥa-ab-du-Ya-an-du (var. Ab-du-Ya-an-du/Ab-di-ya-du) /ʿabdu-Y/ 'Servant-of-Y.' The DN Yaddu appears syllabically at Ugarit: ᵐYa-du-ᵈAddu in which Yaddu is combined with the storm god's name.

The phoneme ḍ is preserved unchanged in classical Arabic and Ethiopic, but is modified elsewhere. In Old Aramaic it becomes q and in Standard Aramaic, ʿ. In Akkadian, Canaanite, and Ugaritic, it is ṣ. The root *rḍw 'to be content, pleased' is well attested in PNs. The Amorite name Ra-ṣa-ᵈDa-gan 'Dagan is content, pleased' was given to the child whose birth shows that the vows of the parent(s) and their gifts to Dagan have pleased the god.

Vocalic variability is especially clear in variant spellings of the same person's name: Sa-mu-A-bi-im/Su-mu-A-bu-um. The different case endings suggest that Sa-mu-A-bi-im means 'Father's Name' while Su-mu-A-bu-um means 'The (deified) Name is the Father'. In any event, 'Samuel' (with a, as in the Greek Septuagint) preserves the a. The primitive Semitic word, which Arabic preserves in sandhi, is -*sm*-. When the word is not joined, it appears as *ismu* in Arabic, as *šum* in Akkadian and Aramaic, and in Hebrew as *ši/em* (in a closed unaccented syllable) or *šēm* (if accented).

The PN *A-du-na-im* (*ʾadōn-naʿīm* 'The Lord is Good') reflects the Canaanite shift *ā* > *ō*, which takes place often, but selectively, in Hebrew. It occurs in most nouns (e.g., Hebrew *ḥămôr* vs. Aramaic *ḥmār*, Arabic *ḥimār* 'ass') and adjectives (e.g., Hebrew *ṭôv* vs. Akkadian/Aramaic *ṭāb* 'good') but not in *nomina agentis* of the *qattāl* and *qātōl* formations, nor in the participles and perfects of hollow verbs (e.g., Hebrew *qâm* which serves as both perfect 'he arose' and sg. m. participle 'rising').

Barth's Law of vocalic sequence in verbs (where **yaqtal* shifts to *yiqtal*, as against **yaqtul* which remains unchanged) is not operative in Amorite. In PNs (such as *Ya-aś-ma-ah* + DN), while the verb could be Yaśmaḥ 'rejoices', it is probably Yasmaʿ 'listens'; i.e., the god has listened to our prayers and given us the child. Here Amorite goes with classical Arabic, against Northwest Semitic (Hebrew, Ugaritic, Aramaic, etc.).

Morphology

The independent pronoun, sg. 1c., can be expressed by *ʾanā* 'I' as in Arabic = *ʾnā* in Aramaic. 'I' in Eblaite is written *a-na* or *an-na* and was probably pronounced *ʾanna* in accordance with the rules of normal orthography (to wit, a singly written consonant can represent a phonetically single or doubled consonant, whereas a doubly written consonant represents a phonetically doubled consonant).

The construct singular of the uniconsonantal noun *p*- 'mouth' ends in a long vowel; nominative -*ū* occurs in the PN *Pu-ú-*ᵈ*Da-gan* meaning that the child was born through 'the word/command/mouth of Dagan'.

The sg. f. absolute ends in -*ā*; e.g., the f. PN *Ṭá-a-bā*. Side by side in Amorite we find the form with the f. -*t* preserved by the case ending (as in Akkadian/Arabic): *Ṭá-ba-tum*.

The PNs *Mu-tu-*ᵈIM and *Mu-tu-*ᵈ*Da-gan* mean 'The Man of (the respective) God'. The noun *mut*- 'man, husband' is familiar from Akkadian. However, such PNs do not establish *mut*- as the normal word for 'man' in Amorite any more than the Hebrew PN *Mĕtū-šā-ʾēl* 'Man-of-God' establishes it for Hebrew. In Hebrew *mĕtê-mispār* 'men of number = a few men' occurs as a rare archaism, but it in no way rivals *ʾîš* as the common word for 'man' nor even *ʾĕnôš* or *ʾādām* as less common synonyms.

Ya-we-AN corresponds to the Hebrew PN *Yôʾēl* 'Joel' in which are combined *Yw* = *yô* (an old form of *Yhwh* /Yahwe/) and *ʾl* = *ʾēl* 'God' (specifically the head of the pantheon).

The conjugations of the verb are familiar from other ancient Semitic languages. For example, forms of the simple (G) conjugation of *šwb* (< **θwb*) 'to return, come back' occur in the PNs: *Šu-ub-*ᵈIM 'Return, O Addu!' (with the sg. m. imperative *šub*) and *Ya-šu-ub*-AN = *Yašūb-ʾIlu* 'El returns (through the birth of this son)' (with the sg. 3m. imperfect *yašūb*).

The Gt conjugation appears in PNs such as *Ya-an-ta-qi-im* (from *nqm* 'to avenge'). 'Avenger' = nominalized sg. 3m. imperfect. A sg. 3f. Gt imperfect appears in the PN *Ta-aḫ-ta-mar*.

Of special interest is the Amorite PN *Ḫa-am-mi-is-ta-mar* = 'Ammistamar because it is also the name borne by kings of Ugarit, where it is written both alphabetically (*ᶜmθtmr*) and syllabically (*ᵐA-mis-tam-ru*). The first element is theophoric = the deified *ᶜAmm*- 'paternal uncle'. The verb is the Gt of *θmr* 'to be fruitful'. The name means that 'Amm has been fruitful in bestowing the son who bears this PN.

The local adverb of interrogation, *ʾayya*, occurs in PNs that express concern for a missing god. Such names were appropriate when the birth was saddened by troubles. Examples: *A-ya-Da-du/Ḫa-la/Ḫa-mu-ú* 'Where is Daddu/Ḫala/ 'Ammu?'. Enclitic *-ma* can be suffixed to *ʾayya*: *A-ya-ma*-AN 'Where is El?'.

Syntax

The verb normally precedes the subject; e.g., the PN *Ḫa-ya-Su-mu-ú-A-bi-im* 'Father's name lives' or simply *Ḫa-a-ya-A-bu-um* 'Father lives (on through the son who bears his name)'. The verbal root is *ḥyy*.

In Amorite PNs, *e-pu-uḫ* (var. *ya-pu-uḫ*) can be the theophoric subject. The root, **wpᶜ*, is known from the Hebrew hiphil *hôfīaᶜ* 'to appear (in splendor)' and Akkadian *Š* 'to cause something to appear brilliantly'. The verbal form is nominalized into the DN *ᵈI-pu-uḫ* in the PN *Ya-šu-ub-ᵈI-pu-uḫ* meaning 'I/E-*pu-uḫ* has returned' (signifying that the benevolent god, who had been missing, has come back). The final consonant is correctly and unambiguously rendered alphabetically in Ugaritic *Nqmpᶜ*; usually spelled *Ni-iq-me-pa* syllabically in Akkadian tablets from Ugarit, but also once *Ni-iq-me-pu*.

Some PNs consist of simple coordination. Thus *Ḫa-bi-ᵈIM* 'Ḫaby + Addu'. *Ḫaby* is the arch-demon of evil and is described in Ugaritic as possessing horns and tail – prefiguring the modern iconography of Satan. The propitiation of the forces of evil is common in ancient Near East religion, as evidenced by the frequency of Nergal/Reshef/Rasap in Akkadian, Amorite and Eblaite PNs. *Ya-we-ᵈIM* (= Addu) is the same type of name, which however invokes a good, creative deity instead of the deified forces of death, sickness and misfortune.

Eblaite

Phonology

The Eblaite system of writing is inherited from Sumerian proto-writing of Early Dynastic II. Semitic phonology includes a threefold repertoire of dental and palatal stops, and sibilants; namely surd (voiceless), sonant (voiced) and emphatic. Thus we find *t/d/ṭ*, *k/g/q* and *s/z/ṣ*. Sumerian lacks the emphatic; so that *da* covers *da* and *ṭa*, *ga* covers *ga* and *qa*, and *za* covers *za* and *ṣa*. However in Eblaite all three grades are lumped together so that DA covers *ta/da/ṭa*, GU covers *ku/gu/qu* and SA covers *sa/za/ṣa*. Neither the doubling of consonants nor the length of vowels is normally indicated. It follows that normalization and etymology cannot be ascertained mechanically. The process requires an extensive and systematic knowledge of the Semitic languages.

In the bilinguals ŠU-TUR (lit. 'little hand') designates 'finger' and its Eblaite form corresponds to the Common Semitic word that appears as *'eṣbaʿ* 'finger, toe' in Hebrew. The Eblaite is written two ways: *i-sa-ba-um* TUR and *iš-ba-um* TUR. Note the open syllable spelling with *sa* for vowelless *s* in the first form and the *š* for *s* in the second form. Eblaite is often written in open syllable orthography (like Linear A and B, or Japanese). A word beginning *'aṣmi-* is spelled *a-za-mi-* or *a-zi-me-*; note that the vowelless *s* is written either *za*, reflecting the vowel of the preceding syllable or *zi*, reflecting the *i* of the following syllable. This open syllable orthography gives the illusion that there are no closed syllables in Eblaite, which is not at all the case.

The mixed character of Eblaite is reflected in the words designating the large numbers: *mi-at* '100' is Common Semitic, *li-im* '1,000' is East Semitic, *ri-bab* '10,000' is West Semitic, and *ma-i-at* '100,000' goes its own way in a new direction. The variant forms of '100,000' are *ma-i-at*, *ma-i-ḫu-at* and *ma-ḫu-at*; all three are probably related phonetically although the details are not yet clear.

It is interesting to note the Eblaite forms of Sumerian names: ^{d}EN-LIL > *I-li-lu*, ^{d}NIN-KAR-DU > *Ni-ka-ra-du*, ^{d}SUMUQAN > *Sa-ma-gan*, ^{d}ASNAN > *A-sa-ma-an*.

The bilingual equation BAḪAR 'potter' = *wa-ṣí-lu-um* (cognate with Hebrew *yôṣēr* 'potter') illustrates that, (1) unlike Northwest Semitic, initial *w- remains in Eblaite (as in Akkadian and Arabic) without shifting to y-; and that (2) *r* may change to *l*. The change of *r* to *l* (which is quite common) is not reversible, for *l* never shifts to *r*. The falling together of *r* and *l* (in the *r* > *l* shift) reflects a common phenomenon. In Linear A and B, and in hieroglyphic Egyptian, *r* and *l* fall together, at least in the orthography. In Chinese and Japanese, they definitely fall together in the spoken language as well.

The geographical name (GN) *Ar-ga*^{ki} /ʾarqa/ has lost the final *-t* of the sg. f. suffix *-at*. In the Amarna Letters this GN is called Arqat. Compare the GN É-*ma*^{ki} = Ḥamāt (modern Ḥama). The final *-t* of the sg. f. suffix is generally dropped in Hebrew, and regularly in spoken Arabic. Final *-t* begins to be dropped in Egyptian in the third millennium.

The GN *Máš-a*^{ki} is to be compared with the GN *Maśśāʾ* (Proverbs 30:1; 31:1). The *-a* accordingly does not reflect the feminine suffix (which would be written with a final *-h* in Hebrew) but final *-ʾ*.

Etymology indicates that *l* frequently loses its normal consonantal character in Eblaite and is not represented in the script. For example, *a-bi-nu-u(m) i-a-ba-nu* SIG₄-GAR /ābinū yabānū libitta/ 'brickmakers will make the brick'. The root of the first two words is **lbn* although no *l* appears in the orthography. We must reckon with vocalic *ļ* (and also vocalic *ŗ*) in the Semitic languages. In Akkadian, the second radical of all quadriconsonantal verbs is either *l* or *r*. This may explain the Arabic conjugation III (*qātala*; cf. Hebrew *pôlēl* with a long vowel representing the absorption of vocalic *l̥* or *r̥*).

Initial *w-* does not undergo the Northwest Semitic shift to *y-*. Eblaite retains *w-* like Akkadian, Arabic and Ethiopic. In addition to the example on p. 105, note (the dual) *wa-ti-a* /wādi-ā/ 'the two wadis'.

Vowels

The script reflects four vowels: *a*, *i*, *u* and *e*. However, *e* may well be non-phonemic but only positionally conditioned by contact with *ḥ* or *ʿ*.

The diphthongs *ay*, *aw* and *ue* can all be reduced to *ā*. In the case of *ay > ā* and *aw > ā*, the shift can be explained as "falling" diphthongs (with the accent on the *a*) as distinct from "rising" diphthongs (with the accent on the *y/w*) whereby **bayt* yields *bīt* 'house' and **mawt* yields *mūt* 'death' in Akkadian. While we find many Eblaite examples of *ay > ā* and several of *aw > ā*, there is only one of *ue > ā*: the Akkadian *Suen* (which comes into Babylonian and Assyrian as *Sin*, is reduced to *San* 'Moon' in *San-Ugāru* 'Moon of the Field' (an epithet of the Moon in an incantation where the reference to the Moon is fixed by duplicate passages which have ITI 'month, moon' instead). *San* also appears instead of *Sin* (the Moon god) in the Hebrew form of the Mesopotamian names *San-ḥērîb* (Sennacherib) and *San-ballaṭ*. In the Palestinian GN 'Beth-shan' the second element (Shan) designates the Moon god. Examples of *ay > a* in Eblaite: *ba-du* /bāt-/ 'house'; *a-na* and *a-na-a* /ʿānā/ 'eyes' (du.); *ba-nu* /bān-/ 'tamarisk' (vs. Akkadian *bīn-* with rising diphthong); *ma-sa-lu-u(m)* /māšalu/ 'justice, uprightness' from **yšr* (note Hebrew *mêšārîm*) and from the Št stem of the same root *uš-da-ši-ir* /uštašir/ 'he prepared, released (lit. 'caused to be right)'. There are fewer examples of *aw > ā*: **ʾaw > ʾā* 'or'; and the PN *Mu-ša-ra-du* (Š participle of **wrd* 'to bring down gods with gifts = to propitiate them successfully'; cf. Arabic and especially Ugaritic).

Cryptic Writings

Cryptic writings were meant to be read by the initiated. We know from a bilingual tablet that ᵈMUL = *Kab-kab* 'Star'; however in an incantation, it is written *ga : ga : ba : bu* /kabkabu/ (ending in nominative *-u*). A similar cryptograph is *ga : ga : li : la* which calls to mind *galgal* 'wheel'; if correct, note that *li* stands for vowelless *l*.

The name *Da-gu-nu* corresponds to Hebrew *Dāgôn* (< Dagān) with *ā > ō* which is frequent in Canaanite. Compare also Minoan *Da-gu-na*.

-dk- is assimilated to *-kk-* in *a-za-me-ga* /ʾaṣmikka < **ʾaṣmid-ka/* 'I bind thee'.

*Sum-ar-rúm*ᵏⁱ 'Sumer' comes into Hebrew as *Šinʿār* 'Babylonia'. Note that AR = *ʿar* and begins a new syllable. Another change in syllabification is inherent in Eblaite and Old Akkadian *en-ma* (> Standard Akkadian *um-ma*), and Hebrew *nʾum* – all meaning 'so says' (followed by direct discourse). The initial *n-* is properly vocalic *n̥*, which has to be written *en-* according to the rules of the Mesopotamian syllabary, and *nĕ* according to the rules of Masoretic Hebrew (Gordon 1993: 109–110).

Vocalic nasals and liquids include *r̥*. The tree called the ᴳᴵˢšU-ME is bilingually rendered in Eblaite as either *ši-rí-mi-nu* or *ša-mi-nu*. Expressed alphabetically, the choice is between *šrmn* and *šmn*. The *r* is vocalic and not represented in the latter.

Philippi's Law (*i* > *a* in an originally closed accented syllable) is operative in Northwest Semitic (Canaanite, Aramaic, Ugaritic). It does not take place in Akkaidan, Arabic, etc. Since Eblaite is a border language between East and Northwest Semitic, it is not surprising that it occurs sporadically. Thus in Eblaite both *libittu* and *libattu* (spelled *li-bi-tum* and *li-ba-tum*) 'brick' occur.

Pronouns

The following independent personal pronouns are attested:

Sg.	1c.	nom.	*an-na, a-na* /ˀanna/ 'I'
	2m.	nom.	*an-da* /ˀanta/ 'thou'
		acc.	*gu-wa-ti* /kuwāti/ 'thee'
		dat.	*gu-wa-si* /kuwāši(m)/ 'to thee'
	3m.	nom.	*su-wa* /šuwa/ 'he'
		acc.	*su-wa-ti* /šuwati/ 'him'
		dat.	*su-wa-si* /šuwāši(m)/ 'to him' ·
	f.	nom.	*si-a* /šiya/ 'she'
Du.	1c.	dat.	*ne-si-in* /nešin/ 'to both of us'
Pl.	2m.	nom.	*an-da-nu* /ˀantanu/ 'ye, you'
	3m.	nom.	*su-nu* /šunū/ 'they'

The following suffixed personal pronouns are attested:

Sg.	1c.	gen.	*-i* /-ī/, or (postvocalic) *-a* /-(y)a/ 'my'
		acc.	*-ni* /-ni/ 'me'
	2m.	gen. acc.	*-ga* /-ka/ 'thy, thee'
		dat.	*-kum* /-kum/ 'to thee'
	f.	gen. acc.	*-gi* /-ki/ 'thy, thee'
	3m.	gen. acc.	*-sù, -su* /-šu/ 'his, him'
		dat.	*-su-um* /-šum/ 'to him'
	f.	gen.	*-sa* /-ša/ 'her'
Pl.	1c.	gen .	*-na* /-nā/, *-nu* /-nū/ 'our'
	2m.	acc.	*-gu-nu* /-kunū/ 'you'
	3m.	gen. acc.	*-su-nu* /-šunū/ 'their, them'
	f.	gen.	*-si-na* /-šina/ 'their'
		acc.	*-si-na-at* /-šināt/ 'them'

The lone occurrence of an unusual pronominal suffix calls for special notice. The meaning of *ši-ne-mu* /šinn-êmo/ 'his teeth' is fixed by context. The ending *-êmō*, known from Biblical Hebrew poetry, is a general possessive suffix that can be applied regardless of person. Here it means 'his teeth' but in another context it could mean 'their teeth' and so forth. An exact (though admittedly clumsy) translation is 'thereof'.

The relative pronoun 'who, which, that' is derived from the noun meaning 'man'. In the Ebla tablets it can be expressed by the Sumerogram LÚ 'man'. The same semantic development has taken place in Semitic. There is an Egypto-Semitic uniconsonantal word for 'man'; it is written *s* in Egyptian; in Old Akkadian it is used as the relative pronoun 'who, which', fully inflected (nom. *šu*, gen. *ši*, acc. *ša*). Later, only *ša* is used regardless of case. In archaic Hebrew, *ša* appears sporadically. From late Biblical Hebrew and in all subsequent stages down to the present, it appears as *še* 'who, which'. In several Ebla PNs, *Šu-* 'he of' is followed by a theophoric element; e.g., *Šu-Na-im*, *Šu-I-lum*, *Šu-Ma-lik*; Na'îm = 'The Good One', Ilum = 'El, God'; Malik 'The (divine) King'. The Eblaite determinative relative pronoun (in agreement with Akkadian and Amorite) is:

		Nominative	Genitive	Accusative
Sg.	m.	*šu*	*ši*	*ša*
	f.	*ša-du* /šātu/	*ša-ti* /šāti/	
Pl.	m.		*šu-ti* /šūti/	*šu-ti* /šūti/
	f.		*ša-ti* /šāti/	*ša-ti* /šāti/

The interrogative pronoun, animate, is nom. *ma-nu* /mannu/ 'who?', acc. *ma-na* /manna/ 'whom?'; inanimate nom. *mi-nu* /mīnu/, acc. *mi-na* /mīna/ 'what, which?', dat. *mi-ne-iš* /mīniš/ 'to which?'.

The preceding pronoun may be generalized by the suffixing of enclitic *-ma*: animate *ma-nu-ma* /mannuma/ 'whoever', inanimate *mi-nu-ma* /mīnuma/ 'whatever'.

The noun has two genders (masculine and feminine), three numbers (singular, dual and plural) and six cases. Mimation is sometimes indicated and sometimes not, so that no rule can be formulated.

The six case endings are: nominative *-u(m)*, genitive *-i(m)*, accusative *-a(m)*, dative locative *-iš*, locative adverbial *-u(m)*, absolute *-a/-Ø*. The three commonest cases (nom., gen., acc.) are often confused. There are some indeclinables in *-a*, especially among the PNs such as *Ra-ba*, *Ba-ga-ma*, *Tab-rí-sá* and the DN ᵈ*Ba-ra-ma*. While a bilingual renders the name of the Sumerian god EN-KI as *É-um* /Ḥayyum/ in Eblaite, the other Eblaite texts regularly render the name *É-a* /Ḥayya/ ending in *-a*. Other DNs in *-a* are: *É-da* /Hadda/ and *Qu-ra* /Qūra/.

The absolute in *-Ø* (zero) is common in some proper names; e.g., the DNs ᵈ*Ga-mi-iš*, ᵈ*Ra-sa-ap*; the GNs *A-da-bi-ik*ᵏⁱ, *A-da-ti-ik*ᵏⁱ and in month names such as ITI *za-É-na-at*.

The construct state is not always expressed in writing: for example, it is not expressed in *ha-za-nu* GN 'the mayor of X', while it is in *ma-lik* GN 'the advisor of Y'.

The suffix marking the dual is *casus rectus* *-ā(n)*, *obliquus* *-ay(n)* (which can shift to *-ā(n)* in accordance with the reduction of the diphthong *ay* to *a*); e.g., *tal-*

da-an /daltān/ 'double doors' and *su-lu-la-a* 'the two horns'. The following citation has the dual suffix in the word designating a pair of deified rivers and a dual
noun in apposition with them: 2 ^{d}*Ba-li-ḫa wa-ti-a* /Baliḫa wādia/ 'the two divine
Baliḫ rivers, the two streams'.

The suffix marking the pl. m. *casus rectus* is *-ū*; *obliquus -ī*. That marking the
pl. f. *casus rectus* is *-ātu/i, obliquus: -āti*. The sg. f. *zi-ne-éb-ti* 'tail' is pluralized
zi-na-ba-ti.

One of the common methods of pluralizing a noun in Sumerian is to repeat it.
When a scribe writes GURUŠ-GURUŠ 'workmen' in an Eblaite tablet it is possible
that he intended the reader to add the Semitic plural suffix *-ū/ī* to a Semitic word
for 'workman'. But that is not necessarily so. Though repeating a noun for plurality is not a normal Semitic usage, we do find the repetition of Semitic words to
pluralize them in Eblaite; e.g., *na-si$_{11}$ na-si$_{11}$* 'patricians' (passive participle of
*nś² 'to lift up'), *maš-maš-sù* 'his sons'.

The doubling of nouns for pluralizing reflects Sumerian usage, because Sumerian has no dual, and therefore plurality starts with two. In Egypto-Semitic, however, there is a dual, so that plurality starts with three. Therefore we find the plural
²ilū 'gods' written DINGIR-DINGIR-DINGIR.

Etymologies, even when correct, do not always supply satisfactory meanings
for Eblaite vocabulary. The title of the head man in the hierarchy of Ebla is EN, an
old term signifying the priest-king of a theocratic Sumerian city-state, with emphasis on his priestly rather than his royal status. A bilingual informs us that NAM-
EN '*en*ship' = Eblaite *ma-li-gú-um*. The abstract noun standing concretely for a
type of person (like the abstract "acquaintance" in the sense of "someone we
know") is common in Semitic (e.g., Akkadian *mūdu* or Hebrew *môdā'* lit.
'knowledge', but in the sense of 'a friend'). Accordingly NAM-EN implies that EN
was pronounced /malikum/. When the king is called *malikum* we are dealing with
the West Semitic sphere; in the East Semitic sphere the king is called *šarrum*. The
noun *nāśí²* 'exalted one' designates 'king, prince' in Biblical Hebrew and 'presi-
dent' in modern Hebrew. At Ebla it designates the full-fledged free citizen (whom
we may call a 'patrician') as distinct from a GURUŠ 'worker' (= 'plebeian' or 'helot') and from the lowest IR$_{11}$ or 'slave'.

There is one pair of words that raises fundamental questions to be pondered
though not definitively answered now. The nouns *ḫrd* 'child' and *ms* 'son, child'
have long been known only from Egyptian. Then both turned up in Ugaritic of the
Late Bronze Age, and now in Eblaite of the Early Bronze Age. Ebla had connections with Egypt; alabaster vessels with the names of Chefren (Fourth Dynasty)
and Pepi I (Sixth Dynasty) have been found at Ebla in the archeological stratum
that yielded the Archives. The meaning of Eblaite *ḫar-da-du* /ḫardātu/ in the sense
of 'young women' is fixed by context; the same form with the same sense occurs
in Old Kingdom Egypt. The situation with Eblaite *maš* (= Egyptian *ms*) is more
complex and tantalizing. It is common in all periods of Egyptian from start to finish. But it also occurs in Sumerian (MÁŠ) with the meaning of a 'kid, young goat'.
Words for young animals are often applied to children.

The adjective has long been known to be inflected like the noun except for the pl. f., *status absolutus* in Syro-Aramaic. Now Ebla shares that exception with Syro-Aramaic. In Hebrew *mĕlākîm*/n 'kings' has its feminine counterpart in *mĕlākôt* 'queens'. But in Aramaic the phonetic equivalent of Hebrew pl. f. construct *malkôt* 'queens (of)', namely *malkât* 'queens (of)', can only serve as the construct. The Aramaic absolute (corresponding semantically to Hebrew *mĕlākîm*/n 'kings') is *malkān* 'queens'. Thus Eblaite *du-na-an* /dunnān/ 'mighty (females)', has the suffix *-ān* for the adjective pl. f. absolute.

Tense

There are two principal tenses: (1) the so-called imperfect with prefixes and some suffixes, and (2) the so-called perfect with suffixes but no prefixes. Verbs are usually classified as strong (with a root of three stable consonants) or weak (with a semivowel: *w* or *y*, functioning as one of the root consonants; or with only two consonants in the root with the second one repeated). A root can be treated within the matrix of several conjugations, all familiar from the other Semitic languages; e.g., G, Gt, D, Š, ŠD, ŠDt. Like Aramaic, Eblaite has no N conjugation. The imperfect has modal suffixes; thus *-u* is the sign of the indicative. In the perfect, the sg. 3m. ends in *-a*. In Akkadian the perfect is for stative or intransitive verbs; in West Semitic the perfect is used for transitive as well as intransitive verbs. Here, Eblaite goes with West Semitic.

The imperfect has *a*, *i* or *u* as the thematic vowel between the last two consonants of the root:

u-class: *Iq-bu-ul-(Ma-lik)* is a PN meaning '(The Divine King) has accepted (the propitiatory offerings of the parents and granted the child who bears the PN)'.

i-class: *Ig-ri-iš-(Li-im)* is a PN meaning '(God) has driven out (the forces of evil)'.

a-class: *Ir-kab-(Ar)* is a PN meaning '(The Deity Ar) rides'.

The prefix vowel gives the impression that there is an isogloss with East Semitic in which we find Akkadian *iprus*, *iddin*, *iṣbat* vs. West Semitic where we find Arabic *yaqtul*, *yajlis*, *yasmaʿ*. Little weight can be attributed to the loss of the *y-* in Akkadian because of the vocalization of the Hebrew in the LXX (Septuagint Greek) tradition and some living traditions like the Arabic. Note LXX *ISAAK* 'Isaac' (vs. Masoretic *Yiṣḥāq*) and Arabic *ʾIshāq*; and vs. Masoretic *Yiśrāʾēl*, 'Israel', note Arabic *ʾIsrāʾīl*. However, *ya-* is preserved in both the LXX and Arabic traditions: Masoretic *Yaʿaqōb*, LXX *IAKOB*, Arabic *Yaʿqūb*.

The attested morphs of the imperfect tense are: sg. 1c. *ʾa*-CCVC; sg. 2m. *ta*-CCVC; sg. 3m. *i*-CCVC; sg. 3f. *ta*-CCVC; pl. 3m. *i*-CCVC-*ū*.

The perfect (sg. 3m. = CaCVCa) is used in PNs such as *Ra-ga-ma-Il* 'God has spoken' (with **rgm* 'to speak' as in Ugaritic) or *Qá-ba-Lum* 'God has spoken' and *Qa-ba-Da-mu* 'The (god) Damu has spoken' (where the verb is familiar from Akkadian *qabū* 'to speak'). East Semitic restricts the perfect to intransitive verbs, whereas Eblaite, like West Semitic, uses it for transitive as well as intransitive verbs. In addition to the above transitive perfects, note also *ba-na-a* 'he has built'.

The following is a D imperfect intensified by an infinitive absolute ending in adverbial -*u* (as in Ugaritic and Akkadian): *i-na-É-áš na-É-su* /ʾinaḫḫaš naḫâšu/ 'I shall verily perform magic'. Note that the D prefix does not go with Arabic and Akkadian ʾ*u-*.

The infinitive absolute in -*u* appears in the *figura etymologica*: *ḫu-mu-zu ḫa-ma-zi, bu-ru₁₂ ba-ra-ru₁₁* (*brr).

The ŠD participle *muška⁽⁽inum* is of interest because it explains Akkadian *muškēnum* 'helot, plebeian' which survives into modern Hebrew *miskēn* and Arabic *miskīn* 'poor'; and French *mesquin* 'shabby, mean'.

The composite interregional nature of Eblaite precluded the modicum of consistency and uniformity that more natural languages have developed through analogic leveling. We thus find the same root (*hlk) with two treatments of the G infinitive in the bilinguals: *É-a-gu-um* /hākum/ and *É-la-gum* /halākum/ 'to go'. There would be little merit in our striving to create a consistency that is not there.

Sundry Particles

En-ma 'so says' introduces direct discourse.

In the PN *A-ku-Da-mu* (meaning 'The god Damu exists'), *a-ku* seems to anticipate colloquial Iraqian Arabic *aku* 'there is'.

What has evolved into the conjunction *wa* 'and' is an Egypto-Semitic particle indicating existence. It serves as an auxiliary verb in an old construction named (though badly so) the *waw*-conversive. It has been known from classical Hebrew and other Canaanite dialects. The *w* + verb must head the sentence or clause; then comes the subject; finally comes the object if the verb is active and transitive. *Wa-*ÍL IGI-IGI EN *wa*-NAM-KU₅ 'The ruler's eyes were raised and he swore'. This construction (*w* + imperfect) is the normal narrative tense in classical Old Testament prose. With the passing of time, it became vestigial and eventually went out of use. Its earliest occurrence so far known is at Ebla.

Besides *wa* (*ú, ú-ma*), *ap* is also used as the conjunction 'and'.

The preposition *al₆* /ʿal-/ means '(up)on'. The dative is indicated by the preposition *si-in* /sin/ 'to'. One and the same root is declined to form three prepositions (as in Akkadian): *áš-du* /aštu/ '(out) from', *áš-ti* /ašti/ 'from', *áš-da* /ašta/ 'on, at, from'. *Mi-in* /min/ 'from' (as in Canaanite, Aramaic and Arabic) also occurs. East Semitic *in* 'in(to), at [local], on [temporal]' occurs more frequently than West Semitic *ba* 'in'. Compare *iš ₓ-ki* /ʿiški/ 'for' with Ethiopic (Geʿez) *ʿaskā* 'into'. The following illustrates the temporal application of *áš-du* and *si-in*: *áš-du* U₄-U₄ *si-in* U₄-U₄ 'from days to days, periodically, annually' patterned after a Northwest Semitic idiom (Hebrew *miy-yāmîm yāmîmā* 'from days to days, periodically, annually').

Syntax

The word order is rather free. Often the verb heads the sentence: e.g. ʾ*aṣmidu hab-habi* 'I bind Ḥabḥaby', ʾ*asmikka* ʿ*al-l* ʾ*abni* 'I bind thee on a stone'.

For emphasis the order can be varied. Note subject–object–verb (+ resumptive accusative suffix) in: *'annā kuwāti-ma 'iṣbaṭeka* 'I thee strike = I strike thee'. Logically the verb *'iṣbaṭeka* expresses the entire subject–object–verb; but the magician is asserting his power, and then emphasizes the specific target of his magic act.

Chronology and Borrowing

The Early Bronze Age date of the Ebla Archives provides an abundance of Semitic documents in Syria a millennium earlier than the Ugaritic tablets and half a millennium earlier than Minoan Linear A. Eblaite words borrowed from Sumerian, such as *mallāḫ-* 'sailor', show that they were already part of Syro-Palestinian speech and did not have to be borrowed much later, as was previously assumed. Words like *kinnār-* 'harp, lyre' > Greek *kinúra*, show how specific elements in Greek culture were already in the Near East before Greece was Greek.

References

Archi, A. 1987. "Ebla and Eblaite. In *Eblaitica 1*, ed. C. H. Gordon. Winona Lake, Ind.: Eisenbrauns. 7–17.
Cagni, Luigi, ed. 1981. *La Lingua di Ebla: Atti del Convegno Internazionale (Napoli, 21– 23 aprile 1980)*. Istituto Universitario Orientale: Seminario di Studi Asiatici. Series Minor 14.
Diakonoff, I. M. 1990. "The Importance of Ebla for History and Linguistics." In *Eblaitica 2*, ed. C. H. Gordon. Winona Lake, Ind.: Eisenbrauns. 3–29.
Gelb, I. J. 1980. *Computer-aided Analysis of Amorite*. Chicago: Oriental Institute, University of Chicago.
Gordon, Cyrus H. 1987. "Eblaitica." In *Eblaitica 1*, ed. C. H. Gordon. Winona Lake, Ind.: Eisenbrauns. 19–28.
—— 1990. "Eblaite and Northwest Semitic." In *Eblaitica 2*, ed. C. H. Gordon. Winona Lake, Ind.: Eisenbrauns. 127–139.
—— 1992. "Notes on the Ebla Exorcisms." In *Eblaitica 3*, ed. C. H. Gordon. Winona Lake, Ind.: Eisenbrauns. 127–137.
—— 1993. "Vocalized Consonants: The Key to *um-ma/en-ma/*םאָ." In *The Tablet and the Scroll: Near Eastern Studies in Honor of William W. Hallo*, ed. M. E. Cohen, D. C. Snell and D. B. Weisberg. Bethesda, Md.: CDL Press. 109–110.
Haldar, A. 1971. *Who Were the Amorites?* Leiden: Brill.
Huffmon, H. H. 1965. *Amorite Personal Names in the Mari Texts*. Baltimore: Johns Hopkins University Press.
Zadok, Ran. 1993. "On the Amorite Material from Mesopotamia." In *The Tablet and the Scroll: Near Eastern Studies in Honor of William W. Hallo*, ed. M. E. Cohen, D. C. Snell and D. B. Weisberg. Bethesda, Md.: CDL Press. 315–333.

Further Reading

A complete bibliography of the Eblaite texts would fill a large volume. The following is instead a list of the publications containing large assemblages of Eblaite texts.

The first group is called MEE (Materiali Epigrafici di Ebla); for the sake of avoiding a glaring gap, MEE 1 is included though it is a catalogue of the texts rather than the texts themselves. MEE is published by the Seminario di Studi Asiatici of the Istituto Universitario Orientale di Napoli.

Pettinato, Giovanni, ed. 1979. MEE-1: *Catalogo dei testi cuneiformi di Tell Mardikh-Ebla.*
—— 1980. MEE-2: *Testi amministrativi della biblioteca L 2769,* volume 1.
—— 1981. MEE-3: *Testi amministrativi della biblioteca L 2769,* volume 2.
—— 1982. MEE-4: *Testi lessicali bilingui della biblioteca L 2769,* volume 3.
Mander, P., ed. 1990. MEE-10: *Administrative Texts of the Archive L.* Rome: Dipartimento di Studi Orientali of the Università degli Studi di Roma "La Sapienza."

This series is also called Materiali per il Vocabulario Sumerico-1. Some of the texts have been published previously, but twenty-three are published here for the first time.

The group that follows is the ARET (Archivi Reali di Ebla– Testi) series, published by the Università degli Studi di Roma "La Sapienza."

Archi, Alfonso, ed. 1985. ARET-1: *Testi amministrazioni: Assegnativi di tessuti.*
—— 1988. ARET-7: *Testi amministrativi: Registrazioni di metalli e tessuti.*
Archi, Alfonso and M. G. Biga, eds. 1982. ARET-3: *Testi amministrazioni di vario contenuto.*
Biga, M. G. and L. Milano, eds. 1984. ARET-4: *Testi amministrativi: Assignazioni di tessuti.*
Edzard, D. O., ed. 1984. ARET-5: *Hymnen, Beschwörungen und Verwandtes.*
Fronzaroli, Pelio, ed. 1993. ARET-11: *Testi reali della regalità.*
Milano, L., ed. 1990. ARET-9: *Testi amministrativi: Assignazioni di prodotti alimentari.*
Sollberger, Edmond. 1986. ARET-8: *Administrative Texts Chiefly Concerning Textiles.*

With the exception of ARET-8, all of the above volumes include indexes which enable the reader to locate details conveniently.

7 *Aramaic*

Stephen A. Kaufman

The Periods and Sources of Aramaic

Aramaic is attested over a period of almost 3,000 years, during which time there of course occurred great changes of grammar, lexical stock, and usage. Although no universally accepted classification scheme for these phases exists and new discoveries regularly alter our picture – especially for the sparsely attested older dialects – the general shape of the outline is clear.

Old Aramaic *c.* 850 to *c.* 612 BCE

This period witnessed the rise of the Arameans as a major force in Ancient Near Eastern history, the adoption of their language as an international language of diplomacy in the latter days of the Neo-Assyrian Empire, and the dispersal of Aramaic-speaking peoples from Egypt to Lower Mesopotamia as a result of the Assyrian policies of deportation. The scattered and generally brief remains of inscriptions on imperishable materials preserved from these times are enough to demonstrate that an international standard dialect had not yet been developed.

The extant texts may be grouped into several dialects:

Standard Syrian (or Western Old Aramaic): These inscriptions, of very limited chronological (mid-ninth to end of eighth century BCE) and geographic spread (within a circle of radius *c.* 100 km centered on Aleppo) include commemorative stelae and international treaties.

Samalian: At modern Zincirli, dynasts of the Neo-Hittite kingdom of Sam'al (also referred to by some scholars as Ya'udi) wrote their dedicatory inscriptions first in Phoenician (KLMW), then in a local, highly idiosyncratic Aramaic dialect (the so-called Hadad and PNMW inscriptions), and, finally, in standard, Syrian Old Aramaic (BR-RKB).

Fakhariyah: On the Upper Habur, a bilingual, Neo-Assyrian and Aramaic inscription on a statue. The script and orthography of this inscription are of major importance for the history of the alphabet.

Mesopotamian: Primarily consists of brief economic and legal texts and endorsements scratched on clay tablets. Not surprisingly, both the Fakhariyah and Mesopotamian dialects evidence a substantial amount of Akkadian influence.

Deir Alla: This important but frustratingly fragmentary text, painted on the plaster walls of a cultic installation in the mid-Jordan valley, recounts a vision of

"Balaam, son of Beor," the trans-Jordanian prophet known from Numbers 22–24. The fact that some scholars classify the language of this text as a Canaanite, rather than an Aramaic, dialect, illustrates that there is no clearly demonstrable division between Canaanite and Aramaic at this time.

Imperial Aramaic (or "Official Aramaic") *c.* 600 to *c.* 200 BCE

During this period Aramaic spread far beyond the borders of its native lands over the vast territories of the Neo-Babylonian and even larger Persian empires – from Upper Egypt to Asia Minor and eastward to the Indian subcontinent. Unfortunately, only a minuscule remnant of the undoubtedly once vast corpus of administrative documents, records and letters that held these empires together has been preserved, for such texts were written in ink on perishable materials, in sharp contrast to the well-nigh imperishable cuneiform clay texts of earlier western Asiatic cultures. (A single syllabic cuneiform Aramaic text, an incantation from Uruk, is known. Though the text itself is from Hellenistic times, its archaizing language may be ascribed to this period.) Isolated, monumental stone inscriptions have been found in the various peripheral regions (e.g. Sheik Fadl in Egypt, Teima in Arabia, Daskyleion in Asia Minor), but none to speak of, surprisingly enough, in the core regions of Syria and Mesopotamia. The bulk of the finds, however, is from Egypt, where the dry climate led to the preservation of papyrus and leather along with the expected ostraca and stone inscriptions. The major finds there are:

1 papyrus archives of the Jewish military garrison at Elephantine/Syene (including deeds of sale, marriage contracts, formal letters to the authorities in Jerusalem, and fragments of literary materials);
2 the correspondence of the Persian satrap of Egypt, Arsames;
3 a packet of letters sent to family members residing at Syene and Luxor, discovered at Hermopolis;
4 Saqqarah: A late seventh-century papyrus letter from a Philistine king (perhaps of Ekron) asking for Pharaoh's help against the king of Babylon; and legal and economic records on papyri and ostraca from the fifth and fourth centuries.

The Aramaic "official" letters in the book of Ezra are almost certainly to be viewed as composed in Imperial Aramaic, for both their language and their epistolary style are appropriate to the period.

From a linguistic perspective, what characterizes this period above all is that it witnessed the development of a literary, standard form of both the language and its orthography – an ideal to be strived for, at least in literary texts and formal documents. The model for this standard appears to have been Babylonian Aramaic as spoken and written by educated Persians. This ideal, in the guise of "Standard Literary Aramaic" (SLA), was to last more than a thousand years.

The semi-demotic language of the personal letters evidences features that are later to appear in the formal language: weakening of the *haf ͨel* (*hktb/yhktb*) to

ʾafʿel (ʾktb/yktb), and substitution of *nun* for final *mem* on the plural pronominal suffixes. The later Western Aramaic features of *-n* on the pl. 3 perfect of IIIy verbs and *mem* preformative of derived theme infinitives are also found. Changes in the formal language include the simplification of the infinitive to a single form (*peʿal mktb*); the use of pl. 3m. forms for pl. 3f.; and the first appearance of the determined plural ending *-ē*. This form appears first on gentilics and collectives, and later, in the Eastern dialects, will replace *-ayyā* as the normal ending of the masculine plural.

Middle Aramaic c. 200 BCE to c. 250 CE

In this period, namely the Hellenistic and Roman periods, Greek replaced Aramaic as the administrative language of the Near East, while in the various Aramaic-speaking regions the dialects began to develop independently of one another. Written Aramaic, however, continued to serve as a vehicle of communication within and among the various groups. For this purpose, the literary standard developed in the previous period, Standard Literary Aramaic, was used, but lexical and grammatical differences based on the language(s) and dialect(s) of the local population are always evident. It is helpful to divide the texts surviving from this period into two major categories: epigraphic and canonical.

Epigraphic

Palmyrene: dedicatory and honorific inscriptions and a decree of duty tariffs from the independent Syrian desert oasis trading city of Tadmor/Palmyra. Many of the texts are Greek bilinguals.

Nabatean: tomb and votive texts from the Arab kingdom of Petra. A hoard of legal papyri from the Bar Kochba period was discovered in one of the Nahal Hever caves.

Hatran: dedicatory inscriptions from the important, second century CE Parthian kingdom of Hatra. A smaller, similar group was found at nearby Assur.

Other: isolated inscriptions from Syria (especially Dura-Europos), Asia Minor, Armenia, Georgia, Media, Parthia, Persia, and Babylonia. Archival materials from the Judean desert are also to be placed here.

Canonical

Daniel

The Aramaic portions of this biblical book (in contrast to the material in Ezra) clearly belong to this dialect rather than to Imperial Aramaic.

Jewish Literary Aramaic

1 Qumran
   Among the Dead Sea Scrolls, much (if not most) of the non-sectarian, parabiblical material is in Aramaic. This includes: the Genesis Apocryphon,

Targum of Job, the Books of Enoch, and the Testament of Levi.
2   Targum Onkelos/Jonathan
    Although the only reliable manuscripts of this Jewish translation/interpre-
    tation of the biblical text stem ultimately from the Babylonian rabbinical
    academies, the consonantal texts of Targum Onkelos to the Pentateuch (To-
    rah) and Jonathan to the Prophets apparently originated in Palestine in this
    period.
3   Legal formulas
    Preserved in Rabbinic literature are texts and formulas of an authentic Ara-
    maic tradition.

Middle Iranian Ideograms
After a brief flirtation with cuneiform for their monumental inscriptions ("Old
Persian"), the Persians adopted the Aramaic script for writing their language and,
perhaps under the cuneiform model, in both Parthian and Pehlevi, Aramaic ideograms were used to indicate Persian lexemes.

Also apparently from the earliest part of this period is the Aramaic material preserved in Demotic script papyrus Amherst 63, consisting of a New Year's ritual
and the lengthy story of the conflict between the two royal Assyrian brothers,
Asshurbanipal and Shamashshumukin.

Late (or Classical) Aramaic *c.* 200 to *c.* 1200 CE

The bulk of our evidence for Aramaic comes from the vast literature and occasional inscriptions of this period. During the early centuries of this period, Aramaic
dialects were still widely spoken. During the second half of this time frame, however, Arabic had already displaced Aramaic as the spoken language of much of
the population, so many of our texts were composed and/or transmitted by those
whose Aramaic dialect was only a learned language. Although the dialects of this
period were previously generally divided into two (Eastern and Western) branches, it now seems best to think rather of three: Palestinian, Syrian, and Babylonian.

Palestinian

Jewish
Inscriptions (mostly from synagogues).
Targumic: the dialect of the Palestinian Targumim (Bible translations: Neofiti,
Genizah fragments (from the storeroom of the Old Cairo Synagogue), and the
Fragment Targum).
Galilean: the dialect of the Talmud and midrashim of the land of Israel (so-called
"Yerushalmi").

Christian
Christian Palestinian Aramaic: a small group of inscriptions, Bible translations,
and liturgical lectionaries from the Judean region written in Syriac script.

Samaritan

Two different translations of the Pentateuch, liturgical poetry, and some literary/ exegetical works are preserved from this group. The reading tradition of the modern Samaritan priests is a valuable linguistic source here, as it is for their Hebrew tradition.

Syrian

Syriac

The liturgical language of Eastern Christianity is by far the best-documented Aramaic dialect. A vast and varied literature in two (Eastern/Nestorian, Western/ Jacobite) dialects and orthographies has been preserved, as well as small collections of epigraphic and archival materials. The orthography of Syriac is based on that of Standard Literary Aramaic, while its lexicon and grammar are primarily that of the city of Edessa.

Late Jewish Literary Aramaic

This literary dialect, only recently recognized, served for the composition of Aramaic parabiblical and liturgical texts (the best known of them being Targum Pseudo-Jonathan, Targum Psalms, and the canonical Targum of Job) and in some cases (Tobit and perhaps others) for the translation into Aramaic of works whose presumed Hebrew or Aramaic original had been lost. Like other literary dialects, it borrows heavily from its forbears, in this case Biblical Aramaic, Jewish Literary Aramaic, Jewish Palestinian Aramaic, and Jewish Babylonian Aramaic. Like most rabbinic materials, the texts have suffered greatly in transmission and often give the impression of massive inconsistency. Recent studies have revealed, however, that this is a real, albeit literary, dialect with its own grammar and lexicon, whose lexical affinities point to a close relationship with the Syriac-speaking region.

Babylonian

Jewish

The spoken language of the Jews of Babylonia, preserved primarily in large parts of the Babylonian Talmud (records of the academies of the fourth and fifth centuries CE). Slightly different dialects are found on "magic bowls" (incantations written on pottery bowls) and in the halakhic literature of the post-Talmudic Babylonian sages (gaonim). The written and oral traditions of the Jews of Yemen are particularly important sources for this material.

Mandaic

The spoken and literary language of a non-Christian gnostic sect. The sect itself is generally thought to have Palestinian origins, but its language is totally at home in Southern Mesopotamia.

Modern Aramaic
See Chapter 16.

Phonology

Consonants

Old Aramaic
In this period the Proto-Semitic phonemic inventory survives virtually unchanged, though some minor changes in articulation seem to be indicated. Since the linear consonantal alphabet used for Aramaic, borrowed from a Canaanite/Phoenician source, had only twenty-two graphemes, several of the characters had to be polyphonous. Thus:

> *Šin* indicates: *š*, *ś*, and *θ*
> *Samek* (at Fakhariyah only) indicates both *s* and *θ*
> *Zayin* indicates *z* and *δ*
> *Ṣade* indicates *ṣ* and *ẓ*
> *Qop* indicates *q* and *ḍ* (probably a velar spirant by this time)
> *Ḥet* indicates *ḥ* and *ħ*
> *ʿayin* indicates *ʿ* and *γ*

That these consonantal phonemes still survived (rather than having merged with their graphic equivalent) is surmised largely on the basis of their independent histories in the subsequent dialects. (See comparative tables of consonantal reflexes.) In the case of *ħ* and *γ*, however, evidence for their existence is extrapolated from the fact that they are still regularly distinguished in the Demotic papyrus (see p. 117). The result of these orthographic choices (with the exception of *qop* for *ḍ*), taken together with the natural affinity between older dialects of closely related languages, gives these texts an appearance very similar to that of Canaanite, a fact that has led some scholars to unwarranted claims of Canaanite influence in grammar, vocabulary, and style.

    Nun is always assimilated to a following consonant in this period: *ʾt* 'you' (< *ʾanta*).

    Metathesis of dental and sibilant in the *t-* verbal stems, regular in the later dialects, is not fully carried through yet in Old Aramaic.

Imperial Aramaic
The graphic representation of consonants begins to change noticeably, presumably as a result of phoneme mergers and the ensuing or concomitant introduction of the spirantization of stops (lenition). Though in this period archaizing orthographies are common (particularly with *z* for original *δ* and *q* for original *ḍ*), the language here starts to take on the appearance it will have in subsequent dialects.

These mergers are: $\theta > t$, $\delta > d$, $\d > $ $^\prime$, $\d > t$, $\d > \d$ (though in some dialects the merger in fact may have been the reverse), $\gamma > $ $^\prime$. The initial tendency for $\check{s}$ to merge with s probably can also be ascribed to this period, since it is common to all subsequent dialects.

A noteworthy feature of the formal language (the base of Standard Literary Aramaic) is "nasalization," namely, the dissimilation of long ("doubled") consonants into *nun* + consonant. In some of these forms (e.g. *ʾnt(h)* 'you') the *nun* is etymologically correct but had assimilated in Old Aramaic. In others (e.g. *mndᶜ* 'knowledge'), it is strictly a phonetic phenomenon. Nasalization is regularly found, not surprisingly, with dental stops, but it also appears, heretofore inexplicably, with the root *ᶜll* 'to enter', e.g. the causative stem infinitive *lhnᶜlh* (Daniel 4:3) vs. *lhᶜlh* (Daniel 5:7). It now appears probable that the latter case merely represents an attempt to indicate the lengthened voiced velar spirant γ.

Classical Aramaic and Syriac

As a result of the above mentioned consonantal mergers, the standard phonemic inventory of classical Aramaic is the twenty-two-element "Hebrew" system as follows:

p	t	s	k	ḥ	h
		š			
b	d	z	g	ᶜ	ʾ
	ṭ	ṣ	q		
m	n	l			
w	r	y			

At the onset of the classical period, lenition of the stops was a productive feature, but it atrophied in the course of the first millennium CE (and is not indicated in our transcriptions here).

Weakening of the laryngeal/pharyngeal consonants is characteristic both of Palestinian dialects (Samaritan and some Galilean) and of Babylonian. In Babylonian, final liquids, nasals, and interdentals also regularly elided.

Vowels

Old Aramaic

The indirect evidence of the morphology of feminine nouns (e.g. **malkatu > malkat > malkah*) suggests that final unstressed vowels had dropped by this period.

Imperial Aramaic

The distinctively Aramaic phonological feature – the reduction of short vowels in open unstressed syllables (using regressive alternation) – seems to have had its start in this period, at least for *i/u* vowels.

Classical Aramaic

Noteworthy features of the later dialects include:

Short vowels in unstressed syllables are first reduced and, ultimately in most dialects, totally elided. The vocalization traditions indicate that by now (i.e. after the loss of final case vowels) stress was generally on the final syllable of the word, though the modern dialects (and some reading traditions) show a strong tendency toward penultimate stress. In Syriac and Babylonian, originally final unstressed **long** vowels are also elided.

In the transcriptions used in this chapter, short vowels reduced in the classical stages of the language are indicated by superscript.

Characteristic of all Aramaic dialects, as of all Semitic dialects, is variation of vowel quality in different environments of stress and syllable length, even though such changes are indicated only irregularly in the schemes of vowel pointing introduced in Late Aramaic. Typically, front and back vowels are raised in stressed or opened syllables and lowered in closed unstressed syllables. In Western Syriac, all mid and low long vowels are raised; thus $\bar{o} > \bar{u}$, $\bar{e} > \bar{\imath}$, and $\bar{a} > \bar{o}$. In some dialects simplification of diphthongs is similarly conditioned; in others (notably Syriac) *ay* and *aw* are tenaciously preserved (or restored?) in the reading traditions.

Morphology

Pronouns

Personal Pronouns

Independent

The following may be ascribed to common Aramaic:

	Singular	Plural
1c.	*ʾanā*	*ʾanaḥnā*
2m.	*ʾattā, ʾantā*	*ʾattūma > ʾattūn, ʾantūn*
f.	*ʾattî, ʾantī*	**ʾattina > ʾattēn*
3m.	*hūʾa > hū*	*humu* (OA), *himmō himmōn, hlʾinnōn*
f.	*hīʾa > hī*	**hina, hlʾinnēn*

These forms are used exclusively in nominative and absolute constructions, except for the pl. 3 forms. The existence of a dual number may be assumed for early Aramaic but is not clearly attested.

In the later dialects, the independent pronouns are typically bound with present tense verbs (1st and 2nd person only) and nouns/adjectives in pronominal predicative constructions, yielding a series of enclitic forms. In Syriac, for example, some of the enclitic forms are: sg. 1c.: *nā* (often written *ʾnʾ*); 2m.: *at*, 2f.: *at* (written *ʾt, ʾty*); 3m.: *ū*, 3f.: *ī* (written *hw, hy*); pl. 1c.: *nan* (written *hnn* or *nn*). Thus *kāteb-nā* 'I am writing'; *šappīr-ū* 'he is beautiful'.

Suffixed
The suffixed pronouns are used as possessives on nouns and objectives on verbs. Typical of these forms is the synchronic "jump" of the color of the distinctive final vowel into the position held by the case vowel at an earlier stage of the language; thus: **malku/a/ika* ('your king') > *malkāk*.

	Singular	Plural
1c.	*-ī* (nominal), *-anī* (verbal)	*-anā* (> *-an*, *-nan*)
2m.	*-āk*	*-kuma* > *kōn*
f.	*-ek*, *-ekī*	*-kina* > *kēn*
3m.	*-eh*, (*-hī* after vowels)	*-huma* > *hōn*
f.	*-ah*, (*-h(ā)* after vowels)	*-*hina* > *hēn*

Interrogatives

'who'   (*mannu* [Uruk incantation]) > *man* (and often with enclitic 3rd person pronoun: *mannū*).

'what'   *mā* (Syriac, more commonly, *mān*, *mānā*).

Relative
dī (spelled *zy* in Old and Official Aramaic) > *d-*. This, the reflex of the Semitic determinative pronoun *δū/ā/ī*, is used as the regular relative marker from earliest time. It also becomes the common genitive particle starting with the Official Aramaic period (see p. 129).

Demonstrative

Near
sg. m. *din* (> *dēn*), *dᵉnā*; sg. f. *dā'* > *dā*; pl. *'illay*, *'illayn*.

Far
In the earlier dialects, far demonstratives *per se*, with the typical Semitic augment *-k*, are regularly used: sg. m. *dnk*, *dk*, *dkn*; sg. f. *dky*; pl. *'lk*, etc. Early on, however, these tend to be replaced by the 3rd person independent pronouns.

In Middle Aramaic, a distinction develops between substantive and attributive demonstratives, the latter formed by combining the older forms with the deictic particle *hā*; thus Jewish Palestinian Aramaic *hādēn*, Syriac *hānā* (< *hā* + *dinā*). Eventually, the new forms are used in substantival constructions as well.

Indefinite or Impersonal
Common to all the dialects is *kull* 'all'. From Imperial Aramaic on *mindaᶜm* > *meddem*, *medde* is 'something'. In the earlier dialects *'īš* is used for 'someone'

(> Babylonian *'iniš*); later on one finds instead *gbar* (literally 'man') and *ḥad* (literally 'one') in pronominal usage, while the relative *d-* alone is used in relative constructions.

Nouns

Case

Samalian shows a distinction between nominative and oblique cases in plural nouns: *-w/-y*. Standard Old Aramaic and Imperial Aramaic regularly spell the pl. m. suffix simply *-n*, so no distinction is apparent. By the time that the vocalic traditions first appear, no case distinction is attested for the plural. In the singular, however, the adverbial case (others "accusative") was apparently regularly used well into the late first millennium BCE, at last in the absolute state. Feminine nouns are spelled with final *-t* (presumably /ata/) instead of the *-h* (/ā/ < *at*) of the nominative case. (As in other Semitic languages, final *-a* of the adverbial was maintained somewhat longer than the *-u/i* of the other cases.) After the complete loss of case marking, the morphology of adverbials in the later dialects preserves relics of the case ending: *-ā, -āt, -āīt, -āūt*. The loss of the Semitic case system was obviously interrelated with the development of the postpositive definite article and the system of nominal states (see State, below). Since adverbials and predicatives are rarely determined, the survival of marking for this case should not be surprising.

State

The most notable difference between Aramaic and the other Northwest Semitic dialects is the presence of the suffixed definite article *-ā(')*. Probably in origin the same form as the Hebrew and Phoenician *ha:-* (cf. *hā'-* 'here'), the suffixation of this deictic element gives the language the appearance of having three noun states (absolute, construct, emphatic (or determined)):

	Absolute	Construct	Emphatic
sg. m.	*mlk*	*mlk*	*mlk'* (*-ā'*)
pl. m.	*mlkn* (*-īn*)	*mlky* (*-ay*)	*mlky'* (*-ayyā'*)
sg. f.	*mlkh* (*-ā(h)*)	*mlkt* (*-āt*)	*mlkt'* (*-atā'*)
pl. f.	*mlkn* (*-ān*)	*mlkt* (*-āt*)	*mlkt'* (*-ātā'*)

In the classical Eastern dialects of the Common Era, the determinate force of the emphatic state is lost, whereby final *-ā* on nouns becomes the unmarked state. The now marked, absolute state is then limited to predicative and distributive constructions in a manner reminiscent of Akkadian, the influence of which on this usage may be suspected. In those dialects, as well as Hatran and sometimes in Palmyrene, the unmarked pl. m. suffix is normally *ē* rather than *-ayyā* (cf. Adjectives, below).

Adjectives

Adjectives probably were originally limited to the passive participles and the related form *kattīb*. In the later dialects, in particular in Syriac, the originally gentilic suffix *-āy* (Note plural emphatic: *-āyē*) is widely and freely used as an adjectivizing morpheme.

Prepositions

A distinctive characteristic of the development of new prepositions is the combination of the simple common Semitic prepositions with specific nouns of place, cf. for example Jewish Palestinian Aramaic *mn ᵓpy* 'from the surface', *mn lwwt* 'from the presence', *mn gb* 'from the top', *mn byny* 'from between' and so on.

Numerals

Cardinals

The Common Aramaic system is as follows:

	Masculine	Feminine
1	*ḥad*	*ḥᵃdā*
2	*trēn*	*tartēn*
3	*tᵃlātā*	*tᵃlāt*
4	*ᵓarbᵃᶜā*	*ᵓarbaᶜ*
5	*ḥamⁱšā*	*ḥᵃmiš*
6	*šittā*	*šit*
7	*šabᶜā*	*šᵃbaᶜ*
8	*tᵉmānⁱyā*	*tᵉmānē*
9	*tišᶜā*	*tⁱšaᶜ*
10	*ᶜesrā*	*ᶜᵃsar*
11	*ḥad ᶜᵃsar*	*ḥᵃdā ᶜasrē*
12	*trē ᶜᵃsar*	*tartē ᶜasrē*
20	*ᶜasᵃrīn*	
30	*tᵃlātīn*	
100	*miᵓā*	
200	*miᵓᵃtēn*	
1,000	*ᵓᵃlip, ᵓālip*	

As is usual in the Semitic languages, the later dialects evidence contraction in the teens, e.g., Syriac *ᵓarbᵉtaᶜsar* '14'; Babylonian *trēsar* '12'. Compound numerals reference the larger units first.

Ordinals

Separate ordinals are used for 1–10. With the exception of 'second', they are simple adjectives in *-āy* with 3–10 using the pattern *kᵃtībāy*: *qadmāy* 'first'; (NB) *tinyān* (Syriac *taryān*) 'second'; *tᵃlītāy* 'third'; *rᵃbīᶜāy* 'fourth', etc.

Fractions

Fractions are nouns with the pattern *kutb* (some *kitb*); e.g., *ḥumš* 'a fifth'.

Verbs

Root Classes

As in the other Semitic languages, the fundamental opposition in the verbal system is that between active verbs (i.e., verbs *per se* in Western languages) and stative verbs (i.e., adjectives in Western languages). Morphologically, that distinction is reflected in the thematic vowel pair ablaut between the "perfect" and "imperfect" finite forms: active *k^{a}tab/yiktub* (termed thus a/u); stative *k^{a}teb/yiktab* and *k^{a}tub/yiktab* (termed thus i/a and u/a). Diachronically, the drift is toward increasing the membership in the active class at the expense of the stative, and many intermediate forms (intermediate in terms of both morphology and semantics) occur in the various dialects.

Derivation Classes

Verbs: The three fundamental themes are the basic theme (*pe^{c}al*: *katab/yiktub*, etc.), factitive theme (*pa^{cc}el*: *kattib*), and causative theme (*haf^{c}el*: *haktib*). In the oldest dialects, passives are expressed by internal vowel modification of the active form (presumably using the vowel pattern *u-a* in the derived conjugations). Middle Aramaic has a basic theme passive *p^{ac}īl* in the perfect – identical with the passive participle. No certain N theme is attested in normative Aramaic, though it does occur at Deir Alla and, possibly, in Samalian. Reflexive/middle derived themes with a *taw* augment (*'tp^{c}l*), that will soon begin to replace the internal passives, are still rare in the earliest period. At Fakhariyah, the reflexive of the basic theme still has infixed *taw*, as in Arabic and Ugaritic.

Morphosyntactic changes in Imperial Aramaic include: limitation of the use of internal passives in favor of the *'t-* preformative themes. (In this period only the *'etp^{ac}el* and *'etpa^{cc}al* are attested. Internal passives seem to have survived longest in the causative conjugation. Biblical Aramaic word initial *ht-* is undoubtedly a Hebraism.)

The *haf^{c}el* reflexive/passive *'ettaf^{c}al* occurs in all later branches of Aramaic, so it must have already existed in the Imperial Aramaic period. After the demise of the internal passives, then, the following symmetrical pattern of theme formation is distinctive to Aramaic:

Basic	*k^{e}tab*	*'etk^{e}teb*
Factitive/Pluralitive	*katteb*	*'etkattab*
Causative	*'akteb*	*'ettaktab*

Though a substantial group of derived themes in *š-* and *s-* occur, some borrowed from Akkadian, others, no doubt survivals from an earlier stage of the language (e.g. *šaklel* 'to complete', *ša^{c}bed* 'to enslave') the *šaf^{c}el* is not a productive causative conjugation in Aramaic.

Aspect and Tense
Formatives for the perfect (suffixed) tense/aspect are:

	Singular	Plural
1c.	-*it* (earlier -*tu*)	-*na*
2m.	-*t(a)*	-*tum* > -*ton*
f.	-*t(i)*	-*tin* > -*ten*
3m.	-*Ø*	-*u*
f.	-*at*	-*u/a/in*

Imperfect (prefixed) formatives are as follows. (The vowel of the prefix varies with theme and root category, of course.):

1c.	ᵓ-	*n*-
2m.	*t*-	*t*- -*ūn*
f.	*t*- -*īn*	*t*- -*ān*
3m.	*y*-	*y*- -*ūn*
f.	*t*-	*y*- -*ūn/ān*

The Eastern dialects of the classical period use *l*- (Babylonian) and *n*- (Syriac and less frequently in Babylonian) preformatives instead of *y*- in the 3rd person. In the late Western dialects, the first person preformative is *n*- in the singular as well as in the plural.

Additionally, a separate jussive form exists in the early dialects, differing orthographically from the imperfect in its absence of "nunation" in the pl. 3m. and pl. 2m. (and, presumably, the sg. 2f., as in later Aramaic) and in final weak roots, where the imperfect ends in -*h* (presumably /e/), the jussive in -*y* (probably, simply /i/!). The two forms are also distinct when they have pronominal suffixes, where (as in Hebrew) the imperfect inserts the so-called "energic" *nun* between the stem and the suffix, while the jussive does not. Samalian uses jussive-like forms for the imperfect as well (cf. standard Hebrew *yiktᵉbû* as opposed to archaic *yiktᵉbûn*). In Fakhariyah, Mesopotamian, and Samalian, the 3rd person jussive takes a *lamed* preformative instead of a *yod* (cf. the Akkadian precative *liprus*), a form apparently ancestral to the later *l-/n-* preformative of the Eastern Aramaic dialects. It is now clear that the so-called "imperfect consecutive" (the old fashioned term "converted imperfect" is a glaring misnomer) narrative tense – an archaic remnant of the old Semitic preformative preterite tense – attested in the Zakkur and Tel Dan ninth-century BCE inscriptions as well as at Deir Alla (but not at Sam'al), was a feature common to Old Syrian, Aramaic and Hebrew, just one of the many grammatical and lexical isoglosses in respect to which Hebrew sides with early Aramaic over against Phoenician.

Verbal Nouns
The classical infinitive of the basic stem is *miktab*. The derived stems show substantial variation, e.g. for the causative:

SLA	*ʾaktābā* (*ʾaktābūt-* before suffixes)
Western	*maktābā* (but *ʾaktābā* as a verbal noun)
Syriac	*maktābū*
Babylonian	*ʾaktōbē* (also in proto-Eastern Neo-Aramaic)

The morphology and syntax of the infinitive in Old Aramaic now appears to be much more Hebrew-like than previously thought. In Syrian Old Aramaic a distinct, suffixless "infinitive absolute" is attested (cf. Sefire III:2 *hskr thskrhm* 'you shall certainly hand them over'; IIIy verbs show final *-e*, cf. III:6 *rqh*), while the "construct" infinitives (verbal nouns) of the derived stems have a feminine ending (*ḥzyh* 'to see'; *lhmtty* 'to kill me' (note the nominal rather than the objective pronominal suffix)). In the basic theme, Fakhariyah has the *mem* preformative known from later Aramaic, whereas the other dialects, again like Hebrew, have so far yielded only forms without the *mem*. On the other hand, at Fakhariyah the derived theme verbal noun seems to be without feminine ending. The *peʿal* passive participle is *paʿīl* (cf. Hebrew *pāʿûl*).

In the Jewish Literary Aramaic dialect ('Targum Onkelos' and 'Jonathan to the Prophets'), a separate "infinitive absolute" form is also used in the basic stem (*miktāb* as opposed to *miktab*) to translate the equivalent Biblical Hebrew form.

As the original participle (*kāteb*) became a true present tense, a new, nominal participle *kātōb* developed.

Adverbs and Other Parts of Speech
True adverbs are originally limited to temporals and modals. Later, adverbs are mostly nouns and adjectives in the adverbial case (see p. 123). Some prepositions and compound prepositions, such as *bᵉgō* 'within', are also used adverbially.

Syntax

Word Order
In Old Aramaic (with the exception of strongly Akkadianizing Mesopotamian texts), word order is generally of the standard Semitic VSO type, allowing for emphasis by the fronting of any element. Imperial Aramaic evinces a tendency toward verb-final order, especially in infinitival verbal clauses. That this tendency reflects literary artifice alone (as an attempt to mimic the Aramaic of native Persian speakers) is evidenced by the fact that it does not continue into later periods, which reflect, rather, the normal Semitic drift from VSO to SVO type. In the classical Eastern dialects in particular, word order in the verbal phrase may be said to be free.

A distinct difference between the Eastern and Western dialects is the synthetic present tense formed by the combination of participle and personal pronoun. In the East, as in Standard Literary Aramaic, the proniminal element follows the verb (see p. 121). In the West, it precedes it: thus 'I am writing' *kātēb-nā* vs. *ᵃnā kātēb*.

Agreement

The unmarked gender is masculine, with gender agreement regular in the singular and lax in the plural. Number agreement is regular except – as in Hebrew – in verb-initial clauses with a compound subject, where singular verbs predominate in the earlier texts.

Assertions, Negations

The 3rd person pronouns are used as copulas from early on, with forms of the verb *hwy* 'to be', used in equivalent verbal (i.e. non-present) contexts (see p. 121). Enclitic forms of *hwy*, both conjugated forms and frozen sg. m. form of the perfect (*hᵉwā > wā*), become widely used as aspectual modifiers in the later dialects.

'There is' is *īt(ay)* (*ʾit + kā* 'here' > *ʾikkā* in Babylonian; 'to have' is expressed with this pseudo-verb plus the proclitic preposition *l-*, as in Hebrew). The negative equivalent is *lāʾ + ʾīt > layt/let* (Babylonian *lekkā*). The negative is regularly conjoined with pronominal suffixes as a negative copula, a usage found, but less frequently, with the positive as well.

The common negative is *lā(ʾ)*, which also replaces the earlier *ʾal* in vetitive use beginning with the Middle dialects (a process coterminous with the demise of separate jussive verbal forms).

Questions

In all dialects, the common Semitic interrogative pronouns are used for explicit information-seeking questions: *māh* 'what' (in Syriac also *mān* and *mōn*), *man* 'who', *ʾay* + demonstratives 'which'. In the earlier dialects, through the Middle Jewish Aramaic period, indicative sentences can be made interrogative by introducing them with the particle *ha-*, as in Hebrew. In Jewish Babylonian Aramaic and Mandaic the equivalent interrogative proclitic particle is *mī-*. The other later dialects apparently made do only with intonation cues and clause fronting of the interrogative focus.

Coordination

Phrasal Coordination

The general and all-purpose conjunction *wa* (> *wᵉ*), 'and', serves for both phrase level and clause level coordination from earliest times. The strictly consonantal orthography of the earliest texts does not allow us to determine if there were any differences of stress or vocalism such as occur between the conjunctive *waw* and the so-called "*waw* consecutive" clause level coordinator in Biblical Hebrew.

Clausal Coordination

In Old and Imperial Aramaic, temporal coordination is regularly expressed, as in Hebrew, by a nominal or participial clause coordinated to the main clause with simple *waw* (e.g. *wlʾ yklwn yqblwn ʿlyk ... wsprʾ znh bydk* 'they shall not be able to bring suit against you **while this document is in your possession**'. In later dialects, explicit temporal conjunctions (see p. 129) are used.

Conditionals

The conditional particle 'if' is *hin* (> *ʾin*), though it need not always be present. 'If not' is *hin + lā(ʾ)* > *ʾillā*, but also *lahin* in early texts. 'Lest' is *lma* and also *dilma*.

In Old Aramaic, the real future conditional is expressed with an imperfect in the protasis and a perfect in the apodosis. Later Aramaic evinces the imperfect both clauses.

Unreal conditions (no early examples are attested!) are expressed by augmenting the verbal form with the perfect of *hwy*.

Subordination

The determinative pronoun *di* becomes an all purpose relativizer *dᵉ*- in the classical dialects. It has four major uses: (1) simple relative (in which case it may be preceded by but rarely replaced by *ma* 'what' and *man* 'who'); (2) substantivizer (i.e. the old determinative function); (3) conjunctivizer – virtually any preposition can be turned into a "conjunction" by adding *dᵉ*- (e.g., *qudam* 'before' (prep.), *qudam dᵉ*- 'before' (conj.); some of these compounds, like *kad* 'when' and *mad* 'after' survive long after the demise of preposition itself); alone as a conjunction it means 'so that'; (4) genitive particle (see Non-verbal Expressions, below).

Among the most varied syntagms in Aramaic (as in Semitic generally) is the choice of verbal form in imbedded object clauses. 'In order to' and 'for the sake of' can be explicitly expressed with a *l*- preposed infinitive from earliest times. For complements of such verbs as 'to be able to' and 'to want to', however, preformative *yktb* is exclusively used in Old Aramaic and in formulaic Imperial Aramaic, presumably reflecting the proto-West Semitic "subjunctive" preformative in final -*a*. With the loss of final short vowels and the concomitant neutralization of the indicative/subjunctive opposition, infinitives generally replace the old subjunctive for a time. The force of drift is strong, however, so by the time of the Late Aramaic colloquials and Modern Aramaic we find that new subjunctives based on the present stem (the old participle *kateb*, *mkatteb*, etc.) have been formed. In all of the later dialects, clauses relativized with *dᵉ*- may also be used.

Non-verbal Expressions

The construct state is used almost exclusively in Old Aramaic for the genitive. As the emphatic/determined state became fixed in the language the need for distinctive levels of determination on the genitive developed, and three constructions are used, which may be illustrated in the following example of 'the king's house', list-ed in the order of presumed increasing determinative force:

1 *bēt malkā*
2 *baytā dᵉmalkā*
3 *bayteh dᵉmalkā*

In pronominal possessive constructions, the use of the pronominal suffixes (as op-posed to independent possessive pronouns) also diminishes over time, until, in Modern Aramaic, it becomes limited virtually to parts of the body and family members (i.e. 'my hand', 'your father'). Independent possessives are formed var-iously in the dialects with *dīl-* (*dī + l-*) and *dīd-* (< *dī + yad* 'hand').

Numerals
The cardinal numeral generally precedes its noun and is in the absolute state. When the noun is definite, however, the numeral is often in the construct state. In enumerative lists and measurements, the noun may precede the numeral. Ordinals are treated like other adjectives.

Further Reading
Valuable, detailed surveys and complete bibliographies can be found in:

Beyer, K. 1986. *The Aramaic Language*, trans. J. F. Healey from revised German of the first chapter of *Die aramäischen texte vom Toten Meer*, 1984. Göttingen: Vandenhoeck & Ruprecht. (Unfortunately, the *ex cathedra* pronouncements of the latter valuable but highly idiosyncratic work must be taken with a large grain of salt.)
Kutscher, E. Y. 1971. "Aramaic." Cols. 259–287 in volume 3 of *Encyclopaedia Judaica*. Jerusalem: Keter.
Segert, Stanislav. 1975. *Altaramäische Grammatik: Mit Bibliographie, Chrestomathie und Glossar*. Leipzig: VEB Verlag Enzyklopadie.

8 Ugaritic

Dennis Pardee

Ugaritic is the only well-attested example known today of the native languages of the Levantine area in the second millennium BCE. Various brief documents exist, as well as Amorite words in the Mari texts, or the "Canaanite glosses" in the texts from El-Amarna, but these highly fragmented sources cannot compare with the data from the Ugaritic language, for Ugaritic is attested in approximately 1,000 reasonably well-preserved texts (with many more fragments). The texts are written in an alphabetic cuneiform script on clay tablets and date to approximately 1400–1190 BCE. Only discovered in 1929 at modern Ras Shamra, ancient Ugarit, located on the north coast of Syria, they provide the sole coherent body of literature from the entire Northwest Semitic area for the period.

There are approximately fifty mythological texts in poetry, with the balance of the corpus in prose: religious (ritual, pantheon, votive); ominological (astral, malformed births, extispicy); epistolary; administrative (contracts, lists of many sorts); medical (hippiatric); and school texts (abecedaries, exercises).

These texts originated largely from the administration of the city of Ugarit. The administration was headed by a king, often in vassal position to a king of a larger political entity, particularly the Hittite king in the period documented. The average territory controlled by the city of Ugarit and where Ugaritic was spoken may have been approximately 2,000 square km.

The place of Ugaritic in the Semitic languages has been a matter of much dispute, in part because of a confusion of categories, namely, between linguistic and literary criteria. Literarily, the poetic texts show strong formal (poetic parallelism), lexical, and thematic affinities to Biblical Hebrew poetry. Linguistically, however, Ugaritic shows archaic features characteristic of old Canaanite and it may be a remnant of a Western "Amorite" dialect.

Finally, it is important to note that the Ugaritic language was only one of at least eight languages and/or writing systems in use at Ugarit, only one other of which is Semitic, namely, Akkadian, the international lingua franca of the time, in which approximately 2,000 texts are written, primarily epistolographic, legal, and administrative. Various numbers of texts have also been found in Sumerian, Hittite (alphabetic and hieroglyphic), Egyptian, Hurrian, and Cypro-Minoan.

The following presentation will constitute an uneasy truce between simple description and reconstruction. This is because the Ugaritic writing system does not represent vowels. The reconstruction of the Ugaritic vocalic system must rely, therefore, on two types of internal sources: (1) the "extra" *ʾaleph* signs in the Ugaritic alphabet (see below); (2) Ugaritic words in syllabically written texts. The latter appear in three distinct forms: (a) the so-called polyglot vocabularies (Ugaritic words written in ancient "dictionary" entries); (b) Ugaritic words in Akkadian texts; (c) proper names (this source is less useful than the others because the bearers of the names may be of non-Ugaritic origin).

There is virtually no problem of periodization of Ugaritic, since it is only attested for approximately 200 years. It is becoming clear that more of the texts previously excavated must be dated to the late years of the city than has previously been believed to be the case and the concept of the evolution of the Ugaritic language towards a Phoenician-like form must be rejected.

Phonology

The vocalization of Ugaritic is largely reconstructed; the consonantal system is described primarily in terms of the graphemes rather than in phonetic terms.

The Abecedaries and the Consonantal Alphabet

The order of the alphabet is known from abecedaries and is similar to that of the later Northwest Semitic languages:

```
UG   å b g ḫ d h w z ḥ ṭ y k š l m δ n ẓ s ʿ p ṣ q r θ γ t ì ù ś
NWS  ʾ b g   d h w z ḥ ṭ y k   l m   n   s ʿ p ṣ q r š   t
```

The basic consonantal inventory consisted of twenty-seven phonemes; the origin of the last three signs is in dispute. The three *ʾaleph* signs are used to indicate /ʾ/ plus following vowel (e.g., ⟨å⟩ = /ʾa/), with ⟨ì⟩ used for syllable-final /ʾ/.

The Consonantal Repertory

By comparison with other Semitic graphic and phonetic systems, the alphabet may be roughly arranged according to phonetic properties as follows:

p	t	θ	s (ś)	k	ḫ	ḥ	h
b	d	δ	z	g	γ	ʿ	ʾ
ṭ	ẓ	ṣ	q				

In addition to these relatively clear two- or three-element sets, there is a series of continuants (*m* = bilabial, *n* = alveolar/palatal, *l* = lateral, *r* = apical or lateral, *š* = sibilant or lateral) and two semivowels (*w* = bilabial, *y* = palatal).

There is no sign for /ḍ/, which has fused with /ṣ/, nor for /ś/ (sign 30 of the alphabet does not correspond to later /ś/) which has probably fused with /š/.

The graphic system does not correspond precisely to the phonetic one. ⟨ẓ⟩ is used for etymological /ẓ/, but certain words containing etymological /ẓ/ are regularly written with ⟨γ⟩. In two texts, *CAT* 24 and RIH 78/14, ⟨ẓ⟩ is used for etymological /ṭ/. Etymological /δ/ is sometimes written ⟨δ⟩, but usually ⟨d⟩.

The Vocalic Repertory
The vocalic system is assumed to have consisted of six primitive vocalic phonemes, /a/, /i/, /u/, /ā/, /ī/, /ū/, to which two long vowels were added by monophthongization, /ê/ < /ay/ and /ô/ < /aw/.

The Writing System
The Ugaritic writing system is consonantal and claimed cases of *matres lectionis* are dubious.

Morphology
In the following tables "Ø" = unattested form; "-ø" = zero element.

Pronouns

Independent Pronouns

Nominative Case

Sg.	1c.	ành/àn	Du.	1c.	Ø	Pl.	1c.	Ø
	2m.	àt		2m.	àtm		2m.	àtm
	f.	àt		f.	Ø		f.	Ø
	3m.	hw		3m.	hm		3m.	hm
	f.	hy		f.	Ø		f.	Ø

Oblique Case
Separate forms are attested for the oblique case of the sg. 3m. (*hwt*), sg. 3f. (*hyt*), du. 3m. (*hmt*), and pl. 3m. (*hmt*).

Proclitic and Enclitic Pronouns
Pronominal elements of verbs were suffixed in the perfective, prefixed in the imperfective.

Pf.	Sg.	Du.	Pl.	Impf.	Sg.	Du.	Pl.
1c.	-t	-ny	-n	1c.	ʾ-	n-	n-
2m.	-t	-tm	-tm	2m.	t-	t-	t-
f.	-t	Ø	-tn	f.	t-	t-	t-
3m.	-ø /-a/	-ø /-ā/	-ø /-ū/	3m.	y-	y-/t-	y-/t-
f.	-t	-t	-ø /-ā/?	f.	y-	t-	t-

The du. 1c. *-ny* (also attested as a genitive enclitic) is an archaic retention.

Enclitic pronouns are attached to nouns, with a genitive function, and to verbs, with an accusative function (occasionally dative). The series is similar to the independent pronouns in the 3rd person only:

	Singular	Dual	Plural
1c.	*-y/-ø/-n*	*-ny*	*-n*
2m.	*-k*	*-km*	*-km*
f.	*-k*	Ø	*-kn*
3m.	*-h*	*-hm*	*-hm*
f.	*-h*	*-hm*	*-hn*

The forms indicated for the 1st person are distributed according to function: *-y/-ø* is genitive (i.e., attached to nouns), *-n* accusative (i.e., attached to transitive verbs). The first set is distributed according to the case of the singular noun to which the genitive suffix is attached (nom. = -ø; gen./acc. = -y).

Most of the dual forms were differentiated from identically written plural forms by vocalic pattern.

Demonstrative Pronouns

Demonstrative pronouns consist of the deictic particle *hn+d* (the same as the relative pronoun) or *k* (of uncertain origin). The forms are identical to those of the demonstrative adjectives (p. 136).

Relative Pronouns

Only the series based on *δ + vowel is used, nearly always written with ⟨d⟩.

d (sg. m.)   *dt* (pl. m. and f.; not used consistently)
dt (sg. f.)

Interrogative Pronouns

The interrogative pronouns attested are: *my* 'who?', *mh* 'what?'.

Indefinite Adjectives and Pronouns

mn and *mnk* designate human entities ('whoever'), *mnm* inanimate ones ('whatever'). The distinction between human and non-human referents was expressed by ablaut (perhaps /man-/ for humans, /mīn-/ for non-humans). *-k* and *-m* are expanding elements of uncertain semantic content.

Nouns

Nouns and adjectives are marked for gender, number, and case, but not for definiteness and only partially for state.

Gender

Sg. m.   = -ø
Sg. f.   = -*t* /-(a)t-/
Pl. m.   = lengthening of case vowel
Pl. f.   = -*t* /-āt-/

Number
Singular, dual, and plural are productive, marked by variations in the case vowel, with affixation of -m to the dual and plural.

Case
A triptotic case system (nominative, genitive, accusative) is used in the singular, a diptotic one (nominative, oblique) in the dual and plural. This system is demonstrated by the use of the *ʾaleph* sign, e.g., sg. m. nom. ⟨ksù⟩ = /kussaʾu/, sg. m. gen. ⟨ksì⟩ = /kussaʾi/, sg. m. acc. ⟨ksà⟩ = /kussaʾa/; pl. m. nom. ⟨rpùm⟩ = /rapaʾūma/, pl. m. obl. ⟨rpìm⟩ = /rapaʾīma/.

There is not a separate vocative case. There are two lexical vocative markers, *l* and *y* (cf. Arabic *ya*), but a noun may be a vocative phrase without the use of a lexical marker.

The accusative case is used both for the object(s) and for various adverbial notions (see p. 141).

Some nouns, particularly those bearing a nominal suffix containing a long vowel (e.g., /-ān/, /-īt/), have a diptotic singular system: /-u/ subject, /-a/ oblique.

The case vowel is preserved in the first word(s) of genitive phrases while in the dual and the plural, the -*m* of the *nomen regens* is usually dropped: /malku/ 'king', /malku qarti/ 'the king of the city', /malkuha/ 'her king'; /mal(a)kūma/ 'kings', /mal(a)kū ʾarṣi/ 'the kings of the earth', /mal(a)kūha/ 'her kings'.

The noun may consist of (1) ROOT + internal vowel(s) (e.g., /MaLK-/ 'king'); (2) nominal prefix + ROOT + internal vowel(s) (e.g., /maLʾaK-/ 'messenger'); (3) ROOT + internal vowel(s) + nominal suffix (e.g., /RaʿaBān-/ 'famine'); (4) combination of 2 and 3 (e.g., /ʾaLʾiYān-/ 'mighty'). It is uncertain whether nouns of the *qatl/qitl/qutl* types had monosyllabic or bisyllabic stems in the plural. There are reduplicated (e.g., *qdqd* 'top of head', *ysmsm* 'beauteous') and quadriconsonantal (e.g. *ʿrgz* 'walnut'?) nominal forms. The most common nominal prefixes are *m-* (concrete entities), *t-* (abstract entities); rarer are *ʾ-* and *y-* (both for concrete entities). The most common nominal suffixes are -*n* (/-an-/ or /-ān-/; usually concrete entities) and -*t* (abstract entities).

Adjectives
Adjectival morphology is like that of nouns (p. 134). Adjectives agree in gender, number, and case with the modified noun.

The primary adjectival suffix is the so-called *nisbe* ending consisting of vowel + -*y* (/-yy-/) + case vowel.

Comparative and superlative adjectival markers do not exist and such notions were expressed lexically (e.g., by forms of the root MꞋD 'much') or syntactically (e.g. nʿmt šnt il 'the best years of El', a substantivized adjective in construct with a noun, literally 'the good ones of the years of El').

A nominal genitive formation is often used in place of an adjectival one, e.g. åθt ṣdqh /ʾaθθatu ṣidqihu/ 'the wife of his legitimacy' = 'his legitimate wife'.

Deictics

Demonstrative adjectives correspond to the demonstrative pronouns (p. 134): hnd/k (sg. m./f.; du./pl. m.), hnd/k + t (sg. f.). 3rd person independent pronouns could also be used as demonstrative adjectives (only the oblique case is attested: mlk hwt 'that king', ḥwt hyt 'that land').

The standard presentative particle is hn, functioning primarily deictically ('behold'), sometimes locally ('here'). The basic element is h-, for alongside hn one finds hnn, hnny, hl, hln, hlny, and ht (< /han+t/).

Numerals

The cardinal numbers are nouns, the ordinals are adjectives. In the numerals 3 through 10, the distribution of forms marked with -ø vs. -(a)t does not observe common Semitic "chiastic concord."

Forms

	Cardinals	Ordinals (where different)
1	åḥd/åḥt and ʿšty	?
2	θn/θt	
3	θlθ/θlθt	
4	årbʿ/årbʿt	rbʿ
5	ḥmš/ḥmšt	
6	θθ/θθt	θdθ
7	šbʿ/šbʿt	
8	θmn(y)/θmnt	
9	tšʿ/tšʿt	
10	ʿšr/ʿšrt	
11	ʿšty ʿšr/ʿšrh	
12	θn ʿšr/ʿšrh	
etc.		
20	ʿšrm	
etc.		
100	mìt (Sg.)/màt (Pl.)	
1,000	ålp	
10,000	rbt	

The only attested forms of the absolute case of the number '2' are θn and θt (θnm is adverbial, 'twice').

The presence of the ⟨h⟩ in the writing system shows that the origin of the element -h in ʿšrh was consonantal.

The ordinals are not formed with the *nisbe* suffix, which would be written -y. Ordinals had a long vowel between the second and third radicals: /θiθθu/ (< /θidθu/) vs. /θadV:θu/.

In the number phrase, the noun denoting the counted entity may either be in the same case as the number or in the genitive case.

The preposition *l* is often used to join the unit to the ten in compound numbers, as in θn l ʿšrm 'twenty-two'.

Verbs

The verbal system represents an archaic form of West Semitic with a variety of "stems."

Verbal Stems

G-stem   (base stem, or simple stem; active and passive voices)

Gt-stem   (-*t*- infixed after first radical of G-stem; middle/reflexive in function)

D-stem   (doubled middle radical; factitive in function; active and passive voices)

tD-stem   (*t*- prefixed to D-stem; middle/reflexive of D in function)

N-stem   (preformative *n*-; middle/passive in function)

Š-stem   (preformative *š*-; causative in function; active and passive voices)

Št-stem   (-*t*- infixed after *š*- of causative stem; middle/reflexive of Š in function; only a few forms are attested and the stem may no longer have been productive)

L-stem   (lengthened vowel after first radical and reduplicated second/third radical; intensive or factitive in function)

R-stem   (reduplication of essential radicals: both radicals of biconsonantal root, second and third radicals of triconsonantal root; factitive in function)

tR- or   (*t* prefixed to first root consonant or infixed after first root consonant
Rt-stem   of R-stem; factitive reflexive in function)

Aspects/Tenses

There are two verbal conjugations marked for person, gender, and number: STEM + PRONOMINAL ELEMENT and PRONOMINAL ELEMENT + STEM + (AFFIX in some forms). In prose texts the former is used for acts viewed as complete (perfective), the latter for acts viewed as incomplete (imperfective). In poetry the distribution of the two forms has to date defied complete description, though the use of the imperfective seems to reflect an older stage of the language, when the zero-ending *yaktub* (see p. 139) functioned as a preterite, like Akkadian *iprus*.

The two forms may be represented as *kataba* and *yaktub*. The perfective may have been characterized by internal ablaut for active (*kataba*) vs. stative (*katiba*, *katuba*), but all extant evidence is for the *katiba* type (⟨lìk⟩, ⟨šìl⟩). The imperfective was characterized by internal ablaut, perhaps for active (*yaktub-*) vs. stative (*yiktab-*). The imperfective is also marked, by affixation to the stem, for mood (see p. 139). The "Barth-Ginsberg" law (*yaktab → yiktab*) was operative.

No certain evidence exists for a present–future form corresponding to Akkadian *iparras*.

Two productive verbal forms are unmarked for aspect or person, the participle and the infinitive. Morphologically adjective and noun, respectively, they may also function verbally, i.e., complementation may be either accusatival or genitival.

The Participle
Each verbal stem has at least one verbal adjective (participle). If the stem is transitive, there was a participle for each voice, the active and the passive. The G-stem probably had two stative verbal adjectives, for a total of four: *kātib-* = active, *katib-* and *katub-* = stative, *katV:b-* = passive. All the derived stems except the N-stem form the participle with a prefixed *m-*.

The Infinitive
The pattern of the abstract verbal noun (infinitive) in the G-stem was not fixed, though *katāb-* was the most common for strong roots (*b šàl* [preposition *b* + infinitive] /bi ša'āli/). The infinitive in the derived stems was formed by ablaut: no *m*-preformative infinitives are attested.

There is a syntactic usage corresponding to the so-called "infinitive absolute" construction, but a productive separate form in contradistinction to the verbal noun did not exist. III-' roots show that the infinitive in absolute usage is in the nominative case: *hm ɣmù ɣmìt* /himma ɣamā'u ɣami'ti/ 'If you are indeed thirsty'.

Voices

Active and Passive
Active verbs are of two primary types, transitive and intransitive (e.g. /maḫaṣa 'êba/ 'he smote the enemy' and /halaka/ 'he went'); passive forms derive only from the transitive type.

Middle
Between the two extremes marked by the transitive and passive forms, there is a middle range of forms denoting reflexivity, reciprocity, advantage or disadvantage to actor, etc. These notions are clearest in the t-stems (Gt, tD, and Št). The primary function of the N-stem is to express patient-oriented acts and it is thus used for both the passive and the middle.

Moods

Moods are marked by variations to the imperfective stem.

The imperative has no preformative element and the stem vowel is the same as that of the imperfective: ROOT + stem vowel (+ AFFIX). To the basic imperative element may be added the /-a(n)(na)/ elements listed below. The imperative existed only in the second person and only for positive commands (negative commands are expressed by *àl* + jussive).

A second series of moods consists of the complete IMPERFECTIVE STEM + suffix. For ease of expression, the stem *yaktub-* will be used below for STEM.

YKTB + ø	= jussive	/yaktub/
YKTB + /u/	= indicative	/yaktubu/
YKTB + /a/	= volitive	/yaktuba/
YKTB + /an/	= energic 1	/yaktuban/
YKTB + /anna/	= energic 2	/yaktubanna/

The consonantal nature of the writing system often makes it difficult to distinguish among these forms.

Table 8.1   G-stem of strong verbs

		Perfective	Imperfective	Jussive	Imperative
Sg.	1c.	/katabtu/	/ʾaktubu/	/ʾaktub/	
	2m.	/katabta/	/taktubu/	/taktub/	/kutub(a)/
	f.	/katabti/	/taktubīna/	/taktubī/	/kutubī/
	3m.	/kataba/	/yaktubu/	/yaktub/	
	f.	/katabat/	/taktubu/	/taktub/	
Du.	1c.	/katabnayā/?	/naktubā/?	/naktubā/?	
	2m.	/katabtumā/	/taktubā(ni)/	/taktubā/	/kutubā/
	f.	Ø	Ø	Ø	Ø
	3m.	/katabā/?	/yaktubā(ni)/ or /taktubā(ni)/	/yaktubā/ or /taktubā/	
	f.	/katabtā/?	/taktubā(ni)/	/taktubā/	
Pl.	1c.	/katabnū/	/naktubu/	/naktub/	
	2m.	/katabtum(u)/	/taktubū(na)/	/taktubū/	/kutubū/
	f.	/katabtin(n)a/	/taktubna/?	/taktubna/??	/kutubā/?
	3m.	/katabū/	/yaktubū/ or /taktubū/?	/yaktubū/ or /taktubū/?	
	f.	/katabā/?	/taktubna/?	/taktubna/??	

Particularly doubtful reconstructions are indicated with one or more question marks. More complete sets with proposed vocalizations can be found in Segert 1984.

Infinitive: /katāb-/ and others.

Participles: active /kātib-/, passive /katūb-/, stative /katib-/ and /katub-/.

Some Details of the Verbal System

3rd person dual and plural imperfectives often have preformative *t-*, rather than *y-*.

The N-stem imperative had /i/ in the preformative syllable (*išḫn* /ʾiššaḫin-/ < /*ʾinšaḫin-/ 'be hot!'), as did the Gt perfective.

The Gt and tD were characterized by different stem vowels in the imperfective: *yštil* (Gt) vs. *yštâl* (tD) 'ask, importune'.

The D-stem had /a/ in the preformative of the imperfective (*arḫp* /ʾaraḫḫip-/ 'I shall have (something) soar') and /u/ in the preformative of the participle (cf. the syllabically spelled proper name *mu-na-ḫi-mu*).

Several nouns, non-participial in form, are formed from the Š-stem: *šʿtqt* 'she who causes to pass on', *šmrr* 'that which causes bitterness (venom)'.

There was no H-causative (*hiphil*) or ʾ-causative (*aphel*) alongside the Š-causative.

Some Peculiarities of "Weak" Roots

Some I-ʾ*aleph* roots show vagaries in orthography that indicate mutation of the ʾ*aleph* (quiescence, "secondary opening"?): *yiḫd* vs. *yuḫd*, both 'he seizes'.

I-*y*/*w* roots have become I-*y* in the perfective. Imperfectives usually show a bi-syllabic stem, with /a/ in the prefix syllable: *ard* /ʾarid-/ 'I descend'.

Hollow roots have no middle consonantal element. Imperfectives usually have preformative vowel /a/: *abn* /ʾabīn-/ 'I understand'.

III-*w* roots have shifted to III-*y* (exceptions are attested for *ašlw* 'I relax' and *atwt* 'you have come'). The ø-ending imperfective (jussive, historical preterite) has monophthongized (/*yabniy/ → /yabni/) but usage is not consistent in the poetic texts and use of historical writing (i.e., /yabni/ = ⟨ybn/ybny⟩) may be at the origin of some forms.

Adverbs, Conjunctions, Prepositions, Enclitic Particles

Adverbs

Adverbials may be expressed by adverbial lexemes or by adverbialization of a noun, i.e., by prefixing a preposition, by use of the accusative case, or by suffixation of an adverbial morpheme.

Local and temporal adverbs:

- Basic local and temporal adverbial notions are expressed by lexemes which may be expanded by enclitic particles: *hn, hnn, hnny* 'here', *hl, hlh, hlny* 'here', *θm, θmn, θmny* 'there', *ʿt* 'now', *ht* rhetorical 'now' (*hn+-t*), *ap* 'also', *ʿln* 'above' (= *ʿl+-n*).
- Interrogative adverbs are *iy* and *an* 'where?', *ik(y)* 'how?', *lm* (probably *l* 'to/for' + *m* 'what?') 'why?'.
- Negative adverbs are *l* (indicative), *al* (volitive).
- Prepositional adverbialization is common, e.g., *l ʿlm* 'for a long time' (*l* = 'to', *ʿlm* = 'long time').

- The accusative case is used for otherwise unmarked nominal adverbials, e.g., *qdqd* 'on the head', *ym* 'for a day', *šmm* 'to the heavens'.
- The two most common adverbial suffixes are *-m* and *-h*. The first appears on virtually all parts of speech and its function has not yet been precisely defined. The second is used in the nominal system and has various functions, local and temporal being most common, e.g., *šmmh* 'to the heavens', *ʿlmh* 'for a long time'.

Conjunctions

The most common coordinating conjunction is *w-*, capable of linking phrases at all levels (word, clause, sentence, paragraph). *p* is much rarer and usually denotes cause-and-effect linkage (see Coordination, p. 143). *ú* functions both independently and correlatively (*ú* ... *ú* = 'either ... or'). Two lexemes are written ⟨ú⟩: (1) /ʾū/ 'and'; (2) /ʾô/ (< /*aw/) 'either/or'. *ảp* 'also' functions most commonly at the paragraph level.

The most common subordinating conjunction is *k* 'because, when, if'. Both *ìm* and *hm* are attested as conditional conjunctions ('if').

Prepositions

The number of primary prepositions is small (*ảẖr* = 'after', *b* = 'in', *k* = 'like', *l* = 'at', *ʿd* = 'up to, until', *ʿl* = 'upon', *ʿm* = 'with', *tẖt* = 'under'); there are also complex prepositions (e.g., *b+yd* = 'in the hand of, under the management of'; *b+tk* = 'in the midst of'; *l+pn*, 'face' = 'in front of'). Each preposition has a variety of translation values, e.g., *b* = 'in, within, through, by the intermediary of, by the price of, from'. There is no specific prepositional lexeme expressing the ablative 'from, away from'; the real-world notion of separation is expressed by verb/preposition idioms in which a number of prepositions are used.

The substantive following a preposition is in the genitive case (*l ksî* /lê kussaʾi/ 'to the chair/throne').

The case system still being in force, no prepositional particle has developed to mark the object (contrast *ʾyt/ʾt/wtyt* in the later Northwest Semitic languages).

Enclitic particles can be joined to all parts of speech and are capable of accretion one to another.

-d = relative pronoun that can function as a compounding element with other particles (e.g., *hnd* 'this')

-h = adverbial (see above)

-y = enclitic particle, particularly as expander to another particle (e.g., *hn+n+y*)

-k = enclitic particle in *hnk* 'that'

-m = enclitic particle used on all parts of speech (see above)

-n = enclitic particle used on all parts of speech.

Syntax

The relative dearth of prose texts makes it difficult to ascertain a normative prose syntax, while the lack of vocalized texts makes some aspects of morpho-syntax difficult to ascertain precisely.

Word Order

Order of Morphemes
Details have been indicated above and only a summary is here provided.

> Pronoun: (deictic element *àn* +) pronoun
> Noun/Adjective: (nominal prefix) + STEM (+ nominal suffix) + gender/
> number/case (+ genitive pronominal element)
> Deictics: deictic + expanding enclitic particles
> Verbs: perfective = STEM + subjective pronominal element (+ objective
> pronominal element)
> imperfective = subjective pronominal element + STEM (+ AFFIX)
> (+ mood marker) (+ objective pronominal element)

Phrase Level
The simple verbal phrase is by definition a sentence: SUBJECT + PREDICATE (imperfective) or PREDICATE + SUBJECT (perfective). The verb phrase may be expanded by addition of an independent pronoun for "emphasis," creating a formal *casus pendens* (e.g., *àtm bštm w àn šnt* 'as for you, you may tarry but as for me, I'm off'). The independent pronoun may precede or follow the verbal unit.

There are two primary nominal phrases: the genitival and the adjectival.

The genitival phrase is the common Semitic "construct state": X of Y. The first element is in the case required by context, the second in the genitive. It can denote the relationships well known elsewhere (subjective genitive, objective genitive, genitive of identification, genitive of material, etc.). No lexical or pronominal element may intervene between the members of a construct chain, only enclitic particles.

The adjectival phrase is of two types, (1) the phrase level or attributive, in which the adjective follows the noun and agrees in gender, number, and case, and (2) the sentence level or predicative, in which the adjective may either precede or follow the noun and agrees in gender, number, and case. An attributive adjective modifying any member of a construct chain must come at the end of the chain (e.g., *ḫbr kθr ṭbm* 'the companions of Kothar, the good ones').

Sentence Level
Word order is essentially free with fronting used for topicalization.

Agreement

Personal pronouns agree in person, gender, and number with an appositional verbal form (*ånk åḥwy* 'I give life'); in gender, number and case with an appositional or predicate noun (*åt ůmy* 'you, my mother') and with predicate adjectives (*dbḥn ndbḥ hw* 'the sacrifice, sacrificed is it'). The relative pronoun agrees in gender and number and probably in case with its antecedent. Demonstrative pronouns and adjectives agree in gender, number, and case with the modified noun.

Assertions, Negations
The primary asseveratives and negatives were written the same but had different vocalizations: *l* = /lāʿ/ 'not', /la/ 'indeed'; *ål* = /ʾal/ 'must not', /ʾallu/? 'must'. These particles are placed immediately before the word they modify, usually a verb, sometimes another part of speech.

Questions
The interrogative pronouns and adverbs are *my* 'who?', *mh* 'what?', *iy/ån* 'where?', *ik* 'how?', *lm* 'why?'. There is no proclitic interrogative particle. The interrogative particles normally come at the head of the sentence.

Coordination
Coordination is indicated most commonly by *w-*, by *p-* when effect is denoted (see Conjunctions, p. 141). Asyndesis is frequent at the sentence (and paragraph) level, common at the phrase level.

Conditions
Conditions may be marked by *hm* or (rarely) *im* and usually precede the main clause. Conditional clauses may be unmarked. A lexical distinction between real and irreal conditions is as yet unknown. The main clause following the conditional clause may or may not be preceded by the so-called *w* or *p* of apodosis.

Subordination
The principal types of subordinate clauses are (1) relative, (2) conditional, and (3) a variety of temporal/circumstantial, causal, resultative, and completative (object) clauses most commonly introduced by *k* /kī/ when lexically marked. The concept of "subordinate" clause is rendered murky by the frequent use of the so-called *w* (or more rarely *p*) of apodosis, i.e., heading the main clause with *w* or *p* when it follows the logically subordinate clause.

Relative clauses
Explicit relative clauses are preceded by *d/dt*. Relative adverbials are usually marked (*ådrm d b grn* 'the leaders who are at the threshing floor'). Unmarked relative verbal clauses are rare.

The relative pronoun functions both at the phrase level (*il d pìd* 'god of mercy') and at the sentence level (*il ... d yšr* 'the god ... who sings'). It may either have an explicit antecedent, or be used absolutely (*d in b bty ttn* 'What is not in my house shall you give').

Lexicon

Ugaritic fits the common Semitic patterns in kinship terms (*àb* 'father', *ùm* 'mother'), tree names (*àrz* 'cedar'), geographical terms (*nhr* 'river'), with some notable peculiarities, e.g., *ḥwt* /ḥuwwat-/ 'land (geographical–political entity)', alongside *àrṣ* 'earth, ground' and *bld* 'homeland'. The primary verbs of movement resemble those of the Hebrew/Phoenician group rather than those of Aramaic or Arabic: *hlk* 'go', *yrd* 'descend', *ʿly* 'ascend', *bʾ* 'enter' (alongside *ʿrb*), *yṣʾ* 'exit', *θb* 'return'. Some verbs of movement that can also denote the state attained are: *qm* 'arise', *škb* 'lie down', *ʿmd* 'stand', *rkb* 'mount'. Motion verbs peculiar to Ugaritic are *tbʿ* 'go away', *mɣy* 'go to, arrive at', and QL Št-stem attested only in poetry, in the imperfective, *yštql* 'he arrives'. Expressions of existence resemble the later Northwest Semitic pattern: there are positive and negative quasi-verbs, *iθ* and *in*, as well as the verb *kn*, which corresponds to the regular verb 'to be' in Phoenician and Arabic.

References

CAT = Dietrich, Manfried, Oswald Loretz, and J. Sanmartín. 1995. *The Cuneiform Alphabetic Texts from Ugarit, Ras Ibn Hani and Other Places (KTU: Second, Enlarged Edition)* (Abhandlungen zur Literatur Alt-Syrien-Palästinas und Mesopotamiens 8). Münster: UGARIT-Verlag.

RIH = text discovered at Ras Ibn Hani

RS = text discovered at Ras Shamra

Further Reading

Bordreuil, Pierre and Dennis Pardee. 1995. "L'Épigraphie ougaritique: 1973–1993." In *Le pays d'Ougarit autour de l'an 1200 av. J.-C.*, ed. Marguerite Yon (Ras Shamra–Ougarit XI). Paris: Éditions Recherche sur les Civilizations. 27–32.

Gordon, Cyrus H. 1965. *Ugaritic Textbook: Grammar, Texts in Transliteration, Cuneiform Selections, Glossary, Indices* (Analecta Orientalia 38). Rome: Pontificium Institutum Biblicum.

Huehnergard, John. 1987. *Ugaritic Vocabulary in Syllabic Transcription* (Harvard Semitic Studies 32). Atlanta, Ga.: Scholars Press.

Segert, Stanislav. 1984. *A Basic Grammar of the Ugaritic Language*. Berkeley: University of California Press.

Tropper, J. 1994. "Is Ugaritic a Canaanite Langauge?" In *Ugarit and the Bible: Proceedings of the International Symposium on Ugarit and the Bible, Manchester, September 1992*, ed. G. J. Brooke, et al. (Ugaritisch-Biblische Literatur 11). Münster: UGARIT-Verlag. 343–353.

Verreet, E. 1988. *Modi Ugaritici. Eine morphsyntaktische Abhandlung über das Modalsystem im Ugaritischen* (Orientalia Lovaniensia Analecta 27). Leuven: Peeters.

9 Ancient Hebrew

Richard C. Steiner

This chapter is dedicated to my esteemed teacher, Professor Henry M. Hoenigswald. (For the system of transliteration employed in this chapter see note p. 172)

Ancient Hebrew was the language of the Israelite tribes who, at the beginning of the first millennium BCE, established a united kingdom in the land formerly known as Canaan. After the reigns of David and his son, Solomon, the united kingdom split into the northern kingdom of Israel and the southern kingdom of Judah, the latter remaining loyal to the Davidic dynasty in Jerusalem, the former being ruled by a series of dynasties until its destruction by the Assyrians in 722 BCE.

The Babylonians conquered Judah in 586 BCE, exiling its people and razing the Temple that Solomon had built in Jerusalem. The Persians, who made Judah a province of their empire, allowed Jewish exiles to return and rebuild the Temple. The Hellenistic period saw the rise of an independent Judean state under the Hasmonean dynasty. The Romans brought an end to this independence, appointing Herod as their governor. Two revolts against the Romans had disastrous results. The first ended in the destruction of the Second Temple in 70 CE. The second, led by Bar-Kokhba in 132–135 CE, emptied Judea of its Jewish inhabitants; those who were not killed or deported fled to Galilee in the north.

The two great bodies of literature in ancient Hebrew, composed during the period when it was a living language, are biblical literature and tannaitic (early Rabbinic) literature, including the code of Jewish law known as the Mishnah and legal commentaries to the Pentateuch such as the Mekhilta, the Sifra and the Sifre. (All of the citations from tannaitic literature in this chapter are from reliable vocalized manuscripts; they may disagree with standard editions and dictionaries.) The oldest dated manuscripts of these works are from the ninth century CE, but almost all of the biblical books are represented among the fragmentary scrolls from the Dead Sea (Qumran), believed to date from around the first century BCE. Among the Dead Sea Scrolls are also Hebrew versions of apocryphal books such as Jubilees (previously known from translations into Greek, Ethiopic, etc.), as well as Hebrew works authored by the Qumran sectarians themselves. There are also hundreds of inscriptions written by native speakers, ranging in time from *c.* 1200 BCE to 132–135 CE (Bar-Kokhba letters). The Canaanite glosses written in cuneiform script in the Akkadian letters found at El-Amarna, Egypt, are from pre-

Israelite Canaan (fourteenth century BCE), but they are so similar to Hebrew that they are regularly cited as evidence for Proto-Hebrew.

The language of the Hebrew Bible is by no means monolithic. There is enough variation to justify distinguishing Standard Biblical Hebrew (SBH; before 500 BCE) from Late Biblical Hebrew (LBH; after 500 BCE) and both of these from the archaic poetic dialect. The relative clause, for example, is introduced in SBH by *ʾăšär* 'that', but there is also an unrelated and more archaic dialectal counterpart *ša+* > *šä+* which becomes increasingly common in LBH; in the poetic dialect, these conjunctions are sometimes replaced by the archaic *zu^w*, and asyndetic relative clauses are common.

Mishnaic (or Middle) Hebrew (MH) used to be viewed as an artificial scholastic jargon, but the prevalent view today is that MH was a colloquial idiom spoken until *c.* 200 CE and that it was descended from an older colloquial idiom (hereafter: Pre-MH) spoken in the biblical period. According to this view, LBH is a purely literary language whose non-SBH features come from Pre-MH.

MH frequently exhibits the culmination of developments begun in SBH and continued in LBH. Thus, the word *ʾe^ykâ^h* 'how' in the archaic poetic dialect changes to *ʾe^yk* in SBH, then to *he^yk* in LBH and finally to *he^yʾâk* in MH. Similarly, the perfective ≠ habitual opposition could be expressed in Proto-Northwest Semitic only in the past tense. In SBH, we find a new habitual future, in LBH, a new habitual infinitive, and in MH, a new habitual imperative (see p. 158).

On the other hand, MH *tăpi^yl:â^h zo^w* 'this prayer' (Berakhot 4:2), with its *t*-less and article-less demonstrative adjective reminiscent of Phoenician, is actually more archaic than its SBH counterpart, *hat:ăpi^yl:â^h haz:oʾt* (2 Sam. 7:27). The same goes for the MH relative conjunction *šä+* in comparison with SBH *ʾăšär* (see above and Relative Clauses, p. 171). The biblical evidence shows that the absence of the article is characteristic of the archaic poetic dialect (see above) and that *zo^h/zo^w* and *šä+* were features of Pre-MH and of the northern dialect(s) of Hebrew. Clearly, MH is not a direct lineal descendant of SBH.

The literature of the Qumran sectarians, despite its being preserved in ancient copies, is, in some ways, a more problematic source for reconstructing the history of Hebrew in ancient times. Most scholars believe that the language of this literature owes more to imitation of the Bible than to the Hebrew vernacular of the period.

Other aspects of the sociolinguistic interplay of dialects (regional and social) and languages in Palestine are reflected in various biblical and Talmudic passages: Judg. 12:5–6, Isa. 36:11–13, Neh. 13:23–24, Bava Ḳamma 82b–83a, ʿAvodah Zarah 58b, Ḥullin 137b, and Pal. Talm. Berakhot 4d, Megilla 71b.

Information about regional dialects can also be gleaned from inscriptions and biblical compositions whose geographic origin is known. It has been shown that the Hebrew of the northern kingdom, unlike that of the southern kingdom, differed from SBH in important respects, at least partly as a result of Phoenician influence. Some "northernisms" (e.g., *šä+* and *zo^h/zo^w* discussed above) are standard features of Pre-MH (especially in Ecclesiastes and Song of Songs) and MH; others (e.g., *šat* 'year' and unconditional monophthongization of *ay* and *aw*) are not.

Orthography and Phonology

Consonants: Phonology
Hebrew exhibits both the loss of old consonants and the creation of new ones. Seven of the Proto-Semitic fricatives were lost by merger at various times: the interdentals *ṯ* (> *š*), and *ḏ* (> *z*) *ṱ* (> *ṣ*), the laterals *ḻ* (> *ṣ*) and *ḻ* (> *s*), and the uvulars *ḫ* (> *ḥ*) and *ɣ* (> *ʿ*). In return, seven new consonantal phones were created. An emphatic *ṗ* was created to render the unaspirated *p* of Iranian and Greek, and six fricatives *ḇ*, *ḡ*, *ḏ*, *ḵ*, *p̄*, *ṯ* [v ɣ ð x f θ] were created as a result of the assimilation of non-emphatic, ungeminated stops to preceding vowels.

These opposing developments did not exactly cancel each other out. Although four of the seven lost fricatives were restored, the old fricatives were phonemes while the new fricatives were all allophones of stops, conditioned by a preceding vowel, at least in the beginning. (Eventually most of them were phonologized via secondary split, when some of the conditioning vowels were deleted.)

In addition, the language was left with a large concentration of labial phones: [p b ṗ f v w m]. Three of these phones were redistributed by a merger of /w/ with /b/, which seems to be attested already in the vulgar spelling of the Copper Scroll. In the Samaritan reading tradition, where the merger was unconditional, the merger product originally had three allophones, distributed roughly as follows: [w] after /u/, [v] after other vowels, and [b] elsewhere. In the Tiberian tradition, the merger was more restricted, but there too *w* retained its original bilabial realization only after *u*, as in the name *Pwh*, read [puw:å] by the Tiberians and [fuw:a] by the Samaritans.

At the other end of the articulatory tract, in the pharynx and the larynx, there was a gradual reduction in the inventory for some speakers. By the tannaitic period, the Hellenized inhabitants of Beisan, Haifa, and Tivon had merged /ḥ/ with /h/ and /ʿ/ with /ʾ/. The mergers seem to have gone further among the Qumran sectarians and the Samaritans, but Jerome's descriptions and Arabic renderings of Hebrew toponyms (including Haifa and Tivon!) show that the loss of these consonants was far from universal.

Vowels: Phonology
Proto-Semitic /i:/ and /u:/ were retained unchanged throughout the history of Hebrew, but /a:/ became raised and rounded by the fourteenth century BCE in all or most environments. The evidence of the Tiberian reading tradition (see pp. 148–9) suggests that there were two raised and rounded allophones of /a:/, which in one instance yielded doublets: *ḳan:oʾ* = *ḳan:åʾ* 'zealous'.

Eventually, the inherited short vowels also developed allophones as did the upgliding diphthongs: [å:] and [ä] from /a/; [o:], [o] and [å] from /u/; [e:], [e], and [ä] from /i/; [o:] from /aw/; [e:] and [ä:] from /ay/. The merger of some of these allophones resulted in a completely reorganized system in which the number of contrastive qualities was doubled and the role of quantity was greatly reduced.

Long [i:] and [u:] are in complementary distribution with [y] and]w], respectively, and alternate with them, e.g., [kǽli:] 'vessel' ~ [kälyɔ̌kǽ] 'your vessel', [pí:hu:] ~ [pi:w] 'his mouth', [šǽ̱ku:] 'lookout point' ~ [šäḵwí:] 'rooster', [yištaḥǽwǽ:] 'he will prostrate himself' ~ [way:ištáḥu:] 'and he prostrated himself'. It is, thus, possible that the semivowels should be viewed as allophones of vowels rather than consonantal phonemes.

Consonants: Orthography

The Israelites adopted unchanged a twenty-two-sign version of the alphabet current in their area, even though they had preserved more than twenty-two of the twenty-nine Proto-Semitic consonants (see p. 147). Consequently, they were forced to use some signs with more than one value.

Only one instance of such polyphony survived long enough to be recorded by the Masoretes (see Vowels, below): ש š representing both /š/ and /ś/, the latter probably realized [ɬ] until it merged with /s/. Thus, škwr was read [šǽ:ḵú:r] < [šaku:r] when it had the meaning 'intoxicated', but [sǽ:ḵú:r] < [ɬaku:r] with the meaning 'hired'.

Recently, there has been confirmation of an old theory positing two additional instances which survived only until the Hellenistic period: ח ḥ representing both /ḥ/ and /ḫ/; ע ʿ representing both /ʿ/ and /ɣ/. Thus, ḥrym, read [ḥo:rí:m] by the Masoretes, originally had two realizations: one with initial [ḥ] corresponding to the meaning 'nobles, freemen' and the other with initial [ḫ] corresponding to the meanings 'holes' and 'Hurrians' (see p. 147).

The polyphony of the letters bgdkpt recorded by the Masoretes has a different origin (see p. 147).

Vowels: Orthography

Another type of polyphony is that of h, w, and y. These three letters represented vowels as well as consonants, but only in a rudimentary, ambiguous fashion, since their use as vowel letters (matres lectionis 'reading aids') was not consistent in all positions, and the number of vowel phonemes was, in most periods, no less than six. Thus, ancient Hebrew had a highly homographic spelling which left much to the reader's imagination.

Such a situation was intolerable in the case of the Bible. Small wonder, then, that the Talmud contains many references to an accepted biblical reading tradition, mastery of which was essential for one who aspired to be a reader in the synagogue.

There were, in fact, a number of accepted reading traditions in use at the time in Palestine and Babylonia. They were reduced to writing in the post-Talmudic period by various schools of traditionists, called "Masoretes," through the insertion of "points" into the received consonantal text. The same signs were used to record reading traditions of MH. Reliable manuscripts show that there were many differences between the reading traditions of MH and of BH – differences which have been partially obliterated in our modern printed editions.

The differences among the Masoretic reading traditions are, for the most part, differences of dialect rather than meaning. The Tiberian and Babylonian systems (each with several subsystems) distinguish seven and six contrasting vowel qualities, respectively, while the various Palestinian systems and subsystems distinguish five, six, or seven.

Stress, Length, and *Shewa*: Orthography and Phonology

The primary stress is normally marked by one of the Masoretic accent signs; secondary stress is frequently marked by the *ga'ya* sign. Both of them lengthen vowels – hence the name *ga'ya* 'lowing, mooing' given by the Tiberians and the alternative names used by later grammarians: *mäṭäḡ* 'bridle' and *ma'ǎmi'd* 'restrainer'. The position of the primary stress – ultimate or penultimate – is contrastive, at least in BH, serving, for example, to distinguish the IIw sg. f. perfect from both its participial and its IIIy sg. m. counterparts (e.g., *šåḇǻʰ* ≠ *šåḇǻʰ* 'she returned ≠ returning; he captured'). The corresponding contrast between the IIw and IIIy plural perfects (e.g., *šåḇúʷ* ≠ *šåḇúʷ* 'they returned ≠ they captured', attested together in 1 Kings 8:48) seems to have been in the process of breaking down due to an increased tendency to stress the final syllable. In sg. 1c. and sg. 2m. forms of the perfect, the position of the stress is a tense marker (e.g., *måšåḥtǻ* ≠ *uʷmåšaḥtǻ* 'you anointed ≠ and you shall anoint' attested together in Exod. 40: 15; see p. 156).

Outside of closed unstressed syllables, which excluded long vowels, Ancient Hebrew had a contrast between long and short vowels. However, between the tannaitic period and the time of the Masoretes, short vowels in stressed syllables lengthened, erasing the contrast in those syllables. Thus, while Hebrew was still a spoken language, the *o* of infinitival *yåḵó(ʷ)l* 'be able' was long, while the *o* of sg. 3m. perfect *yåḵól* 'he was able' was short, like the ancestor of *å* in *yǝḵåltåm*. In the Pre-Tiberian reading tradition, the *o* of sg. 3m. perfect *yåḵól* lengthened, splitting off from the ancestor of *å* in *yǝḵåltåm* and merging with the long *o* of infinitival *yåḵóʷl*.

As a result of this change, length became to a large extent conditioned by stress. Outside of open unstressed syllables (where a length contrast survived), there was a simple rule: stressed vowels are long and unstressed vowels are short.

Non-systematic representation of vowel length through the use of *matres lectionis* (see p. 148) developed in SBH. These vowel letters are used to mark not only etymologically long vowels but also stressed vowels in pre-pausal position. In the Tiberian reading tradition, such vowels were probably no longer than other stressed vowels, but morphophonemic alternations show that a length difference had once existed, e.g. *tiškaḇ* ~ *tiškåḇ* < *tiškab* ~ *tiškāb*, *yǝšal:aḥ* ~ *yǝšal:eaḥ* < *yišal:eḥ* ~ *yišal:ēḥ*.

Consonant length (like vowel length) was phonemic in Proto-Hebrew, but it was not represented in the biblical period, not even in an unsystematic way. Thus, the spelling ʿrwmym was used for both members of the minimal pair Job 5:12 [ʿăru:mi:m] ≠ Job 22:6 [ʿărum:i:m] 'crafty (pl. m.) ≠ naked (pl. m.)'. And the spelling ntnw was used for both [nå̄tan:u:] 'we gave' and [nå̄tå̄nu:] 'they gave', even though the long n of the former results from the coalescing of the final n of the stem and initial n of the suffix ([nå̄tan+nu:]). It was only in MH that representation of consonant length began to appear, and even then, only in cases like [nå̄tan+nu:] and [kå̄rat+ti:], where a morpheme boundary was spanned. Thus, the citation of 2 Chron. 14:10 in the Mekhilta has nšʿnnw for Masoretic nšʿnw = [nišʿan+nu:] 'we have relied'.

Most of the Proto-Hebrew minimal pairs are no longer valid for the Tiberian system. Many of the new pairs are problematic in some way, since a difference in consonant length normally entails some other difference – in vowel length, secondary stress, or type of *shewa* (see below). There is a kind of vicious circle involved in phonemicizing the words [yig:ŭʿú:] ≠ [yì:ḡʿú:] ≠ [yiḡʿú:] 'they will touch ≠ they will be weary ≠ they will moo': any pair one selects will differ in two or more features.

The fact remains, however, that the Masoretes considered consonant length important enough to create a sign for it ("strong" *dagesh*). Two minimal pairs noted by the Masoretes themselves are Job 5:12 ʿăruʷmiʸm ≠ Job 22:6 ʿăruʷm:iʸm (see above) and Lev. 7:30 tǝbiʸʾäʸnåʰ ≠ Lev. 6:14 tǝbiʸʾän:åʰ 'they (f.) shall bring ≠ you/she shall bring it'. Although Arabic transcriptions suggest that, in the first pair, the vowel preceding the lengthened consonant was shorter than the vowel preceding its unlengthened counterpart, the Masoretes clearly considered this difference to be secondary, unworthy of being represented.

The same goes for a pair like [ḥizḳú:] ≠ [ḥiz:ăḳú:] 'be strong ≠ they strengthened': the Masoretes use the same sign (whose name, *shewa*, comes from the word for 'nothingness') to represent the absence of a vowel following [z] in the first word that they use to represent the [ă] following [z:] in the second, thereby suggesting that [ă] (together with its positional variants: [ĭ], [ŭ], [ĕ], and [ŏ]) is an allophone of Ø. (Later grammarians use the terms "quiescent" for *shewa* realized as Ø and "mobile" for vocalic *shewa*.)

It is certainly true that [ă] (with its positional variants) is completely predictable in some environments: those where it is needed to break up a consonant cluster. In other environments, matters are far more complicated. For one subset of nouns, the most reliable sources seem to describe a form of metrical conditioning requiring that the secondary accent be separated from the primary accent by two syllables, one of them containing [ă], e.g., [hà:măhal:é:ḵ] ≠ [hà:mhal:ăḵí:m] 'the walker ≠ the walkers'. But this is, at best, just a tendency, for there are also free variants like [hà:mḏab:ărí:m] / [hà:măḏab:ărí:m] 'the speakers' (the former in Exod. 6:27 and the latter in 2 Chron. 33:18 according to Aaron ben Asher; vice versa according to other Masoretic sources).

Such complex conditioning and free variation was completely eliminated by the increasingly schematic rules for the realization of the *shewa* sign promulgated by later grammarians. According to one of those rules, a *shewa* preceded by a long vowel and a single consonant must have a vocalic realization (a zero realization would create an extra-heavy syllable); the closest counterpart to this in a masoretic treatise is a tendency rather than a categorical rule, and is largely restricted to *shewa* preceded by an *r*. Despite these differences, the Masoretes seem to agree with the later grammarians on the basic point: the vocalic realizations of *shewa* do not contrast with Ø.

Morphophonemic Alternations

The Tiberian reading tradition has an unusually large number of alternations, most involving vowels (usually the historically short ones) or semivowels. The great majority are – or were originally – conditioned by differences in stress, syllable structure, and/or the proximity of a laryngeal (/ʾ h ḥ ʿ/). A sample of some of the most common alternations among vowels other than shewa are shown below. The main stress is marked by ´ in context and by ″ in (pre-)pause. Forms without either sign are proclitic.

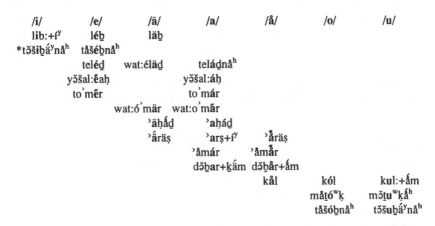

/i/	/e/	/ä/	/a/	/å/	/o/	/u/
lib:+fʸ	léḇ	läḇ				
*tɔ̌šiḇáʸnåʰ	tåšéḇnåʰ					
	teléḏ	wat:éläḏ	teláḏnåʰ			
	yɔ̌šal:ēaḥ		yɔ̌šal:áḥ			
	toʾmḗr		toʾmár			
		wat:óʾmär	wat:oʾmár			
		ʾäḥáḏ	ʾaḥáḏ			
		ʾắräṣ	ʾarṣ+fʸ	ʾå̃räṣ		
		ʾåmár	ʾåmắr			
		dɔ̌ḇar+ḵám	dɔ̌ḇắr+å̃m			
			kål	kól	kul:+å̃m	
				måṭóʷḵ	mɔ̌ṭuʷḵắʰ	
				tåšóḇnåʰ	tɔ̌šuḇáʸnåʰ	

Alternations of the above vowels with *shewa* result from two opposite processes: reduction and epenthesis. Thus, the alternation of *å* in *mǎlåḵiʸm* 'kings' with quiescent *shewa* in *malḵeʸ* < **malakay* 'kings of' (note the spirantized *ḵ*) is a product of reduction, while the alternation of the second *ä* in *mäläḵ* < **malk* 'king' with quiescent *shewa* in *malkiʸ* 'my king' (note the unspirantized *k*) reflects epenthesis.

Reduction affected short vowels in certain kinds of unstressed open syllables, turning them into *shewa*. The most sonorous of the short vowels, *a*, was the most resistant to reduction. It survived in pretonic open syllables where it was later lengthened to *ā* > *å* (e.g., **šanatu* 'year' > **šānā* > *šånåʰ*) except in the construct state (e.g., *šǎnaṯ* 'year of'; see p. 153); as a rule, it did not survive in propretonic ones (e.g., *šǎnåṭoʷ* 'his year'). Short *i* sometimes behaves like *a*, surviving in open pretonic syllables (e.g., **šinatu* 'sleep' > *šenåʰ*), except in the construct state (e.g., Jer. 51:39 *šǎnaṯ* 'sleep of' homonymous with Jer. 48:44 *šǎnaṯ* 'year of'). At other times, it is reduced in open pretonic syllables (e.g., **nāšibāt* > Sifre Devarim

40 *no^wšəḇo^wṭ* 'blowing', contrasting with Ezek. 38:12 *no^wšåḇoṭ* settled').

Epenthesis affected word-final consonant clusters, breaking them up through the insertion of *ä* (*segol*, hence the term "segolation"), *a* (in the vicinity of *h*, *ḥ* or *ʿ*) or *i* (in the vicinity of *y*). It occurred both in nouns (e.g., *rägäl* < **ragl* 'foot', *naʿal* < **naʿl* 'shoe') and verbs (e.g., *way:ägäl* < **way:agl* 'and he exiled', *wan:aʿal* < **wan:aʿl* 'and we went up'). Qumran Hebrew and the Tiberian Massorah preserve evidence of a different, no doubt earlier, rule of epenthesis in the construct form of nouns (see p. 153).

Morphology and Morphosyntax

Nouns and Adjectives

Gender and Number

Masculine singular nouns and adjectives are unmarked. Feminine singular nouns and adjectives usually take one of two endings: + *å^h* or + *ṭ* (> +*ä/aṭ* if the stem ends in a consonant). In BH, the allomorph + *å^h* is often in free variation with + *ṭ* (e.g., *moʾåḇiy:*+ *å^h* ~ *moʾåḇṭ^y*+ *ṭ* 'Moabitess', *ḥaṭ:åʾ*+ *å^h* ~ *ḥaṭ:ǻ*+ *ṭ* 'sin') or with *(ä/a)ṭ* (e.g., *ʾoḵəl*+ *å^h* ~ *ʾoḵä́l*+ *äṭ* 'consuming', *tiṗʾår*+ *å^h* ~ *tiṗʾár*+ *äṭ* 'glory').

Masculine plural nouns and adjectives take the ending + *í^ym* (> + *í^yn* in MH), feminine plurals, the ending + *ó^wṭ*. Apart from a few tree names, noun stems with the underlying form CVCC+ ("segolates") change in the plural to CVCåC+ (→ CəCåC+ by reduction; see p. 151), a very archaic alternation of which only traces remain in the other Semitic languages. Interchange of + *í^ym* and + *ó^wṭ* is common, but not their total absence. Probably the only true plurals without a suffix among the nouns are *ṣoʾn* and *båḵår* – the suppletive, suffixless plurals of *šä^h* 'sheep/goat' and *šo^wr* 'ox', respectively. Semitists use the term "collective" to describe these nouns and mass nouns, as well as true collectives.

Dual number is restricted to a small set of nouns, mainly those denoting units of measurement and counting; it is not found with adjectives (or pronouns or verbs). When used with nouns denoting paired body parts, the dual ending + *ayim* is structurally a plural ending, for it does not contrast with the regular plural endings and it cooccurs with numerals greater than 1. This "pseudo-dual" remained unchanged in MH, while the true dual was partially replaced by the word for 2 (cf. already 2 Sam. 1:1 *yåmi^ym šənåyim* 'two days' instead of *yo^wmayim*).

Definiteness

Definiteness is expressed by the definite article *ha* +, which is prefixed to nouns and adjectives. A more precise transliteration would be *haC:*, for this morpheme has three (unstable) components: (1) the consonant *h*; (2) the vowel *a*; and (3) lengthening of the following consonant (the initial consonant of the word). The third component, which is discontinuous with the first two, is not found with the consonants *ʾ*, *ʿ*, *h*, *ḥ*, *r*, due to a sound change. In such cases, the second component may undergo compensatory lengthening. The first component is normally elided following the prefixes *bə̆* + 'in', *kə̆* + 'like' and *lə̆* + 'to' (but not *me* + 'from' or *wə̆* + 'and'). For example, when *bə̆* + is added to *hab:ayiṭ* 'the house', the result is *b+ab:ayiṭ*. In the Bar-Kokhba letters, the accusative marker *ʾeṭ* (see below) has been reduced to a prefix which produces the same elision, e.g., *tslʿ hzwʾ* < *ʾāṭ-has:äläʿ haz:o^w* 'this *selaʿ*' (alongside *ʾt hšṭr hzʾ* 'this document'), *tšbt hzw* < *ʾāṭ-haš:ab:āṭ haz:o^w* 'this Sabbath'.

Indefiniteness is usually expressed by the absence of the definite article, but occasionally *ʾäḥāḏ* 'one' serves as an indefinite article with nouns.

Case and State

The Proto-Semitic case system has broken down in BH, largely as a result of sound change. The old accusative ending **+a* is gone, leaving only a few frozen relics behind; its functional heir, the preposition *ʾeṭ ~ ʾäṭ-*, normally governs only **definite** objects, and even with them it is not obligatory. Also gone is the old genitive ending **+i*, used in Pre-Hebrew to mark the second (attributive) constituent of noun phrases like *šämän zayiṭ* 'olive oil', *ze^yṭ šämän* 'oil olive', *ʿeṣ pə̆ri^y* 'fruit tree', *pə̆ri^y ʿeṣ* 'tree fruit'.

In Hebrew, it is the first constituent (the head) of these phrases which sets them apart. That constituent, said to be in the "construct state," undergoes a number of distinctive modifications. Two of them are illustrated by Exod. 38:21 *ham:iškån, miškan hå^ʿeḏuṭ* 'the Tabernacle, the Tabernacle of the Pact', where the *å* in the closed final syllable of *ham:iškån* is replaced by *a* in *miškan*, and the definite article is omitted (see p. 161). Another two are illustrated by Exod. 22:4 *biśḏe^h ʾaher* 'in another's field', where the *å* of *śåḏä^h* has been reduced to *ə̆* (p. 151) and then deleted entirely, and word-final *ä^h* has been replaced by *e^h*; contrast Ruth 2:8 *bə̆śåḏä^h ʾaher* 'in another field'. Finally, in Gen. 44:14 *be^yṭåh yo^wsep* '(and Judah came) to Joseph's house', the word for 'house' has [ay] contracted to [e:] (written *e^y*) and lacks the definite article, in contrast to Gen. 43:26 *hab:ayṭå^h* '(and Joseph came) to the house'. In cases where the head does not change in the construct state and the genitive noun is indefinite, ambiguity may arise. Thus, the Mekhilta feels the need to prove that Exod. 21:2 *ʿäḇäḏ ʿiḇri^y* means 'a Hebrew slave' rather than 'a Hebrew's slave'.

The sg. f. ending *+å^h* has the allomorph *+åṭ* in the construct state; the pl. m. ending *+i^ym* has the allomorph *+e^y*, imported from the pseudo-dual, instead of the historically expected *+i^y*. Thus, the construct of *šåni^ym* 'years' is *šə̆ne^y* 'years of', the same as the construct of *šə̆nayim* 'two'.

Pronouns

There are three major sets of pronouns: "nominative" independent pronouns, "accusative" pronouns attached to verbs, and "genitive" pronouns attached to prepositions and nouns. The attached pronouns have one set of allomorphs beginning with a vowel for stems ending in a consonant and another set beginning with a consonant for stems ending in a vowel, e.g, Esther 2:7 *ʾåḇi^y+hå wə̆ʾim:+åh* 'her father and her mother' and Jer. 29:5 = 29:28 *piry+ån ~ pri^y+hän* 'their (f.) fruit'.

The same pronouns were originally used with plural nouns, e.g., *bǎne^y+häm* 'their sons' (stem ending in a vowel, like *pri^y+hän*) and *bǎno^{w}ṯ+åm* 'their daughters' (stem ending in a consonant, like *piry+ån*), but at an early period *+e^y+häm* was reanalyzed as a single morpheme – a suffix to be used with any plural noun – and new forms like *bǎno^{w}ṯ+e^{y}häm* were created. The variation between *+o^{w}ṯ+åm* and *+o^{w}ṯ+e^{y}häm* was lexically conditioned. In Jeremiah's time, *bǎno^{w}ṯ+åm* was obsolete, but *ʾǎḇo^{w}ṯ+åm* 'their fathers' was still the normal form, *ʾǎḇo^{w}ṯ+e^{y}häm* replacing it only occasionally (e.g., Jer. 9:15 ~ 19:4, in the same expression).

In SBH, a few of the independent pronouns have long allomorphs ending in *å^h* alongside short allomorphs, e.g., *hem ~ hem:å^h* 'they'. In Qumran Hebrew more of the independent pronouns and a few of the suffixed ones have the long allomorphs, and in the Samaritan reading tradition these forms predominate. In Qumran Hebrew, the original conditioning of the allomorphs *+m ~ +må* 'them' has been partially preserved: the long suffix *+må* is never attached to a verb ending in (long) *u* or *i*.

Numerals and Quantifiers

The word for 1 is an adjective; it occasionally appears in the plural, e.g., Gen. 11:1 *såpå^h ʾäḥåṯ u^{w}ḏḇåri^{y}m ʾăḥåḏi^{y}m* 'one language and one$_{pl.}$ (set of) words'. Numerals above 1 are nouns, as are the quantifiers *kol ~ kål-* 'all' (lit. 'totality') and *mǎʿaṭ* 'a bit'. Like those quantifiers, they normally precede the counted noun in BH and MH. However, *harbe^h* 'a lot' normally follows the quantified noun in BH and MH, and behaves more like an adjective. With rare exceptions, the three quantifiers do not agree with their nouns, while many numerals (3–10, 13–19, 23–29, etc.) exhibit a kind of reverse agreement (polarity), taking a feminine ending with masculine counted nouns (e.g., *šǎloš+å^h båni^{y}m* 'three sons') and vice versa (e.g., *šåloš båno^{w}ṯ* 'three daughters').

Counted nouns normally stand in apposition to the numeral, but there are exceptions. In all periods, the numerals 2–10 normally form a genitive phrase with the word for 'days' (e.g., *šǎlošäṯ yåmi^{y}m* 'three days'), with definite nouns (e.g., 1 Sam. 31:8 and Bet She‘arim inscriptions *šǎlo(^{w})šäṯ bånå^{y}w* 'his three sons') and with other numerals (*šǎloš me^{ʾ}o^{w}ṯ* '300', *šǎlošäṯ ʾǎlåpi^{y}m* '3,000'). With most nouns, it is definiteness which determines the state of the numeral which precedes them, e.g., Num. 28:19 *šiḇʿå^h kǎḇåśi^{y}m* 'seven sheep' vs. 28:21 *šiḇʿaṭ ha+k:ǎḇåśi^{y}m* 'the seven sheep' (also: 'seven of the sheep'; cf. Exod. 26:9, Num. 35:14).

Ordinals exist only for 1–10; beyond that, cardinal numbers are used in one of four constructions. For 'the Xth year', the Bible has (1) *šǎnaṭ ha+X šånå^h*; (2) *šǎnaṭ ha+X*; (3) *šǎnaṭ X*; (4) *X šånå^h*; only (3) is found in the Mishnah. Construction (4) also has the meaning 'X years'; the two meanings are found side by side in Gen. 14:4.

Conjunctions, Prepositions, Postpositions, and Adverbial Endings

The underlying form of the coordinating conjunction is normally *wə̆+*. When prefixed to a word whose initial consonant is a labial or is followed by *ə̆*, it has the allomorph *u*^w+ in the Tiberian reading tradition. In binomials like *šå̆mayim wå̆ʾå̆rä̱ṣ* 'heaven and earth', the underlying form is *wå̆+*.

The most primitive prepositions are *bə̆+* 'in', *kə̆+* 'like', and *lə̆+* 'to'. When prefixed to nouns, their underlying vowel is *ə̆*, but with suffixed pronouns, it is *å̆*. With *kå̆+*, unlike *bå̆+* and *lå̆+*, the particle *mo*^w+ (~ *mo*^w*ṯ* in MH) is normally inserted before the suffixed pronoun. In the poetic dialect, that particle may be added to any of these three prepositions before nouns. Most of the longer prepositions can be seen to be derived from nouns in the construct state.

BH has a postposition +*å̆*^{*h*} 'to', which alternates with the prepositions *lə̆+* and *ʾäl*, e.g. *hå̆ʿaynå̆*^{*h*} ~ *ʾäl-hå̆ʿå̆yin* 'to the spring' found side by side in Gen. 24. Eventually, it became a meaningless ossified relic, used in forms like *la/ə̆+ḥu*^w*ṣå̆*^{*h*} 'to the outside' (LBH, Qumran Hebrew) and even *me+ḥu*^w*ṣå̆*^{*h*} 'from the outside' (MH).

Another ending which could be viewed as a postposition is +*å̆m*, generally equivalent to *bə̆+* and used to form adverbs, e.g., *ʾå̆mn+å̆m* 'really' < *ʾomän* 'truth', *ḥin:+å̆m* 'gratis' < *ḥen* 'favor', *yo*^w*m+å̆m* 'by day' < *yo*^w*m* 'day'. For the most part there is no specific affix or pattern for adverbs. For the adverbial use of verbs, see below.

Verbs

Verbs do a great deal of work in BH. The finite verbs inflect for number, gender and person, and thus contain their own pronominal subjects. Moreover, verbs are frequently used to express concepts which English expresses with adjectives ("be old," "be big," "be strong," etc.) and adverbs ("greatly," "well," "increasingly," "really").

The Root

Lexical morphemes composed solely of consonants can be isolated in members of virtually all syntactic categories, but only in the verb are these "roots" free to "interdigitate" with a large number of contrasting "patterns."

The verbal root is usually triconsonantal, occasionally quadriconsonantal, rarely quinqueconsonantal. Synchronically biconsonantal roots like *l-d* and *b-n* (see below) occur chiefly as allomorphs of triconsonantal ones. The sg. 3m. imperfect verbs in Table 9.1, p. 156, once assigned to the roots *š-b* and *s-b*, are analyzed today as representing five distinct triconsonantal roots. The three positions within the triliteral root are numbered I, II, and III; thus, a I*n* root is a root with *n* in the first position.

From a diachronic point of view, the biconsonantal allomorphs are probably relics of a very ancient stage in which biconsonantal verbs were fairly common. Viewed in this light, most, if not all, of the verbs in Table 9.1, p. 156 are seen to be originally biconsonantal verbs which were "triconsonantalized" through the

Table 9.1 Roots with "weak" radical

Verb	Meaning	Root	Class
yiš:ób	blow (wind)	n-š-b	I*n*
yaš:í^{y}b	cause to blow	n-š-b	I*n*
yeséb	sit, dwell	y-š-b	I*y*
yo^{w}ší^{y}b	cause to sit/dwell	y-š-b	I*y*
yåšú^{w}b	return	š-w-b	II*w*
yåší^{y}b	cause to return	š-w-b	II*w*
yišbá^{ʰ}	capture	š-b-y	III*y*
yåsób/yis:ób	go around	s-b-b	II=III
yåséb	cause to go around	s-b-b	II=III

addition of a semi-vowel or consonant length. It is not uncommon to find alternation between two triconsonantalizations of a single biconsonantal original, e.g., *y-g-r ~ g-w-r* 'be afraid' and *ṭ-w-b ~ y-ṭ-b* 'be good' (both Perfect ~ Imperfect). The spread of triconsonantalization continued in the historical period via analogy, e.g., BH *bån+åh/åm* > MH *bĕnåy+åh/åm* 'he built it/them' and BH *yim:aḏ* > MH *yim:åḏeḏ* 'it may be measured'.

Tense and Aspect

BH has six paradigms with temporal and/or aspectual value, listed below together with conventional sg. 1c. examples from the root *k-t-b* 'write':

A   Perfect: *kåṯáḇti^y* 'I wrote, I (now) write' (penultimate stress)

B   Imperfect: *ʾäḵtóḇ* 'I will write, I used to write, I (habitually) write'

C   Perfect + *waw* consecutive/conversive: *wĕkåṯaḇtí^y* 'and I shall write' (final stress; see p. 149)

D   Imperfect + *waw* consecutive/conversive: *wåʾäḵtóḇ* 'and I wrote'

E   Participle: *koṯéḇ* 'writing' (also: 'writer')

F   Participle + auxiliary: *(wĕ)håyí^{y}ṭi^y/(wå)ʾähyä́^{ʰ} koṯéḇ* '(and) I used to / will (habitually) write'

E is etymologically and morphologically nominal; accordingly, it inflects only for number and gender. The others inflect for person, as well.

The "converted" forms C and D are very common in BH, but they function mainly as markers of formal style. They are virtually nonexistent in MH. They both contain the conjunction 'and'; accordingly, they are restricted to clause-initial position. In that position, C alternates with B, and D alternates with A.

In an utterance whose first verb is B, the subsequent verbs may be either B or, if clause initial, C. Jer. 49:22 *hin:e^ʰ kan:äšär yaʿälä^ʰ wĕyiḏʾä^ʰ wĕyipʿroś kĕnåpå^{y}w* 'behold, like an eagle, he flies up and soars and spreads his wings' is a B–B–B sequence, while *hin:e^ʰ kan:äšär yiḏʾä^ʰ u^{w}pårás kĕnåpå^{y}w* 'behold, like an eagle, he soars and spreads his wings' in Jer. 48:40 is a B–C sequence. Similarly, in an utterance whose first verb is A, the subsequent verbs may be either A or, if clause initial, D. Thus the phrase *ʿåru"m rå'åh rå'å^h wystr/wǝnistår* 'the shrewd man saw trouble and hid' in Prov. 22:3 is written as an A–D sequence (*wystr = way:is:åṭer*) but read as an A–A sequence (cf. also Jer. 7:30–31 vs. 32:34–35). Once a verb from paradigm C or D is selected, all subsequent verbs will normally be from the same paradigm, until the sequence is broken by the introduction of a non-clause-initial verb (see p. 166).

According to some scholars, paradigms A–D have temporal meaning in SBH; according to others, aspectual meaning. The question has been debated furiously and inconclusively for more than a century.

The examples below show that collocations of A and B may be used to express the past/future distinction, irrespective of the event/habit/state distinction, while the process/event distinction is expressed by collocating A and B not with each other but with E. Although A, B, and E have a bewildering variety of uses, these particular uses seem to be at the core of the system.

Expressing Distinctions of Tense and Aspect in Biblical Hebrew

	Past	Future		
Event	A	B		

ka'åšär   *ʿåśiyṭi^y*   *lǝšomro"n* ...   *ken*   *'å'åśä^h*   *li^yru"šålayim* ...
'as   I did   to Samaria ...   so   shall I do   to Jerusalem ...'
(Isa. 10:11; cf. also Exod. 10:14 and 2 Kings 10:18)

Habit   A   B

'åbi^y   *yis:ar*   *'äṭkäm*   *baš:o"ṭi^ym*   *wa'åni^y*   *'åyas:er*   *'äṭkäm*
'my father   flogged you   with whips,   but I   will flog   you
                    bå'akrab:i^ym
                    with scorpions'
(1 Kings 12:11; cf. also Josh. 1:17a and Jer. 44:17)

State   A   B

ka'åšär   *håyi^yṭi^y*   *ʿim*   *mošä^h*   *'ähyä^h*   *ʿim:åk*
'as   I was   with   Moses   I shall be   with you'
(Josh. 1:5; cf. also Josh. 1:17b and Jer. 2:36)

	Process	Event				
Future	E	B				

hin:e^h'o"ḏåk   *mǝḏab:äräṭ šåm*   *ʿim*   *ham:äläk wa'åni^y*   *'åbo'*
    'you will still be speaking there with the king,   and I   will come'
    (1 Kings 1:14; cf. also 1 Sam. 10:5 and Isa. 65:24)

Past   E   A

wǝhin:e^h   *ʿo"ḏän:å^h*   *mǝḏab:äräṭ*   *ʿim*   *ham:äläk*   *wǝnåṭån* ...   *bå'*
'and   she was still speaking   with   the king,   and Nathan ...   came'
(1 Kings 1:22; cf. also Jud. 13:9 and Job 1:13–19)

When one considers the full range of uses of these paradigms in SBH, it becomes clear that A and B need to be described in terms of both tense and aspect.

Only for E is it possible to give a simple description, namely, imperfective aspect.

The complexity of the tense/aspect system is due, in part, to the fact that it was constantly in flux. E and F gradually took on the functions of B, in the following order:

1   progressive: complete replacement already in SBH except in present tense questions; without exception in LBH;
2   habitual: partial replacement in BH completed in MH;
3   future: large-scale replacement in MH outside of subordinate clauses;
4   modal: partial replacement in MH.

At the same time, E took on two of the functions of A: perfective present (including the performative) and present of transitive statives.

One result of this expansionism was that E lost its aspectual value and became a tense (present in LBH (?), nonpast in MH). Moreover, thanks to the spread of F, Hebrew developed the ability to distinguish habitual aspect in the future (rare in SBH, common in Qumran Hebrew and MH), the infinitive (rare in LBH, common in MH), and the imperative (MH).

Mood

The BH imperfect distinguishes, in part of its paradigm, a volitive mood (representing diachronically the conflation of the Proto-West Semitic subjunctive, imperative and jussive) from the indicative mood, e.g., *ʾåmú^{w}ṭ+å^h* 'let me die', *mú^{w}ṭ* 'die!', *yåmóṯ* 'let him die'; *ʾåšíʾ^{y}ḇ+åh* 'let me bring back', *håšéḇ ~ håšíʾ^{y}ḇ+å^h* 'bring back!', *ʾal-tåšéḇ/tåšåḇ* 'do not turn back'. In the first person, singular and plural, the volitive is expressed by the +å^h (cohortative) ending, which can be used with all verbs except, normally, those ending in a vowel (IIIy and IIIʾ verbs). In the third person singular, m. and f., the volitive has a distinct (jussive) form in only three categories of verbs: *hip̄ʿil* (see p. 159), IIIy, and IIw,y *ḳal*. There was also an energic mood with some kind of emphatic force, e.g. *yåḵab:ə̆ḏ+ån+ni^y* 'he does honor me'.

This distinction did not survive very long. Already in SBH, the volitive forms are sometimes replaced by their indicative counterparts. In Qumran Hebrew, the breakdown of the system is virtually complete; the old volitive forms are still in use, but they no longer have their old meaning. In MH, cohortative forms are virtually nonexistent, and jussive forms are uncommon and largely restricted to certain literary genres. Thus, Deut. 13:7 *nelə̆ḵå^h wə̆naʿabdå^h* 'let us go and worship' is paraphrased as *neleḵ wə̆naʿăḇo^{w}ḏ* in Sanhedrin 7:10. However, the ability to distinguish volitive future from indicative future has been regained through a restructuring of the tense system.

Binyan

Hebrew, like the other Semitic languages, has an elaborate system of morphological patterns (Medieval and Modern Hebrew *binyanim* 'buildings, verbal stems or derivational classes') used, for the most part, to derive verbs from other, more basic, verbs. Thus, one root can generate a number of morphologically distinct verbs referring to related activities. In the case of human reproduction, the root *y-l-d* yields a verb *yålad* 'give birth' usually referring to the role of the mother, a second verb *ho*ᵂ*liyd* 'sire' referring to the role of the father, a third verb *no*ᵂ*lad* 'be born' referring to the role of the baby, and a fourth verb *yil:ed* 'deliver' referring to the role of the midwife. A fifth verb *hityal:ed* refers to declaring oneself to be someone's offspring.

The meaning of a given *binyan* cannot be stated in absolute terms, but only relative to a more basic *binyan*. Hence, it makes no sense to ask for the meaning of the most basic *binyan* (*kal*), nor does it make sense to attempt to relate the meaning of a specific "derived" verb to the meaning of its *binyan* in cases where a basic counterpart is not attested.

Despite many irregularities and nuances, perhaps produced by semantic change, the relationships in the table below are fairly typical for BH: *hitpaʿel* is often and *puʿal* is always the reflexive–reciprocal and medio-passive, respectively, of *piʿel*, which, in turn, is frequently a causative of *kal*; and *hupʾal* is always the medio-passive of *hipʿil*, which itself frequently functions as a second causative of *kal*. *Nipʿal*, although normally the medio-passive or reflexive of *kal*, sometimes interchanges with *hitpaʿel*.

Table 9.2   Biblical Hebrew *binyanim*

		Perfect	Imperfect	Participle
Kal	'be(come) holy/taboo'	kådáš	yikdáš	(kådóᵂš adj.)
Nipʿal	'reveal oneself as holy'	nikdáš	yik:ådéš	nikdáš
Piʿel	'sanctify/purify'	kid:áš	yəškad:éš	məkad:éš
Puʿal	'be sanctified/purified'	kud:áš	yəškud:áš	məkud:åš
Hipʿil	'consecrate/devote'	hikdíʸš	yakdíʸš	makdíʸš
Hupʿal	'be consecrated/devoted'	hukdáš	yukdáš	mukdáš
Hitpaʿel	'sanctify/purify oneself/ reveal oneself as holy'	hitkad:éš	yitkad:éš	mitkad:éš

The MH chart for *k-d-š* would be much the same except in *nipʿal*, *puʿal*, and *hitpaʿel*. *Nipʿal* is no longer attested with this verb, no doubt because that *binyan* is no longer used for reflexives. The *puʿal* perfect and imperfect have ceased to exist for virtually all verbs in MH, their function as medio-passive of the *piʿel* perfect and imperfect being taken over by the *hitpaʿel* perfect and imperfect (the former altered in form to *nitkad:aš*, with preformative *n+*, by analogy with the *nipʿal*). Concomitantly, the rare ingressive use of the *puʿal* participle has been transferred to the *hitpaʿel* participle (which in the case of *k-d-š* has retained its initial *m+* but in other verbs has preformative *n+*). As a result, the *piʿel* participle has two medio-passive counterparts in MH: the stative *puʿal* participle and the ingressive *hitpaʿel* participle. *Hitpaʿel* continues to function as a reflexive, as well.

Valence: *Increase and Decrease*

Most of the above relationships correspond to oppositions of valence. *Pi'el* and *hip̄'il*, when functioning as causatives, add an argument to the verb, while *nip̄'al*, *pu'al*, *hup̄'al*, and *hitpa'el*, functioning as medio-passives, reflexives or reciprocals, subtract an argument, as shown below:

Binyanim	Root	Valences	Example
Ḳal, Nip̄'al	r-p-ʾ	2, 1	Jer. 17:14 *rǝp̄āʾeniʸ Y. wǝʾerāp̄eʾ* 'heal me, O Lord, that I may be healed' (cf. Jer. 31:3)
Hitpa'el, Pi'el	ḳ-d-š	1, 2	2 Chron. 29: 5 *hitḳad:ǝ̄šuʷ wǝḳad:ǝ̄šuʷ ʾät-beʸṭ Y.* 'sanctify yourselves and sanctify the House of the Lord' (cf. Lev. 14:11)
Pi'el, Pu'al	b-r-k	2, 1	2 Sam. 7:29 *uʷb̄āreḵ ʾät-beʸṭ 'ab̄dǝ̄ḵā ... yǝb̄oraḵ beʸṭ 'ab̄dǝ̄ḵā* 'and bless your servant's house ... may your servant's house be blessed'
Hip̄'il, Hup̄'al	b-w-ʾ	3, 2	Gen. 43:17–18 *way:āb̄eʾ hǎʾiʸš ʾät-hǎʾǎndši̇ʸm beʸṭāʰ yoʷsep̄ ... huʷb̄ǎʾuʷ beʸṭ yoʷsep̄* 'and the man brought the men to Joseph's house ... they were brought to Joseph's house'
Pi'el, Ḳal	ṭ-h-r	2, 1	Ezek. 24:13 *ṭihartiʸḵ wǝloʾ ṭāhart* 'I purified you, but you would not be purified' (cf. 2 Kings 7:4)
Hip̄'il, Ḳal	š-w-b	2, 1	Jer. 31:17 *hǎši̇ʸb̄eniʸ wǝʾǎšuʷb̄āʰ* 'bring me back that I may come back' (cf. 2 Sam. 15:20, 2 Kings 7:4, and Jer. 11:18)

In BH, valence decrease can take place with rearrangement of the remaining arguments (type 1) or without it (type 2). The process which derives medio-passive verbs normally deletes the subject of their active counterparts rather than allowing it to remain in a prepositional phrase – hence the medieval Hebrew description of medio-passive verbs as "those whose agent is not mentioned." Type 1 medio-passives advance the original direct object by making the derived verb agree with it and deleting the accusative marker *ʾeṭ*, while type 2 medio-passive verbs are impersonal (i.e., invariably sg. 3m. and subjectless) and are used with *ʾeṭ*, e.g., Num. 26:53–55 *teḥāleḵ hǎʾǎrāṣ ... yeḥāleḵ ʾät-hǎʾǎrāṣ* 'the land shall be divided ... the land shall be divided'. Intermediate types, with partial advancement, exist as well. With oblique objects, type 2 is the norm (as in Arabic), e.g., Ezek. 10:13 *lǎ+häm ḳoʷrǎʾ* 'they were referred to (lit. to them it was called)', 16:34 *ʾaḥǎrayi+ḵ loʾ zuʷn:āʰ* 'you were not sought after (lit. after you it was not whored)', Song 8:8 *yǝḏub:ar-bǎ+h* 'she shall be spoken for (lit. it shall be spoken about her)'. In MH, type 2 has virtually disappeared, although there is at least one example of it in reliable manuscripts: Pesaḥim 7:7 *šä+n:izraḳ ʾäṭ dāmoʷ* 'whose blood was sprinkled' (cf. also Sanhedrin 7:5 and Kelim 7:3 in the Naples edition of the Mishna).

Change of *binyan* and change of valence do not always coincide. There is a

whole class of verbs (intransitive statives) which either have the same valence in
$hip^c il$ that they have in kal or else have two meanings in $hip^c il$ – one with valence
increase and one without it, e.g., $hikri^yb$ 'come near (= $kårab$); bring near', $hib^ʾi^yš$
'stink (= $bå^ʾaš$); cause to stink'. Conversely, intransitive pi^cel verbs have a causative in the same *binyan*, e.g., BH *miher* 'hurry (intrans. and trans.)', MH *ķil:aḥ*
'gush, cause to gush', *me^ʾen* 'refuse, instruct to refuse'. There are also a few *ķal*
verbs of this type, e.g., BH–MH $rå^cå^h$ 'pasture (trans. and intrans.)' and BH *råḥaṣ*
'take a bath (= MH *råḥaṣ*), wash (part of the body = MH $hirḥi^yṣ$)'. And BH *nåṭan*
'give' and *śåm* 'put' function as suppletive causatives of $håyå^h$ 'be' without
change of *binyan*.

Denominatives
Verbs derived from triconsonantal nouns may occur in any *binyan*, and sometimes
occur in several unrelated *binyanim*. Thus, we have BH–MH $hišri^yš$ 'become root-
ed' contrasting with BH–MH *šeraš* 'uproot' and MH $hiṭli^ya^c$ 'become wormy' (=
BH $way{:}årum\ to^{w}lå^ci^ym$ 'and it became infested with worms') contrasting with
MH $ṭil{:}a^c$ 'de-worm'. In these examples, the $hip^c il$ denominatives are intransitive
stative verbs, while the *pi^c el* ones are transitive privative verbs, reminiscent of English "skin a cat" and "worm a dog."
   Triconsonantal denominative verbs normally have the same morphology as other verbs, but the MH stative $hip^c il$ meaning 'become poor', derived from $^cåni^y$
'poor (man)', is irregular: imperfect ya^cni^y, perfect $hä^cni^y$, participle ma^cni^y. The
expected $ya^cänä^h$ was avoided, apparently to prevent confusion with $kal\ ya^cänä^h$
'he will answer'.
   Quadriconsonantal denominatives cannot be accommodated in most *binyanim*.
In LBH and MH, the problem was solved through a modification of pi^cel, pu^cal
and $hiṭpa^cel/niṭpa^cal$ – a modification used earlier for reduplicated quadricon-
sonantals like *k-l-k-l*. Thus, in LBH we find the participles $måṭurgåm$ 'translated'
and $måķurbål$ 'bemantled', derived from quadriconsonantal Aramaic nouns for
'translator, dragoman' and 'mantle', respectively. These participles have the pattern $måCuCCåC$, which differs from the $måCuC{:}åC$ pattern of the *pu^c al* participle
only in that the doubled medial radical has been shortened to make room for an
additional consonant.

Syntax

Modification of Nouns
Nouns may be modified attributively by adjectives, quantifiers, nouns (genitive
and appositive), pronouns (possessive and demonstrative), prepositional phrases,
or clauses (see p. 171).
   Nominal attributes of the genitive type are distinguished from adjectival ones
in three ways: they put their heads in the construct state (see p. 153), e.g., $^cåre^y$
mibṣår 'fortress cities' (contrast $^cåri^ym\ båṣuro^wṭ$ fortified cities'), they do not

agree with their heads, and they normally prevent their heads from taking a definite article, e.g., *ʿåreʸ ha+m:iḫṣår* 'the fortress cities' (contrast *hä+ʿåriʸm ha+b:ǎṣuroʷṭ* 'the fortified cities').

The distinction between the two types of attributes is often blurred. Thus, in adjectival *šaʿar hå+ʿälyoʷn* 'the upper gate' (Ezek. 9:2), the head lacks the definite article, a feature which becomes common in MH, while in the genitive construction *ha+š:aʿar ha+d:åroʷm* 'the south gate' (Ezek. 40:28), the head has the definite article. In adjectival *malʾäḵeʸ råʿiʸm* 'evil emissaries' (Ps. 78:49) the head is in the construct state. In Deut. 25:15 *ʾäḇän šǎlemåʰ wåṣädäḵ* 'a full and righteous weight', an adjective is conjoined with an abstract genitive noun, no doubt on the analogy of interchanges like Ps. 9:5 *šoʷp̄eṭ ṣädäḵ* 'judge of righteousness' with Ps. 7:12 *šoʷp̄eṭ ṣad:iʸḵ* 'righteous judge'. There is also a tendency to make the genitive noun agree in number with its head (see below).

In true compounds like *ʿåreʸ ha+m:iḫṣår* and Deut. 13:4, 6 *ho(ʷ)lem ha+ḥăloʷm*, the definite counterpart of Deut. 13:2 *holem ḥăloʷm* 'a dream dreamer', the definite article prefixed to the genitive noun serves to make the entire phrase definite. With other genitive phrases, especially possessive ones, a definite article prefixed to the genitive noun belongs to it alone, and there is no way to mark the definiteness of the head. Thus, *malʾaḵ hå+ʾălohiʸm* has the same form whether it means 'an angel of God' (Judg. 13:6, etc.) or 'the angel of God' (Judg. 13:9, etc.), and *kǎnap̄ ha+k:ǎruʷḇ* has the same form whether it means 'a wing of the cherub' (1 Kings 6:27) or 'the wing of the cherub' (1 Kings 6:24).

The rule which places the definite article on the genitive noun of compounds produces bizarre results when it is applied to gentilic nouns derived from compound names (of places, tribes, or clans). The toponym *beʸṭ-ʾel/beʸṭʾel* 'Bethel', literally 'house of God', is treated in SBH as a genitive construction – even after it is converted to a gentilic through the addition of +*iʸ*. Thus, *beʸṭ hå+ʾäl+iʸ* 'the Bethelite', the definite form of **beʸṭʾäl+iʸ*, is split in the middle by the definite article, as if it meant 'house of the godly'. Small wonder that, in the later period, Bar-Kokhba calls the people of En-Gedi (lit. 'kid spring') *hʿngdyn* rather than *ʿyn-hgdyyn*.

In SBH, the plural ending is normally attached only to the head of the genitive phrase, but a second plural ending is sometimes attached to the genitive noun. This **redundant plural ending**, which becomes increasingly common in LBH and MH, is used with both mass nouns (even those which are otherwise unattested with a plural ending, e.g., Isa. 42:22 *båt:+eʸ kǎlåʾ+iʸm* 'houses of detention', Bava Batra 10:4 *šǎṭår+eʸ ʾäriʸsiy:+oʷṭ* 'contracts of tenantship', Sifra Nedava 8:2 *båt:+eʸ dǎšǎn+iʸn* 'receptacles for fatty ash') and count nouns (even when ambiguity is created, e.g., Deut. 1:15 *śår+eʸ ʾälåp̄+iʸm* 'chiefs of a thousand').

The process which creates the genitive construction is **iterative** and a number of long chains are attested, e.g., Lev. 13:59, 2 Kings 18:24, Isa. 21:17, 28:1, 2 Chr. 36:10, Copper Scroll XI, 16. In 1 Chr. 9:13 [*gibʸoʷreʸ heʸl*] [[*mǎläʸkät ʿăḇoʷdat*] [*beʸṭ-håʾălohiʸm*]] '[men of valor of] [[the work of the service of] [the House of God]]', the constituent phrases are easily recognizable because they are frequently attested in the Bible. In the end product, all nouns but the last are in the construct state; hence *ḥayil* → *ḥe*^{y}*l* and *ʿăḇo*^{w}*ḏậ*^{h} → *ʿăḇo*^{w}*ḏaṭ*.

All nouns in the chain but the last normally dispense with the definite article. In 2 Kings 23:17, we find two exceptions in a single sentence quoting the people of Bethel: *ha+ḳ:äḇär* ʾ*i*ʾ*š̌* *hậ+*ʾ*ălohi*ʾ*m* 'the grave of the man of God' and *ha+m:izbaḥ be*ʾ*ṭ-*ʾ*el* 'the altar of Bethel'. This may be a syntactic allusion to Gen. 31:13 *hậ+*ʾ*el be*ʾ*ṭ-*ʾ*el* 'the God of Bethel'.

A process which serves some of the same functions as the one which creates genitive phrases and which sometimes alternates with it is the insertion of the preposition *lə+* 'to, belonging to' (e.g., 2 Kings 5:9, Ruth 2:3), usually preceded by relative ʾ*ăšär/šä+*. This **circumlocution** permits the use of the definite article with the head noun, e.g., Gen. 29:9 *ḥaṣ:o*ʾ*n* ʾ*ăšär lə+*ʾ*äḇi*ʾ*hậ* 'the flocks which belong(ed) to her father' (also 31:19) vs. Gen. 37:12 *ṣo*ʾ*n* ʾ*äḇi*ʾ*häm* 'their father's flocks'.

In some contexts, circumlocution of the genitive construction with (ʾ*ăšär/šä+*) *lə+* is more than just a stylistic option. In MH, it is obligatory for the second genitive construction in constructions of the form "A of B ..., but (that) of C ..." (e.g., Berakhot 4:1, Sanhedrin 10:5), "... A of B; also (that) of C" (e.g., Ṭevul Yom 1:1, 2), and "A of B is more ... than (that) of C" (e.g., Terumot 5:9), where the second occurrence of A is deleted by a gapping transformation.

In all periods, circumlocution is obligatory when the noun phrase to be modified contains a conjunction, e.g., Gen. 40:5 *ham:aš̌kä*^{h} *wə̌hậ*ʾ*opä*^{h} ʾ*ăšär lə̌mäläḵ miṣrayim* 'the butler **and** the baker of the king of Egypt' instead of **maš̌ke*^{h} *wə̌*ʾ*ope*^{h} *mäläḵ miṣrayim*, 2 Kings 11:10, Benei Ḥezir tomb inscription *ḳbr whnpš̌ š̌lʾlʿzr* '(the) tomb **and** the monument of Eleazar', Copper Scroll III, 2–3 *kly ksp wzhb š̌ldm*ʿ 'vessels of [silver **and** gold] of *terumah*', Pe'ah 4:9, Shevi'it 1:4, Terumot 11:4. The genitive construction may be used only if the coordinate noun phrase is first broken up, e.g., Gen. 40:1 *maš̌ke*^{h} *mäläḵ miṣrayim wə̌hậ*ʾ*opä*^{h} 'the butler of the king of Egypt and the baker', Deut. 22:15 ʾ*äḇi*ʾ *han:a*ʿ*ărậ*^{h} *wə̌*ʾ*im:ậh* 'the girl's father and her mother', Sanhedrin 11:1, Menaḥot 7:4. The genitive constituent, on the other hand, is often a coordinate noun phrase, e.g., Exod. 32:2, Lev. 13:59, Num. 20:5, Deut. 8:8, Josh. 6:19, Terumot 11:4, Ḥagigah 1:8.

In MH, the phrase *š̌ä+l:ə+* 'that belongs to' has been reanalyzed as a single morpheme: a new preposition *š̌äl* with the meaning 'of'. This is evident in the phrase *š̌hyw š̌l hgw*ʾ*yn* 'which belonged to the gentiles' (Bar-Kokhba letters), for the first half of a bimorphemic *š̌+l+* would be redundant following *š̌+hyw* and the second half would elide the [h] of the definite article (see pp. 152–153) and be written as part of the next word, without a space. Chains with more than one occurrence of *š̌äl* are attested, e.g., Kelim 12:3, 6, Zavim 4:2 (*bis*), Bet She'arim inscriptions (cited below).

Suffixed pronouns, unlike genitive nouns, are normally possessive. Thus *be*ʾ*ṭ+ o*^{w} 'his/its house' can be equivalent to *be*ʾ*ṭ hậ*ʾ*i*ʾ*š̌* 'the man's house' but not to *be*ʾ*ṭ haḳ:ayiṣ* 'the summer house'. Another difference is that the suffixed pronoun cannot normally serve as the head of another genitive noun or any other non-appositive modifier. Nouns modified by suffixed pronouns, like those modified by genitive nouns, do not normally retain their definite article, unless the pronoun is separated through the insertion of (*ăšär/šä*+) *lǎ*+, e.g., 1 Sam. 25:7 *hǎroᶜiʸm* *ǎšär lǎ*+*kǎ* vs. Gen. 13:8 *roᶜäʸkǎ* 'your shepherds'.

The tendency of these pronouns to be attached to the last noun of a genitive construction often conflicts with the syntactic bracketing required by the sense, e.g., Prov. 24:31 [*gädär₁ ʾǎbǎn₂*] [*ǎʸw₃*] 'his₃ stone₂ fence₁', Prov. 10:15, 18:11 [*kiryat₁ ᶜuz:₂*][*oᵂ₃*] 'his₃ mighty₂ city₁' (contrast the purely poetic Ps. 71:7 *mahs₁+iʸ₂-ᶜoz₃* 'my₂ mighty₃ refuge₁'), Yoma 5:1, Negaᶜim 12:5. The conflict is sometimes resolved through the use of a circumlocution, e.g., Gen. 44:2 *gǎbiʸᵏiʸ* *gǎbiʸaᶜ hak:äsäp* 'my silver goblet (lit. my goblet, the silver goblet)', 2 Kings 25:30; Exod. 35:16 *mikbar han:ǎhošät ʾǎšär-loᵂ* 'its copper grating (lit. the copper grating that belongs to it)', Lev. 9:8, Judg. 3:20.

The first constituent of the genitive construction may take a suffixed pronoun referring to the second constituent. In MH, where this **anticipatory pronoun** is common, its referent must be governed by *šäl*, e.g., Sanhedrin 8:5 *miʾtǎt+ǎn* *šäl:ǎrǎšǎᶜiʸn* 'the death (of them,) of the wicked', Bet Sheᶜarim inscriptions *ʾrwn+n šlšlwšt bny+w šlrby ywdn bn+w šlrby myʾšh* 'the ossuary (of them,) of the three sons (of him,) of Rabbi Judan, the son (of him,) of Rabbi Myʾšh'. In BH, where it is rare, its referent is (with one exception, in Song 3:7) not governed by a preposition, e.g., Ezek. 42:14 *bǎboʾ+ǎm hak:ohǎniʸm* 'upon the entering of (them,) the priests'.

Modification of Verbal Nouns and Adjectives

Verbal nouns can also be modified by genitive nouns, which may be underlying subjects or objects; in 2 Sam. 1:26, *ʾahǎbat nǎšiʸm* 'love of women' is ambiguous. Adjectives, too, may be used in the genitive construction, whether they function as nouns (e.g., 2 Kings 10:6 *gǎdoleʸ hǎᶜiʸr* 'the grandees of the city') or not (e.g., Gen. 41:2 *yǎpoᵂt marʾäʰ* 'beautiful of appearance', Ezek. 17:7 *gǎdoᵂl kǎnǎpayim* 'great of wing', Gittin 9: 8). Here too, the definite article which logically belongs to the whole phrase is attached to the genitive noun (see pp. 161–2). Thus, when *yǎpoᵂt marʾäʰ* (Gen. 41:2) and *gǎdoᵂl kǎnǎpayim* (Ezek. 17:7) modify definite nouns, they become *yǎpot ham:arʾäʰ* (Gen. 41:4) and *gǎdoᵂl hak:ǎnǎpayim* (Ezek. 17:3), literally 'beautiful of the appearance' and 'great of the wing'.

The comparative degree of adjectives is expressed by means of an adverbial phrase introduced by the preposition *min/miC*: 'from, away from', e.g., Judg. 14:18 *mǎtoᵂk mid:ǎbaš* 'sweet beyond honey', Niddah 2:7. In MH, this adverbial may be strengthened by placing the word *yoᵂter* 'more' before it (not before the adjective, as in Modern Hebrew).

The superlative, too, is expressed syntactically, e.g., Song 1:8 *hay:ǎpǎʰ* *ban:ǎšiʸm* 'the fair(est) among women', Deut. 28:54. In MH and sometimes in BH, the relative conjunction is inserted before the preposition, e.g., 2 Sam. 7:9, Pesahim 9:8 *hay:ǎpäʰ šä+b:ǎhän* 'the fair(est) among them'.

Word Order

Within the Noun Phrase

Attributive modifiers (with the exception of some quantifiers; see p. 154) follow their heads in a fairly predictable order: (1) genitive nouns; (2) possessive pronoun; (3) adjectives; (4) demonstrative pronoun/adjective; (5) relative clauses. In LBH, (3) and (4) may be reversed, e.g., 2 Chron. 1:10, Esther 9:29.

Put differently, adjectives and relative clauses may not separate the immediate constituents of a genitive phrase; they must follow the last genitive noun or pronoun. Thus, both the wide scope modifier of 1 Kings 6:24 $kănap̄_f$ $hak{:}ăru^w\underline{b}_m$ $haš{:}eni^y\underline{t}_f$ 'the second$_f$ wing$_f$ of the cherub$_m$.' and the narrow scope modifier of 1 Kings 6:27 $u^w\underline{k}nap̄_f$ $hak{:}ăru^w\underline{b}_m$ $haš{:}eni^y{}_m$ 'and a wing$_f$ of the second$_m$ cherub$_m$.' come after the word for 'cherub'. However, adjectives which are inside the genitive noun phrase and, thus, do not separate it from its head are permitted, at least in MH, e.g., Bava Meṣi'a 1:5 $meṣi^{y\jmath}a\underline{t}$ $bĕno^w$ $u^w\underline{b}it{:}o^w$ $hag{:}ă\underline{d}o^w li^y m$ $wă^\varsigma a\underline{b}do^w$ $wăšip̄hă\underline{t}o^w$ $hă^\varsigma i^y\underline{b}ri^y m$ 'an object found by (lit. the find of) his big son or daughter or his Hebrew manservant or maidservant'.

When both wide and narrow scope modifiers are present, the latter come first (as in Arabic), e.g., Deut. 5:24, 21:6, 28:58, 31:16 [$\jmath ălohe^y$ $ne\underline{k}ar$] [$h\mathring{a}\jmath\mathring{a}räṣ$] [$\jmath ăšär$ $hu^{w\jmath}$ $b\mathring{a}\jmath$ $šăm{:}\mathring{a}^h$] [$bă\underline{k}irbo^w$] '[the alien gods]—[of the land] [which they are about to enter]—[in their midst]' ('in their midst' modifies 'the alien gods'!), Ps. 86:2.

With some genitive types, the phrase-final placement of adjectives managed to survive the transition to circumlocution with šäl. Thus, some of the MH counterparts of Esther 8:15 $\varsigma ă\underline{t}äräṭ$ $z\mathring{a}h\mathring{a}\underline{b}$ $gă\underline{d}o^w l\mathring{a}^h$ 'a large crown (made) of gold' (genitive of material) exhibit the old order, with the adjective at the end: Rosh Hashanah 2:3 $kălo^w nso^w\underline{t}$ $šäl{:}\mathring{a}\jmath äräz$ $\jmath äru\underline{k}{:}i^y m$ 'long poles of cedar', Nega'im 14:1. Others have the adjective after the first noun: Tamid 3:6, Kelim 25:7 $\varsigma äre^y\underline{b}\mathring{a}^h$ $gă\underline{d}o^w l\mathring{a}^h$ $šäl{:}\mathring{a}^\varsigma eṣ$ 'a large kneading-trough of wood'. This order is found already in Ezek. 40:40 $hak{:}\mathring{a}\underline{t}ep̄$ $h\mathring{a}\jmath a\hbar äräṭ$ $\jmath äšär$ $lă\jmath ul\mathring{a}m$ $haš{:}a^\varsigma ar$ 'the other side of the gate's vestibule'.

Within the Non-verbal Clause

In BH (and sometimes in MH too), predicative adjectives come before their subject in verbless clauses, except in those beginning with wă+ (circumstantial, concessive, and parenthetical clauses, e.g., Gen. 13:13, 18:11, 29:17, Yevamot 13:1) or the presentatives $hin{:}e^h/hălo^\jmath$. Thus, in asking Jacob for lentils Esau says ki^y $\mathring{a}yep̄$ $\jmath \mathring{a}no\underline{k}i^y$ 'for I am famished' (Gen. 25:30) with the adjective first, but in the previous verse (25:29) the account of Esau returning home uses a circumstantial clause with the adjective second: $way{:}\mathring{a}\underline{b}o^\jmath$ $\varsigma eś\mathring{a}w$ $min\text{-}haś{:}\mathring{a}\underline{d}\mathring{a}^h$ $wă{+}hu^w$ $\mathring{a}yep̄$ 'and Esau came in from the field famished (lit. and he was famished)'.

When the predicate adjective is modified by an adverbial, the predicate is often split, with the adjective preceding the subject and the adverbial following, e.g., Gen. 3:6, 12:14, Deut. 7:17, Josh. 9:22, 1 Sam. 29:9, Avot 4:17. This order seems

to be very ancient, since it is also reflected in the morphology of the stative perfect. Thus, 1 Sam. 15:17 *ḳåṭon ʾat:åʰ bǝ̆ʿeʸnäʸḳå* 'small are you in your (own)
eyes' would have had the same order and meaning had it been expressed by a stative verb in the perfect: *ḳåṭon+tå bǝ̆ʿeʸnäʸḳå* (not attested, but see Gen. 32:11).

Within the Verbal Clause

BH verbal sentences are basically VSO, but there are numerous exceptions. Verbal circumstantial and concessive clauses, like the non-verbal ones discussed on
p. 165, begin with the conjunction *wǝ̆+* followed by the subject (e.g., Gen. 18:13,
24:31).

Other exceptions involve **focused elements,** which are moved to the beginning
of the clause, e.g., Gen. 37:4, Deut. 6:13 *ʾäṭ-Y. ʾǎlohäʸkå tiʸrå ̓ wǝ̆ ̓oṭoʷ taʿåbod
uʷbišmoʷtiš:åbeaʿ* 'it is the Lord your God that you shall revere, and Him that you
shall worship, and His name that you shall swear by', 13:5. When the focused element is the subject of the verb, a redundant independent pronoun may be inserted
before the verb, e.g., Deut. 1:38–39 *yǝ̆hoʷšuaʿ ... **huʷ ̓** yåbo ̓ šåm:åʰ ...
wǝ̆ṭap:ǝ̆käm ... **hem:åʰ** yåbo ̓uʷ šåm:åʰ* '(... you will not come there) Joshua ...
he will come there ... and your children ... **they** will come there', Ḳiddushin 3:7.

Similar devices are used to signal **contrast** between two clauses. In some cases,
the inversion or independent pronoun is found only in the second of the two
clauses, e.g., Gen. 12:12 *wǝ̆hårǝ̆ĝuʷ ̓oṭiʸ wǝ̆ ̓oṭåk yǝ̆hay:uʷ* 'and they shall kill
me, but **you,** they will let live' (contrast Num. 22:33), Gen. 33:16–17, Exod.
33:23, Gen. 42:8 *wayak:er yoseꝑ ̓äṭ-ʾähåʸw wǝ̆hem lo ̓ hik:iruhuʷ* 'Joseph recognized his brothers but **they** did not recognize **him**'. In other cases, the first clause
mimics the second, e.g., Gen. 41:13 *̓oṭiʸ hešiʸb ʿal-kan:iʸ wǝ̆ ̓oṭoʷ ṭålåʰ* 'me, he
restored to my post, and **him,** he hanged' (contrast Gen. 40:21–22), Gen. 34:21,
Deut. 23:21, 1 Kings 12:11, Judg. 14:16, Ezek. 33:25, Jon. 4:10–11 (for the last
three, see p. 167). Sometimes, the inverted second clause exhibits the topic–comment construction, e.g., Exod. 9:20–21, 2 Chron. 10:16–17; see p. 168.

Agreement

Verbs and predicate adjectives agree with their subjects in number and gender; attributive adjectives agree with their heads in definiteness as well. Demonstrative
adjectives, being inherently definite, differ from most other attributive adjectives
in discriminating between two kinds of definite heads: those with the definite article and those with a suffixed pronoun. Demonstratives take a redundant definite
article with the former type but not with the latter, e.g., *had:ǝ̆båriʸm håʾel:äʰ*
'these words' vs. *dǝ̆båray ̓el:äʰ* 'these words of mine'.

In all periods, collectives may take either singular or plural concord, but in LBH
and MH the plural prevails. In SBH, there is much variation, even within a single
verse or adjacent verses, e.g., Josh. 6:20, Judg. 9:36–37; attributive adjectives are
consistently singular even when other modifiers are plural, e.g., Num. 14:35,
Judg. 2:10, 2 Sam. 13:34 *ʿam-rab holǝ̆kiʸm* 'a large crowd was (lit. were) coming'. For the non-agreement of passive verbs, see p. 160.

In BH, the rules of agreement often depend on the word order, i.e., on whether the verb comes before the subject or not. This is the case with coordinate noun phrases (compound subjects). In the book of Esther, the phrase *ham:äläḵ wǝhåmån* 'the King and Haman' appears five times as a subject, four times **following a singular** verb and once **preceding a plural** verb. There is no categorical rule requiring a verb preceding a compound subject to be singular, but when it is, it agrees in gender with the closer conjunct, e.g, Esther 9:29, 31, Gen. 33:7, Shabbat 11:6, and Sanhedrin 1:6.

The clearest evidence of the influence of word order on agreement in BH comes from the many cases where we find singular verbs preceding the subject and plural verbs following it (in a subsequent clause). This is found with compound subjects (e.g., Gen. 9:23, 14:8, 21:32, 24:50, 61, 31:14, 33:7 [*bis*], 34:20, 44:14, Num. 12:1–2, 1 Sam. 27:8) and with collectives (e.g., Exod. 1:20, 4:31, 17:2 [contrast 17:3], 20:14, 32:1, 31, 33:10, Lev. 9:24, Josh. 6:20, 1 Kings 18:39).

Modifiers of genitive phrases occasionally exhibit the force of attraction, agreeing with the adjacent genitive noun instead of its head, e.g., Exod. 26:26 (contrast 26:27), Josh. 7:21, 1 Sam. 2:4, 2 Kings 1:13 *śar ḥămiš:iʸm šǝliši ʸm* 'a third captain of fifty'.

Interrogation, Affirmation, and Negation

Yes–no questions are introduced by *hă+ ~ Ø*, e.g., 1 Kings 2:13 *hăšålo ʷm bo ʾ äḵå* 'do you come in peace?' vs. 1 Sam. 16:4 *šålom bo ʷʾ äḵå* 'you come in peace?'. Omission of the particle is especially common in astonished rhetorical questions which follow from a premise, e.g., Judg. 11:23, 14:16 *hin:e ʰ lǝ ʾ åḇi ʸ u ʷl ʾ im:i ʸ lo ʾ hig:aḏti ʸ wǝlåḵ ʾ ag:i ʸḏ* 'my father and my mother I haven't told and you I should tell?!', 1 Sam. 25:10–11, 2 Sam. 11:11, 2 Kings 19:11, Jer. 25:29, 45:4–5, 49:12, Ezek. 18:11–13, 33:25, Jon. 4:11 vs. Num. 32:6 and Ezek. 20:30–31. Such questions serve as the apodosis of *a fortiori* arguments, substituting for assertions introduced by *ʾap ki ʸ* 'all the more so'.

Hebrew originally had no word for 'yes'; MH *hi ʸn* 'yes' is an Aramaic loanword, while in Gen. 30:34 *hen* is an Aramaism in the mouth of an Aramean. Affirmative answers to yes–no questions consist of a restatement of the question in positive terms with change of person (first to second and vice versa) but not of word order. The answer is often simplified through deletion of all but its first word; thus, the affirmative reply to *hayḏa ʿtäm ʾ äṭ-låḇån bän-nåḥo ʷr* 'do you know Laban son of Nahor?' (Gen. 29:5) is just *yåḏå ʿnu ʷ* 'we know' (not 'we know him') and the answer to *hăḵo ʷlǝḵå zä ʰ* 'is that your voice, (my son David)?' (1 Sam. 26:17) is *ḵo ʷli ʸ* 'my voice, (my lord king)'.

Answers to other types of questions follow the word order of the question, in which the questioned element comes first, e.g., Gen. 37:15–16, Josh. 9:8–9, Judg. 15:10, 1 Sam. 28:11, 13, 2 Sam. 1:3, Jer. 1:11, Yadayim 4:4.

In all periods, the most common negation is *lo ʾ*. In addition, there are a number of specialized negations, including *ʾe ʸn* for verbless clauses, *ʾal* for volitives, BH *bilti ʸ* for infinitives (see p. 170), BH *ṭäräm* 'not yet' (normally takes the imperfect, regardless of the tense), MH *lå'w* 'not so' (in *'im lå'w* 'otherwise') and MH negative polarity words like *kəlu*^{w}*m* 'anything' and *me*^{c}*o*^{w}*låm* 'ever (in the past)'.

The scope of *lo'* is highly variable in BH. We find it negating single words, e.g., Deut. 32:21 *lo'-'el ... lo'-'åm* 'a non-god ... a non-folk', Jer. 5:7. We also find it negating compound and complex sentences with a scope so wide that it is difficult to reproduce in normal English, e.g., Gen. 31:27 *låm:å*^{h} *... lo'-[hig:aḏtå l:i*^{y} *wå'ăšal:ehåkå bəśimhå*^{h} *u*^{w}*bširi*^{y}*m]* 'why ... did (it) not (happen that) [you told me (you were leaving) and so I sent you off with festive music]', Lev. 10:17 *mad:u*^{w}*a*^{c} *lo'[-'ăkaltäm 'äṯ-haḥaṭ:å*^{t} *bimko*^{w}*m hak:oḏäš ki*^{y} *koḏäš kåḏåši*^{y}*m hi*^{w}*]* 'why did (it) not (happen that) [you ate the sin offering in the sacred area because it is most holy]?', 2 Sam. 18:11, 19:22, Jer. 20:17.

Scope ambiguity of the negation is common. The phrase *lo' yu*^{w}*maṯ X ki*^{y} *...*, which occurs in 2 Sam. 19:22 with wide scope *lo'* ('it is not the case that [X shall be put to death because ...]'), occurs in 1 Sam. 11:13 and Lev. 19:20 with narrow scope *lo'* ('X shall not be put to death, because ...') (cf. also Gen. 31:27 vs. Ps. 81:12–13). Word order can sometimes be used to disambiguate. Thus, the semantic difference between Ps. 9:19 *lo' långṣaḥ yiš:åkaḥ* 'not forever will he be forgotten' and Ps. 119:93 *lə*^{c}*o*^{w}*låm lo'-'äškaḥ* 'forever will I not forget = I will never forget' is made clear by word order, but not the semantic difference between Ps. 74:19 *'al-tiškaḥ långṣaḥ* 'do not forget forever' and Ps. 15:5 *lo' yim:o*^{w}*ṭ lə*^{c}*o*^{w}*låm* 'he will never be shaken'. In MH, there is no ambiguity: *lo' ... lə*^{c}*o*^{w}*låm* always means 'never'.

Conjunction

Coordination

The boundary between coordination and subordination in BH is not as sharp as in English. Semantic relations which are normally made explicit through subordination are occasionally expressed less precisely in BH by coordination, e.g. Gen. 44:22 *wə*^{c}*åzab 'äṯ-'åbi*^{y}*w wåmeṯ* 'he will leave his father and he will die' (entailment; contrast 1 Chron. 28:9 *wə'im ta*^{c}*azbän:u*^{w} 'and if you leave him'), Exod. 10:13 *hab:okär håyå*^{h} *wəru*^{w}*aḥ hak:åḏi*^{y}*m nåśå' 'äṯ-hå'arbä*^{h} 'morning came and the east wind brought the locusts' (simultaneity; contrast Exod. 19:16 *bihyot hab:okär* 'as morning came').

The ubiquitous *wə*+ is normally considered the main coordinating conjunction, but it is not restricted to that role. In all periods, it frequently serves to connect a main clause to a previous subordinate clause (e.g., the *waw* apodosis in Lev. 6:21 and Soṭah 8:1) and a comment to its topic (e.g., Jer. 6:19 *wəṯo*^{w}*råṯi*^{y} *way:im'åsu*^{w}*-båh* 'and as for my Torah, they rejected it', Shabbat 16:6). And in all periods, it is used regularly to connect subordinate clauses of one type (circumstantial) to the main clauses which they modify (see Circumstantial Clauses, p. 169). If it is used less commonly to introduce subordinate clauses of other types, that is only because they have their own, more specific, conjunctions which pre-empt it. But when for some reason those other conjunctions are not used, it is always on hand to fill the void, e.g., Gen. 11:4 (instead of relative *'ăšär*), Gen. 42:10 (instead of adversative *ki*ʸ; cf. 42:12), and Gen. 47:6 (instead of complementizing *ki*ʸ). Finally and most remarkable of all, BH *wə+* is not uncommon at the beginning of utterances or even whole books.

Subordination

Circumstantial Clauses

In all periods, a clause may serve as a temporal adverbial even though it contains no word meaning 'while' but simply *wə+* or nothing at all (e.g., Exod. 22:13). In such a clause, the subject, if definite, will come first, whether the predicate is a perfect (e.g., Gen. 24:31), an active participle (e.g., Gen. 18:1, Bava Meṣi'a 4:10), a stative participle/adjective (e.g., Gen. 18:12, Giṭṭin 8:2, Yevamot 13:1), or a prepositional phrase (e.g., Lev. 7:20, Jer. 2:37, Ketubbot 12:3, Giṭṭin 8:1).

Conditional Clauses

The most common conditional particle in all periods is *'im* 'if'. Others include BH *lu*ʷ > MH *'i*ʸ*l:u*ʷ (counterfactual), BH *lu*ʷ*le'/lu*ʷ*le*ʸ > MH *'i*ʸ*l:u*ʷ*le*ʸ (negative counterfactual), and MH *'api*ʸ*l:u*ʷ 'even if'.

Omission of the apodosis is permissible in contexts which allow the hearer to reconstruct it. When the speaker lays out two antithetical alternatives in conditional form, the apodosis of the first conditional may be omitted if it is the one preferred by the speaker and requires no further action, e.g., Gen. 4:7, Exod. 32:32 *'im-tiś:ă' ḥaṭ:ă' ṭăm wə'im 'ayin măheni*ʸ *nă' mis:iprəkă 'ăšär kătăbtă* 'if You will forgive their sin; but if not, erase me from Your book which You have written', 1 Sam. 12:14–15, Makkot 1:1 (cf. also Dan. 3:15). In all of these cases, the apodosis of the first conditional is to be understood as *ṭo*ʷ*ḇ* 'well and good' and/or a volitive formed from the verb of the protasis, as in Ruth 3:13 *'im-yiḡ'ălek ṭo*ʷ*ḇ yiḡ'ăl wə'im lo' yaḥpoṣ ləḡă'ălek u*ʷ*ḡ'alti*ʸ*ḵ 'ănoḵi*ʸ 'if he will redeem, good – let him redeem; but if he does not want to redeem for you, I will redeem for you myself'.

Complement Clauses

Complement clauses occur commonly as subjects of equational sentences and as objects of verbs and prepositions, but only rarely as subjects of verbs (except for those modified by the adverbial *bə'e*ʸ*ne*ʸ *X* 'in the eyes of X'). Finite and non-finite types coexist in all periods, with the latter becoming relatively less frequent in MH.

As subjects of equational sentences and objects of prepositions, the finite and non-finite types are in free variation (cf. Gen. 27:44–45 *'ad 'ăšär-tăšu*ʷ*ḇ ḥămaṭ 'ăḥi*ʸ*ḵă, 'ad-šu*ʷ*ḇ 'ap 'ăḥi*ʸ*ḵă mim:əḵă* 'until your brother's fury turns back, until the turning back of your brother's anger from you', where the two are in apposition) or complementary distribution (see below). However, *lipne*ʸ 'before' takes only non-finite complements in all periods, while BH *bə+ṭäräm* 'before (lit. when not yet)' usually takes finite complements. Verbs, too, generally select one type or the other.

When a compound or complex noun sentence with two finite verbs is transformed into the complement of a preposition, and the first verb turns into an infinitive, the second verb normally remains finite in BH, even though it is also governed by the preposition. It continues to bear the same relationship to the infinitive that it did to the finite verb, whether it be consecutive (e.g., Gen. 39:18 *kahări'mi'ko^wli'wǎ'äkrǎ'* 'when I raised [lit. upon my raising] my voice and cried out'; cf. 39:15 *hări'moti' ko^wli' wǎ'äkrǎ'* 'I raised my voice and cried out'), circumstantial (e.g., Gen. 44:30 *kǝbo'i' 'äl-'abdǝkå 'åbi' wǝhan:a'ar 'e'nän:u^w 'it:ånu^w* 'upon my coming to your servant, my father, the boy not being with us'; cf. 44:34 *'e'k 'ä'älä^h 'äl-'åbi' wǝhan:a'ar 'e'nän:u^w 'it:i'* 'how can I go up to my father, the boy not being with me'), adversative (e.g., Exod. 12:27 *bǝnågpo^w 'ätmiṣrayim wǎ'ät-båt:e'nu^w hiṣ:i'l* 'when he smote [lit. at the time of his smiting] the Egyptians but saved our houses [lit. our houses he saved]' [note the inverted word order], 1 Sam. 24:11 [12]) or repetitive (e.g., Ezek. 13:8; contrast Ezek. 25:6).

BH grammars do not distinguish those non-finite usages that correspond to the English verbal noun from those that correspond to the English infinitive, calling them all infinitives. The complementizer *lǎ/ǝ+* (etymologically, but not syntactically, identical to the preposition *lǎ/ǝ+* 'to, for') is not considered an adequate basis for distinguishing, since, in most of the environments which permit it, it is only optional (contrast Prov. 21:9 *to^wb lǎ+šäbät 'al-pin:at-gåg* 'to dwell on the corner of a roof is better …' with 25:24 *to^wb šäbät 'al-pin:at-gåg* 'dwelling on the corner of a roof is better …' and Deut. 22:19 with Deut. 22:29).

The MH situation is quite different, a sharp distinction having developed between two types of non-finite complements: an infinitive and another type reminiscent of the English verbal noun. The latter, frequently on the patterns *CǝCi'Cå^h* (in *kal*) and *CiC:u^wl* (in *pi'el*), is more noun-like than the former, appearing already in the Bible with the definite article and even the plural ending. The infinitive is the direct descendant of the old BH infinitive with the complementizer *lǎ/ǝ+*. That complementizer has become obligatory and inseparable: BH *mi+b:o^w* > MH *mi+l:åbo^w* '(prevent/refrain/delay) from/in coming', BH *lǝ+bilti' 'äšo^wt* 'to not do' > MH *(šä+)l:o' la'äšo^wt* 'not to do'.

The use of the infinitive rather than a finite complement in the imperfect was optional with some matrix verbs (contrast Demai 6:8 with Ketubbot 6:2, below, and Yevamot 9:3 with 13: 12) and obligatory with others; either way, it created a good deal of alternation between the infinitive and the imperfect, which, in turn, led to morphological contamination of the former by the latter. Thus, BH *lǎ+tet* > MH *li'ht:en* 'to give', due to alternations like Makkot 1:1 *ro^wṣä^h li'ht:en* 'wants to give' ~ Avot 5:13 *ro^wṣä^h šä+y:it:en* 'wants that he give'. Similarly, BH *le+'mor* > MH *lo^wmar* 'to say', due to alternations like Demai 6:8 *yåko^wl hu^w lo^wmar* 'he is able to say' ~ Ketubbot 6:2 *yåko^wl hu^w šä+y:o'mar* 'he is able that he say'.

Relative Clauses

In the fullest case relative clauses have a head, a relative conjunction (not a pronoun) and a so-called "resumptive" pronoun, e.g., Gen. 9:3 *kål-rämäṣ ʾăšär hu"-ḥay* 'every mobile thing such that it is alive', Deut. 18:21, 22 *had:åḇår ʾăšär loʾ-ḏib:ǝroʷ Y.* 'the thing such that the Lord did not say it', Gen. 28:13, Kil'ayim 5:1, Pe'ah 2:7.

Under certain conditions, one or more of these may be omitted. When the nouns *ʾiʸš* 'person', *dåḇår* 'thing', and *måḵoʷm* 'place' serve as the head, they may be omitted, leaving behind any preposition which governed them and/or the word *kol* 'every', e.g., Exod. 35:23–24 *wǝkål-ʾiʸš ʾăšär nimṣåʾ ʾit:oʷ ... wǝkol ʾăšär nimṣåʾ ʾit:oʷ* 'and every person such that there was found with him ... and every [person] such that there was found with him ...', Num. 31:23 *kål-dåḇår ʾăšär-yåḇoʾ båʾeš ... wǝkol ʾăšär loʾ-yåḇo båʾeš ...* 'every thing such that it withstands fire ... and every [thing] such that it does not withstand fire ...', Ruth 1:16, Berakhot 6:7, Yevamot 2:3.

Resumptive pronouns which function as subject or object of the relative clause are commonly omitted in all periods, yielding the gap type of relative clause. This can create syntactic ambiguity. Thus, 2 Kings 19:12 *hag:oʷyim ʾăšär šiḥătuʷ ʾăḇoʷṭay* 'the nations that my ancestors destroyed' can also mean 'the nations that destroyed my ancestors', since the use of the direct object marker is not obligatory (see p. 153).

Resumptive pronouns attached to nouns (e.g., the possessive pronoun in Deut. 28:49 *goʷy ʾăšär loʾ-ṭišmaʿ lǝšonoʷ* 'a nation such that you do not understand its language', Ketubbot 4:3) may not be omitted, but resumptive pronouns attached to prepositions are occasionally omitted, especially in biblical poetry. When this occurs, the stranded preposition is normally omitted as well, e.g., Deut. 28:27, 35 *šǝḥiʸn ... ʾăšär loʾ-ṭuʷkal lǝheråpe* 'an inflammation such that you will not be able to recover [from it]', Isa. 51:1 *ṣuʷr ḥuṣ:aḇtäm ... mak:äḇäṭ boʷr nuk:artäm* 'the rock [such that] you were hewn [from it] ... the quarry [such that] you were dug [from it]', Terumot 1:2. In rare instances, we find the stranded preposition moved out of a headless relative clause and placed in front of *ʾăšär*, e.g., Gen. 31:32 *ʿim ʾăšär timṣåʾ ʾäṭ-ʾălohäʸkå* 'with [the person] such that you find your gods (will not live) = the person such that you find your gods with him (will not live) vs. Gen. 44:9 *ʾăšär yim:åṣe ʾit:oʷ* '[the person] such that it is found with him (will die)', Num. 22:6, Ezek. 23:40.

Asyndesis with a finite verbal predicate is common in biblical poetry, especially when the antecedent of the relative clause is indefinite, e.g., Jer. 5:15 *goʷy loʾ-teḏaʿ lǝšonoʷ wǝloʾ ṭišmaʿ maʰ-yḏab:er* 'a nation [such that] you do not know its language and you do not understand what they are saying' (contrast Deut. 28:49, above). It is far less common in biblical prose and non-existent in the Mishnah. In the linguistically modernized version of Isaiah found at Qumran many of the asyndetic relative clauses of the Masoretic version have been eliminated through the activity of MH-speaking scribes who found them difficult to understand.

Hebrew has considerable flexibility in forming relative clauses. It allows types whose English counterparts are ungrammatical, e.g., Exod. 33:1, Josh. 13:21–22 *si'hoᵂn mäläḵ hå'ămoriʸ 'ăšär* [*hik:åʰ mošäʰ 'oṭoᵂ wə'äṯ-nəśiʸᵉʸ miḏyån ... wə'äṯ-bilᶜåm bän-bə⁽ᶜ⁾oᵂr ... hårəḡuᵂ bəneʸ-yiśrå'el* ...] 'Sihon king of the Amorites such that [Moses smote him and the Midianite chiefs ... and the Israelites slew Balaam son of Beor]', 1 Sam. 25:11 *'ănåšiʸm 'ăšär lo' yåḏaᶜtiʸ 'eʸmiz:äʰ hem:åʰ* 'men such that I know not where they are from'.

It also allows relative clauses to contain multiple resumptive pronouns, e.g. Deut 8:9 *'äräṣ 'ăšär 'ăḇånäʸhå ḇarzäl uᵂmehăråräʸhå taḥsoḇ nəḥošäṯ* 'a land such that **its** rocks are iron and from **its** hills you shall hew copper', 11:6, Avot 3:17, and – with asyndesis – Jer. 5:15 (see above). Sometimes the first of these pronouns will be omitted but not the second, yielding a hybrid of the gap and pronoun retention types, e.g., Gen. 26:18, Deut. 4:46–47, Jer. 28:3, Ezra 1:7.

BH permits the formation of relative clauses with two different antecedents, as long as they are immediate constituents of the same genitive noun phrase, e.g., Gen. 24:24 *bän-milkåʰ 'ăšär yåləḏåʰ* 'the son of Milkah such that **she** bore [**him**]', 2 Sam. 16:23 *ᶜăṣaṯ 'ăḥiʸṭopäl 'ăšär yåᶜaṣ* 'the advice of Ahithophel such that **he** gave [**it**]' (contrast 17:7 *håᶜeṣåʰ 'ăšär yåᶜaṣ 'ăḥiʸṭopäl* 'the advice such that Ahithophel gave [**it**]), Gen. 45:27, Exod. 5:14, Deut. 5:24, 1 Kings 15:30, 2 Kings 17:22, Ps. 107:2.

In addition, BH does not require the resumptive pronoun to be in the 3rd person. In syndetic relative clauses modifying the nominal predicate of a 1st or 2nd person pronoun, the resumptive pronoun is normally in the same person, e.g., Judg. 13:11 *ha'at:åʰ hå'iʸš 'ăšär-dib:artå 'äl-hå'iš:åʰ* 'are you the man such that **you** spoke to the woman?' The same is true of syndetic relative clauses modifying a vocative noun but not asyndetic ones; contrast Isa. 41:8 with 44:1.

Finally, it is worth noting that biblical style has no aversion to sentences crammed full of relative clauses. Deut. 11:2–7, with its ten relative clauses embedded at four different levels within a complement clause embedded at a fifth level, is probably about as close as one can come to infinite recursion in the real world.

Notes

Our italicized transliteration of the Masoretic pointing is based on the views of the Masoretes themselves rather than those of later theoreticians like Joseph Ḳimḥi. Thus, we distinguish seven vowel qualities: *ˌi, ˌe, ˌä, ˍa, ˌå, ˙o, ˌu.* (The choice of Swedish *å* and *ä* to represent ˌ and ˌ is based, in part, on parallels in the historical development of these vowels.) We indicate quantity in *ˌə, ˌˌä, ˍˌä, ˌă,* and *ˌˌå,* but the superscript letter in *ˈ ˌiʸ,* etc. does not represent length. Whenever a letter is left unpointed in the Masoretic text of the Bible (mainly א *',* ה *h,* ו *w,* and י *y,* but in several instances צ *ṣ* and שׁ *š*), we indicate that fact using superscript signs: *', ʰ, ᵂ,* and *ʸ.* The Masoretes viewed all such letters as quiescent, unlike Ḳimḥi, who considered some of them to be markers of vowel length.

Acknowledgments

I am deeply indebted to Professors Moshe Bar-Asher, Joshua Blau, Bernard Comrie, W. Randall Garr, and Robert Hetzron for their encouragement and their repeated attempts to improve this chapter, which has been expanded from my 'Hebrew, Ancient' entry in *International Encyclopedia of Linguistics* (ed. William Bright, New York, 1992), vol. 2, pp. 110–18, published by Oxford University Press. The English renderings of many biblical excerpts are adapted from the translation of The Jewish Publication Society.

Further Reading

Azar, Moshe. 1995. *The Syntax of Mishnaic Hebrew.* Jerusalem: Academy of the Hebrew Language. (In Hebrew.)

Ben-Ḥayyim, Zeev. 1977. *The Literary and Oral Tradition of Hebrew and Aramaic Amongst the Samaritans*, vol. 5: *Grammar of the Pentateuch.* Jerusalem: Academy of the Hebrew Language. (In Hebrew.)

Bergsträsser, Gotthelf. 1918–1929. *Hebräische Grammatik.* 2 vols. Leipzig: Vogel.

Blau, Joshua. 1972. *Phonology and Morphology.* Tel Aviv: Hakibbutz Hameuchad. (In Hebrew.)

Davidson, A. B. 1901. *Hebrew Syntax.* Edinburgh: T. & T. Clark.

Garr, W. Randall. 1985. *Dialect Geography of Syria-Palestine, 1000–586 B.C.E.* Philadelphia: University of Pennsylvania Press.

Gesenius, Wilhelm, Emil Kautzsch, and A. E. Cowley. 1910. *Gesenius' Hebrew Grammar.* Oxford: Clarendon Press.

Haneman, Gideon. 1980. *A Morphology of Mishnaic Hebrew According to the Tradition of the Parma Manuscript.* Tel Aviv: Tel-Aviv University. (In Hebrew.)

Joüon, Paul, and T. Muraoka. 1991. *A Grammar of Biblical Hebrew.* Rome: Pontificium Institutum Biblicum.

Kutscher, Eduard Yechezkel. 1982. *A History of the Hebrew Language.* Jerusalem: Magnes.

Lambert, Mayer. 1946. *Traité de grammaire hébraïque.* Paris: Presses Universitaires de France.

Malone, Joseph L. 1993. *Tiberian Hebrew Phonology.* Winona Lake, Ind.: Eisenbrauns.

Qimron, Elisha. 1986. *The Hebrew of the Dead Sea Scrolls.* Atlanta, Ga.: Scholars Press.

Ridzewski, Beate. 1992. *Neuhebräische Grammatik auf Grund der ältesten Handschriften und Inschriften.* Frankfurt am Main: Peter Lang.

Segal, Moses H. 1927. *A Grammar of Mishnaic Hebrew.* Oxford: Clarendon Press.

Yeivin, Israel. 1985. *The Hebrew Language Tradition as Reflected in the Babylonian Vocalization.* 2 vols. Jerusalem: Academy of the Hebrew Language. (In Hebrew.)

10 Phoenician and the Eastern Canaanite Languages

Stanislav Segert

Hebrew (see Chapter 9), Phoenician, languages of the area east of the Jordan River: Ammonite, Moabite and Edomite, moreover Ugaritic (see Chapter 8) and early Canaanite words and constructions in the Akkadian texts of El-Amarna, Egypt, constitute the Canaanite branch of Semitic. Except for Hebrew, they all died out in antiquity and were forgotten till the inscriptions were deciphered, from the eighteenth century on (many were found in the nineteenth century, some recently). In the Eastern Mediterranean, Phoenician was used until the first century BCE. In North Africa it survived until the fifth century CE.

As against the well-attested Hebrew, its Canaanite neighbors are only known from a few hundreds of epigraphic sources (i.a. seals) from the first half of the first millennium BCE, many of them fragmentary or short. From the presumably rich literature of the Phoenicians, the inventors of the alphabetic script, nothing survived in the original. Many thousands of inscriptions, most of them the same type of votive formulae, have survived in North Africa, mostly at Carthage (in today's Tunisia), destroyed by the Romans in 146 BCE, written in the late Phoenician dialect, Punic. A few of these are in Greek or Latin letters. The Roman playwright Plautus inserted a Punic conversation, in Latin script, in his play *Poenulus* (about 200 BCE).

The Phoenicians lived roughly in the territory which is Lebanon today. Through colonization, they exported their language to other areas of the Mediterranean. Besides the ancient dialect of Byblos and the conservative homeland Phoenician, written in a strictly consonantal spelling, the dialect of Cyprus shows some differences. The Punic dialect developed in Carthage around the middle of the first millennium BCE. After its destruction, Late Punic (or Neo-Punic) was used for many more centuries in North Africa and in Sardinia. Two inconsistently used writing systems were introduced for Punic, where vowels were indicated by originally consonantal letters.

174

All the languages mentioned in this chapter were forgotten. Only in the eighteenth century was the Phoenician alphabet deciphered. The close relationship of these languages to Biblical Hebrew helped a great deal. Many important texts were discovered in the nineteenth century, e.g. the inscription of Mesha, king of Moab, but even recent times enriched the inventory, such as the Ammonite inscriptions.

The following abbreviations will be used below: Ph. (Phoenician), Pu. (Punic), LPu. (Late Punic), OBy. (Old Byblian), Cy. (Cyprus dialect), A (Ammonite), Mo. (Moabite), E (Edomite), Heb. (Hebrew), Ug. (Ugaritic). Italics are used only for words attested in the ancient texts, while reconstructed forms are indicated by roman letters. Greek and Latin sources are distinguished by using lower case and capital letters respectively.

Semitic characters: *italic*
Greek and Latin characters: *sans serif italic*

Phonology

The Consonants
The twenty-two letters of the alphabet invented by the Phoenicians are adequate to render the Canaanite consonant system tabulated below:

		ʾ	h			
		ʿ	ḥ			
q	g	k				
		š				y
ṣ	z	s	l			
ṭ	d	t	r	n		
	b	p		m	w	

Changes of Consonants
Spirantization can be observed only in Punic: for 'I', both *anec* and *anech* appear in the Poenulus text. Preconsonantal *n* was mostly assimilated to the following consonant, even if *-n* belonged to a preceding closely connected word: *mn* 'from', A *mʾlt* 'from Elat [goddess]', Mo. *mʿlm* 'from the age', also in Byblian: *bn* 'son of' – *byḥmlk* 'son of Yeḥimilk'; Late Punic has exceptions: *mnṣbt* 'stela'.

The laryngeal *h* could be changed to *y* by partial assimilation to a contiguous *i* in Phoenician and Punic as in the causative prefix *hi- > yi-*, e.g. Cy. *yqdšt* 'I consecrated', or some forms of the sg. 3m./f. suffix pronoun: *-h- > -iy-*, OBy. *mšpṭh* 'of his rule', but Cy. *ʾby* 'his father'.

Evidence of Vowels
Phoenician used no signs for vowels. In the latest period of Punic two systems of

using consonantal letters for vowels were introduced. One used phonetically related consonants: *y* for /i/, *w* for /u/, ' for /a/ and ' for various vowels. The other system followed the Latin model of using originally consonantal Semitic letters: *y* for /i/, *h* for /e/, ' for/a/, ' for /o/ and *w* for /u/.

The Moabite and Ammonite vowel marking corresponds to the Hebrew use of *matres lectionis*: *y* for /i:/, *w* for /u:/ and -*h* for long final vowels /-a:/ and /-e:/.

Diphthongs

It is not always clear where -*w*- or -*y*- between two consonant letters indicate diphthongs /-aw-/ or /-ay-/, or the results of their monophthongization: /-o:-/ or /-e:-/ respectively. Even information available in other scripts may be ambiguous, e.g. the Phoenician words quoted from Sanchuniatōn in the Greek book by Philo of Byblos: *mōt* and *mouth* 'death', *baitylon* and *bētylon* from **bayt-* > **bēt* 'house'. The sg. 3m. pronoun suffix /-o:/ developed from **-a(h)u*: By. '*dtw* 'his lady', Pu. *ql'*, *koylō* 'his voice'.

Reduced and Assimilated Vowels

Some Greek and Latin transcriptions of Punic words may point to the existence of reduced vowels, indicated by the Greek letter *Y*: *ys*, *sy* 'which'. Assimilation of vowels to vowels may be observed as well: *u-ulech* 'the visitor' (< **(h)a-*).

The Canaanite Shift

Primary and secondary long **a:* led to /o:/ as in Hebrew. In the alphabetic script this marked by·the letter *w*: A '*mwn* 'Ammōn', proper name E '*qbwr* 'Aqbōr'; place name Mo. *daibōn*. The element -*u*- in the Assyrian cuneiform writing also indicates the pronounciation [o:].

This shift went farther in Phoenician. **a* > *o:* and long **a:* > *u:*. A convenient example is the word for 'Aion, eternity' /'u:lo:m/, written in Greek letters as *oulōmos*, cf. Heb. '*ōlām* (< **'a:lam*), cf. *sufet(es)*.

Morphology

Pronouns

Independent Personal Pronouns

- Sg. 1 appears in the longer form: Ph., Pu. '*nky*, Ph., Mo. '*nk*, Pu. *anec* and *anech*.
- Sg. 2m./f. are written in Ph. '*t*.
- The written form *h*' is used for sg. 3m./f. in Phoenician, Punic and Moabite. In Late Punic *hy* is attested for sg. 3f. The Punic form of sg. 3m. *hy* may be understood as an indication of **hu* > [hü:]. Old Byblian has *h*'*t* for 'he' in

the nominative (cf. Ug. *hwt*).
- Pl. 1 *ʾnḥn* does not indicate the character of the final vowel.
- No pl. 2 forms are attested.
- Pl. 3 *hmt* is used for m. in Phoenician, f. in Cyprus dialect. Moabite *hm* appears as an object after a verb.

Personal Pronoun Suffixes after Nouns and Prepositions

- Sg.1 written as -*y* may be reconstructed as /i:/ in Moabite, Ammonite and in Punic *donni* 'my lord', with pl. f. *bynuthi* 'my daughters'. In Northern Phoenician the pronoun is not written in the nominative, e.g. *ʾab* 'my father' (*/-i:/), but it is in the genitive: *ʾby* 'of my father' (*/i(y)a/).
- Sg. 2m. Ph. and E -*k*. Sg. 2f. LPu. -*ky*.
- The sg. 3m. is written -*h* in Moabite and Ammonite, but Phoenician and Punic have -*h* *-ih* for the genitive, zero in the accusative in Northern Phoenician, perhaps *-o:* written -*w* in Old Byblian. In later Phoenician and Punic -*y* may stand for *-yu* < *-hu*. The Punic form -*o:* is written as *ʾ*; *koylō* 'his voice'; in Late Punic also -*ʿ*. Late Punic also has -*yʾ* and often *-im*: *bnm*, *binim* 'his son'.
- Sg. 3f.: Mo. and By. -*h*, Ph. -*y*, MPh. zero (*-a*?), Pu. -*ʾ*, LPu. *ʾ* (*ʿ*), *byne* 'her son', -*m*.
- Pl. 1c. Ph. and Pu. -*n*, LPu. *rbtn* and *rybathōn* 'our lady'.
- Pl. 2 not attested in Phoenician, -*km* in Moabite.
- Pl. 3m. -*m* in Phoenician and Punic; Late Punic *bunom* 'their son'; Cy. and Pu. -*nm*, e.g. Cy. *nḥtnm* 'their repose'.

Forms attached to duals and plurals with masculine ending may differ in writing from those with singular and feminine plurals: sg.1c. -*y*; *-ay*. Sg. 2m. LPu. *(b)aiaem* 'in his life'.

Personal pronouns suffixed to particles are the same as above: *li* 'to me' (Ph. *ly*), *(syl)lohom* '(which belongs) to them'.

Object pronouns attached to verbs differ from the possessive suffixes in sg. 1: -*n* (* -*ni:*), e.g. Ph. *pʿlt-n* 'she made me'.

Deictic Pronouns

Demonstratives
Near demonstratives are derived from the base *ð- > z- in both Phoenician and other Canaanite languages. In later Phoenician and Punic other sibilants are also written: sg. m. 'this' *z*, *ʾz*, Cy. *zʿ*, later *s*, *st*, *syth*. The same forms are used for sg. 2f. in Phoenician and Punic, but *zʾt* in Moabite. Older Phoenician dialects have *zn*. The pl.c. 'these' is written Ph. and Pu. *ʾl*, LPu. *ily*.

Distant demonstratives are identical with the 3rd person personal pronoun: *h* 'that', *hmt* those'.

The Definite Article

Its original form was **ha* with doubling of the subsequent consonant. This doubling is attested in LPu. *'mmqm* for *ham-m-* 'the place'. In older stages of Phoenician, Punic, Moabite, Ammonite and Edomite the article is written as *h-*.

In Ammonite the initial **ha-* was weakened or eliminated, as indicated by the use of other letters, *'-*, *'-*, *ḥ-* or by the initial vowel in Greek and Latin transcriptions *amathēd* 'the gift', *aelichot* 'the hospitality'. Vowel assimilation is found in Punic: *uulech* 'the guest'.

Determinative/Relative Pronouns

Phoenician and Punic have *'š, YS, ys, š', sy, si*, OBy. *z-* 'which'.

Interrogative Pronouns

The pronoun 'who?' is *m-* in Phoenician (cf. Old Canaanite El-Amarna *mi-ya*), *my mi* in Punic.

'What' is also written *m-* in Phoenician. The Punic form in Latin letters and prosthetic vowel *ymu* points at an original **ma: > mu:*.

The Indefinite Pronoun

The form *mnm* 'anything' in Phoenician and Punic resembles Ug. *mnm* and Akkadian *mi:numme:*.

Nouns

Formation

Short Roots

This is a very limited set.

- Monoconsonantal: Ph. *p(y)* 'mouth', *š* 'sheep'.
- Biconsonantal: kinship terms Mo., A, E, Ph. *'b* 'father'; Ph., Mo., A *bn*, Pu. *bn, byn* (**bün*) 'son'; body parts: Mo., A, Ph. *yd*, LPu. *yadem* (du.) 'hand'.

Triconsonantal Roots

The monosyllabic base CVCC survived before a vowel; otherwise an anaptyctic vowel was inserted between the last two root consonants: **šurš > syris* 'root'.

Due to the very rare use of vowel letters in the Canaanite script, the various types of triconsonantal groups cannot be recognized; some information is provided in other scripts, e.g. the pattern *qu:tel* used for active participles: *špt*, pl. *sufet(es)* 'judge'. Likewise, doubled consonants cannot be identified, but Late Punic has *ymman(ai)* 'craftsman'.

Quadriconsonantal Roots

Reduplicated biconsonantal base in Phoenician: *glgl* 'wheel', with reduced second radical *kbkb (as in Ugaritic) > kkb (cf. Heb. ko:ka:b) 'star', E proper name blbl.

Nouns with Prefixes and Afformatives

The most common prefix, with various functions, is m(V)-: LPu. myqdš 'sacred place', Mo. mslt (f., root sll) 'road'. Ph. mqm. Pu. macom 'place' (root qwm), Ph. mmlkt 'kingdom'. A mqn- 'possession' (root qny).

The prefix t- is used mostly in feminine nouns: LPu. tkl'tt, thycleth 'expense'.

Initial ' may indicate a prosthetic vowel: Ph. 'gdd(m) 'band(s)', or a prefix: Ph., Pu. 'rbᶜ 'four'.

The prefix ᶜ probably indicates intensity, "very numerous" used as in the word for 'mouse' ᶜkbr; it serves as a proper name in Phoenician, Punic and Ammonite.

The most frequent afformative is -n: *-a:n > -o:n, later -u:n: Ph. 'dn, Pu. donn(i), LPu. adoyn 'lord'.

The Feminine Ending

The ending -t may directly follow a consonant or be preceded by a vowel: -a/-i:/-u:t.

After a consonant: Pu. mysyrth 'righteousness', Pu. passive participle byrychth, berict 'blessed'; assimilating a preceding -n-: Ph. 'lmt 'widow'); Ph. and Mo. (as in the North Israelite ostraca of Samaria): št 'year' (< *šnt).

In Moabite and most probably in Ammonite, -t appears in the absolute state, Mo. (h)mslt 'the highway'. In Phoenician and Punic -at becomes -o:t: -mil-ku-ut-ti (for -milko:t) 'queen'. Construct state Ph. khnt 'priestess', Pu. amot- 'maid servant'.

Abstract nouns have the ending: -V:t, Ph. 't: r'št 'first quality', 'bt 'fatherhood'.

States

The written forms of the construct state ('NOUN of') and the absolute state (other contexts) can be clearly distinguished in the duals and masculine plurals, see pp. 179–180 for examples.

Number

Singular
No special marker.

Dual

The original marker *-ay was monophthongized to -e:. In the absolute state, Phoenician has a further -m, Mo.: -n. Ph. construct state ᶜn 'two eyes of', Pu. absolute state iadem 'two hands'; Ph. šnm, Pu. (l)isnim 'two'. The feminine marker precedes this: Pu. m'tm, Mo. m'tn '200', NL qrytn 'twin cities'.

Plural

Masculine absolute state has the ending Ph., Pu., A -i:m, Mo. -i:n: Ph., A 'lm 'gods', Pu. *gubulim* '(boundaries >) territory'; Mo. *ymn* 'days'. Phoenician of Arslan Tash has both: 'lm 'gods', *qdšn* 'the holy ones'.

The noun for 'heaven' is a plural with endings similar to those of the dual, Ph. *šmm*, *sa-ma-me*, LPu. *samen*.

The pl. m. construct state ending is the same as the dual -e:: Mo. *ymy* 'days (of)', Pu. *phene*, LPu. *pnˁ/pnʾ* 'faces (of)'.

The pl. f. has -t in both states, for -o:t in Moabite and Ammonite, -u:t in Phoenician: Mo. abs. *gbrt* 'women', A abs. and Ph. *šnt*, LPu. *sanuth* 'years'. In Punic the plural of words for deities can be extended by -o:n-: 'lnm, *alunim* 'gods', *alon(i)uth* 'goddesses'.

Normally, nouns have endings of the same gender in the singular and in the plural. For some nouns, both kinds of endings are attested. Some feminine nouns with no feminine marker have feminine plurals: Ph. 'rṣ/'rṣt 'land/s', Mo. *mgdl* 'tower', *mgdlt(h)* 'its towers'. Masculine nouns with pl. f. endings: Ph. *šm* 'name', pl. LPu. *šmˁt*. Feminine nouns with pl. m. endings: Ph. 'bn 'stone' (f. with no f. ending), pl. Pu. 'bnm. Masculine nouns with both endings: Ph. *ym* 'day', pl. Ph. *ymm*, Mo. *ymn*, but OBy. *ymt*, Pu. *ymmoth*, A *ywmt*. Note Ph. *pˁm* 'foot', pl. Pu. *pˁmm* 'feet', but *pˁmʾt* '(14) times'.

Case Endings

Case endings are indicated (1) in proper names in the cuneiform script: *ma-ti-nu-ba-ˁ-li*, lit. 'Gift of Baal', with nominative -u and genitive -i, from the ninth century BCE; cf. *ma-ta-am-ba-a-al* with no case marking, from the seventh century BCE; (2) with a sg. 1c. possessive ending: Ph. nominative 'b 'my father' for *[abi:], genitive 'by 'of my father' for *[abiya]. (3) Punic words in Latin and Greek letters show case distinctions as well: genitive (governed by a preposition) *li-binim* 'to his son', accusative *koylō* 'his voice' (ō < -ahu).

Adjectives

Morphologically they behave like substantives, e.g. Pu. *lbn*, *labon* 'white', pl. m. Ph. A *rbm*, Mo. *rbn* 'great, numerous'. They can be derived from geographic names by means of the nisbe *-iy: Ph. *ṣdny/ṣdnt/ṣdn(y)m* 'Sidonian (m./f./pl.)', Cy. *qrtḥdšty* 'Carthaginian'.

Numerals

Cardinal Numerals

Numbers are mostly spelled out in words in Phoenician and Moabite. The short Ammonite and Edomite texts have number signs.

  1 (an adjective) m.: Pu. 'ḥd, LPu. ḥd; f.: Pu. 'ḥt
  2 (nouns in the dual) m. abs. Ph. *šnm*, LPu. *(l)isnim*, construct state Pu.

       šn. For the gender of numerals 3–10 see Agreement Rules, p. 185 for polarity.

3	Ph. m. *šlšt*, f. *šlš*, LPu. *šʿlš*, *salus*
4	Ph. *ʾrbʿ(t)*
5	Ph. *ḥmš(t)*
6	Ph. *šš(t)*
7	Pu. and Mo. *šbʿt*
8	Ph. *šmn*, *šmnh*
9	Pu. *tšʿ*
10	Ph. and Pu. *ʿšr(t)*, LPu. *ʿšrt*
20	Pu. *ʿsrm*, LPu. *ysrim*
30	Ph. *šlšm*, Mo. *šlšn*
100	Ph. and Mo. *mʾt*
200	Pu. *mʾtm*, Mo. *mʾtn*
300	Ph. *šlš mʾt*
1,000	Ph. and Mo. *ʾlp*

Composite numbers were in Phoenician most often connected by *w-* 'and', e.g. Pu. *ʾsr wšnm* '12'. A numeral may take a suffixed pronoun: LPu. *ʾrbtnm* 'four of them'.

Ordinal Numbers
In Phoenician, ordinal numbers were formed by means of the derivational suffix *-iy*: (cf. Adjectives, above): Ph. *šny* 'second', Pu. *ʾrbʿy* 'fourth'.

Expression for 'all'
The substantive for 'all' appears in the absolute state in Ph. *kl*, more frequently in the construct state Ph. and Mo. *kl*, Pu. *chll*, *chyk*, also with suffixed pronouns: LPu. *klʾ* 'all of him'.

Verbs

Categories
Verbal roots consist of three consonants. They are preserved in strong verbs. In various classes of weak verbs either some root consonants were changed or eliminated, or, some classes had only two root consonants and a long vowel as a third radical.

    The "verbal patterns" express both "manner of action" – simple, intensive (or factitive), causative – and verbal voice – active, passive, reciprocal, reflexive.

    The finite verbal forms exhibit person and number; in most forms of the 2nd and 3rd person grammatical gender is also distinguished.

    The indicative has two tenses: perfect for past and imperfect for nonpast. The other moods are: jussive, *modus energicus* and imperative.

    The verbal nouns are the two infinitives: absolute and construct, and the verbal adjectives: the participles.

Verbal Classes

Strong Verbs
All consonants are preserved in all forms of the verb.

Weak Verbs

Assimilation of *n* The consonant *n* assimilates to an immediately following consonant: in most prefix forms of I*n* verbs: Ph. *yš'n* 'they will bring' (√*nš'*) and also in some forms with *n* as the third radical. In the verb Ph., Mo. √*lqḥ* 'to take', the liquid assimilates to the following *q*, e.g. Ph. *yqḥ* 'he will take'.

The laryngeal ' may occur in any position. At the end of a syllable it may be dropped, e.g. Pu. *corathi* 'I invoked' (root √*qr'*). In Late Punic, the original root consonant ' could be dropped and the verb made "weak" as in verbs with ', e.g. Ph. √*p'l* 'to make', Pu. *fel* 'he made'.

Initial *y* Whether original or coming from *w*, initial *y* disappears in forms with personal prefixes, in imperatives and infinitives: Pu. *lech* 'go', *ytn* 'he may give' (√*ytn*).

Last two radicals identical (√1-2-2) In some forms there is contraction: Ph. *tm* 'it was accomplished'.

Final semivowel The weak consonant ~ semivowel survives in some forms. In contact with vowels, it assimilates yielding a long vowel: OBy. *bny*, Ph. *bn* 'he built', LPu. *avo* 'he lived'.

Mid semivowel *w* and *y* appear in some forms. This middle element may have originally been a long vowel. This class differs the most from the strong verbs.

Verbal Forms with Suffixed Pronouns
Object pronouns are like the possessive ones (see p. 177) except for sg. 1c. which is -*n* (*-*ni:*).

Verbal Forms

Perfect Forms
Using afformatives, they express the past.

- Sg. 1c. -*t*/-*ti*: Pu. *corathi* 'I called', Mo. *mlkty* 'I reigned'
- Sg. 2m./f. both written with -*t*: m. LPu. *šm't* 'you heard', f. Ph. *šlḥt* 'you sent'
- Sg. 3m. -Ø, Pu. *p'l* 'he made'; Ph., Pu., A *ndr*, Pu. *nadōr* 'he vowed'; IIIy: Mo. *bnh* 'he built', Pu. *avo* 'he lived'; IIw: Pu. *chon* 'he was'

- Sg. 3f. Pu. *-a: > *-o:: ndr' 'she vowed'; before a pronoun suffix the original *-t is preserved: Ph. p'ltn 'she made me'
- Pl. 1c. -n: LPu. p'ln 'we made'
- Pl. 3c. *-u:: Pu. p'l', felu 'they made'

Imperfect Forms

These express the present or the future. All persons have prefixes, sg. 2f. and pl. 2/3 m./f. use further afformatives.

- Sg. 1c. '-: Ph. 'p'l 'I shall make', Pu. ythmum 'I shall accomplish'
- Sg. 2m. and 3f. t-: Ph. tšm' 'you hear', Pu. tšm' 'she hears'
- Sg. 3m. y-: yp'l 'he makes', Mo. y'np 'he is/has been angry'
- Pl. 2m. t- ... -u:: LPu. tšm' 'you hear'
- Pl. 3m. y- ... -u: (A: -n): Pu. yzbḥ 'they offer', Pu. (pi'el) ibarcu 'they (may) bless', A ymtn 'they will die'

In Moabite, the imperfect preceded by w- expresses the past (see Chapter 9, Ancient Hebrew, p. 156).

Volitive Moods

The **jussive** forms look similar to the imperfect; they can be identified mainly by the context: sg. 2m. Ph. ('l) tšm' '(don't) listen!'.

The energic mood has a suffix -n: Ph. 'pqn 'may I get!' (√npq), Ph. yš'n 'may they bring' (√nš').

Imperative: sg. m. Ph., E 'mr 'say!', Pu. lech and Mo. lk 'go!' (√hlk), pl. m. pi'el LPu. brk' 'bless'.

Infinitives

Absolute infinitives strengthen the meaning of a subsequent finite verb with the same root in Phoenician and Moabite: Ph. ptḥ tptḥ 'you will indeed open!'

Construct infinitives take prepositions and suffixed pronouns referring to the subject: Pu. lictor 'to approach' (√ktr), Ph. lp'l and Pu. liful 'to make'; sibitthim (√yšb) '[the fact of] his dwelling'.

Participles

- Basic active: sg. m. Ph., Pu. p'l 'making/maker'; Ph. Pu. špt, Pu. sufet(es) 'judge(s)', Pu. rp' and rufe 'physician (< healer)'; sg. f. škbt 'lying'; pl. m. Ph. p'lm 'making (ones)' and Pu. dobrim 'saying (ones)'.
- Basic passive: Pu. brk 'blessed', Pu., NP buruc, baric /barük/.
- Participles of the nip'al have the prefix n-; the intensive and the causative have m- in Phoenician (see Intensive active, p. 184).

Derived Patterns

Basic internal passive marked by the vowel *-u-* after the first consonant: sg. 3m. perfect LPu. *qybr* ([qü-?] < **qu* …) 'he was buried'.

Basic reflexive marked by an infixed *-t-*: OBy. *thtpk* 'may she be turned over!', Mo. *hlthm* 'fight!'.

Reciprocal/passive (*nip'al*) marked by a prefix *n-*: LPu. *np'l'* for sg. 3f. and pl. 3m. 'she was/they were made'

Intensive active (*pi'el*): The geminate mid radical is marked in Punic only: *balsil-lec* 'Baal saved'. After the first root consonant, the vowel is *i* in the perfect: LPu. *ḥydš* 'he renewed', *dyburth* 'I spoke'. Imperfect: Pu. *ibarcu* 'they bless', imperative LPu. *brk'* 'bless_{pl}!'. Participle: Pu. *m'rḥ, merre* 'guiding'. In verbs with weak or repeated mid consonant ($\sqrt{1\text{-}2\text{-}2}$), the type *pōlel* may be reconstructed: participle Ph. *mtpp* 'drummer'.

Intensive passive (*pu'al*): perfect Ph. *ksy* 'he was covered'.

Intensive Reflexive (*hitpa'el*) marked by a prefixed *-t-*: perfect *htqdš* 'he sanctified for himself'. In verbs with *w/y* as mid consonant or $\sqrt{1\text{-}2\text{-}2}$, as above, the last consonant is repeated with *ō* between the first two: Ph. *ytlnn* 'they grumble (to themselves)' ($\sqrt{lwn}$).

Causative active (*hip'il*): Eastern Canaanite kept the prefix *h-*: Mo. *hr'(ny)* 'he let (me) look down', E *(w)hbrkt(k)* '(and) I blessed (you)'. In Phoenician, assimilation produced **hi* > *yi-*: Cy. *yqdšt* 'I consecrated', LPu. *'yqdš* 'he consecrated'.

Causative passive (*hop'al*): perhaps *ypqd* 'they were commissioned'.

Adverbs
Some are derived from nouns: LPu. *mt'* 'below'.

Existence, Negation
Mo. *'n* 'there is not'; *'d*, Pu. *(b)od(i)* 'there is yet'; Ph. *bl* 'not', also *'y*, prohibitive *'l*.

Prepositions
Common to all Canaanite languages are *l-*, Pu. *la-*, *li* 'to'; *b-*, Pu. *bi-*, *by* 'in'; *k-* 'as'; *'l* 'to'; *'t* 'with'; *mn*, Pu. *min* where *n* is often assimilated 'from'; *'l*, Pu. *aly* 'upon'.

The preposition introducing the direct object was shortened in Late Punic: By. *'yt*, Ph. and Mo. *'t*, Pu *yth*, LPu. *t*, *th-*.

Compound prepositions: Ph. *bd* 'through' (lit. 'in + hand'); Ph. *l* + *m(n)* + *b(ḥyy)* 'during' ('my life time').

Conjunctions
Coordination: *w-*, Pu. *u-* 'and'; Ph. *'p*, Pu. *p*, Mo. *gm* 'also'.
Subordination: Mo. *ky*, Ph. *k chy* 'because'; compound Ph. *km 'š* 'like'.
Conditional Ph. *'m* 'if'.

Interjections
Rare instances: OBy. *hn* 'behold', Ph. *l-* perhaps for vocative. Precative perfect, Pu. *ḥwʾ*, *avo* 'may he live' was also used as an interjection.

Syntax

Word Order
In nominal clauses, the subject–predicate order prevails: Ph. *ʾnk yḥmlk* 'I (am) Yeḥawmilk', Mo. *wbr ʾn* 'and there was no cistern'; also when the verb is a perfect: Mo. *ʾby mlk* 'my father ruled', but also PS Ph. *pʿln bʿl* 'Baal made me'.

PS is found in subordinate clauses: Ph. *k mlk ṣdq hʾ* 'for he (is a) righteous king'; also with a verb in the perfect: Mo. *ʾrn z pʿl ʾtbʿl* 'the sarcophagus that Itobaal made'; Pu. *ʾš ndr mgn/ys nadōr sōsipatios* 'which Magon/Sosipatios pledged'.

In sentences with prefix-conjugated verb, the subject follows the predicate: Mo. *wyʾmr ly kmš* 'and Kamosh said to me', Ph. *ytlnn mškbm* 'the settlers grumbled'; jussive: *thttpk ksʾ* 'may the throne be overturned!', also with the absolute infinitive: *wqrʾ ʾnk* 'and I invoked'. Yet the word order is flexible and topics are put in the front.

Appositions, attributes and adnominal adjuncts follow the governing nouns.

Agreement Rules
Agreement rules involve number, gender and person from the subject to the predicate. Additionally, adjectives also agree in definiteness: *hʾlnm hqdšm* 'the holy gods', cf. older Ph. *lʾlm ʾdrt ʾš* 'to the noble deity$_{abstract plural}$ Isis'.

The principle of polarity applies to numerals 3–10: Pu. *ʾšrt hʾšm* 'ten men' (numeral with *-t*) vs. *šnt šlš* 'three years'.

Questions
There is an optional initial sentence-question particle *h-*: E *h-šlm* 'is there peace/well-being?', vs. Ph. *w-šlm ʾt* 'and are you healthy?'.

Interrogative pronouns: Pu. *mi … ianna* 'who will answer?'; A, PN *mnr* 'who is Light?'; impersonal Pu. *mu phursa* 'what is the meaning?'.

Coordination, Conditional
Clause constituents or components of the same function are coordinated by *w-* 'and'. The "and" clause may express subsequent action or situation, or be adversative: Ph. *wkn ʾb … wkn ʾḥ … wʾnk* 'and there was my father … and (then) there was my brother … , but(!) I …'.

In conditional constructions, the apodosis is introduced by *w-*. The protasis is introduced by *ʾm* or *ʾl* 'if' or the relative particle; real conditional has the imperfect, the unreal one the perfect: *wʾl mlk ʿly gbl* 'and if a king should go up against Byblos'.

Subordination

Subordinate clauses are introduced by conjunctions or particles. Complement clauses have *k, chy: yd*ᶜ ... *k yd*ᶜ 'may they know that (the community) knows'. Comparative clauses begin with Ph. *k* or *km* ʾ*š*. The conjunction Ph. *k*, Mo. *ky* introduces temporal and causal clauses: Mo. *ky.y*ʾ*np.kmš* 'because Kamosh was angry'. Purpose clauses have Ph. *lkn* 'in order that', negative *lm* 'lest': Ph. *lm ys-grnm* 'so that they may not deliver him'.

Relative clauses, often very short, serve mostly as appositions to nominal constituents: Ph. *b*ᶜ*l* ... ʾ*š lgbr* 'B. that is of G.', Pu. *amma silli* 'mother of mine'. A relative clause may be attached to an incomplete clause consisting of a subject only or may stand alone in votive texts: *ndr* ʾ*š ndr* 'vow that he vowed', *ys nadōr* 'which he vowed'.

Other Syntactic Phenomena

In Phoenician, the verb 'to be' √*kwn* is used for the past and the plusquamperfect, but not in the present: ʾ*š kn lpnm nšt*ᶜ*m* 'what had been feared earlier'. The same verb with *l-* expresses possession: ʾ*l ykn lm mškb* 'may they have no resting place'. This may be also expressed by *l-* alone: *lkhnm ksp* 'the priests (shall have) money'.

Prepositions are governed by the verb, hence some special meanings: for ᶜ*l*, usually 'upon', OBy. *wnḥt trbh* ᶜ*l gbl* 'and may peace flee **from (above)** Byblos'; for *b-* usually 'in' Ph. *w*ʾ*l y*ᶜ*msn bmškb z* 'and may he not carry me **from** this resting place'.

Lexicon

The majority of Phoenician inscriptions are monotonous, repeating one formula. Inscriptions in Eastern Canaanite languages are rare and mostly short. Thus the information about lexicon is scarce. The common verb for 'to make' is Ph. *p*ᶜ*l*, Mo. and Heb. √ᶜ*šy*, A √ᶜ*bd*. 'To give' is Ph. and Ug. √*ytn*, but Mo., A and Heb. √*ntn*.

Further Reading

Friedrich, Johannes, Röllig, Wolfgang. 1970. *Phönizisch-punische Grammatik* (Analecta Orientalia 46). Rome: Pontificium Institutum Biblicum.

Garr, W. Randall. 1985. *Dialect Geography of Syria-Palestine, 1000–586 B.C.E.* Philadelphia: University of Pennsylvania Press.

Harris, Zellig S. 1936. *A Grammar of the Phoenician Language* (American Oriental Series 8). New Haven, Conn.: American Oriental Society.

Segert, Stanislav. 1976. *A Grammar of Phoenician and Punic.* Munich: C. H. Beck.

11 Classical Arabic

Wolfdietrich Fischer

Historical Background

Classical Arabic before Islam

Pre-Islamic Inscriptions

Centuries before the rise of Islam, Arab tribes had already immigrated into the regions of Palestine, Syria and Mesopotamia. Arabs formed the dominant group among the inhabitants of Palmyra, which was controlled for a long time by a dynasty of Arab origin until the Romans destroyed their kingdom in 273 CE. Between the first century BCE and the third century CE the Nabateans established a state reaching from Sinai in the west to northern Hejaz in the east and from Madā'in Ṣāliḥ in the South to Damascus in the North, with Petra as its capital. The Arabic-speaking tribes of Palmyra and the Nabateans both used Aramaic in writing, but the influence of Arabic is clearly attested in their inscriptions by the occasional use of Arabic vocabulary and in particular by numerous Arabic proper names.

Ancient Arabic Dialects

The text corpus of preislamic Classical Arabic (CA), for the most part poetry going back to the sixth and seventh centuries CE, was recorded by Arab philologists in the eighth and ninth centuries. At the same time these philologists composed works about grammar and gathered vocabulary. Pre-Islamic CA was not the uniform language that it seems to be in the obviously standardized form of the transmitted texts. The Arab philologists speak about a dialect split between the western area of Hejaz and the eastern area of the Tamīm and other bedouin tribes. The phonemic glottal stop preserved in the eastern dialects had been replaced in the dialects of Hejaz by vowels or semivowels, e.g. Eastern *ra'sun* 'head', *su'a:lun* 'question', *ka'i:bun* 'sad' versus Hejaz *ra:sun*, *suwa:lun*, *kayi:bun*. With respect of the status of the glottal stop, the CA standard is based on the eastern dialects, but the CA spelling reflects the Hejaz dialect.

Classical Arabic after the Rise of Islam

The Qur'an, the first literary text written in CA, is composed in a language broadly identical to that of the ancient poetry. After the spread of Islam CA became the ritual language of the Muslims and the language of learning and administration. The increasing number of non-Arabs who struggled to participate in the new civilization on the one hand, and the will of the Muslims to protect the purity of the revelation on the other hand, made the establishing of grammatical norms and institutions of language teaching inevitable. The development of grammatical norms took place in the course of the eighth century, linked with a process of unification and standardization of the educated language. Forms and expressions peculiar to pre- and early Islamic poetry as well as the Qur'an disappeared from prose during the second half of the eighth century, albeit they continued as archaic features in poetry to a certain extent. After the creation of a CA standard by the Arab grammarians, the language basically remained unchanged in its morphology and syntactic structures. Afterwards, as CA became the educated language of the Islamic world, syntactic features slightly deviating from the old models arose. Thus we may distinguish a pre-Classical period and a post-Classical period. Pre-Classical texts show, in spite of their transmission in a standardized shape, some archaic features; post-Classical texts show deviating syntactic features which gradually infiltrated the CA standard.

In its standardized form CA became the educated language of the Muslim elites and was also adopted by religious minorities, mainly Jews and Christians. Since the Arabic vernaculars very early had become widely different from the language of educated elites, CA gained the status of a scholarly and purely literary language even in Arabic-speaking regions. This linguistic situation, in which two different variations of the same language, a high one and a low one, are used side by side is called by Ferguson (1959) diglossia. The question of when this diglossia arose in the Arabic-speaking community is very controversial. The traditional Arab view states that it developed as late as the first Islamic century as a result of the Arab conquests, when non-Arabs began to speak Arabic. This view is also held by Nöldeke (1910), Fück (1950) and Blau (for the last time 1986). Others (Vollers 1906, Wehr 1952 or Diem 1973) have come to the conclusion that diglossia is an old phenomenon going back to pre-Islamic times. But we must note that the early Arab grammarian Sībawaih (d. 793 CE) claims that he took linguistic information immediately from native speakers of correct, i.e. Classical Arabic.

The training in CA grammar was for many centuries the domain of Muslim scholars. Jews and Christians, and many Muslims as well, did not always take a full share in this philological education. Their language, showing more or less deviations from CA, is often called Middle Arabic.

Modern Standard Arabic

As a language of poetry and scholarly literature, CA continues to the present day. In the nineteenth and twentieth centuries, new elites that emerged under the influence of Western civilization and power revitalized CA and thus formed a linguistic medium, usually called Modern Standard Arabic (MSA), appropriate for all subjects of modern life. Through modern communication media, MSA has a broad effect on the public and is now the official language of all Arab countries including Somalia and, with Hebrew, Israel. It is also in wide use as a second language throughout the Muslim world, in particular among the religious representatives of Islam. MSA is first of all a written language. However, in formal situations such as academic education, political interviews etc., it gains increasing importance as a spoken language too. Since the speakers of MSA do not always observe the intricate rules of CA grammar and tend to give way to colloquial expressions, this sort of language is sometimes called Intermediate Arabic.

MSA differs from CA only in vocabulary and stylistic features. The morphology and the basic syntactic structures have remained untouched, but there are some innovations on the periphery and in sections not strictly regulated by the classical authorities. On the whole, MSA is not homogeneous; there are authors who write in a style very close to the classical models and others who try to create new stylistic patterns. Add to this, regional differences in the vocabulary depending upon the influence of the local dialects and the influences of foreign languages, such as French in North Africa or English in Egypt, Jordan and other countries.

Phonology

Phoneme Inventory

Consonants

b				t d	ṭ ḍ		k q		ʾ
						j			
	f		ð θ	s z	ṣ ẓ	š	x γ	ḥ ʿ	h
m				n					
				l					
				r					
w						y			

CA shares with Ethiopic and South Arabian the shift *p > f; in loanwords p is represented by f, if it comes from or through Aramaic, e.g. ka:fu:run 'camphor' < Malayan kapur, and mostly by b, if it comes from Persian, e.g. ba:latun 'flask' < Persian piya:lah 'cup'. Semitic *g is palatalized to j. The three Semitic sibilants preserved in Hebrew and Epigraphic South Arabian are reduced: *s and *š became CA s, whereas *ś became š (cf. Hebrew ḥameš CA xamsun 'five', Hebrew ʿeśer CA ʿašrun 'ten').

The transliteration given above reflects the modern pronunciation of CA according to the standard of the Qur'an readers. Its phonemic system probably corresponds to that of earlier periods with exception of ḍ (ḍa:d) which may have been pronounced as an emphatic lateral. The so-called emphatics are nowadays articulated with velarization or pharyngealization, their articulation in earlier times may have been different.

Vowels

short	i		u	long	i:		u:
		a				a:	

Short *i* and *u* are distinct, but the number of minimal pairs is very small: *yaḥullu* 'he unties' : *yaḥillu* 'it is allowed'. Often *i* and *u* can alternate: *yastiru* / *yasturu* 'he covers'. The long vowels *i:* and *u:* can be interpreted as *uw*, *iy*, thus classed with the diphthongs *aw*, *ay*. This becomes evident in the case of vocalic suffixes: *ʾal-wa:di:* : *ʾal-wa:diya:ni* 'the wadi : the two wadis', *yadʿu:* : *yadʿuwa* 'he calls' (ind. : subj.). The combinations *ʾiw*, *ʾuy* do not occur; where they should for morphological reasons they are changed to *iy* or *uw*: *ʾmiwza:nun* (pattern *mifʿa:l* to the root *w-z-n*) > *mi:za:nun* 'balance', *ʾbuyḍun* (pattern *fuʿl* to the root *b-y-ḍ*) > *bi:ḍun* 'white' (pl.).

Syllable Structure

CA has two types of syllable, open CV and closed CVC or CV:. Therefore syllables of the form CVCC or CV:C are not permitted. There is one exception; in geminate verbs geminated consonants can occur after CV:, e.g. *ma:ssun* 'touching'. Word forms beginning with CC must add a prosthetic vowel when they come after a consonant or at the beginning of an utterance (in this case preceded by a glottal stop): *ʾktub* > #*ʾuktub* 'write!', *ʾqraʾ* > #*ʾiqraʾ* 'read!', but #*ʾuktub wa-qraʾ* 'write and read!'. *ʾa-* of the definite article *ʾal-* is dropped within an utterance; after a consonant an auxiliary vowel takes its place: *lam ʾaqraʾ* + *ʾal-kita:ba* > *lam ʾaqraʾ-i l-kita:ba* 'I did not read the book'.

Shortening of CV:C to CVC is frequent in the last syllable of the inflectional base: *qu:mu:* 'stand up!' (pl. m.), but *qum* (sg. m.) 'stand up!'; *ʾal-wa:di:* 'the wadi', but *ʾwa:di:+n* > *wa:din* 'a wadi'; *ʾaṣ-ṣada:* 'the echo', but *ʾṣada:+n* > *ṣadan* 'an echo'. Otherwise shortening of v:C is avoided by means of a paragogic vowel: *hayha:t* > *hayha:ti*, *hayha:ta*, *hayha:tu* 'but oh!', *ʾsa:riqa:+n* > *sa:riqa:ni* 'two thieves', *ʾsa:riqu:n* > *sa:riqu:na* 'thieves' (the shortened forms *ʾsa:riqan*, *ʾsa:riqun* would be identical with the nom. and acc. sg.). Shortening of CVCC is rare: *ḍalla* 'he passed the day', but *ʾḍall+tu* > *ḍaltu* 'I passed the day'; *laysa* 'he is not', but *ʾlays+tu* > *lastu* 'I am not'. Word-final VCC, where CC is geminate, is protected by adding a paragogic vowel: *jurru:* 'draw!' (pl. m.), but *ʾjurr* > *jurra*, *jurru*, *jurri* 'draw!' (sg. m.).

Stress in the modern pronounciation of CA is conditioned by the syllabic sequence. Most speakers observe the following stress rules: (1) stress does not fall on a final syllable; (2) stress falls on the penultimate syllable, if closed, otherwise on the antepenult: *katábahu:* 'he wrote it', *kátabu:* 'they (m.) wrote', *katábna* 'they (f.) wrote'.

Morphophonemics

CA derivational and inflectional patterns are described in terms of three or some-times four "sound," i.e. stable consonants which appear unchanged in all deriva-tives. Forms derived from "weak" roots, however, fail to have a complete set of root consonants. About the pecularities of the weak root classes see p. 204. In this chapter, morphological patterns are demonstrated, as usual, by the root *f-ʿ-l* for three-consonantal, and *f-ʿ-l-l* for four-consonantal roots.

Pausal Forms

At the end of an utterance the last or the two last phonetic segments of the word fall silent and are dropped. Thus all final short vowels, but also the indefinite case endings *-un, -in* disappear: *kataba* 'he wrote' > *katab#, kita:bun, kita:bin* 'book' > *kita:b#*. Long vowels are shortened: *katabu:* 'they wrote' > *katabu#, kita:bi:* 'my book' > *kita:bi#*, but *-a:* becomes sometimes *-ah: ma:* 'what' > *mah#*. In the case of the accusative ending *-an* as well as in cases of final *-an, -in* of nouns de-rived from roots with *w* or *y* as third radical, only *-n* is dropped: *kita:ban* > *kita:ba#, ṣadan* 'echo' > *ṣada#, wa:din* 'wadi' > *wa:di#*. The pausal form of the femine ending is *-ah#*, equally for *-atu(n), -ati(n), -ata(n)*. Final *-CC* is shortened to *-C* (in this case the otherwise required paragogic vowel is superfluous): *murr(a)* 'pass!' > *mur#*.

Nominal Morphology

Derivation

Most nouns are derived from verbal roots, but verbal roots also develop from nouns. In the case of two-consonantal nouns, the root is enlarged to a three-consonantal root by adding a weak radical or *h: damun* 'blood' > *damiya* 'to bleed', *ma:ʾun* 'water' > *ma:ha, yamu:hu* 'to abound in water'. There are roots de-rived from loanwords: *qa:labun* 'mold' (< Greek καλοπόδιον) > *qalaba* 'to turn about' and others which owe their origin to internal reorganization: *ʾiša:ratun* 'in-dication' (*š-w-r*) > *ʾaššara* 'to indicate' (*ʾ-š-r*).

Every derived noun is modeled on a certain pattern consisting of a discontinu-ous morpheme which determines the distribution of the vowels and affixes across the consonantal root. As derivation affixes act:

suffixes: *-a:n, -iyy* (for adjectives of relation and origin), *-u:t* (from Aramaic)
prefixes: *ma-, mi-, mu-; ta-, ti-, tu-; ʾa-, ʾi-, ʾu-*

The prefixes *mi-, mu-* are variants of *ma-*. The vowel depends upon the following vowel which is regularly elided: *mafʿu:l < *ma-faʿu:l* (passive participle), *mifʿa:l < *ma-fiʿa:l, mufʿul < *ma-fuʿul*.

CA has an immense number of nominal patterns in part because of the integra-tion of several dialects into the language of pre- and early Islamic poetry. There are variants such as *faʿl / faʿal / faʿil, fuʿl / fuʿul, fiʿla:n / fuʿla:n, faʿa:l / fiʿa:l / fuʿa:l*. Sometimes a single lexeme is realized in different patterns as *xariʿun, xari:ʿun, xaru:ʿun* 'soft', but in many other cases the same patterns are used to distinguish different lexemes. Borrowings from Aramaic like *xa:tamun* 'seal ring' and *ra:wu:qun* 'filter' introduced the patterns *fa:ʿal* and *fa:ʿu:l* which then became productive in Arabic.

The clear distinction between patterns specific for adjectives and those specific for substantives, as existing in Akkadian (Kienast 1990), is given up in CA. Although the old adjective patterns *faʿal, faʿil, faʿul* still exist, most of them are replaced by *faʿi:l* (corresponding to the passive participle *qti:l* in Aramaic). Nearly every nominal pattern is used as substantive and adjective as well:

faʿl	*sahlun*	'easy'	*harbun*	'war'
fuʿl	*ṣulbun*	'hard'	*ṣulḥun*	'peace'
fiʿl	*rixwun*	'loose'	*silmun*	'peace'
faʿal	*ḥasanun*	'good'	*ṭalabun*	'claim'
faʿil	*ḥaδirun*	'cautious'	*kabidun*	'liver'
fuʿul	*junubun*	'impure'	*ʿunuqun*	'neck'
fuʿa:l	*ʿuja:bun*	'marvelous'	*nuḍa:run*	'pure gold'
faʿi:l	*qali:lun*	'little'	*qali:bun*	'well'
faʿu:l	*ʾamu:nun*	'trusty'	*ʿamu:dun*	'pillar'

Every adjective may be employed as a substantive: *baṭalun* 'brave' and 'hero'. Conversely, there are substantives that serve as adjectives: *θiqatun* 'trust, confidence' and 'trustworthy'. Some adjectives which do not agree in gender with the noun they qualify, for instance those which are modeled after *faʿu:l*, have originally been substantives.

Notwithstanding the semantic ambiguity of many derivational patterns, there also are patterns clearly associated with certain semantic classes:

faʿl makes verbal nouns of stem I: *faʿala: darsun* 'learning' to *darasa* 'he learned';

faʿal makes verbal nouns of stem I: *faʿila: saharun* 'sleeplessness' to *sahira* 'he was sleepless';

fuʿayl is the pattern of diminutives: *kulaybun* to *kalbun* 'dog';

faʿa:lat makes abstract nouns of quality: *basa:ṭatun* 'simplicity';

fuʿu:lat makes abstract nouns: *buru:datun* 'coldness', *ruju:latun* 'masculinity';

faʿʿa:l makes intensive adjectives: *bakka:ʾun* 'weeping much', but also nouns of profession: *xayya:ṭun* 'tailor' (in the latter function it is borrowed from Aramaic);

ʾafʿal makes adjectives of eye-catching qualities such as colors and defects (see Elative, p. 197);

mafʕal,   are patterns for nouns of place and time: *mašrabun* 'drinking place',
mafʕil   *mawʕidun* 'time and place of an appointment', with suffixed *-at:*
  maɣa:ratun 'cave';
mifʕal,   make nouns of instruments: *mibradun* 'file', *miknasatun* 'broom',
mifʕa:l   *mifta:ḥun* 'key';
tafʕa:l,   occur as verbal nouns of the basic stem: *takra:run* 'repetition'; derived
tifʕa:l   from roots with *w* as first radical, **tiw-* must be changed to **tu:-* which
  is then shortened to *tu-*: **tiwra:θun > turaθ:un* 'legacy'.

In some cases a certain noun was likely to be the nucleus that attracted others
of similar meaning to its pattern:

fiʕl   for paired things such as *qismun* 'part', *šibhun* 'something similar to
  another thing';
fiʕa:l   for tools as *ḥiza:mun* 'belt', *ʕina:nun* "bridle', *sila:ḥun* 'weapon';
fuʕa:l   for diseases as *suʕa:lun* 'cough', *ṣuda:ʕun* 'headache';
fuʕa:l,   for names of plants and animals such as *ʕuqa:bun* 'eagle', *ɣura:bun*
fuʕʕa:l   'crow', *tuffa:ḥun* 'apple';
ʔufʕu:l-at for literary genres such as *ʔuḥdu:θatun* 'talk', *ʔuɣni:yatun* 'song'.

Patterns with gemination of the second as *fuʕʕa:l*, *fuʕʕu:l*, *fiʕʕi:l*, but also
mifʕa:l, *mifʕi:l* and others express an intensive meaning: *kurra:mun* 'very noble',
quddu:sun 'most holy', *širri:run* 'very bad', *miṭʕa:mun* 'eating much', *miʕṭi:run*
'using perfumes permanently'.

Nominal Inflection
Nouns are marked with reference to definiteness/indefiniteness, case, gender and
number. Adjectives normally distinguish the same categories in agreement with
the noun they qualify. Quantifying nouns do not distinguish gender and number.

Gender
Gender distinction is a grammatical category, but feminine markers include natural gender. Natural gender is sometimes lexically differentiated: *ʔabun* 'father' :
ʔummun 'mother'; *ḥima:run* 'ass' : *ʔata:nun* 'she-ass'. In good CA some specific
female qualities are not marked by the feminine ending *-at*: *ḥa:milun* 'pregnant
(woman)', *ʕa:qirun* 'barren (woman)'. Besides, there are unmarked nouns that
are grammatically feminine: *šamsun* 'sun', *na:run* 'fire' *yadun* 'hand', *ʕaynun*
'eye' etc. On the other hand nouns denoting outstanding (male) persons are
marked by the feminine ending: *xali:fatun* 'caliph', *ʕalla:matun* 'most erudite
scholar'. In the majority of cases, however, nouns denoting females are marked by
-at: *šayxun* 'old person' : *šayxatun* 'old woman'. An archaic form *-t* is preserved
in *ʔuxtun* 'sister', *bintun* (along with #*ʔibnatun*) 'daughter', *kilta:* 'both', *θinta:ni*
'two'.
The most frequent of the three feminine markers is *-at*; *-a:* and *-a:ʔ* are mainly

reserved for adjectives. The basic function of -*at* is to denote the particular, distinguishing it from the general; it marks the female in contrast to the generic term which includes the male gender, the outstanding person in contrast to the common one, and the singulative in contrast to the collective: *šajaratun* 'a single tree' : *šajarun* 'tree, trees'; *baqaratun* 'a cow' : *baqarun* 'cows, cattle'; *darbun* 'beating' : *darbatun* 'a single beat'. Substantives derived from adjectives are sometimes marked by -*at*: *ḥasanun* 'good' : *ḥasanatun* 'good deed', in connection with the so-called *nisbe* ending -*iyy* with the meaning of an abstract: *ṣu:fiyyun* 'sufi' : *ṣu:fiyyatun* 'sufism'.

Number
CA distinguishes singular, plural and dual. The singular is unmarked except for singulatives: *ḥadi:dun* 'iron' : *ḥadi:datun* 'a piece of iron', *jinnun* 'demons' : *jinniyyun* 'demonic, a demon'. Dual and "sound" plural have only two cases, the nominative, and the oblique for genitive and accusative.

The dual marker is -*a:* followed by *n* with a paragogic vowel *i*, e.g. *malik-a:ni* 'two kings', *malikat-a:ni* 'two queens'. In the oblique case, the plural ending -*i:n* is affixed to -*a:* (*-*a:*-*i:n* > -*ayni* with final *i* as a paragogic vowel): *malik-ayni*, *malikata-ayni*.

There are two kinds of plural formation, the sound plural marked by suffixes and the "broken" plural marked by internal vocalic change. For marking the sound plural, the last vowel of the inflectional base is lengthened; a final paragogic vowel is added to preserve the lengthening:

Masculine	Sg. nom.	-*un*	Pl. nom.	-*u:na*
	Sg. gen.	-*in*	Pl. obl.	-*i:na*
Feminine	Sg. nom.	-*at-un*	Pl. nom.	-*a:t-un*
	Sg. gen.	-*at-in*	Pl. obl.	-*a:t-in*

The broken plural forms are lexicalized. One noun may be accompanied by several plural forms. The large number of plural patterns can be divided into three groups: (1) patterns derived by lengthening; (2) patterns occuring as singular as well; (3) patterns exclusively used for plural.

1   In this group singular patterns *faʿl-at*, *fiʿl-at*, *fuʿl-at* are in plural lengthened to *faʿal*, *fiʿal*, *fuʿal* (the plural marker -*a:t* is normally added, but may be absent on *fiʿal* and *fuʿal*): *lamḥatun* 'a glance' : *lamaḥa:tun*, *ḥikmatun* 'wisdom' : *ḥikamun*, *rukbatun* 'knee' : *rukabun*, *rukaba:tun*. Singular patterns containing four consonants or a long vowel, mostly in combination with the feminine ending, make the plural by changing the vowel sequence of the singular into *a-a:-i/i:* (the quantity of *i/i:* corresponds with the last vowel of the singular pattern):

ʾiṣbaʿun	'finger'	Pl. ʾaṣaːbiʿu
faːrisun	'horseman'	Pl. fawaːrisu
manzilun	'station'	Pl. manaːzilu
miːzaːnun	'balance'	Pl. mawaːziːnu

2   The second group originates in abstract nouns that were interpreted as collectives. The most frequent patterns are: *fuʿul, fuʿuːl, fiʿaːl, faʿiːl, fiʿlaːn, fuʿlaːn, faʿalat, fiʿlat*.

fuʿul	ṣaḥiːfatun	Pl. ṣuḥufun	'leaf'
fiʿaːl	rajulun	Pl. rijaːlun	'man'
fuʿuːl	malikun	Pl. muluːkun	'king'
fiʿlaːn	γazaːlun	Pl. γizlaːnun	'gazelle'

3   From the patterns mentioned under (2) plural patterns have been derived which were used for a multiplicity of individuals. Most of them show the prefix *ʾa-*: *ʾafʿul, ʾafʿaːl, ʾafʿilat, ʾafʿilaːʾ*, e.g. *ṣaːḥibun* 'companion' : *ṣaḥbun* 'companionship, a group of companions' : *ʾaṣḥaːbun* 'companions (as individuals)'.
With this group one may also class patterns like *fuʿʿaːl* and *fuʿalaːʾ* which are specialized as plurals of persons: *kaːfirun*, pl. *kuffaːr* 'unbelievers'; *faqiːrun*, pl. *fuqaraːʾu* 'poor men'.

Definiteness/Indefiniteness: The Three States of the Noun

Definiteness is normally marked by the definite article *ʾal-* which assimilates before apical consonants, the so-called "sun" letters (*t, d, θ, δ, s, z, ṣ, ḍ, ḏ, š, n, l, r*), all others are called "moon" letters (*ʾaš-šamsu* 'the sun', *ʾal-qamaru* 'the moon'). *ʾ* and the initial vowel is elided within an utterance (see p. 190). The indefinite noun is marked by *-n*: *kitaːbun* 'a book'. Nouns lack *-n* as head of a genitive construction and when personal pronouns are suffixed: *kitaːbu-hu:* 'his book'. The three possible forms of a noun are called 'states': definite state (*ʾal-kitaːbu*), indefinite state (*kitaːbun*), construct state (*kitaːbu* 'book of').

A number of nouns, called diptotic, and the vocative (see p. 203) have no *-n* in the indefinite state: *ṣaḥraːʾu* 'a desert' : *ʾaṣ-ṣaḥraːʾu* 'the desert'. Conversely, masculine dual and plural forms have in both states, *-ni, -na*, respectively: *muʾminaːni, ʾal-muʾminaːni* '(the) two believers', *muʾminuːna, ʾal-muʾminuːna* '(the) believers'.

Case Inflection

The case system in singular consists of nominative marked by *-u*, genitive marked by *-i*, and accusative marked by *-a*. In the sound plural and dual there are only two cases, the nominative and an oblique case. The broken plural forms are inflected like the singular. Diptote nouns, both singular and plural patterns, have in the indefinite state only one form for genitive and accusative marked by *-a*.

Table 11.1   Triptotic inflection

			Definite state	Indefinite state	Construct state
Sg.	m.	nom.	ˀal-muˀminu	muˀminun	muˀminu
			'the believer'		
		gen.	ˀal-muˀmini	muˀminin	muˀmini
		acc.	ˀal-muˀmina	muˀminan	muˀmina
Du.	m.	nom.	ˀal-muˀmina:ni	muˀmina:ni	muˀmina:
		obl.	ˀal-muˀminayni	muˀminayni	muˀminay
Pl.	m.	nom.	ˀal-muˀminu:na	muˀminu:na	muˀminu:
		obl.	ˀal-muˀmini:na	muˀmini:na	muˀmini:
Sg.	f.	nom.	ˀal-muˀminatu	muˀminatun	muˀminatu
		gen.	ˀal-muˀminati	muˀminatin	muˀminati
		acc.	ˀal-muˀminata	muˀminatan	muˀminata
Du.	f.	nom.	ˀal-muˀminata:ni	muˀminata:ni	muˀminata:
		obl.	ˀal-muˀminatayni	muˀminatayni	muˀminatay
Pl.	f.	nom.	ˀal-muˀmina:tu	muˀmina:un	muˀmina:tu
		obl.	ˀal-muˀmina:ti	muˀmina:tin	muˀmina:ti

Diptotic Inflection

	Definite state	Indefinite state	Construct state
Nom.	*ˀal-ˀaswadu*	*ˀaswadu*	*ˀaswadu*
	'the black'		
Gen.	*ˀal-ˀaswadi*	*ˀaswada*	*ˀaswadi*
Acc.	*ˀal-ˀaswada*	*ˀaswada*	*ˀaswada*

In a few nouns derived from bi- and monoconsonantal roots, the case marker of the construct state is a long vowel which may be understood as compensation for the incompleteness of the root:

	Definite state		Indefinite state		Construct state	
Nom.	*ˀal-ˀabu*	*ˀal-famu*	*ˀabun*	*famun*	*ˀabu:*	*fu:*
	'the father'	'the mouth'				
Gen.	*ˀal-ˀabi*	*ˀal-fami*	*ˀabin*	*famin*	*ˀabi:*	*fi:*
Acc.	*ˀal-ˀaba*	*ˀal-fama*	*ˀaban*	*faman*	*ˀaba:*	*fa:*

The diptotic inflection includes (1) the elative *ˀafʕalu* (see p. 197), (2) two adjective patterns, *ˀafʕalu*, f. *faʕla:ˀu* and *faʕla:nu*, f. *faʕla:* and some other patterns ending in -*a:ˀu*, (3) the plural patterns *faʕa:lilu/faʕa:li:lu*, (4) feminine proper names and place names such as *Fa:ṭimatu*, *Zaynabu* and *Makkatu* (Mecca), *Miṣru* (Egypt) and also some masculine proper names such as *ʕUmaru* (Omar).

Quantifying Nouns

Common Pecularities

CA possesses a noun class distinct from substantive and adjective. It includes the elative *ʾafʿalu*, numerals, *kullun* 'whole', the interrogative *ʾayyun* 'which'. Basically these nouns occur in the construct state quantifying a noun following in the genitive:

kullun	'all'	*kullu rajulin*	'every man'
xamsun	'five'	*xamsu siniːna*	'five years'
ʾayyun	'which one?'	*ʾayyu rajulin*	'which man?'
kullu r-rijjaːli	'all the men'	*kullu-hum*	'all of them'
		xamsu-hunna	'those five (f.)'
ʾayyu r-rijaːli	'which of the men?'	*ʾayyu-hum*	'which of them?'

These nouns do not occur in definite attributive position, but do occur as appositives: *ʾar-rijaːlu kullu-hum* 'all the men' (lit. the men – all of them), *ʾar-rijaːlu l-xamsatu* 'the five men'. In post-Classical Arabic they were partially accommodated to the other noun classes. As a subclass one may consider *ɣayru-* 'anybody/anything different from …' and *miθlu-* 'somebody/something like …': *miθlu haːða: l-qurʾaːni* 'something like this Qur'an'. *ɣayru* is also a negative of adjectives: *ʾal-qurʾaːnu ɣayru l-maxluːqi* 'the uncreated Qur'an'.

Elative

The elative has the diptotic pattern *ʾafʿalu* in both genders and all numbers. It is directly derived from the three-consonantal root and may refer to different nominal patterns: *ʾakramu* 'extremely noble' in relation to *kariːmun* 'noble', *ʾaḥaqqu* 'extremely true' in relation to *ḥaqqun* 'truth' or 'extremely worthy' in relation to *mustaḥiqqun* 'worthy'. Depending on the context, the elative expresses a unique high degree of quality, the comparative or the superlative: *ʾallaːhu ʾakbaru* 'God is of unique greatness', *huwa ʾaṭwalu min naxlatin* 'he is taller than a date palm'. The genitive which follows the elative is either indefinite, then explicative, or definite, then partitive:

ʾaʿla: jabalin	'the highest mountain'
ʾaʿla: l-jabali	'the highest part of the mountain'
ʾaʿla: l-jibaːli	'the highest (one or ones) of the mountains'

From *ʾafʿalu* two kinds of nouns developed which turned to adjectives:

1   Elatives of relative contrast which take a feminine *fuʿla:*, e.g. *ʾal-ʾaxu: l-ʾakbaru* 'the elder brother', *ʾal-ʾuxtu l-kubra:* 'the elder sister', *ʾal-ʾaxu: l-ʾaṣɣaru* 'the younger brother', *ʾal-ʾuxtu ṣ-ṣuɣra:* "the younger sister', and

also *'awwalu*, f. *'u:la:* 'first', *'a:xaru*, f. *'uxra:* 'last'.

2 Adjectives of eye-catching qualities which take a feminine *fa'la:'u* and a plural *fu'lun*: *'azraqu*, f. *zarqa:'u*, pl. *zurqun* 'blue', *'aṭrašu*, f. *ṭarša:'u*, pl. *ṭuršun* 'deaf'.

Two nouns, *xayrun* 'good, better, best' and *šarrun* 'bad, worse, worst' are employed like elatives without taking the pattern *'af'alu*. In substandard texts they often appear as *'axyaru*, *'ašarru*.

The formula of admiration *ma: 'af'ala* with a following accusative or suffixed pronoun: *ma: 'aḥsana s-sama:'a* 'what a beautiful firmament there is!', *ma: 'aḥla:-ha:* 'how sweet she is!', originates in the elative. If derived from hollow roots, elative and formula of admiration show a consonantal second radical: *'aṭwalu* 'extremely long', *ma: 'aṭwala ha:ða:* 'how long this is!'.

Numerals

Like other Semitic languages CA has a double set of cardinal numerals which are used in gender opposite to the noun denoting the thing counted. This noun follows after the numbers from 3 to 10 in the genitive plural: *xamsatu 'ayya:min* 'five days' (*yawmun* sg. m.), *xamsu laya:lin* 'five nights' (*laylatun* sg. f.), after the numbers from 11 to 19 in the accusative singular: *xamsata 'ašara yawman* 'fifteen days', *xamsa 'ašrata laylatin* 'fifteen nights'. There is no distinction of gender in the tens, hundreds, and thousands. After the hundreds and thousands nouns follow in genitive singular: *mi'atu laylatin* '100 nights', *mi'ata: laylatin* '200 nights', *'alfu laylatin* '1,000 nights'. The tens are marked by the plural suffix *-u:na*; nouns follow in the accusative singular, because the genitive would require the construct state and abolish the characteristic of the marker *-u:na*: *xamsu:na laylatan* 'fifty nights' (not **xamsu: laylatin*).

Numerals have case inflection like other nouns except the numbers from 11 to 19:

1	*wa:ḥidun*, f. *wa:ḥidatun*
2	*('i)θna:ni*, f. *('i)θnata:ni*, *θinta:ni* (du.)
3	*θala:θatun*, *θala:θun*
4	*'arba'atun*, *'arba'un*
5	*xamsatun*, *xamsun*
6	*sittatun*, *sittun*
7	*sab'atun*, *sab'un*
8	*θama:niyatun*, *θama:nin*
9	*tis'atun*, *tis'un*
10	*'ašaratun*, *'ašrun*
11	*'aḥada 'ašara*, *'iḥda: 'ašrata*
12	*('i)θna: 'ašara*, *('i)θnata: 'ašrata*
13	*θala:θata 'ašara*, *θala:θa 'ašrata*
14	*'arba'ata 'ašara*, *'arba'a 'ašrata* etc.

20 *ʿišru:na*, 30 *θala:θu:na*, 40 *ʾarbaʿu:na*, 50 *xamsu:na*, 60 *sittu:na*, 70 *sabʿu:na*, 80 *θama:nu:na*, 90 *tisʿu:na*.

100 *miʾatun*, 200 *miʾata:ni* (du.), 300 *θala:θu miʾatin*, 400 *ʾarbaʿu miʾatin* etc.

1,000 *ʾalfun*, 2,000 *ʾalfa:ni* (du.), 3,000 *θala:θatu ʾa:la:fin* etc.

wa:ḥidun and *(ʾi)θna:ni* are adjectives: *ʾaxun wa:ḥidun* 'one brother', *ʾuxtun wa:ḥidatun* 'one sister'. Both are used in counting: *wa:ḥid#*, *ʾiθna:n#*, *θala:θah#*, *ʾarbaʿah#*, *xamsah#* etc. In compound numbers from 21 to 100 the units precede the tens. All numerals are connected with *wa-* 'and': *sabʿu-miʾatin wa-xamsatu wa-xamsu:na* '755'.

The ordinal numerals from 2 to 10 are derived with the pattern of the active participle *fa:ʿil*: *ʾawwalu* 'first' (see Elative, p. 197), *θa:nin*, f. *θa:niyatun* 'second', *θa:liθun*, *ra:biʿun*, *xa:misun*, *sa:disun*, *sa:biʿun*, *θa:minun*, *ta:siʿun*, *ʿa:širun*. From 11 to 19 they are not inflected: *ḥa:diya ʿašara*, f. *ḥa:diyata ʿašrata* 'eleventh', *θa:niya ʿašara*, f. *θa:niyata ʿašrata* 'the twelfth'. The tens have no special form for ordinals: *ʾal-laylatu l-ʿišru:na* 'the twentieth night'.

Prepositions
There are two kinds of prepositions, old prepositions inherited from Common Semitic and others derived from nouns. Both govern the genitive. The old prepositions are: *bi-* 'on, by means of', *li-* 'for, to' (with a variant *la-* connected with suffixed personal pronouns), *fi:* 'in' (maybe cognate to *fu:* 'mouth'), *ʾila* 'toward', *ʿala* 'upon', *lada:* (rarely *ladun*) 'at, near', *maʿa* 'together with' (Hebrew *ʿim*, Aramaic *ʿam*), *ʿan* 'off', *min* 'of, from', *ka-* 'like'. In connection with suffixed personal pronouns, *ʾila:*, *ʿala:*, *lada:* 'get' *ʾilay-*, *ʿalay-*, *laday-*, e.g. *ʾilay-ya* 'to me', *ʿalay-kum* 'upon you', *laday-hi* 'at him'. *ka-* and *min* often imply a substantival meaning: *ka-* 'someone like, something like', *min* 'some of, a part of', e.g. *ka-l-ʾasadi* 'someone like a lion', *min-a l-ma:ʾi* 'some water'.

Every noun of place or time which is employed in the adverbial accusative, may serve as a preposition too: *xa:rijan* 'outside', *xa:rija l-madi:nati* 'outside the town'. CA has had secondary prepositions like these from its beginning, such as: *bayna* 'between', *ʿinda* 'by, in the opinion of', *taḥta* 'under', *du:na* 'below, without', *baʿda* 'after', *qabla* 'before', etc. Their number has increased with time. Some of the prepositions can be marked by *-u* which is assumed to be the remnant of an old local case: *ʿalu* 'above', *taḥtu* 'below', *baʿdu* 'later', *qablu* 'before'. This marker is also found with the relative *hayθu* 'where'.

Temporal adverbs of this kind are used as prepositions and conjunctions as well: *yawma ða:ka* 'on the day of that', *yawma qutila ʿUθma:nu* 'on the day when Othman was killed'. The same is found with *ḥatta:* 'until, up to' (< *ʿad-kay*) and *li-* 'to': *ḥatta: maṭlaʿi l-fajri* 'till the break of day', *ḥatta: ṭalaʿat-i š-šamsu* 'until the sun rose', *tub li-yaɣfira la-ka lla:hu* 'repent, that God may forgive thee'.

Pronouns and Particles

Demonstrative Pronouns

'This' and 'That'
The simple demonstratives are seldom found. Referring to the near, the deictic particle *ha:-* is normally added, referring to the far, the suffixes *-ka* or more often *-lika* are attached.

Sg. m.	*ha:ða:*	'this'	f. *ha:ðihi:*	*ða:ka, ða:lika*	'that'	f. *tilka*
Du. m. nom.	*ha:ða:ni*		f. *ha:ta:ni*	*ða:nika*			*ta:nika*
obl.	*ha:ðayni*		*ha:tayni*	*ðaynika*			*taynika*
Pl. c.	*ha:ʾula:ʾi*			*ʾula:ʾika*			

The far demonstratives occur sporadically with *ha:-* prefix too: *ha:ða:ka, ha:ði:ka, ha:ʾula:ʾika.*

Demonstrative pronouns include the elements *ða:, ði:* for masculine and feminine, *ta:, ti:* for feminine and *ʾula:* for plural. Gender distinction is expressed either by the contrast of *a:* and *i:* or the contrast of *ð* and *t:* sg. m. *ða:*, sg. f. *ði:* or sg. m. *ða:* sg. f. *ta:, ti:* (cf. The Relative, p. 201). The CA demonstratives show pausal forms which penetrated into the regular forms used in junction: *ðih#* > *ðihi, ðihi:*, *ʾula:ʾ#* > *ʾula:ʾi*. In *ðihi:* the long *i:* may be understood on the analogy of the personal pronoun sg. f. *-hi:*.

The reference to the far is marked by the suffixes *-ka* 'you' or *-lika* 'for you': sg. m. *ða:ka, ða:lika* 'that', f. *ði:ka, ta:lika*, **ti:lika* > *tilka*, pl. *ʾula:ʾika, ʾula:lika.* Other forms of the pronoun of the 2nd person such as *ða:-ki, ða:-kum* or *ða:-likuma:, ða:-likunna* are attested in pre-Classical texts.

Combined with a noun the demonstrative pronouns precede the definite noun: *ha:ða: r-rajulu* 'this man', *ha:ðihi: l-marʾatu* 'this woman', *ʾula:ʾika l-muʾminu:na* 'those believers', but they follow a nominal phrase which is not marked by the definite article: *kita:bi: ha:ða:* 'this book of mine', *Fa:ṭimatu ha:ðihi:* 'this Fatimah'. When they are used as presentatives (*ha:ðihi: Fa:ṭimatu qad ʾatat* 'here is Fatimah, having come'), the personal pronouns can be inserted after *ha:-: ha:-ʾana:-ða:, ha:-ʾanta-ða:, ha:-ʾanti-ði:, ha:-ʾantum-ʾula:ʾi* 'here I am, here thou art, here you are'.

With a following genitive the demonstrative pronoun means 'this one of ...' and takes nominal inflection: *ðu:* is taken as nominative, *ði:* as genitive, *ða:* as accusative: *ðu: ma:lin* 'this one of wealth, a wealthy man'. The feminine is enlarged by *-(a)t, ða:tu*, pl. *ðawa:tu*, and the masculine plural takes the plural marker *-u:*, nom. *ʾulu:*, obl. *ʾuli:*.

The Relative
CA has attributive clauses which are equivalent to the relative clauses of Indo-European languages. As with other attributes they must be in agreement in defi-

niteness/indefiniteness with the head noun. Indefiniteness is unmarked; definiteness is marked by *ʾal-laδi:*. The relative is not a part of the attributive clause, but a connecting link governed by the head noun. It agrees in gender and number with the head noun.

kita:bun qaraʾtu-hu: 'a book I read it', i.e. 'a book which I read'
ʾal-kita:bu l-laδi: qaraʾtu-hu:'the book that I read it', i.e. 'the book which I read.'

It is also used as a head noun of the relative clause in the sense of 'the one who' or 'that which': *ʾayyuha: l-laδi:na ʾa:manu:* 'O you who believe'. The relative is composed of the definite article, the deictic *la*, and a demonstrative pronoun:

Sg. m.		*ʾal-laδi:*	f. *ʾal-lati:*
Du. m. nom.		*ʾal-laδa:ni*	f. *ʾal-lata:ni*
	obl.	*ʾal-laδayni*	*ʾal-latayni*
Pl. m.		*ʾal-laδi:na*	f. *ʾal-la:ti:*, *ʾal-lawa:ti*

In the dialect of Tayyiʾ, the relative particle was *δu:* invariable in gender and number: *biʾri: δu: ḥafartu* 'my well which I dug'.

Demonstrative Adverbials and Particles
Local demonstratives are *huna:*, *ha:huna:* 'here', *huna:ka*, *huna:lika* 'there', *θamma* 'there' (corresponding to Hebrew *ša:m*), and in pre-Classical texts *hanna:*, *hinna:* 'there'. Modal demonstratives are formed with the preposition *ka-* 'like': *ka-δa:*, *ha:-ka-δa:* 'thus, so' and *kayta wa-kayta*, *kayti wa-kayti* 'so and so' which comes from **ka-ta:*, **ka-ti:* and is transformed to *kayta*, *kayti* on the analogy of *kayfa* 'how'.

Temporal demonstratives show an element *ʾiδin: yawma-ʾiδin* 'that day' (final *-in* seems to be a pausal feature). It is also found in the particles: *ʾiδ*, *ʾiδa:* 'at that moment, then' (both are used as conjunctions too), and in *ʾiδan* 'hence', *ʾiδ-δa:ka* 'at that time'.

The particle *ʾinna*, etymologically cognate to Hebrew *hen*, *hinne:* 'behold', emphasizes that the speaker's utterance is true. It comes at the head of the sentence and is followed by a noun in the accusative: *ʾinna lla:ha ʿala: kulli šayʾin qadi:run* 'indeed, God is powerful over everything'. The shortened form *ʾin* comes with a similar function, but mostly it serves as a conjunction of the conditioning clause.

Interrogatives
Interrogative pronouns do not distinguish gender and number: *man* 'who?', *ma:* (pausal form *mah#*) 'what?', *ʾayyun* 'which?' (see p. 197). To *man* and *ma:* the demonstrative *δa:*, functioning as a presentative, may be added: *ma:-δa: taṣnaʿu* 'what you are doing here?'. In combination with prepositions *ma:* is shortened to *ma* or even *m: li-ma* (sometimes *lim*) 'why?', *ʿala:-ma* 'what about?' , **ka-ma:* >

kam 'how much?'. Adverbial interrogatives are *'ayna* 'where?', *'anna:* 'where ... from?', *kayfa* (< **ka-'ayyin fa-*)'how?', *mata:* 'when?', *'ayya:na* (< **'ayya-'a:na*) 'what time?'. In post-Classical texts one finds *'ayšin* (< *'ayyu-šay'in*) 'what?'.

Interrogatives serve as relatives: *ya: man la: yamu:tu* 'O the one who does not die (God)'. As a suffixed particle *ma:* marks indefiniteness: *'amrun-ma:* 'a certain affair', in particular, combined with relatives: *mahma:* (< **ma:-ma:*) 'whatever', *'ayna-ma:* 'wherever', *mata:-ma:* 'whenever'. From rhetorical questions there developed the use of *ma:* as a negative (see Nominal Sentences, pp. 212 and 214). Interrogative sentences are marked by *'a-* or *hal* (< **ha-la* [?], see Questions, p. 213).

Personal Pronouns

Independent Pronouns

	Singular		Dual	Plural			
1	*'ana:*			*nahnu*			
2m.	*'anta*	f. *'anti*	*'antuma:*	m. *'antum*	f.	*'antunna*
3m.	*huwa*	f. *hiya*	*huma:*	m. *hum*	f.	*hunna*

Dual forms are derived from plural by means of the dual marker *-a:*. The feminine plural is marked by *-na* which is also found as a feminine plural marker in the verbal inflection: *'antunna* < **'antum-na*, *hunna* < **hum-na*. The plural marker *-u:*, despite its redundance, is sometimes added to the plural forms: *'antum-u:*, *hum-u:*.

Independent personal pronouns occur as subject of a nominal sentence and in order to emphasize a suffixed pronoun: *'antuma: kari:ma:ni* 'both of you are generous', *nasi:b-i: 'ana:* 'my (and not your) share'.

Suffixed Personal Pronouns

	Singular		Dual	Plural			
1	*-i:, -ya, -ni:*			*-na:*			
2m.	*-ka*	f. *-ki*	*-kuma:*	m. *-kum*	f.	*-kunna*
3m.	*-hu:, -hi:*	f. *-ha:*	*-huma:*	m. *-hum*	f.	*-hunna*

In the 1st singular, *-i:, -ya* is added to nouns, *-ni:* to verbs and particles. Before *-i:* final short vowels disappear: *kita:bu+i:, kita:bi+i:, kita:ba+i: > kita:bi:* 'my book' (nom., gen., acc.). To long vowels, *-ya* is suffixed with assimilation of *-u:* to *-i:* and *-aw* to *-ay*: *'ammata:-ya* 'both my aunts', *mu'allimu:ya > mu'allimi:-ya* 'my teachers'. The second person is characterized by *k* as against the *t* of the independent pronoun and the personal markers of the perfect. The suffixes of the third person singular masculine are shortened after closed syllables (CVC and

CV:): *kita:bu-hu:* 'his book', but *ʾabu:-hu* 'his father'. After *-i:* and *-y*, *-hu:* turns into *-hi:*, e.g. *kita:bi:-hi:* (gen.), *ʿammatay-hi* 'both of his aunts (obl.)'. In the dialect of Hejaz, this assimilation did not take place: *kita:bi-hu:*.

Pronominal suffixes are suffixed to the construct state of the noun, mostly with possessive meaning. Attached to verbs, they denote the object: *raʾayta-ni:* 'you saw me', *tuʿjibu-hum* 'you appeal to them'. Two suffixes can be added to one verb: *ʾaʿṭaytu-ka-hu:* 'I gave thee it'. The suffixes of the 2nd and 3rd person plural masculine take the plural marker *-u:*, when a second suffix is attached: *ʾaʿṭayna:-kumu:-ha:* 'we gave you her'. There is another way to combine two pronominal objects with one verb, namely, by means of the particle *ʾiyya:-*, e.g. *ʾaʿṭaytu-ka ʾiyya:-hu* 'I gave thee it'; it also makes it possible to place the pronominal object before the verb: *ʾiyya:-ka naʿbudu* 'thee we worship'.

Other Particles

The most frequent are connective particles and interjections.

Connective particles: *wa-* 'and', *fa-* 'and then, and so', *θumma* 'then, thereupon', *ʾaw* 'or', *ʾam* (< **ʾa-ma:*) 'or' in alternative questions: *ʾa-ha:ða: ʾam ða:ka* 'this or that?'.

Particles of agreement or disagreement: *naʿam* 'yes indeed' (cognate to *naʿama* 'may he feel happy!'), *la:* 'no', *bal* 'nay', *bala:* 'certainly!', *ʾajal* 'yes indeed'.

Interjections: *ya:* 'O', *ʾayyuha:* 'O' (both for vocative). After *ʾayyuha:* the noun follows with the definite article: *(ya:) ʾayyuha: l-muslimu:na* 'O you Muslims!', after *ya:* in the nominative of the definite state without article: *ya: rajulu* 'O man!' or, in case of a construct state, in the accusative: *ya: rasu:la lla:hi* 'O apostle of God!'. *ya: la-* is used for an exclamation of surprise: *ya: la-d-da:hiyati* 'O the misfortune!', or for a call for help: *ya: la-qawmi:* 'help, O my people'.

Verbal Morphology

Root Classes

ʾ or w as First Radical

Roots with *w* as first radical partly originate in biconsonantal roots. The initial *w* is absent in the imperative, the imperfect active and in the verbal noun: *wasama* 'he branded', imperative *sim*, imperfect *yasimu*, verbal noun *simatun*. The verbal stem with infixed *-t-* (stem VIII) shows an unstable initial cluster **wt-* which is regularly replaced by *tt-*: **wtasama > (#ʾi)ttasama* 'he was branded'. The number of roots with sound *w* is very small: *wajila, yawjalu* 'to be afraid'. From the VIIIth stem with **wt- > tt-* new roots with *t* as first root consonant were sometimes developed: *taqi:yun* 'God-fearing' (root *t-q-y*) from *(#ʾi)ttaqa:* 'he feared God' (root *w-q-y*).

In roots with ʾ as the first radical, after prefixes with ʾ, the ʾ of the root is dis-

similated with concurrent lengthening of the preceeding vowel: *ʔaʔmana >
ʔaːmana 'he believed', *ʔiʔmaːnun > ʔiːmaːnun 'belief'. In the imperatives of the
frequently employed verbs ʔakala 'he ate', ʔaxaδa 'he took', ʔamara 'he com-
manded' the dissimilation ends in the loss of the first radical: kul, xuδ, mur.

ʔ, w, y as Second Radical

Roots with w or y as second radical show in many patterns a long vowel between
the first and the third root consonant, and therefore are traditionally called hollow
roots. If the long vowel is high it usually, but not always, coincides in quality with
the underlying weak radical: yaluːmu 'he blames' (l-w-m), yabiːʿu 'he sells' (b-
y-ʿ), yaxaːfu 'he is frightened' (x-w-f).

In patterns with a long vowel or a geminated second radical, w and y appear as
consonants: qawaːmun 'straightness', xawwafa 'he frightened', bayyaːʿun 'deal-
er'; w is frequently assimilated to i: qiyaːmun 'standing', *qiwmatun > qiːmatun
'value'. From such cases a separate root with y instead of w sometimes derived:
qayyama 'he evaluated'. In the active participle faːʿil the second radical is replaced by a glottal stop: baːʔiʿun 'selling'. Derivatives of later origin frequently
exhibit w and y as consonants: qawadun 'retaliation', hayafun 'slenderness'.

As a second radical, ʔ remains unchangeable with the exception of ʔaraː 'he
showed' which is dissimilated from *ʔarʔaː. raʔaː 'he saw' loses ʔ only in the imperfect: yaraː 'he sees'.

w or y as Third Radical

Nominal and verbal derivatives from roots with a weak third radical have a final
long vowel equivalent in its quality to the last vowel of the inflectional base pattern.

daʿaː, yadʿuː	'to call'	=	faʿala, yafʿulu	
ramaː, yarmiː	'to throw'	=	faʿala, yafʿilu	
laqiya, yalqaː	'to meet'	=	faʿila, yafʿalu	
daːʿiː-, raːmiː-, laːqiː-		=	faːʿil- (active participle)	
but talaqqiː-	'receipt'	=	tafaʿʿul	

When suffixes are annexed, some phonetic alternations take place: the homogeneous vowels (i.e. iː and uː) are displaced by the affixed vowel: *tadʿuː+iːna
> tadʿiːna 'thou (f.) call', *tarmiː+uːna > tarmuːna 'you call'. When aː is af-
fixed, aː+iː, aː+uː are contracted to ay, aw: *talqaː+iːna > talqayna 'thou (f.)
meet', *talqaː+uːna > talqawna 'you meet'. Before aː or consonantal suffixes, -aː
is changed to ay or aw according to the vowel of the imperfect stem.

daʿaː+aː	> daʿawaː	'both of them called'
daʿaː+tu	> daʿawtu	'I called' according to yadʿuː
ramaː+aː	> ramayaː	'both of them threw'
ramaː+tu	> ramaytu	'I threw' according to yarmiː

Identical Second and Third Radicals

The roots with geminated second radical may partly be of biconsonantal origin. In the derivatives geminated consonants alternate with separated second and third root consonants, since gemination only takes place in the sequence CVCV : *madda, yamuddu* 'to extend' = *faʿala, yafʿulu,* but *madadtu* 'I extended', *yamdudna* 'they (f.) extend'.

In order to avoid the alternation, forms ending in -CVC can take a paragogic vowel: apocopate *yamudda, yamuddu* beside *yamdud = yafʿul.* In the perfect some dialects inserted *a:* or *ay* before the consonantal suffixes: *madda:tu, maddaytu* instead of CA standard *madadtu.* Forms corresponding to *maddaytu* became common in the modern dialects.

Derivational Patterns ("Stems")

Most verbs follow ten derivational patterns, the so-called "stems": a basic stem and nine derived stems formed by root-internal and prefixal modification. Every stem has two inflectional bases, one for the suffix conjugation (perfect) and one for the prefix conjugation (imperfect). The difference is marked by vowel change except for the stems V and VI. Vocalic differentiation within the perfect base occurs in the basic stem (I). All others have *a-a* as base vowels.

In **stem I,** *faʿala* contains transitive and intransitive verbs of action: *qatala* 'he killed', *qa:ma* 'he stood up'; *faʿila* contains intransitive verbs, often denoting a temporary state: *raḍiya* 'he became satisfied', but there are exceptions like *šariba* 'he drank'. *faʿula* is reserved for qualities: *ṣaʿuba* 'he is difficult'; in this function *faʿila* is found too: *ʿawija* 'he is crooked'.

Stem II *faʿʿala, yufaʿʿilu* expresses an iterative as against the single action: *kasara* 'he broke', *kassara* 'he fragmentized', as well as causativity and factitivity: *ʿallama* 'he caused to know, he taught', often in an appellative sense: *kaδδaba* 'he called somone a liar' (*kaδaba* 'he lied'); it is frequently denominative: *lawwana* 'to color' (from *lawnun* 'color').

Stem III *fa:ʿala, yufa:ʿilu* is a verbalization of the active participle *fa:ʿil.* It denotes the attempt to achieve an action directed towards someone: *qa:tala* 'he tried to kill (*qatala*)' > 'he fought', *sa:ʿada* 'he attempted to achieve happiness for someone' > 'he helped' (*saʿida* 'he is happy').

Stem IV *ʾafʿala, yufʿilu* makes a causative of the basic stem: *ʾadxala* 'he let enter' (*daxala* 'he entered'), *ʾaɣa:ra* 'he made jealous' (*ɣa:ra* 'he was jealous'). Frequently it denotes the action versus the state: *ʾaḥsana* 'he acted well' (*ḥasuna* 'he is good'). Derived from nouns, it denotes direction towards something: *ʾanjada* 'he went to Nejd (*ʾan-najdu*)', *ʾaṣbaḥa* 'he began to do something in the morning' or 'he entered into the morning (*ṣaba:ḥun*)'.

Stem V *tafaʿʿala, yatafaʿʿalu* is the reflexive of stem II: *taʿallama* 'he taught himself, he learned'. It denotes actions which come to pass without an agent (pseudo-passive): *tadawwara* 'it (m.) is circular' (*dawwara* 'he made round'), as a reflexive of the appellative stem II pretense: *tanabbaʾa* 'he claimed to be a prophet'.

Stem VI is the reflexive or pseudo-passive of stem III: *taṣa:dafa* 'it happened by chance' (*ṣa:dafa* 'he met by chance'). In most cases it denotes reciprocity: *taʿa:wanu:* 'they assisted one another' (*ʿa:wana* 'he attempted to assist'), sometimes pretense: *tama:raḍa* 'he pretended to be sick'.

Stem VII (*ʾi)nfaʿala, yanfaʿilu* is a pseudo-passive of the basic stem: (*ʾi)nhadara* 'he descended' (*ḥadara* 'he brought down').

Stem VIII (*ʾi)ftaʿala, yaftaʿilu* is a reflexive of the basic stem: (*ʾi)ḥtajaba* 'he veiled himself' (*ḥajaba* 'he veiled'). Often it denotes an action done in favor of the agent: (*ʾi)ktašafa* 'he disclosed for his own sake, he detected' (*kašafa* 'he disclosed') or pseudo-passive: (*ʾi)ḥtaraqa* 'he took fire' (*ḥaraqa* 'he burnt something'). The infixed *-t-* is assimilated to preceding dentals: (*ʾi)ḍṭaraba* 'he got agitated', (*i)zdaḥama* 'he got crowded'.

Stem X (*ʾi)stafʿala, yastafʿilu* is a reflexive of the stem IV: (*ʾi)staʿadda* 'he prepared himself' (*ʾaʿadda* 'he prepared'), (*ʾi)staʿlama* 'he asked for information' (*ʾaʿlama* 'he gave information'). If the causative is appellative, then the reflexive means considering something to be such and such: (*ʾi)staxaffa* 'he thought it light' (*xaffa* 'he was light').

Stem IX (*ʾi)fʿalla, yafʿallu* and **stem XI** (*ʾi)fʿa:lla, yafʿa:llu* are related to the adjectives of color and eye-catching qualities of the pattern *ʾafʿalu*: (*ʾi)swadda* 'he became black' (*ʾaswadu* 'black'). Outside that group this stem is very rare: (*ʾi)rfaḍḍa* 'he scattered'.

The patterns of four-consonantal roots correspond with those of the three-consonantal ones: (I) *faʿlala, yufaʿlilu* is equivalent to stem II, (II) *tafaʿlala, yatafaʿlalu* is equivalent to stem V, and (III) (*ʾi)fʿalalla, yafʿalillu* is formally equivalent to stem IX, but not bound to a specific nominal pattern. There are verbs outside these patterns such as *haydala, yuhaydilu* 'he cooed' (root *h-d-l*), (*ʾi)rʿawa:, yarʿawi:* 'he looked after' (root *r-ʿ-w*), (*ʾi)xḍawḍara, yaxḍawḍiru* 'he became green' (root *x-ḍ-r*), (*ʾi)ʿlawda:, yaʿlawdi:* and (*ʾi)ʿlawwada, yaʿlawwidu* 'he is strong' (root *ʿ-l-d*). They are classed among the following patterns: (*ʾi)fʿawʿala, (*ʾi)fʿawwala, (*ʾi)fʿanlala, (*ʾi)fʿanla:* (stems XII–XV).

Verbal Inflection

Morphological Categories
All verbs except a few defective ones make a perfect; an imperfect, including three moods, indicative, subjunctive and jussive (or apocopate); an imperative; an active and a passive participle; as well as a verbal noun. In both perfect and imperfect, there is a passive voice distinguished from the active by internal vocalic change.

The perfect, which originates in a stative as preserved in Akkadian, is inflected with suffixes. The stative function is retained in verbs of quality (*faʿila, faʿula*). The jussive (apocopate) is of twofold origin: it continues the old Semitic preterite (Akkadian *iprus*) on the one hand, and is an inflected imperative, i.e. jussive, on the other. As a past tense it is confined to conditional sentences and the use after the negative *lam*. The imperfect indicative is derived from the apocopate forms by the markers *-u* and *-n(a)* which originally denoted simultaneity. The subjunctive is restricted to subordinate clauses and has become more and more bound with particular conjunctions such as *'an, kay, ḥatta:*, and the negative *lan*. The so-called *energicus* is formed by adding *-anna*, (rarely) *-an*, to the imperfect inflectional base. It is employed in order to emphasize statements or wishes relating to the future: *la-'uɣwiyanna-hum 'ajmaʕi:na* 'I will surely lead them all astray'.

Both perfect and imperfect refer to time and aspect. The perfect denotes a single complete action, mainly with reference to the past: *jalasa ḥayθu jalasa 'abu:hu* 'he sat where his father had sat', but also to the present or future, as in wishes and vows: *'a:laytu la: xa:marat-ni: l-xamru* 'I swear, wine shall not have made me intoxicated'. The imperfect denotes an action in its process and is normally interpreted as referring to the actual or habitual present or to the future: *qul-i lla:hu yuḥyi:-kum θumma yumi:tu-kum θumma yajmaʕu-kum 'ila: yawmi l-qiya:mati* 'say: God lends life to you, then He makes you die, thereupon He will gather you to the day of resurrection'. Future is made definite by adding *sawfa* or *sa-: sawfa 'astaɣfiru la-kum rabbi:* 'I shall ask my Lord to forgive you'. If the context indicates past, the imperfect expresses an actual or habitual action in the past, *ka:na* 'he was' being the most frequently used means of indicating the past: *ka:na n-nabi:yu yaʕu:du l-mari:ḍa wa-yuja:lisu l-fuqara:'a* 'the prophet used to visit the sick and to sit with the poor'. To mark the pluperfect, *ka:na* can be compounded with the perfect: *qad ka:na rasu:lu lla:hi baʕaθa -hu: 'ila: Makkata* 'the apostle of God had sent him to Mecca'.

Suffix Inflection (Perfect)
The suffix inflection is illustrated below with the verb *kataba* 'he wrote'.

	Singular	Dual	Plural
1	*katab-tu*		*katab-na:*
2m.	*katab-ta* f. *katab-ti*	*katab-tuma:*	m. *katab-tum* f. *katab-tunna*
3m.	*katab-a* f. *katab-at* m. *katab-a:*	f. *katab-at-a:*	m. *katab-u:* f. *katab-na*

The suffixes of the 2nd person are identical with those of the personal pronoun. The 3rd person is marked by the nominal suffixes sg. f. *-at*, pl. m. *-u:*; pl. f. *-na* is also found in the imperfect and personal pronoun. The masculine singular is unmarked (*-a* originates in an auxiliary vowel). The dual forms of the 3rd person are derived by adding the nominal marker *-a:* to the singular forms.

The inflectional base of weak verbs undergoes phonetic changes mentioned above (see p. 204). In the basic stem, there are four types of inflectional bases, those ending in *-a:/-ay, -a:/-aw, -iy* and very seldom *-uw*.

1   *rama:* 'he threw', *ramat, ramaya:, ramata:, ramaw, ramayna* etc.
2   *daʕa:* 'he called', *daʕat, daʕawa:, daʕata:, daʕaw, daʕawna* etc.
3   *nasiya* 'he forgot', *nasiyat, nasiya:, nasiyata:, nasu:, nasiyna* etc.
4   *saruwa* 'he is high-minded', *saruwat, saruwa:, saruwata:, saru:, saruwna*
    etc.

All derived stems behave as *rama:*.

The inflectional base of hollow verbs (see p. 204) shows a long *a:*, which is shortened when consonantal suffixes are added. The shortened forms have a high vowel agreeing in roundness with the vowel of the imperfect base: *ka:na* 'he was', *ka:nat, ka:nu:*, but *kuntu* 'I was' (*yaku:nu* 'he is'); *sa:ra* 'he marched', *sa:rat, sa:ru:*, but *sirtu* 'I marched' (*yasi:ru* 'he marches'); *na:ma* 'he slept', *na:mat*, but *nimtu* 'I slept' (*yana:mu* 'he sleeps'). A single verb, *ma:ta* (*yamu:tu*) 'he died', has the irregular vowel change *a: ~ i* (*mittu* 'I died'). In the derived stems, there is no vowel change: *'aqa:ma* 'he straightened', *'aqamtu* (root *q-w-m*); *('i)xta:ra* 'he chose', *('i)xtartu* (root *x-y-r*). In a similar way the negative *laysa* 'he is not' is inflected: *laysa, laysat, laysa:, laysata:, laysu:*, but *lasna, lastu* etc.

Prefix Inflection (Imperfect)

The inflectional prefixes mark person and gender. Number and, in the 2nd person singular, gender, is marked by suffixes. There are two sets of prefixes. One with the vowel *a* (*ya-, ta-* etc.) is used with the basic stem and the reflexive stems, another with the vowel *u* (*yu-, tu-* etc.) is used with the transitive causative stems and in the passive voice. The prefix *'a-* of stem IV is deleted by the inflectional prefixes.

	Singular		Dual			Plural	
1	*'-...-Ø*					*n-...-Ø*	
2m.	*t-...-Ø*	f. *t-...-i:*	*t-...-a:*			m. *t-...-u:*	f. *t-...-na*
3m.	*y-...-Ø*	f. *t-...-Ø*	m. *y-...-a:*	f. *t-...-a:*		m. *y-...-u:*	f. *y-...-na*

The above affixes form the jussive (apocopate):

malaka 'he possessed' (stem I)

1st	*'amlik, namlik;*
2nd	*tamlik, tamliki:, tamlika:, tamliku:, tamlikna;*
3rd	*yamlik, tamlik, yamlika:, tamlika:, yamliku:, yamlikna.*

'amlaka 'he put in possession' (stem IV)

1st	*'umlik, numlik;*
2nd	*tumlik, tumliki:, tumlika:, tumliku:, tumlikna;*
3rd	*yumlik, tumlik, yumlika:, tumlika:, yumliku:, yumlikna.*

In the subjunctive, the suffix *-a* takes the place of *-Ø*:

1st	*'amlika, namlika;*
2nd	*tamlika, tamliki:, tamlika:, tamliku:, tamlikna;*
3rd	*yamlika, tamlika, yamlika:, tamlika:, yamliku:, yamlikna.*

In the indicative *-u* replaces *-Ø* and *-na* is added to the suffixes *-i:* and *-u:*, *-ni* to the dual ending *-a::*

1st	*ʾamliku, namliku;*
2nd	*tamliku, tamliki:na, tamlika:ni, tamliku:na, tamlikna;*
3rd	*yamliku, tamliku, yamlika:ni, tamlika:ni, yamliku:na, yamlikna.*

The inflectional bases of hollow verbs must be shortened when consonantal suffixes or -Ø are added: *yaqu:mu* 'he stands up', *yaqu:mu:na, yaqu:ma* etc., but *yaqum, yaqumna; yasi:ru* 'he marches', *yasi:a,* but *yasir; yana:mu* 'he sleeps', *yana:ma,* but *yanam.* Verbs with *w* or *y* as third radical also form the jussive by shortening the vowel: *yansa:* 'he forgets', *yadʿu:* 'he calls', *yarmi:* 'he throws', *yuṣalli:* 'he prays'; jussive *yansa, yadʿu, yarmi, yuṣalli.*

Imperative
The imperative has the shape of the 2nd person of the jussive, but without inflectional prefix:

| Jussive sg. 2m. *ta-qum* f. *ta-qu:mi:* du. *ta-qu:ma:* pl.m. *ta-qu:mu:* f. *ta-qumna* |
| Imperative | *qum* | *qu:mi:* | *qu:ma:* | *qu:mu:* | *qumna* |

The causative prefix *ʾa-* (stem IV), which is deleted after the inflectional prefixes, is restored in the imperative: *yuqi:mu* 'he straightens' (*ʾaqa:ma*) has the jussive *tuqim, tuqi:mi:* etc., but in the imperative *ʾaqim, ʾaqi:mi:* etc.

As a result of the omission of the prefix, many verbs have an initial consonant cluster. Therefore a prosthetic vowel is added. It is *i,* if the inflectional base contains *a* or *i* but *u* in case of *u* in the inflectional base:

jalasa 'he sat down'	jussive *ta-jlis*	imperative #ʾijlis
nasiya 'he forgot'	jussive *ta-nsa*	imperative #ʾinsa
kataba 'he wrote'	jussive *ta-ktub*	imperative #ʾuktub
daʿa: 'he called'	jussive *ta-dʿu*	imperative #ʾudʿu
(*ʾi)xta:ra* 'he chose'	jussive *ta-xtar*	imperative #ʾixtar

As for verbs with geminated second radical, there is a choice between geminated and ungeminated forms: *madda* 'he extended', jussive *ta-mdud/ta-mudd-a,* imperative #ʾumdud/mudd-a. Some verbs with *ʾ* as first radical lose it in the imperative (see p. 203).

Internal Passive
All verbs which can be supplied with direct or indirect objects are able to form an internal passive. In the suffix inflection, it is made by shifting the vowel sequence *a–a/i* to *u–i*:

I: *qatala* 'he killed' : *qutila* 'he was killed', *rama:* 'he threw' : *rumiya* 'he was thrown', *samiʿa* 'he heard' : *sumiʿa* 'he was heard';
III: *wa:jaha* 'he faced' : *wu:jiha* 'he was faced';

IV: *ʾadxala* 'he introduced' : *ʾudxila* 'he was introduced';

V: *talaqqa:* 'he received' : *tuluqqiya* 'he was received';

X: (*ʾi)stašhada* 'he quoted' : (*ʾu)stušhida* 'he was quoted'.

Hollow verbs replace *a:* of the inflectional base by *i:*, e.g. *qa:da* 'he led' : *qi:da* 'he was led', (*ʾi)staša:a* 'he asked for advice' : (*ʾu)stuši:ra* 'he was asked for advice'.

The passive of the prefix inflection is formed by changing the vowels of the inflectional base to *a* or *a:*. The prefixes are vocalized with *u*: *yaksiru* 'he breaks' : *yuksaru* 'he is broken, *yadʿu:* 'he calls' : *yudʿa:* 'he is called', *yuʿi:du* 'he brings back' : *yuʿa:du* 'he is brought back'. The *w* as first radical which is lost in the active forms, is restored in passive: *yajidu* 'he finds' (from *wajada*) : *yuwjadu* 'he is found, he exists'.

The CA passive is strictly agentless. The expression of a known agent is excluded. In transforming an active sentence structure to a passive one, the first object gets the position of the subject, other complements remain untouched: *wajadtu l-kita:ba mufi:dan* 'I found the book useful' > *wujida l-kita:bu mufi:dan* 'the book was found useful'. If a verb which governs a prepositional phrase is put into the passive, the prepositional phrase remains in place: *ʾaθiqu bi-kum* 'I place my confidence in you' > *yuwθaqu bi-kum* 'one's confidence is placed in you'.

Participles

The active participle of the basic stem is formed by *fa:ʿil*: *ka:tibun* 'writing', *da:ʿin* 'calling' (root *d-ʿ-w*), *qa:ʾidun* 'leading' (root *q-w-d*), *ma:ssun* 'touching' (root *m-ss*). The passive participle is derived by *mafʿu:l* (< *ma-faʿu:l*): *maktu:bun* 'written', *mamsu:sun* 'touched'. As for weak and hollow verbs, the vowel *i:* of the imperfect displaces the *u:* of *mafʿu:l*: *marmi:yun* 'thrown' (*yarmi:*), *madʿu:wun* 'called' (*yadʿu:*), *mabi:ʿun* 'sold' (*yabi:ʿu*), *maqu:dun* 'led' (*yaqu:du*), but *maxu:fun* 'feared' (*yaxa:fu*).

The participles of the derived stems are formed by prefixed *mu-*. Active participles have *i*, passive participles *a* in the inflectional base: (II) *mufaʿʿilun* – *mufaʿʿalun*; (III) *mufa:ʿilun* – *mufa:ʿalun*; (IV) *mufʿilun* – *mufʿalun*; (V) *mutafaʿʿilun* – *mutafaʿʿalun*; (VI) *mutafa:ʿilun* – *mutafa:ʿalun*; (VII) *munfaʿilun* – *munfaʿalun*; (VIII) *muftaʿilun* – *muftaʿalun*; (IX) *mufʿallun* (only active); (X) *mustafʿilun* – *mustafʿalun*.

Stative verbs do not form participles, instead, adjectives of various patterns derived from them, e.g. *danisun* 'soiled' to *danisa* 'he is soiled', *ʾali:mun* 'painful' to *ʾalima* 'he is in pain', *jawa:dun* 'openhanded' to *ja:da* 'he was openhanded'. Prepositional phrases governed by verbs can accompany the passive participle: *mawθu:qun bi-hi:* 'someone who is trusted', *muḍa:fun* 'a thing that is added to something', *muḍa:fun ʾilay-hi* 'a thing to which something is added'. Passive participles derived from pseudo-passive verbs are used as *nomina loci*: *munḥanan* 'bend, curve'.

Verbal Nouns

Every verb except defective ones such as *'asa:* 'it could be that ...' has a verbal noun (often called infinitive). It behaves like other nouns, taking case markers and definiteness/indefiniteness and may be the head of a genitive construction. Whereas the formation of the verbal nouns of derived stems is regular and predictable, there are numerous patterns of abstract nouns associated as verbal nouns with the basic stem:

fa'l is the most common: *darbun* to *daraba* 'he beat', *qawlun* to *qa:la* 'he said';
fa'al mainly belongs to *fa'ila*: *'amalun* to *'amila* 'he acted', but also to verbs
    with *r* or *l* as second radical: *talabun* to *talaba* 'he demanded',
    harabun to *haraba* 'he fled';
fa'ala:n to verbs of iterative action: *xafaqa:nun* to *xafaqa* 'it (m.) vibrated';
fi'l to verbs of remembrance: *ðikrun* to *ðakara* 'he remembered', *'ilmun* to *'al-
    ima* 'he knew';
fu'u:l to verbs of movement: *xuru:jun* to *xaraja* 'he went out', *duxu:lun* to *dax-
    ala* 'he entered';
fu'a:l to verbs of sound-making: *nuba:hun* to *nabaha* 'he barked', *su'a:lun* to
    sa'ala 'he asked';
fi'a:lat to verbs of cultural activities: *kita:batun* to *kataba* 'he wrote',
    qira:'atun to *qara'a* 'he read';
fa'a:lat and *fu'u:lat* to verbs of quality: *suhu:latun* to *sahula* 'it (m.) easy'.

The formation of verbal nouns by lengthening the last vowel of the inflectional base to *a:* is characteristic of the stems III, IV and VII–X and is also used for a few basic stems such as *ðaha:bun* to *ðahaba* 'he went away', *'iba:'un* to *'aba:* 'he refused'; the derived stems have: (III) *fi'a:lun*, (IV) *'if'a:lun*, (VII) *('i)nfi'a:lun*, (X) *('i)stif'a:lun* showing the vowel sequence *a–a:*.

Stem V and VI have *tafa''ulun*, *tafa:'ulun*, a formation which has no parallel in CA nominal or verbal morphology, but has to be compared with Akkadian verbal nouns of the derived stems such as *purrusum* to *uparris* (preterite), *pitarrusum* to *iptarras* etc. Stem II is associated with *taf'i:l/taf'ilat* as its regular verbal noun: *takði:bun* to *kaððaba* 'he called a liar', *tajliyatun* to *jalla:* 'he made clear'.

Syntax

Nominal Sentences and Verbal Sentences

CA has three types of sentences: (1) verbal sentences with the word order verb–subject–object; (2) nominal sentences with a nominal phrase as predicate; (3) enlarged nominal sentences consisting of a subject and a verbal or nominal clause as predicate. In all cases the subject is marked by the nominative.

Verbal Sentence

Word order in the verbal sentence is modeled on the suffixal inflection in which
the pronominal subject marker immediately follows the inflectional base:

xaraja – Zaydun   according with   *xaraj-tu*
'went out – Zayd', i.e. 'Zayd went out'   'went out-I', i.e. 'I went out'

Since the basic form (*faʿala*) is devoid of any subject marker, an agreement in
gender and number with the following subject is not required. This situation is still
recognizable in the earliest texts: *baka: bana:tuhu:* 'his daughters cried', *kayfa
ka:na ʿa:qibatu l-mukaδδibi:na* 'how was the outcome of the disbelievers?'. The
feminine form (*faʿalat*) came up in accordance with a following feminine subject:
qa:lat-i mraʾatu ʿImra:na "Imra:n's wife said'. Agreement in number never became established in CA.

Thus verbal sentences follow the following models: *xaraja/yaxruju rajulun,
rajula:ni, rija:lun* 'a man, two men, some men went out/go out', *xarajat/taxruju
mraʾatun, mraʾata:ni, nisa:ʾun* 'a woman, two women, some women went out/go
out'. Reference to the plural of nouns denoting nonhuman beings requires the feminine singular: *ʾila: lla:hi tarjiʿu l-ʾumu:ru* 'to God return (all) matters'. On the
other hand, if a verb refers to a noun mentioned before, it agrees not only in gender, but also in number: *naδara baʿḍu-hum ʾila: baʿḍin θumma nṣarafu:* 'they
looked at one another, then they turned away', *ʾaṣbaḥat-i l-imraʾata:ni tanu:ḥa:ni*
'both of the women began to lament'. In this case gender and number markers of
the verb have to be considered as pronominal exponents of the subject, i.e.
(ʾi)nṣarafu: 'turned away-they', in the example given above, is a complete sentence.

Nominal Sentences

The predicate of a nominal sentence is a nominal phrase (noun or prepositional
phrase). There is no copula. The nominal predicate is normally indefinite and
takes the nominative. It agrees in gender and number with the subject like an attribute: *ʾar-rija:lu qawwa:mu:na ʿala: n-nisa:ʾi* 'men are preeminent over wom-
en'. If the predicate is definite, a personal pronoun of the 3rd person intervenes
between subject and predicate in order to prevent the interpretation as an attributive phrase: *kalimatu lla:hi hiya l-ʿulya:* 'the word of God is the most superior'.

The nominal sentence refers to the present. With non-present time reference
ka:na, yaku:nu 'to be' is used. It requires the predicative noun to take the accusative: *kuntum qawman musrifi:na* 'you were an immoderate people'.

The nominal sentence is negated by *ma:* or *laysa. laysa* governs, like a verb, the
accusative or the preposition *bi-*: *lasta mursalan* 'thou art not a messenger', *lasta
ʿalay-him bi-muṣayṭirin* 'thou art not a commander over them'. After the negative
ma: too the predicate occurs with or without *bi-*: *ma: Muḥammadun ʾilla:
rasu:lun* 'Muhammad is not but a messenger', *ma: hum bi-muʾmini:na* 'they are
not believers'. A characteristic of the Hejazi dialect is the construction of *ma:*

analogous to *laysa* with an accusative: *ma: ha:ða: bašaran* 'this is not a human being'.

The negative *la:* followed by a noun in the accusative without nunation negates the existence of something: *la: ḥawla wa-la: quwwata ʾilla: bi-lla:hi* 'there is no power and no strength save in God'.

Enlarged Nominal Sentences

Sentences consisting of a subject in the first position and a predicative verbal or nominal clause in the second position have to be considered as topic–comment sentences. The predicative clause contains a reference pronoun which links the predicate with the subject. It may be embodied in the verb or in any other part of the predicative clause: *ʾinna rusula-na: yaktubu:na ma: tamkuru:na* '(certainly) our messengers: they write down the tricks you have used', *ʾaz-za:niyatu la: yankiḥu-ha: ʾilla: za:nin* 'the female fornicator: only a fornicator shall marry her', *ʾal-baɣyu marta⁽u-hu: waxi:mun* 'the outrage: its pasture is unhealthy'.

Questions

Interrogatives take the head position of the sentence: *ma: ʾantuma: wa-min ʾayna jiʾtuma:* 'what sort of people are you both, and from where did you come?'. They occur in genitive position: *ʾabu: man ʾanta* 'whose father are you?', *bi-ʾayyi ḥadi:θin ba⁽da-hu: yuʾminu:na* 'in which report do they believe after that?', and may take the position of an object: *ʾayya ʾa:ya:ti lla:hi tunkiru:na* 'which of God's signs do you deny?'.

Interrogative sentences are introduced by an interrogative particle. Lack of the particle is very rare. The most frequent of the particles is *ʾa-*: *ʾa-yaḥsabu ʾan lam yara-hu: ʾaḥadun* 'did he think that no one has seen him?'. The particle *hal* introduces questions which are often rhetorical and imply a negative sense: *hal yastawi: l-ʾa⁽ma: wa-l-baṣi:ru* 'are the blind and the seeing equal?'.

The Nominal Phrase

Nominal Attributes

Attributes follow the noun and agree with it in definiteness/indefiniteness, case and gender: *ja:run ḥasanun* 'a good neighbor', *ʾal-ja:ru l-ḥasanu* 'the good neighbor'; *ja:ratun ḥasanatun* 'a good neighbor (f.)', *ʾal-ja:ratu l-ḥasanatu* 'the good neighbor (f.)'. Agreement in number takes place in the dual and, if the head noun denotes a human being, in the plural: *ja:rata:ni ḥasanata:ni* 'two good neighbors (f.)', *ji:ra:nun ḥisa:nun* 'good neighbors', *ja:ra:tun ḥsana:tanun* 'good neighbors (f.)'. Relating to a plural denoting non-human beings the adjective takes the feminine singular: *ʾal-ʾa⁽ma:lu l-ḥasanatu* 'the good deeds'.

Attributive Clauses

Nominal sentences as well as verbal sentences occur as attributes or predicates. If the head noun is definite and its attendant clause is indefinite, the clause is interpreted as predicate. If both have the same status of definiteness, the attendant clause is an attribute. Definite attributive clauses are marked by the relative (see p. 200), indefinite attributive clauses remain unmarked. The attributive clause normally contains a reference pronoun which combines it with the head noun.

> *ʾar-rajulu bi-yadi-hi: sayfun* 'the man: in his hand is a sword', i.e. 'the man holds a sword in his hand'
> *ʾar-rajulu l-laδi: bi-yadi-hi: sayfun* 'the man in whose hand is a sword'
> *rajulun bi-yadi-hi: sayfun* 'a man in whose hand is a sword'

Attributive clauses undergo a transformation if the predicate is an adjective or a participle. Then the predicate is attracted to the head noun and agrees with it in definiteness/indefiniteness and case, but in gender/number it agrees with its following subject:

> **fi: rijja:ln nifa:qu-hum maʿru:fun > fi: rija:lin maʿru:fin nifa:qu-hum* '(accompanied) by men whose hypocrisy is well known'
> **fi: r-riija:li l-laδi:na nifa:qu-hum maʿru:fun > fi: r-rija:li l-maʿru:fi nifa:qu-hum* '(accompanied) by the men whose hypocrisy is well-known'.

Genitive Construction

The head noun of a genitive construction is in the construct state (see p. 195), the noun depending on it follows in the genitive. Between the two nouns no other word is permitted; an attribute referring to the head noun has to follow after the annexed genitive. The phrase as a whole is definite or indefinite according to the state of the genitive noun: *kita:bu ʿa:limin qayyimun* 'a valuable book of a scholar', *kita:bu l-ʿa:limi l-qayyimu* 'the valuable book of the scholar' and *kita:bu ʿa:limin na:bihin* 'a book of an eminent scholar', *kita:bu l-ʿa:limi n-na:bihi* 'the book of the eminent scholar'. The genitive expresses either a possessive or a partitive relationship: *kita:bu l-ʿa:limi* 'the book of the scholar (possessed or written by him)', *ʾawwalu l-ḥika:yati* 'the first part (i.e. the beginning) of the story'. Notice also the constructions on p. 197, Quantifying Nouns.

Annexed to adjectives, the genitive expresses limitation: *ṭa:hiru l-qalbi* 'pure of heart', *ʿaδi:mu l-qadamayni* 'big with respect to his two feet'. Although the genitive has always the definite article, the whole phrase is not definite; it takes the definite article if attributed to a definite head noun: *rajulun ṭa:hiru l-qalbi* 'a man having a pure heart', *ʾar-rajulu ṭ-ṭa:hiru l-qalbi* 'the man having a pure heart'.

The Accusative in Nominal Phrases

To specify quantities, the indefinite accusative comes within verbal as well as nominal phrases: *miθqa:lu δarratin xayran* 'the weight of a dust particle in good'. The accusative of specification comes with quantifying nouns and pronouns: *kam kita:ban* 'how many books?', *ʾakbaru-na: sinnan* 'the oldest of us in age', *ʾaṭharu qalban* 'purer/purest in heart' (elative to *ṭa:hiru l-qalbi* 'pure of heart', see above, p. 214).

The Verbal Phrase

Accusative and Prepositional Objects

There are intransitive verbs without any object such as *rakaʿa* 'he bowed in prayer' and others that get transitivity by means of prepositions, such as *jalasa* 'he sat down': *jalasa ʾila: ʾaḥadin* 'he sat down with someone'. Especially the preposition *bi-* 'with' gives the verb a transitive meaning: *qa:ma* 'he stood up': *qa:ma bi-fiʿlin* 'he stood up with doing something', i.e. 'he undertook something'. The transitive verb may govern objects in the accusative and/or objects annexed by prepositions. e.g. one accusative object: *ʾata: ʾaḥadan* 'he came to someone', two accusative objects: *ʾa:ta: ʾaḥadan šayʾan* (causative stem IV of *ʾata:*) 'he brought someone something', one preposition: *raɣiba fi: šayʾin* 'he desired something' etc.

Negatives of the Verbal Phrase

CA has a complex system of negatives: *ɣayru* is employed with nouns (see p. 197), *ma:*, *la:*, *ʾin*, and *laysa* with both nominal and verbal phrases, *lam* and *lan* only with verbs.

la: is the negative of the imperfect (indicative and subjunctive): *la: yaktubu* 'he does not write', *li-kay-la: yaktuba* 'in order that he does not write'. With the jussive *la:* serves for prohibition: *la: tajlis* 'don't sit down!', with the perfect for a negative wish: *la: fuḍḍa fu:-ka* 'may thy teeth (lit. mouth) not be broken!'.

lam with the jussive (apocopate) denotes a negative past tense: *lam yaktub* 'he did not write'.

lan followed by the subjunctive, marks a negative future: *lan yakutba* 'he never will write'.

ma: is more expressive than *la:* or *lam* and negates the occurence of an action as a whole, not only in a certain case: *li-tunδira qawman ma: ʾata:-hum min naδi:rin min qabli-ka* 'in order that thou warnest a people to whom before thee never a warner has been come', *ma: yuzakka: l-ʾinsa:nu bi-šaha:dati ʾahli bayti-hi:* 'a man is not declared righteous by the evidence of his own household'.

ʾin as a negative is rarely used; it is sometimes combined with *ma:* (*ma: ʾin*).

laysa may be combined with verbs: *lastu ʾaqṣidu l-ḥarba* 'I do not intend to make war'.

Optional Accusatives Governed by the Verb

The Internal Object

Every transitive or intransitive verb can take an internal object which consists of a verbal noun in the accusative, usually belonging to the same verb. When it stands alone, it lays emphasis on the action itself: *na:ma nawman* 'he slept a (real) sleep', also with the passive: *ḍuriba ḍarban* 'he was struck (with) a striking'. Often the internal object is connected with a complement that expresses a special quality of the action: *ḍarabtu-hu: ḍarbatayni* 'I struck him two strikes', *ḍarabtu-hu: ḍarban šadi:dan* 'I struck him (with) a violent striking', *naðartu ʾilayhi naðrata l-maɣḍu:bi* 'I look at him the look of the angry, i.e. I gave him an angry look'.

Adverbial Accusatives

The function of the internal object has been enlarged by using verbal or abstract nouns as well as nouns denoting time, place or measure. This sort of accusative may be interpreted as an adverbial phrase, denoting

1 time: *sa:ra yawman* 'he traveled for a day';
2 place and direction: *waḍaʿa sayfa-hu: ja:niban* 'he put his sword aside';
3 motivation: *(ʾi)nṣaraftu maxa:fata š-šarri* 'I turned away from him for fear of evil';
4 mode: *ðahaba mašyan* 'he went away walking';
5 specification: *za:dat-ni: ruʾyatu-hu: ɣaḍaban* 'looking at him increased me in rage'. This usage of the accusative has been transferred to the nominal phrase (see p. 214).

Additional Predicative Clauses

The verbal phrase may be enlarged by an additional predicative phrase which describes an attendant contemporaneous circumstance. The additional predicative phrase, traditionally called circumstance clause, is basically an enlarged nominal clause connected with the main clause by *wa-* 'and': *ʿa:dat Zaynabu wa-hiya tab-ki:* or *ʿa:dat Zaynabu wa-hiya ba:kiyatun* 'Zaynab returned (and she is) weeping'.

In most cases, it is possible to transform the basic structure by deletion of *wa-* together with the following reference pronoun. Then the predicative adjective or participle is changed into the accusative: *ʿa:dat Zaynabu tabki:* or *ʿa:dat Zaynabu ba:kiyatan* 'Zaynab returned weeping'.

The immediate annexation of the predicative verb is possible, in particular after verbs of motion as well as verbs of beginning and continuation. Some of such verbs lost their intrinsic meaning and gained the function of modifiers: *fa-ʾaṣbaḥa yuqallibu kaffay-hi* 'then he came into the morning wringing his hands', i.e. 'then he got into a situation that he wrung his hands!'.

There exist two other types of circumstance clause. One describes a situation simultaneous with that of the main clause, but resultant from an anterior action; it is annexed with *wa-qad* plus perfect: *ma: la-na: ʾalla: nuqa:tila wa-qad ʾuxrijna: min diya:ri-na:* 'why should we not fight, since we have been driven out of our dwellings?'. The other describes a subsequent action intended at the time to which the main clause refers: *θumma nazaʿat θiya:ba-ha: taɣtasilu* 'then she took off her clothes in order to wash herself'.

The circumstance clause may also refer to the object: *ʾaxrajna: l-ʾasa:ra: wa-hum muṭriqu:na ruʾu:sa-hum* 'we brought out the prisoners while they bowed their heads', *marartu bi-l-mar'ati wa-hiya ja:lisatun* 'I passed by the woman while she was sitting'. A similar construction is found with verbs denoting 'make, let be, find, regard, call someone/something such and such'. They take an accusative object and an attendant predicative noun or a predicative verb referring to the object: *ma:-ða: huwa l-laði: yaj'alu-ki tabki:na* 'what is it that makes you (f.) cry', *wajadna: l-qawma ra:ji'i:na min-a š-ša'mi* 'we found the people returning from Syria'.

Subordinate Clauses
Beside the attributive and predicative clauses, CA mainly distinguishes three kinds of subordinate clauses: (1) adverbial clauses annexed by a conjunction; (2) object, subject and other complement clauses which may be replaced by a verbal noun; (3) conditional clauses.

Adverbial Clauses
There are some conjunctions followed by a subordinate clause : the temporal conjunctions *lamma:* 'after', *'ið* 'when, as', *ḥatta:* 'as long as, until', *bayna-ma:* 'while', the final conjunctions *li-* (*li-'an*), *kay* (*li-kay*) 'in order that' and the relative *ḥayθu* 'where, inasmuch as'. In most cases a verbal clause follows: *yaḍiba lla:hu 'alay-him ḥayθu lam yatta'iðu:* 'God was angry with them inasmuch as they did not accept warning'. In a final clause after *li-*, *kay* and *ḥatta:*, the verb comes in the subjunctive: *fa-ṣbiru: ḥatta: yaḥkuma lla:hu bayna-kum* 'so take patience until God will decide between you!'.

Clauses Replacing a Verbal Noun
Clauses headed by *'an*, *'anna* or, sometimes, *ma:* substitute verbal nouns in every possible position within the sentence and may be substituted by them. The particle *'an* introduces a verbal clause, *'anna* a nominal clause of which the subject noun immediately follows in the accusative: *balaɣa-ni: 'anna 'aba:-ka qad ma:ta = balaɣa-ni: mama:tu 'abi:-ka* '(the message) that thy father died has reached me' = '(the message of) the death of thy father has reached me'. An action which is expected is introduced by *'an* plus the subjunctive: *'uri:du 'an 'aðhaba = 'uri:du ð-ðaha:-ba* 'I want to leave'. In connection with prepositions these particles form conjunctions such as *li-'anna* 'because', *ba'da 'an* or *ba'da-ma:* 'after', *qabla 'an* 'before', *'ila: 'an* 'until', *ka-'anna* 'as though'. The latter introduces subordinate and independent clauses as well: *ka'ann-i: 'anðuru 'ila: man la: ḥaya:'a la-hu:* 'I seem to look at one who has no shame' and *ka:na n-na:su ka'anna-hum la: ḥaya:'a la-hum* 'the people behaved as if they were shameless'.

Conditional Sentences
The conditional sentence consists of two interdependent clauses asyndetically bound together. It has a characteristic structure in that the reference of the perfect verb to the past is neutralized for both of the two component clauses. Instead of the perfect the apocopate occurs with the same shift in time reference. The protasis

is marked by *'in* 'if' or *'iða:* 'if, when, whenever' (after the latter the apocopate is excluded).

> *'in taxallafta ʿan-i n-nafi:ri yaʿtabir bi-ka γayru-ka*
> 'if you stay away from departing into the battle, others will follow your example',
> *'inna-ma: l-mu'minu:na l-laði:na 'iða: ðukira lla:hu wajilat qulu:bu-hum*
> 'The believers are just those who whenever God's name is mentioned are afraid in their hearts'.

The particle *law*, also used for wish sentences, introduces hypothetical conditions. Normally in both component clauses the perfect or its negative counterpart *lam yafʿal* is used. The apodosis is frequently introduced by *la-*: *law ka:na ʿinda-na: ma:lun la-'aʿṭayna:-ka* 'if we had money we would give you it', *law wajada-ni: na:'iman la-ma: 'ayqaða-ni:* 'had he found me sleeping he would not have woken me'.

The above-mentioned structure of conditional sentences comprises all interdependent clauses which imply a conditional relationship, i.e. clauses introduced by indefinite pronouns like *mahma:*, *man* and adverbials like *mata:(-ma:)*, *'ayna(-ma:)*, *ḥayθu-ma:* belong here, but also *kulla-ma:* 'whenever', and *ma:* 'as long as'. Some examples: *man daxala da:ra 'abi: Sufya:na fa-huwa 'a:minun* 'whoever enters Abu Sufyān's house will be protected', *wa-huwa maʿa-kum 'ayna-ma: kuntum* 'and he is with you wherever you are'.

References

Blau, Joshua. 1977. "The Beginnings of the Arabic Diglossia: A Study of the Origins of Neoarabic." *Afroasiatic Linguistics* 4: 175–202.

—— 1986. "The Jahiliyya and the Emergence of the Neo-Arabic Lingual Type."*Jerusalem Studies in Arabic and Islam* 7: 35–43.

Diem, Werner. 1973. "Die nabatäischen Inschriften und die Frage der Kasusflexion im Altarabischen." *Zeitschrift der Deutschen Morgenländischen Gesellschaft* 123: 227–237.

Ferguson, Charles A. 1959. "Diglossia."*Word* 15: 325–340.

Fischer, Wolfdietrich. 1987. *Grammatik der klassischen Arabisch*, 2nd edn. Wiesbaden: Harrassowitz. English edn. forthcoming.

Fück, Johann. 1950. *Arabiya: Untersuchungen zur arabischen Sprach- und Stilgeschichte* (Abhandlungen des Sächsischen Akademie der Wissenschaften zu Leipzig, Philologisch-historische Klasse 45/1). Berlin.

Kienast, Burkhardt. 1990. "Zur Nominalbildung im Semitischen." In *Festschrift Å. Sjöberg*. Uppsala.

Nöldeke, Theodor. 1910. "Zur Sprache des Korans." In *Neue Beiträge zur semitischen Sprachwissenschaft*. Strassburg.

Vollers, Karl. 1906. Volkssprache und Schriftsprache im alten Arabien. Strassburg.

Wehr, Hans. 1952. Review of Fück (1950). *Zeitschrift der Deutschen Morgenländischen Gesellschaft* 102: 179–184.

Further Reading

Bakalla, M. H. 1983. *Arabic Linguistics: An Introduction and Bibliography.* London.

Blau, Joshua. 1965. *The Emergence and Linguistic Background of Judaeo-Arabic: A Study of the Origins of Middle Arabic.* (2nd ed. 1981.) Oxford.

Corriente, Federico. 1976. "From Old Arabic to Classical Arabic through the Pre-Islamic Koine: Some Notes on the Native Grammarians' Sources, Attitudes, and Goals." *Journal of Semitic Studies* 21: 62–96.

Denz, Adolf. 1982. "Die Struktur den Klassisch-Arabisch." In *Grundriss der arabischen Philologie*, vol. 1: *Sprachwissenschaft.* Wiesbaden. 58–82.

Fleisch, Henri. 1968. *L'Arabe classique, esquisse d'une structure linguistique.* Beirut.

—— 1961, 1979. *Traité de philologie arabe*, vols. 1 and 2. Beirut.

Rabin, Chaim. 1951. *Ancient Westarabian.* London.

Wright, William. 1896–1898. *A Grammar of the Arabic Language. Translated from the German of Caspari and edited with numerous additions and corrections.* 3rd edn. revised W. Robertson Smith and M. J. de Goeje, vols. 1 and 2. Cambridge.

12 Sayhadic (Epigraphic South Arabian)

Leonid E. Kogan and Andrey V. Korotayev

A group of languages known from numerous inscriptions and graffiti from South Arabia is traditionally called Epigraphic South Arabian (ESA). A. F. L. Beeston proposed to denote them as Sayhadic, (*Ṣayhad* being the name used by medieval Islamic geographers for the desert now called Ramlat al-Sab'atayn). It was along the edge of this desert that most of the earliest attestations of these languages were found.

This group is usually thought of as consisting of four languages: Sabean (Sab.), Qatabanian (Qat.), Hadramitic (Hadr.) and Minean. The latter is now also called Madhabic, as it was used not only by the Mineans but also by other communities of the Wadi Madha:b (here traditionally abbreviated as Min.).

The earliest Sayhadic (Sayh.) documents can be dated to the beginning of the first millennium BCE. Some sherds with South Arabian letters have been found in Raybu:n (Ḥaḍramawt) in the layers which could be dated by radiocarbon to the twelfth century BCE. A considerable number of informative Sayhadic (Sabean and Minean) texts are attested for the eighth century BCE. In the seventh century BCE the number of Sabean inscriptions rapidly increases. In this period Sabean was used not only on the Sabean mainland (i.e. in the region of Ma:rib), but also throughout the Ṣayhad region and even outside of it – in the Wadi Ḥaḍramawt, near the Red Sea coast and in Ethiopia.

The end of Sabean control over most Ṣayhad regions led to the growing use of the local Sayhadic languages (Minean, Qatabanian, Hadramitic) retaining sometimes a certain Sabean influence for a while.

The Minean mainland was situated in the Wadi Madha:b. However, Minean was also used in the other kingdoms of this wadi. The fact that the Mineans were heavily engaged in the incense trade with the Mediterranean world, led to the appearance of Minean texts in areas very distant from the Minean mainland itself, first of all in the territory of ancient Dida:n (modern al-'Ula:), but also even in Egypt and the island of Delos.

The Qatabanian mainland is the area of the wadis Bayha:n and Ḥari:b at the edge of the inner Ṣayhad desert. In the second half of the first millennium the area

220

under the control of the Qatabanian kings expanded significantly. As a result, the Qatabanian language area included the Southern Highlands adjacent to the Qatabanian mainland.

Hadramatic was used in the Wadi Ḥaḍramawt itself, as well as in the area of the Hadrami capital, Shabwah, outside the wadi. The Hadrami kingdom controlled the main frankincense producing area in Dhofar (present-day Oman), where an important Hadrami colony *S¹mhrm* (*Kho:r Ro:ri:*) was established.

At the end of the first century BCE, most of the western part of South Arabia was unified within the "empire" of the kings of Saba' and dhu:-Rayda:n. Its creators were most likely the Himyarites (*Ḥmyrm* of the inscriptions), a tribe in the Southern Highlands which started playing a very important role in South Arabian political (and linguistic) history from that time. Sabean became the official language of the Himyarites and came into use in most of the Southern Highlands. There is no doubt, however, that Sabean was not a vernacular of the Himyarites.

The late second century BCE saw the end of the use of the Minean connected with the end of the Minean Kingdom. We can observe the formation in the former Minean linguistic domain (mainly in the area of Haram), of a specific dialect of Sabean with a rather weak influence of the Minean substratum and a stronger influence of the Arabic adstratum (see e.g. pp. 237–239). By the end of the second century ce the use of Qatabanian also ceased due to the destruction of the Qatabanian kingdom under the blows of the Himyarite, Sabean and Hadrami kingdoms. In the fourth century the Hadrami kingdom came to an end, conquered by the Himyarites, who brought their official language, Sabean, to this area too.

In the second half of the first century BCE, beside the monumental script of the inscriptions, another, "cursive" (or "minuscule"), script of everyday documents – private letters, contracts, magic texts etc. – developed. Discovered only in 1973, this script has been extremely difficult to decipher. Only about two dozen minuscule documents have been published and interpreted, out of an estimated number of more than 1,000. Almost all published minuscule texts are Sabean and date from the second–third centuries CE. Most of them come from the city of Nasha:n in the Wadi Madha:b.

In the late fourth century CE the monotheistic period started. Because the pagan practice of dedications to the temples ceased, the available Sayhadic documentation from the fifth–sixth centuries is considerably reduced. The lexicon of monotheistic (mainly Judaic and Christian) texts exhibit foreign influences, first of all Hebrew/Aramaic and Greek. The most recent Sayhadic (Sabean) documents were produced in the second half of the sixth century, the last dated Sabean inscription (C 325) being dated to the year 669 of the Himyarite era (559 or 554 CE).

By now, a widely acknowledged linguistic periodization has been worked out, for Sabean only. Its history may be subdivided into archaic (the first millennium BCE), middle (first century BCE – late fourth century CE) and late or monotheistic – (up to the late sixth century CE) periods.

Since, on the one hand, Sabean is by far the best-documented among Sayhadic languages and, on the other, they are all relatively close to each other, we thought it convenient to take Sabean as the base of our description. Accordingly, linguistic phenomena quoted below without any special mark belong to Sabean monumental texts. Otherwise they are marked as Min., Qat., Hadr. or minuscule.

Where sources of quotations are indicated, they are given according to the abbreviations in Beeston et al. 1982.

Phonology

Consonants

Since we deal here with dead languages without oral tradition, it is practically impossible to reconstruct the phonetic value of Sayhadic graphemes. Accordingly, we shall content ourselves with a conventional table of Sayhadic consonants based on their Semitic correspondences:

	b			w	m
f					
t	d	ṭ		n l r	
θ	δ	θ̣			
s³	z	ṣ			
s²		ḍ			
				y	
s¹					
k	g	ḳ			
x	γ				
ḥ	ʕ				
h	ʔ				

One of the most acute problems of Sayhadic phonology is that of non-emphatic unvoiced sibilants, transcribed here as s^1, s^2 and s^3. Traditional Sabeology was deeply influenced by Arabic studies and believed that Sayhadic was especially close to Classical Arabic. Accordingly, these graphemes received the phonetic value observed in the corresponding Arabic cognates. Thus, s^1lm 'peace' was transcribed as *slm* because of Arabic *sala:m-* and $s^{2c}b$ 'tribe, commune' as *š^cb* because of Arabic *ša^cb-*. Since Arabic has no third unvoiced sibilant, s^3 was conventionally transcribed *ś*; most scholars thought it to have had a phonetic value close to *š* (our s^2), but even a lateralized articulation was sometimes proposed.

Nowadays, most scholars think that there is no special relationship between Sayhadic and North Arabian dialects. At the same time, the system described above obviously contradicts the data of those languages which do have three unvoiced sibilants, namely Hebrew and Modern South Arabian (MSA):

Sayhadic	Hebrew	MSA
s¹	š	š
s²	ś	ś
s³	s	s

Examples: Sayh. *dbs¹* 'honey' ~ Heb. *dəbaš*, Jibba:li *dɛbš*; Sayh. *s²bᶜ* 'abundant, abundantly' ~ Heb., Mehri *śbᶜ* 'to be satiated'; Sayh. *ʾs³r* 'to be bound with an obligation' ~ Hebrew *ʾsr* 'to tie', Jibba:li *ʾsr* 'to hobble an animal'. Though some sporadic exceptions should not be neglected (see, e.g., Sayh. *ᶜs¹y* 'to do, make', which is obviously to be compared with Hebrew *ᶜśh*), in the great majority of cases these correspondences are valid, and this is the notation that we shall follow in our chapter.

Vowels

Since the South Arabian system of writing is purely consonantal, we cannot draw any direct information about Sayhadic vowels. The existence of an *u* (most likely long) may be proved by Sabean variant spellings of the pl. 3 pronominal suffix -*hmw*/-*hm* (see p. 224). It is likely that beside the six vowels typical for many of Old Semitic languages (*a, i, u, a:, i:, u:*), there existed also *e:* and *o:* resulting from the contraction of -*ay* and -*aw*-. It may be evidenced by such pairs of variant spellings (belonging to the same period and often even to the same text) as *byn*/*bn* 'between' or *θwr*/*θr* 'bull', in which the latter represent the historical spelling of the actual [*be:n* (< *bayn*-), *θo:r*- (< *θawr*-)].

Peculiar Phonetic Phenomena

Sabean *h* corresponds to *s¹* of other Sayhadic languages in the prefix of the causative verbal theme and in pronominal morphemes of the 3rd person (-*hw* versus -*s¹w* etc.).

A comparatively frequent merger of *θ* and *ṣ* is attested, e.g. *ḳṣ* 'summer season' beside (the etymologically correct) *ḳyθ*; *θlm* 'statue' versus *ṣlm* etc. (However, it may be explained partly by a mere confusion of letters for *ṣ* and *θ*.) In minuscule documents etymological *θ* is reflected as *ḍ*, e.g. *ḍbyt* 'young she-camel > sack made of its hide' (~ monumental *θbyt*), *mfḍr* 'a measure of capacity' (~ monumental *mfθr*). It seems that minuscule script had no letter for *θ* at all.

s³ is often reflected as *s¹* in late Sabean, e.g. *ms¹nd* 'inscription' instead of *ms³nd*, *s¹n* 'up to, next to, by' instead of *s³n* etc. This process is also attested for the Haramic dialect of middle Sabean (e.g. *ʾks¹wt* 'clothes' vs. standard Sabean *ks³wy* 'clothing').

n is sporadically assimilated to the following consonant, e.g. *yδrn* (beside *ynδrn*) – impf. from *nδr* 'to atone'; *mḍḥ* (beside *mnḍḥ*) 'tutelary deity', *ʾfs¹* (beside *ʾnfs¹*) – broken plural of *nfs¹* 'soul'.

Sayhadic *θ* is often reflected as *s³* in Hadramitic texts (especially from Wadi Ḥaḍramawt itself), e.g. *s²ls³* 'three' (~ Sab. *s²lθ*).

Some cases of Hadramitic *θ* corresponding to Sayhadic *s³* are also attested (e.g. *mθnd* 'inscription' vs. Sayh. *ms³nd* or *kθʾ* 'to command' versus Qat. *ks³ʾ*).

Metathesis is a comparatively frequent phenomenon in Sayhadic, e.g. variant forms *ʾwld*/*ʾlwd* and *ʾwyn*/*ʾywn*, both broken plurals from *wld* 'child' and *wyn* 'vineyard' respectively. See further *ḳlmt*/*ḳmlt* 'kind of insects', Min. *s²mʾl*/*s²ʾml* 'northwards' etc.

An interesting phenomenon is the so-called "parasitic" *h*, i.e. non-etymological glide *h* appearing in a number of morphemes (mainly affixes and particles). In Minean it is typical of the affixes of external plural (masculine and feminine), e.g. *ymhn* 'days' (pl. m. abs. < *ywm* (*ym*) 'day'), *ʿhrhn* < *ʿhr* 'noble', *ʾnθht-n* (pl. f. determined < *ʾnθt* 'woman'), *ʿδbht-y* 'reparations' (pl. f. const. < *ʿδbt*) etc.; it is often found at the end of nouns in singular and broken plural in *status constructus* (see p. 227). Though it remains uncertain under what conditions this *h* appears, it is thought that it was caused by a peculiar character of the stress (possibly even pitch). As for the examples attested outside of Minean, see *bhʾ* 'to enter' (cf Semitic *bwʾ* 'to come, to enter'); *mhn* (beside *mn*) 'who, which' (relative), which may be compared with Arabic dialectal *mi:n* etc.

Morphology

Pronouns

Personal Pronouns (Independent)
Independent personal pronouns of the 1st person are only doubtfully attested in the texts (sg. 1 *ʾn* in *bnhw ʾn*, *bnhw ʾn* 'I am his son, I am his son' [Gl 1782]; *brʾk-h ʾn* 'it was myself who built it' [J2353,3]; pl. 1 (?) in *sʾṭrw δn msʾndn ʾn ʾbrh* 'we, Abraha, wrote this inscription' [C541,3–4]).

Forms of the 2nd person are extremely rare in monumental inscriptions (perhaps *ʾt* in *Rḥmnn rḥmk mrʾ ʾt* 'O Raḥma:n! You are merciful; you are the lord!' [Ry508,11]), but they are frequent in minuscule documents. Forms attested in published texts are as follows: sg. m. *ʾnt* (variant *ʾt*): *w-ʾt sʾxln l-Frʿn nkt-hw* 'and you, take care about *Frʿn*, his she-camel' [A-40-4,3–5]; pl. m. *ʾntmw*; *w-ʾntmw f-l tsʾtʿddnn l-hmw* 'and you (pl.), you should verify the calculations for them' [YM11732,3].

Forms of the 3rd person are identical with the nominative forms of remote deictics: *w-tʾwlw b-wfym hwʾ w-kl sʾwʿ-hmw* 'and they returned in safety, he (himself) and all their companions' [J631,13–14]; *w-hmw f-nθrw mwʿd ʾgrn* 'as for them, they remembered the promise of the Najranites' [J577,10].

A number of 2nd person pronominal enclitics are attested in minuscule documents: sg. *-k*, pl. *-kmw* (see below; *-k* also in monumental Qatabanian [J 367; 2439,1] *ʿbd-k* 'your /sg./ servant', *ʾδn-k* 'your /sg./ authority').

The suffix *-n* in a number of theophoric names may be regarded as the object enclitic of 1st person singular, e.g. *Ḥm-n-nsʾr*, which probably means 'Protect-me-Nasr' (imv. sg.) or pf. sg. 3m. from *ḥmy* 'to protect' + *-n*, see p. 235).

Attached to nouns, enclitic pronouns denote possession *ʾxt-hn* 'their (f.) sisters', minuscule *bt-k* 'your (sg.) house' etc. Attached to verbal forms, enclitic pronouns denote the direct object (*mtʿ-hmw* 'he has saved them', Min. *l-ysʾṣfd-s¹ tθfṭ* 'let the judgment bind him' [R4728,1]), but they are also widely used for the indirect object: *δbḥ-hw δbḥm* 'he offered him [i.e. the god] a sacrifice' [e.g. C461,2], *xmr-*

Table 12.1   Attested forms of pronominal enclitics

		Singular	Dual	Plural
Sab.	m.	-hw, -h	-hmy	-hmw, -hm
	f.	-h, -hw		-hn
Min.	m.	-s¹, -s¹w	-s¹mn	-s¹m
	f.	-s¹		-s¹n
Qat.	m.	-s¹, -s¹ww	-s¹my	-s¹m
	f.	-s¹, -s¹yw		
Hadr.	m.	-s¹, -s¹ww	-s¹mn, -s¹myn, -s¹my	-s¹m
	f.	-θ (-s³), -θyw (-s³yw)	-s¹my	

hmw δnmm 'he [a deity] granted them rain' [J563,11–12].

Pronominal enclitics are extensively employed, with prepositions: *b-ʿm-hmw* 'with them,' Min. *b-ʿbr-s¹mn* 'regarding them both'; minuscule *l-k* 'for you', *ʿbrn-kmw* 'to you (pl.)'.

Relative Particles

Table 12.2   Attested forms of relative particles

		Singular	Dual	Plural
Sab.	m.	δ-	δy-	ʾlw, ʾly, ʾlht, ʾl
	f.	δt, t-	δty	ʾlt
Min.	m.	δ-	δy-	ʾhl-, hl-, δl-
	f.	δt	δtyn	
Qat.	m.	δ(m)-, δw-	δw-, δn	δtw, ʾwlw, ʾl (?)
	f.	δt(m)-		δtw
Hadr.	m.	δ-		
	f.	δt		

These particles are used to introduce relative clauses (see p. 239) and in periphrastic genitive constructions: *bkrtn δt δhbn* 'the bronze young she-camel' [C579,4–5]; *ʾmθln ʾly δhbn* 'the bronze images' [J558,2]; *fnwt-hw δt ts¹ qyn-hw* 'his canal, which irrigates it [the palm grove]' [C657,3]. They may agree in gender and number with the antecedent, but δ- often becomes generalized: *ʾbdtm δ-kwnw byn xms¹nhn* 'irregulars who were between the two armies' [J633,7–8], *ṣlmtn ... δ-s²ftt mrʾhmw* 'the statuette ... which she promised to their lord' [J706,3–4].

Of interest are some nouns with δ- which are used without an antecedent like δ-ʾʿδr 'distant relatives', δ-gbʾn 'document of property transfer', δ-ʾmnt 'person or thing under protection' (cf. Geʿez *za-manfas* 'spiritual', *za-lamṣ* leprous' etc).

Indefinite Pronouns

mn (δ ...) 'somebody', someone', *mhn* 'something', *ʾhnn (ʾhnm)* 'whatever, whenever, wherever': *w-mn-mw ys²tr-hw* 'whoever destroys it ...' [R4091,1–3] (with enclitic *-mw*, see p. 237).

Nouns

Nominal Patterns
Examples of primary nouns:

> monoradical: *f* 'voice, authority';
> biradical: *s²h* 'sheep', *gw* 'community, group', *'b* 'father;
> triradical: *rgl* 'foot', *b'r* 'well', *s²ms¹* 'sun';
> from "geminated" roots: *ˁm* 'uncle' (pl. *'ˁmm*), *ˁr* 'mountain, hill-fortress' (pl. *'ˁrr*);
> from "hollow" roots: *ywm/ym* 'day' (pl. *'ywm*), *θwr/θr* 'bull' (pl. *'θwr*), *byt/bt* (pl. *'byt*) 'house', *kyθ kṣ* 'summer season';
> quadriradical (not very frequent): *'rby* 'locusts', *ˁglm-t* 'breakwater', *kwkb* 'star', *glgl-n* 'sesame' (minuscule) and some others.

The following types of derived nouns are recognizable (*ṣhf* 'to write' is the sample root):

ṣhf: *s²rh* 'safety, deliverance' < *s²rh* 'to deliver'; *δbh* 'victim' < *δbh* 'to slay' etc. It is often augmented with *-t*: *nfl-t* 'accident' < *nfl* 'to fall in battle', *blw-t* 'funerary monument' < *blw* 'to construct a tomb'. In nouns derived from roots with the first radical *w* this consonant may be dropped, and *-t* is usually added: *zˁ* 'control' < **wzˁ*, cf. *wzˁ* 'title of commander', *kh/kh-t* 'order, command' < *wkh* 'to command'; *hb-t* 'gift' < *whb* 'to give, to grant'.

ṣ-y-hf: 'seal' in *xytmn* 'two seals' (minuscule); *ṣh-y-f* – attested in *ṣlym* 'statuette', probably a diminutive [**kutayl-*] from *ṣlm* 'statue'.

t-ṣhf(-t): some verbal nouns (presumably from the themes **ṣahhafa* and **taṣahhafa*: *t-hrm* 'ritual prohibition' < *hrm* 'to prohibit'; *t-θwb* 'completion of a work' < *θwb* 'to complete'; *t-kdm* 'attack' < *tkdm* 'to attack'; *t-nxy(-t)* 'confession' < *t-nxy* 'to confess'; cf. also some concrete nouns like *t-bkl* (*t-bkl-t*) 'plantation' < *bkl* 'to lay out ...'; *t'nθ* 'women', Qat. *thmy* 'wall'.

n-ṣhf: *n-hkl* 'specially'.

ṣhf-': *δfr'-n* 'ill-smelling plants'.

m-ṣhf(-t): denotes a large range of meanings (place, time , instrument, etc.) *m-s¹'l* 'oracle' < *s¹'l* 'to ask'; *m-ṣdk* 'documentary proof of ownership' < *ṣdk* 'to claim proprietorial rights over something'; *m-s¹ky* 'irrigation' < *s¹ky* 'to irrigate'; *m-δbh-t* 'altar' < *δbh* 'to slay'. Active and passive participles of various themes, *m-nṣf* 'servant, temple personnel' < *nṣf* 'to perform rites' etc.

ṣhf-n: *xmṭ-n* 'disorder', *xmr-n* 'concession, gift', Min. *rgl-n* 'time(s) [multiplied]'. *ṣhf-y(t)* – (?) *ghmy* 'last part of the night', *grby* 'worker in stone', Qat. *ywm-y-t* 'date'.

Gender
The two genders are masculine and feminine. The latter is usually unmarked. The most common feminine ending is *-t*. It is used for deriving nouns denoting female

beings from the masculine: *ʾbl-t* 'she-camel' < *ʾbl* 'camel'; *ʾl-t* 'goddess' < *ʾl* 'god'; *bn-t* 'daughter' < *bn* 'son' etc. A number of feminine nouns have no *-t*: *yd* 'hand', *ʿyn* 'eye', *hgr* 'city' etc. A number of nouns without *-t* are feminine since they may be applied to females only (*ḥyḍ* 'menstruating woman', *nfs¹* 'woman in childbed'). For the masculine with the ending *-t* see *xlf-t* 'viceroy' which may be a loanword from Arabic *xali:fat-*. Grammatical gender is very stable and only very few nouns are suspected to be attested in both genders: *nxl* 'palm grove'; *nfs¹* 'soul' (attested mostly as f., but apparently m. in *l-ymtn nfs¹-hw* 'let him die' [Ra42,13]). Note that the word *frs¹* certainly denoted both 'horse' and 'mare' (*ymtn frs¹-hw* 'his horse would die' [J649,21–22]/*frs¹m δt δhbm* 'a mare of bronze' [J752,7–8), thus belonging to the same group. In Qatabanian *ywm* 'day' and *ʿm* 'year' may be used as feminine (*ṭt.* (f.!) *ywmm* 'one day' [e.g. R3854,6–7], *ʿmm s²lθtm* 'third year' [Bron/MB8,2]).

State

Three states of noun are attested in Sayhadic: absolute, construct and determinate.

1   A noun which is neither the possessed in the genitive construction nor determined by the article is in the absolute state. It may have no special marker (*ʾs¹d* 'soldiers'), but much more often (especially in Sabean) it is marked by *-m*, "mimation" (*ṣlm-m* 'a statue').

The mimation is unpredictable in many cases, so that only some trends of its use may be detected. Thus, it is usually lacking in words denoting the seasons of the year: *nʾd ʾθmr-m ... bḵyθ w-dθʾ w-ṣrb* (but!) *w-mly-m* 'abundance of crops in summer, and spring, and autumn and winter' [C174,3]; contrast *nʾd ḵyθ-m w-ṣrb-m* abundance of summer and autumn harvests' [J651,48].

Numerous adverbial expressions derived from nouns very often exhibit *-m* (e.g. *dwm-m* 'forever'; *δr-m* 'to saturation', *s²bʿ-m* 'abundantly' etc.).

2   A noun which is either the possessed of the genitive construction or is followed by a pronominal suffix appears in its bare form, the construct state: *ʾbʿl byt-hmw* 'the lords of their house' [e.g. R3991,21–22]. Qat. *rdʾ s²ms¹-s¹* 'the help of his sun-goddess' [R3856,4], Hadr. *wld-θ* 'her children' [e.g. Rb645,3]. Minean may have a special marker of the possessed, namely *-h*: *b-ʾmr-h Nkrh* 'by the order of [the deity] *Nkrḥ*' [MAFRAY/Darb aṣ-Ṣabil,5], *b-ʾwθn-h mḥrm-h ḍlʿn* '(with)in the boundary stones of the sacred enclave of (= for) the ill people' [lines 6–7]. In such cases the possessed itself is in the genitival position as above (cf. in the same text *ykwn ʾwθn* (without *-h*!) *mḥrmn* 'the boundary stones of the sacred enclave are established' [lines 2–3]). Nouns in the construct state are also found before relative clauses (see p. 240). Unlike Arabic, more than one possessed can precede a possessor, e.g. *xl w-mkm Tʾlb* 'the strength and the power of *Tʾlb*' [C2,8].

3   In the definite state the marker of definiteness for singular nouns, broken plurals and feminine external plurals is a postpositive article *-n* (in Hadramitic mainly *-hn*): *hgr-n* 'the city', Hadr. *ʿkbt-hn* 'the fortification'. Nouns in the definite state are used independently (*b-wθn-n* 'at the border stone'), after deictics

(see p. 230), before relative clauses introduced by relative particles (see p. 240), before proper names (Hadr. *s'r-hn ʿrmw* 'the valley ʿrmw' [Ingrams 1,2]). Note that nominal subject is usually definite while nominal predicate is in the absolute state.

Number
Sayhadic has three numbers: singular, dual and plural (external and internal or broken).

Forms of the Dual
Absolute state:

> Sab. *-n (-yn)*: (θny) *ʾs'n, ʾs'yn* 'two men'
> Min. *-ny*: *ṣḥftny* 'two curtain walls'
> Qat. *-myw*: *ywmmyw* 'two days'
> Hadr. *-nyw*: *fhd-nyw* 'two cheetahs'

Construct state:

> Sab. *-y*: *mlky S'bʾ* 'two kings of Saba''
> Min. *-y*: *rs²wy ʾlhn* 'two priests of the deity'
> Qat. *-w, -y, -h (?)*: *mlkw Ḳtbn* 'two kings of Qataba:n'; *bḥty blḳm* 'two votive phalli of limestone', (?) *nfs'h-s'yw* 'two funerary monuments of hers'
> Hadr. *-y, -hy*: *ḳtby mlkn* 'two camel-riders of the king', *gs'mhy gnʾ Ḳlt* 'two constructions of the wall of Ḳlt'

-y may disappear when pronominal suffixes are added: *bn-hw* X *w-*Y 'his two sons X and Y', Hadr. *ʿyn-s'ww* 'his two eyes'.

Determinate state:

> Sab. *-nhn, -ynn, -nn, -ynhn, -ynhyn*: *hgrnhn* 'the two cities', *ṣlmynn* 'the two statues', *bytnn* 'the two houses', *s²ʿbynhn, s²ʿbynhyn* 'the two communities'
> Min. *-nhn, -nyhn*: *ʿynnhn* 'the two eyes', *s²wʿnyhn* 'the two (temple) servitors'
> Qat. *-nyhn*: *mkmnyhn* 'the two meetings'
> Hadr. *-yhn, -yn*: *hndyyhn* 'the two Indians', *ʿrbytyn* 'the two Arab women'

The External Plural
The masculine external plural is very rare in Sayhadic. In Sabean more or less certain cases are restricted to the construct state, e.g. *bn-w/bn-y* 'sons of ...', *ʾx-y* 'brothers of ...', *xrf-y* 'years [in which] ...'; possibly also *ḥwr-w* 'citizens of ...', *ʿhr-w* 'nobles of ...' (the last two may be regarded, alternatively, as broken plurals). Forms of the absolute and determinate state are less certain, partly because

they often formally coincide with the respective forms of the dual (e.g. *bn-n* 'sons', *ʾm-n* 'cubits' < sg. *ʾmt*, *ʾrbʿtn mʾnhn* 'the four hundred' < sg. *mʾt*).

Masculine external plural is more common in Minean: absolute *ywm-hn* 'days', *xrf-hn* 'the years'; construct *ʾb-hw/ʾb-hy* 'fathers of ...', *xlf-hy* 'gates of ...'. Note Qat. *bn-w/bn-y* 'sons of ...', *ʾlh-w/ʾlh-y* 'gods of ...', *ʾx-y/ʾx-h* 'brothers of ...', Hadr. *ʾlh-y* 'gods of ...'.

The feminine external plural ending in Sabean attested also in Qatabanian is -*t* (graphically indistinguishable from the singular and presumably differentiated by the quantity of the vowel, *-*a:*t-* vs. *-*at-* or *-*t-*):

ʾnθt 'woman' – pl. *ʾnθt*, *tkdm* 'attack' – pl. *tkdmt* etc.

-*ht* (abs. and det.) in Minean and Hadramitic: *ṣrḥht-m* 'upper parts of build-
    ings', *bḥ-ht-m* 'votive phalli', *nθ-ht-n* 'the women'

-*hty* (const.) in Minean Qatabanian and Hadramitic: *ʾrḍ-hty* 'lands of ...'

Broken Plurals

The following forms of the broken plurals are attested:

ṣhf < *ṣhf*, *ṣhft* (the first case homographic with the singular, but may have had a different vocalism, e.g. **ṣV̆ḥaf-* or **ṣiḥa:f-*: *ʾhl* < **ʾhl* 'kind of cistern', *ʾlm* < *ʾlm* 'feast'; *fnw* < *fnwt* 'secondary canal'. Note *ʾmm*, a plural of *ʾmt* 'cubit', which certainly points to an apophonic change like [**ʾammatu ~ *ʾamamu*].

ṣhf-w: *ḥwr-w* (< *ḥwr* 'citizens' (coll.), *ʿhr-w* 'nobles' (cf. Qat. sg. *ʿhr*); note that at least some of these forms may be considered external plurals.

ṣ-w-ḥf(-t): *ʾ-w-mr* 'signal stations'; Qat. *x-w-ll-t* 'orders'; *ṣ-y-ḥf(-t)*: *x-y-tm-t* 'plots of cultivated land'; *ṣhf-n*: *ḥyr-n* < *ḥyr-t/ḥr-t* 'camp'; *ṣh-w-f*: *δk-w-r* < *δkr* 'male'; often in Qat.: *xd-w-r* < *xdr* 'place of business', *xr-w-f* < *xrf* 'year'; *ṣh-y-f*: *xm-y-sʾ* < *xmsʾ* 'main army force'; *xṭ-y-ʾ* < *xtʾ* 'sin'; *xr-y-f* < *xrf* 'year'; *ṣh-w-f-t*: *ʾd-w-m-t* 'groups of serfs, dependent persons'; *ṣh-y-f-t*: *xr-y-f-t* 'autumn seasons', *ʾd-y-m-t* 'groups of dependent persons'.

ʾ-ṣhf: the most widespread pattern of broken plurals; it is probable that several patterns are behind this consonantal form (e.g. **ʾaṣha:f-*, *ʾaṣhuf-*, *ʾaṣhu:f-*, *ʾaṣa:hif* etc.). Examples: *ʾ-hgr* < *hgr* 'city'; *ʾ-mlk* < *mlk* 'king'; *ʾnmr* < *nmr* 'leopard'.

ʾ-ṣhf-t: *sʾbʾt* < *ʾ-sʾbʾ-t* 'military expedition', *ʾ-xrf-t* < *xrf* 'year'; *ʾ-ṣhf-w*: *ʾ-δkr-w* < *δkr* 'male'.

mṣhf: most often from *mṣhft*, e.g. *mybb* < *mybt* 'defensive work', *mṣdk* < *mṣdkt* 'documentary proof'; also from *mṣhf*: *msʾbʾ* < *msʾbʾ* 'way, road'; *mṣhf-t*: from *mṣhf – mhfḍ-t* < *mhfḍ* 'tower', *mkbr-t* < *mkbr* 'grave, tomb'.

External and internal plural markers may combine as in *ʾ-ḥrr-t* 'freeborn wom-
en' < **ḥr-t* (cf. m. *ʾhrr* < *ḥr*), (?) *ʾ-mlk-t* 'queens' < *mlk-t* 'queen'. A noun often has two or more broken plurals. Thus, about seven (!) forms of plural of *xrf* 'year' are attested; many of them are quoted above. A few nouns are thought to have sup-pletive plurals (*ʾdm* < *ʿbd* 'client', possibly *ʾsʾd* < *sʾ/ʾysʾ* 'man'). Some "plural of plurals" are probably attested, in *ʿbd* 'client' ~ *ʾdm* 'clients' ~ *ʾd-y-m-t/*

ʾd-w-m-t 'groups of clients'.

Case

The Sayhadic case system remains practically unknown since in most cases the writing system did not mark case endings. We are strongly inclined to think that *-w* of the Sabean external plural construct *bnw* 'sons' is in most cases a nominative marker, while *-y* in *bny* (not followed by a pronominal suffix) marks the oblique case: *bnw Grt ... hqnyw* 'the sons of (the clan) *Grt* ... have dedicated' [J561,1–2] vs. (in the same inscription): *wfy ʾdm-hw bny Grt* 'the well-being of his servants, the sons of (the clan) *Grt*' [lines 14–15]. Some exceptions are attested (though still less than ten percent), but most of these exceptions appear either to come from peripheral areas or to be relatively late (since the third century CE only). The same distribution might be supposed with respect to Qatabanian *ʾlhw/ʾlhy* (const.) 'gods of'.

Adjectives

The most frequent adjectival pattern is *ṣhf*, e.g. *rḥḳ* 'far', *ṭhr* 'pure', *fs²ʾ* 'contagious, epidemic'. *Nisbas* in *-y*, derived from common nouns, toponyms and ethnonyms, are also common, *ḳyl-y* 'that belonging to *ḳayls* (heads of tribes)' < *ḳyl*, *mʿrb-y* 'western' < *mʿrb* 'west', *s¹bʾ-y* 'Sabean' < *s¹bʾ* 'Saba'' The singular feminine marker *-t* is attested in adjectives mostly in *nisbes*, e.g. *s²ms¹-hw ms²rḳy-t-n* 'his sun-goddess, the eastern one' [C572,2–3], but see also *ḳdm-t* in *b-ʿδθt-hmw ḳdm-t-n* 'according to their previous demand' [C541,94].

Both external and broken masculine plurals are attested for adjectives, thus *ʾwld-m hnʾ-m* [e.g. C352,10] beside *ʾwld-m hnʾ-n* [e.g. F88,4] 'healthy children'. Broken plurals from *nisbas* are very widespread; most of them employ triconsonantal roots even when the adjective has more than three consonants, e.g. *ʾḥmr* 'Himyarites' < *ḥmyry*; *ʾṣrḥ* 'Sirwahites' < *ṣrwḥy* and even *ʾʾδn* 'Maʾdhinites' < *mʾδny*. Feminine external plural in *-t* is probably attested in *hnʾ-t bn ʾθrbhmw* 'pleasing [crops] from their lands' [R3966,9].

Forms of gradation are not found, with a possible exception of Minean *ʾ-ṣnʿ* 'the strongest' in *kwnt δt gzytn ʾṣnʿ kl gz[...]* 'this decree is the strongest among all the de[crees]' [R3307,3]. For this pattern cf. also *ʾ-ʾxr* 'other' > 'another time' and *ʾ-ḳdm* 'previous' (beside *ḳdm*).

Deictics

There are two sets of forms for remote demonstratives. The first series is employed when the noun is syntactically in the nominative.

In non-nominative position a *-t* ending appears, thus *hgbʾy l-ʾlmḳh hy-t ʾrḍn* 'they (du.) handed over to [the god] *ʾlmḳh* that land' [C376,10–11]; *bn hw-t brθn* 'from that campaign' [J636,38-39]; Qat. *b-s¹my-t mḳmnyhn* 'at those two meetings' [R3566,10].

Demonstratives precede the nouns they qualify (usually definite). *hʾ θyln* 'that lava flow' [C323,3]; Qat. *δtn ʾs¹ṭrn* 'these inscriptions' [e.g. R3856,5]. They may

Table 12.3 Nearer demonstratives

		Singular	Dual	Plural
Sab.	m.	ẟn	ʾln, ẟyn	ʾln
	f.	ẟt		ʾlt
Min.	m.	ẟn		ʾhl, ʾhlt, ʾhlty
	f.	ẟt		
Qat.	m.	ẟn		ẟtn, ẟtw
	f.	ẟt		

Table 12.4 Remote demonstratives

		Singular	Dual	Plural
Sab.	m.	hʾ, hwʾ	hmy	hmw
	f.	hʾ, hyʾ	hmy	hn
Qat.	m.	s¹w	s¹my	s¹m
	f.	s¹y		
Min.	m.	s¹w-t (? oblique)		s¹m
	f.			s¹mt (?)

be the subjects in nominal clauses (the nominal predicate usually in the absolute state): *ʾlt ʾhgrm w-ʾbḍʿm gnʾ ... Krbʾl* 'these are the towns and territories which *Krbʾl* walled' [R3946,1]; Qat. *w-ẟn ʾbyt wʾrḍt ḳny w-ʿs¹y w-s²ʾm Yẟmrmlk* 'and these are houses and lands which *Yẟmrmlk* has acquired, and took into possession and bought' [R3858,5–6].

Numerals

Cardinals

Sayhadic cardinal numerals from one to ten exhibit two forms, namely with *-t* ending and without it; in the list quoted below the former is given first.

1 *ʾḥd/ʾḥt, ʾḥdy*. In Qatabanian *ṭd/ṭt* and *ʿs¹tn-m*, in Minean *ʿs¹t* (beside *ʾḥd*; treated as 11 by some scholars).

2 *θny/θnty, θty, θt*; Qat. *θnw*. Note also *klʾy* (*kly*), f. *klʾty*, e.g. *kly tʾdmynhn* 'the two rebellions' (*tʾdm* in the dual det.).

3 *s²lθ/s²lθt* (archaic Sab., Qat., f. *s²hlθt* in Min.); the rest of Sab. *θlθ/θlθt*; Hadr. *s²lθ* (*s²ls³*)/*s²lθt* (*s²ls³t*).

4 *ʾrbʿ/ʾrbʿt*.

5 *xms¹/xms¹t*.

6 *s¹dθ/s¹dθt* (archaic Sab., Min. and Qat.; *s¹θ/s¹θt* the rest of Sab.).

7 *s¹bʿ/s¹bʿt*.

8 *θmny/θmnyt* (archaic Sab.); *θmn/θmnt, θmt* (the rest of Sab.).

9 *ts¹ʿ/ts¹ʿt*.

10   ‘s²r/‘s²rt.
11   ’hd ‘s²r.
12   θny ‘s²r etc.

Note that ‘s²r in these forms is invariable and does not depend on the gender of the enumerate (e.g. ’rbᶜ-‘s²r and ’rbᶜt-‘s²r).

Twenty is ‘s²ry, the rest of the decades are formed by adding -y to the respective form in the first decade (θlθy ‘30’, xms¹y ‘50’) etc. In Minean forms endings in -hy are attested, thus ’rbᶜhy ‘40’; cf. also Hadr. ts¹ᶜhy ‘90’. The order of elements in compound numerals (each preceded by w-) ascends from units to thousands (see examples below).

Forms with -t occur with masculine nouns, forms with zero ending with feminine ones (exceptions are 1, 2, 11 and 12). The noun counted, always in the plural (except for 1 and 2), appears after the numeral. As a rule, numerals up to 100 are in the construct state, the noun in the absolute with mimation: θlθt ’wrxm ‘three months’, θlθ ’brkm ‘three rainy seasons’ < brk (f.), Qat. ṭd ‘s²r ’nxlm ‘eleven palm groves’; the noun without -m: Min. xms¹ ’mh ‘five cubits’ (sg. ’mt), Hadr. θmnwt ’fhd ‘eight cheetahs’. If the noun is definite (rarely found) the numeral also has a -n: θlθt-n ’ṣlm-n ‘the three statues’. ‘100’ is m’t (pl. m’, m’n, m’t, m’nhn; Min. m’t, m’h, Hadr. m’h, Qat. m’t). ‘1,000’ is ’lf (pl. ’’lf). In most cases hundreds and thousands are in the absolute state with mimation, so that the numeral should not be regarded as the possessed, but rather as an apposition: xms¹ m’tm w-θlθt ’’lfm ’s¹dm ‘3,500 men’ [J665,29–30]. Note an opposite case (the hundred in the construct state) in xms¹ w-ᶜs²ry wm’t ’frs¹m ‘125 horsemen’ [J665,30–31].

Ordinals

The syntax of ordinals, which in most cases look like the corresponding cardinals (i.e. s²lθl-t, xms¹/-t etc.; ‘first’ – kdm – is an exception), is in all respects identical to that of adjectives. However, they may precede the noun which they qualify (especially if it is in the absolute state), cf. θnym/θlθm ywmm ‘second/third day’ versus xms¹n rbᶜn ‘the fourth district’ [C435,3–4], xrf Wdd’l … s¹dθn ‘the sixth year of [the eponym] Wdd’l’ [NNAG11,11–12].

Fractions and Distributives

‘Half’ is probably attested as fkh in fkhm w-θlθ blṭm δ-rḍym ‘three and a half’ blṭ-coins of full weight’ [G11361,2]. Other fractions are used extensively. Their form is ṣhf from the consonantal root of the respective cardinal, e.g. rbᶜ ‘one-quarter’, s¹bᶜ ‘one-seventh’ etc. (note Min. s²lwθ in ᶜd s²lwθ hgrn ‘up to one-third of the city’ (?) [R2774,2]). The plural of this pattern is ’ṣhf; it seems that fractions may agree both as masculine and feminine: contrast ’ht ‘s²r ‘one-tenth’ [R4995,1]and (Qat.) s²lθt ’xms¹m ‘three fifths’ [J343A,3–4]. Of interest is Sab. mxms¹t ‘one-fifth (pl.)’. An interesting way of expressing fractions consists in using ’ṣbᶜ ‘finger’, e.g. ’ṣbᶜm bn θmny ’ṣbᶜ ‘one finger from eight fingers’, i.e. ‘one-eighth’ [C640,2].

Distributives are expressed by the repetition of the cardinals, e g. (Qat.) $'s^2r$ $'s^2r$ *xbṣtm mṣ'm l-ṭt ṭt ywmm* 'ten coins of full value for each day' [R3854,6–7]. Note $s^2l\theta t$-$'\delta$ 'for the third time' [e.g. C366] (cf. Arabic *ḥi:na-'iδin* 'at that time').

Verb

Root

Consonantal roots may be classified into "sound" and "weak." Sound verbs have three permanent radicals though a few have four (Qat. *fdfd* 'to expand, improve'). Weak verbs contain *w* or *y* as one of the radicals, namely I*w/y*, II*w/y* and III*w/y*. Verbs I*n* and verbs with the second and third radicals identical also exhibit some special features.

Themes

Of course, neither *ṣaḥḥafa* nor *ṣa:ḥafa* themes can be distinguished in writing from the basic theme *ṣhf*. The existence of at least one of them can easily be proved by many semantically contrasting pairs like *yf'* 'to raise up, to set up' ~ *yf'* 'go up, rise', *xṭ'* 'to commit a sin, an offense' ~ *xṭ'* 'to make amends for a sin'; *kwn* 'to be, to exist' ~ *kwn* 'to go to help'.

A theme *ṣḥḥf* is attested in Minean: *'xxr* 'to impose' (also *'xr*); *'lly* 'to raise, to lift', *fnnw* 'to send, to credit goods', *frr'* 'to lift', s^1kky 'to irrigate fields', *ẓwwr* 'to wall something', impf. *ymhhr-* 'to make a payment'. This theme is sometimes compared with the Arabic theme II (*kattaba*, reconstructed also for Sayhadic, see above); according to this suggestion, the graphic doubling of the second radical may represent its phonetic gemination (as in Arabic). We know, however, that a theme *kata:taba* (*kätatäbä*) is attested in Ethiopian (the so-called "frequentative"), but the scarcity of Minean examples prevents us from drawing definitive conclusions.

The basic meaning of the *h*-theme (s^1- in non-Sabean Sayhadic) is the causative: *h-s¹ṭr* 'to commit to writing' ~ *s¹ṭr* 'to write'; *h-wrd* 'to bring troops into the field' ~ *wrd* 'to go down; to fall upon the enemy', Qat. s^1-*gzm* 'to cause to decide' ~ *gzm* 'to decide'. If the simple theme denotes a state, the *h*-theme may have a resultative causative meaning: *htlf* 'to destroy' ~ *tlf* 'to be struck dead, to perish'; Min. s^1mlk 'to make/proclaim a king' ~ Qat. *mlk* 'to rule, to be a king'.

Two *t*-themes are attested, namely *ṣ-t-ḥf* and *t-ṣhf*. Their primary significance is reflexive and passive, presumably for **ṣaḥafa* and **ṣaḥḥafa* respectively.

Reflexive: *ḥ-t-my* 'to protect oneself' (~ *ḥmy* 'to protect'); *γ-t-s¹l* 'to wash oneself'; *t-ṣn'* 'to fortify oneself' (~ *ṣn'* 'to fortify'); *s¹-t-ky* 'to quench one's thirst' (~ *s¹ky* 'to irrigate').

Passive: s^2-*t-rḥ* 'to be saved' (~ $s^2rḥ$ 'to deliver, to save'), *t-'tml'-t-tm* 'to be mustered (~ *'tm* 'to bring together'); s^1-*t-my* 'to be named' (~ s^1my 'to name').

These themes often appear as medial: *x-t-dm* 'to get fields cultivated'; ts^2ym 'to appoint somebody (direct object) for oneself' (~ s^2ym 'to appoint'), $t-s^1ṭr/s^1$-*t-ṭr* 'to write an inscription (direct object) for oneself' (~ $s^1ṭr$ 'to write'). Sometimes the meaning is only slightly differentiated from that of the basic theme, e.g. s^1-t-kf 'to build a roof [for oneself]' (~ s^1kf 'to roof'). Some t-shf and s-t-hf forms are reciprocal and may represent a *$tasa:hafa$ theme: $thrg$ (also $htrg$) 'to beat one another, to fight' (~ hrg 'to kill'); t^csr 'struggle with one another'.

The original (causative reflexive) meaning of the s^1t- theme may be found in Minean s^1t-s^ck 'to inform oneself' (~ s^1-s^ck 'to announce'). However, much more often this theme denotes seeking, asking for something e.g. s^1t-yd^c 'to seek oracular knowledge' (h-yd^c 'to make known'); s^1t-ws^{2c} 'to seek favor' (~ h-ws^{2c} 'to grant favor'); s^1t-$ml^{\jmath}$ 'to demand oracular response (~ h-$ml^{\jmath}$ 'to grant a request'), s^1t-zr 'to ask to visit' (~ Arabic zwr 'to visit').

Voice
The distinction between active and passive must have been expressed by internal apophonic changes, thus having no representation in writing. Yet it is easily detected syntactically: $mktr$ s^1rk bn $mhrmn$ 'incense altar which was stolen from the temple' [C30,4–5] vs. δ-ys^1rkn $mhrm$-hw 'one who robs his temple' [C522,2]; wld l-hmw bnm δkrm 'a male child was born to them' [J669,8-9] vs. γlm $wldt$-hw $Mgd^{\jmath}lt$ 'a boy to whom $Mgd^{\jmath}lt$ gave birth' [C19,7–8].

Tenses
There are two basic types of conjugation, prefixal and suffixal, traditionally called "imperfect" and "perfect." Only forms of the 3rd person are found in monumental texts; some 2nd person forms are attested in minuscule documents. The 3rd person forms are as follows (on N-imperfects see p. 235):

	Singular			Dual			Plural		
	Pf.	Impf.	N-impf.	Pf.	Impf.	N-impf.	Pf.	Impf.	N-impf.
m.	-Ø	y-	y-..-n	-y	y-..-y	y-..-nn	-w	y-..-w	y-..-nn
				(Qat. -w)				(Qat. y-..-wn)	
f.	-t	t-	t-..-n	-ty	t-..-y	t-..-nn	Qat. -n		t-..-nn

Plural and dual endings of the perfect are extremely rare in Minean so that the respective forms coincide with the singular. After l- (see p. 236) prefixal y- is occasionally dropped (e.g. minuscule l-$hslhnn$ 'may they both put in order ...' [YM11729,2–3], contrast l-$yhslhnn$ [YM11732,2] in a completely identical context).

No 1st person forms are attested (see, however, $br^{\jmath}$-k-h $^{\jmath}n$ (?) 'it is myself who built it' etc. in a peculiar (Sab.?) inscription from the Wadi Shirja:n [J2353]). The following 2nd person verbal forms are attested in published minuscule texts: pf. s^1tr-k 'you wrote', shf-kmw 'you (pl.) wrote' etc.; impf. t-$ml^{\jmath}$ 'you pay', t-shf 'you write' etc.; with -n: t-s^1tnhr-n 'you make a sacrifice'; t-s^1t^cdd-n-n 'you (pl.) check your calculations'.

The perfect denotes both immediate and historical past action: $Yhd^{\jmath}$ Ykf ... $br^{\jmath}$ ... byt-hw 'Yehuda Yakkuf has built his house' [B.Ašwall,1], $hl\theta$ ... $bwrx$ δ-$Mlyt$

δ-xrf Wdd'l 'he was ill in the month δ-Mlyt of the year of [the eponym] Wdd'l'
[J613,9–10]; a durative action in the past hws¹y-hmw b-ml't s¹b't xryftm 'they
gave [French donnaient] them assignments during seven years' [J647,26–27]; seldom a state without restriction of time: rḥkt b'rm δt bn-hw ys¹t'bnn 'the well from
which they take water, is far' [Hakir 2 = Gr40,2]. An example of optative perfect
may be found in w-nkrm kwn δn mṣdḳn 'and let this document be annulled' [Gl
1533,11–12]. For the perfect in prohibitions, see p. 238.

The imperfect denotes an action in the future: w-yz'n hwfyn 'ṣlmm 'and he will
continue giving statues [J736,11] (also future in the past, e.g. w-s²ft-hmw 'lmkh
θhwn k-y'thdn brwy-hw 'and 'lmkh θhwn promised them that he would protect his
two sons' [J716,6–7]); an action without restriction of time: s¹ṭrnhn yrmyn b'rn
'the two inscriptions overlook the well' [J539,4–5]. The imperfect preceded by w-
is widely used to denote actions in the past which are regarded as consequences of
other past actions (the so-called "consecutive construction"): w-b'ww b-llyn ḥyrt
'ḥbs²n w-yhrgn bn 'ḥbs²n 'rb' m'nm 's¹dm 'they attacked the camp of the Habashites at this night and killed of the Habashites 400 men' [J631,29–31]. In middle Sabean the imperfect without w- sometimes denotes past actions without any
consecution: w-l-θlθm ywmm ybrrn 'and on the third day [some of the tribe ...]
came into the open [to fight]' [J631,28].

In Qatabanian the indicative imperfect is usually preceded by b-: b-ys¹fd
xr[f]myw 'he will complete two years [in office]' [R3688,3–4].

Moods

Monumental texts yield no imperative forms (a possible exception may be tḳṣw in
tḳṣw 'brm wθnn 'avoid surpassing the boundary stone' [R4088,1–2]). A few imperative forms (sometimes augmented with -n) may be found in minuscule documents: f-hmy hfn-k f-t'lm-n b-hmy 'as for these two [documents], sign them both
[t'lm-n b-hmy] as soon as they reach you' [YM11749,2]; w-'nt f-s³xl-n 'bd δ-
Dwrm 'and you, take care about the client of δ-Dwrm' [YM11742,2].

In Sabean the imperfect is often augmented with -n (exact forms on p. 234).
Though the exact distribution of N-forms and simple imperfects is still a matter of
dispute, it may be observed that the N-forms are predominant in subordinate
clauses (including relative), and in the jussive (see below): 's²r y's²rnn-hw 'the
tithe which they cede to him' [G11438,5], w-mẓ'-hmw mnδrm ... k-yhṣrn b-'ly-
hmw Krb'l Byn 'and a warning reached them ... that Krb'l Byn was marching off
against them' [J643,26–27]; but see also w-bn-hw f-ybḥḍn mlkn 'and it was from
it that the king made a sortie' [J576,4].

The prefix conjugation (alone or preceded by l- (k in Minean, l or h- in
Hadramitic)) is often used as jussive–optative. It is impossible to say whether
there was some formal difference between forms employed in such cases, and the
normal forms of the imperfect. Examples: w-b-δt ys³fn-hmw 'lmkhw wldm 'and
because of that, may 'lmkhw grant them more children' [J558,4]; w-l-yz'n 'lmkh
hwfyn-hmw 'and may 'lmkh continue protecting them' [J584,4]; w-l-yr'y θwrm
'let the bulls be pastured' [Gr/Hadaka:n,l].

An example of negative imperative (*'l* + *n*-impf.): *w-'l t'yrn 'ys'n* 'do not do harm to this man' [minuscule YM11742,3].

Infinitives and Participles
The infinitive usually looks like the sg. 3m. of the perfect (e.g. *ṣhf, hṣhf, tṣhf* etc.) with the exception of **ṣahhafa*-theme, the infinitive of which is *tṣhf(-t)*. In Sabean *-n* is sometimes added to this bare stem, but its use is in most cases optional. Mimated infinitives are attested in Qatabanian: *bn wfr w-'s²k w-s¹kh-m w-s¹'hd-m θrbt-s¹* '... from cultivating, and tilling, and setting in order, and taking care of his field' [R3854,4–5].

The infinitive may appear in the position of the direct object: *xmr-hw 'lmkh hrg lb'n 'lmkh* 'allowed him to kill the lion' [Ry538,28] and with prepositions (very often with *l* to denote purpose: *w-yns²' 's¹m l-mt' kny-hw* 'and every man rose in order to protect his property' [R3945,2]).

Much more often, however, the infinitive functions as a finite verbal form. In this case the (nominal or pronominal) subject which follows it seems to be in the nominative: *xmr₁-hmw₂ 'tw₃ w-s¹twfyn₄ hw' ₅ brkn₆ b-wfym₇* 'he [the deity] granted₁ them₂ the coming₃ and the taking place₄ of that₅ monsoon₆ without accidents₇' [E22/1]; *s¹t'wln hw' w-'kwl-hw* 'the return of him and his kayls' (lit. 'the returning, he and …') [J577,15].

The infinitive is used in the so-called "infinitive chain," a series of homogeneous verbal predicates, in which only the first member is a finite verbal form. The remaining verbs are in the infinitive, with or without *-n* (the last member of the infinitive chain usually has *-n*). Examples: *t-nxyt w-tnδrn l-'lh-h* 'she confessed and did penance to her god' [R3957,2–4]; *w-ykm'w w-hb'ln hgrnhn* 'and they overthrew and seized the two cities' [J576,8]; *w-θbrw w-hb'ln w-km' w-hs¹b'n* 'and they destroyed, seized, overthrew and forced to capitulate' [J576,4].

The patterns of active and passive participles of the basic theme are *ṣhf* and *mṣhf* respectively: *s¹b'm l-sm Rhmnn* 'fighting for the name of [the god] Rahma:n' [Ry520,8], *mhmy* 'irrigated' [in J550,1]. For a passive participle *ṣhf* see probably Hadramitic *m'ltn* in *s¹b' bhhtm w-'rktm m'ltm* 'seven [votive] phalli with torn out testicles' [RbI/84no. 253a–e,2–4] (cf. Arabic *m'l* 'to castrate'). Both active and passive participles of derived themes are poorly attested. For the causative theme see Qat. *ms¹nkrm bn brθ-s¹* 'one moving [the object] from its place' [e.g. J350,4], Min. *ms¹mt'm W[nh]s¹tb w-kny-s¹w k-Wd* 'consecrating Wnhs¹tb and his property to Wadd' [R3602,6–7]. *mtrhm* in *Rhmnn mtrhmn* 'the Merciful Rahma:n' [F74,3], might be considered a participle of the *t*-theme, but it is likely to have been borrowed from Hebrew/Aramaic.

Verbal Forms from Weak Roots
In the imperfect of the basic theme from roots Iw, the first radical is dropped: *yhb < whb* 'to give'; *yrd < wrd* 'to go down' etc. Conversely, the first radical is preserved in corresponding forms from roots Iy, e.g. *yyf' < yf'* 'to go up'. As for the derived themes, where we deal with contraction rather than with simple deletion,

forms with and without *w* are attested indiscriminately, though forms preserving *w* are somewhat more frequent: *hwfy/hfy* 'to grant', *hwθḳ/hθḳ* 'to guarantee' etc.

In verbal forms from roots II*w/y* the weak radical may or may not be preserved. The distribution of these forms is still under review. Those with *w/y* dropped are evidently more common: *gz* 'to flow, pass' (contrast sg. 3f. *gwzt*); *hḵḥ* (also *hḵwḥ*) 'to finish off'; *tḵwm* 'to rise with a claim', *ts²m* 'to appoint' (the root *s²ym*); *s¹tᶜn* 'to seek help' (the root ᶜ*wn*). In the imperfect of the basic theme non-contracted forms do occur (*ykwn* 'to be', *ymwt* 'to die') but not in the causative theme (see, however, Min. *ys¹ḥwr* 'to ordain').

Weak consonants are usually preserved in verbal forms with roots III*w/y*: pf. *ʾtw* (pl. *ʾtww*) 'to come', *ḵny* (f. *ḵnyt*, pl. m. *ḵnyw*) 'to acquire'; impf. *yʾtw*, *yḵny*; *h*-theme: pf. *hʾtw*, impf. *yhʾtw* 'to bring', pf. *hḵny*, impf. *yhḵny* 'to dedicate'. Forms with last radical dropped are relatively rare; see *yʾt* (beside *yʾtw*); *hrḍ* (beside *hrḍw*) 'to satisfy', *hgd* 'to make a grant of land' < *gdy* (cf. *gdyt* 'grant of land').

Adverbs and Other Parts of Speech

Nouns (presumably in the accusative with -*m*) used as adverbs are discussed on p. 227. Adverbs proper are very rare (probably *θmt* 'there').

The following are the most common prepositions: *l-* 'for, to, until', (*k-* in Minean, *h-* in Hadramitic); *b-* 'in (local, temporal), by , with', *bn* 'from' (*mn* in inscriptions from Haram: *mn mḥrmn* 'from the temple' [= 548,8] (see p. 221), *byn* 'between', ᶜ*m* '(together) with', ᶜ*ly* 'on, above', *ḥ(n)g* 'according to', ᶜ*d(y)* 'until, in', ᶜ*br* 'towards'. Compound prepositions (mostly with *b-* and *bn*) are very widespread in Sayhadic, e.g. *b-*ᶜ*ly* 'above', *bn-*ᶜ*m* 'from' etc. In Sabean -*n* is often added to some prepositions without appreciable difference in meaning, e.g. ᶜ*m-n*, *ḥg-n*, ᶜ*br-n* etc. In Qatabanian forms with -*w* generally correspond to Sabean forms with -*y*, thus ᶜ*lw*, ᶜ*dw*.

Some enclitic particles are attested (especially often in Qatabanian): -*mw* (-*m*), Min., Qat. -ʾ*y*. Though in most cases their exact function remains obscure, some examples of evident semantic contrast between forms with and without enclitics may be quoted: *b-mw hwt wrxn* 'in that very month' [e.g. J653,13–14] versus *b-hwt wrxn* 'in that month' [e.g. J627,8]. Note the deictic particle *rʾ* 'behold!'.

Syntax

Word Order

In sentences with a non-verbal predicate (which may be a noun, an adjective, a deictic pronoun or a prepositional phrase), the first position is most often occupied by the subject, though the opposite is not infrequent, especially in decrees. Examples:

(Qat.) *w-ṭbnn s¹m s²ᶜbn ms³ wdn w-ṭbnn* 'and the landowners are (*s¹m* 'they' is used as a copula) the community, the council and the landowners [themselves]' [R3566,5];

θhrn … s¹xlm w-nfḳm 'the document … is binding and having legal force' [C376,12–13];

b-ᶜly-hw θwrm 'there is a [bronze] bull on it' [J713,6];

vs. (Qat.) *ʾs¹dm ᶜlmw b- δn ftḥn … Yṣrᶜm δ-yrbm* [etc.] 'Yṣrᶜm δ-yrbm etc. are the people who signed this decree' [R3566,23–24];

f-brʾm mhš̌ʾmn 'and the seller is not guilty' [R3910,6].

In verbal sentences the subject usually heads the sentence if it is at the beginning of an inscription: *ʾmtʾlmḳh s¹bʾytn … hḳnyt … ʾʾmtʾlmḳh*, the Sabean woman, has dedicated …' [J706,1–2]. Otherwise the normal word order is VSO: *w-tḳnᶜ Yrm … ʾmr-hw* 'and Yrm convinced his lords' [C315,8–9]. The indirect object usually comes before the direct one: *hwfy l-mrʾ-hmw hḳnyt-hw* 'he has given to their lord his offering' [J664,7–8].

Any part of the sentence may be put before the verbal predicate for topicalization. The verb in this case is usually introduced by *f-*: *w-hmw f-ḥmdw xl w-mḳm Tʾlb Rymm* 'as for them, they praised the strength and the power of *Tʾlb Rymm*' [C2,7–8]; *w-bᶜd-hw f-yṣbʾw b-ᶜly ʾrḍ Mhʾnfm* 'it was after this that they waged the war against the land of [the tribe] *Mhʾnfm* [J576,6].

Agreement Rules
Qualifiers agree with nouns they qualify in gender, number and state (see pp. 225, 230, 230 and 232).

An agreement in gender and number between subject and predicate is normally observed: *s²ftt-hw ʾmt-hw* 'his maidservant promised him' [J717,4–5]; *tʾwly mrʾy-hmw* 'their two lords returned' [J581,5].

Pluralis majestatis is common in Himyarite (but not Sabean) royal inscriptions: *S²rḥbʾl Yᶜfr mlk S¹bʾ w-δ-Rydn … ᶜδbw ᶜrmn ᶜS²rḥbʾl Yᶜfr*, the [Himyarite] king of Saba' and Dhu:-Rayda:n etc. have repaired the dam' [C540,1–6]. Verbs in the plural instead of the dual occur sporadically in archaic Sabean (*w-ḳwlnhn … l-ykwnw b-ᶜly mbᶜl Tʾlb* 'and let the 2 ḳayls be in charge of the property of [the god] *Tʾlb*)' [R4176,5], whereas in middle Sabean this becomes a marked trend, thus *ʾgrm w-S²rḥm δy δ-Byn hqnyw … ʾʾgrm and S²rḥm*, both of (dual!) [the clan] *δ-Byn*, have dedicated (pl.) …' [J720,1–2]. The verb *kwn* 'to be, to occur' is often used without agreement with the subject, e.g. *xwm w-ᶜws¹ w-mwtt kwn b-ʾrḍn* 'pestilence, plague and epidemic which took place in the land' [J645,13–14].

Assertions/Negations
Sabean *kn*, Minean *s²kn* introducing legal documents might be regarded as asseverative 'thus, certainly'. The same may be assumed for such combinations of particles as *l-k-δ(y), k-δ-m* etc. See further *l-* in *mn l-yhmr[n]* 'indeed, whoever sells corn' [C603a,3]; Qat. *n-* in *n-l ys¹tfḥwn* 'indeed, let them be governed' [R3691,5].

The most common negative particle is *ʾl*. It is used with the narrative perfect and imperfect (*ʾl ḥyw l-hw wldm* 'a child of his did not survive' [Ry375,4]; Qat. *ʾl s¹knw w-ʾl b-ys¹knwn* 'they have not enforced and they will not enforce' [R3566,14]); in indirect prohibitions, also both with the perfect and the imperfect (*ʾl s¹ʾlw* 'let them not lay claim' [e.g. C611,5], *ʾl yʿtnn* 'let them not neglect' [R4176,1], Qat. *ʾl b-ys²tyt* 'may it not be sold' [R4337B,19]). For the so-called "generic negation" see *ʾl ʾs¹* [e.g.F70,3] followed by a verb 'nobody should ...' (lit. 'no man should ...'); also *ʾl l-hmw b-hw kl mwm* 'there is no water for them in it [the besieged castle]' [E13/10].

The negative *lhm/lm* is found in Minean: *lhm ʿrb* 'let him not enter' [R2803,1]. In texts from Haram the negative *lm* is attested (*lm yγts¹l* 'he did not wash himself' [e.g. C533,4–5]), which is thought to be a loan from Arabic. The negative particle *dʾ* (probably borrowed from Himyaritic) in some late texts: *dʾ gbʾw* 'they did not return' [C541,50]. Sab. *γyr* in *γyr ṯhrm* 'not pure' [C523,6] also deserves mention.

A possible example of an indirect question may be *mrḍm fs²ʾm δ-ʾl mn s²ʿr k-m-hn hʾ ḥgr-hw* 'a contagious disease about which nobody knew what (*k-m-hn*) its remedy was' [J720,12–14].

Coordination, Conditionals
Coordination (both between single words and clauses) is expressed by *w-* which practically always precedes every element of the chain (except the first one): *b-wfym w-ḥmdm w-yhrm ...* 'in safety, glory, renown etc.' [J616,29]. Only for Qatabanian do we have some exceptions: *S²hr Hll ... kθr kyn rs²w ʿmm θntm* 'S²hr Hll collected [sacred] taxes, was a *kyn*-official, performed priestly functions for a second year' [e.g. R3540,1–3]). *w-* is also used as disjunctive and adversative: *δ-rḥq w-qrb* 'which is far or near' [e.g. J578,41]. Note also disjunctive *ʾw* (*f-ʾw*): *ʿbdm f-ʾw ʾmtm* 'a male or female slave' [R3910,3].

Conditional clauses are introduced by *hm/hmy* (the latter especially in minuscule) 'if'. Apodoses may be preceded by *w-* or *f-*: *hm ʾl tʾxδ f-ḥlt nfs¹-hw l-δ yhrgn-hw* 'and if he is not arrested, anyone may kill him' [R4088,4–6]; minuscule *hmy krb l-k s¹lʿm δ-glglnm ... l-tmlʾ s¹lʿtn ʾbdlm* 'if he delivers to you cargoes of sesame ... may you pay for this merchandise with an equivalent' [YM11738,4–7]. Indefinite pronouns (see p. 225) may imply some shade of conditionality: *w-l-wzʾ ʾlmkh xmr ʿbd-hw ... γmmm ʾhn-mw ys¹bʾnn* 'and may *ʾlmkh* grant his servant booty wherever they go on campaign' [C407,27–28]; *w-yzʾn hwfyn ʾṣlmm k-mhn-mw yxmrn-hw ʾδkrm hnʾn* 'he will continue giving statues whenever (*k-mhn-mw*) he (the deity) grants him healthy male (children)' [J736,11–13].

Subordination
The conjunction *k-* (also combinations like *k-δ, k-n* etc.) is employed to introduce object clauses: *kwmw k-ʾl kwnw l-bny ʿθkln* 'they claimed that they did not belong to the clan ʿθkln' [F76,7]. Final and causal clauses may be introduced in the same way: *tkhw ... s²ʿbn δ-hgrn Mdrm ... k-yhgrnn ... δt brktn l-Nws²m* 'the community of the city *Mdrm* ... has ordered that they should reserve ... this cistern ... to the

exclusive use of [the goddess] *Nws²m*' [Rob Mašl,1–4]; *w-ḳds¹w bᶜt Mrb k-b-hw qs¹s¹m* 'they held a mass in the church of [the city] Maᵓrib, as there was a priest in it' [C541,66–67]. A widespread causal conjunction is *l-ḳbly* 'since, because': *l-ḳbly δ-hxbt brḳ xrf δ-xrf Tbᶜkrb* 'because the autumn monsoon of the year of (the eponym) *Tbᶜkrb* failed to come ...' [J653,5–6].

The following are the most common conjunctions of time and place:

> *ywm* 'when' (*ywm hwṣt kl gwm* ... 'when [lit. the day in which ...] he gave legal status to every community ...' [e.g. R3949])
>
> *mty* 'when' (Min., Qat.) (*mty yxdr xdrm* 'when someone establishes a trading stall' [R4337A,13])
>
> *bᶜdn δ-* 'after' (*bᶜdn δ-ᵓδnw b-ᵓs²ᶜbn* 'after they allowed the communities to depart' [C541,76])
>
> *ᶜdy* (*δ.../δt* ...) 'until' (*f-hṣrw ᶜdy δt mθᵓw ᶜdy brrn* 'and they marched until they reached the plain' [J576,5–6])
>
> *brθ* 'where' (*bn bhrm brθ hs²k-hw mrᵓ-hmw* 'from overseas where their lord sent him' [E28/1])

Relative clauses may be introduced by relative particles (see additional examples pp. 225 and 235) or be asyndetic. In the first case the antecedent is in the determinate state (or in the absolute state with mimation) while in the second it is usually in the construct state. Examples:

> *kl ᵓs¹dn w-ᵓnθn ᵓlw ys¹tmynn ᵓs¹lm w-*... 'all the men and women who are called *ᵓs¹lm* and ...' [F76,2–3]
>
> *ᵓḳny-hmw δ-ḳnyw w-yḳnynn* 'their possessions which they have acquired and will acquire' [C94,6]
>
> *hlθ ymrn-hw drm b-xrfm* 'disease which strikes him once a year' [J711,5–6]
>
> *kl ms¹bᵓ s¹bᵓw* 'all campaigns in which they took part' [e.g. C2,10–11]

If the antecedent is an indirect object (more seldom also a direct one) it may be reflected in the relative clause by the "resumptive pronoun": *b-mw ywmn δ-b-hw θhb-hmw* 'on the very day in which he returned (the answer) to them' [J616,19–20]; Qat. *kl ᵓfthm b-s¹m-ᵓl fth ... mlkn* 'all decrees which the king has not decreed ...' [R3566,15].

Copular and Possessive Expressions

In addition to personal pronouns (see p. 237), the verb *kwn* 'to be' often appears in the function of copula: *w-kwn δn wθnn wθn byn* ... 'and let this boundary stone be the boundary stone between ...' [C975,1–2]. For zero copula in nominal sentences see p. 237. Some possessive constructions with *l-* (also with *kwn* 'to be') are attested:

wtfn ... l-δ-S'mwy 'the land possession belongs to [the god] *δ-S'mwy*' [Ist7626,1];

l-kwn hmw ʾs'dn ... w-ʾnθn ... l-byt ... ʾ[m]rʾ-hn 'so that those men and women should belong to the house of their lords' [F76,4–5].

Acknowledgments

We are deeply grateful to Professor Dr. I. M. Diakonoff who kindly agreed to read our contribution and made many valuable suggestions and corrections. Our gratitude goes to Dr. S. A. Frantsuzoff for some important remarks concerning Hadramitic.

Reference

Beeston, A. F. L., M. A. Ghul, W. W. Müller, and J. Ryckmans. 1982. *Sabaic Dictionary (English–French–Arabic)*. Louvain-la-Neuve: Peeters; Beirut: Librairie du Liban.

Further Reading

Arbach, M. 1993. "Le Maḏābien: Lexique – Onomastique et Grammaire d'une langue de l'Arabie méridionale préislamique." Ph.D. dissertation, Université de Provence Aix Marseille I.

Bauer, G. M. 1966. *Jazyk južnoaravijskoj pis'mennosti* [The language of the South Arabian inscriptions]. Moscow: Nauka.

Beeston, A. F. L. 1984. *Sabaic Grammar*. Manchester: Manchester University Press.

Biella, Joan C. 1982. *Dictionary of Old South Arabic (Sabean Dialect)*. Chico, Calif.: Scholars Press.

Höfner, Maria. 1943. *Altsüdarabische Grammatik*. Leipzig: Harrassowitz.

Nebes, Norbert. 1987. "Zur Konstruktion von Subjekt und Objekt abhängiger Infinitive im Sabäischen." In *Ṣayhadica*, ed. C. Robin and M. Bāfaqīh. Paris: Paul Geuthner. 75–98.

Ricks, S. D. 1989. *Lexicon of Inscriptional Qatabanian*. Rome: Editrice Pontificio Istituto Biblico.

Ryckmans, Jacques, W. W. Müller and Y. M. Abdallah. 1994. *Textes du Yemen antique inscrites sur bois*. Louvain-la-Neuve: Institut Orientaliste.

13 Ge'ez (Ethiopic)

Gene Gragg

Ge'ez (*gə'əz*, self-designation, etymology uncertain) is the oldest attested member of the Ethiopic Semitic language family. It is presumably derived from one or more forms of South Semitic brought from Yemen, probably in the first half of the first millennium BCE. We know in fact that there were trade relations between the South Arabian city states and the Ethiopian coastal and highland regions, and a South Arabian colony existed not far from the later Ethiopian capital Aksum, paleographically dated to around 500 BCE by monumental inscriptions of the Sabean type. However it is not possible to derive Ethiopic Semitic from any attested form of Old South Arabian. One may presume that Ethiopic Semitic evolved out of a South Arabian-based trade lingua franca. The substratum languages in this development presumably belonged to the Cushitic language family, and a number of important early loanwords from Cushitic are evident in Ge'ez – but these are far from approximating the level of penetration of, say, English vocabulary by that of French at the time of Chaucer. Processes of piginization and creolization familiar from differentiation and development of language families elsewhere in the world undoubtedly played a role in the development of Ge'ez – for example in the systematization of the weak verb system and the regularization and partial lexicalization of the derivational class system noted below. However Ge'ez maintains a level of morphological complexity inconsistent with any radical pidginization: maintenance of a (reduced) case system, a large inventory of internal plurals, most of the major inflectional and derivational categories of South Semitic.

Ge'ez disappeared as a spoken language probably some time before the tenth century CE. However it continues today as the liturgical language of the Ethiopian Orthodox Church, and was the only official written language of Ethiopia practically up to the end of the nineteenth century. The corpus of written Ge'ez material can be conveniently divided into three periods.

Aksumite Inscriptions
The core of this corpus is formed by about a dozen longish royal inscriptions in Ge'ez (plus six in Greek), the most important of them from the king Ezana (perhaps mid-fourth century CE). Six of the Ge'ez inscriptions are written in the Old South Arabian alphabet, two in non-vocalized Ethiopic, and four in the earliest attestation of vocalized Ethiopic script. The earliest inscriptions of Ezana are pagan,

while the last few attest to the introduction of monotheism (presumably Christian) to the court at Aksum. There are also about thirty other short Aksumite inscriptions in vocalized and unvocalized Ethiopic – at least nine of them from a period before Ezana.

Ge'ez: Pre-1000 CE

Although there are few if any extant manuscripts earlier than the twelfth century, scholars have isolated a core of Ge'ez literature – the first texts drawn up to define and propagate Christianity in Ethiopia. These include the Ge'ez translation of the Bible and accompanying apocrypha, liturgical texts, some lives of saints, some patristic fragments, and a version of the monastic Rules of Pachomius. The texts are almost completely ecclesiastical in nature, and most of them are translations or adaptations from the Greek (which in turn may be a rendering of a Hebrew or Aramaic original). The linguistic value of these texts arises from the fact that they were drawn up when Ge'ez was still a spoken language, and they thus set the stylistic, lexical, and syntactic parameters for all subsequent use of Ge'ez.

Ge'ez: Post-1000 CE

After a very obscure period of isolation starting with the collapse of Byzantium in the Near East, and continuing during the first centuries of Islam, Ethiopia reestablished contact with Egypt – from that time until 1945 the Metropolitan (*abuna*) of the Ethiopian Church would be an Egyptian cleric appointed by the Patriarch of Alexandria. There was a new flourishing of ecclesiastical literature of all genres (much of it translated from the Arabic, in turn translated from Greek, Coptic, Syriac, or other sources). In addition, an original secular or court literature arose in the form of royal chronicles, legal texts, even a sort of national epic (the *Kəbrä Nägäst* 'Glory of Kings', an elaboration of the legend of Solomon and Sheba). A more popular magic literature also took shape, centered around the production of amulets and "magic scrolls" – a productivity that continued into the present century. Given the necessity of some knowledge of Ge'ez for many court and ecclesiastical careers, a church- and monastery- based standard curriculum of studies was established, to which we owe, among other things, our knowledge of the pronunciation tradition of Ge'ez.

Phonology

Our most direct source of evidence for Ge'ez phonology is the pronunciation tradition, supplemented by what is known about the phonologies of the Ethiopian Semitic languages still spoken today. Neither of these sources guarantees accurate information about the pronunciation of Ge'ez in the earliest sources. For the consonants at least, the fact that the writing system contains symbols for three consonants ($\acute{s}$, $\underline{h}$, $\d{d}$) which are distinguished neither in the traditional pronunciation nor in any of the modern languages makes it clear that the traditional pronunciation shows a state of the language later than that of the earliest writing system. Moreover, the traditional pronunciation, which, since the Middle Ages, has represented a court-influenced Amharicizing tradition, does not have a distinct phonological representation for two characters, *ḥ* and ʿ (pronounced as *h* and ʾ), which are preserved in Tigrinya and Tigré. (Anecdotal evidence indicates that distinct pronunciation of these consonants was considered, at least by literati and the clerical elite, as "rustic" and "peasant-like".) See p. 245 for the transcription values and probable nature of these consonants.

Three important aspects of phonological representation, however, are not accounted for in the writing system: stress, consonantal gemination, occurrence of /ə/ (as opposed to absence of vowel). No graphic representation of stress or gemination was ever developed in native Ge'ez texts; and the vocalic system uses the same modification of the basic consonantal signs to represent consonant followed by /ə/ and consonant followed by no vowel. For these phenomena we must rely wholly on a still imperfectly studied pronunciation tradition. In this chapter we will follow Leslau 1987 for stress, gemination, and shwa, to the extent that they are indicated there, otherwise Cohen 1921 and Makonnen 1984; Mittwoch 1926 notes a large number of additional gemination patterns which still need to be investigated.

Consonants
The consonant system of Ge'ez is shown below.

p	t		k	kʷ	ʿ	ʾ	
ṗ	ṭ		q	qʷ			
b	d		g	gʷ			
f	s	ś	ḫ	ḫʷ	ḥ	h	
	ṣ	ḍ					
	z						
m	n						
	r l						
w	y						

Labials: /f/ is the basic voiceless labial in Ge'ez (as in Arabic and South Arabian). /ṗ/, and the even more rare /p/, occur almost exclusively in loanwords, where they usually correspond to Greek π.

Emphatics: /ṗ, ṭ, ṣ, ḍ, q/ are all glottalized in Ge'ez, as in Ethiopic Semitic generally.

Sibilants: The consonants corresponding to the graphemes ⟨ś⟩ and ⟨ḍ⟩ have merged respectively with /s/ and /ṣ/ in the phonological system represented by the traditional pronunciation – and indeed in all modern Ethiopic Semitic. These two consonants are reflexes of a lateralized series (voiceless and glottalized) in Proto-Semitic, also attested in South Arabian. There is however no evidence either in the tradition or in Ethiopic Semitic what value these consonants may have had in Ge'ez. For ⟨ḍ⟩ the transcription value comes from the conventional representation of the etymologically corresponding segment in Arabic and Old South Arabian. *ś* is an older conventional representation of the Proto-Semitic voiceless lateral, and also of the grapheme which represents it in Hebrew. In some grammars and dictionaries, ⟨ś⟩ is transcribed as *š*, since it frequently corresponds etymologically to Arabic /š/. There are however some major problems with this. In the first place, it is not certain whether, or at what periods ⟨ś⟩ might have been pronounced as [š]. More seriously, this transcription could lead to confusion, since a genuine /š/ **did** develop in Ethiopic Semitic (mostly from palatalization of /s/), and a new grapheme for it, properly transcribed as *š* was created by adding a diacritic to the grapheme ⟨s⟩. Moreover, this ⟨š⟩ grapheme can occur in late Ge'ez texts, usually in contemporary personal or place names.

Laryngeals: /ḫ/ corresponds etymologically to a velar or uvular spirant in Akkadian, Arabic, and South Arabian. However in the Ge'ez pronunciation tradition and in Ethiopic Semitic generally, it has merged with /ḥ/. Presence or absence of glottal stop is not distinctive in initial position, although there is no way in the writing system to write a syllable-initial vowel without a preceding glottal stop (or glide if the preceding syllable ends in a vowel). Since it is not phonetically salient in the traditional pronunciation, no representation of initial glottal stop is given in this description. Note however the non-existence of a contrast between initial /ä/ and /a/ in the pronunciation tradition; the putative sequence # + /'/ + low vowel is usually written ⟨'ä⟩, but pronounced /a/. This is possibly connected with the laryngeal ("H") effect: /äH/ → /aH/ in syllable-final position (*yəsmaʿ* 'may he hear', versus paradigmatic *yəlbäs* 'may he wear'). The other important laryngeal effect is low vowel harmony across laryngeals: /əHä/ → /äHä/ (*yäḥärrəs* 'he plows', /äHə/ → /əHə/ (*yəməḥḥər* 'he is merciful') – both versus paradigmatic *yənäggər* 'he speaks'. These two effects account for most of the differences in the inflectional behavior of verbs whose roots contain a laryngeal radical.

Labiovelars: All the velars of Ge'ez developed a corresponding labio-velar phoneme. In some cases there is an unambiguous conditioning environment with a (long) rounded vowel: the denominal verb *tärgʷämä* 'translate' comes ultimately from the Aramaic loanword *targūm* 'translation'; *əḥʷ* 'brother' shows the influence of the Proto-Ethiopic, and Proto-Semitic, long stem vowel in **aḥū-*. In other cases derivation from a form with such an environment must be assumed: *ḥʷälläqʷä* 'count' must have involved an analogical extension from some environment such as **ḥul(l)ūq-* 'counted' (cf. Arabic *ḥalaqa* 'measure').

Glides also interact with vowels in a characteristic but highly patterned way, which accounts for a number of the inflectional differences between paradigmatic verbs and verbs whose root has a glide radical. Using the roots *ftw* 'love' and *sty* 'drink', these can be exemplified: /äw/ → /o/ (*fätäwkä ~ fätokä* 'you loved'), /äy/ → /e/ (*sätäykä* [*sätekä* rare] 'you drank'), /əw/ → /u/ (**yəfättəw > yəfättu* 'he loves'), /əy/ → /i/ (**yəsättəy > yəsätti* 'he drinks').

Vowels

Ge'ez has the following seven-member system:

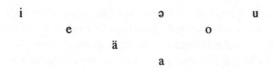

Assuming a Proto-Ethiopic Semitic system with three short vowels /*i, *a, *u/, three long vowels /*ī, *ā, *ū/, and two diphthongs /*ay, *aw/, then it is clear that the Ge'ez system is the result of a series of changes which started with a merger of the short high vowels /*i, *u/ into a high central /ə/, and a shift of the low short /*a/ to /ä/. The quantity of the long vowels was thus made redundant, and they became simply the unmarked low, high front, and high back vowels of the system (even if they are sometimes phonetically longer than /ə, ä/). Note that the use of macrons in the transcription of Ge'ez, which one can still find, should be taken as having diacritical, or at best etymological function only. The monophthongizing of the diphthongs to /e, o/ rounded out the system, which is attested in the earliest vocalized texts, and remains remarkably stable even in many of the modern Ethiopian Semitic languages.

Stress
Stress, for which we are completely dependent on traditional pronunciation, has yet to be completely analyzed. However some general rules seem clear.

1 Verbs are stressed on the penultimate except in pl. 2f.: *yə́ngər, yənä́ggər, nägä́rä, yənäggə́ru* 'may he speak, he speaks, he spoke, they speak', but *nägärkə́n* 'you (pl. 2f.) spoke'.
2 Nouns and pronouns have stem-final stress (i.e., not on the suffix vowel of the accusative): *nəgús, nəgúsä* 'king' (nom., acc.).
3 Personal pronouns and verbs and nouns with pronominal suffixes follow special patterns, giving rise to minimal pairs like *yənäggərá* (< *yənäggər+ha*) 'he speaks to her' versus *yənäggə́ra* 'they (pl. 3f.) speak' (see pronominal paradigms p. 247).

Morphology

Pronouns
The paradigms of the independent and suffix pronouns are given below. As can be readily seen, the 1st and 2nd person independent pronouns are fairly straightforward representatives of Common Semitic, whereas a certain amount of idiosyncratic innovation has taken place in the 3rd person independent pronouns. The suffix pronouns, on the other hand, object and possessive, show predictable Semitic forms. Note that the sg.1 suffix is *-Vyä* with nouns and *-Vni* with verbs. The stressed or unstressed V with 1st and 2nd person forms is, for nouns, the stem-final vowel, or vocalic suffix, if there is one, or /ə/ if the noun form ends in a con-

sonant; for verbs it is /ä/ (except for 2nd person object suffixes with jussive verb forms, compare *yənäggərä́kkä* 'he speaks to you' vs. *yəngə́rkä* 'may he speak to you'). The data of Cohen 1921 and Makonnen 1984 consistently show after a short vowel gemination of the first consonant of an object suffix (*nägärätänni* 'she spoke to me'), or the last consonant preceding the object suffix (*nägärätto* 'she spoke to him'; note also jussive *yəngə́rro* 'may he speak to him' versus present–future *yənäggəró*). In the 3rd person, in nouns and verbs /ä/ + *hú/há/ hómu/hón* gives *ó/á/ómu/ón* (as in *nägärä+hú > nägäró* 'he spoke to him' *betä+ hú > betó* 'his house (acc.)'). In nouns C+hV gives CV (as in *bet+hú > betú* 'his house (nom.)'). The gemination which occurs after a short vowel when the suffix refers to an object is given in parentheses below.

		Independent	Singular	Plural
	1	*ánä*	*nə́ḥnä*
	2m.	*ántä*	*antə́mu*
	f.	*ánti*	*antə́n*
	3m.	*wəʾə́tu*	*wəʾətómu/əmuntú*
	f.	*yəʾə́ti*	*wəʾətón/əmantú*
Suffix	1	-V*yä*/-V(*n*)*ni*	-V(*n*)*nä*
	2m.	-V(*k*)*kä*	-V(*k*)*kə́mu*
	f.	-V(*k*)*ki*	-V(*k*)*kə́n*
	3m.	-*hú* ~ -*ú* ~ -*ó*	-*hómu* ~ -*ómu*
	f.	-*há* ~ -*á*	-*hón* ~ -*ón*

The independent pronouns can only be used in subject or predicate nominal function. Quasi-independent and emphatic pronouns for other functions can be obtained by adding possessive suffixes to the pronominal or prepositional bases: genitive *ziʾä-* (*ziʾäkä* 'yours, your own'); direct object *kiya-* (*kiyayä* 'me myself'); emphatic reflexive *lälli-* (*lällihu* 'he himself, he alone').

Nouns

The relevant morpho-syntactic categories are gender (masculine, feminine), number (singular, plural) case (unmarked, accusative construct). Of these, gender is not systematically marked in the nominal morphology, although feminine nouns occasionally have a suffix -*t*: *bəʾsi* 'man', *bəʾsit* 'woman'; *əgziʾ* 'lord', *əgziʾt* 'lady'.

The unmarked pluralizing process is by suffixation of -*at* (from common Semitic feminine plural, used in Ge'ez for both genders): *may* 'water', pl. *mayat*; *ṣəge* 'flower', pl. *ṣəgeyat*; *ʿaṣa* 'fish', pl. *ʿaṣat*. Nouns with feminine formative -*t* may or may not drop this before the suffix: *śərəʿt* 'law', pl. *śərəʿtat*, but *ʿäzäqt* 'well', pl. *ʿäzäqat*. However many Ge'ez nouns form their plural according to one of the internal (so-called "broken") plural patterns, if necessary using "underlying" glides or supplemental consonants to make up the canonical consonants of the pattern. The vast majority of triconsonantal internal plurals follow one of the five patterns:

aCCaC	ləbs	'garment'	albas
	färäs	'horse'	afras
	bet	'house'	abyat
	ṣom	'fast'	aṣwam
	səm	'name'	asmat
aCCuC	adg	'ass'	aʾdug
	hägär	'city'	aḥgur
aCCəCt	rəʾs	'head'	arʾəst
	gäbr	'slave'	agbərt
aCaCəC(t)	bägʾ	'sheep'	abagəʾ
	ganen	'devil'	aganənt
CVCäC	əzn	'ear'	əzän
	əgr	'foot'	əgär
CVCäw	əd	'hand'	ədäw
	ab	'father'	abäw
	əḫʷ	'brother'	aḫäw

Most noun stems with four consonants, and a number of nouns with three consonants and at least one "long" stem vowel /i, e, o, u/, build their plural according to the so-called quadriliteral pattern:

CäCaCəC(t)	dəngəl	'virgin'	dänagəl
	mäsfən	'prince'	mäsafənt
	kokäb	'star'	käwakəbt
	mäskot	'window'	mäsakut (< mäsakəwt)
	dorho	'chicken'	därawəh
	lelit	'night'	läyaləy
	bəḥer	'earth'	bähawərt
	wəḥiz	'river'	wäḥayəzt
	qäsis	'priest'	qäsawəst

Note from the above that the inserted glide is not generally predictable from the nature of the vowel. Note also that in spite of numerous exceptions, there is a general tendency toward polarity in forms with optional -t: -t is added in the plural if it is absent in the singular (unless the noun is feminine), and dropped in the plural if it is present in the singular. Finally, an additional morphological plural marking occurs with all plural forms (suffix or internal) followed by possessive suffixes: an /i/ is inserted between the noun and the suffix. Thus corresponding to ṣəgeyat 'flowers', abyat 'houses' we have ṣəgeyatina 'our flowers', abyatina 'our houses'.

There is only one morphologically marked case form in Ge'ez, the accusative construct. (Henceforth simply "accusative," it will be designated by "of" in glosses when it marks the "(possessive)" construct" configuration, otherwise by "acc.") The accusative is formed by suffixation of *-ä* (*-hä* with certain non-Ge'ez proper names) to the unmarked (henceforth "nominative") form of the noun: thus, nominative *bet* 'house', accusative *betä*. This form is used both for the direct object of a verb, as in: *särhä nəgus bet-ä* 'the/a king built the/a house' ('built king[nom.] house-acc.'), and for the head (first) noun in the so-called "(possessive) construct" configuration, as in: *bet-ä nəgus* 'the/a house of the/a king' ('house-of king[nom.]').

In both constructions, morphological indication of case can be replaced by syntactic paraphrase. In the case of the direct object, the construction 'Verb Noun[acc.]' can be replaced by 'Verb + Obj.-Suff. *lä*-Noun[nom.]', where *lä* is the preposition 'to'. Thus instead of *särhä betä* 'he made the/a house' one can have *särho* (< *särhä+hu*) *lä bet* 'he made the house' (lit. 'he + made-it to-house'; note that the prepositional paraphrase tends to be preferred for definite direct object). For the (possessive) construct 'Noun₁[acc.] Noun₂[nom.]' there are two possibilities. Either 'Noun₁ *zä* Noun₂' (where *zä* is the relative pronoun), or 'Noun₁ + Poss.-Suff. *lä*-Noun₂'. Thus instead of *betä nəgus* one can have either *bet zä nəgus* or *betu* (< *bet+hu*) *lä nəgus* (where the last variant may be preferred for a definite head noun).

Adjectives and Participles

This morphological class includes: (1) general adjectives of many canonical shapes, for which we will use *šänay* 'beautiful' as typical; (2) a special class of quality adjectives of the base form sg. m. *CäC(C)iC* (*ħäddis* 'new', *'äbiyy* 'big'); (3) the present or active participle of the verb *CäCaCi* (*nägari* 'speaker'); (4) the passive or intransitive participle of the verb *CəCuC* (*nəgur* 'spoken').

In general, adjectives form the sg. f. by suffixing *-t*, pl. m. by suffixing *-an*, and pl. f. by suffixing *-at*, according to the following paradigm:

	Sg.	Pl.
m.	*šänay*	*šänayan*
f.	*šänayt*	*šänayat*

The active participle has a special pl. m. form:

	Sg.	Pl.
m.	*nägari*	*nägärt*
f.	*nägarit*	*nägariyat*

The passive participle and the *CäCCiC* adjectives have a special sg. f. form:

	Sg.	Pl.
m.	nəgur	nəguran
f.	nəgərt	nəgurat
m.	ḥäddis	ḥäddisan
f.	ḥäddas	ḥäddisat

Some CäCCiC have a pl. c. like the active participle:

	Sg.	Pl.
m.	ʿäbiyy	ʿäbbäyt
f.	ʿäbbay	ʿäbbäyt

Case marking is as in the noun.

Deictics

The deictic relative paradigms are built on the stem series z- (singular, mostly masculine), ənt- (most feminine singulars), əll- (plural). Far deixis adds the element -(k)ku. Both near and far have a long form with suffix -tu~ti~tä, which can be used independently. The paradigm of the whole deictic–relative–interrogative series is given in Table 13.1.

Table 13.1   Ge'ez deictics

		Singular Nominative	Accusative	*Plural* Nominative	Accusative
'this'	m.	zə-	zä	əllu	
	f.	za	za	əlla	
'this (long)'	m.	zəntu	zäntä	əllontu	əllontä
	f.	zatti	zattä	əllantu	əllantä
'that'	m.	zəkku	zəkkʷä, zəkku	əlləkku	
	f.	əntəkku	əntəkkʷä, əntäkku	əlləkku	
'that (long)'	m.	zəktu	zəktä	əlləktu	əlləktä
	f.	əntakti	əntaktä	əllaktu	əllaktä
relative	m.	zä-		əllä	
	f.	əntä		əllä	
'who?'		männu	männä		
'what?'		mənt	məntä		
'which?'		ay		ayat	ayatä

Numerals

The Ge'ez cardinal numbers show the expected Semitic polarity switch, with a *t*-suffixed form in the masculine, and an unmarked form in the feminine. In addition to these forms, Ge'ez has a great variety of derived forms, the most important of which are the ordinals (mostly of the CaCəC pattern), day-of-week/month forms

(*CäCuC* pattern), and adverbial forms ('once', 'twice' etc.; of the *CǝCCä* pattern). For the numbers 1–10, these forms are as in Table 13.2. Note that for the numeral '2', except for the day nominalization, which uses the inherited Semitic root **θny*, the root has been replaced by **kilʾ*-, the Semitic word for 'both'. Other nominalizations involving '2' call upon lexical items *dgm* 'repeat' and *k'b* 'double'. The ordinal for '1' uses the lexical item *qdm* 'precede'. The ordinals are the only place in Ge'ez morphology where one finds a survival of the common Semitic active participle of the form **Ca:CiC > CaCǝC*. The masculine cardinals have an accusative form in *-tä*, and have *-ti-* before suffix pronouns: *šälästä* 'three[acc.]', *šälästihomu* 'the three of them'. Feminine cardinals are usually treated as invariants. For numbers above ten the order is "Ten *wä* Unit": *'äšärtu wä-šälästu, 'äšru wä-šälas* '13 m., f.'. The tens units are: *'ǝšra* '20', *šälasa* '30', *arb'a* '40', *hämsa* '50', *sǝssa* '60', *säb'a* '70', *sämanya* '80', *tǝs'a* or *täs'a* '90'; '100' is *mǝʾǝt*, '10,000' is *ǝlf* ('1,000' is *'äšärtu mǝʾǝt*). The form cited for the ordinals is the sg. m.; there are alternate masculine forms in *-awi, -ay* (*hamsawi, hamsay* 'fifth[m.]'). Feminine ordinals end in *-it* or *-awit* (*hamsit, hamsawit* 'fifth[f.]').

Table 13.2   Ge'ez numerals

	Cardinal m.	f.	Ordinal	Day	Adverbial
1	ahädu	ahati	qädami	ǝhud	mǝ'rä, ahätä
2	kǝlʾe, kǝlʾetu	kǝlʾeti	dagǝm, kalǝʾ, ka'ǝb	sänuy	ka'bä, dagmä
3	šälästu	šälas	šaləs	šälus	šǝlsä
4	arba'tu	arba'	rabǝ'	räbu'	rǝb'ä
5	hämǝstu	häms	hamǝs	hämus	hǝmsä
6	sǝdǝstu	sǝssu	sadǝs	sädus	sǝdsä
7	säb'ätu	säb'u	sabǝ'	säbu'	sǝb'ä
8	sämäntu	sämani	samǝn	sämun	sǝmnä
9	tǝs'ätu, täs'ätu	tǝs'u, täs'u	tasǝ'	täsu'	tǝs'ä
10	'äšǝrtu	'äšru	'ašǝr	'äšur	'ǝšrä

Verbs

Following a general Semitic pattern, a Ge'ez verb form is basically a combination of one entry from each of two series of paradigms, here referred to as the Affix Paradigms and Stem Paradigm. The Affix series, given below, is a set of two subject paradigms for personal affixes agreeing in person, number, and gender with the subject. One of these is entirely suffixing and is used with past tense verb stems; important here is the characteristic Ethio-Semitic *-k* formative of the sg. 1 and 2nd person forms. Pre-object suffix forms are in parentheses (optional for sg. 2m.). The other subparadigm is predominantly prefixing, and is used with the nonpast and jussive verb forms.

		Singular	Plural
Past	1	*-ku*	*-nä (-na-)*
	2m.	*-kä (-ka-)*	*-kəmu*
	f.	*-ki*	*-kən*
	3m.	*-ä*	*-u*
	f.	*-ät*	*-a*
Nonpast	1	*ə-*	*nə-*
	2m.	*tə-*	*tə-...-u*
	f.	*tə-...-i*	*tə-...-a*
	3m.	*yə-*	*yə-...-u*
	f.	*tə-*	*yə-...-a*

The Stem series of paradigms governs the stem form to which the subject markers are affixed. There are four basic morphological categories involved, which we will refer to as "root class," "tense," "derivational class," and "lexical class." The root class categories are: "weak": verbs whose roots have a glide or vocalic radical and "strong" verb roots whose radicals are fully consonantal. The primary "tense" categories are past, nonpast, jussive, imperative. The imperative stem is identical with the jussive stem in Ge'ez, and hence will not be noted in the paradigms (see Table 13.3). Infinitives and converbs are not tense categories in any usual morpho-syntactic sense of the term, but it will be useful to display infinitives in the paradigm as a fourth "tense" form. The derivational classes are: Base (zero affix), Causative (prefix *ä-*), Passive Reflexive (prefix *tä-*, if not preceded by a subject prefix, otherwise *t-*), Causative Passive (prefix *astä-*). These derivational classes are formed, with more or less idiosyncratic semantics, with all verbs in the lexicon, although not all verbs occur in all derivational classes.

Historically related to the various Semitic verbal derivation systems, but almost completely lexicalized in Ge'ez, are the categories of lexical class, conventionally designated in Ge'ez with the letters A, B, and C. A is the unmarked class. In the Base past and jussive there are two subclasses: A1 has stem vowel /ä/ in the past and stem vowel /ə/ in the jussive, whereas A2 has stem vowel /ə/ in the past and /ä/ in the jussive. Recalling that Ge'ez /ə/ represents Semitic /*i, *u/, this clearly corresponds to the common stem vowel alternations (e.g., in Arabic): past CaCaC ~ present jussive CC*u*C, past CaC*i*C ~ present jussive CC*a*C. Note that some verbs can be A1 in the past and A2 in the jussive, and vice versa. B is the class of verbs with geminating middle radical (*pi'el* in Hebrew, D-stem in Akkadian, Form II in Arabic); C is the class of verbs with stem vowel /a:/ after the first radical consonant (Form III in Arabic). Unlike other Semitic languages, these do not occur in Ge'ez as derived forms of the unmarked base, but as a lexically determined class. A verbal entry must be marked in the lexicon as either class A, class B, or class C in Ge'ez, and if it occurs in one class, will not occur in another (the few cases where this occurs are usually counted as homophonous). An exception to this general rule is the class of passive reflexive C (*tänagärä*, cognate with

Form VI of Arabic) and causative passive C (*astänagärä*) which occur with many verbs, the former frequently as a reciprocal, the latter with widely varying semantics. Given the existence of this set of lexically determined categories, it is convenient to enter quadriradical verbs (verbs with four root consonants) under this general heading as lexical class D. These verbs are especially frequent in Ethiopic Semitic. There are only a few cases where they can be etymologically linked to triradical verbs, but phonologically most of them are either of the form $C_1RC_2C_3$ (R = /n, l, r/) or of the form $C_1C_2C_3C_3$, where C_1, C_2, C_3 otherwise follow the cooccurrence constraints of triconsonantal roots. As is often the case in Semitic, these D (quadriradical) verbs closely resemble B (middle-geminating) verbs in their morphological structure.

Table 13.3 gives the stem paradigms for the so-called strong verbs. The lexical items used are: *ngr* 'speak (Class A1)', *lbs* 'wear (Class A2)', *fṣm* 'finish (Class B)', *msn* 'perish (Class C)', *dngṣ* 'surprise (Class D, quadriradical)'. Note that the infinitive forms in /t/ are functionally equivalent to the short forms, but are more likely to be used when the infinitive requires a suffix pronoun or an accusative case marker. As in all other Semitic languages, Ge'ez has a smaller but important class of weak verbal roots (including a number of high frequency, basic lexical items such as "stand," "die," "drink," "put") which deviate from the pattern of the strong paradigms by showing a glide or vocalic configuration at one or more of the root consonant positions. In Ge'ez these roots can be schematized according to glide variant, /w/ or /y/, and root position, 1, 2, or 3: thus "W_2", "Y_3" – note that "Y_1" verbs are very few in number, and have been largely regularized. Table 13.4, p. 254 gives the stem paradigm for the finite Base A form of triconsonantal glide roots, using the lexical items *wrd* 'descend', *wdq* 'fall', *mwt* 'die', *šym* 'appoint', *ftw* 'love', *bdw* 'be desert', *bky* 'cry', *sty* 'drink'. The other lexical and derivational classes are straightforward extensions of the Base A form. Note that for W/Y$_2$ A, there is no distinction between subclass 1 and 2.

Verbs which have a laryngeal (henceforth H = /ʾ, ʿ, ḫ, ḥ, h/) as a radical largely follow the strong pattern, as modified by the special vowel–laryngeal sequence constraints noted in Phonology, p. 245. Thus for H$_1$: sg. 3m. past *ʿaqäbä* 'he kept', present *yäʿäqqəb* (< *yəʿäqqəb*, by laryngeal vowel harmony). Many H$_2$ behave completely like strong roots, as *sähäbä*, *sähäbkä* 'he/you[sg. m.] pulled', however an important subclass of these verbs have a past stem vowel pattern with /ə/ throughout: *səḥtä*, *səḥətkä* 'he/you[sg. m.] erred' (contrast non-laryngeal *läbsä* < *läbəsä* < *labisa, but *läbäskä*). The present shows the regular laryngeal modification of the strong pattern, and jussive is with /ä/ for both of these subclasses: *yəsäḥḥəb*, *yəsḥäb*; *yəsäḥḥət*, *yəsḥät*. H$_3$ verbs of the A class have the idiosyncracy that they are all of the A2 (*läbsä*) subclass: *wäḍʾä*, *wäḍaʾkä* 'he/you[sg. m.] left'. In addition H$_3$ verbs of the B, C, and D class have the unique property in the Ge'ez conjugation system of also having a *läbsä*-like pattern in the past: *läqqəḥä*, *läqqaḥkä* 'he/you[sg. m.] lent', *baləḥä*, *balaḥkä* 'he/you[sg. m.] rescued', *zängəʿä*, *zängaʿkä* 'he/you[sg. m.] raved'.

Finally, there are a dozen or so verbs, most with glide or laryngeal radicals (see

Table 13.3 Strong verb stem paradigms

		Base	Causative	Passive Reflexive	Causative Passive
Past	A1	nägär-	angär-	tänägr-	astängär-
	A2	läbs-	albäs-	täläbs-	astälbäs-
	B	fäṣṣäm-	afäṣṣäm-	täfäṣṣäm-	astäfäṣṣäm-
	C	masän-	amasän-	tämasän-	astämasän-
	D	dängäṣ-	adängäṣ-	tädängäṣ-	astädängäṣ-
Present–	A	-näggər(-)	-anäggər(-)	-tnäggär(-)	-astänäggər(-)
Future	B	-feṣṣəm(-)	-afeṣṣəm(-)	-tfeṣṣäm(-)	-astäfeṣṣəm(-)
	C	-masən(-)	-amasən(-)	-tmasän(-)	-astämasən(-)
	D	-dänäggəṣ(-)	-adänäggəṣ(-)	-tdänäggäṣ(-)	-astädänäggəṣ(-)
Jussive	A1	-ngər(-)	-angər(-)	-tnägär(-)	-astängər(-)
	A2	-lbäs(-)	-albəs(-)	-tläbäs(-)	-astälbəs(-)
	B	-fäṣṣəm(-)	-afäṣṣəm(-)	-tfäṣṣäm(-)	-astäfäṣṣəm(-)
	C	-masən(-)	-amasən(-)	-tmasän(-)	-astämasən(-)
	D	-dängəṣ(-)	-adängəṣ(-)	-tdängäṣ(-)	-astädängəṣ(-)
Infinitive	A	nägir(ot)	angəro(t)	tänägro(t)	astänägro(t)
	B	fäṣṣəmo(t)	afäṣṣəmo(t)	täfäṣṣəmo(t)	astäfäṣṣəmo(t)
	C	masno(t)	amasno(t)	tämasno(t)	astämasno(t)
	D	dängəṣo(t)	adängəṣo(t)	tädängəṣo(t)	astädängəṣo(t)
Converb	A	nägir-	angir-	tänägir-	astänägir-
	B	fäṣṣim-	afäṣṣim-	täfäṣṣim-	astäfäṣṣim-
	C	masin-	amasin-	tämasin-	astämasin-
	D	dängiṣ-	adängiṣ-	tädängiṣ-	astädängiṣ-

Table 13.4 Weak verb stem paradigms

		Past	Present	Jussive
W$_1$	A1	wäräd-	-wärrəd(-)	-räd(-)
	A2	wädq-	-wäddəq(-)	-däq(-)
W$_2$	A	mot-	-mäwwət(-)	-mut(-)
Y$_2$	A	śem-	-śäyyəm(-)	-śim(-)
W$_3$	A1	fätäw/fäto-	-fättu(-)	-ftu(-)
	A2	bädw-	-bäddu(-)	-bdäw(-)
Y$_3$	A1	bäkäy-	-bäkki(-)	-bki(-)
	A2	säty-	-sätti(-)	-stäy(-)

the convenient list in Lambdin 1978: 450f.), which show one or more idiosyncratic irregularities in stem paradigm. The only one we will mention here is the unique (and archaic) conjugation pattern of the verb *bhl* 'say' in its base form (the derived class forms are conjugated regularly). Instead of an expected past tense *bəhlä (compare kəhlä from khl 'be able') this verb has a **prefixing** past tense, the only survival of this archaic form in Ethiopic Semitic, with stem -be in non-suffixed forms, -bel- in suffixed: yəbe, yəbelu 'he/they said'. The present stem of this verb is -bəl(-), and its jussive is -bal(-): yəbəl 'he says', yəbal 'let him say' (compare *yəkəl* 'he can', *yekal* 'let him be able').

Adverbs and Prepositions

A number of adverbs are productively formed from accusatives (suffix *-ä*) of nouns and adjectives: *lelitä* 'by night', *qədmä* 'in front', *rəḥuqä* 'afar', *märirä* 'bitterly'. The same suffix (*-ä*), this time from a construct-like configuration, is also the norm for many conjunctions: *əmmä* 'if', *sobä* 'when', *änbälä* 'except', *ənzä* 'while', *əskä* 'until', *əsmä* 'because'. On the other hand, an adverbial (hence nominal) origin seems probable for some prespositions: *maʾkälä* 'between' (from 'middle'), perhaps also *mängälä* 'towards' (nominal form of some root '*ngl*' – etymology not clear. Most of the usual prepositions end in *-ä* before nouns, and *-e* before pronominal suffixes: *ḫäbä* ~ *ḫabe-* 'to, towards', *dibä* ~ *dibe-* 'on', *məslä* ~ *məsle-* 'with' (e.g., *məslä säbʾ* 'with (the) man', *məslehu* 'with him'). Special cases: *əmännä* (proclitic form *əm-*) ~ *əmənne-* 'from', *kämä* ~ *käma-* 'like', *wəstä* ~ *wästet-* 'in', *ʿäwdä* ~ *ʿäwdä-* 'around'; *əskä* 'until, up to' and *əntä* 'through' do not occur with pronominal suffixes. The monosyllabic prepositions are proclitic: *bä-* 'in' (*bə-* before 1st and 2nd person pronouns, 3rd person singular *bo* ~ *bottu*, *ba* ~ *batti*), *lä-* 'to' (except *litä* 'to me', *lottu* 'to him', *latti* 'to her', *lon* ~ *latton* 'to them[pl. f.]'). Compound prepositions such as *bä-qädmä* 'in front of' are common.

Syntax

The examples in the following section are almost all from the Ge'ez Bible, still on the whole our most reliable source of Ge'ez language data. Most of these examples can be found in the context of a larger collection of data in the excellent syntax section of Dillmann (1907). After each translation will be found a word for word (and to a certain extent morpheme for morpheme) gloss; syntactically relevant morphological material which cannot be conveniently "linearized" will be given in square brackets ("[ ]").

Word Order

The unmarked main clause word order in Ge'ez is Verb Subject Object: *wä-räkäbä Yosef mogäs-ä bäqädmä əgziʾ-u* 'and Joseph found favor before his lord (and-found-sg. 3m. Joseph favor-acc. before lord-his)'. Ge'ez however has a large repertory of word order possibilities. Subject Verb Object order can correspond to emphasized subject: *əgziʾäbḥer wähäb-ä-kəmu z-ä-ʿəlät-ä sänbät* '**God** has given you this Sabbath day (God gave-sg. 3m.-you this-acc.-day-of sabbath)'. The fronted subject is often marked with the enclitic conjunction *-s(s)ä*: *abäw-i-na-ssa bä-zəntu däbr sägäd-u* '**our fathers** worshiped on this mountain (fathers-pl.-our-as-for in-this mountain worshiped-pl. 3m.)'. This word order occurs often in subordinate, for example in *əsmä* clauses: *əsmä ab yafäqqəd wäld-o* 'for the father loves his son (for father loves son[acc.]-his)'. Verb Object Subject order can occur where there is verb-first word order, and at the same time the verb and its object form a tight semantic, quasi-lexical unit, as in the expression 'cast one's eyes' in: *wä-wädäy-ät a⁽yənt-i-ha la⁽lä Yosef bə⁾sit-ä əgzi⁾-u* 'and the wife of his lord cast her eyes upon Joseph (and-cast-sg. 3f. eyes-pl.-her upon Joseph woman-of lord-his)'. In the following case of Verb Object Subject order, noted by Dillmann, there may be a question of an overlapping syntactic configuration in which "Noah" is subject both of the first (main) clause and of the second (relative): *a-rḥäw-ä mäskot-a lä-tabot Noḥ əntä gäbr-ä* 'Noah opened the window of the Ark which he had made (cause-open-sg. 3m. window-her to-ark Noah rel.-sg. f. made-sg. 3m.)'. Finally, Object Verb word order may be conditioned by the topic role of the object: *ḥäṭi⁾ät-əyä ə-zzekkär yom* 'I remember today my sin (sin-my sg. 1-remember today)'. Object Verb word order can also be found more frequently in various kinds of relative clause – *wä-zä-ssä ṣədqä yə-gäbbər* 'and whoever does justice (and-rel.-but justice-acc. sg. 3m.-do)'.

The word order in the noun phrase generally follows the pattern seen in many Subject Object Verb languages, according to which quantifiers, numerals, and demonstratives precede the head noun, and adjectives and relatives follow. Here also a good deal of variation is possible: thus *⁽äbiyä ṣəqayä* 'great torment' in Genesis 12:17, but *ḥəzbä ⁽äbiyä* 'great people' in Genesis 18:18. Note especially a tendency for short stative relative clauses (see below), which are frequently used as quasi-adjectival modifiers, to occur in pre-nominal position: *zä-yä⁽äbbi bərhan wä-zä-yənə⁾⁾əs bərhan* 'a greater light and a lesser light (rel.-be + great light and-rel.-be + small light)', *zä-yäṣenni wäyn-ä* 'the good wine (rel.-be + good wine-acc.)', *kʷəllo zä-wəstä sämay gəbrä* 'all creation in heaven (all[acc.] rel.-in heaven creation[acc.])'.

Agreement

As a rule, as can be seen in many examples in this section, modifiers agree with head nouns in gender, number and case. For numbers, note that beyond the number 2, the masculine form of the numeral has the *-t-* formative characteristic of feminines, which in turn is uniformly absent from the feminine forms: *säb⁽ätu aḥäw* 'seven brothers', *säb⁽u dänagəl* 'seven virgins'. Note also that while the head noun in numeral phrases is usually in the plural, as in the preceding examples, it can sometimes be in the singular (especially with inanimate or mass nouns): *säb⁽u ḥəbəst* 'seven loaves (seven loaf)'. In general, although grammatical gender is very much a feature of the language, Ge'ez seems to be developing toward a system of natural gender. While genders are consistently distinguished for animate beings, even the best texts show a certain amount of fluctuation where inanimates are concerned: *mədr šänayt* '(land beautiful[f.])' in Mark 4:8, but *mədr šänay* '(land beautiful[m.])' in Mark 4:13.

The general rule for verbs is that they agree with their subjects in person, gender, and number: *tä-wäld-a l-omu awaləd šänay-at* 'beautiful daughters were born to them (passive-born-pl. 3f. to-them children beautiful-pl. f.)'. Here also, a tendency to natural gender can be seen: *wä-konä dəqät-u ⁽äbiy-ä* 'and his fall was great (and-was-sg. 3m. fall[sg. 3f.]-his great[sg. 3m.-acc.])', *ra⁾yat dibe-yä wädäqu* 'visions fell upon me (visions[pl. 3f.] upon-me fell-pl. 3m.'. On occasion plural subjects can have a verb in the sg. 3f.: *ḫäṭawə'-i-homu ʿäby-ät* 'their sins were great (sins[pl. f.]-pl.-their be + great-sg. 3f.)'; and, as noted by Dillmann, in a number of instances a sg. 3m. verb in initial position is found with a plural sub-ject: *ḫäläf-ä mäwaʿəl-i-hu* 'his days passed (passed-sg. 3m. days-pl.-his)'.

Negation

The usual negation, both of simple propositions and commands, is with the parti-cle *i* (< **'al* by palatalization > *'ay* reduced to *'əy* – a form attested in the Aksum inscriptions), usually procliticized to the main verb of the clause: *nəḥnä i-nə-kəl ḥäwir-ä* 'we cannot go (we not-pl. 1-can[pr.] go[inf.]-acc.)', *i-təqtəlu näfs-o* 'do not kill him (not-kill[pl. 2m. juss.] soul[acc.]-his)'. This particle can also be used to negate individual clause constituents, or non-verbal predicate elements: *i-kon-kä Krəstos-ha wä-i-Elyas-ha wä-i-näbiy-ä* 'you were not Christ nor Elias nor a prophet (not-were-sg. 2m. Christ-acc. and-not-Elias-acc. and-not-prophet-acc.)', *i-qätil-ä näfs i-tämaḥzo i-säriq* '[list of commandments] not to kill, not to commit adultery, not to steal (not-kill[inf.]-of soul not-commit + adultery[inf.] not-steal[inf.])'. It is also productive in the formation of negative lexical items: *iya'məro* 'ignorance (< *i-a'məro* 'not-knowledge'). A stronger negation of non-verbal constituents is possible with *akko*, which can also be used in conjunction with *kəmmä* 'only, just': *akko bä-ḥəbəst kəmmä* 'not by bread alone'. Note that an emphatic negation of a clause can be obtained by using *akko* with a relativized verb: *akko zä-motät ḥəḍan* 'the child has **not** died (not rel.-died child)' versus a possible *i-motät ḥəḍan* 'the child did not die (not-died child)'. The usual lexical items for negation and affirmation are: *əwwä* 'yes (general)', *oho* 'yes (to com-mand)', *ənbiyä* 'no'. See p. 260 on the negative expression *albo*.

Questions

Yes–no questions are formed by suffixing *-nu* or *-hu* to the first constituent of the sentence, which thereby becomes the foregrounded element: *zänt-ä-nu gäbär-ki* 'did you do this? (this-acc.-interr. did-sg. 2f.)', *əmənnä säb'-ä zi'ä-nä-nu antä aw əmənnä ḍärr-nä* 'are you **from our own men** or from our enemy? (from man-of own-our-interr. or enemy-our)'. The interrogative particle after the verb in un-marked clause-initial position in principle corresponds to interrogation over the whole clause: *yəqäśśəmu-hu əm-aśwak askal-ä* 'do they gather grapes from thorns? (gather[pl. 3m.]-interr. from-thorns grapes-acc.)'. However, to signify unambiguously that the whole clause is in the scope of the interrogation, the clause can begin with *bonu* 'is it that (exists-interr.)' with a normal or relativized verb: *bo-nu əbn-ä yəhub-o* 'will he give him a stone? (exists-interr. stone-acc. gives-him)', *bo-nu kalə'-ä zä-nə-sseffo* 'shall we look for another? (exists-interr. other-acc. which-we-look + for[< *-tseffäw* passive B])'.

   WH-questions are formed with the interrogative pronouns (*männu, mənt*, see p. 250) or the interrogative adverbs (principally: *ayte* 'where', *əfo* 'how', *ma'ze* 'when' – 'why' is *lä-mənt* [to-what]). Note the use of the pronouns as "governing" noun in a construct configuration: *wälätt-ä männu anti* 'whose daughter are you (daughter-of who you[sg. 2f.])', and its quasi-adjectival use in apposition to a head noun: *mənt-ä ʿäsb-ä bəkəmu* 'what reward will you have? (what-acc. reward-acc. in-you [see p. 260])'.

Coordination, Condition

The usual coordinating particle for conjunction in Ge'ez is *wä-*, which procliticizes onto the following lexical item (many examples above). In addition to a lexical inventory of particles for other relations of coordination (including *aw* 'or', *alla* 'but', *ənga, ənka* 'then, so'), a characteristic feature of Ge'ez syntax is the use of enclitic coordinating and foregrounding particles which, frequently in conjunction with *wä-*, set off and relate clauses and clause constituents: *-(s)sä* 'but, on the one hand', *-hi* 'also', *-ni* 'even', *-mä* '(emphasis)', *-ke* 'thus' – where the glosses are meant simply to give an approximate idea of the particles' syntactic and discourse functions. Two well-known examples: *bäkämä bä-sämay wä-bä-mədr-ni* 'on earth as it is in heaven (as in-heaven and-in-earth-also)', *qal-(ə)ssä qal-ä Yaʿqob wä-ʾədäw zä-ʿesaw* 'as for the voice, it is the voice of Jacob, but the hands are those of Esau (voice-but voice-of Jacob and-hands rel.-Esau)'.

For constructions of the form "Clause₁ and Clause₂" where "and" means "and then", and not arbitrary conjunction ("he opened the door **and** walked in" vs. "he spoke French **and** rode horseback") Ge'ez uses a construction type widespread in Semitic and non-Semitic Ethiopian languages sometimes called "conjunctive" or "converb" ("perfective active participle" in Lambdin 1978). In Ge'ez it consists of the infinitive-like converb form of the verb (see the paradigm for the strong verb in Table 13.3, p. 254) in the accusative, with possessive suffix for subject in one of the clauses (usually the first) and a finite verb form in the second; the tense and mode interpretation of the converb verb are those of the finite. The construction is most frequently used to signify temporal priority of the converb clause: *wä-sämiʿ-o Herodəs dängäd-ä* 'and Herod heard (this) and was alarmed; and having heard this, Herod was alarmed (and-hear[converb, acc.]-his Herod be + alarmed-sg. 3m.)', *ḥäwir-ä-kəmu täsäʾäl-u* 'go and ask (go[converb]-acc.-your[pl. 2m.] ask[imp.]-pl. 2m.)'. But the construction can also be used for relations of simultaneity and manner: *täʿägiś-ä-kä aḍməʾ-(ä)ni* 'hear me patiently (be + patient[converb]-acc.-your[sg. 2m.] hear[imp., sg. 2m.]-me)'.

Finally, clauses can be coordinated in a conditional relationship. Real conditions introduce the protasis clause with *əmmä*, and usually uses the past tense form: *əmmä ḥädäg-o yə-mäwwət* 'if he leaves him, he will die (if leave[past, sg. 3m.]-him sg. 3m.-die[pr.])'. Contrary-to-fact conditionals use *sobä* (usually 'when') and the past tense in the protasis, and *əm-* with a past tense verb in the apodosis, if it comes after the protasis, otherwise a simple past tense verb: *sobä nägär-kä-ni əm-fännäw-ku-kä* 'if you had told me, I would have sent you (when tell[past]-you[sg. m.]-me then-send[past]-I-you[sg. m.])', *ḥäyäs-ä-nä sobä mot-nä bä-bəher-ä Gəbṣ* 'it would have been better for us if we had died in the land of Egypt (be + better-sg. 3m.-us when die[past]-we in-land-of Egypt)'.

Subordinate Constructions

In certain circumstances, especially with perception verbs, object clauses can be put in simple parataxis with main clauses: *rə'y-ä tä-säṭq-ä sämay* 'He saw the heavens split (saw-sg. 3m. passive-split[past]-sg. 3m. heaven)', *räkäb-o yə-qäwwəm* 'he found him standing (find[past, sg. 3m.]-him sg. 3m.-stand[pr.])'. Otherwise object clauses with verbs of speech, cognition have are introduced by one of a number of conjunctions, the most common of which are *kämä* 'that', *əsmä* 'because', *ənzä* 'while': *a'mär-ä kämä tä-nätg-ä may* 'he knew that the waters had receded (knew-sg. 3m. that passive-recede-sg. 3m. water)'. The verb *mäsälä* 'seem', which takes a relativized verb, is exceptional: *mäsäl-omu zä-tä-ḥäwwər ḥäbä mäqabər* 'it seemed to them that she was going to the tomb (seemed[sg. 3m.]-them rel.-she-go[pr.] to tomb)'.

Ge'ez, unlike some other Semitic languages, does not restrict the jussive to main clauses; object clauses of verbs of volition and purpose usually have their verbs in the jussive. The clause may or may not be introduced by *kämä*: *fäqäd-ä kämä tə-ba'* 'he wanted you to come (wanted-sg. 3m. that sg. 2m.-come[juss.])', *fätäw-u yər'äyu* 'they desired to see (desired-pl. 3m. see[juss. pl. 3m.])', *mäṣ'-ä yə-r'äy* 'he came to see (came-sg. 3m. sg. 3m.-see[juss.]'. Finally, a number of verbs, notably *kəhlä* 'be able', *dägämä* 'repeat, do again' use the accusative of the infinitive in their object clauses: *i-yə-kəl ḥädig-ä abu-hu* 'he cannot leave his father (not-sg. 3m.-can leave[inf.]-acc. father-his)', *dägäm-ku nägirot-ä-kəmu* 'I spoke to you again (repeated-I speak[inf.]-acc.-you)'.

Relative clauses, as have been seen above, are related in a rather straightforward fashion to the head noun of their noun phrase by a relative particle, which may agree with it in gender and number (sg. m. *zä-*, sg. f. *əntä*, pl. *əllä*), or use the sg. m. *zä-* as an invariant. However there are a number of different patterns of agreement between the head noun and pronominal elements within the relative clause. When the head noun is also subject of the verb, it of course shows concord with the verb's subject marker: *bə'si zä-yä-ḥäwwər* 'the man who comes (man rel.[sg. m.]-sg. 3m.-come)'. When the head noun is the object of the relative verb, it is normally represented by an object suffix on the verb: *aḥzab zä-antəmu tə-twärräs-əw-omu* 'the peoples which you will inherit (peoples rel.[sg. 3m.]-you[pl. 2m.] you-inherit[pr.]-pl. m.-them)'. However this is not obligatory; in the following example the choice of an indirect object suffix on the verb makes the inclusion of a direct object suffix impossible in any case: *mədr əntä wähäb-ä-kä* 'the land which he gave you (land rel.[sg. f.] gave-sg. 3m.-sg. 2m.)'.

Similarly, when the head noun is object of a preposition in the relative clause, it is normally represented by a pronominal object: *mədr əntä bä-wəstet-a tä-wäld-ä* 'the land in whose midst he was born (land rel.[sg. f.] in-midst-her passive-born-sg. 3m.)'. Here also the pronominal object can be dropped, leaving a "dangling" preposition: *mədr əntä ḥäbä mäṣa'-nä* 'the land to which we have come (land rel.[sg. f.] to come-we)'. Perhaps as a consequence of this, we find rather frequently in Ge'ez relative clauses with the preposition shifted in front of the relative pronoun: *mäwa'əl-i-hu bä-zä astär'äy-omu kokäb* 'the days on which the star appeared to them (days-pl.-his in-rel.[sg. m.] appeared-them star)'. And there are even instances of use of the shifted preposition and preposition with object pronoun in the same clause: *bäträ-kä bä-zä bott-u zäbäṭ-kä* 'your stick with which you beat (stick-acc.-your in-rel. in-it beat-you)'.

'Be' and 'Have'

For simple present tense predication, the independent pronoun functions as copula in Ge'ez: *märet antä* 'you are dust (dust you)', *männu wə'ətu zəntu* 'who is this? (who he this)', *zati yə'əti ŝər'ät-əyä* 'this is my law (this she law-my)'. Sometimes the sg. 3m. pronoun can function as a default copula: *antəmu wə'ətu bərhan-u lä-'aläm* 'you are the light of the world (you[pl. 2m.] he light-his to-world)', *ana wə'ətu* 'it is I (I he)'. When tense or modal distinctions are necessary, the verbs *konä* and *hälläwä* are used. Note that the nominal or adjectival complement of these verbs is in the accusative case: *ə-käwwən nəsuḥ-ä* 'I will be pure (I-be pure-acc.)'.

These later verbs are used also for 'be in a place' and 'exist', but a characteristic feature of Ge'ez is the use of the preposition *bä-* 'in' plus the sg. 3m. suffix pronoun, *bo* or *bottu*, literally 'in it' to signify 'exists' (with predicate in the accusative): *b-o ḥəḍwan-ä* 'there are eunuchs (in-it eunuchs-acc.)'. The negative form of this expression, *albo* 'there is not (not-in-it)', contains the only survival in Ge'ez of the Proto-Ethio-Semitic form of the negative particle: *albo sədq-ä* 'there is no justice (not-in-it justice-acc.)'. Both the positive and negative forms are widely used in forming indefinite expressions: *bo zä-yəmäṣṣä'* 'someone is coming (exists rel.-comes)', *albo zä-tärfä* 'no one was left (not-exists rel.-remained)'.

In an extension of this existential expression *bä-* plus pronominal suffix yields the ordinary Ge'ez construction for 'have': *mäṣḥaf-ä bə-nä* 'we have a book (book-acc. in-us)', *b-ati əhw-ä* 'she has a brother (in-her brother-acc.)', *bə'si b-ottu kəl'et-ä wəlud-ä* 'a man has two sons (man in-him two-acc. sons-acc.)'. The negation of 'have' is simply *al + bä +* pronominal suffix: *ganen-ä al-bə-yyä* 'I do not have a devil (devil-acc. not-in-me)'.

References

Cohen, Marcel. 1921. "La Pronunciation traditionnelle du guèze (éthiopien classique)." *Journal Asiatique* 11/17: 217–269.

Dillmann, August. 1907. *Ethiopic Grammar*, translation by James Crichton of *Grammatik der äthiopischen Sprache*. Leipzig: Tauchnitz (1857). 2nd edition enlarged and improved by Carl Bezold (1899). London: Williams & Norgate.

Lambdin, Thomas. 1978. *Introduction to Classical Ethiopic (Ge'ez)*. Missoula: Scholars Press.

Leslau, Wolf. 1987. *Comparative Dictionary of Ge'ez*. Wiesbaden: Harrassowitz.

Makonnen Argaw. 1984. *Matériaux pour l'étude de la prononciation traditionnelle du guèze*. Paris: Éditions Recherche sur les Civilizations.

Mittwoch, Eugen. 1926. *Die Traditionelle Aussprache des Äthiopischen* (Abessinische Studien 1). Berlin and Leipzig: de Gruyter.

PART III

MODERN SEMITIC

14 Arabic Dialects and Maltese

Alan S. Kaye and Judith Rosenhouse

All the data cited are in a uniform IPA-based transcription with the exception of Maltese, which is cited in its standard orthography.

When dealing with dialects, a fundamental question is how they should be defined. Exactly which and how many features are sufficient for a language's many subsystems to be described as distinct dialects or languages? Occasionally, when languages are in contact, they diverge through pidginization and creolization as, e.g., creole Arabic in East Africa, Ki-Nubi, and Juba Arabic of the southern Sudan. According to Versteegh (1984), all the modern Arabic sedentary dialects stem from pidgin Arabic.

Arabic dialects may be considered languages, comparable to the Romance situation. Peripheral Arabic dialects such as Uzbeki Arabic, Maltese, Juba Arabic and Ki-Nubi, Afghan Arabic, the extinct Andalusian (Spanish) Arabic, are more divergent than the mainstream Middle Eastern or North African dialects. Maltese, though often called Maltese Arabic, has in fact developed into a new language in its own right, unlike all other Arabic dialects, in that it is a national language with a non-Arabic writing system. Due to its isolation since the thirteenth century, it is also free from diglossia (see p. 267). (Modern South Arabian languages such as Jibbaali (Sheri) or Soqotri belong to a different group within Semitic, i.e., South Semitic, whereas Arabic is Central Semitic.)

It is usually believed that the larger the intercommunal geographical distance or isolation among dialects, the greater the linguistic differences among them, too. These are not the only factors, however, in dialect development as sociolinguistic factors also have come into play (see pp. 265–267). Mutual intelligibility remains, however, the **most** important consideration in dialect recognition.

Most comprehensive bibliographies available in comparative Arabic dialectology include Sobelman (1962) and Bakalla (1975, 1983). This chapter presents comparative Arabic dialectology from a double perspective, namely the major structural phenomena of Arabic dialects which form their internal makeup, as well as traits which set them apart. Map 2 shows the main dialect groups. We focus on the synchronic rather than the historical perspective. Each section first depicts the

Map 2 The main dialect groups

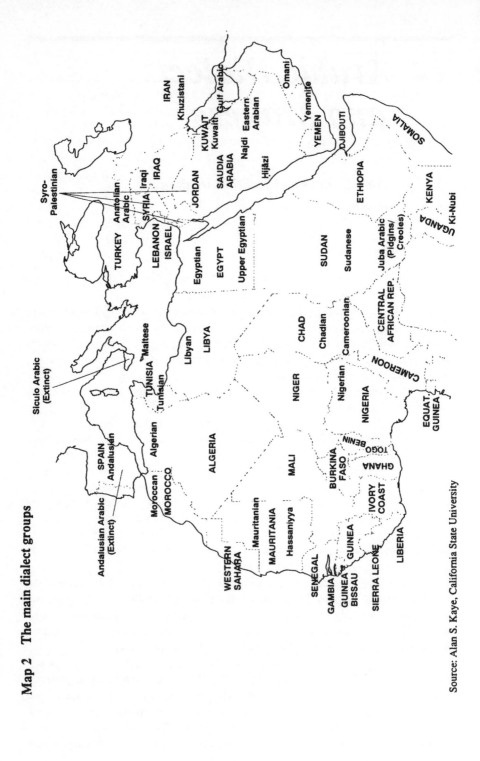

Source: Alan S. Kaye, California State University

common features of the major dialects and then discusses and illustrates linguistic issues pertaining to phonology, morphology, syntax and lexicon.

Our starting point is often Cairene, which is in a central location in the Arabic world and has much prestige among speakers of other Arabic dialects. We also consider the major dialects of Syria–Lebanon, Mesopotamia, the Arabian Peninsula, North Africa and elsewhere. Features of sub-Saharan African dialects and Maltese are also mentioned.

Dialect Geography: Eastern vs. Western Dialects

Though Arabic originally developed in Arabia, its speakers spread it eastward, northward and westward, along with Islam, from the seventh century CE. Following the doctrine of the "wave theory," dialects nearer the original center are more similar among themselves than ones at more distant locations. Much of the literature describes Arabic dialects from the viewpoint of the East–West dichotomy.

The Eastern dialects include the Arabian Peninsula (Saudi Arabia, Yemen, Kuwait, Oman and the United Arab Emirates), along with Mesopotamia (Iraq), the Syrian–Lebanese–Palestinian area as well as Jordan, Israel and Egypt. There are also some Arabic dialects quite distinctly removed and with few speakers; e.g., in Afghanistan and Uzbekistan. The isolated and nearly extinct Arabic dialect of Kormakiti (Cyprus) has been assumed to be related to Lebanese.

The Western group includes the dialects to the west of Egypt, namely Libyan, Tunisian, Algerian, Moroccan, and Mauritanian. Andalusian Arabic and Siculo Arabic (both extinct) also belong to this group. In Eastern Arabic are included, however, also the dialects of the Sudan, Chad and even Nigeria. In the latter there are many Arabic dialects spoken by parts of the respective populations with varying amounts of influence by local (e.g., Nilo-Saharan) languages, although a few affinities are shared with Western Arabic. As a whole, Sudanese dialects, at least those in the north, form one macro-grouping with the Egyptian dialects. Maltese is normally considered Western for it seems to be genetically related to Tunisian Arabic; however, some Eastern features (e.g., ʾ for the *qaaf*, *ʾimaala*) complicate the picture.

Differences among Eastern and Western dialects exist on all linguistic levels. Phonetically, the latter have lost many short vowels and reduced long vowels (as a result of Berber substratum). This change is typical of Tunisia, Algeria, Morocco, but rarely occurs elsewhere in Africa (Libya, the Sudan or Egypt). In addition, in many of these Western dialects the phonemic distinction between *s* and *ṣ* as well as between *z* and *ẓ* has been lost, unlike their parallels in the East. The main morphological difference lies in the imperfect prefixes: in the West (up to the Delta in Egypt) there is an innovative symmetrical *n-* for the sg. 1 and pl. (*nəktəb-nəktəbu* 'I/we write', respectively), while in the East only the pl. has *n-* (*ʾaktib-niktib*, id.). Furthermore, in the West, pl. verbs (including pl. 1f.) end with *-u*, which is missing from the parallel pl. 1 in the East. Syntactic differences are not numerous and often relate to lexical items used in certain syntactic roles; e.g., *illi* vs. *(id)di* 'that, which' (relative particles), or *ʾiza*, *ʾiδa* vs. *ʾila* 'if' in the East and West respectively.

The Basic Dichotomy: Bedouin vs. Sedentary Dialects

Even in olden times Arabic was a conglomerate of different dialects. The modern varieties continue the two basic sociolinguistic elements, namely the speaker's nomadic or sedentary backgrounds. On the one end there are typical urban (sedentary) dialects, and on the other, the bedouin ones. Between these two extremes exist degrees of bedouin/sedentary mixtures. The complex features of a dialect often reflect its bedouin/sedentary-type history.

The sedentary dialects, in all likelihood, evolved from a mixture of some original (Arabian) Arabic variety with a non-Arabic substratum while the bedouin-type dialects are of "less mixed" origin. Modern bedouin dialects in the Arabian Peninsula consist of a number of different groups. Such groups also existed in pre-Islamic times, with at least the Hijaaz and Tamiim dialects.

Bedouin remained more isolated from external influences than sedentary dwellers. Thus bedouin dialects preserve many old features, which are also similar to those of Classical Arabic (CA), and are today more conservative than sedentary dialects. One example of this cleavage is the Mesopotamian split between the *gələt* and *qəltu* groups, named after basic phonetic and morphological characteristics (see Blanc 1964).

Among the basic features of bedouin dialects there are the voicing (and fronting) of old Arabic *q (which usually becomes *q*, *j*, or *dz*); the tendency toward emphasis; the "*gahawa/bṣala* syndrome" of syllable structure (see p. 280), which affects verbs, nouns and adjectives more or less alike, and residues of syntactic case endings. Also, in bedouin dialects gender is usually kept more intact in plural pronouns than in sedentary dialects. Syntactic differencs are few; e.g., modal structures and distributions. Lexical variation between sedentary and bedouin dialects is considerable (see p. 308). Identical lexemes may have different meanings in sedentary and bedouin dialects (e.g., *daḥraj* 'see' in Galilean bedouin vs. 'roll something' in the sedentary Palestinian dialects, as in MSA (Modern Standard Arabic); Rosenhouse, 1984). Also, many bedouin lexemes are known in CA and are not used in sedentary dialects (e.g., *ḥusaam* 'sword', *an-nišaama* 'the brave men, warriors', *baʿiir* 'camels' in the Galilean bedouin dialects).

Communal Dialects: Muslim, Christian and Jewish Dialects

Religion (Islam, Christianity, Judaism) is the basis for the communal sociolinguistic division of Arabic dialects. As each of the religions has in the course of history split into sects, there are more than three communal dialects. Thus in Lebanon, e.g., Shiite dialects differ from those of the Sunnis, Druze, or Maronites.

Blanc (1964) discussed the issue of communal dialects and distinguished three degrees of interdialectal differentiation: minor, medium and major. Jerusalem Arabic was an example of the first, with differences noted in the frequency of certain phonemes or intonation patterns, or in the use of religion-specific lexemes.

A medium line was drawn for various North African towns where only Muslims and Jews lived. Algiers, e.g., displayed differences in (1) *s, j, r, q, h, e*; (2) the form of the feminine ending in nouns (*a* by Muslims and *e* by Jews); and (3) certain forms of bound prepositions. Clearer differences can be felt in the use of certain basic lexemes (e.g., adverbs of place and time, prepositions) and borrowed words. Such communal properties are systematic but few. Baghdad served as the major example of communal distinctions when it had Muslim, Jewish and Christian communities. Baghdadi dialects reflected the underlying division into sedentary and bedouin (Christians and Jews came earlier while the ex-bedouin Muslims sedentarized there later.)

Diglossia

The term "diglossia" was made popular for Arabic by W. Marçais in 1930, though K. Krumbacher already used it in 1902. Ferguson (1959) discussed other languages besides Arabic since elements of diglossia frequently occur in many languages. Thus, diglossia is probably a linguistic universal, though Arabic is unique in its "grand scale." Arabic diglossia is a sociolinguistic fact which unites most of the Arab world. Cypriot Arabic, Maltese, and most varieties of Juba and Chadian Arabic, however, do not have it. The phenomenon is ancient, dating from the pre-Islamic period; however, it is assumed that its Neo-Arabic form arose in the seventh century CE.

Diglossia involves two basic varieties of the same language living side by side, each performing different functions. While colloquial Arabic is always an acquired system, i.e., informally learnt, MSA is studied in school. Diglossia is best viewed as a continuum from the highest or most prestigious CA (fuṣḥaa) to the lowest or most colloquial dialect ('aammiyya). Thus MSA ʾalaysa kaδaalika 'isn't it so?' is Cairene (Ca.) muš/miš kida. A striking feature of diglossia is paired vocabulary; e.g., MSA ḥiδaaʾun 'shoe' = Ca. gazma, or MSA raʾaa 'see' = Ca. šaaf.

Generally, MSA is used in written texts, sermons, university lectures, most political speeches and news broadcasts, while colloquial Arabic is used conversing with family or friends, also in radio and TV soap operas. Since there is no clear delimitation between MSA and colloquial Arabic, native speakers often mix the two to various degrees using the so-called "middle" language.

Since the Qur'an is written in CA, it is admired as more beautiful, logical, elegant and eloquent than any colloquial dialect, and therefore also "better" than colloquial dialects. MSA is the mark of ʿuruuba or pan-Arabism, since there can be a high degree of mutual unintelligibility among various colloquial varieties such as Moroccan and Iraqi.

Gender-based Differences

Material is being accumulated attesting to the linguistic differences between Arabic-speaking men and women in the various dialects. Differences have been found on all levels – phonology, morphology, syntax, and vocabulary and discourse types and structures.

Table 14.1 Arabic consonant phonemes

	Bilabial	Labio-dental	Inter-dental	Dental	Emphatic	Palatal	Velar	Uvular	Pharyn-geal	Laryn-geal
Stops	b			t d	ṭ ḍ		k	q		ʾ
Affricates						ǰ š				
Fricatives		f	θ ð	s z	ṣ ð̣ (ẓ)			x ɣ	ḥ ʿ	h
Nasals	m			n						
Liquids (lateral and trill)				l r	ḷ					
Approximants	w					y				

Source: Alan S. Kaye, "Arabic," in *The World's Major Languages*, ed. B. Comrie. Oxford University Press, Oxford 1987, p. 666. Reproduced by permission of Oxford University Press.

Table 14.2 Reflexes of Classical Arabic *q* in some dialects

Place	CA qalb 'heart'	baqara 'cow'	waqt 'time'	qaal 'said'	qamar 'moon'	qahwa 'coffee'	quddaam 'in front of'
Jugari (Uzbek.)	qalb	baqara	waqt/†waḥt	qaal	qamar		giddaam
Mus.Bag.	galub	šbaqar	wagut/šwaket	gaal	gumar	gahwa	geddaam/jeddaam
J.Bag.	qalb			qaal	qamaɣ		jeddaam
Mosul	qaalb			qaal			
ʿAanah		†bagra	waqet	qaal		gahwa	
Rural Lower Iraq	galub	bgura/bagra	wakit	gaal	gumar	ghawa/gahwa	jiddaam
Judeo-Ar. Iraqi Kurdistan	qalb	baqara	waqt/waxt	qaal	qamar	ghawe	qoddaam
Mardin (Anatolia)	qalb	baqara	waqt/waxt	qaal	qamar	qaḥwe	qeddaam
Sheep nomads, Mes., NE Ara.	galb/galub	bgara	wagt/wakit	gaal	gumar	ghawa	jeddaam
Camel nomads, Mes., NE Ara.	galb/galub	bgara	wagt	gaal	gumar	ghawa	dˤˤeddaam
Aleppo	ʾalb	baʾara	waʾt	ʾaal	ʾamar	ʾahwa	ʾeddaam
Damascus	ʾalb	baʾara	waʾt	ʾaal	ʾamar	ʾahwe	ʾeddaam

Table 14.2 Reflexes of Classical Arabic *q* in some dialects (*continued*)

Place	CA	*qalb* 'heart'	*baqara* 'cow'	*waqt* 'time'	*qaal* 'said'	*qamar* 'moon'	*qahwa* 'coffee'	*quddaam* 'in front of'
Beirut		ʾalb	baʾara	waʾt	ʾaal	ʾamar	ʾahwe	ʾəddaam
NW Jordan		galib	bagara	wagət	gaal	gamar	gahwah	giddaam
Druze		qalb	baqara	wakt	qaal	qamar	qahwe	kuddaam
Nazareth		kalb	bakara	wakt	kaal	kamar	kahwe	ʾuddaam
Jerusalem		ʾalb	baʾara	waʾt	ʾaal	ʾamar	ʾahwe	kuddaam
Biir Zeet		kalb	bakara	wakt	kaal	kamar	kahwe	guddaam
Yemen (Sanʿaʾ)		galb	bagara	wagt	gaal	gamar	gahweh	ʾuddaam
Cairo		ʾalb	baʾara	waʾt	ʾaal	ʾamar	ʾahwa	giddaam
Sudan		galib	bagara	wagt	gaal	gamra	gahwa/gahawa	giddaam
Ouaday(Chad)		galəb	beger	wagt	gaal	gamar	gahwa	
E. Libyan (Benghazi)		galəb	əbgəra	wagət	gaal	gəmaṛ	gahawa	giddaam
Tunis		qalb	†bagra	waqt	gaal			quddaam
El Hamma de Gabes		galᵇ§			gal			
Marazig		galab		wəʾt	gal		gahwa/qahwa	geddaam
J. Algiers		ʾəlb				ʾəmr		ʾəddam
Bou Saada			bigar	weqt		gimar		
Djidjelli		qelb		weqt		qmer		qeddam
Casablanca		qelb	bqʌr/bgʌr	wʌqt		qemr		qoddam
N. Taza				waqt †wax		gəmra		
Maltese		qalp	bakar	waqt	qaal	qamar		quddiem
Andalusian (low register)		kalb	bakar	wakt		kamar		kuddim

† Only in one or two isolated places.

§ An irregular reflex.

Phonology

Consonants and Vowels
The consonantal segments of a "fairly typical" educated pronunciation of MSA are shown in Table 14.1, p. 268, although one can always argue about the precise definition of "typical."

The Arabic alphabet provides for a rough depiction of some of the phonological facts of CA and, on the whole, reflects consonantism better than vocalism. Arabic dialects, however, are not well served by the orthography because the pronunciation of some consonants differs from those presented in Table 14.1. Among the most conspicuous consonantal differences between CA and the dialects are the developments of Old Arabic *qaaf and *jiim (PCA [Proto-Colloquial Arabic] *žiim but PS [Proto-Semitic] *g). Somewhat less varied, yet important, is the development of Old Arabic *kaaf. Table 14.2, p. 268, gives the details of the reflexes of CA q for seven common illustrative words. Table 14.3 shows the correspondence for five lexemes with CA k. Some generalization to the data presented in the tables follows.

Qaaf
Bedouin (or those descended from speakers of bedouin or bedouinized dialects) have a voiced reflex of the qaaf, while sedentary dialects, such as Cairene and Damascene, have a voiceless one – ' < q. Many city/rural and sedentary/non-sedentary distinctions thus tend to cut across areas displaying a geographic unity.

The Old Arabic *q survives unvoiced in parts of Iraq, Lebanon, Syria, Yemen, Tunisia, Algeria and Morocco. In the case of (Muslim) Baghdadi it is ordinarily thought of as associated with more formal speech (or with that of Christians and Jews), whereas the g and j variants are associated with colloquial speech. The word for 'near' may be heard there as as jiriib, griib, giriib or qariib, and ṣidq 'truth, honesty' is pronounced as ṣigid (with metathesis), ṣidig, ṣidug, or ṣidiq.

The shift q > ' occurs in a geographically wide area: Aleppo, Damascus, Beirut, Jerusalem, Cairo, Jewish Algiers, Tlemçen, etc. The fact that it occurs also in Maltese is strong evidence that the latter cannot be considered a Maghrebine (North African) dialect, as has been its usual classification (along with Sicilian and Andalusian Arabic).

The loss of the emphatic nature of q has caused it to develop into k in e.g., Charmuuch (Iraq), some rural Palestinian dialects, Djidjelli (Algeria), Msirda and Andalusia.

Many bedouin dialects have a voiced qaaf, i.e., IPA [ɢ], which may even be its original pronunciation. Others have a g/j alternation as in Muslim Baghdadi, whereas others have a g/dz reflex. This alternation often depends on a front vowel environment. The affrication of qaaf as dž (and k > tš) in Yemen and Central Najd occurs in some dialects of southern Iraq and the Arabian Peninsula, too. See Map 3, p. 272. Other developments occur sporadically in various dialects as, e.g., ḥ in addition to q/g in Jugari Arabic (Uzbekistan) and x < q in Iraq.

Table 14.3 Reflexes of Classical Arabic *k* in some dialects with CA correspondences

Place	CA kaan 'he was'	kabiir 'big'	kalb 'dog'	kull 'all'	kitaab 'book'
Jugari (Uzbek.)	koon	kabiir	kalb	kul	ḳitaab
Mus. Bag.	čaan	čebiir	čaleb	kull	†ketaab
Jewish Baghdad	kaan	kbiiɣ	kalb	kell	
Mosul	ḳaan			kell	
ʿAanah	†čaan	kbiir	†čaleb		
Rural Lower Iraq	čaan	čebiir		kill	
Judeo-Ar. Iraqi					
Kurdistan	kaan	gəbiir	kalb	kəll	
Mardin (Anatolia)	kaan	gbiir	kalb	kəll	kteeb
Sheep nomads,					
Mes. NE Ara.	caan	čebiir	čalb	kill	ktaab
Camel nomads,					
Mes. NE Ara.		cebiir	calb		
Aleppo	kaan	kbiir	kalb	kull	ktaab
Damascus	kaan	kbiir	kalb	kəll	ktaab
Beirut	kaan	kbiir	kalb	kəll	ktaab
Horan	kaan	čebiir	čal^{e}b/†kelb		
Druze	kaan	kbiir	kalb	kull	ktaab
Nazareth	kaan	kbiir	kalb	kull	ktaab
Jerusalem	kaan	kbiir	kalb	kull	ktaab
Biir Zeet	čaan	čbiir	čalb	kəll	čtaab/ktaab
Yemen	kaan	kabiir	kalb	kull	kitaab
Cairo	kaan	kibiir	kalb	kull	kitaab
Sudan	kaan	kabiir	kalib	kull	kitaab
Ouaday(Chad)	kaan	kebiir	kelb	kull	kitaab
E. Libyan					
(Benghazi)	kaan/kien	kibiir	kalib	kill	ktaab/ktieb
Tunis	kaan	kbiir	kalb	kul	ktaab
Marazig	kaan	kebiir	kalb	kul	kataab
J. Algiers	kan	kbir	kəlb	kəll	ktab
Bou Saada					k^{u}taab
Djidjelli	kan	kbir	kəlb	kəll/k^{s}ell	
Casablanca	kan	kbir	kəlb	kəl	
Maltese	kien	gbiir	kelp	kol	ktiep
Andalusian	kin	kibiir	kalib	kill	ktaab/ktieb

† An irregular reflex.

j *vs.* dz

The following examples demonstrate Old Arabic **q > j/dz* in Kuwaiti and ʿAnaiza dialects (Eastern Arabian Peninsula): Ku. *ṭiriij* vs. ʿAnaiza *ṭiriidz* 'road', Ku. *θijiil* vs. ʿAnaiza *θidziil* 'heavy', Ku. *dijiij* vs. ʿAnaiza *didziidz* 'flour', Ku. *jiddaam* vs. ʿAnaiza *dziddaam* 'in front of, forward'.

Other Developments

Other developments occur in limited circumstances and sporadically in various dialects. Thus, e.g., Jugari Arabic (Uzbekistan) has *ḥ* in addition to *q/g*, Iraqi

Map 3   The approximate distribution of the affricated variants of ك and ق

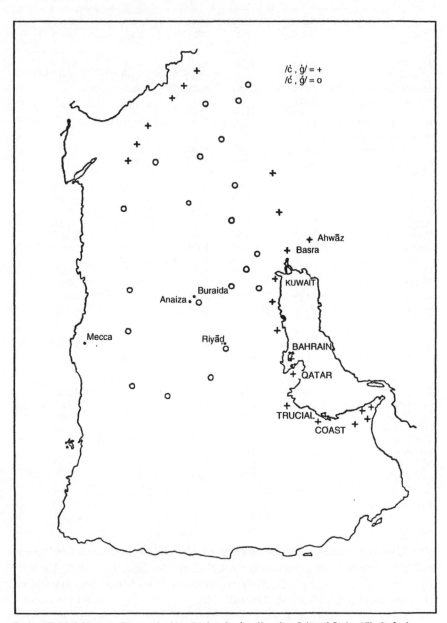

Source: T. M. Johnstone, *Eastern Arabian Dialect Studies* (London Oriental Series 17). Oxford University Press, London 1967, p. 5. Reproduced by permission of Oxford University Press.

Arabic has $x < q$ in some lexemes, e.g., *ṭaqm* (MSA) = *ṭaxim* (Baghdadi) 'suit (clothes), set'. (Some developments might be due to effects of bilingualism and/or substratum, as with the above example, cf. Persian *väqt* 'time' < Arabic *waqt* > colloquial Persian *väx*.)

Kaaf

The development of PS (Proto-Semitic) *k*, through Old Arabic **k*, is described in this section. It remains *k* in most of the sedentary dialects, including Jugari, Christian and Jewish Baghdadi, Mosul, Aleppo, Laodicea, Hama, Homs, Beirut, Damascus, Jerusalem, Cairo, Yemen, the Sudan, Ouaday (Chad), Oran, Bou-Saada, Marazig, Morocco and Andalusia.

It has palatalized to *kʸ* in many areas such as in the Arabian Peninsula (e.g., Oman) and in Djidjelli. The affrication of *k* into *č* is noteworthy in the contiguity of front vowels in all positions among many bedouin dialects in Saudi Arabia, Syria, Iraq and Muslim Baghdadi and among the Bahraini Sunnis, and as unconditioned articulation in other dialects in the Syro-Palestinian area, including some rural Samaria and Galilee ones, as well as those of the Shiites in Bahrain. At present, the affricate articulation tends to occur more frequently in the speech of the older generation; e.g., *šibbaač* 'window' for *šibbaak* due to the undergoing processes of leveling and koineization and the spread of MSA. The situation in the Arabian Peninsula demonstrated by Kuwaiti *č* and 'Anaiza (Najdi) *ts* is fairly typical as the affricates occur in the environment of front vowels. The symmetry of both dialects is such that also *j* and *dz* regularly occur for the *qaaf*. Consider a few examples of the opposition *č/ts* between Kuwaiti Arabic and 'Anaiza Arabic: Ku. *inčaan* vs. 'Anaiza *intsaan* 'if', Ku. *čabda* vs. 'Anaiza *tsabda* 'liver', Ku. *ḥinč* vs. 'Anaiza *ḥanats* 'jaw', and Ku. *čiθiir* vs. 'Anaiza *tsiθiir* 'much'.

In Yemenite dialects and in Bahrain, however, one finds also *š* for *k* in the sg. 2f. (see Table 14.5, p. 288). This may probably have led to the change of *šaaf* 'he saw' into *čaaf* in this area (Holes 1983). Many North African dialects affricate *t* and *k* to *ts* (*tsbiir* 'big' for *kbiir*). The latter is a Judeo-Arabic isogloss and exists (see p. 270) in the Arabian Peninsula, too (for *q*).

In Maltese *g* occurs for Old Arabic **k* (via regressive assimilation) and *ċ* and *ts* for Old Arabic **g*, e.g., *gibiir* 'big', *ħriġt* [hričt] 'I went out'. A typical example of the variations in one region (Eastern Arabian Peninsula) is the modal particle *tsid* ('Anaiza), *čid* (Abu Dhabi), *qid ~ jid* (Qatar), *dzid* (Najd).

In modern Yemenite dialects, as in CA, *kaskasa/kaškaša* occurs. This phenomenon is the suffixation of *s(i)* or *š(i)* to the sg. 2f. bound pronoun -*ki*, or its replacement by such an element.

Root Alternation and Morphological Doublets

Phonological rules affect the structuring of the root and yield allomorphy or suppletive structures. The following illustrations are from Muslim Baghdadi: *čaan/ykuun* 'be', *čibiir/ kbaar* 'big', *čarra* 'he gulped', but *karʿa* 'a gulp'. Examples of morphological doublets from Muslim Baghdadi are: *mčammal* 'complete' vs. *mkammal* 'someone perfect', *čiwa* 'to scorch' vs. *kiwa* 'to iron', *kital* 'to hit' vs. *qital* 'to kill', *fariq* 'parting (of hair)' vs. *farig* 'difference'.

Jiim

Another major consonantal isogloss in Arabic dialects is the reflex of CA *jiim*. The historical development yields three major productions of this phoneme in the dialects: *g*, *ž*, *j (dž)*. In some dialects *jiim* has been fronted to g^y (Yemenite, some other Arabian dialects) or d^y (in Sudan). In a few others (notably, Sunni dialects in Bahrain) *y* has entirely taken over. The following examples may be taken as representative but not exhaustive. Asterisked forms indicate PCA.

Cairo /g/
*/ž/ → /g/   */žamal/ >   /gamal/ 'camel'
Damascus /ž/
*/ž/ → /ž/   */žamal/ >   /žamal/ 'camel'
Aleppo /j/
*/ž/ → /j/   */žamal/ >   /jamal/ 'camel'
Baghdadi (Muslim) /j /
*/ž/ → /j/   */žild/ >   /jilid/ 'skin'
Yemenite /j /
*/ž/ → /j/   */žild/ >   /jild/ 'skin'
Medina (Saudi Arabia) /d^y/
*/ž/ → /d^y/   */žamal/ >   /d^{y}amal/ 'camel'
Khartoum /d^y/
*/ž/ → /d^y/   */žabal/ >   /d^{y}abal/ 'mountain'
Jugari (Uzbekistan) /j/
*/ž/ → /j/   */žawaab/ >   /jawoob/ 'answer'
Moroccan /ž/, /g/
*/ž/ → /ž/   */žuuʕ/ >   /žuʕ/ 'hunger'
*/ž/ → /g/   *#So MI (mirror image)   So {s, z} So#
                                 */žibs/ >   /gəbs/ 'plaster'
                                 */žazzaar/ >   /gzzar/ 'butcher'

Exceptions to this rule may exist; thus /gləs/ 'he sat', /gales/ 'sitting' but /mažles/ 'parliament' (the latter is probably a MSA loanword).

Maltese /j/ /š/ /č/
*/ž/ → /j/   */žabal/ >   *ġebel* 'mountain'
*/ž/ → /š/ /__ t   */xiražt/ >   *ħriġt* 'I went out'
*/ž/ → /č/ (by dissimilation)
                  */zawž/ >   *zewġ* 'two'
Algiers (Jewish) /j/ /ž/
*/ž/ → /j/   */jamal/ >   /jamal/ 'camel'
*/ž/ → /ž/ /__ t   */ħaažati/ >   /ħažti/ 'my thing'

Tunis /ž/, /z/
*/ž/ → /ž/   */žabal/ >   /žbal/ 'mountain'
*/ž/ → /z/   *#So MI So {s, z} So#
                  */žibs/ >   /zibs/ 'plaster'
                  */žewza/ >   /zuuza/ 'nut'
                  */zawž/ >   /zuuz/ 'two'
Djidjelli (Algeria) /ž/
*/ž/ → /ž/   */žamal/ >   /žamal/ 'camel'
Gulf (Abu Dhabi) /y/ /j/
*/ž/ → /y/ ~ /j/ */rižl/ >   /riil/ 'foot'

(Some speakers have free variation of /y/ ~ /j/: /ya/ ~ /ja/ 'he came'.)

Labials

CA and MSA do not have *p* or *v*, yet some dialects have developed these in native words in addition to their occurrence in loanwords. The following examples are from Yemenite Arabic (Ṣanʿāʾ): *sappaak* 'pipe fitter', *ðuppi* 'fly'. In Iraq there is even an emphatic *p*. Certain Moroccan dialects have *b > v*. Also Maltese, Anatolian and Cypriot Arabic use *v*, e.g., Cypriot *zava* for *jawwa* 'inside'.

Interdentals

One can dichotomize Arabic dialects into those which preserve fricative *θ, δ* and those which merge them with their corresponding stops. As a rule of thumb, those which keep them have *δ* as the reflex of the *ḍaad*, originally probably an emphatic lateralized dental [ḍl]. Yemenite Arabic is typical of an interdental preserving dialect: *θalaaθa* '3', *ʾaxδar* 'green', *ðippaal* 'wedding celebration'. However a *ḍ* has also developed there by way of voicing of *ṭ*. Consider *maḍar* 'rain', *baḍḍa* 'duck' and *maḍaabix* 'kitchens' (pl. of *maṭbax*). (This probably represents the original state of affairs, as the emphatics were voiced.)

Developments of interdentals include *θ > f* (*falaafa* '3' in Shiite Hasaawi Arabic, Eastern Saudi Arabic and Bahraini), *famma* ('there is', Tunisia) and Anatolian *δ > v* (*vahab* 'gold'). Among other changes are *θ > s*: in Uzbekistan, Chad, Cameroon: Jugari *salaas* '3', Cameroonian *salaasa* '3'; *δ > ḍ* in Chad *ḍahab* 'gold'; *δ > z* and even *δ > ẓ* in *ʿaẓiim* 'great' in many dialects (e.g., Egyptian).

The development of interdental fricatives to stops distinguishes between bedouin and sedentary dialects in that the former tend to preserve the fricative articulation. In Dathina (Yemenite Arabic), e.g., the emphatic *δ* is preserved as an interdental while the *ḍaad* is an emphatic *ḷ*.

Emphatics

Most Arabic dialects today contain emphatic (*mufaxxama*) vs. non-emphatic (*muraqqaqa*) contrasts (except for a few dialects such as Maltese, Chadian, and Nigerian Arabic (some speakers), Juba Arabic, Ki-Nubi, and Cypriot Arabic. The emphatic consonants basically include *ṣ, ḍ, ṭ, δ*, depicted herein with a dot underneath them. Thus a word such as Cairene *ṣeef* 'summer' has a non-emphatic minimal pair *seef* 'sword'. The vowels around an emphatic as a rule tend to become lower, retracted or more centralized than those around non-emphatics. The usual phonological explanation for this feature lies in the opposition between emphatic and non-emphatic parallel consonants.

Emphatics are often called velarized or pharyngealized due to difficulties in their phonetic description. (The IPA indicates both pharyngealization or velarization with a wavy bar through the consonant, i.e., [ɫ].) Indeed, this is a very controversial area in the Arabic phonological literature as to description and functioning. They correspond to ejectives in Ethio-Semitic languages, but there it is probably due to the Cushitic substratum.

Since Modern South Arabian languages have ejectives as the phonetic realization of emphasis, many Semitists hypothesize that the PS emphatics were ejectives as well. Consequently, the Arabic type today seems to be secondary, although not all Semitists agree. In the CA period the existence of emphatics in the language was noted, as the name *luɣat al-ḍaad* 'the language of *ḍaad*' for Arabic indicates (cf. *luɣat muḍar* 'the language of Muḍar', also containing a *ḍaad*).

The Debate about Emphasis

Blanc (1953) in his fundamental study of Druze dialects in the Galilee area discussed the basic issues of the debate between the twin series of non-emphatic and emphatic consonants therein. Blanc (1953: 53) maintains: "The difference between them is distinctive in some cases and non-distinctive in others, but it is in all cases acoustically striking and *characteristic of the dialect*, and even non-distinctive *tafxiim* [emphasis] plays an important role in phonetic change on both the historical and the synchronic levels."

Roman Jakobson (1957) attributes some of the phonetic characteristics of emphasis to a contraction of the upper pharynx. Velarization (or "darkness," among other terms) refers in essence to a decrease in the volume of the back orifice of the vocal tract (buccal cavity) serving as a resonator. In addition to the above, emphasis may also involve some degree of protrusion and rounding of the lips. This explains why emphatics are often perceived as labials by non-Arabs and why they have labial correlates when Arabic words with them are borrowed into other languages (e.g., Swahili). Jakobson (ibid.) called this feature [+flat] which he considered also present in labials and labialized phonemes. In terms of acoustic phonetics (and as seen in spectrograms), emphatics reveal lower second formant frequency ranges compared to the non-emphatics (cf. Obrecht 1968).

Emphasis has been problematic for phonologists, particularly because of difficulties in defining "emphasis spread." Walter Lehn (1963) suggested that at least for Cairene, the minimum domain of emphasis is the syllable and the maximum domain is the utterance. He suggested that emphasis should not be treated as a distinctive feature of the consonantal or vocalic system but as a redundant feature of both and proposed underlining all emphatics, e.g., _darab_ 'he hit', _darabit_ 'she hit'. (We do not use this transcription.)

Other Developments of the Emphatics
The existence of emphatics is remarkably stable throughout the Arab world, although they have been lost in some dialects (see p. 275). In addition to the primary emphatics noted there, found also in CA and MSA, many dialects developed new secondary ones. Some sedentary dialects have only single, isolated words with secondary emphasis; cf. Galilee Druze *baaba* 'father', *yamma* 'mother', *ʾalla* 'God'. In other sedentary dialects emphasis is more widespread, mainly for *r, l, m, n*; e.g., MSA *raʾs* vs. Ca. *raaṣ*, MSA *daar* vs. Mor. *ḍaaṛ*. However, emphatic *f, b, w, p, ġ* are also to be noted. Much emphaticization is characteristic of bedouin dialects; thus cf. bedouin *ġaaδi* vs. sedentary *ʾaaḍi* 'judge'. Consider, however, also Nigerian Arabic *karra* 'he tore', *karra* 'he dragged'; *gallab* 'he raced', *gallab* 'he got angry'; *amm* 'mother' and *emm* 'uncle'.

In many varieties of Nigerian Arabic the *t* has become a voiced pharyngealized implosive (symbolized here as *ḍ*; e.g., *xaḍḍa* 'put'). Also, in Zabiid (Yemenite Arabic) the reflex of *t* and *q* is glottalized *t̉, k̉*, respectively.

Differentiated use of emphatics is also characteristic of male speech having more emphasis than female speech. Whether this is true for the whole Arab world remains to be investigated.

Pharyngeals

h and *ʿ* are basic characteristics of Arabic, although they have usually been lost in, e.g., Maltese, Cypriot and Chadian Arabic. They have totally disappeared in Nigerian Arabic, Juba Arabic and Ki-Nubi. Maltese merged *x > h* and *h*, and *γ > ʿ* as happened also in NW Semitic, but has subsequently lost *ʿ*. In Cypriot Arabic *h > x* (*paxr < bahr* 'sea') and *γ > ʿ*, as in Maltese. In North Yemen (Zabiid) *ʿ* is not a pharyngeal fricative but a pharyngeal plosive. J. C. Catford calls both of these Semitic phonemes "pharyngeal approximants," whereas Ladefoged and Maddieson (1996: 168) refer to them as "epiglottals."

Laryngeals

ʾ already began to weaken in Old Arabic, cf. the CA imperative of *ʾaxaδa = xuδ* 'take!' or the possible imperfect of *saʾala*, namely, *yasʾalu ~ yasalu* 'he will ask'. In many dialects one finds many more such cases; e.g., MSA *al-marʾah/imraʾah* > colloquial *mara* 'woman' (in Cairene), or active participle MSA *naaʾim* > colloquial *naayim* 'asleep'. (This process does not occur with *ʾ < *q*.) Original *ʾ* is often replaced in the dialects by *w, y* or by compensatory vowel lengthening; e.g., colloquial *raaṣ* for CA *raʾs*. III-*ʾ* verbs have merged with III-*y* ones: *bada* (CA *badaʾa*) 'he began' is in the same class with *bana* (CA *banaa*) 'he built'.

h, too, has been lost in many dialects, particularly in the 3rd person suffixes (CA *-hu/-ha/-hum/-hunna* 'sg. m., sg. f., pl. m., pl. f.' respectively. Some conservative dialects (e.g., bedouin and Yemenite ones) have, however, preserved the feminine *-h*.

Vowels

Though the CA and MSA vowel system have the classical triangular shape preserving PS *a–i–u* vocalism, many Arabic dialects have developed other vowels such as *ə, e, o*, etc. As in CA and MSA, the vowels may be short or long (geminated) in most dialects. Many analyses of Moroccan Arabic, for example, do not contrast long vs. short vowels.

Vowel allophonics are quite rich because vowels take on the coloring of adjacent consonants; emphatics (and back consonants such as *r*) push them down and back, while non-emphatics raise them to higher and front positions; however, not all dialects (e.g., Nigerian Arabic) have such *a* vs. *ä* variation. Many of the mainstream dialects follow similar or identical rules. They are presented in the following rule series (the lack of a line in the environment means that the segment may occur on either side of the motivating feature or segment):

1 /i/ → [ɨ] /   – [+ emphatic] –
    → /ɪ/   – {ʿ, γ} –
    → /i/   (elsewhere)

2 /ii/ → [ɨɨ] /   – [+ emphatic] – (except /ļ/)
    → /ɪɪ/   – {ʿ, γ} –
    → /ii/   (elsewhere)

3 /u/ → /ʊ/ /   – [+ emphatic] –
    → /u/   (elsewhere)

4 /uu/ → /ʊʊ/ /   – [+ emphatic] – (except /ļ/)
    → /uu/   (elsewhere)

5 /a/ → /ə ~ ä/ __ #   (but not next to /q, ʿ, r, γ/)

$$\rightarrow /a/ \quad / \quad \left[\left\{ \begin{matrix} - + \text{emphatic} - \\ \left\{ \begin{matrix} -q- \\ -r- \end{matrix} \right\} \end{matrix} \right\} \right]$$

    → /ʌ/ /   – {ʿ, γ} –
    → /æ/ /   (elsewhere)

$$6 \quad /aa/ \rightarrow /aa/ \quad / \quad \left[\left\{ \begin{matrix} - + \text{emphatic} - \\ \left\{ \begin{matrix} -q- \\ -r- \end{matrix} \right\} \end{matrix} \right\} \right]$$

    → /ʌʌ/ /   – {ʿ, γ} –
    → /ææ ~ ää/   (elsewhere)

In the dialects the short vowels are more susceptible to change than the long ones. CA *i, u* merge in many Eastern and Western dialects into one central vowel *ə* (as in Geʿez). The most stable and conservative of the three short vowels is usually *a*, but in many dialects, it, too, is subject to change. Many Maghrebine dialects shortened CA *aa*, while unstressed CA *a* has been deleted and vocalic length ceased to be relevant.

The short vowels often do not match up in the dialects. (This can also be noted for Old Arabic dialects.) CA had many doublets and even triplets in its short vowel configuration, e.g., *laṣṣ*, *liṣṣ*, *luṣṣ* 'thief'. Many modern vocalic discrepancies may be attributed to this feature. Compare Nigerian Arabic *himirre ~ humurre* 'donkeys' in which we can posit either assimilation or dissimilation processes.

CA possessed two diphthongs *aw* and *ay*: *yawm* 'day' and *bayt* 'house'. Some dialects preserve them; e.g., Lebanese or Yemenite *bayt* 'house' (yet in some dialects of both also *beet*). In most of the Eastern dialects the diphthongs have monophthongized into *oo*, *ee*, respectively, and into *uu*, *ii* in the Maghreb. Some Syro-Lebanese dialects delete the second element of the diphthong, yielding *aa* or *a* (e.g., *jaᶜaan* 'hungry', *lamuun* 'lemon').

ᵓimaala: /a/-Raising

ᵓ*imaala* (literally 'inclination') refers to *a*-raising (*a > e/i/ie*) due to the umlauting influence of *i*. This phonetic feature is typical of Iraq, Syria and Lebanon. Maltese has it, too; e.g., *bieb* 'door' (= MSA *baab*), *kelmiet* 'words' (= MSA *kalimaat*).

ᵓ*imaala* may be internal (cf. above) or final, in which it is mainly an allomorph of the feminine ending *-a*, (cf. Syrian *madrase* 'school' vs. *riyaaḍa* 'sport'). Basically *a* occurs after all back consonants including emphatics and *e* elsewhere. The height of the vowel (*e, i*) depends on the dialect in question.

Standard Maltese has no final ᵓ*imaala*: *kalba* 'bitch', *tfajla* 'young woman', but Gozo Maltese has it: *sitte* 'six' for standard *sitta*. Maltese can be regarded as a *Mischsprache*, since it has undergone heavy ᵓ*imaala* in other positions; e.g., *tiegħi* 'my' (but *tagħha* 'hers').

Phonotactics

Changes in syllable structures had far-reaching ramifications in the dialects. While CA does not allow for long vowels in closed syllables (except *aa*) or before consonant clusters in general, the dialects allow both, although there are different phonotactic systems for consonant clusters and epenthetic rules to break them up. Elision of the short unstressed vowels *i* and *u* is similar to developments in Hebrew, Aramaic or Ethiopic, i.e., the "normal" development one might have expected. A major feature in the dialects is anaptyxis; e.g., Ca. *il-bint-ĭ-di* 'this girl' in which *ĭ* is inserted to break up the triple consonant cluster. Some dialects have degemination (e.g., Galilean and Iraqi). Multi-consonantal clusters are, however, typical of Maghrebine dialects.

Consonantal assimilations occur in all Arabic dialects. Nigerian Arabic is typical: *albiddi* 'this girl' < *albitt + di* (lit. the + girl + this (f.)), or *benna* 'our house' < *beet+-na*, Mor. *srqunna* 'they stole from us' < *srgu+ lna*, Maltese *tagħha* 'hers' < **taᶜha*. Some assimilations point to consonantal losses in final positions such as with *-h* (cf. p. 277) which is observed, e.g., in Cairene *wišš* or Maltese *wiċ* 'face' < PCA **wiẑh* (final devoicing). Cf. Nig. Ar. *juwaap* 'answer' (with final nasal plosion) < **jawaab*, Cyp. Ar. *taep* 'good' < **tayyib*.

Some Egyptian and Sudanese dialects are known for final consonant deletion: Sud. Rubatab *kitaa* for *kitaab* 'book', Upper Eg. *diggee* < *dilgeet* 'now', or *kee* 'how' for *keef*, *raaˤ albeet* for *raaḥ ˤalbeet* 'he went home' in Galilean, Lebanese and Anatolian dialects. This process exists in some Eastern bedouin dialects and the rural forms of Juba Arabic and Ki-Nubi as well (e.g., *ye-wéle* 'boy sg.' *yewelé* 'boy pl.' < Eg. *yaa walad*, 'oh, boy'). It is also known elsewhere in Semitic; cf. e.g. Syriac *bee* 'house'.

Vowel Deletion and Vocalic Assimilation

The most apparent difference between MSA and the dialects is the loss of vowels. The loss of case and mood marking (*ˀiˤraab*) in the dialects is alone responsible for many final consonant clusters making vowel epenthesis common. So, too, various phonological rules have resulted in many long vowels shortening and short vowels deleting in various environments. The following example from Cairene is typical: *kaatib* 'writer, having written' yields f. *katba*, pl. *katbiin*. The extreme in vowel loss are Moroccan dialects. (Berber languages with their multi-consonantal clusters make substratum the likely explanation.)

Vocalic assimilation is common in all Arabic dialects. Consider Cairene *ḥaˀˀ* + *-ku(m)* 'your (pl. m.) right' > *ḥaˀˀúku(m)* (Yemeni *ḥaggukum*), but *ḥaˀˀ* + *-ha* > *ḥaˀˀáha* 'her right'. Other cases are bedouin *ubuuna* 'our father' < *ˀabu* 'father'; Nig. Ar. *usum* 'name' occurs also in Palestinian Arabic, though in most dialects it is *ˀisim/ˀasim*, or Nig. Ar. *bagarikki* 'your (sg. f.) cow' vs. *bagarukku* 'your (pl. m.) cow'.

Stress

The Arab grammarians never wrote about stress in the Old Arabic dialects. We can only assume that it was not phonemic and thus irrelevant to their concerns. Stress in the modern dialects is, however, one of the most involved topics in Arabic phonology.

As illustrative, in Cairene *ḥaˀˀúku(m)* 'your (pl.) right', the stressed vowel is originally anaptyctic, whereas in Yemenite the same vowel is unstressed (see p. 280). The diachronic explanations for such developments have been unsatisfactory.

Stress in the dialects may be considered phonemic since there are minimal pairs establishing this. Ca. *ḍárabu* 'they hit' vs. *ḍarabúu* 'they hit him', or Pal. *ˀaxádna* 'we took' vs. *ˀaxadnáa* 'we took it', and *ˀábila* 'before her' vs. *ˀabíla* 'receive her!'.

In many dialects word stress rules place the main stress on long syllables, especially at the end of the word, or on the penultimate or antepenultimate where there is no long syllable; long vowels are thus stressed, but the stress shifts to the second of two long vowels in a word as the first shortens. In Cairene the penult is typically stressed in, e.g., *madrása* 'school' whereas Damascene stresses the antepenultimate (*mádrase*).

Arabic dialects can be be bifurcated *vis-à-vis* stress: Eastern with *kátab* 'he wrote', vs. Western with *ktáb*, *ktǝb*. Also Eastern bedouin dialects (in Syria and Arabia) show the two stress patterns. This indicates that the dichotomy probably arose when Arabic dialects developed syllable stress. Maltese is in this regard clearly Eastern (*kísar* 'he broke', *tálab* 'he asked') unlike Maghrebine dialects. The Chadian–Nigerian area is complicated as there is a major dichotomy between *kátab* 'he wrote' (Gawalme) vs. *katáb* (Balge).

The same situation occurs in CVCVCV words. The original PCA stress on the first syllable, has been preserved in Ca. *sámaka* 'fish', Sudan *bágara* 'cow', Chad. *séjera* 'tree', Bag. and Jugari *hájara* 'stone' (cf. Ki-Nubi *sámaga* 'fish'). The unstressed vowel is usually elided in dialects which elide various medial vowels of the perfect plural, e.g.: Maur. *sádga* 'alms', Moroccan *bə́gra*, Alg., Tun., Mal. and Hadramawt *bágra* 'cow', Omani *šéjre* 'tree'.

Many bedouin dialects and some sedentary descendants thereof in the Arabian Peninsula are known for the "*ghawa* syndrome" (< g/*qahwa*) in which the first vowel of this word pattern is elided while stress moves to the following vowel. This shift usually depends on the presence of a "guttural" around the first vowel; e.g., *ghawa* 'coffee' (hence its name), *ɣnima* 'ewe', *bṣala* 'onion' and *yʿarf* 'he knows'.

Some bedouin dialects stress initial CVC syllables even if they are prefixed; e.g. *álaxu* 'the brother', *ʾáštaɣal* 'he worked'. This phenomenon may be used to prove the originally bedouin nature of Nigerian Arabic (*álme* is 'water' with an originally frozen definite article vs. *alálme* 'the water').

An unusual form is to be noted in Nigerian Arabic in which the 1st pronominal suffix -*i* is stressed; e.g., *úṣubi* 'finger' vs. *uṣubí* 'my finger'. This occurs elsewhere (Egypt, Chad, and the Negev bedouin dialects), cf. Chadian Arabic *ligiiní* 'he found me' and Sinai Arabic *maṭlabii* 'my cow'. These cases may be used as evidence that the object suffixes attract the stress, i.e., that stress is also morphologically conditioned.

Morphology

Arabic morphology deals mainly with the nominal and verbal elements. The adjective is included in nominal morphology, for morphologically it is not distinct from the noun.

Nominal Morphology

Nouns
Certain nouns are inflected for gender (m., f.) and most of them for number (sg. du., pl.). Still, there are some differences among dialects concerning the gender of certain nouns; e.g., *raas* 'head' which is f. in Cairene but m. in Jerusalem Arabic.

Noun structures may be simple (e.g., C*a*CC, C*u*CC, C*i*CC) or augmented by affixes. Quadriradical roots seem to be more abundant in the Maghrebine dialects than in Eastern ones; e.g., *sərwal* 'trousers', *zərbiya* 'rug', *sərduq* 'cock'. A clear tendency is to make biconsonantal nouns triconsonantal via *Systemzwang*; e.g., *dam* > *damm* 'blood'(possibly an archaism), *yad* > *ʾiid* 'hand' (making the root triconsonantal *'yd*), *'ibn* > *'iben* 'son', *hum* > *humma* 'they', etc. Bedouin and sedentary dialects are distinguished by the "*gahawa* syndrome," e.g., sedentary *ɣaname* ~ bedouin and bedouinized *ɣnima* 'ewe'.

Verbal Nouns

Verbal nouns (except for Form I, which has many patterns) are directly related to the verb forms themselves (cf. p. 293). Thus in Cairene: *taCCiiC* is for Form II (e.g., *tanziil* 'lowering of prices'), *miCaCCa* or *CiCaaC* for Form III (e.g., *mi'aksa* 'quarrel', *firaaq* 'parting from someone'); *'iCCaaC* for Form IV (*'ikraam* 'respect, hospitality'); *taCaCCuC* for Form V (*takabbur* 'self-satisfaction'); *taCaaCuC* for Form VI (*tafaahum* 'mutual understanding'); *'inCiCaaC* for Form VII (*infigaar* 'explosion'); *iCtiCaaC* for Form VIII (*'i'tiraaf* 'confession'); *'iC-CiCaaC* for Form IX (*'ihmiraar* 'turning red', and *'istiCCaaC* for Form X (*'isti'maal* 'use, applying something').

Some new verbal noun patterns have evolved in certain dialects, mainly in the Maghreb; e.g., *t'aniid* 'rivalry' for Form III in Algeria, *metgaarsa* 'wrestling' (for Form VI) and *tmesxiir* 'making of oneself a laughing stock' in Morocco, *tkebbir* 'self-importance, enlarging' (for Form V), *tqabid* 'fighting' (for Form VI) and *stenbih* 'awakening' (for Form X) in Maltese.

In general, verbal nouns of the derived Forms are rare and are often substituted by verbal nouns of Forms I–III of the same roots.

Gender

For gender distinction a suffix marks the feminine while the unmarked noun (and adjective) is considered masculine. This method applies when the feminine form implies natural sex, grammatical gender, or unit (in cases of 'unit nouns'). Thus in Ca. *malik* 'king' : *malika* 'queen'; *kalb* 'dog' : *kalba* 'bitch': *kibiir* 'big (m.)' : *kibiira* 'big (f.)': *maktab* 'office' : *maktaba* 'library'.

The feminine ending of a free noun is in most dialects *a/e* (according to dialect-specific phonological rules – cf. p. 278); however, in Negev bedouin *-ih* also occurs; e.g., *himuulih* 'clan', *girbih* 'water skin'. (This ending occurs also in other noun patterns which have a short or long final *a*.) In many Yemenite dialects the feminine ending is *-at/-it*, e.g. *ak-kahalat* 'the old woman' (Gumar), *in-niswaanit* 'the woman' (An-Nadiir). This *-t* appears in the other dialects only in bound environments. (This *t* is called *taa' marbuuṭa* in MSA and carries the case ending and is therefore never omitted except in pre-pause position.)

Some body parts, natural elements etc. (which vary among the dialects) are feminine though not overtly marked; e.g., Cairene *ṛaaṣ* 'head'; *šams* 'sun'; *ḥarb* 'war'; *riiḥ* 'wind'; *suu'* 'market'; *bint* 'girl' etc. (In Maghrebine dialects *swiiqa* 'holiday market' and *bnita* 'little girl' also occur.) Rarely, a masculine noun may take the feminine ending, e.g., Ca. *'umda* 'mayor'.

Some animate entities use a suppletive system, both in the dialects and CA/MSA; e.g., Ca. *gamal* 'camel (m.)', *naa'a* 'camel (f.)', *raagil* 'man', *mara* 'woman'.

Number

Number categories include the singular, dual and plural. The singular is considered the "base pattern." A dual is formed by suffixing *-een* to the singular noun. Thus in Ca. *walad* 'boy' : *waladeen* 'two boys', *širka* 'company' : *širkiteen* 'two companies'. However, Nigerian Arabic prefers *uṣubi tineen* 'two fingers'; this structure exists elsewhere as a variant for the dual; cf. Jerusalem Arabic *waladeen* ~ *wlaad tneen* 'two boys'.

In contrast to the wide use of the dual in CA, Arabic dialects preserve it only in nouns, and even here it is not used at the same rate everywhere. Mainly, dual body parts and certain time and quantity expressions take the dual but there are syntactic, morphological and semantic distinctions between the "real dual" and the "pseudo-dual." Thus Ca. *rigleen* and Moroccan *rəjliin* are not necessarily 'two legs' but rather the plural of 'leg', while Jer. Ar. *ʾižirteen* means 'two legs'. Usually the "real dual" retains the morpheme *-ayn* while the "pseudo dual" forms vary among the dialects. The real dual tends not to take bound pronouns, thus retaining the *-n* (Jer. Ar. *ʾalameenak* 'your two pens', vs. *ʾižreehum* 'their legs').

As in MSA, there are two major types of plural:

1 The sound plural, where the pl. m. *-iin* or pl. f. *-aat* is suffixed to the singular base form as in, e.g., Jer. Ar. *falla(a)ḥiin* 'farmers', *ʿanzaat* 'goats'. The sound pl. m. is usually used with nouns indicating humans whereas the pl. f. is much less restricted.
2 The broken plural, where a different pattern is formed from the same root as the singular noun. The patterns (which are not restricted to humans) may include affixed vowels and consonants. Most broken plural patterns are common to all the Arabic dialects; however, some are typical of certain ones. Thus, Maghrebine dialects prefer the patterns with *-a*, *-an*, which exist elsewhere; e.g., *mγarba* 'Moroccans', *tlamda* 'students', *qdadša* 'servants', *dyuba* 'jackals', *jbala* 'mountain dwellers', *fərsan* 'mares', *ʿəmyan* 'blind (pl.)', *biban* 'doors'. The quadriradical patterns with a long vowel after C2 also occur frequently; e.g., *mjaləs* 'meetings', *braməl* 'buckets', *slaləm* 'ladders', *srawəl* 'trousers (pl.)', etc. Bedouin and sedentary dialects may also be distinguished by their use of plural patterns. Cf. Maghrebine bedouin *bramiil* vs. sedentary *braməl* 'buckets'.

The plural CVCVC*a* in *dubúʿa* 'hyenas', *numúra* 'tigers', stresses quite exceptionally the penultima in Cairene. This pattern is used elsewhere; cf. Galilean bedouin *nmura* 'tigers'. $C_1uC_2uC_3C_3e$ is clearly Nigerian, Chadian and Darfurian (Western Sudanese) and Upper Egyptian; e.g., Nig. Ar. *digin* 'beard', pl. *dugúnne*.

A third method of pluralization combines the sound and broken plurals by suffixing the sound plural to the broken plural. This structure probably exists in most of the dialects, but is infrequent. Cf. Ca. *ʾuṭuraat* 'trains', Dam. *ṭərʾaat* 'roads', *šhabiin* 'friends', Gal. bedouin *ziʿamaat* 'leaders', *furugaat* 'differences', Mag. *xwataat* 'sisters', *dmuʿaat* 'tears', *yaamaat* 'days', and Mal. *elufijiet* 'many thousands'.

Some suppletive plurals are probably found in all dialects; e.g., Dam. *niswaan* for *mara* 'woman, wife'.

Case Endings (Nunation)

Case endings survive in Arabian bedouin and Yemenite dialects. Even in these they are functionally limited (cf. p. 298) and take the form *-en, -in*, rarely *-an*, without direct association of the case and its form. This is unlike MSA where the three syntactic cases – nominative, accusative/adverbial, genitive – have clear morphological forms, i.e., *-un, -an, -in* respectively. This fact has led to the insertion of anapyctic vowels in many dialects. (See p. 279.) Residues of case endings exist, however, in highly frequent words in many dialects, as e.g., *daayman* 'always', *'ahlan* 'welcome', *'abadan* 'never' or in less frequent ones, such as *kullan* 'all, the whole of'. In such cases the ending *-an* stands for the adverbial case suffix.

Diminutives

Diminutives are used mainly in Maghrebine and bedouin (and bedouinized) dialects in both nouns and adjectives. Three basic patterns, C*u*C*ai*C, C*u*C*ayyi*C, CC*ay*C*uun*, are illustrated by bedouin *kleeb* 'small dog', *wleed* 'small child', *rwee'iy* 'a young shepherd'(< *raa'iy* 'shepherd'), Mor. *bnita* 'little girl', Ca. *gnejna* 'a little garden', *xayya* 'little sister', *ṣuɣayyar* 'small', Mal. *xwejjah* 'old man', bedouin *grayyib* 'near', *glayyil* 'a little', Bag. *zɣayruun* 'small'. Other examples from Negev bedouin are *aḥaymir* 'slightly red' (< *aḥmar* 'red'), *xrayrifih* 'a little story' (< *xurraafa* 'story, tale'). Diminutive forms may also be used as caritative, often in female speech in Maghrebine dialects (cf. p. 267).

Adjectives

Most verb forms have active and passive participles which may be used as adjectives. Still, the adjectives–participles do not always share the same meaning as the inflected verb forms. Cf. Jerusalem *faateḥ* (Form I) 'light (color)' (the basic meaning of the root is 'open'); *naayim* (Form I) 'lying down' (the basic meaning is 'sleep'); *mit'allem* (Form V) 'educated' (the basic meaning of the root is 'learn').

Some adjectives exhibit different morphophonemic alternations in the dialects. Noteworthy are active participles of the verbs 'eat' and 'take'. The former in Damascene is *'aakil*, Ca. *waakil*, Jer. *maakil ~ meekil* while the latter is *waaxuδ* in Eastern Libyan.

Adjectives of colors and defects take the pattern *'a*CC*a*C or *'i*CC*a*C with their f. C*a*CC*a* and pl. C*u*C(*v*)C patterns; e.g., Ca. *'aḥmar* (m.), *ḥamra* (f.) *ḥum(o)r* (pl.) 'red'. Cf. Gal. *'iṣfar* 'yellow (m.)', *'iswad* 'black (m.)'. One notes, however, *'aswid* 'black (m.)' (Bišmizziin), *'əswəd* 'black' (Mardin), Ca. *iswid*, and *ḥamar* (Arabian bedouin, bedouin elsewhere and bedouinized dialects due to the "*gahawa* syndrome" noted on p. 282), *'amyi* 'blind (f.)', *ṭaršiy* 'deaf (f.)' (Negev bedouin), *biiδa* 'white (f.)' (J. Bag.) vs. *beeδa* (Mus. and Chr. Bag.), *ʾaṣfar* 'yellow (m.)', *ṣtafraay* 'yellow (f.)', *ṣtufriin* 'yellow (pl.)' (Yemenite), *ḥmor* 'red (pl.)' (Mag.).

The *ʾaCCaC* pattern is also used for the elative (e.g., *ʾaṭwal* 'longer'). The distinction between elatives and superlatives in the dialects is syntactic and not morphological, unlike MSA. For 'good' some Yemenite dialects use *xayr* rather than *ʾaxyar* 'better', just like CA and MSA. However, many dialects use suppletion: *mniiḥ* (Jer.), *kuwayyis* (Ca., Sud., Nig.), *zeen* (Arabian bedouin, Mor., Nig.) and *ʾaḥsan* 'better' (all, but with appropriate phonological adjustments).

'First' and 'last' use the superlative pattern; *ʾawwal* (m.) *ʾawwala* (f.) 'first', *ʾaaxar* 'last' in many dialects. But cf. Maghrebine *l-axoor*, and Iraqi *l-axx* 'last'.

Relational (*nisba*) adjectives exist in all Arabic dialects. They are formed mostly by suffixing *-i(y)* or *-aani* (m.)/*-iyye, -aaniyye* (f.) to a noun, e.g., Dam. *šaami* 'Syrian, Damascene', *ḥaʾiiʾi* 'real, true,' *fooʾaani* 'upper', etc.

Numerals

Cardinal Numbers

'1' is *waaḥad* (Jer.), *waaḥid* (Ca.), *wieḥid* (Mal.), *waaḥi(d)* (Mor.), *waaḥit* (Nig.) '1 (m.)'. It follows the noun as an adjective, unless used as pronoun, meaning 'someone'. The feminine ending is *a* or *e* (see p. 282).

'2' is often substituted by the dual noun (see p. 283). In the Eastern sedentary and bedouin dialects (also in the bedouin dialects of Tunisia and Libya, and in Nigeria) the forms are related to CA *ʾiθnayn*; e.g., *ʾitneen* (Ca.), *θneen* (Bag.) and the f. *tinteen* (Ca.). Yemenite dialects have *iθnee, θatte*. The Maghrebine dialects use *žuuž* (CA *zawj*) or the like (*zuuj, jowj, zowž*) though *θniin, θnein* also occur. Maltese has both *tniin*, and *zewġ* or *ġiex*. 2 follows the dual noun in some dialects (e.g., Jerusalem Arabic) for emphasis (cf. p. 283), though in others it may precede the plural noun. In Nigerian it follows the singular noun.

3–10: these numbers are inflected by adding the pseudo-feminine suffix to the masculine (long) form as other adjectives (see p. 282). The long form is used when it does not govern any noun, i.e., when counting (alone); the short form is used when the counted noun follows. Some Iraqi and Anatolian dialects use *f, s* or *t* instead of *θ, t*; e.g., *snayn* '2', *saase, saasi, faafe* (Anat.) '3', *θneen* '2', *tlaaθa* '3' (Bag.). *flaafa* '3' is also used in Algerian and Hasawi Arabic. Jewish Baghdadi uses its usual *γ* for *r* in *aγbaʿ* '4' and *ʿašeγ* '10'. Maltese has the usual strong *ʾimaala* in *tlieta, tliet, tlitt* '3' and *tmienja* '8' as well as *tlit elef* '3,000', but *tlettax* '13' and *tletin* '30'. A special Syrian bedouin *samḥa* '7' for *sabʿa* is used "against the evil eye." For similar sociolinguistic reasons, '9' is *təsʿood* in Oran and *t(ə)sʿuud* in Morocco. Maltese voices the *t* in *disgha* '9', *dsatax* '19', and *disgħin* '90'.

11–19 consist of the unit numbers + *-ar* 'teen'. The morphological distinction in the two paradigms (with or without *-ar*) is, like 3–10, syntactically conditioned; i.e., when the numeral is followed by the counted noun *-ar* is omitted, when it is not followed by the counted noun the form with *-ar* is used. From '11' on, the head noun of the number is always singular. A special set is found in Nigerian Arabic; e.g., *ašara-haw-waahit* '10 + 1', *ašara-haw-tineen* '10 + 2' etc. Baghdadi Arabic loses *h* in *da'aš, ida'š, ida'eš* '11'. *xmuṣṭa'eš* '15' is peculiar in Muslim Baghdadi and Arabian dialects. In Yemenite *ç* is used for *š* in the "teens"; e.g., *ḥida'aç* '11', *'iθna'aç* '12'. Note *tlettaaš-en-marra* 'thirteen times', *ḥdaš-en-mya* '1100' in Algerian, Tunisian and Libyan dialects; and *tnaaš-el-'aam* 'twelve years' in Tlemçen, and *ḥdax-il-elf* '11,000' *sbatax-il-elf* '17,000' in Maltese via analogy to the indefinite article *waḥd-el-*.

Tens are formed by suffixing the pl. m. to the units; e.g., Ca. *'išriin*, Maltese *għoxrin* '20'.

'100' is *miyya* (Ca.) *miyye* (Dam.) *mija* (Mal.) *imya* (Arabian dialects), *mya* (Mag.). 3–9 usually form a construct with 100; however, it is not in the plural (unlike the rule for nouns after 3–10). In the Maghreb the annexation between the number and the noun may be explicit; cf. *arba'-mya d-el-jmaal* and *arba'-myat-jməl* '400 camels'. In Cairene the unit numbers of the hundreds are like the fractions; e.g., *tultu-miyya* '300', *tumnu-miyya* '800'.

Thousands in the plural form a construct state with the unit numbers. In this case some sedentary dialects prefix to the 'thousands' a *t* (historically the *taa'* *marbuṭa* ending for masculine nouns); e.g., *xams-talaaf* '5,000' (Syr. and Pal.) as in other cases when the noun begins with a weakened *'* (e.g., *saba'-tiṣnaaf* '7 kinds' (Ca.), *tmen-tiyyaam* (Bag.), and *tmin-tirġiil* '8 men' (Mal.)).

Ordinal Numbers

Ordinal numbers are syntactically adjectives, following the noun. For 'first' Cairene, Damascene and other Eastern dialects have *'awwal* and *'awwalaani* (cf. Mor. *lowwel* and Mal. *l-ewwel*).

Ordinal numbers 2–10 take the CaaCiC pattern yielding in Jewish Baghdadi, due to *'imaala*, *tiini, tiilit, γiibe', xiimes*, etc. and Maltese *it-tieni, it-tielit, it-tiemin*. In Lebanese and Tunisian (e.g., Suusa) the *'imaala* is lower (*e*), yielding *it-teeni, it-teelit*. The *t* of 'sixth' is voiced to *saadis* (as in CA and MSA) in Syro-Palestinian, Iraqi and many Arabian dialects, though not 'Anaiza which has *as-saatt*, but remains in Cairene *as-saatit*, in Suusa *is-seetit*, and in Nigerian *saati*. In the Maghreb *saat(ə)t* is common, but in Morocco and Algeria *saadəs* occurs as well. Above 'tenth' ordinals use definite cardinal numbers, but cf. Moroccan *ḥadeš* 'eleventh', *taneš* '12th', Suusa *el-ḥaadiš* 'eleventh', *it-taaniš* 'twelfth'.

Fractions

Fractions have the pattern CuC(*u*)C. CA 'half' shows metathesis in Tripoli (Lib.) and Suusa *nufs* and Maltese *nofs*; however, it is *nuṣṣ* in most dialects. 'one-sixth' is in Cairene *suds*, pl. *'asdaas* 'sixths'. In Suusa *tluut* 'one-third' and *zduus* 'one-sixth' show vowel reshuffling. Maltese may use the Italian loanwords *terz* 'one-third', *kwart* 'one-quarter', *kwint* 'one-fifth', but also, e.g., *mis-sitt waḥda* 'one-sixth' up to *mil-għaxra waḥda* 'one-tenth', etc.

Independent Personal Pronouns

Table 14.4, p. 288 lists pronouns, some of which are distinguished for gender. Sg. 1 and pl. normally have a common gender, but 'Adeni *'ana/'ani* 'I (m./f.)' is an exception. In sedentary dialects plural gender differentiation is usually more limited than in bedouin and rural ones (also in the verbs). In some Maghrebine dialects an *n* is added *humman* (Berber substratum?). Yemenite dialects have distinct pronouns in pause and juncture; e.g., nasalized *'antīn* 'you (sg. f.)' vs. *'anti* respectively.

Bound Personal Pronouns

The bound pronouns have numerous allomorphs, especially in the Yemenite and bedouin dialects (e.g., in Galilean bedouin the pl. 2m. is -*kam*). In Baghdadi *n* is added (for pl. 3m.) as in some other Iraqi and Anatolian dialects (Aramaic substratum?). In some Arabian bedouin, Syrian, and Yemenite dialects the system prefixes an anaptyctic -*a* to the bound pronoun; e.g., *beetakam* 'your (pl. m.) house' (similar to CA case endings, but not syntactically conditioned).

Demonstratives

All Arabic dialects have two paradigms of demonstrative for closer and further objects. Both inflect for gender and number, though dialects vary as to gender distinction. In the plural some dialects use the element *'uulaa* but cf. Galilean bedouin *haaδam* (pl. m.), *haaδan*, *haδiičan* (pl. f.). Some of the dialects use one of the elements only ("short" or "long" forms), and even reduplicatively, in the pattern *ha l-walad haaδa* 'this boy' (lit. 'this the boy this one'). This pattern is mostly found in bedouin dialects but also in some sedentary Eastern and Western ones, such as the Syro-Lebanese and Moroccan dialects. Tables 14.6 and 14.7 demonstrate the richness of dialects such as Yemenite and the uniformity of the large urban centers.

Relative Particles

Compared with CA, the dialects are poor in relative particles, using mainly *illi*, which inflects neither for gender nor for number. Bedouin dialects typically have *alli*. Other dialects use the second element of the CA form (*allaδii*), namely *δii*, yielding *(ad)di* in Moroccan. In limited cases *'aš* 'what' occurs in the Moroccan dialects. In the Iraq–Anatolia area (including Baghdad) and in the Sudan, Chad and Nigeria, the definite article is often used as a relative.

Cairene: *'illi*
Damascene: *'illi, yalli*
Iraqi (Jewish Baghdadi): *elli, l-*
Negev bedouin: *alliy*
Yemenite: *δii, δaa; δee, δeeleh*
Moroccan: *lli, di; aš*
Maltese: *illi, li*

Table 14.4 Independent pronouns in seven Arabic dialects

		Cairene	Dam.	Ir. (J. Bag.)	Negev bedouin	Yemenite	Mor.	Maltese
Sg.	1c.	ʾana	ʾana	ana	ana/anaa	ʾanaa/ʾani	ana	jien
	2m.	ʾinta	ʾɔnte	enta	int/intih	ʾanta/ʾinta	nta	int(i)
	f.	ʾinti	ʾɔnti	enti	intiy	ʾanti/ʾinti	nti(ya)	int(i)
	3m.	huwwa	huuwe/huu	huwwi	huu	huuwa/huu	huwa	hu/huwwa
	f.	hiyya	hiiye/hii	hiyyi	hii	hiyya/hii	hiya	hi/hiya
Pl.	1c.	ʾiḥna	nəḥna	neḥna	aḥna	niḥna/ʾihna ʾaḥna/ʾaṇḥa	ḥna	aḥna
	2m.	ʾintu	ʾɔntu	entem	intuw	ʾantuu/ʾintu ʾantum/ʾantim	ntuma	intom
	f.	ʾintu	ʾɔntu	entem	intin	ʾantu/ʾintu ʾantunna/ʾantin	ntuma	intom
	3m.	humma	hɔnne	hemmi	hum	hum/him	huma	huma
	f.	humma	hɔnne	hemmi	hin	him/hin/hinna	huma	huma

Table 14.5 Bound pronouns in seven Arabic dialects

		Cairene	Dam.	Ir. (J. Bag.)	Negev bedouin	Yemenite	Mor.	Maltese
Sg.	1c.	-i/-ya	-i/-yi	-i/-yi	-i/-y	-i(i)-ya	-i/-ya	-i/-ja
	2m.	-ak/-k	-ak/-k	-ak/-k	-ak/-k	-ak/-ča/-ša/-ik	-ek/-k	-ok/-ek
	f.	-ik/-ki	-ek/-ki	-k/-ki	-kiy	-aki/-či/-ši/-iš/-ič	-ek/-k	-ok/-ek
	3m.	-u(h)	-h/-o	-u/-nu	-ih/-ah/-uh	-eh/-uh/-huuh	-u/-h/-eh	-u/-h
	f.	-ha	-(h)a	-a/-ha	-ha(-hiy)	-ha(a)	-ha	-ha
Pl.	1c.	-na	-na	-na	-na	-na	-na	-na
	2m.	-ku(m)	-kon	-kem	-kuw	-kum/-čum	-kom	-kom
	f.	-ku(m)	-kon	-kem	-kin	-kum/-čunna/-činna	-kom	-kom
	3m.	-hum	-hon	-(h)em	-hum	-hum/-hin/-aam	-hom	-hom
	f.	-hum	-hon	-(h)em	-hin	-een/-oon/-aam	-hom	-hom

Table 14.6 Demonstratives in seven Arabic dialects: near objects

		Cairene	Dam.	Ir. (J. Bag.)	Negev bedouin	Yemenite	Mor.	Maltese
Sg.	m.	da	haad(a)	haaða	haaða	haaðaa ðaa/ðiih/ðayy	had(a)	dan(a)
	f.	di	hayye/haadi	haayi	heeðiy	haaðihii/taa tih/ðiih/tay	hadi	din(a)
Pl.	m.	dool	hadool(e)	hadooli	hoolal(ðah)	hawla/ʔulaa	hadu	dawn(a)
	f.	dool	hadool(e)	hadooli	hoolal(ðah)	hawla/ʔulaa	hadu	dawn(a)

Table 14.7 Demonstratives in seven Arabic dialects: far objects

		Cairene	Dam.	Ir. (J. Bag.)	Negev bedouin	Yemenite	Mor.	Maltese
Sg.	m.	dukha	hadaak(e)	haðaak	haðaak(ah)	ðaak/ðiiyak haaðaak	hadak	dak(a)
	f.	dikha	hadiik(e)	hadiik	heeðiik(ih)	taak/tiyaak ðiik/haðiik	hadik	dik(a)
Pl.	m.	dukham	hadenk(e) hadooliik	haðoolak	hooðallaak(ah)	ʔawlaak/ ʾoolaak (haa)ðolaak	haduk	dawk(a)
	f.	dukham	hadenk(e) hadooliik	haðoolak	hooðallak(ah)	ʔawlaak ʾoolaak	haduk	dawk(a)

Table 14.8 Interrogative pronouns in seven Arabic dialects

Gloss	Cairene	Dam.	Ir. (J. Bag.)	Negev bedouin	Yemenite	Mor.	Maltese
who	miin	miin	mani	min	man/min	(a)škun	miin
what	ʾeeh	šuu(we)	aškuun	eeš/iiš/wiš	maa/maadi	š/šnu, aš	xi
		ʾeeš	aš/eeš		weyš/weeššu		
which	ʾaay/ʾanhu	ʾayy/ʾanu	hayyi	yaat	ʾayyan	ina	liema
why	leeh	leeš	leeš	leeš/liiš/leeh/	limaaða/lama/lima/	ʿlaš	għala
				liih/ʿalaamah	leyš/maalak		
when	ʾimta	ʾeemta	eemta	mitaa(h)	mataa/matee	waqtaš	meta
where	feen	ween	ween	wagteeš	wayyħiin/ʾeeħiin	fuqaš	xħin
		feen		ween	weyn/ween	fain	fejn
how	izzaay/keef	kiif/šloon	ašloon	keef/kiif/kayf	waan/yaanhaa	kiifaš	kif
					keef/keyf		
					čeef		
how much	ʾaddiʾ eeh	ʾaddeeš	ašqad	gaddayš/gaddeeš	gadar eeš/gadar kam	šħal qeddayš	kemm
how many	kam	kamm	kem	kam	min kam/mikkam/kam	šħal	kemm

Interrogative Pronouns

Interrogative pronouns include "wh-" question words and others. A yes–no question is introduced in some dialects by *'ayy*, or the sg. 3 at the head of the sentence (e.g., in Cairene) or *waš, yak* (Maghrebine dialect). Other dialects (e.g., Jerusalem Arabic) have no interrogative pronoun for this kind of question, which is indicated by rising intonation. Table 14.8, p. 290 compares several particles in some Arabic dialects.

Verbal Morphology

Arabic is typologically a synthetic language with quite an involved morphology; however, the modern dialects, as can be seen in the evolution of the Semitic languages elsewhere, have all drifted towards a reduction ("simplification") of the system, i.e., they have become more analytic. (The variation of the genitival exponent is proof *par excellence* of their analytic structure as the construct state tends to be used less and less.) Further, Arabic sticks out in comparative Semitic linguistics because of its almost (too perfect) algebraic-looking grammar, i.e., root and pattern morphology. It is so algebraic that the medieval Arab grammarians have been accused of contriving some artificiality about the CA system.

Arabic dialects, on the whole, preserve CA root and pattern verbal (and nominal) morphology. All lexical items can be extracted from roots which are augmented by the discontinuous morphology of prefixation, suffixation or infixation processes. In the Arabic dialects verbs indicate time partly by conjugations. Thus, *faʿal* is used for the past, preterite, or perfect, and *yifʿal* for the imperfect which may indicate the present or future time. For the present time – including momentary, continuous, general, and perfect aspects – participles are often used. There is also an imperative mood. (See details about conjugations on pp. 292–4, and p. 304 about syntactic apsects.)

The dialects, as opposed to MSA, have innovated certain autonomous morphological markers for expressing tenses and moods. These are usually affixed to the imperfect, while the perfect does not take affixes, e.g., *bi-, qa-, da-, ku-, ka-, ta-,* for the indicative, *ha-, raah-, γa-* for the future, *ʿammaal, ʿam(ma)-* for the present progressive. Thus the imperfect is often prefixed by one of them.

Some dialects are quite conservative in that they agree with CA and MSA in several respects rather than with the general tendencies attributed to either the Arabic *koiné* or drift (the norms of diachronic evolution). One of the best examples of this is the preservation of the pan-Semitic *raʾaa* 'see' in Maltese, Cypriot Arabic, Mardiin, Diyarbakir, various Judeo-Arabic colloquials, etc. To illustrate further, Sudanese Arabic preserves the *a* as the preformative of the imperfect *yaktib* 'he writes' vs. *i* in, e.g., Cairene *yiktib*. So does Nigerian Arabic *tamiš* 'you (sg. m.) go'. Sudanese Arabic also retains the internal passive; e.g., *harag* 'burn' but *hirig* 'got burnt'. This situation is paralleled exactly by many Arabian dialects e.g., Najdi, which supports the thesis that Sudanese dialects are to be subgrouped together with them. Most dialects have, however, resorted to the external passive (see further p. 304).

Table 14.9   Perfect and imperfect affixes in Arabic dialects

	Perfect Singular Ca.	Bag.	Plural Ca.	Bag.	Imperfect Singular Ca.	Bag.	Plural Ca.	Bag.
1c.	-t	-et	-na	-na	'a-	a-	ne-	ne-
2m.	-t	-et	-tu	-tu	ti-	te-	ti ... u	te ... uun
f.	-ti	-ti	-tu	-tu	ti ... i	te-iin	ti ... u	te ... uun
3m.	-Ø	-Ø	-u	-aw	yi-	ye-	yi ... u	ye ... uun
f.	-it	-at	-u	-aw	ti-	te-	yi ... u	ye ... uun

Juba Arabic and Ki-Nubi, as can be understood due to their pidgin genesis, have totally lost the traditional Arabic morphological system and have one basic unin-flected form of the verb, such as *ašurubu* 'drink' for all numbers and tenses (there is no gender), although a new passive has been innovated there: *áakulu* 'eat' vs. *aakulú* 'be eaten' (< 'they eat it'). Uzbeki Arabic has a verbal morphology which is different from what is presented in the following, whereas another peripheral dialect, Cypriot Arabic, has kept the basic system intact.

Subject Markers and Conjugations
Cairene and Muslim Baghdadi will be used here to illustrate the perfect and im-perfect. The affixes for these two basic stems express tense–aspect, person, gender and number (Table 14.9). In general, subject markers are suffixed to the perfect and both prefixed and suffixed to the imperfect.

In rural and bedouin dialects pl. 2 and 3f. suffixes differ from the pl. m. forms, unlike many sedentary urban dialects. Thus for pl. 2f. one uses *-tan* and pl. 3f. *-an* in the former dialects. The following tables (14.10 and 14.11) are comparative.

Although all the dialects herein noted have *-t*, or *-k* (perhaps due to Modern South Arabian substrata) as 1st and 2nd person markers in the perfect, Nigerian Arabic has Ø; e.g., *tammam* 'I/you finished' (for *tammamt). However, the *-t* is present before object suffixes; e.g., *tammamta* 'I finished it'.

Table 14.10   Perfect conjugation in seven Arabic dialects

Dam.	Gulf	Yemenite (Ḍafaar)	Yemenite (Al-Maḥall)	Tunisian (Marazig)	Moroccan	Maltese
katabt	k(i)tabt	katabt	katabk	ktəbt	ktəbt	ktibt
katabt	k(i)tabt	katabt	katabk	ktəbt	ktəbti	ktibt
katabti	k(i)tabti	katabti	katabš	ktəbti	ktəbti	ktibt
katab	kitab	katab	katab	ktəb	ktəb	kiteb
katbet	ktibat	katabat	katabat	kətbət	kətbət	kitbet
katabna	k(i)tabna	katabna	katabna	ktəbna	ktəbna	ktibna
katabtu	k(i)tabtu	katabtu	katbakum	ktəbtu	ktəbtu	ktibtu
katabtu	k(i)tabtin	katabtan	katabkun	ktəbtan	ktəbtu	ktibtu
katabu	ktibaw	katabu	katabu	kətbu	kətbu	kitbu
katabu	ktiban	kataban	kataban	kətban	kətbu	kitbu

Table 14.11 Imperfect conjugation in seven Arabic dialects

Damascene	Gulf	Yemenite Ḍafaar + Al-Maḥall	Tunisian Marazig	Moroccan	Maltese
bəktob	aktib	ʾaktub	nəktəb	nəktəb	nikteb
btəktob	taktib	tuktub	təktəb	təktəb	tikteb
btəktbi	taktəbiin	tuktubi	təktəbi	təktəbi	tikteb
byəktob	yaktib	yuktub	yəktəb	yəktəb	yikteb
btəktob	taktib	tuktub	təktəb	təktəb	tikteb
mnəktob	naktib	nuktub	nəkətbu	nəkətbu	niktbu
btəktbu	taktəbuun	tuktubu	təkətbu	nəkətbu	tiktbu
btəktbu	taktəban	tuktubayn	təkətban	nəktəbu	tiktbu
byəktbu	yaktəbuun	yuktubu	yəkətbu	yəktəbu	yiktbu
byəktbu	yaktəban	yuktubayn	yəkətban	yəktəbu	yiktbu

In some dialects the pl. 2m. and 3m. endings are *-um* or *-am* (Yemenite, Galilean bedouin) rather than *-u*. Even in Cairene one can say *katabu* or *katabum* 'they wrote', *tiktibu* or *tiktibum* 'you write (pl., m., f.)', perhaps on the analogy of *humma* 'they', though Cairene *gum* 'they came' is more common than *gu* (cf. pl. 2m. object – *ku(m)*). Many bedouin and bedouinized dialects have the *-n* form for pl. f. persons (perfect *-in ~ -an*, *-tin ~ -tan*, imperfect *-in ~ -an*).

The f. *-iin* (also *-ayn ~ -een*) and *-uun* (also *-awn*, *-oon*), as in MSA, are found in bedouin and bedouinized dialects, and it is a common feature of the *qəltu* dialects. They are not present in Meccan Arabic, demonstrating that it is closer to the urban Egyptian–Levantine dialects than to Gulf Arabic. Cf. Tikrit *ykətbawn*, Jewish Baghdadi *ykətboon*, Mosul *yəkətbuun* and Muslim Baghdadi *yikitbuun* 'they write'.

The Verb Forms

Most dialects have preserved the system of the CA derived stems. Even a peripheral dialect, such as Nigerian Arabic, preserves the distinction between Forms I and II; e.g., *širib* 'he drank' and *šarrab* 'cause to drink' as in *šarraba alme (leyya)* 'he caused him to (made him) drink water'. In Chadian Arabic only Forms II and VII are productive; however, this situation is somewhat rare. Form II is probably the most common, statistically, of all the derived stems in many dialects; however, not all the meanings of Form II are "derived," in the sense that Form I is not used with the same roots. In Sudanese Arabic, for example, the following are basic: *gannub* 'sit', *ʿarras* 'marry'. Sometimes an MSA derived stem becomes a basic one; e.g., *ʾaraad* 'want' (Form IV) > *raad* (Form I). Form IV has thus been lost in many dialects, while Form II has often become a productive causative stem. Some dialects have innovated new patterns, notably Egyptian *ʾitwagad* 'it/he was found' (with preformative *t-* affixed to Form I), and *istaxaffa* 'he disguised himself' (with preformative *ist-* affixed to Form II of C-*w/y* roots), Moroccan *ttajraḥ* 'was wounded' (with a geminated preformative *tt-* and Form I), and Maltese *in-*

steraq 'was stolen' (affixing both *in-* of Form VII and *t-* of Form VIII to the root).

Form I
Form I applies only the root consonants. The dialects, however, diverge by vowel variations. Thus, Yemenite has four major types (one more than MSA): *ragad* 'he slept', *širib* 'he drank', *wugif* 'he stopped', and *ʿuṭus* 'he sneezed'. The last type usually contains an emphatic or is a passive; e.g., *kumul* 'it was completed'. (Many dialects still preserve the internal passive, e.g., *ksir* 'it was broken'; see p. 297.) Damascene has two types: *katab* 'he wrote' and *šəreb* 'he drank'. These two merge in Moroccan Arabic to one: *ktəb*, and *šrəb*. Maltese has six basic patterns: *talab* 'he asked', *qatel* 'he killed', *fehem* 'he understood', *seraq* 'he stole', *ġibed* 'he pulled', and *ħolom* 'he dreamt'.

Form II
Many verbs in this category are transitive causatives of Form I. Thus in Yemen *daras* 'he studied' contrasts with *darras* 'he taught'; but some are basic, e.g., Yem. *xazzan* 'he chewed qat'. In Juba Arabic *derisu* can be either 'study' or 'teach' (note the degemination). Moroccan *nuwwe ḍ* has a causative sense: 'to cause to get up, get out of bed' contrasts with *naḍ* 'get up, get out of bed', whereas an intensive and denominative meaning can be illustrated by Damascene *kassar* 'he smashed' and *ṣawwar* 'he took a picture' (cf. *ṣuura* 'a picture'). Maltese follows the others: *kisar* 'he broke' vs. *kisser* 'he smashed'; *xemmex* 'he exposed to the sun' from *xemx* 'sun'. In all derived Forms (II–X) in Cairene *a* follows C2 when it or C3 is emphatic or guttural while other roots take *i*; e.g., *labbis : yilabbis* 'dress someone', *naḍḍaf : yinaḍḍaf* 'clean something'.

Form III
Form III verbs are often derived from nouns or from Form I verbs. In Yemenite *ħaaka* 'he engaged someone in conversation' contrasts with *ħaka* 'he talked'. Moroccan has very few verbs in this category, for which the pattern is *ṣafef* 'he lined up'; however, the final vowel may elide giving *ṣaff*. Damascene serves as illustrative of the conative or participative meanings: *kaatab* 'he wrote to someone' vs. *katab* 'he wrote', *laaħaʾ* 'he pursued someone' vs. *ləħeʾ* 'he caught up with someone'. Maltese shows *ʾimaala* in *bierek* 'he blessed' (= MSA *baaraka* 'he blessed'), *biegħed* 'he put at a distance' (cf. *bogħod* 'distance').

Form IV
Yemenite still has this form though it is not common. It is characterized by an optional *ʾi-* or *ʾa*: *(ʾi)bṣar* 'he saw' or *(ʾi)xraj* 'he excluded'. It is still very much alive in bedouin dialects. Form IV usually occurs in MSA borrowings or classicisms. It has often been replaced in dialects by Form II. There are only remnants of it in Maltese and many other dialects. Mauritanian Arabic dialects use *sa-* as prefix instead of *ʾa*, e.g., *saħmar* 'he made red, reddened'.

Form V

Often a reflexive counterpart of Form II, Form V prefixes *t-* to a Form II verb. Thus, e.g., Yemenite *ɣadda* 'he gave someone lunch' vs. *tɣadda* 'he ate lunch', *twaṭṭa* 'he/it lowered himself/itself' vs. *waṭṭa* 'he lowered something'; some verbs in Form V are really passive (see directly below). Some verbs in this class are basic (not derived from Form I): *tšaggar* 'he peeked'. In Syrian–Lebanese–Palestinian dialects Form V is most often a passive or reflexive of Form II; thus most of these verbs are intransitive; e.g., *ɣayyar* 'he changed something' : *tɣayyar* 'it changed, was changed'. Compare Cairene *ʿallim* 'teach' : *itʿallim* 'he learned', *ḥabb* 'love' : *itḥab* 'it was loved', or *itʾal* 'it was decreased'. The situation in Moroccan Arabic is quite different from the Eastern dialects. Here *t-* or *tt-* is prefixed to Form I or II verbs with possible assimilation; from *šaf* 'he saw' one obtains *(t)tšaf* 'he was seen'. Consider also: *zad* 'he added' and *dzad* 'it was added', *ṭehher* 'he circumcised' vs. *ṭṭehher* 'he was circumcised'. Maltese prefixes *t* to Form II and assimilates it before *ċ, d, ġ, n, s, x, ż* and *z*; e.g., *ċaħħad* 'he denied' and *iċċaħad* 'he denied himself'. The Egyptian and Maghrebine dialects have preserved the reflexive passive *t* which is possibly reinforced by substratum (cf. Aramaic *ʾeθpǝʿel*). In some bedouin dialects the preformative *t* may be omitted in the imperfect (by haplology); e.g., Galilean bedouin *yinaggaluun* 'they roam' for *yitnaggaluun*.

Form VI

Form VI verbs often denote reciprocity, pretense or are passive or denominative. In Yemenite one prefixes *t(a)* to Form III verbs. Thus from *ʿaafa* 'he cured someone' we derive *tʿaafa* 'he recuperated'; from *mayyit* 'dead' there is *tamaywat* 'he pretended to be dead'; from *gaabal* 'he met someone' *tgaabal* 'he had a meeting with someone'. Damascene is similar; e.g.: Dam. *tbaarak* 'he was blessed', *tkaatabu* 'they corresponded with each other'. So do also Moroccan and Maltese; from Moroccan *ḍay(ǝ)f* (III) 'receive as a guest' : *ḍḍay(ǝ)f* 'be received as a guest' with assimilation of the *t*. From Maltese *biegħed* 'he placed far off', *tbiegħed* 'he went far away'. Here, too, there is an assimilation of *t* before *ċ, d, ġ, s, ż* and *z*. Cf. in Ca. *itbaarik* 'he was blessed', *itʿaamil* 'he was treated' (due to the phonological rule mentioned on p. 294).

Form VII

Form VII is formed by prefixing *(i)n* to C1 of the verb. There is a phenomenal variation among the dialects here. In Damascene it borders on being a productive passive of Form I; e.g., from *ḥabas* 'he imprisoned', *nḥabas* 'he was imprisoned', from *saʾal* 'he asked', *nsaʾal* 'he was asked'. But in Yemenite Form VII does not occur and it is rare to non-existent in the Maghrebine dialects in general. Two examples are, however, *ndfǝn* 'he was buried' from *dfǝn* 'he buried', and *nšmǝt* 'he was cheated' from *šmǝt* 'he cheated'. Examples from Maltese include the reflexive and passive meanings of Form I; e.g., *indaħal* 'he interfered' from *daħal* 'he entered' and *inqabad* 'he was caught' from *qabad* 'he caught'.

Form VIII

Form VIII is formed by infixing *t* after the first radical of a Form I verb. In Yemenite these are mostly passive; from *kassar* 'he broke' *ktasar* 'it was broken'. Some are reflexive, while others are denominative or derived from Form IV. Cf. *btall* 'he wet himself' vs. *ball* 'he made something wet'. Damascene is again similar; e.g., *nta'al* 'he was transported' from *na'al* 'he transported something'. Moroccan and other dialects seem to have independent and/or idiosyncratic meanings associated with this form; e.g., *xtarᵊ⁽* 'he invented, imagined'. In Maltese one often encounters a reflexive or passive meaning; e.g., *ftaqar* 'he became poor' from *faqar* 'poverty' and *intesa* 'it (he) was forgotten' from *nesa* 'he forgot'.

Form IX

This Form, reserved in CA and MSA for colors and defects, is not common in the dialects which use Form II instead; e.g., Yemenite *ḥammar* 'it turned red'. It still occurs in Damascene, though rarely; e.g., *ḥmarr* 'it turned red'. Moroccan has no reflex of this form. Rather it uses Form XI (also in CA exclusively for colors and defects); e.g., *sman* 'he became fat', *byaḍ* 'it became white'. Maltese is remarkably similar to Moroccan; cf. *ḥdar* 'it turned green' from *aḥdar* 'green (sg. m.)' or (with *'imaala*) *swied* 'it grew black' from *iswed* 'black (sg. m.)'. (Cf. the striking similarity in vowels to Cairene *'iswid*.)

Form X

This form is formed by prefixing *sta-* to Form I, but is also derived from nouns or adjectives. Cf. Yemenite *stajaab* 'he responded' from *jaawab* 'answer'; *starxaṣ* 'he found something cheap', from *raxiiṣ* 'cheap'; *sta'nas* 'he had a good time', from *winseh* 'fun, good time'. Damascene is similar; e.g., *staṭwal* 'he considered something long' from *ṭawiil* 'long'. Moroccan prefixes *stᵊ-* before a CC- stem, or *st-* before a CV- stem; e.g., *stᵊxbᵊr* 'make inquiries', *styᵊll* 'take use of'. Likewise Maltese: *stagħġeb* 'he was amazed' from *għaġeb* 'a marvel' or *stkerrah* 'he loathed' from *ikrah* 'ugly (sg. m.)'.

The Quadriliteral Verb

As in other Semitic languages, CA and MSA, the dialects have quadriliteral roots. There are four basic types, as illustrated by Yemenite Arabic: (1) 1234, *qambar* 'he sat down'; (2) 1233, *qardad* 'it gnawed'; (3) 1232, *ⁿanwan* 'he addressed (a letter)'; and (4) 1212, *rašraš* 'he sprayed'. Some derived quadriliterals have no base forms; e.g., *tšawraⁿ* 'he walked in the street', *tgambaⁿ* 'he jumped for joy'. Maltese has five possible vowel patterns: *qahqah* 'he hacked', *qarmeč* 'he crunched', *temtem* 'he stuttered', *tertaq* 'he shattered', and *bixkel* 'he cheated'. Passives/reflexives are formed by prefixing *t* to the root; e.g., Damascene *taržam* 'he translated' : *ttaržam* 'it was translated'.

The Weak Verb

The Semitic languages have intricate morphophonemic rules for the conjugation of the weak verb. Arabic dialects, like MSA, are not exceptions. There are irregularities of the defective, hollow and doubled verbs which need not concern us here. The sedentary dialects have evolved differently from CA in that some differences have been neutralized; e.g., III-*w* > III-*y* verbs (so, too, in Hebrew and Syriac). The doubled (geminate) verbs have, due to *Systemzwang*, also merged with III-*y* roots. The other Semitic languages also merged doubled roots (e.g., Akkadian and Ethiopian) with the strong ones.

The Passive

n- and *t*- passives have already been mentioned. Let us turn to the various geographical areas in which internal and external *n*, *t* passives occur. In Syro-Palestinian dialects, more than half of all Form VII verbs are passive in nature. Form VIII verbs are lexicalized and only 20 percent are passive. Internal passives are cited in the literature (e.g., *tuḍrab* 'may you be hit' reported for Damascene by G. Bergsträsser), yet it remains unclear to what extent they are not the result of MSA influence in this region. Verbs in Forms V and I occur also with passive sense in all dialects.

Many examples of Form VII passives can be cited for the Iraqi *qəltu* dialects. There are also a few cases of Form VIII passive, but only a few examples of internal passives: *xalṣət lə-fluus* 'money was used up'. The Iraqi-area *gələt* dialects use Forms VII and VIII extensively to mark the passive. There are also a few cases of an internal passive; e.g., *xluṣet el-ḥičaaya* 'the story is finished'.

Uzbeki and Afghan Arabic use Form VII for the passive and no cases of an internal passive are attested with either.

Forms VII and VIII are common in Egyptian Arabic. A few cases of the internal passive occur: *xiliṣ ~ xuluṣ* 'it was finished', *ṣuɣur ~ ṣiɣir* 'it became small' and *ximir ~ xumur* 'it fermented' (Form I).

Chadian Arabic uses Form VII for the passive. Internal passives also exist there; e.g., *sirig* 'it was stolen' (cf. Nigerian Arabic *xalaaṣ ~ xuluṣ* 'it finished'). It has probably also developed into an *l*- type, documented also for the Egyptian cases and for Nigerian Arabic in which *al*- also shows up commonly for the more "normal" *t*-: *alkallam* 'he spoke' and *alqadda* 'he had lunch'. There are also in Nigerian Arabic, however, clear-cut cases of *al*- passives: *alkarfaš* 'become wrinkled', *alkaršam* 'wither (intr.)', and *alkassar* 'be broken'.

Maghrebine sedentary dialects are divided into those that use *n*- and those that use *t*-. The latter prefix *t*- or *tt*- to Form I. This group includes Muslim and Jewish Tunisian, Susa and Takrouna and the large cities of Morocco. The *n*- dialects are those of Fez (J.), Tetwan, Tlemçen, Oran, Cherchell and Algiers. Finally, there are some dialects which normally use a combination of both *n*- and *t*-. Two such are Djidjelli and Maltese; cf. Maltese *instab* 'was found' from *sab* 'find'. Maltese also uses phrases with *kien* 'be' or *safaʾ* 'was reduced to the condition of', or even *ġie* 'come' + passive participle, e.g., *safaʾ maqtul* 'he was killed'.

There are a few documented cases of internal passives for the Maghrebine area: *xlaq, yaxloq* 'create', *xluq, yuxluq* 'be created'. A few verbs across the Maghreb use an internal passive in CC*a*C: *xlaq* 'was born', *'waž* 'become bent, twisted'. Fez (J.) also has *xla'at* 'she was born'.

Algerian Hilali dialects have generally *t-* passives; however, *n-* occurs sporadically. There are examples of an internal passive in Bou Saada, Mzaab, 'Ain Madi and Arbaa': *ksur* 'he went bankrupt'.

Mauritanian Arabic shows a unique development which could be the result of Berber substratum (or result by analogy from the *u* of the imperfect). Although the productive passive marker with Form I is *n-*, there are some Form VIII passives as well. However, with Forms II and III, including the unique *s-* causative stem (e.g., *saḥmar* 'make red'), there is an *u-* passive in the perfect as well as the imperfect. Thus (Form II) *ubaxxar* 'he was perfumed with incense', impf. *yubaxxar*, imp. *ubaxxar*, part. *mubaxxar*, and (Form III) *gaabal* 'he met' : *ugaabal* 'he was confronted with', and with quadriliterals: *säkräf* 'he bound' : *usäkräf* 'it was bound'; *sägbäl* 'he guided towards the south' : *usägbäl* 'he was guided towards the south'.

In the Arabian Peninsula, urban Hijazi and Yemenite use both *t-* and *n-*. The internal passive is more frequent in bedouin(ized) dialects. Cf. *sugii* 'it was irrigated'. Southern Arabian has VII and VIII; the internal passive was alive and well during C. de Landberg's fieldwork in Dathina and Hadramawt. According to C. Holes (1995), *n-* is now replacing the internal passive all over Oman; he observes that Forms I and II internal passives are still common and are a feature keeping them apart from Eastern Arabian while aligning them with Najdi (see below). Thus, e.g., *kaan* 'he was', vs. *giṣṣat* 'was cut'(imperfect *yigaal* 'it is said').

The Northern Arabian dialects, including parts of Jordan, Syria and the Gulf, use both Form VII and the internal passive. Najdi and Qatari dialects are reported to use the internal passive more than the external one. According to P. Abboud (1964), there is even a difference in meaning between the two: *inkisar* means 'it got broken by some outside unspecified force', whereas *ksir* means 'it was broken by an outside agency known but not indicated'. For the derived stems in this area most verbs use *t-* or *n-*.

Syntax

Much of the syntax of Arabic dialects is similar to that of CA and MSA. The basic structures include nominal and verbal clauses which may be simple, compound or complex, but spontaneous speech may diverge from the fixed patterns yielding types such as cleft sentences and holophrases. We start with basic syntactic categories – definiteness, concord and word order, followed by NP, VP sentence types and "deviant" structures.

Definiteness

Definiteness is a feature of the NP (see pp. 300–300). A noun may be indefinite or definite. The explicit marker of nominal definiteness is the definite article *il-*, *el-*, *al-* (the latter is typical of bedouin dialects) or *l-*, which is prefixed to the defined noun. Definiteness is implied when a noun is bound, i.e., when a personal pronoun is suffixed to it, when it is the first noun in a construct state and its second noun is definite or is a proper noun. Free personal pronouns are also implicitly definite.

The indefiniteness of a noun is usually unmarked. Some dialects, however, mark this state: in Moroccan dialects, e.g., the particle *waḥd el-* (lit. 'one of the') is prefixed to the noun (see Fischer and Jastrow 1980: 88); in Iraqi Arabic *fard*, *fadd* (lit. 'single') has a similar role while Maltese *wieħed* (lit. 'one') marks indefiniteness.

Residues of CA nunation are still used productively in some bedouin dialects (mainly in the Arabian Peninsula). The occurrence of this nunation is limited in its distribution to certain nominal phrase structures, mainly nominals + adjectives, where the nunation affects the first member of the phrase, i.e., the nouns or the active participles only. It also occurs in complex conjunctions such as *yoomin ma* 'when' (e.g., Bahraini Arabic). In Najdi Arabic this *-in* denotes "one single but undefined member of a class whereas the absence of the marker means purely 'a member of the class in general'" (Ingham 1982: 53–54).

Noun Phrases: Genitival Exponents

In Arabic dialects the genitive is often indicated by the construct state between two nouns or by suffixing a bound pronoun to the noun. The definition of a construct is normally done by *el-* prefixed to the second noun, e.g., Jer. Ar. *bint el-malik* 'the king's daughter'. A suffixed pronoun prevents the use of the definite article; e.g., Jer. Ar. *beeti* 'my house', *ṣuurti* 'my picture'.

Most of the dialects developed analytical possessive particles from various nouns, which led to a functional distinction between the construct state and phrases with the genitival exponent. Most dialects prefer the construct state with inherent possession of body and kinship members; e.g. Ca. *ibn el-ʿamm* 'cousin (m.)' or Jer. *ižr el-walad* 'the boy's leg', and lexicalized compounds; e.g., Mor. *ma l-ward* 'rose water'. The more "external" or "temporary" possession is indicated by the genitival exponent. This is useful to: (1) control each noun for definiteness, emphasis, adding adjectives or a personal pronoun to the whole compound or any of its parts; (2) form genitival phrases with more than two words (the "default" in a construct state); and (3) use the construct state with words which have irregular syllabic structures often due to their foreign origin. These features increase the flexibility of the structure along with its distribution. Some dialects inflect the particle for number and gender and make it agree with its head noun.

The following list is illustrative of the diversity:

Bag. Ar. *maal* (< *maa li-* 'what to, what he has');
Mes. and Anatolia *δiil* (lit. 'which to, what he has'), *δiila, δeel, δeela, leel, lee, liit, laat* ;
Syr. *tabaʿ* (lit. 'following' or metathesized form of **bataʿ*), *šeet* (lit. 'thing of'), *šyaat*;

Pal. *tabaᶜ*, *btaaᶜ*, *šuɣl* (lit. 'work of'); *šeet*; *šiit*;
Negev bed. *šuɣl*;
Galilee bed. *ḥagg* (lit. 'the right of');
Ca. *bitaaᶜ*, *bituuᶜ*;
Eg. (except Ca.) *ihniin* (m.) *ihniit* (f.);
Chad. *hana* (inflected *hanay*, *hanaak*, etc.), *hine(e)*; these also occur in Nig. Ar.
    besides *hiil*, *hille*;
Sud. Ar. *huul*, *hiil*;
Oman and Zanzibar *haal*;
Mag. *mtaaᶜ* ('the property of'), *ntaaᶜ*, *taaᶜ*, *ddi*, *di*, *d*, *dyaal*;
Mal. * taʾ*, *tagħ-*, *tiegħ-*.

Noun Phrases: Nouns + Attributes

Normally in Arabic dialects, nominal attributes (such as adjectives) follow the N-head. They are usually definite according with their N-head, cf.: *beet kbiir* 'a big house' vs. *el-beet el-kbiir* 'the big house' in Jerusalem Arabic. In some dialects (mainly Iraqi, Maltese, and Moroccan) either the noun or the attribute may be definite under certain conditions; e.g., Moroccan *jaamaᶜ-l-kbiir* 'the great Mosque' (lit. 'mosque the great'), *baab-l-jdiid* 'the new gate' (lit. 'gate the new').

Demonstratives (deictics) show partly conditioned fluctuations between pre- and post-nominal position, as also in MSA. When in attributive role the demonstrative normally precedes the (definite) head noun. However, when the head noun itself is a construct or includes a bound pronoun suffix, the demonstrative follows the NP.

Mainly in Syro-Palestinian, Tunisian and Moroccan dialects (with apparently ex-bedouin origins) there is a double demonstrative structure of the pattern *ha(d)* + definite NP + *haaδa* 'this + def. NP + this'. The first part is often short (e.g., *ha-*) and seems to have lost much of its deictic power so that the demonstrative meaning is supplied by the full form following the NP:

Dam. Ar. *ḥal-banaat həlwiin ktiir* 'these girls are very pretty';
Yem. (North) Ar. *lihaaδa s-sabab* 'for this reason';
Tun. Ar. *ummi lkbiira haadi* 'this grandmother of mine';
Mal. *dawn it-tfal maltin* 'these (pl. dem.) children are Maltese';
Ca. *xalla l-ḥayyi-da farḥaan* 'he left this person happy';
Mor. Ar. *had-ar-ražel*; also: *had-ar-raajel-haada* 'this man';
Gal. bed. Ar. *fallet ha-l-ᶜabed-haaδa* 'she said: let this slave go free'.

Word Order

Unlike CA and MSA a frequent and unmarked (i.e., unstressed) word order in sentences in Arabic dialects is subject–predicate for both nominal and verbal clauses, though also VS and V(S)O are also frequent. Since normally the number and/or gender of a V(P) are morphologically marked, its referent subject can be understood from the context (unless first mentioned). If not at the head, the verb seems to prefer the second place in a clause after a subject or an adverb, e.g.:

Subject–Predicate

Ca. *wu di ʾabriiʾ* (lit. 'and this jug') 'and this is a water jug';
Druze (Gal.) *turkiyya nkasrat* 'Turkey has been defeated';
Dam. Ar. *ʾana jibt-al-kutub* 'I brought the books';
Mor. Ar. *wəl-ʿaadaat əl-ʿaṣriyya dyal l-mdina šəkl axor* 'and the modern urban habits are different';
Mal. *il-Maltin jistudjaw ħafna l-ingliz* 'the Maltese study English a lot'.

Verb–(Predicate)–Subject

Ca. *bassi-karr-riiḥ kuwayyis* 'but there was a good wind';
Dam. Ar. *ʾəli ʾaxxeen kbaar tneen* 'I have two big brothers';
Aleppine Ar. *xalṣet el-ḥafle hayye* 'this feast ended';
Arabian Ar. *maa fiih xuðratin halḥeel* 'there is not much grass';
Yem. Ar. *lagyuu ðaak im-ðiib* 'they met this wolf';
Lib. (Eastern) Ar. *naadir yaakil f il-laḥam* 'he rarely eats meat';
Mal. *Iħobb ʾl-Alla* 'he loves God'.

An interesting inversion type exists in, e.g., Cairene, Jerusalem and Moroccan dialects: *ʾabel huu ma yišrab* 'before he drinks' for *ʾabel-ma*, where the subject precedes *ma* of the subordinate particle instead of following it. Similarly, in Damascene *laazem tkammlu ʾana lli ḥtaramt menno* 'you must finish what I have been hindered from', the subject pronoun precedes its subordinate relative clause particle.

Agreement (Concord) Rules

As in CA, an adjective agrees with its head noun in definiteness, gender and number and a verb agrees with its subject in number and gender. A non-human head noun governs a sg. f. form; e.g., Mor. Ar. *mšat ʾiyyaam ujat ʾiyyaam* 'days went (sg. f.) and days came (sg. f.)', Mal. *sitt bajdiet moqlija* 'six fried (sg. f.) eggs'.

Dialects which do not distinguish gender in the plural of verbs and adjectives may deviate from the above "general Arabic"; e.g. Ca. *banaat il-beet il-ḥilwiin* 'the beautiful girls of the family'; Lib. Ar. *binaat ikbaar/kibiiraat* 'big girls'. Unlike CA, "real dual" nouns do not govern dual agreement in the dialects but rather the pl. and sg. f. for pseudo-duals; e.g., Ca. *biteen kubaar* 'two big houses' vs. *ideen ṭiwiila* 'long hand, arms'.

In Arabic dialects the real-life number category often overrules the formal rules, not only when the noun is animate:

Ca. *fareen miṣaḥbiin baʿḍ* '(there were) two mice (who) were friends (pl. m.)';
Gal. bed. Ar. *buu miʿza li insargan* 'there are goats of mine which were stolen

(pl. f.)';

Arabian Ar. *alkanabah wa assariir aljudud* 'the new (pl. m.) sofa and bed';

Mor. Ar. *utəlbs ħwaiž mzyanin nqiyin* 'and she wears good, clean (pl. m.) clothes';

Mal. *dawn huma l-flus li bihom ħallast il-ħaddiem* 'this (pl. m.) is the money with which (pl. m.) I paid the worker'.

Negation

Verb negation is usually marked by *ma(a)* in both Eastern and Western dialects, but *muu-b* is typical of many Arabian bedouin dialects. *muu* or *mii* negates nominal members in Syrian as well as many bedouin dialects and *moo* in Mesopotamian and Anatolian. Often *š* (< *šay'* 'thing') is suffixed to the negating particle yielding, e.g., *muš, miš*. Compare:

Ca. *muš ilwalad* 'not the boy';

Dam. *'əntu muu wlaad* 'you are not children';

Mes. *qaal mana joo'aan* 'he said, I am not hungry';

moo yešrab 'he does not drink';

Mor. *maa fiiha* (+ *š*) *baas* 'there is nothing wrong in it';

Mal. *hi m'hix ~ m'hijiex marida* 'she is not ill'.

Negation of the imperative (= inhibition) or two coordinated nouns uses *maa* and in some dialects *laa*. Thus Ca. *ma txaaf! ma yi'daršĭ yiḍḥak 'alayya* 'don't worry! he can't get the better of me'; Dam. Ar. *ma bəstəɣni 'annak wəla bxalliik truuħ* 'I can't do without you and I won't let you go'; Mor. *laa truuħ* 'don't go!'.

laa is also the absolute negation particle which in some Eastern dialects (Cairene, Jerusalem, Galilean and Syro-Lebanese) is often lengthened into *la'('a)* or *la'('a)* (Yem.). Demonstrating diversity here is the Yemenite case in which 'no' can be *la', la', laas, lawm, loom(i), da(w)', duwwayy, ma', ma', ma'h, maašii, maa'/ah, lees, lays, 'aba', 'abe'*.

Interrogation

The two main types are sentence (yes–no) and pronominal (wh-) questions. For confirmation only a few Arabic dialects use an interrogative at the head of the sentence; e.g., Ca. *huww-anti za'laana?* 'are you (sg. f.) angry?'; in Moroccan there are *waš, yak*; e.g., *yak-ana qult-lkum 'intu ta-taklu 'en-diyalkum?* 'didn't I tell you you were eating on your own?'. In Cairene and Libyan Arabic *š, ši* or *šu* may be suffixed to the end of a sentence for interrogation of yes–no questions; e.g., *'andakši sagaayir?* 'have you any cigarettes?'.

Interrogative particles usually come sentence initially:

Dam. *šloon bəddak tbaṭṭlo?* 'how do you want to fire him?';

Yem. *maalak maa jiitan?* 'why haven't you come?';

Mor. *škun l-qlb bla hmm?* 'who is the Untroubled Heart?';
Mal. *liema ktieb?* 'which book?'

In Egyptian and Sudanese these particles take their place within the clause in the normal word order:

Ca. *bitiʿmil eeh?*
(lit. 'you are doing what?')
'What are you doing?';
ma byištaɣaluuš leeh?
(lit. 'they aren't working why?')
'Why aren't they working?';
Sud. Ar. *ʿaawza nahaḍḍir šinu?*
(lit. 'you (sg. f.) want me to prepare what?')
'What would you like me to prepare?'

The Use of Copulas
Usually independent pronouns of the 3rd person (sg./pl., m./f.) serve as copulas indicating the present both in nominal and verbal clauses, or are the base for the copulas. In most dialects nominal copulas come between subject and predicate; e.g., Dam. *haada **huwwe** zzalame* 'this is the man'; Mal. *l'Italia **hi** art sabiħa* 'Italy is a beautiful land'.

In the *qəltu* dialects as well as Uzbekistan a special post-positional copula developed; e.g., Bag. *kalebna kelleš zeen **yaanu*** 'our dog is very nice'(copula: *yaanu*); Anat. *haada mešṭi-**we*** 'this is my comb' (copula: *we*); *naayme-**ye*** 'she's asleep' (copula: *ye*); *hawya lɣanam mən haak əlbayt-**ən*** 'these sheep are from that house'(copula: *ən*). This *ye* in Nigerian is an intensifier which follows independent pronouns: *humma-**ye*** 'they themselves'.

Possessive Clauses ("Have")
Unlike some non-Semitic languages, Arabic (including both written and colloquial) uses a prepositional phrase structure to indicate possession which elsewhere is expressed by a verb such as "have."

The phrase is based on inflected prepositions such as *ʿind-*, *maʿa-* or *ʾil-* which may be translated into English by 'by, with, to (someone)', respectively (but are perhaps more similar to the structure in Russian).

Word order in such sentences usually requires that this phrase should precede the subject:

Jer. Ar. *ʾili waladeen ubint* 'I have two children (boys) and a girl (daughter)';
ʿindi talat ɣuraf 'I have three rooms';
Ca. *ʿandak tiffaaħ, min faḍlak?* 'Have you any apples, please?'
Mor. Ar. *ʿndu flus bzzaf* 'he has a lot of money';

Since prepositions do not carry temporal meanings, the verb *kaan* 'be' is used as an auxiliary to indicate possession in the past or the future, as in other cases of prepositional phrases in Arabic. Thus, e.g.: Yem. Ar. *kaan ma'na baṭṭaariyya* 'we had a battery'; Mor. Ar. *kaan mrra jha 'ndu waḥd-l-bqra* (lit. 'it was once, Juha has a cow') 'once Juha had a cow'.

Verb Phrases: Tenses, Moods, Aspects

Three important syntactic categories of the verb are tenses, aspects and moods. The perfect refers to a completed action which usually occurred in the past (preterite). The imperfect is an action which is nonpast or not yet completed. But the perfect is used also in conditionals or optatives without necessarily referring to time, and the imperfect can appear in narrating past events. In Jerusalem and Syrian dialect the negation particle + imperfect with an additional stress on the verb denotes the jussive; e.g., *ma túktub* 'well, write then!'.

Aspects are mainly the indicative and subjunctive. The latter is unmarked morphologically, while the former is marked by prefixes (cf. p. 291). The indicative prefix occurs mainly in sedentary dialects, while bedouin ones hardly use it. Though some exceptions occur (e.g., the Negev), this may be considered a highly characterizing syntactic feature for the bedouin/sedentary dichotomy.

As the imperfect indicates an aspect rather than a tense, some dialects have developed time particles. For the future these are: *raaḥ, raayiḥ, ḥa-* (< 'going') in Cairene and Syro-Palestinian dialects, *di-, d-* in Iraqi, *b, bba-, bbi-, yabi-* (< 'want') (and its inflection) in some Arabian, Yemenite and Libyan dialects, and *γa, γadi* (< 'going') in Moroccan, while *'am-, 'ammaal* (< 'working') in the Syrian–Lebanese–Palestinian area and *taw* (< 'immediately') in the Maghreb denote the present progressive.

Other verb aspects are expressed by an auxiliary followed by the (semantically) main verb. Tense differences between the auxiliaries and the main verb affect structural meaning. The lexical meaning of the auxiliary gives the phrase its precise aspectual role:

> Ca. *yimkin ḥa-yḥibbǐ yiigi yšuufna*
> (lit. '(sg. 3m.) possible future particle will-want (sg. 3m.) will-come (sg. 3m.) will-see-us (sg. 3m.)')
> 'Maybe he will wish to come to see us';
> *yiẓhar kaan yi'uuz yiruuḥ yaakul*
> (lit. 'seems (sg. 3m.) was (sg. 3m.) will-want (sg. 3m.) will-go (sg. 3m.) will-eat (sg. 3m.)')
> 'It seems that he wanted to go to eat';
> Dam. *xalliina ne''od ma'ak*
> (lit. 'let (sg. 2m.) us will-sit (pl. 1) with-you (sg. 2m.)')
> 'Let us sit with you';
> *beddi ḥeṭṭek tet'allami lexyaaṭa*
> (lit., 'wish-my will-put (sg. 1) you (sg. 2f.) will-learn (sg. 2f.) the-sewing')

'I wish to have you learn sewing';
Gal. bed. *yiṣiiruun yijirruun bal-xeeṭ*
(lit. 'will become (pl. 3m.) will pull (pl. 3m.) with-the-string')
'They start pulling the string';
Ara. *hiyya gaaʿda tilʿab*
(lit. 'she sitting (sg. f.) will-play (sg. 3f.')
'She is playing';
Lib. *tibbi tixrij*
(lit. 'will want (sg. 3f.) will-go-out (sg. 3f.)')
'She wants to leave';
Mal. *kont ~ qed naqra l-gazzetta xħin wasal*
(lit., 'was (sg. 1) (or: particle) will-read (sg. 1) the-paper when arrived (sg. 3m.)')
'I was reading the paper when he arrived'.

Reference to the present is complex, due to the partial overlap between the active participle and the imperfect. In, e.g., Syro-Lebanese and Egyptian bedouin and sedentary dialects, the active participle refers to the present in verbs of motion, spatial location and senses, while in other verbs the participle may indicate resultative, perfective, static or progressive.

The imperative is used for commands. A pre-imperative prefix *de* is used in the Mesopotamian dialects; e.g., *detnaawal ṭareeqek* 'get off (on) your way'. The "imperative of narration" is frequent in bedouin dialects, as well as in some sedentary ones (according to Piamenta), and appears in various narrative genres instead of the perfect; e.g., *falleel lamma lkull rawwaḥ, gum yaa xaaḷah, wuugd an-naar* 'at night, when everyone had gone home, his uncle got up, kindled the fire … ' (Blanc 1970).

Verb Phrases: Transitivity and the Active and Passive Voice

Though the rate of use of the passive is much lower in Arabic dialects than in MSA (or English), transitivity is a basic syntactic feature of verbs with semantic as well as morphological implications. Active–passive transformations are possible with transitive verbs. Passive sentences in the dialects can be classified into two groups: (1) transformations of active agentive sentences, and (2) agentless sentences, or rather sentences where the agent is unspecified due to its being unimportant or unknown.

Transitivity is normally expressed in the presence of a "direct" object. In Mesopotamian *qəltu* dialects, however, as well as in the Syro-Palestinian area and Maltese, under certain conditions, a pronoun suffixed to the verb form "anticipates" the direct object (and makes it "indirect"); e.g., Baghdadi Jewish Arabic *hezzu lγaasak* 'shake your head'. A related phenomenon is found in Libyan Arabic: under certain conditions only an object marked by *fii* is allowed – *šaayfa isakkar f il-baab* 'I saw him closing the door'.

Topicality and Cleft Sentences

Certain syntactic members may be marked by movement to positions which are not their usual ones by, e.g., fronting. In addition to movement, other means of topicalization include use of relative clause structures and pronouns; e.g., Arabian *zamiilak huwwa alli kaan hina* 'your colleague, he was the one who was here' or the copula in, e.g., Arabian *haada huwwa alwalad azzaki* 'this is the smart boy'. In all likelihood, the most frequently occurring type of structure is based on a simple or complex fronted member later referred to by a bound pronoun:

> Egyptian *waaḥid ʿandína insaraʾ minnu gamuusa*
> 'One of us, a buffalo was stolen from him';
> Arabian *ʾaṣ-ṣabr, ʾal-ḥayaah tiʿallimuh li-nnaas*
> 'Patience, life teaches it to people';
> *illi ja šifta*
> 'He who came, I saw him';
> Maltese *l-għonja għandhom igħniu l-faqr*
> 'The rich, (they) must help the poor'.

Holophrases and Formulas

Holophrases ("minor sentences") carry full information value (including whole intonation contours) of sentences, though they do not have the conventional SV(O) structure. Ever since CA, many such structures have been used as greetings and expressions of anger, hope, surprise, admiration, etc. Many of these "formulas" express religious awareness by allusions to or by explicit mention of the name of Allah. Syntactically, "formulas" may take the form of phrases, subordinate clauses or whole sentences. Their function in the communicative act is often not related to their literal meanings. Their exact phrasing and meaning often depend on the dialect; e.g.: *ṣbaaḥk* (lit. 'your morning') 'good morning' in Maghrebine and Yemenite dialects, while in Muslim Baghdadi one may salute *alla bilxeer* (lit. 'God with goodness') 'may God (bless your day) with goodness'. Eastern dialects have *maa šaa ʾalla* 'it's God's will' while Maghrebine dialects express this notion by *tsbaark alla* 'blessed (is) God'. In the Eastern dialects *baarak allaahu fiik* is used when thanking, whereas in the Maghreb it is used for entreating. Taking refuge in God by Eastern *daxiil ʾalla* when entreating someone is not common in Egypt or further west; instead *fi ʿarḍ alla* is used. A bedouin invoking God when thanking the host for a meal may say *alla yxallif* 'may God recompensate' while a non-bedouin would say *alla yixlif*. In Iraq and Sudan one conjures *ʿaleek alla* 'by God (do/don't do something)', while in other Eastern dialects one says just *balla* or *balla ʿaleek*. *yiftaḥ alla* is an expression of negation in the Eastern dialects, while it connotes 'please!' in Algerian. In the East *il-barake* 'the blessing' is a prophylactic expression, whereas it means 'enough' in Moroccan.

Major Clause Types

Clause types are (probably) predominantly the same in all Arabic dialects, and similar to CA structures. Differences among dialects may appear in use of subordinating particles, in relative frequency of certain patterns and in a few innovations.

Relative Clauses

Relative clauses are governed by a subordinating particle if the antecedent noun is definite or by null particle if the antecedent is indefinite, e.g.: Ca. *huwwa raagil yistaḥa'' ittar'iya* 'he is a man who deserves promotion'; *huwwa-rraagil illi yistaḥa'' ittar'iya* 'he is the man who deserves promotion'. More than in CA and MSA, relative clauses in the dialects are often governed by the syntactic subordinating particle even when the antecedent noun is indefinite. Thus, e.g., bed. Gal. *yijiik yoom elli tə'uuzo* 'a day will come that you need him'.

Object Clauses

The particle *'an* which introduces complement clauses (subjunctive object clauses) in CA, is practically lost in the Arabic dialects, probably due to the loss of the distinction between the imperfect conjugations of the subjunctive, the jussive and the indicative. Compare, e.g. Arabian *'uxti alkibiira tiḥubb tizuurna* 'my elder sister likes to visit us'. (Cf. p. 304 for more examples.)

Reflexes of *'inna*, i.e., *'enno, 'inno* 'that, (object particle)' function in the Eastern dialects and reflexes of *aš* 'what' and *illi* 'that which', in the Maghrebine dialects; e.g., *bain, bin, baš, belli*, with *li* in Maltese. Moroccan Muslim dialects tend to use asyndetic clauses when possible, while Jewish dialects there prefer the syndetic patterns. In Moroccan, *baš* is typical of Jewish dialects, while *b(a)in* is Muslim. In all Arabic dialects asyndetic object clauses appear at least (1) when the governing verb is an auxiliary requiring the subjunctive mood; (2) when the object clause is a transformed question, or (3) when it is transformed "indirect speech." The following examples demonstrate some of the wealth involved:

Ca. *simi'̆t innĭ 'ali (ḥa)yiwṣal bukra*
'I hear(d) that 'Ali is arriving tomorrow';
'inta mit'akkid innak muš 'awzu(h)?
'Are you sure you don't want it?';
Ara. *hiyya gaalat inn aljaww baarid*
'She said that the weather is cold (it is cold)';
Mor. Ar. *ma 'raf baš mat*
'he did not know that he (had) died';
qalo li bain ražlek baɣi idžuwuž 'alik
'They told me that your husband wants to marry another woman'.

Circumstantial Clauses

Circumstantial syndetic and asyndetic clauses differ. In the latter, the circumstantial member is an imperfect following the main verb. The syndetic pattern, however, is [w + clause] (with the predicate often in the present participle) following the main clause. Cf. Ara. *annaas xaraju yitfassaḥu* 'the men went out picnicking'; Ca. *ʾabilna ṣaaliḥ f-issikka w-iḥna mrawwaḥiin* 'we met Saalih in the street as we were going home'.

A new structure in many Arabic dialects is the "inverted" circumstantial clause where a syndetic circumstantial clause precedes the main clause. Dam. Ar. *w-ana raaže', žtama't bi-ʾabuu naḅiil* 'as I was going back, I met Abu Nabil'; bed. (Gal.) Ar. *uhu gaaʿad ʿal-ḥajar, ja ʿalee d-dubb* 'as he was sitting on the stone, the bear came unto him'; Mal. *hu u jitkellem inḥanaq f dqqa* 'while (he was) speaking he suddenly grew hoarse'.

Conditional Clauses

Conditional clauses in MSA and the dialects use the finite verb without necessarily referring to time. But unlike CA, they may freely use the imperative. Asyndetic conditions also exist in the dialects, often in double conditions. Conditional particles include *iza, ila, in*, but many dialects developed particles from *kaan* 'be' in a fossilized perfect or imperfect form, at times combined with another lexical element. Combinations of particles + verb yield real or hypothetical conditions (with particles such as *law*) in the past, present or future. Also non-verbal conditions occur, e.g.:

Ara. *loo ʿindana fišag, čaan gaanṣiin*
'If we had cartridges, (we) would be away hunting';
Dam. Ar. *ʾen ʿažabek ha-š-šarṭ bteži taani yoom*
'If this condition suits you, you will come tomorrow';
Ca. *ʾiza (ʾin/law) kuntĭ ruḥt imbaariḥ, kunt iddetlak ilfiluus*
'If you had gone yesterday, I would have given you the money';
Mor. *ila čaanu waldiha f-xeer ʿaleehum, tšʿabbi čil-ši*
'If her parents were well to do, she would bring everything';
Mal. *li għidtli li tixtieq tiġi, kont nistiednek*
'If you told me that you wished to come, I would have invited you'.

Lexicon

More than phonological, morphological or syntactic differences, it is in the lexicon that some of the major discrepancies among Arabic dialects can most easily be spotted. One can predict a Mauritanian, Moroccan, Algerian or Tunisian background by *atay* or the like for 'tea', whereas elsewhere 'tea' is usually *šaahi, šaay*, or *čaay*. Similarly, Maghrebine dialects use *ḥəll* 'he opened', for *fataḥ* occurring in Eastern dialects. Lexicon also marks the sedentary/bedouin dichotomy and other communal dialects. The following tables illustrate some major types of lexical variation among the Eastern and Western dialects.

Table 14.12 Comparison of glosses in Nigerian, Cairene, Damascene, Iraqi, Meccan, Maltese and Lebanese dialects

Gloss	Nigerian	Cairene	Damascene	Iraqi	Meccan	Maltese	Lebanese
now	hatta/hassadug(g)ut	dilwa'(t)(i)	halla'	hassa	daḥḥiin	issa	halla'
good	zeen	kuwayyis	mniiḥ	xooš/zeen	zeen	tajjeb	mliiḥ/mniiḥ
bad	fasil/maknuushawaan	wiḥiš	fii	muzeenmuu-maaleḥ		mhux tajjeb	manno mniiḥ
there is	fi	fii	fii	'aku	fii	(h)emm	fii
there is not	ma fii/mifi	mafiiš	maa fii	maaku	maafiiš	ma-emm-x	maa fii
how much	kam	kam	'addeeš	čam	kam	kemm	'addeeš/kam
much/many	bil(h)eenkatiir	kitiir	ktiir	hwaayakθiir/r	waajid	ḥafna	ktiir
very	bil(h)een	'awi	ktiir	kulliš	katiir	ḥafna	ktiir
to do	amal/xadam	'amal	'əmel/saawa	sawwa/'amal	sawwa	hadem/ghamel	sawwa/'imel
eggs	beed/ṣ/dahii	beed	beed	beeḍ	beed	bajdiet	beed
rain	almatara	matar	maṭar	muṭar	maṭara	xita	šita
nothing	ma-še	wala ḥaaga	maa-ši	wala šii	walašay	ma ... xaji	wala šii

Table 14.13 Comparison of glosses in Anatolian, Israeli, Mauritanian, Moroccan, Algerian, Tunisian and Libyan dialects

Gloss	Anatolian	Israeli	Mauritanian	Moroccan	Algerian	Tunisian	Libyan
now	issaa'/hassaa'	'essa/halla'hal'eet	dark	daba	delwoq druuk	tawwa	alaan
good	baas (Kurd.)	mniiḥ	zeen	mezyan/waxxa	(a)mliiḥ	baahi	ṭayyeb
bad		'aaṭel		'aṭel/xayeb			šeen
there is	aku/kooku	fii	xalag	kayn	kan	famma	fiih
there is not	maaku	maa fii(š)	maxalagši	makanš	makaanš	mafammaš	mafiiš
how much	kam	'addeeš/kam	kamm	(a)šhal	gaddaaš	qaddaaš	kam
much/many	kəθiir	ktiir		bezzaf	bezzaaf	barša	
very	kəθiir/booš	ktiir	ḥatta	bezzaf			yaaser
to do	sawwa	saawa/'imel	waasa	dar	xdam	'mal	sawa
eggs	bayz/bayd	beed	beez	awlad žaaž	biid	'ḍaam	deḥii
rain	maṭar	šita	šhaab	naw/nu	šhab/naw	šṭaa	mṭar
nothing	laa šee	wala 'iši	ši	walu	ši	šay	kaan-l-barka

Acknowledgments

The authors extend their grateful thanks to F. Corriente, B. Ingham, O. Jastrow, J. Owens, M. Piamenta, H. Qafisheh and R. Hetzron for helping them with some data.

References

Abboud, P. F. 1964. "The Syntax of Najdi Arabic." Ph.D. dissertation. University of Texas.
Bakalla, M. 1975. *Bibliography of Arabic Linguistics.* London: Mansell.
—— 1983. *Arabic Linguistics: An Introduction and Bibliography,* 2nd rev. edn. London: Mansell.
Blanc, H. 1964. *Communal Dialects in Baghdad.* Cambridge, Mass.: Harvard University Press.
Ferguson, C. A. 1959. "Diglossia." *Word* 15: 325–340.
Fischer, Wolfdietrich and Otto Jastrow, eds. 1980. *Handbuch der arabischen Dialekte.* Wiesbaden: Harrassowitz.
Holes, C. 1983. "Bahraini Dialects: Sectarian Differences and the Sedentary/Nomadic Split." *Zeitschrift für arabische Linguistik* 10:7–38.
Ingham, Bruce. 1982. *North East Arabian Dialects.* London: Kegan Paul International.
Jakobson, Roman. 1957. "'Mufaxxama': The 'Emphatic' Phonemes in Arabic." In *Studies Presented to Joshua Whatmough on his 60th Birthday,* ed. Ernst Pulgram. The Hague: Mouton. 105–115.
Ladefoged, Peter and Ian Maddieson. 1996. *The Sounds of the World's Languages.* Oxford: Blackwell.
Lehn, W. 1963. "Emphasis in Cairo Arabic." *Language* 39: 29–39.
Obrecht, D. 1968. *Effects of the Second Formant in the Perception of Velarization in Lebanese Arabic.* The Hague: Mouton.
Rosenhouse, Judith. 1984. *The Bedouin Arabic Dialects: General Problems and Close Analysis of North Israel Bedouin Dialects.* Wiesbaden: Harrassowitz.
Sobelman, H., ed. 1962. *Arabic Dialect Studies.* Washington, D.C.: Center for Applied Linguistics and the Middle East Institute.
Versteegh, K. 1984. *Pidginization and Creolization: The Case of Arabic.* Amsterdam: Benjamins.

Further Reading

Aquilina, J. 1970. *Maltese.* 2nd edn. (Teach Yourself Books). London: The English Universities Press.
Behnstedt, P. 1984. "Zur Dialektgeographie des Nord-Jemen." In *Jemen Studien,* ed. Otto Jastrow. Wiesbaden: Harrassowitz. 261–288.
Blanc, Haim. 1953. *Studies in North Palestinian Arabic* (Oriental Notes and Studies 4). Jerusalem: Israel Oriental Society.
—— 1970. "The Arabic Dialect of the Negev Bedouins." *Proceedings of The Israel Academy of Sciences and Humanities* 4/7. Jerusalem: Jerusalem Academic Press. 112–150.
Borg, A. 1985. *Cypriot Arabic.* Stuttgart: Kommissionsverlag Steiner.
Brockelmann, Carl. 1913. *Grundriss der vergleichenden Grammatik der semitichen Sprachen,* volume 2. Hildesheim: Georg Olms.
Cantineau, Jean. 1955. "La dialectologie arabe." *Orbis* 4: 149–169.
Cohen, David. 1963. *Le Dialecte arabe Ḥassaniya de Mauritanie.* Paris: Klincksieck.
Corriente, F. 1977. *A Grammatical Sketch of the Spanish Arabic Dialect Bundle.* Madrid:

Instituto Hispano-Árabe de Cultura.

Cowell, M. W. 1964. *A Reference Grammar of Syrian Arabic (Based on the Dialect of Damascus)*. Washington, D.C.: Georgetown University Press.

Diem, Werner. 1973. *Skizzen jemenitischer Dialekte* (Beiruter Texte und Studien). Beirut: Orient Institut der deutschen morgenländischen Gesellschaft. Distributed by Franz Steiner Verlag.

Feghali, M. T. 1919. *Le parler de Kfar ʿabida (Liban-Syrie)*. Paris: Klincksieck.

Fischer, Wolfdietrich. 1961. "Die Sprache der arabischen Sprachinsel in Uzbekistan." *Der Islam* 36: 232–263.

Harrell, Richard S. 1962. *A Short Reference Grammar of Moroccan Arabic*. Washington, D.C.: Georgetown University Press.

Holes, C. 1995. "The Passive in Omani Arabic." *Proceedings of the Second AIDA (Association Internationale pour la Dialectologie Arabe) Conference, Fall 1995*. University of Cambridge, UK, Faculty of Oriental Studies. 69–74.

Jastrow, Otto. 1978. *Die Mesopotamisch-arabischen Qeltu Dialekte*. Volume 1: *Phonologie und Morphologie*. Wiesbaden: Steiner.

Jiha, M. 1964. *Der arabische Dialekt von Bišmizzin: Volkstumliche Texte aus einem Libanesischen Dorf mit Grundzugen der Laut- und Formenlehre*. Beirut: Imp. Catholique.

Johnstone, T. M. 1967. *Eastern Arabian Dialect Studies* (London Oriental Series 12). London: Oxford University Press.

Kaye, Alan S. 1976. *Chadian and Sudanese Arabic in the Light of Comparative Arabic Dialectology*. The Hague: Mouton.

Marçais, Ph. 1956. *Le parler arabe de Djidjelli (Nord constantinois, Algerie)*. Paris: Klincksieck.

—— 1977. *Esquisse grammaticale de l'Arabe Maghrebin*. Paris: Maisonneuve.

Mitchell, T. F. 1962. *Teach Yourself Arabic: The Living Language of Egypt*. London: The English Universities Press.

Owens, Jonathan. 1984. *A Short Reference Grammar of Eastern Libyan Arabic*. Wiesbaden: Harrassowitz.

—— 1993. *A Grammar of Nigerian Arabic* (Semitica Viva 10). Wiesbaden: Harrassowitz.

Piamenta, M. 1979. *Islam in Everyday Arabic Speech*. Leiden: Brill.

—— 1983. *The Muslim Conception of God and Human Welfare*. Leiden: Brill.

Qafisheh, H. A. 1992. *Yemeni Arabic Reference Grammar*. Kensington, Md.: Dunwoody Press.

Tübinger Atlas des Vorderen Orients (= TAVO). 1977–1994. Wiesbaden: Dr. Ludwig Reichert Verlag.

Tomiche, Nada. 1964. *Le parler arabe du Caire*. The Hague: Mouton.

Addenda and Corrigenda (with thanks to W. Heinrichs)

p. 265, 1.19: Read Syro-Lebanese for Lebanese. p. 266, 1.20: Read: usually becomes *g*; 1.24: Read: pronouns and the plural verb. p. 275, 1.21: Read: reflex of the *ẓaaʾ* and *ḍaad*; ll. 25-6: Read: (... voiced in some older Arabic dialects.); 1.31: Read: even *ẟ̣* . p. 278, rules 1–6: Read [ ] after ➔ (not / /); in rules 5 and 6, read [ʌ] in 3rd and [ʌʌ] in 2nd environments. p. 282, 1.1: Read: *ibn* >; 1.19: Read: Forms IV–X. p. 283, 1.15: Read: tends to retain the *n*-. p. 284, 1.6: Read: p. 299. p. 285, ll. 1–2: Read: *s* (no dots); *stufrin* 'yellow'; 1.3 up: Read: + (ᶜ)(*a*)*šar* 'teen'. p. 296, 1.3: Read: *kasar* 'he broke'. p. 298, 1.19 up: Read: e.g. *gaṣṣat* 'she cut' vs. *giṣṣat* 'was cut'. p. 304, 1.14: Read: Moods for Aspects.

15 Modern Hebrew

Ruth A. Berman

The term "Modern Hebrew" is applied to two different time-spans. Both postdate Medieval Hebrew, which followed the ancient Hebrew of the Biblical and Mishnaic periods (see p. 145, Chapter 9), and both refer to a special kind of linguistic revival (Blau 1981). In one sense, Modern Hebrew arose in the late eighteenth century, first in Central and later in Eastern Europe. The main innovators in this development were Jewish writers and intellectuals associated with the *Haskala* (Enlightenment) movement who advocated the use of ancient Hebrew in literary and publicist writings. Their motivation was a renaissance of Jewish culture, for which they favored the ancient language of classical Hebrew over the parochial Yiddish vernacular, and their efforts were critical for the emergence of contemporary Hebrew writing and culture (Harshav 1990). They set the modernist background for the rich literature, both original and in translation, which flourished in Hebrew in the 1900s, and provided the basis for the creation of Hebrew-language schools and a Hebrew-language press.

In another sense, the direct antecedents of Modern Hebrew date to its revival as a spoken language, starting some hundred years later, in the late nineteenth century. This development was motivated by the Zionist movement for national resettlement of Jews in the area which became established as the State of Israel in 1948 (Cooper 1983, Fellman 1973, Morag 1988: 3–127). The motivation for this unique sociolinguistic development was nationalist. Hebrew constituted a focal point of commonality between the different sectors of the Jewish population in Palestine: devout Jews scattered around the Holy Land, pioneers of Zionist immigration (mainly from Eastern Europe) from the late nineteenth century, and large influxes of Jewish refugees from Europe and the Middle East before and after World War II and in the early years of Israeli statehood. Recognized in 1922 as one of the three official languages of the British Mandate in Palestine (with English and Arabic), Hebrew has come to serve all the functions of a language identified with a given politico-geographical entity in modern times.

The present chapter deals with this latter version of "Modern Hebrew," a language which serves some five million Israelis in their everyday spoken intercourse, for official purposes in government, law, and formal education, and as the medium of literature, drama, the press, and other media. As such, Israeli Hebrew is like any other contemporary language with a documented history, since it is the first and major, if not only, language of its native speakers, and it has both spoken and written versions. But Modern Hebrew has unique underpinnings, due to the fact that Hebrew did not function in this manner for a period of some 1,700 years. From around 200 CE, Hebrew no longer served as the sole or even major means of communication in any speech community. Jews continued to use Hebrew for various purposes, largely liturgical and ritual, but Hebrew was no longer their mother tongue, and it thus had no monolingual speakers. Until the late nineteenth century, Hebrew served in conjunction with local vernaculars (Aramaic and subsequently Arabic in Palestine), or together with the Jewish languages that evolved in the Diaspora, like Judeo-Arabic, Ladino (Judeo-Spanish), and Yiddish (Judeo-German).

This lack of continuity in the evolution of spoken Hebrew has affected its development in both structural and sociolinguistic terms. Contemporary Hebrew derives from multiple sources of variation. It incorporates concurrent use of linguistic forms deriving from different periods in the history of the language (Bendavid 1967, 1971, Rubinstein, 1980); conservative norms prescribed by the Hebrew language establishment together with rapidly changing colloquial usages (Ravid 1994, Schwarzwald 1981); and the impact of non-Semitic contact languages – originally mainly Yiddish and Slavic, currently largely Western European (Fisherman 1986, Wexler 1990). Yet Modern Hebrew shows almost no regional variation, since it is the language of a small country, characterized by a centralized system of government, education, and broadcasting media, and multiple points of contact between different sectors of the population.

Israeli Hebrew usage ranges from the normativist requirements stipulated by such institutions as the Hebrew Language Academy (established by law in 1954, based on the prestate Language Committee) to substandard, nonliterate varieties. Between these two extremes lie "standard" forms of usage, the language of educated, native-born Israelis who are literate but nonspecialist speakers and writers (Berman 1987a). This is the variety described in the present chapter. Forms which are labeled as "non-normative" may be so widespread that they have become part of a new standard, and they are noted here as such. Forms termed here "substandard" characterize the usage of less literate speakers: immigrants for whom Hebrew is a second or foreign language, native-born Israelis with a lower level of education, and preschool children from standard-speaking backgrounds. In pronunciation, the variety of Modern Hebrew described here is similar to what Blanc (1964) described as "General Israeli," with occasional mention of an "Arabicized Israeli" pronunciation used by people of Near Eastern background.

Phonology

The phonemic inventory of General Israeli Hebrew reflects the mixed linguistic origins of its speakers at the turn of the century. The consonants are in general similar to those used by Jews of Ashkenazi (Central and Eastern European) extraction, whereas the vowel system was in the main adapted from the Sephardi reading pronunciation of speakers of Arabic/Judezmo background. As a result, many distinctions attested to in earlier periods and in other ethnic traditions, such as the Yemenite, are neutralized in mainstream Israeli Hebrew.

Vowels

The five vowels are close to cardinal vowels in pronunciation: *i, e, a, o, u.* There is no phonetic contrast between long and short (or tense versus lax) vowels in Modern Hebrew, although in some environments speakers may distinguish between two versions of *e,* the usual short *e* represented by the diacritic "segol" compared with the offglided *ey* represented by "tsere" (e.g., the free form of the singular noun *more* 'teacher' versus the bound form of the plural *morey* 'teachers-of'). The historical schwa *mobile* usually results from phonological rules of elision (e.g., before a stressed suffix) or insertion (e.g., between two homotopic word-initial consonants), and is pronounced like the front vowel *e,* sometimes even raised to *i* by younger speakers. There are three diphthongs, *uy, oy, ay,* created by a nonfront vowel followed by a front offglide, only in word-final position, e.g. *kanuy* 'bought', *goy* 'gentile', *elay* 'to-me'.

Consonants

The consonantal inventory of 'General Israeli' is shown below. The *r* phoneme is pronounced in two ways: a normative front rolled *r* is used in the theater, broadcasting, and in some varieties of Arabicized Hebrew, while the uvular version is typical of standard Israeli speech.

As shown, the major dialect of Modern Hebrew does not include two typically Semitic sets of elements: the historical pharyngeals, *ḥ* and ʿ have been neutralized to velar *x* and to glottal stop or zero respectively, and they are pronounced distinctly only in Arabicized Hebrew; and the historical emphatics, *q, ṭ, ṣ,* are pronounced as *k, t, c* respectively. The consonants listed also reflect several asymmetries. Only three of the six stop consonants, *p, b, k,* have fricative counterparts today, while the voiceless fricatives *š, x* and the voiceless affricate *c* lack voiced counterparts. The class of affricates has been extended to accommodate loanwords, including *č* as in Arabic *čizbat* 'tale', Italian *ciao,* English *chips;* and *ǧ* as in Yiddish *nidžes* or English (plus Russian) *jobnik.*

The orthography of Modern Hebrew uses the same twenty-two consonant letters as Biblical Hebrew (from the Phoenician alphabet). Vowels are indicated only in special contexts such as the Bible, poetry, and learners' texts, by means of the diacritic marks established in the Tiberian system around the ninth century. In contrast, the phonemic system of Modern Hebrew involves numerous levelings of historical distinctions. For example, historical ', ', h are often not pronounced, except in Arabicized Hebrew. They are never realized in word-final position, ' and ' are rare in word-initial position, where h occurs only in careful speech, and all three are pronounced as a glottal stop, if at all, in word-medial position. The same sound [v] is used for both the spirantized version of b and the historical glide w; [x] is used for both the spirantized version of the velar stop k and the historical pharyngeal ḥ; and [k] for both the velar stop k and the historical emphatic q.

This reduction of historical alternations has led to considerable morphophonological opacity and variability in environments that are phonetically unmotivated (Berman 1985, Ravid 1994, Schwarzwald 1981). For example, the same surface form [arim] represents orthographic '*rym* 'I will pick up'; *hrym* = *har* 'mountain' in the plural; and also '*rym* = *ir* 'city' in the plural. And the single surface phonetic string [kara] is a past tense 3rd person masculine verb form which stands for five different lexemes *qrh* = 'happened', *qr*' = 'read', *qr*' = 'tore', *kry* = 'mined', and *kr*' = 'knelt'. But the historical alternations neutralized in the past tense verb *kara* are manifested in other words derived from the same roots; compare, for example, the infinitives *li-kro* 'to-read', *li-króa* 'to-tear', *li-xróa* 'to-kneel', and the nouns *mikre* 'happening', *mikra* 'scripture', *mixre* 'a mine'.

Morphophonology

Three issues deriving from such neutralizations of historically distinct segments and processes are noted here: vowel lowering, vowel reduction, and spirantization. In the first case, the environments which require vowels to be lowered to *a* are often opaque, and speakers tend to extend the process to noncanonic contexts. For example, the infinitive forms of '-initial verbs in the *qal* verb pattern are rendered as *la'aroz* 'to-pack', *la'atom* 'to-seal' for normative *le'eroz*, *le'etom* (cf. '-initial *la'azov* 'to-leave'), and the feminine of *x*-final verbs yield *somáxat* 'to rely', *oráxat-din* 'woman-lawyer' for normative *soméxet*, *oréxet* (cf. ḥ-final *lokáxat* 'takes'). Such processes are widespread, but do not apply across the board, since some words, for reasons of transparency or high frequency, retain their historically normative forms (e.g., *le'exol* 'to-eat' with initial ', *holexet* 'goes' with stem-final *x*).

Second, stem-penultimate nonhigh vowels are reduced in nouns and adjectives before stressed suffixes, only in syllables which were historically open, e.g., *gadol* 'big'/feminine *gdola*, *nicaxon* 'victory'/plural *nicxonot*, *matos* 'airplane'/plural *mtosim*. This is blocked by historical medial geminates, e.g., *gamad* and *gamadim* 'dwarf/s', *ganav* and *ganavim* 'thief/ves'. In such cases, speakers have no phonological basis for deciding when to apply vowel reduction (Berman 1985: 260–263). In word-initial position, in contrast, vowel reduction varies between a schwa-like vowel or zero on phonetic grounds: with two initial consonants which are homotopic or homorganic, a schwa-like element is retained, as normatively required, but when the two consonants are phonetically dissimilar, they are pronounced as a cluster. (Compare *metixa* 'stretching', *betixut* 'safety', where a schwa-like element blocks consonant clustering, with *šmira* 'guarding', *kriʾut* 'readability'.) Modern Hebrew thus differs from its historical antecedents in allowing initial consonant clusters. Final clusters, in contrast, are still prohibited, except with the 2nd person feminine suffix *-t* on verbs, e.g. *šamart* 'guarded 2f.', *mataxt* 'stretched 2f.'. Elsewhere, they occur only in foreign loanwords, and are constrained by phonetic dissimilarity (e.g., *test* versus *fílim* 'film').

The third issue, spirantization or lenition, has received considerable attention in studies of Modern Hebrew. Current Hebrew has three stop-spirant alternations: $p \sim f, b \sim v, k \sim x$. The rules governing these alternations are generally opaque today, for the reasons noted earlier. For instance, intervocalic spirantization was historically blocked by geminate medial consonants, as in the verb *saval* 'suffered' versus the noun *sabal* 'porter', or the verb *safar* 'counted' versus *siper* 'told'. These distinctions are not phonetically motivated today. Hence speakers who use the normative form *li-šbor* 'to break', *nišbar* 'got-broken', with a medial stop *b* in syllable-initial position, may produce either normative *šavur* or substandard *šabur* for 'broken', *šavár-ti* or non-normative *šabár-ti* for 'broke sg. 1 = I broke'. In the opposite direction, speakers may spirantize when not required, yielding substandard forms like *xibásti* 'washed-sg. 1' (cf. *le-xabes* 'to-wash'), *xase oti* 'cover me' (cf. *le-xasot* 'to-cover') in place of required *kibásti, kase oti*. Overextension of spirantization also occurs in infinitives of verbs in the *qal* pattern, e.g., forms like *li-tfor* 'to sew', *li-gvor* 'to increase' commonly replace required *li-tpor, li-gbor* (cf. *li-šbor* 'to break'). Here the reason is the phonetic pull to dissimilation, where a root-initial stop tends to elicit a following spirant, counteracting the classical blocking of syllable-initial spirants.

Stress

Word-stress follows the Sephardi reading tradition and is typically on the final syllable (called *milraʿ*). Exceptions to this generalization are indicated throughout this chapter by an acute accent on the vowel of a nonfinal stressed syllable. As in classical usage, penultimate stress applies to the "segolate" class of derivative nouns, e.g. Biblical *mélex* 'king', Modern *méser* 'message', Mishnaic *nóhag* 'custom', Modern *nóhal* 'procedure' and to unstressed past tense suffixes, which leave main stress on the stem-final syllable (e.g., *tafár-ti* 'sewed sg. 1', *tafár-ta* 'sewed sg. 2), which has been extended to the 2nd person plural suffix *-tem* to yield *tafár-tem* in place of normative *tfar-tém*, and so regularized the past tense paradigm. In contemporary casual usage, Ashkenazi-type penultimate stress is used in proper names and in children's games. Compare, for example, the plural noun *rexovót* 'streets' with the name of the city *rexóvot* (Rehoboth), the action-nominal *širá* 'singing' with the girl's name *šíra* (Shira), or the plural noun *klafím* 'cards' with the name of the children's game of *kláfim*; and the ordinals *rišon* 'first', *šeni* 'second', *šliši* 'third', etc. also get penultimate stress in children's counting out. Finally, loanwords often have nonfinal stress, e.g. *profésor, modérni,* or antepenultimate in words like *univérsita, akadémiya.*

Morphology

Modern Hebrew has retained much of the inflectional morphology of its classical antecedents (see p. 318). In new-word formation, too (p. 320), all verbs and many nouns and adjectives are formed by the classically Semitic devices of consonantal roots plus associated affixal patterns. However, the system of grammatical formatives described below includes many levelings of earlier distinctions, as well as extensions to more analytical forms of expression.

Pronouns

Personal pronouns are marked for person, number, and gender. In the nominative, they occur as free forms, and elsewhere are suffixed to case marking or adverbial prepositionals. These suffixes take either a singular or plural form when attached to a bound prepositional stem, as shown in Table 15.1. The pronouns suffixed to *šel* 'of' are those used for singular nouns in Biblical and in Modern Hebrew, those used with *al* 'on' occur with plural nouns.

Table 15.1 Personal pronouns

	Nominative Singular	Plural	Genitive *šel* 'of' Singular	Plural	Locative *al* 'on' Singular	Plural
1	ani	anáxnu ~ ánu	šel-i	šel-ánu	al-ay	al-énu
2m.	ata	atem	šel-xa	šel-axem	al-éxa	al-eyxem
f.	at	aten	šel-ax	šel-axen	al-áyix	al-eyxen
3m.	hu	hem	šel-o	šel-ahem	al-av	al-ehem
f.	hi	hen	šel-a	šel-ahen	al- éha	al-ehen

The basic prefixal prepositions typically take singular pronominal suffixes, e.g., dative *li, lexa, lax* 'to me, to you (m.), to you (f.)', and locative or instrumental *bi, bexa, bax* 'in/with me, you'. Several prepositions have suppletive stems before a pronominal suffix, e.g., accusative *et* takes forms like *oti, otxa, otax* 'me, you (m.), you (f.)', comitative *im* changes to bound *iti, itxa, ito* 'with me, with you'. There are also paradigm-internal alternations; for example, the comparative preposition, *kmo* 'like' has the bound forms *kamóni* 'like me', *kamóxa* 'like you', and ablative *mi(n)* 'from' alternates between *miméni, mimxa, mimex, mimeno, mimena* with singular pronouns and *miménu* (or *me'itánu*), *mikem, miken, mehem, mehen* in the plural. Paradigm regularization is common in colloquial usage, e.g., *eclehem* for *eclam* 'at them' (cf. *lahem* 'to them'), *bišvilax, otex* for *bišvilex, otax* 'for you, f.', 'you, acc. f.'.

Inflectional Morphology

Verbs alternate across five categories of tense and mood, as shown below for masculine singular forms in three conjugations.

		Nonfinites			Tensed	
Root	Gloss	Infinitive	Imperative	Participial	Past	Future
g-m-r	'finish'	*li-gmor*	*gmor*	*gomer*	*gamar*	*yi-gmor*
s-p-r	'tell'	*le-saper*	*saper*	*me-saper*	*siper*	*ye-saper*
p-s-q	'stop'	*le-hafsik*	*hafsek*	*ma-fsik*	*hifsik*	*ya-fsik*

Infinitives take prefixal *l-* 'to' and are otherwise uninflected in Modern Hebrew. Imperatives are listed here in their normative form, but these are rare in casual usage. Juvenile and intimate peremptory style uses infinitives for imperative injunctions; future tense forms serve for requests in causal style (as is normative in the negative, e.g., *al tafsik* 'not 2nd-will-stop = don't stop!'), and a new imperative form has evolved out of the future stem minus the 2nd person prefix (Berman 1985, Bolozky 1979). Participials (traditionally termed *benoni* 'intermediate') also serve for present tense reference, contrasting with past and future tense (Gordon 1982). Future forms function both as colloquial imperative and for other modalities such as jussives and optatives.

Table 15.2   Verb inflections

		Imperative	Participial	Past	Future
Sg.	1			sipár-ti	a-saper
	2m.	saper		sipár-ta	te-saper
	f.	sapr-i		sipár-t	te-sapr-i
	3m.		me-saper	siper	ye-saper
	f.		me-sapér-et	sipr-a	te-saper
	1			sipár-nu	ne-saper
	2m.	sapr-u		sipar-tem	te-sapr-u
	f.	saper-na		sipar-ten	te-saper-na
	3m.		me-sapr-im	sipr-u	ye-sapr-u
	f.		me-sapr-ot	sipr-u	te-saper-na

Except for infinitives, verbs take agreement suffixes (see p. 326) for plural number and feminine gender, and past and future tense verbs are also marked for person. These inflections are illustrated in Table 15.2 for the verb *saper* 'tell (a story)'.

Masculine gender is the basis for neutralizations, particularly in the plural, as in Modern Hebrew leveling to masculine plural forms of 2nd and 3rd person in future tense. The participial, present tense forms differ from the past and future tense in not being marked for person, with a single form used with 1st, 2nd, and 3rd person pronouns. Past and future tense forms observe the classical asymmetry of suffixal versus prefixal person markings.

Nouns have natural, sex-linked gender if animate, with a feminine suffix in the form of stressed *-a*, *-it*, or unstressed *-et*, e.g., *iš* 'man' ~ *iša* 'woman', *saxkan* 'actor' ~ *saxkanit* 'actress', *tarnegol* 'cock' ~ *tarnególet* 'hen'. Inanimate nouns are either masculine or feminine. Grammatically feminine nouns are generally marked as such by their endings, e.g., masculine *aron* 'closet'/feminine *mita* 'bed', masculine *mazleg* 'fork'/feminine *kapit* 'teaspoon', masculine *séfer* 'book'/ feminine *maxbéret* 'notebook'; but there are exceptions, e.g., feminine *kos* 'glass', *eš* 'fire'. Noun plurals depend on the singular gender, *-im* for masculine, *-ot* for feminine, e.g., *sal-im* 'bags', *amud-im* 'pillars', but *mit-ot* 'beds' from singular *mita*, *tmun-ot* 'pictures' from singular *tmuna*. Lexical exceptions exist in both directions, e.g., masculine *šulxan* 'table', *av* 'father' take the feminine plural *-ot*, while feminine *mila* 'word', *šana* 'year' form their plural with *-im*. The dual suffix *-áyim* is lexically restricted; used mainly for body parts and clothing, e.g. *sfatáyim* 'lips' versus *safot* 'languages, edges', it may be extended, for instance to time-periods, as in *švuʾáyim* 'two weeks', *šnatayim* 'two years' (cf. *šavuʾot* 'weeks', *šanim* 'years'). Complex phonological and morphological processes condition the bound form of different classes of noun stems before a stressed suffix. These include vowel reduction e.g., *gamal* ~ *gmalim* 'camel-s', *nicaxon* ~ *nixconot* 'victory/ies' and other contractions, e.g., *áyin* ~ *enáyim* 'eye-s', *báyit* ~ *batim* 'house-s', *láyla* ~ *lelot* 'night-s', and numerous morphologically conditioned alternations, e.g. *dégel* ~ *dgalim* 'flag-s', *šixva* ~ *šxavot* 'layer-s'.

Nouns also have a bound form in the construct state before a possessive suffix or as the head noun of bound construct state genitive. In everyday speech, the suffixed possessives are typically replaced by a more analytical form with the genitive particle *šel*, thus *ha-sal šel-i* 'the-basket of-me' for 'my basket', *ha-mita šel-axem* 'the-bed of-you' for 'your bed'. The bound pronominal suffixes are restricted to formal high style and to a few lexically frozen expressions, e.g. *tor-i* 'turn-my' = 'my turn' (in games), *ma šlom-xa?* 'what peace-your' = 'how are you?'. Nonlexicalized construct state genitives are common in formal usage (see p. 330), but also tend to be replaced by more analytical forms with *šel* 'of' in spoken Hebrew.

Free nouns and construct state bound head nouns have a distinct inflectional form in the masculine plural, the free suffix *-im* versus bound (Aramaic) *-ey*, e.g., *salim* 'baskets'/*sal-ey kaš* 'baskets-straw' = 'straw baskets', *mtosim* 'planes'/ *mtosey krav* 'war planes'. Examples of a single bound stem form in different morpho-syntactic environments are shown below.

Free form	Gloss	Plural	Possessive suffix		Construct state N + N	
davar	'word'	*dvar-im*	*dvar-a*	'her word'	*dvar haʾel*	'God's word'
láyla	'night'	*lel-ot*	*lel-i*	'my night'	*lel xóref*	'winter night'
xéder	'room'	*xadar-im*	*xadr-o*	'his room'	*xadar óxel*	'dining room'
tmuna	'picture'	*tmun-ot*	*tmunat-i*	'my picture'	*tmunat šáʿar*	'cover picture'

Adjectives pattern morphologically like nouns in most respects, and they agree with their head nouns in number, gender, and definiteness, e.g. *ha-xéder ha-gadol* 'the-room the-big = the big room', feminine *ha-tmuna ha-gdola* 'the big picture'.

Adjectives can also have bound, construct state forms, but these are rare in spoken usage, except where they have become lexicalized in set expressions, e.g., *kcar-re'iya* 'short-of sight = short-sighted'.

Derivational Morphology

Modern Hebrew relies largely on the classical Semitic means for constructing new words, from consonantal roots plus associated affixal patterns: *binyanim* 'conjugations' for verbs and *miškalim* 'weights' for nouns and adjectives. This process has also been extended in several ways to allow for rapid and effective vocabulary expansion.

New-verb Formation: Roots and Conjugations (Binyanim)

All verbs are constructed in one of the seven *binyan* conjugation patterns, labeled here as P1 *qal* or *pa'al*, P2 *nif'al*, P3 *pi'el*, P3$_{ps}$ *pu'al*, P4 *hitpa'el*, P5 *hif'il*, P5$_{ps}$ *hof'al*. (Verbs are cited here in the morphologically simple 3rd person masculine past tense form.)

P1 = *qal*, *pa'al*: This is the most basic pattern, with the highest frequency of distribution for both type and tokens at all levels of usage. Morphologically, it is highly variable, since it lacks a single unequivocal stem form, and it disallows roots of more than three elements. Lexically, it is the least productive pattern, with almost no new verbs formed from denominal or loan sources (e.g., *taxam* 'delimit' from *txum* 'range'). Syntactically, it is the only pattern which is equally open to both intransitive and transitive agentive activity verbs (e.g., *halax* 'walk', *yašan* 'sleep', *caxak* 'laugh') compared with *daxaf* 'push', *tafas* 'catch', *šavar* 'break'), and also to stative verbs (e.g., *ra'a* 'see', *xašav* 'think', *ahav* 'love'). Transitive verbs in this pattern have passive or change-of-state equivalents in P2 *nif'al*, e.g., P1 *lakax* 'take' ~ P2 *nilkax* 'be-taken', P1 *ganav* 'steal' ~ P2 *nignav* 'be-stolen' and P1 *šavar*, trans. ~ P2 *nišbar*, intr. 'break' , P1 *šafax* ~ P2 *nišpax* 'spill'. Occasional alternations between activity verbs in P1 and the P3 *pi'el* pattern are idiosyncratically related (e.g., P1 *patax* 'open' ~ P3 *pitéax* 'develop').

P2 = *nif'al*: Verbs in this pattern are marked by the prefixal *ni-* in present and past tense. They are typically intransitive, since they cannot govern direct objects with the accusative marker *et*. This pattern serves mainly as a change-of-state or passive reflex of transitive verbs in P1. It also contains a large, though closed class of verbs which have transitive causative alternants in P5, e.g., P2 *ne'elam* 'disappear' ~ P5 *he'elim* 'make disappear, hide', P2 *nivhal* 'be startled' ~ P5 *hivhil* 'startle, frighten'.

P3 = *pi'el*: This pattern (traditionally termed "strong" or "heavy" because of the historical gemination of the medial root consonant) includes mainly transitive activity verbs, and a few intransitives, e.g., *xiyex* 'smile', *tiyel* 'take a walk'. Its most productive function in Modern Hebrew is for new-verb formation, either from native nouns (e.g., *kixev* 'star' from the noun *koxav* '(a) star', *'irpel* 'befog' from *arafel* 'fog') or from loanwords (e.g., *siben* from *sabon* 'soap', *tirped* 'torpedo'). In addition, affixal consonants of established nouns are incorporated in this pattern to derive new root elements by a process of "secondary root forma-tion," e.g., *mikem* 'locate' from *makom* 'place' derived from the historical root *q-w-m*, *tifked* 'function' from the noun *tafkid* based on the root *p-q-d*. For exam-ple, the historical root *x-š-b* 'think' has been extended to create two new sets of formatives, with prefixal *m-* to form *m-x-š-v* from the noun *maxšev* 'computer', as in *mixšev* 'computerize', and a suffixal *-n* from *xešbon* 'arithmetic' underlying *x-š-b-n* as in *xišben* 'calculate'. In morphophonological terms, the *pi'el* pattern (like the other two strong patterns, *pu'al* and *hitpa'el*) is particularly accessible to roots with more than the classical three consonants, and can thus accommodate the large number of verbs coined in Modern Hebrew with quadriliteral roots (Yan-nai 1974). These include extension of prefixal elements such as the Aramaic-based *šaf'el* (e.g., *šixzer* 'reconstruct', *šixtev* 'rewrite'), Mishnaic *ʾaf'el* (e.g., *ʾišpez* 'hospitalize', *ʾivtéax* 'secure', and contemporary *taf'el* (e.g., *tidlek* 'refuel', *tiskel* 'frustrate').

P3ps = *pu'al* functions as the syntactically, lexically, and morphologically pro-ductive passive counterpart of transitive P3 *pi'el* verbs, e.g. *sudar* 'be-arranged', *šuxtav* 'be-rewritten'. As such, it forms part of inflectional rather than derivational morphology in Modern Hebrew.

P4 = *hitpa'el* is multifunctional in Modern Hebrew. It never governs the accu-sative marker *et*, and so takes no direct objects, nor does it have a passive coun-terpart. It contains the few lexical reflexives, e.g. *hitraxec* 'wash oneself' and reciprocals, e.g. *hitkatvu* 'correspond (with one another)'. More productively, it is the favored means of expressing inchoativity, based on verbs or adjectives, e.g. *hitragez* 'get angry', *hit'ayef* 'get-tired', *hizdaken* 'grow-old'. Primarily, P4 con-stitutes the intransitive, change-of-state reflex of P3 activity verbs, e.g. *histader* 'settle down', *hitpazer* 'scatter', and so it is also commonly used in denominals, e.g. *histaben* 'soap oneself', *hit'aqlem* 'become acclimatized'. Verbs like *hizdaken*, *histader*, *histaben* show that the classical process of metathesis and voicing assimilation of the prefixal *-t* before a root-initial sibilant in this verb pat-tern has been maintained in Modern Hebrew.

P5 = *hif'il* contains mainly transitive verbs in Modern Hebrew, except for its classical use as both the causative and inchoative form of a restricted set of adjec-tives (e.g. *he'edim* 'redden' = 'make-red' and 'become red', *hivšil* 'ripen' = 'make ripe' and 'become ripe'). P5 is used far less for denomination than in Biblical He-brew, and in such cases, it is often phonologically conditioned, e.g. *hišpric* 'spray' from the loan noun *špric* (although see, too, neologisms like *hilxin* 'put to music' from *láxan* 'tune', *hiklid* 'enter (on keyboard)' from *kalid* 'key'). The most pro-ductive contemporary function of P5 *hif'il* is as the causative counterpart of (mainly intransitive) activity verbs in P1, e.g. P1 *rac* versus P5 *heric* 'run ~ make-run', P1 *caxak* 'laugh' versus P5 *hicxik* 'make-laugh = amuse', and of adjectives, e.g. *gamiš* 'flexible' yields P5 *higmiš* 'make flexible', *kiconi* 'extreme' yields P5 *hikcin* 'extremize'.

P5ps = *hof'al* is the passive alternant of P5 *hif'il* to which it relates much as the other strictly passive binyan pattern P3ps *pu'al* to transitive verbs in *pi'el*, e.g.

hurac 'be (made to)-run', *hugmaš* 'be-made-flexible = elasticized', *hulxan* 'be-put-to-music'.

Passive Participles

The three *binyan* patterns which contain strictly transitive verbs, i.e. verbs which take accusative marked direct objects, have regular passive participial counterparts, as follows. Verbs in P1 *qal* take the form CaCuC, e.g. *sagur* 'closed', *šavur* 'broken', *katuv* 'written'; P3 *piʿel* transitives take the form *mefuʿal*, e.g. *mesudar* 'arranged, tidy', *mefuzar* 'scattered, disorderly', *mešuxtav* 'rewritten'; those in P5 *hofʿal* take the form *mufʿal*, e.g. *mušprac* 'sprinkled', *mustar* 'hidden', *munxe* 'directed' (Berman 1994). These alternations reflect the dual nature of the *qal* pattern in Modern Hebrew, as shown below.

Active transitive	Passive	Perfective Participle
P1 *qal*	P2	*nifʿal* ~ CaCuC
P3 *piʿel*	P3$_{ps}$	*puʿal* = meCuCaC
P5 *hifʿil*	P5$_{ps}$	*hofʿal* = muCCaC

The *u* vowel is a distinctive marker of these passive participles, which have an end state, resultative meaning (e.g., *neʾum katuv* 'speech written = a written speech', feminine *safa medubéret* 'spoken language'). They also create new adjectives from verbs, e.g. *yadúa* 'known = familiar', *mefursam* 'publicized = famous', *mufšat* 'undressed = abstract' and also from nouns, e.g., *meʾuban* 'fossilized' from *éven* 'stone', *menumas* 'polite' from *nimus(in)* 'manners'.

Noun and Adjective Formation: Conversion, Affixation, and Juxtaposition

Conversion from one lexical category to another is another common device for new-noun derivation in Modern Hebrew, under the following constraints. It is based only on the participial ("present tense") form of verbs, active or passive, and it forms only two semantic classes, agent and instrument nouns, e.g., P1 *porec* 'burglar', P2 *neʾeman* 'trustee', P3 *menahel* 'director', P4 *mitʾagref* 'wrestler', P5 *madrix* 'guide'; and P1 *mone* 'meter', P2 *nispax* 'appendix', P3 *meʾavrer* 'ventilator'.

Affixation of classical patterns to consonantal roots remains the favored means of new-noun formation in Modern Hebrew. Internal-vowel patterns are used for new agent nouns, e.g. CaCaC in words like *tayas* 'pilot', *sapak* 'supplier', *pasal* 'sculptor'; for possibility adjectives in CaCiC, e.g., *kavis* 'washable', *kavil* 'acceptable', *axil* 'edible'; and the CéCeC segolate pattern serves for numerous noun coinages, e.g., *méser* 'message', *pélet* 'output', *šéder* 'broadcast'. Classical patterns with prefixal and/or suffixal elements are also widely used in expanding the noun stock of Modern Hebrew, e.g. *maCCeC* for instrument nouns such as *maxšev* 'computer', *macber* 'battery'; CaCéCet for diseases, e.g. *šaʿélet* 'whooping cough', *kalévet* 'rabies' or for collectives, e.g. *canéret* 'pipeworks'; *miCCaCa* for place or collective nouns such as *minhala* 'administration', *mifkada* 'headquarters'; or *tiCCóCet* for abstract nouns such as *tixtóvet* 'correspondence', *tismónet* 'syndrome'.

Modern Hebrew also relies heavily on external affixation to the bound stem form of words. For example, the Mishnaic attributive pattern CaCCan is widely used in modern agent nouns like *karyan* 'broadcaster', *saxyan* 'swimmer', as is the suffix *-an* attached to established nouns in new words like *mišpetan* 'jurist', *psantran* 'pianist', *harpatkan* 'adventurer'. The abstract suffix *-ut* derives abstract nouns by agglutination to existing nouns e.g. *yaldutiyut* 'childishness' or to passive participles, e.g. *meʿuravut* 'involvedness = involvement'. Suffixal *-i* is a major device for denominal adjective formation, e.g. *beʿayati* 'problematic', *taʿasiyati* 'industrial'. A device not attested to in earlier phases of the language are innovative prefixes used to form complex adjectives, e.g., *ben-leʾumi* 'international', *xad-cdadi* 'uni-lateral', *du-mašmaʿi* 'ambiguous', *kdam-akadémi* 'pre-academic'.

Blended words are derived by merging two bound stems or parts of words, e.g. Pl *li-rmoz* 'to signal' plus the noun *or* 'light' yields *ramzor* 'traffic light', *xamiša* 'five' plus *šir* 'song, poem' yield *xamšir* 'limerick'; *midraxa* 'sidewalk' plus *rex-ov* 'street' yield *midraxov* 'pedestrian mall' (Berman 1989). Lexicalized compound nouns are derived from a bound head noun followed by a free form of a second, adjunct noun, e.g., *yošev-roš* 'sitter-head = chairman', *orex-din* 'conductor-law = lawyer'; *tapúax-adama* 'apple-earth = potato'.

Methods for new-adjective formation include use of classical *miškal* patterns such as CaCiC; semantic extension of active participial patterns, e.g. *benoni* forms such as Pl *bolet* 'stands out = conspicuous', P3 *meʿacben* 'annoys = maddening', P5 *macxik* 'amusing = funny'; extension of passive participial form CaCuC, *meCuCaC*, and *muCCaC*; and suffixal *-i* as a productive means for incorporating denominal and loan adjectives, e.g. *xinuxi* 'educational', *cimxoni* 'vegetarian', *modérni, akadémi*.

Modern Hebrew has thus been able to expand its vocabulary effectively to meet the needs of casual everyday intercourse, of science and technology, of journalism and *belles lettres*, while retaining much of the flavor of its ancient Semitic origins.

Syntax

The syntax of Modern Hebrew contains constructions which have been taken over from the two major historical periods in the history of spoken Hebrew, Biblical and Mishnaic, while also showing the impact of different contact languages to which its speakers have been exposed over the past hundred years.

Word Order

Modern Hebrew is predominantly SVO in basic word order: with pronominal and lexical subjects, with copular and main verb predicates, and in main as well as subordinate clauses. Like classical Hebrew, however, Modern Hebrew manifests the syntactic properties associated with verb-initial languages, as follows. It is prepositional rather than postpositional in marking case and adverbial relations; auxiliary verbs precede main verbs; main verbs precede their complements, nominal or sentential; noun modifiers – adjectives, determiners, and noun adjuncts – follow the head noun; hence, too, in genitive constructions the possessee noun precedes the possessor.

Moreover, Modern Hebrew allows, and in some cases requires, sentences which are predicate initial. In possessive and existential constructions (see p. 329), the copula verb *haya* 'be' or the existential particle *yeš* are typically sentence initial. VS order is common though not mandatory with certain other kinds of predicates, particularly those which refer to existence or coming into being and are syntactically unaccusative, e.g. *parca šam srefa* 'broke-out (a) fire there', *hofia dmut ba'ófek* '(there) appeared (a) figure on-the-horizon'. Moreover, verbs with person-marking affixes in past and future tense do not need a separate subject pronoun in noncontrastive contexts, so that the verb is again sentence initial (see further p. 326).

Various kinds of impersonal constructions are also typically subjectless. These include

1 the canonic "strictly subjectless" impersonals with 3rd person plural verbs without any pronoun, e.g., *šotim hamon mic ba-káyic* 'drink + pl. lots juice in-the-summer = people drink a lot of juice in summertime', *yodíu et hatoca'ot bekarov* 'will-announce + Pl. ACC. the-results soon = the results will be announced shortly';

2 "circumstantial predicates" relating to time and weather, e.g. *me'uxar axšav* '(it's) late now', *yihye lexa xam šam* 'will-be to-you hot there = you'll be hot there';

3 impersonal passives with sentential complements, e.g. *ne'emar šehu hevi ota* '(it) was-said that he brought her', *huxlat še ha'inyan yetupal* '(it) was-decided that the matter would-be-treated';

4 modal and other evaluative predicates with sentential complements, e.g. *kday la'azor lo* 'worthwhile to-help him = he should be helped', *xaval še hu lo ba* '(it's a) pity that he did not come', *haya xašuv še-dibárnu ito* '(it) was important that we-talked to-him'.

A major change in colloquial Hebrew is the introduction of an expletive subject, the impersonal pronoun *ze* 'it, this, that', not in the context of (1) and (2) above, but optional with sentential complements of type (4), e.g., *ze lo yafe ledaber kax* 'it (is) not nice to-talk that way', *ze haya xašuv še azárnu lo* 'it was important that we helped him'.

Major constituent order in current Hebrew is thus variable, since the basic SVO order of tensed clauses alternates with a range of VS and subjectless constructions. In addition, various fronting operations allow change of focus or topicalization of a nonsubject element. These more marked orders include left dislocation, in which a topicalized element is fronted, leaving a pronominal copy in its original position, as in (b) below. Spoken usage also allows right dislocation, with case marking retained on both the dislocated nominal and the pronominal trace, as in (c), with nominals case-marked for the accusative, free *et* or bound *otam* 'them'.

(a)	Unmarked SVO:	*ani*	*makir*	*tov me'od*	*et*	*haKohenim*
		I	know	very well	ACC.	the Cohens
(b)	Left-dislocation:	*haKohenim,*	*ani*	*makir*	*otam tov me'od*	
		the Cohens,	I	know	them very well	
(c)	Right-dislocation:	*ani*	*makir*	*otam tov me'od,*	*et*	*haKohenim*
		I	know	them very well,	ACC.	the Cohens

Along with the classical topicalization of (b) and colloquial right dislocation as in (c), Modern Hebrew also allows simple fronting of nonsubject constituents, as shown below.

(a)	Direct object:	*et*	*haKohenim*	*ani*	*makir*	*tov me'od*
		ACC.	the Cohens	I	know	very well
(b)	Oblique object:	*im*	*haKohenim*	*anaxnu*	*nifgašim*	*harbe*
		with	the Cohens	we	meet (up)	a lot
(c)	Locative:	*el*	*haKohenim*	*anaxnu*	*nos'im*	*kol šavua*
		to	the Cohens	we	drive	every week

Internal SV order tends to be retained after such frontings. Where classical inversion to VS occurs in such cases, it is applied to all three tenses, present, past, and future (normatively, the present ~ participial forms, considered nominal, blocked this inversion). The grammar of Modern Hebrew permits a variety of constituent reorderings, but there is a tendency in spoken usage to rely mostly on the unmarked, neutral, or basic SV(O) order.

Determiners

(See Agmon-Fruchtman 1982, Glinert 1989). Definiteness is marked by the morpheme *ha-* prefixed to nouns and their associated adjuncts (see p. 326). Nondefinite noun phrases lack special marking, but colloquial style uses a contracted, unstressed form of the numeral *exad* 'one', feminine *axat*, for nondefinite, specific nouns. Deictic *ze* 'this, that, it' has several functions, and is today commonly used as a pleonastic or expletive pronoun (Berman 1980, 1990). Postnominal demonstratives alternate between Biblical *ha-ze* (m.), *ha-zot* (f.) 'this, that' in spoken usage and Mishnaic *ze, zo* in more formal style, with a suppletive plural *ha-éyle*. There is little use of the contrastive distal paradigm *ha-hu, ha-hi, ha-hem* 'that' (sg. m., pl. m.), and the bound accusative 3rd person forms *oto, ota, otam* meaning 'him, her, them' and also 'the same' are increasingly used as anaphoric demonstratives.

Quantifiers occur before the head noun (see p. 323); they have both bound (construct state) and free forms, e.g., *hu lakax **shney** sfarim, ve ani gam lakáxti **shnáyim*** 'he took two books, and I also took two', and both masculine and feminine gender, e.g., masculine *šney sfarim* 'two books', *šloša baxurim* 'three boys', feminine *štey mapot, šaloš banot* 'two cloths, three girls'. This system is highly variable in juvenile and other substandard usage, since the *-a* endings of masculine numerals typically mark feminine gender in other areas of the grammar, and speakers tend to neutralize numbers to the feminine form without the *-a* ending (Ravid 1995).

Grammatical Agreement

Modern Hebrew has a broad array of inflectionally marked categories of agreement. Past and future tense verbs agree with the grammatical subject in number, gender, and person; present tense forms agree with the grammatical subject in number and gender; and adjectives and determiners agree with the head noun in number, gender, and definiteness. Compare:

(a)	*xaruz*	*gadol*	*ze*	*nofel*	
	bead	big	this	fall	= this big bead + m. is falling
(b)	*kubiya*	*gdola*	*zo*	*nofélet*	
	block	big	this	fall	= this big block + f. is falling
(c)	*ha-kubiyot*	*ha-gdolot*	*ha'éle*	*noflot*	
	the-blocks	the-big	the-these	fall = these big blocks + f. are falling	

The system is asymmetrical along several dimensions (see p. 318). Tense marked verbs have person affixes in 1st and 2nd, not in 3rd person. In the absence of a lexical noun subject, surface pronoun subjects are normally mandatory with 3rd person verbs in all tenses, and in all persons in the present tense, but they are optional in 1st and 2nd person in past and future tense. In spoken usage, 1st and 2nd person pronouns are typically omitted in the past tense in non-contrastive or neutral contexts, but they are retained in future tense, except where these forms function as imperative or optative mood rather than future tense. In subordinate clauses and in extended discourse, 3rd person pronouns are often omitted under conditions of topic maintenance (Berman 1990).

Masculine agreement marking tends to be preferred across the board over the normative feminine in plural forms. This is officially sanctioned for 2nd and 3rd person future, and it is increasingly common in other contexts, too. Neutralizations are usually in the unmarked masculine form except for the numeral system, where there is widespread, as yet substandard, preference for feminine forms, since these lack the *-a* suffix which elsewhere marks feminine gender (Ravid 1995). Agreement also tends to vary between normative and casual usage in VS constructions and in definiteness marking on construct-state nominals (see p. 330).

Definiteness agreement attaches the *ha-* definite morpheme to the head noun and the adjective and demonstrative modifiers which follow it, as in (c) above. In construct state constructions, however, *ha-* attaches only once, to the following adjunct noun, thus:

(a)	Noun + Adjective NP:	*ha-kufsa*	*ha-gdola ha-zot*	
		the-box + f.	the-big the-this	= this big box
(b)	Noun + Noun Construct:	*kufsat-*	*ha-gafrurim ha-zot*	
		box-	the-matches the-this	= this box of matches

Speakers often prepose the definite marker to the entire construct state construction, to yield non-normative combinations like *ha-kufsat gafrurim*, particularly but not only in highly lexicalized construct state compound nouns. As a result of difficulties in online processing, the definite marker is sometimes attached to both the head and adjunct noun, as in ungrammatical *ha-kufsat ha-gafrurim*. In general, however, the classical requirement of number and gender agreement on the head noun and its associated adjuncts is preserved for adjectives and demonstratives, and avoided with noun adjuncts in construct state constructions.

Classes of Simple Clauses: Interrogatives, Negatives

Imperatives and passives are formed through verb inflections (see pp. 318–323). Interrogatives take two main forms. Yes–no questions are marked simply by rising intonation. A special interrogative particle *ha'im* 'whether' is rare in current usage. In information questions, sentence-initial question words replace the questioned constituent with otherwise basic clause structure; the normative requirement for SV inversion with a preposed question word is generally not observed, and one hears both *le'an ha-yéled halax?* 'to-where the-child went?' and *le'an halax ha-yéled?* 'to-where went the child?' (see p. 323). Prepositional markers of case and adverbial relations are fronted with the question word, since Hebrew disallows stranded or orphan prepositions, e.g. *im mi hu halax?* 'with who(m) did he go?', *al ma hem medabrim?* 'on what they talk = what are they talking about?'

Modern Hebrew has three main negative morphemes, the basic *lo* 'no, not', and more restricted *eyn, al*. The morpheme *lo* serves for general denial as the opposite of *ken* 'yes', and also for sentence negation in main and subordinate clauses. It is located immediately preceding the verb phrase, e.g. *hu lo yada* 'he not knew = he did not know' , *hu bevaday lo yada* 'he certainly did not know', *hu lo raca ladá'at* 'he did not want to-know', *ha-yéled ha-ze af pa'am lo haya yodea* 'that boy never not was know = that boy would never have known'. The last example shows that lexical negation and constituent negation require *lo* to be used with the negative adverb or indefinite pronoun, e.g. *af-pa'am lo* 'never not', *ani lo hikárti šam af exad* 'I not knew there nobody = I did not know anybody there'.

Normatively, the negator *eyn* is required in present tense. Modern Hebrew uses *lo* in present as well as past and future tense, e.g., *ani lo yodéa* 'I not know = I don't know'. This is rendered by forms like *eyn ani yodéa* or with a pronominal subject-agreeing suffix, *ani eyn-éni yodéa* only in highly formal, self-conscious usage. The negator *eyn* has, however, been retained in present tense existential and possessive constructions as the negative counterpart of the existential particle *yeš*, e.g. present tense *eyn kša'im itam* 'not difficulties with-them = there are no difficulties with them' compared with past tense *lo hayu kša'im itam* 'not were difficulties with-them = there weren't any difficulties with them' (see p. 329).

In imperatives, the special negator *al* is used with a future tense form of the verb in 2nd person, thus: *al tedaber!* 'Neg. 2nd-will-speak = don't talk!', *al te'ézu* 'Neg. 2nd-will-dare + pl.' = 'don't dare +pl.'.

Subordination

Modern Hebrew has extended the Mishnaic morpheme *še-* 'that' to meet nearly all its subordinating functions, as follows. It serves as the major marker of complement clauses both in subject and postverbal position, for instance following verbs of saying and of cognition. The only exception is with indirect questions, which take question words (see p. 327), except for yes–no questions, which are embedded by means of the particle *im* 'if, whether', e.g. *hu lo yada še/im hi tavo* 'he not knew that/if she will-come = he did not know that/whether she would come'. As this example shows, the tense of embedded complement clauses is relative to that of the matrix verb, e.g. *hu lo yodea še hi ozevet/azva/ta'azov* 'he does not know that she is-leaving/has-left/will-leave' compared with *hu lo yada še hi ozevet/ azva/ta'azov* 'he did not know that she was leaving, had left, would leave'. And the same applies to embedded questions, that is, complements introduced by question words.

Relative clauses, too, rely mainly on the single relative subordinator *še-*, which alternates with *ha-* before *benoni* form verbs or with Biblical *ašer* in formal style only. The internal construction of relative clauses depends on the grammatical relation which is relativized. Subject relatives typically contain only *še-* with no overt pronoun, e.g. *ha-baxur še azav* 'the-boy that left', *ha-kis'ot še naflu* 'the-chairs that fell; accusative object relatives may but need not take a pronominal copy, e.g,. *ha-baxur še Miryam ohevet (oto)* 'the-boy that Miriam loves (him)', *ha-kis'ot še xašavnu liknot (otam)* 'the chairs that we-thought of-buying (them)'; and oblique object relatives require a pronominal copy suffixed to the case marking or adverbial preposition, e.g. *ha-baxur še dibarnu ito* 'the-boy that we-talked to-him, *hakis'ot še yašavnu aleyhem* 'the-chairs that we-sat on-them'. The order of elements in these last two examples is considered normative, but current usage often preposes the pronominal copy, with or without elision of the relative marker *še*, e.g., *hakis'ot še aleyhem yašavnu, hakis'ot aleyhem yašavnu*. In casual usage the oblique pronoun copy may be omitted, e.g. substandard *ha-šita še hištamašnu* 'the-method that we-used' in place of required *ha-šita še hištamšnu ba* '... that we-used with-it'. Another substandard or juvenile but widespread tendency in adverbial relative clauses is to replace personal pronoun copying by question words subordinated by *še-*. Compare normative *ze kara ba-makom še yašavnu bo/šam* 'it happened in-the-place that we-sat in-it/there' with casual *ha-makom efo še yašavnu* ' the place where that we-sat'.

Adverbial clauses are typically introduced by prepositions subordinated by *še*, e.g., *ze kara lifney ha'aruxa* 'it happened before the-meal' versus *ze kara lifney še axalnu* 'it happened before (that) we-ate'. An exception is the subordinating particle *kiy*, originally used to mark complement clauses, today confined primarily to reason clauses, e.g. *ha-tinok baxa kiy (hu) nafal* 'the-baby cried because (he) fell'. Extension of *še* to non-normative contexts occurs in the common use of prepositional *biglal* 'owing-to' as an adverbial conjunction, e.g. *ha-tinok baxa biglal še nafal* 'the-baby cried owing-to that (he) fell'. In contrast, the conjunction *ve-* 'and' is favored over normative *še* for subordination with morphemes which do not also function as prepositions, e.g. normative *yitaxen še yavo* 'likely that (he) will come = 'it's likely he will come' is replaced by *yitaxen ve-*, *me'axar še nafal* 'since that (he) fell = because he fell' becomes *me'axar ve nafal*, evidently as a hypercorrection. This group of formatives seems to be undergoing reorganization, so that *še* and *ve-* are in complementary distribution in these non-normative environments.

Different morphemes are used in **conditional clauses:** *im* 'if, whether' in realis conditionals, e.g. *egmor bazman im ta'azor li* 'I'll finish on-time if you will-help me', and *(i)lu* elsewhere, e.g. *hayiti gomer bazman lu azarta li* 'was-1st finishing = I would have finished on time if you-(had) helped me', or negative *hayiti gomer bazman luley hifrata li* 'I would have finished on time if not you-bothered me = if you had not interfered'. Spoken usage tends to neutralize the distinction, extending *im* to irrealis contexts, e.g. *im hayita ba, ze haya ozer* 'if you were-coming (= would come ~ would have come), it would help ~ have helped me'.

Copular, Possessive, and Existential Constructions

Modern Hebrew is a non-*habere* language, with no separate verb meaning 'have' or 'possess'. The copular verb *haya* 'be' functions in equational, possessive, and existential constructions, nonfinite, and past and future tense, but it has different realizations in present tense contexts. The first set of examples below are of different types of equational sentences. These are typically subject initial, and the predicate may be either a noun phrase, an adjective phrase, or a locative, as in (a), (b), and (c) respectively.

(a) *Dan haya xaver šeli*
    Dan was friend of-me   'Dan was my friend'
(b) *Dan yihye mat'im me'od*
    Dan will-be suitable very   'Dan will be very suitable'
(c) *Dan asuy lihyot baxeder haze*
    Dan may to-be in that room   'Dan is liable to be in that room'

Existential and possessive constructions use an invariable particle *yeš* in present tense, and a form of *haya* elsewhere, with *eyn* in the negative. These constructions typically take the surface form *yeš/haya* + NonDefinite Subject + (Locative) for existentials, as below.

(a) *yeš/eyn talmidim ba-kita*
    be/not students in-class   'There are/aren't any students in class'
(b) *hayu/lo hayu talmidim hayom*

	were/not were	students today	'There were/weren't any students today'
(c)	*yihyu/lo yihyu*	*talmidim*	
	will-be/won't be	students	'There will/won't be any students'

As in many languages, the existential copula also serves in possessive constructions. The possessor is marked by dative case, the possessee is traditionally nominative. However, where the possessee is definite, there is a tendency to treat it as accusative, with the object-marking prepositional *et*, as in (b) below.

(a)	*yeš le-Dan/lo*	*talmidim tovim*	
	be to-Dan/to-him	students good	= Dan/he has good students
(b)	*yeš lanu/la-talmidim*	*(et) hasfarim*	
	be to-us/to-the-students	(ACC.) the-books	= we/the students have the books
(c)	*haya li/la-horim šeli*	*(et) hakesef*	
	was to-me/to-my parents	(ACC.) the-money	= I/my parents had the money

The possessor in (a) above can be fronted to yield *le-Dan yeš talmidim tovim* or right dislocated to *talmidim tovim yeš lo, le-Dan*.

Nominal Constructions

This heading deals with two classes of constructions which are of considerable interest in Modern Hebrew. In the first, construct state genitives traditionally termed *smixut* 'adjacency', Modern Hebrew has taken over devices from both Biblical and Mishnaic Hebrew, and has extended these by constructions found in European languages (see p. 330), while in the case of verbal nouns, Modern Hebrew prefers Mishnaic to Biblical forms of expression (see p. 331).

Construct State and Genitive Constructions

The traditional *smixut* structure in which two nouns are strung together, an initial, bound head noun and a following, free adjunct noun, is an instance where Modern Hebrew has absorbed and adapted elements from different periods in its past. This bound form is used for two main purposes: for vocabulary extension by lexicalized compounds (see p. 322) and, in formal style, for syntactic combination of strings of nouns. In casual style, Modern Hebrew prefers the analytic version with the genitive particle *šel* of the Mishnaic period, particularly, but not only, to express possession, e.g., bound, lexicalized *kova-gerev* 'hat-stocking = balaclava cap', *kova'ey-yam* 'hats-sea = bathing caps', compared with *ha-kova šel Dan* 'the hat of Dan = Dan's hat', *kova'im šel xayalim* 'soldiers' hats'. A third option, the so-called double *smixut*, with a pronominal copy of the adjunct noun suffixed to the initial, head noun, is rare in spoken usage, but common in newspaper and other written styles, e.g. *kova'o šel Dan* 'hat-his of Dan = Dan's hat', *sipurav šel ha-zaken* 'stories-his of the-old man = the old man's tales'.

Modern Hebrew relies on two other options for juxtaposing nominals in a head plus adjunct relation. The first is use of prepositions rather than the genitive particle *šel* to provide a more analytic means of combining nouns. Compare, for example, *kova léved* 'hat felt = a felt hat' with ablative *kova mi-leved* 'a hat from felt', *simlat pasim* 'dress- stripes' with *simla im pasim* 'a dress with stripes', *xanut basar* 'store-meat' with *xanut le-basar* 'a store for meat'. The second is reliance on denominal adjective formation (see p. 322); compare construct *sixat telefon* with noun–adjective *sixa telefonit* 'telephone(y) conversation', *avodat misrad* with *avoda misradit* 'office(y) work', *tiyul layla* with *tiyul leyli* 'night(ly) walk'. These two devices are not normatively sanctioned, but like many of the departures from classical norms noted above, they provide Modern Hebrew with a richly varied set of options for expressing the relationship between two nouns.

Gerunds and Derived Nominals

Modern Hebrew has extended a structure introduced in Mishnaic times, the forms termed *šem pe'ula* 'action noun', for nominalization, e.g. *ha-baxur diber* 'the-boy spoke' > *dibur(o šel) ha-baxur* 'the-speech (of) the boy', *ha-baxur azav* 'the-boy left' > *azivat(o šel) ha-baxur* 'the-boy's departure'. These provide formal, written Hebrew with a productive means of nominalization, through forms which are morphologically related to the *binyan* pattern of the associated verbs. The case relations of the underlying clause are maintained, but the subject is postposed to the nominalized verb, thus: *ha-baxur daxa et hara'ayon* 'the boy rejected ACC. the-idea' > *dxiyat ha-baxur et hara'ayon* 'the-rejection (of) the boy ACC. = of the-idea = the boy's rejection of the idea' compared with *ha-baxur serev la-haca'a* 'the boy refused to the-offer' > *seruv habaxur la haca'a* 'the boy's refusal to = of the offer'. Such constructions, like nominalizations in general, are typical of more formal style and of newspaper and media usage, rather than everyday speech. But they represent a productive set of devices in current Hebrew syntax.

In contrast, nominalization by the Biblical *šem po'al* 'verbal noun' or gerund is highly restricted. Stylistically, these forms are confined to formal and newspaper usage; and semantically, they function only as temporal adverbials. Moreover, syntactically, unlike the *šem pe'ula* action nominals which can stand alone without an overt agent nominal, and so can be lexicalized as independent nouns, gerunds demand a surface postposed subject. Compare the gerund *be-cet ha-baxur meha-xeder* 'on-leaving the-boy ACC. from the-room' = 'on the boy's departing from the room' with the action nominal form *ba-yeci'a (šel ha-baxur) meha-xeder* 'on the departure (of the boy)/exit from the room'.

Language Variation

The preceding notes on nominalizing constructions in Modern Hebrew illustrate how the language has taken over different devices from different strata in its history. This has allowed for differentiation between more classical norms and bound morphological forms of formal or literary style and the kind of nominalizing and other constructions preferred in "medium-level" journalistic and academic writing. And these in turn contrast with the preference for more analytic, simple clause structure with overt subjects and tensed verbs of colloquial speech. Current

Hebrew usage reflects an increasing diglossia between the formal, written norms stipulated by the language establishment and the schools, on the one hand, and the way young people graduating from these schools in fact use the language in their everyday spoken communication, on the other.

References

Bendavid, Abba. 1967, 1971. *Leshon miqra uleshon haxamim* [Language of the Bible and language of the sages], 2 vols. Tel Aviv: Dvir.

Berman, Ruth A. 1980. "The Case of an (S)VO Language: Subjectless Constructions in Modern Hebrew." *Language* 56: 759–776.

—— 1985. *Acquisition of Hebrew*. Hillsdale, N.J.: Erlbaum. (Also in *Crosslinguistic Study of Language Acquisition*, volume 1, ed. D. I. Slobin. 255–272.]

—— 1990. "Acquiring an (S)VO Language: Subjectless Sentences in Children's Hebrew." *Linguistics* 28: 1135–1166.

Blanc, Haim. 1964. "Israeli Hebrew Texts." In *Studies in Egyptology and Linguistics in Honour of H. J. Polotsky*. Jerusalem: Israel Exploration Society. 132–152.

Blau, Joshua. 1981. The *Renaissance of Modern Hebrew and Modern Standard Arabic: Parallels and Differences in the Revival of Two Semitic Languages* (University of California Publications in Near Eastern Studies 18). Berkeley: University of California Press.

Bolozky, Shmuel. 1979. "The New Imperative in Colloquial Hebrew." *Hebrew Annual Review* 3: 17–24.

Cooper, Robert L., ed. 1983. *A Sociolinguistic Perspective on Israeli Hebrew* (International Journal of the Sociology of Language 41). Amsterdam: Mouton.

Fellman, Jack. 1973. *The Revival of a Classical Tongue: Eliezer Ben Yehuda and the Modern Hebrew Language*. The Hague: Mouton.

Fisherman, Haia. 1986. "Milim zarot ba'ivrit bat zmanenu" [Foreign words in contemporary Hebrew: Morphological, developmental, and social aspects]. Ph.D. dissertation. Hebrew University.

Harshav, Benjamin. 1990. "Masa al tehiyat halashon ha'ivrit." [An essay on the revival of the Hebrew language]. *Alpayim* 2: 9–54.

Morag, Shelomo, ed. 1988. *Ha'ivrit bat-zmanenu: mehqarim ve'iyunim* [Studies on contemporary Hebrew], 2 vols. Jerusalem: Academon Press.

Ravid, Dorit. 1994. *Language Change in Child and Adult Hebrew: A Psycholinguistic Perspective*. Oxford: Oxford University Press.

—— 1995. "Death of a Rule: Neutralization of Gender Distinctions in Modern Hebrew Numerals." *Language Variation and Change* 7: 79–100.

Rubinstein, Eliezer. 1980. *Ha'ivrit shelanu ve ha'ivrit haqeduma* [Contemporary Hebrew and Ancient Hebrew]. Tel Aviv: Israel Defence Forces.

Schwarzwald, Ora. 1981. *Diqduq umeci'ut bapo'al ha'ivri* [Grammar and reality in the Hebrew verb system]. Ramat Gan: Bar-Ilan University.

Wexler, Paul. 1990. *The Schizoid Nature of Modern Hebrew: A Slavic Language in Search of a Semitic Past*. Wiesbaden: Harrassowitz.

Yannai, Yigael. 1974. "Pe'alim meruba'ey 'icurim balashon ha'ivrit" [Quadriconsonantal verbs in Hebrew]. *Leshonenu* 35: 119–194.

Further Reading

Agmon-Fruchtman, Maya. 1982. *Hayadua vehasatum* [Definite and indefinite]. Tel Aviv: Papyrus.

Ariel, Mira. 1990. *Assessing NP Antecedents*. London: Routledge.

Berman, Ruth A. 1978. *Modern Hebrew Structure.* Tel Aviv: Universities Publishing.

—— 1982. "Dative Marking of the Affectee in Modern Hebrew." *Hebrew Annual Review* 6: 35–59.

—— 1987a. *Al habeᶜatiyut beheqer haᶜivrit hahadasha.* [Issues and problems in Modern Hebrew research]. *Praqim* 7: 84–96.

—— 1987b. "Productivity in the Lexicon: New-word Formation in Modern Hebrew." *Folia Linguistica* 21: 425–461.

—— 1994. "Formal, Lexical, and Semantic Factors in the Acquisition of Hebrew Resultative Particles." In *Berkeley Linguistic Society, no. 20,* ed. S. Gahl, A. Dolbey, and C. Johnson. 80–92.

Borer, Hagit and Yosef Grodzinsky. 1986. "Syntactic Cliticization and Lexical Cliticization: The Case of Hebrew Dative Clitics." In *Syntax and Semantics,* volume 19, ed. H. Borer. New York: Academic Press. 175–215.

Glinert, Lewis. 1989. *The Grammar of Modern Hebrew.* Cambridge: Cambridge University Press.

Gordon, Amnon. 1982. "The Development of the Participle in Biblical, Mishnaic, and Modern Hebrew." *Afroasiatic Linguistics* 8/3: 121–179.

Kutscher, E. Y. 1982. *A History of the Hebrew Language,* ed. R. Kutscher. Jerusalem: Magnes Press.

Nir, Raphael, 1993. *Hayecira hamilonit ba'ivrit bat-zmanenu* [Lexical innovation in contemporary Hebrew]. Tel Aviv: Open University.

16 The Neo-Aramaic Languages

Otto Jastrow

Western Neo-Aramaic

Western Neo-Aramaic (WNA) has been preserved only in three villages in the Qalamūn mountains north-east of Damascus, Syria, namely Ma'lūla, Bax'a and Ğubb'adīn. Ma'lūla to this day is a predominantly Christian place, but the inhabitants of Bax'a and Ğubb'adīn are now all Muslims. Nevertheless they continue to speak Neo-Aramaic, which is a unique fact in the history of Aramaic. Although each of the three villages has a distinct dialect of its own (henceforward referred to as Ma., Ba. and Ğ) the overall structure of the language is much the same. The present sketch of WNA relies heavily on the work of Werner Arnold (see Further Reading).

WNA has been exposed only to a single adstrate/superstrate language, namely Arabic. It is flooded with Arabic vocabulary which has, however, except for very recent loans, been adapted to WNA phonology and morphology so as to become almost indistinguishable from the inherited stock. In phonology and morphology WNA is very conservative, reflecting closely the language structure of Middle Aramaic (between 500 and 1000 CE approximately).

The description focuses on the dialect of Ma'lūla (Ma.); diverging forms of the other two dialects are cited as seems appropriate.

Phonology
Consonants

p b	t [d]	ṭ	k	ḳ [g]		[']
	(c)		(č) (ǧ)			
f	θ δ	δ̣	x γ		ḥ '	h
	s z	ṣ ẓ	š (ž)			
m	n					
	l					
	r					
w			y			

334

The consonant system of the three dialects is on p. 334 (phonemes not occurring in all three dialects are put in parentheses, phonemes only occurring in unassimilated loans are put between square brackets).

k is a palatalized prevelar to plainly palatal stop [c], *ḳ* a distinctly postvelar but not uvular stop [k], *c* a dental affricate [ts], *č* a palatal affricate [tʃ]. *ṭ*, *ṣ*, *ḏ*, *ẓ* are "emphatic" (velarized) consonants, the latter two occurring only in Arabic loans. Arabic *ǧ* is realized as *ǧ* [dʒ] in Baxʿa but as *ž* [ʒ] in Maʿlūla and Ǧubbʿadīn, reflecting rural and urban Arabic usage respectively.

In Middle Aramaic each of the six stops *p, b, t, d, k, g* was split into two positional variants (allophones), an initial, postconsonantal and geminate one continuing the older stop and a postvocalic one yielding the corresponding fricative, e.g. *p̄, ḇ, ṯ, ḏ, ḵ, ḡ*. In WNA the fricative allophone was generalized to initial position. The resulting twelve consonants later acquired phonemic status. They have been preserved rather well in WNA, as can be seen below. (The diachronic/synchronic symbols *p̄/f*, *ḇ/v*, *ṯ/θ*, *ḏ/δ*, *ḵ/x*, *ḡ/γ* denote the same sound.)

Middle Aramaic	Ma.	Ba.	Ǧ	Examples Ma./Ba./Ǧ	
*p >	*f*	*f*	*f*	*affek affek affek*	'he took out'
*p̄ >	*f*	*f*	*f*	*foγla foγla foγla*	'radish'
*b >	*p*	*p*	*p*	*zappen zappen zappen*	'he sold'
*ḇ >	*b*	*b*	*b*	*δēba δēba δēba*	'wolf'
*t >	*č*	*c*	*č*	*berča berca berča*	'daughter'
*ṯ >	*θ*	*θ*	*θ*	*ḥōθa ḥōθa ḥōθa*	'sister'
*d >	*t*	*t*	*t*	*γelta γelta γelta*	'leather, hide'
*ḏ >	*δ*	*δ*	*δ*	*δōδa δōδa δōδa*	'uncle'
*k >	*k*	*k*	*č*	*malka malka malča*	'king'
*ḵ >	*x*	*x*	*x*	*xarma xarma xarma*	'vineyard'
*g >	*k*	*k*	*č*	*θelka θelka θelča*	'snow'
*ḡ >	*γ*	*γ*	*γ*	*γerma γerma γerma*	'bone'

Vowels
WNA has a system of five long and five short vowels; there are also two diphthongs:

The phonemic status of the short vowels *i, e* and *u, o* is shown by minimal pairs like Ma. *fθoḥla* 'open (m.) to her!' vs. *fθuḥla* 'open (f.) to her!', Ma. *čṭuʿnenna*

'that you (m.) carry her' vs. *čṭuʿninna* 'that you (f.) carry her', Ma. *čaḥref* 'that you (m.) answer' vs. *čaḥrif* 'that you (f.) answer'.

Distribution

Long vowels occur only in stressed syllables; consequently there can be only one long vowel in each word. Long vowels occur both in open and closed syllables. Short vowels occur in stressed and unstressed, open and closed syllables. Thus, long and short vowels can contrast both in open and closed syllables, e.g. Ma. *ḥōčma* 'judge' vs. *ḥočma* 'judgment', Ba. *īδa* 'hand' vs. *iδa* 'when'.

Long vowels are replaced regularly by short ones when the stress is shifted to the following syllable, e.g. Ma. *ḥūya* 'snake' but *ḥuyō* 'snakes'; *ō* which historically derives from **ā* is replaced by *a*, e.g. Ma. *fallōḥa* 'peasant' but *fallaḥō* 'peasants'. Long vowels are **not** shortened when the stressed syllable is closed by a morphological process such as derivation or inflection. This latter fact distinguishes WNA from Eastern Neo-Aramaic (ENA).

Umlaut

The vowels *ē, e, ō, o* are raised to *ī, i, ū, u* when a suffix containing *ī/i* (or whose older form contained *ī/i*) is added, e.g. Ma. *kommax* 'in front of you (m.)' but *kummiš* 'in front of you (f.)', *berčax* 'your (m.) daughter' but *birčiš* 'your (f.) daughter'. In some cases the vowel which triggered the umlaut is no longer there so that the umlaut itself has taken over morphemic function. Compare the following imperatives in which the suffix **-ī* of the feminine has already been lost during the Middle Aramaic period: Ma. *fθōḥ* 'open (m.)!' vs. *fθūḥ* 'open (f.)!', *aḥrēf* 'answer (m.)!' vs. *aḥrīf* 'answer (f.)!'

Reduction of Geminates

In Ǧubbʿadīn historical word-final geminates (long consonants) were reduced to simple consonants; the preceding vowel was lengthened in compensation, e.g. **ḥačč > ḥāč* 'you (sg. m.)', **θarʿayy > θarʿāy* 'their doors'.

Word Stress

Word stress is usually on the penultimate; the last syllable is stressed if it has a long vowel or ends in two or more consonants. Thus (stress indicated by bold vowel): Ma. *zappen* 'he sold', but *zappēn!* 'sell (m.)!', Ma. *yifθuḥʾl* 'he opens for me'. Any divergence from this rule is indicated by an acute (´) on the stressed vowel.

Schwa

Groups of two or more consonants may be alleviated by the insertion of a nonphonemic, functionally non-syllabic ultra-short vowel *ʾ*, e.g. Ǧ *ḥačʾx* 'you (pl. m.)', Ma. *yifθuḥʾl* 'he opens for me'.

Morphology

Pronouns

Table 16.1   Independent personal pronouns

		Ma'lūla	Bax'a	Ğubb'adīn	
Sg.	1c.	ana	ana	ana	'I'
Pl.	1c.	anaḥ	anaḥ	anaḥ	'we'
Sg.	2m.	hačč(i)	hacc	hāč	'you (sg. m.)'
	f.	hašš(i)	hašš	hāš	'you (sg. f.)'
Pl.	2m.	hačxun	hacxun	hačᵊx	'you (pl. m.)'
	f.	hačxen	hacxun	hačxen	'you (pl. f.)'
Sg.	3m.	hū	hū	hū(h)	'he'
	f.	hī	hī	hī(h)	'she'
Pl.	3m.	hinn(un)	hinn	hīn	'they (m.)'
	f.	hinn(en)	hinn	hinnen	'they (f.)'

Bax'a has given up gender distinction in the plural. The form of the original masculine has been generalized.

Pronominal Suffixes
Pronominal suffixes are joined to nouns to express possession, to prepositions to express relation and to verbs to express a pronominal object. Before the pronominal suffixes the nominal suffix *-a* of the singular is dropped, the suffix *-ō* of the plural shows an older form *-ōy* which is shortened to *-ay* before the plural suffixes. The singular and plural of the noun *tarba* 'way, path' with pronominal suffixes in Ma'lūla is shown below; sg. 1c. *-(i)* is optional.

		tarba	*tarbō*
Sg.	1c.	*tarb(i)*	*tarbōy(i)*
Pl.	1c.	*tarbaḥ*	*tarbaynaḥ*
Sg.	2m.	*tarbax*	*tarbōx*
	f.	*tarbiš*	*tarbōš*
Pl.	2m.	*tarbxun*	*tarbayxun*
	2f.	*tarbxen*	*tarbayxen*
Sg.	3m.	*tarbe*	*tarbōye*
	f.	*tarba*	*tarbōya*
Pl.	3m.	*tarbun*	*tarbayhun*
	f.	*tarben*	*tarbayhen*

In Ğubb'adīn there is a facultative variant of the sg. 3f. suffix in which a final *-h* is preserved: *tarba ~ tarbah* 'her path'. Otherwise the noun with sg. 3f. pronominal suffix is identical with the simple noun.

Demonstrative Pronouns
WNA has two sets of demonstrative pronouns denoting closeness and remoteness respectively. Maʿlūla has:

	Close	Remote
Sg. m.	*hanna*	*hōθe*
f.	*hōd(i)*	*hōθa*
Pl. m.	*hann(un)*	*haθinn(un)*
f.	*hann(en)*	*haθinn(en)*

Interrogative Pronouns

	Maʿlūla	Baxʿa	Ǧubbʿadīn
'who?'	*mōn*	*man*	*mūn*
'what?'	*mō*	*mā ~ ma*	*mā(h) ~ ma(h)*

Nouns

Nominal Endings
Inherited Aramaic nouns as well as the majority of adapted foreign (Arabic) nouns are characterized by the ending *-a* in the masculine, *-θa ~ ča* (Baxʿa *-ca*) in the feminine:

Maʿlūla	Baxʿa	Ǧubbʿadīn	
θarʿa	*θarʿa*	*θarʿa*	'door'
warʾḳθa	*warʾḳθa*	*warʾḳθa*	'(piece of) paper'
bisnīθa	*bisnīθa*	*bisnīθa*	'girl'
ḥōlča	*ḥōlca*	*ḥōlča*	'maternal aunt'

A number of nouns, e.g. parts of body, are treated as feminine although they don't have a feminine ending, e.g. *eδna* 'ear', *šenna* 'tooth' etc.

Plural
There are two kinds of plural: a regular plural and the so-called count plural (*Zählplural*) which is used after numerals. The regular plural has the ending *-ōya* (mostly in Ǧubbʿadīn) ~ *-ō* for the masculine, *-ōθa ~ yōθa* for the feminine. In the count plural the nominal endings are dropped; Maʿlūla has preserved an archaic count plural *-an* for the feminine, thus:

	Maʿlūla	Baxʿa	Ǧubbʿadīn	
singular	*θarʿa*	*θarʿa*	*θarʿa*	'door'
plural	*θarʿō*	*θarʿō*	*θarʿō(ya)*	'doors'
count plural	*θarʾʿ*	*θarʾʿ*	*θarʾʿ*	'doors'

singular	war²ḳθa	war²ḳθa	war²ḳθa	'paper'
plural	warḳōθa	warḳōθa	warḳōθa	'papers'
count plural	warḳan	war²ḳ	war²ḳ	'papers'

Status and Definiteness

The nominal endings continue the *status emphaticus* of Middle Aramaic, the *status absolutus* survives only in the count plural. The adjective, however, has preserved both statuses. The forms reflecting the old *status absolutus* express indefiniteness, while those reflecting the old *status emphaticus* – i.e. those identical with the endings of the noun – express definiteness, e.g. *ifḳer* 'poor' (forms given for Maʿlūla only):

	Indefinite	Definite
Sg. m.	*ifḳer*	*fḳīra*
f.	*fḳīra*	*fḳīrča*
Pl. m.	*fḳīrin*	*fḳirō*
f.	*fḳīran*	*fḳirōθa*

Thus, e.g., *fḳīra* can mean 'the old one (m.)' or 'an old one (f.)'; 'the old one (f.)' would be *fḳīrča* etc.

There is no definite article in WNA. A noun can be marked as definite or indefinite by an attributive adjective:

psōna ifḳer	'a poor boy'
psōna fḳīra	'the poor boy'
bisnīθa fḳīra	'a poor girl'
bisnīθa fḳīrča	'the poor girl'

Other than by the attributive adjective, indefiniteness of a noun can also be marked by the preceding numeral for '1', e.g. *aḥḥaδ psōna* 'one boy; a boy', *eḥδa bisnīθa* 'one girl; a girl'. Definiteness can be marked by using the close demonstrative (see Demonstrative Pronouns, p. 338), e.g. *hanna psōna* 'this boy; the boy'. A noun which is the direct object of a verb is marked as definite by a special suffix *-il* on the verb (see p. 344):

| *šattar γabrōna* | 'he sent a man' |
| *šattril γabrōna* | 'he sent the man' |

Annexation

Annexation of nouns (also called genitive construction) is analytical, the suffix *-il* ~ *-lʾ* ~ *-ʾl* being joined to the first noun after the nominal ending *-a* has been dropped, e.g. Ma. *berčil γabrōna* 'the daughter (*berča*) of the man', *sōblʾ blōta* 'the mayor (*sōba*) of the village'. In Ǧubbʿadīn final *-l* is usually dropped, unless the following noun has an initial vowel, e.g. Ǧ *berči zalˀmθa* 'the daughter of the man'.

Numerals

WNA is unique among all Neo-Aramaic languages in having preserved different masculine and feminine forms for all numbers from 1 to 19. The forms are given for Maʿlūla only:

	Masculine	Feminine		Masculine	Feminine
1	*aḥḥaδ*	*eḥδa*	11	*eḥδaʿasˀr*	*aḥḥaδaʿsar*
2	*iθri ~ iθˀr*	*θarč*	12	*θarčʿasˀr*	*θleʿsar*
3	*θlōθa*	*eθlaθ*	13	*eθlaθʿasˀr*	*θlečʿaʿsar*
4	*arpʿa*	*arpaʿ*	14	*arpaʿʿasˀr*	*arpʿačaʿsar*
5	*ḥamša*	*ḥammeš*	15	*ḥammešˀasˀr*	*ḥammešʿaʿsar*
6	*šečča*	*šeθθ*	16	*šeθʿasˀr*	*šečʿaʿsar*
7	*šobʿa*	*ešbaʿ*	17	*ešbaʿʿasˀr*	*šobʿaʿaʿsar*
8	*θmōnya*	*θmōn*	18	*θmōnʿasˀr*	*θmōnyačaʿsar*
9	*ṭešʿa*	*eṭšaʿ*	19	*eṭšaʿʿasˀr*	*ṭešʿačaʿsar*
10	*ʿasra*	*eʿsar*			

With numerals above 1, nouns appear in the count plural, thus e.g. *θlōθa θarˀ<* 'three doors', *eθlaθ warkan* 'three pieces of paper'.

Tens, hundreds and thousands (only Maʿlūla):

20	*ʿisri ~ ʿisˀr*	100	*emʿa*
30	*θlēθ(i)*	200	*θarč emʿa*
40	*irpʿi ~ irpˀ<*	300	*eθlaθ emʿa* etc.
50	*ḥimši ~ ḥimˀš*		
60	*šiččʿ(i)*	1000	*ōlef*
70	*šubʿi ~ šubˀ<*	2000	*θarč ōlef*
80	*θmēn(i)*	3000	*eθlaθ ōlef* etc.
90	*ṭišʿi ~ ṭišˀ<*		

Verbs

Generalities

Verbal roots consist of three or, more rarely, four consonants. "Weak" roots comprise one or two of the "weak" consonants ˀ, *w* and *y* which may not show on the surface of every inflected form.

The two old Semitic tenses, perfect and imperfect, have been preserved; they are here called past tense and subjunctive. The two old participles, the active participle *qāṭel* and the passive participle *qṭīl*, have provided the basis for two new tenses, the present (from *qāṭel*) and the perfect (from *qṭīl*), a development already observable in the Middle Aramaic period.

Derivation

The six derivational classes or stems of Middle Aramaic have been preserved in WNA. Arabic verbs with fitting canonical forms have been adapted into these stems (e.g. Arabic stem I verbs into stem I etc.). In addition a number of stems from Arabic have been integrated into the system.

Table 16.2   Verb Derivation

Present designation	Reflects Aramaic	Reflects Arabic	Example	
I	peʿal	stem I	iḳṭal	'to kill'
II	paʿʿel	stem II	zappen	'to sell'
III		stem III	sōfar	'to travel'
IV	afʿel	stem IV	aḥref	'to answer'
I₂	eθpeʿel		iččxel	'to be eaten'
II₂	eθpaʿʿal	stem V	čḥayyaṭ	'to be sewn'
III₂		stem VI	čḥōṣar	'to be encircled'
IV₂	ettafʿal		ččarnaḥ	'to be put'
I₇		stem VII	inᵊfθah	'to be opened'
I₈		stem VIII	inᵊčyab	'to be stolen'
I₁₀		stem X	sčaṣʿeb	'to find difficult'

Two of the above stems, I₂ and IV₂, are quite rare and will be left out in the following table. The table shows, for each of the remaining stems, the basic form of the four tenses. In the two old tenses, past tense and subjunctive, the sg. 3m. is given as a base; in the two new tenses, present and perfect, the sg. 3m. and sg. 3f. are given. All forms are Maʿlūla. For the inflection see below.

Stem I has several different vocalizations. Beside the past tense *iḳṭal*, WNA has also inherited an intransitive type with *e* in the second syllable, e.g. *iδmex* 'he slept'. In the subjunctive the second syllable can have *u* or *a*. The following combinations occur in Maʿlūla:

iḳṭal	:	yiḳṭul	'to kill'
iskaṭ	:	yiskaṭ	'to fall'
iδmex	:	yiδmux	'to sleep'
išmeʿ	:	yišmaʿ	'to hear'

Inflection

The two archaic tenses, the past and the subjunctive, are still inflected pretty much as in Middle Aramaic. The two newly formed tenses, the present and the perfect, are inflected in a completely different way which is similar to the "predicative inflection" of Eastern Neo-Aramaic; however, the subject marker is **pre**fixed, not **suf**fixed. Compare WNA *n-fōθeḥ* vs. ENA (Ṭuroyo) *fōtăḥ-no* 'I open'.

The **past tense** is inflected by means of suffixes. Below is the past tense of *ifθaḥ* 'he opened' (stem I), *zappen* 'he sold' (stem II), *sōfar* 'he traveled' (stem III) and *arkeš* 'he woke up' (stem IV). These are all from Maʿlūla.

Table 16.3 Tense formation

Stem	Past	Subjunctive	Present	Perfect	
I	iḵtal	yiḵṭul	m. ḵōṭel	m. iḵtel	'to kill'
			f. ḵōtla	f. ḵtīla	
II	zappen	yzappen	m. mzappen	m. zappen	'to sell'
			f. mzappna	f. zappīna	
III	sōfar	ysōfar	m. msōfar	m. sōfar	'to travel'
			f. msafīra	f. safīra	
IV	aḥref	yaḥref	m. maḥref	m. aḥref	'to answer'
			f. maḥr°fa	f. aḥrīfa	
II₂	čḥayyaṭ	yičḥayyaṭ	m. mičḥayyaṭ	m. čḥayyeṭ	'to be sewn'
			f. mičḥayyṭa	f. čḥayyīṭa	
III₂	čḥōṣar	yičḥōṣar	m. mičḥōṣar	m. čḥōṣer	'to be encircled'
			f. mičḥaṣīra	f. čḥaṣīra	
I₇	in°fθaḥ	yin°fθaḥ	m. min°fθaḥ	m. in°fθeḥ	'to be opened'
			f. minfaθḥa	f. in°fθīḥa	
I₈	in°čɣab	yin°čɣab	m. min°čɣab	m. in°čɣeb	'to be stolen'
			f. minčaɣba	f. in°čɣība	
I₁₀	sčaṣʿeb	yisčaṣʿeb	m. misčaṣʿeb	m. sčaṣʿeb	'to find difficult'
			f. misčaṣ°ʿba	f. sčaṣʿība	

Sg. 1c.	faθḥiθ	zappniθ	safīriθ	arkšiθ
Pl. 1c.	faθḥinnah	zappninnah	safirinnah	arkšinnah
Sg. 2m.	faθḥič	zappnič	safīrič	arkšič
f.	faθḥiš	zappniš	safīriš	arkšiš
Pl. 2m.	faθḥičxun	zappničxun	safiričxun	arkšičxun
f.	faθḥičxen	zappničxen	safiričxen	arkšičxen
Sg. 3m.	ifθaḥ	zappen	sōfar	arkeš
f.	faθḥaθ	zappnaθ	safīraθ	arkšaθ
Pl. 3c.	ifθaḥ	zappen	sōfar	arkeš

The older plural endings of the 3rd person have been dropped; they resurface, however, when a pronominal object is added (see p. 345):

	(Sg. 3m.)	→	faθḥe	'he opened it (m.)'
ifθaḥ	(Pl. 3m.)	→	faθḥunne	'they (m.) opened it (m.)'
	(Pl. 3f.)	→	faθḥanne	'they (f.) opened it (m.)'

The **subjunctive** is inflected by a combination of prefixes and suffixes. Below is the subjunctive of *yifθuḥ* 'that he open' (stem I), *yzappen* 'that he sell' (stem II), *ysōfar* 'that he travel' (stem III) and *yaḥšem* 'that he eat dinner' (stem IV). These are all from Maʿlūla.

Sg. 1c.	nifθuḥ	nzappen	nsōfar	naḥšem
Pl. 1c.	nifθuḥ	nzappen	nsōfar	naḥšem

Sg. 2m.	čifθuḥ	čzappen	čsōfar	čaḥšem
f.	čifθuḥ	čzappin	čsōfar	čaḥšim
Pl. 2m.	čfuθhun	čzappnun	čsafīrun	čaḥᵊšmun
f.	čfuθḥan	čzappnan	čsafīran	čaḥᵊšman

Sg. 3m.	yifθuḥ	yzappen	ysōfar	yaḥšem
f.	čifθuḥ	czappen	čsōfar	čaḥšem
Pl. 3m.	yfuθhun	yzappnun	ysafīrun	yaḥᵊšmun
f.	yfuθḥan	yzappnan	ysafīran	yaḥᵊšman

Present and **perfect:** The inflectional bases for present and perfect are old participles which have four different forms, namely sg. m., sg. f., pl. m., pl. f. Without any subject prefix added they function as 3rd persons, e.g. in the present:

Sg. 3m.	ṭōᶜen	'he carries'
f.	ṭōᶜna	'she carries'
Pl. 3m.	ṭōᶜnin	'they (m.) carry'
f.	ṭōᶜnan	'they (f.) carry'

With a prefixed subject marker č- these forms become 2nd person, and with a prefixed subject marker n- they become 1st person, e.g.:

Sg. 2m.	čṭōᶜen	'you (m.) carry'
f.	čṭōᶜna	'you (f.) carry'
Pl. 2m.	čṭōᶜnin	'you (pl. m.) carry'
f.	čṭōᶜnan	'you (pl. f.) carry'

Sg. 1m.	nṭōᶜen	'I (m.) carry'
f.	nṭōᶜna	'I (f.) carry'
Pl. 1m.	nṭōᶜnin	'we (m.) carry'
f.	nṭōᶜnan	'we (f.) carry'

Thus, due to the origin of these forms, there is gender distinction not only in the 3rd and 2nd person but also in the 1st person, which is a rather rare feature in a Semitic language.

The perfect is inflected in the same way. Thus, e.g., the perfect of the verb 'to carry' is iṭᶜen, with the following forms of the 3rd person:

Sg. 3m.	iṭᶜen	'he has carried'
Sg. 3f.	ṭᶜīna	'she has carried'
Pl. 3m.	ṭᶜīnin	'they (m.) have carried'
Pl. 3f.	ṭᶜīnan	'they (f.) have carried'

The remaining persons are inflected as shown, except that the subject markers are či- and ni- rather than č- and n- because the base begins with a cluster of two consonants: niṭᶜen 'I (m.) have carried', niṭᶜīna 'I (f.) have carried' etc.

Imperative: By detaching the inflectional prefix *y-* from the sg. 3m. of the sub-junctive, one arrives at the sg. m. of the imperative, e.g. *yifθuḥ* → *ifθuḥ*, *yzappen* → *zappen* and so on. Usually the imperative has two variants, one with the stress on the penultimate, and another one, now used more frequently, with stress on the last syllable and concomitant lengthening of the vowel, thus *zappen ~ zappēn* 'sell (sg. m.)!'. If the vowel of the final syllable of the masculine form is *e/ē* or *o/ō* it is raised to *i/ī* or *u/ū* in the feminine: *zappin ~ zappīn* 'sell (sg. f.)!'. The plural endings are *-un* for the masculine and *-en* for the feminine; they can also be stressed and their vowel lengthened. The plural endings cause the same reshuf-fling of the syllable as the plural suffixes of the subjunctive, the initial vowel *i* in open syllable is elided, thus *ifθuḥ* 'open (sg. m.)!' but *fuθḥun* 'open (pl. m.)!' (cf. in the subjunctive *yifθuḥ*, *yfuθḥun*). The imperatives of stems I–IV are shown in Table 16.4.

Table 16.4 Imperative

Stem	Subjunctive		Imperative	
I	yifθuḥ (yfuθḥun)	sg. m. sg. f. pl. m. pl. f.	ifθuḥ ~ fθōḥ ifθuḥ ~ fθūḥ fuθḥun ~ fuθḥōn fuθḥen ~ fuθḥēn	'open!'
II	yzappen (yzappnun)	sg. m. sg. f. pl. m. pl. f.	zappen ~ zappēn zappin ~ zappīn zappnun ~ zappnōn zappnen ~ zappnēn	'sell!'
III	yšōreṭ (yšarīṭun)	sg. m. sg. f. pl. m. pl. f.	šōreṭ ~ šarēṭ šōriṭ ~ šarīṭ šariṭōn šariṭēn	'bet!'
IV	yaḥref (yaḥrᵊfun)	sg. m. sg. f. pl. m. pl. f.	aḥref ~ aḥrēf aḥrif ~ aḥrīf aḥᵊrfun ~ aḥᵊrfōn aḥᵊrfen ~ aḥᵊrfēn	'answer!'

Weak Verbs
WNA is very rich in weak and irregular verbs. A detailed description is impossible within the limits of the present sketch. The following table shows the most impor-tant types for stem I. For each inflectional paradigm two forms are cited: for the subjunctive sg. 3m. and pl. 3m., for the remaining tenses sg. 3m. and sg. 3f.

Verb with Nominal Accusative Objects
A noun which is the direct (accusative) object of a verb follows the unmodified verb form if indefinite: *šattar* 'he sent', *šattar γabrōna* 'he sent a man'. Definite-ness of the object noun is marked by a special suffix *-il* on the verb: *šattril γabrōna* 'he sent the man'.

Table 16.5 Weak verbs

Root	Past	Subjunctive	Present	Perfect	Imperative	
1y	ilef	yīlaf	lōyef	layyef	lfā	'to learn'
	ilfaθ	yilfun	lōyfa	layyīfa	lfāy	
1'	axal	yīxul	ōxel	ixel	xōl	'to eat'
	axlaθ	yūxlun	ōxla	xīla	xūl	
2w	aḵam	yīḵum	ḵōyem	ḵayyem	ḵōm	'to stand'
	ḵōmaθ	yḵūmun	ḵōyma	ḵayyīma	ḵūm	
2y	ameθ	yīmuθ	mōyeθ	imeθ	mōθ	'to die'
	mīθaθ	ymūθun	mōyθa	mīθa	mūθ	
2=3	alam	yillum	lōmem	ilmem	lōm	'to gather'
	lammaθ	ylummun	lōmma	lmīma	lūm	
3y	iḥ°m	yiḥ°m	ḥōm	ḥamm(i)	ḥmā ~ iḥma	'to see'
	iḥmaθ	yiḥmun	ḥōmya	ḥammīya	ḥmāy ~ iḥmay	
1' 3y	īf(i)	yīf(i)	ōf(i)	īf(i)	ifā ~ īfa	'to bake'
	īfaθ	yīfun	ōfya	ifīya	ifāy ~ īfay	
2w 3y	išw	yišw	mišw	šaww(i)	šwā ~ išwa	'to do'
	išwaθ	yišwun	mišwa	šawwīya	šwāy ~ išway	

Verb with Accusative Object Suffixes

The different origin of the four tenses is also transparent in the way in which suffixes expressing a pronominal accusative object are joined to the verb.

Past and subjunctive take the following set of pronominal object suffixes (not all allomorphs indicated):

Sg. 1c.	-Ø ~ -i	Sg. 2m.	-ax	Sg. 3m.	-e
		f.	-iš	f.	-a
Pl. 1c.	-aḥ	Pl. 2m.	-xun	Pl. 3m.	-un
		f.	-xen	f.	-en

A suffix with initial vowel leads to a reshuffling of the last syllable of the verb, e.g. *ifθaḥ* + *-e* → *faθḥe* 'he opened it (m.)'. Frequently a verb form with object suffix is more archaic than when it stands alone, thus *faθ°ḥčunne* 'you (pl. m.) opened it (m.)' reflects **faθ°ḥčun* which is older than present-day *faθḥičxun*. In the following table the past and subjunctive of *ifθaḥ, yifθuḥ* 'to open' (see Past Tense and Subjunctive, pp. 341–3) in Ma'lūla are repeated with the sg. 3m. suffix *-e*. The suffix has the allomorphs *-ne, -enne* and (rarer) *-nu*.

Present and perfect receive the accusative pronominal suffixes through the intermediary preposition *-l*, resulting in the following set (not all allomorphs indicated):

Table 16.6 Verb with object suffixes

		Past	+ -e	Subjunctive	+ -e
Sg.	1c.	faθhiθ	faθhičče	nifθuḥ	nfuθhenne
Pl.	1c.	faθhinnaḥ	faθˀḥlaḥle	nifθuḥ	nfuθhenne
Sg.	2m.	faθhič	faθhīčne	čifθuḥ	čfuθhenne
	f.	faθhiš	faθhīšnu (!)	čifθuḥ	čfuθhinnu (!)
Pl.	2m.	faθhičxun	faθˀḥčunne	čfuθhun	čfuθhunne
	f.	faθhičxen	faθˀḥčanne	čfuθhan	čfuθhanne
Sg.	3m.	ifθaḥ	faθhe	yifθuḥ	yfuθhenne
	f.	faθhaθ	faθhačče	čifθuḥ	čfuθhenne
Pl.	3m.	ifθaḥ	faθhunne	yfuθhun	yfuθhunne
	f.	ifθaḥ	faθhanne	yfuθhan	yfuθhanne

Sg. 1c.	-l(i)	Sg. 2m.	-lax ~ -x	Sg. 3m.	-le
		f.	-liš ~ -š	f.	-la
Pl. 1c.	-laḥ ~ -ḥ	Pl. 2m.	-lxun	Pl. 3m.	-lun
		f.	-lxen	f.	-len

Adding the suffixes to the inflected forms of the present and perfect causes the word stress to move to the following syllable. In an unstressed syllable $\bar{o}$ is replaced by a, $\bar{\imath}$ by i; in turn unstressed a, when receiving the stress, is replaced by $\bar{o}$, e.g. $n\bar{o}\check{s}ka$ + -le → $na\check{s}k\bar{o}le$ 'she kisses him'. In the plural the final n assimilates to the initial l of the suffix to yield ll.

'kiss'	Present	+ -le	Perfect	+ -le
Sg. 3m.	nōšek	našekle	inšek	nšīkle
Sg. 3f.	nōška	naškōle	nšīka	nšikōle
Pl. 3m.	nōškin	naškille	nšīkin	nšikille
Pl. 3f.	nōškan	naškalle	nšīkan	nšikalle

As shown on p. 343, the 2nd and 1st persons are arrived at by prefixing č- (2nd person) or n- (1st person) to the above forms.

Verb with Dative Pronominal Suffixes

The pronominal suffixes with *l*- shown above express a dative pronominal object. Since in the two new tenses, present and perfect, they also express an accusative object the two cannot be distinguished, e.g. *ṭaˁenle* = (1) 'he carries him'; (2) 'he carries to him/for him'. In the two old tenses, however, *l*-suffixes always express a dative object. Final -*θ* and final -*n* assimilate to *l*- to yield *ll*. The vowel *u* of the subjunctive is replaced by *o* under stress.

Order of Elements

The preferred word order is SVO.

Table 16.7   Verb with dative pronominal suffixes

'open'		Past	+ -le	Subjunctive	+ -le
Sg.	1c.	faθhiθ	faθhille	nifθuḥ	nifθohle
Pl.	1c.	faθhinnaḥ	faθˀḥlaḥle	nifθuḥ	nifθohle
Sg.	2m.	faθhič	faθhičle	čifθuḥ	čifθohle
	f.	faθhiš	faθhišlu (!)	čifθuḥ	čifθuḥlu (!)
Pl.	2m.	faθhičxun	faθˀḥčulle	čfuθhun	čfuθhulle
	f.	faθhičxen	faθˀḥčalle	čfuθhan	čfuθhalle
Sg.	3m.	ifθaḥ	fθaḥle	yifθuḥ	yifθohle
	f.	faθhaθ	faθhalle	čifθuḥ	čifθohle
Pl.	3m.	ifθaḥ	faθhulle	yfuθhun	yfuθhulle
	f.	ifθaḥ	faθhalle	yfuθhan	yfuθhalle

Eastern Neo-Aramaic

Eastern Neo-Aramaic (ENA) comprises an as yet unknown number of languages and dialects which, until the beginning of our century, were spread over an enormous territory covering southeastern Turkey, northern Iraq, northwestern Iran and, detached from the bulk of ENA, the territory of Mandaic in the Shaṭṭ el-'Arab, which is divided between Iraq and Iran. Apart from Mandaic, most ENA languages were situated within the Kurdish language area in which they formed larger or smaller language islands; only the northernmost languages were situated in a Turkish (Azeri)-speaking area. Apart again from Mandaic, whose speakers adhere to the Mandean religion, ENA languages are spoken by Christians and Jews.

Unfortunately, practically all ENA-speaking groups have been subjected to severe religious persecution since the beginning of the twentieth century. As a result, few ENA speakers still live in their original homeland anywhere in the Middle East. The large majority have been turned into refugees and are dispersed over five continents. The Iraqi and Iranian Jews are safe in Israel but their ENA speech is already in severe danger of extinction. All taken together, the future is very dark for the ENA languages, and the greatest effort has to be made to investigate as many of them as possible while they are still to be found.

Hoberman (1989: 3ff.) divides ENA into three main groups: (1) Ṭuroyo (with Mlaḥsô); (2) Northeastern Neo-Aramaic (NENA); (3) Mandaic. Ṭuroyo is the westernmost ENA language; it is spoken in the Ṭūr 'Abdīn area in the Turkish province of Mardin, to the west of the Tigris river. The language of Mlaḥsô, now virtually extinct, was spoken even further to the northwest, in the vicinity of Diyarbakir. Ṭuroyo and Mlaḥsô are quite distinct from all ENA languages east of the Tigris. Whereas both Ṭuroyo and Mandaic comprise small language areas with only minor dialectal differentiation, NENA is the cover term for an amazing variety of languages and dialects, many of which are still unexplored or even undiscovered. There are, within the NENA group, many varieties which are not mutually comprehensible, so that some of the NENA dialect subgroups should perhaps be set up as different languages. Interestingly enough, one of the main divisions in NENA runs along religious rather than geographical lines. Whereas in the western part of Northern Iraq the ENA dialects of the Christians and Jews are relatively close and mutually comprehensible, they become less and less so as one moves to the east. In Iran the respective NENA speech of Christians and Jews of the same town (e.g. Urmi, Sanandaj) was, to all intents, mutually unintelligible.

Among the several adstrate/superstrate languages which have influenced the ENA languages, Kurdish is the most important. National languages such as Persian in Iran, Turkish in Turkey and Arabic in Iraq, have exercised considerable influence, especially in the lexicon. Regional languages, such as Azeri in Iranian Azerbaijan and Arabic in southeastern Turkey, have also contributed to the complex structure of present-day ENA languages.

I am indebted to Simon Hopkins who contributed the Kerend data quoted in this chapter. He also read the whole text and suggested many important improvements. It goes without saying that the responsibility for all remaining imperfections is entirely mine.

Phonology

Consonants

p b	t d		k g	q (uvular)		(ʾ)
	ṭ (ḍ)					
		č ǧ				
f v	θ δ		x γ		ḥ ʿ	h
	(δ̱)					
	s z	š ž				
	ṣ					
m	n (ṇ)					
	l (ḷ)					
	r (ṛ)					
w		y				

Ṭuroyo exhibits a rather conservative consonant system as shown above (rare phonemes are in parentheses, the "emphatic" consonants – marked by a subscript dot – are velarized).

ḍ and δ̱ occur mostly in loans from Arabic and are not distinguished by all speakers. ʾ is distinctive only word internally and it is rare; word initially it is an automatic juncture marker. ṇ, ḷ, and ṛ occur in verb inflection as a result of the assimilation of stem-final -r to suffix-initial n, l or K, e.g. *komắr-no → komắṇṇo 'I say', *mĭr-le → mĭḷḷe 'he said', *mĭr-Ke → mĭṛṛe 'they said'.

In Middle Aramaic each of the six stops p, b, t, d, k, g was split into two positional variants (allophones), an initial, postconsonantal and geminate one continuing the older stop and a postvocalic one yielding the corresponding fricative, i.e. $\bar{p}$, $\underline{b}$, $\underline{t}$, $\underline{d}$, $\underline{k}$, $\bar{g}$. The resulting twelve consonants later acquired phonemic status. They have been preserved rather well in Ṭuroyo, as can be seen below. (The diachronic/synchronic symbols $\bar{p}/f$, $\underline{t}/\theta$, $\underline{d}/\delta$, $\underline{k}/x$, $\bar{g}/\gamma$ denote the same sound.)

Middle Aramaic >		Ṭuroyo	Examples			
*p	>	f	*pāṭā	>	foθo	'face' (noun)
*p̄	>	f	*mawlep̄>		molĭf	'he teaches'
*b	>	b	*brīṭā	>	briθo	'world'
*ḇ	>	w	*ḥārʾḇīn >		ḥŭrwi	'they perish'
*t	>	t	*taʿlā	>	tăʿlo	'fox'
*ṯ	>	θ	*āṯē	>	oṯe	'he comes'
*d	>	d	*deḇšā	>	dăwšo	'honey'
*ḏ	>	δ	*eḏnā	>	ăδno	'ear'
*k	>	k	*karmā	>	kărmo	'vineyard'
*ḵ	>	x	*bāḵē	>	boxe	'he weeps'
*g	>	g	*gaḇrā	>	găwro	'man'
*ḡ	>	γ	*reḡlā	>	răγlo	'foot'

Middle Aramaic *ḇ, which may have been pronounced [v] originally, appears as w in Ṭuroyo, but as v in Mlaḥsô. *p and *p̄ have been collapsed into f. Otherwise all the the fricatives resulting from the split of p, b, t, d, k, g have been preserved in Ṭuroyo, whereas in Mlaḥsô ṯ and ḏ have been shifted to s and z, e.g. Mlaḥsô ose 'he comes', ezno 'ear'. The pharyngal fricatives, voiceless ḥ and voiced ʿ, have been preserved both in Mlaḥsô and Ṭuroyo.

A few consonants were introduced by loanwords from Turkish, Kurdish and Arabic, such as č, ǧ and ž.

As one moves from Ṭuroyo eastward into the domain of NENA the following simplifications and/or modifications of the consonant system occur:

1 f (< *p/p̄) shifted back to p.
2 θ and δ were retained in some dialects but shifted back to t and d in the majority of the dialects. More rarely (e.g. in the dialect of the Jews of Zaxo) they shifted to s and z. In the Jewish dialects of Azerbaijan there is an asymmetrical development θ > l, δ > d; in Persian Kurdistan both θ and δ shifted to l. In the dialects of Tiari and Txuma δ was retained but θ shifted to š in many instances.
3 ḥ was merged with x, except for the westernmost NENA dialects (Hertevin group) where x was merged with ḥ. ʿ shifted to ʾ and yielded Ø in some dialects. γ did not usually survive but may be represented by ʾ/Ø, presumably after an intermediate change to ʿ.

4   *k* and *g* are palatalized and in some dialects became plain palatal stops [c],
    [ɟ]. In Christian Urmi these palatal stops shifted to *č* and *ǧ*, while *č* and *ǧ* in
    loanwords shifted to *ts* and *dz*. Again in Christian Urmi *q* was fronted to *ḵ*
    [ḵ].

Neo-Mandaic has preserved all the six fricative consonants resulting from the
earlier split: *f*, *v*, *θ*, *δ*, *x*, *γ*. Middle Aramaic *ḇ* has yielded *v*. The pharyngeals have
been lost, ʿ yielding Ø in all positions, and *ḥ* merging with *h* (not with *x* as in
NENA).

Vowels

Mlaḥsô and Ṭuroyo
The Mlaḥsô vowel system is considerably more conservative than that of Ṭuroyo.
In Mlaḥsô there are six vowels: *i*, *u*, *e*, *o*, *a*, *ǝ*. The first five vowels can occur in
all types of syllables. The status of *ǝ* is not yet completely clear. It occurs only in
stressed non-final syllables, e.g., the definite article for both masculine and feminine singular: *ɔ́-gavro* 'the man', *ɔ́-brato* 'the daughter'. The "tense" vowels *i*, *u*,
e, *o*, *a* are close to the five IPA cardinal vowels. The only "lax" vowel, *ǝ*, is always
short. The tense vowels are long in syllables carrying the main stress, long to half-
long in syllables carrying secondary stress and half-long to short in unstressed syllables. The phonetic vowel length is independent of openness or closedness of the
syllable, e.g. *dozo* [doːˈzoː] 'maternal uncle', *doḥlo* [doːħˈloː] 'she fears'.
Ṭuroyo has a more evolved system of five tense and three lax vowels:

i		u		ĭ		ŭ
	e	o				
	a				ă	

The tense vowels are usually phonetically long in syllables carrying main stress,
long to half-long in syllables carrying secondary stress and half-long to short in
unstressed syllables; in unstressed word-final position they are usually short. The
three lax vowels are always short. The phonetic values are:

[iː]		[uː]		[ɪ]		[ʊ]
	[eː]	[oː]				
	[aː]			[æ]		

In Ṭuroyo, if a syllable is closed through a morphological process such as derivation or inflection, a tense vowel is replaced by a lax vowel, whereas in Mlaḥsô no
such change occurs. Note that word stress, unless otherwise indicated, falls on the
last syllable in Mlaḥsô but on the second to last syllable in Ṭuroyo (see p. 353).

	Mlaḥsô	Ṭuroyo	
*i	yarixo	yarixo	'long (m.)'
	yarixto	yarĭxto	'long (f.)'
*u	zʿuro	zʿuro	'small (m.)'
	zʿurto	zʿŭrto	'small (f.)'
	mun	mĭn	'what?'
*e	kefo	kefo	'stone'
	domex	domĭx	'he sleeps'
	doméxno	domăxno	'I sleep'
*o	nofeq	nofĭq	'he comes out'
	nofqi	nĭfqi	'they come out'
*a	zaben	mzabĭn	'he sells'
	zabno	mzăbno	'she sells'

NENA and Neo-Mandaic

The most frequent vowel system found in NENA is identical with the one described for Ṭuroyo (except for diachronic correspondences, see p. 352), namely: i, u, e, o, a, ĭ, ŭ, ă, with similar phonetic realizations and similar rules for vowel length. The lax vowels ĭ and ŭ may be phonetically closer to [e] and [o] than to [ɪ] and [ʊ] respectively, in which case they may be written ĕ, ŏ. Tense a [aː] is more open and retracted than lax ă [æ]; in some dialects (e.g. Hertevin, NENA dialects of Iranian Kurdistan) it is back [ɑː], creating a marked contrast [æ] : [ɑː], reminiscent of Persian. Note in Hertevin:

kpina   'hungry (m.)'
kpĕnta   'hungry (f.)'

ʾămuqa 'deep (m.)'
ʾămŏqta 'deep (f.)'

beʾe   'eggs'
bĕʾta   'egg'

ărmone 'pomegranates'
ărmŏnta 'pomegranate'

ḥwara   'white (m.)'
ḥwărta 'white (f.)'

In the scholarly literature there are many divergent and complex practices for writing the vowels of NENA languages and dialects. For the present chapter, however, tense vowels are always noted as i, u, e, o, a etc., and lax vowels always as ĭ, ŭ, ĕ, ŏ, ă etc.

Diachronic Correspondences

1   In Ṭuroyo the old diphthongs *ăw* and *ăy* have been preserved while in the majority of NENA dialects and in Neo-Mandaic they have been monophthongized and merged with *o* and *e*. Examples: Ṭuroyo *băyto*, Hertevin *beta*, Neo-Mandaic *beθa* 'house'; Ṭuroyo *măwto*, Hertevin *mota* 'death'. In Christian Aradhin, *ăy* has yielded an open /ɛ/ which contrasts with /e/, e.g. *bɛθa* ['bɛːθa] 'house' vs. *beta* ['beːta] 'egg', while *ăw* has been preserved: *măwta* 'death'.

2   One of the most characteristic features distinguishing Ṭuroyo and Mlahsô from the remaining ENA languages is the shift of old *ā to o* [oː], e.g. Ṭuroyo *hoze*, but Hertevin *haze*, Christian Aradhin *xaze*, Neo-Mandaic *hazi* 'he sees'. In some NENA dialects the phonetic realization of *a* is a back and sometimes even rounded vowel: [aː] ~ [ɒː] ~ [ɔː], however, in closed syllables it is replaced by *ă* [æ ~ a] whereas in Ṭuroyo *o* in closed syllables is mostly replaced by *ŭ ~ ĭ*, e.g. *hŭzyo ~ hĭzyo* but ENA *hăzya, xăzya*, Neo-Mandaic *hăzya* 'she sees'.

3   In some NENA dialects the monophthongization of *ăy* and *ăw* to *e* and *o* (see 1 above) has pushed older *e* and *o* to *u* and *i*. In Christian Urmi we find *beta* 'house', *mota* 'death', but *tili* 'he came', *kipa* 'stone', *kuma* 'black', *axuna* 'brother' (cf. Hertevin *ɔeta, mota, tele, kepa, koma, ăhona*). Older *u* has become *ü* [yː] in some dialects, e.g. Hassana *xăbüša* 'apple' (cf. Tkhuma *xăbuša*). In the northernmost Christian dialects of Iranian Azerbaijan (e.g., Urmi, Salamas) older *i* and *u* have been diphthongized to *iy* [ɪj] and *uy* [ʊj] and in some dialects the glide element of these new diphthongs has become a spirant, yielding [ɪç] and [ʊx]. Some instances of a similar process are also found in Neo-Mandaic, e.g. *moxta* (< **mōta < mawtā*) 'death'.

"Synharmonism"

In some of the northernmost NENA dialects the two velarized consonants, *ṭ* and *ṣ*, tend to spread their velarization over the whole syllable or, more frequently, the whole word. In the Jewish and Christian dialects of Persian Azerbaijan not only all the consonants in a velarized ("flat" or "hard") word become more or less velarized but all the vowels have allophones which are lowered, retracted and/or centralized. This synharmonism or "flatting" is a long component since the phonemic contrast no longer resides in a single segment but in the whole word. Thus in the Jewish dialect of Persian Azerbaijan the contrast between the words for 'she says' and 'wool' lies in the flatting, marked by a raised +, of the second word: *ămra* vs. *⁺ămra*.

In dialects where flatting or synharmonism exists, the whole vocabulary and all morphological forms are divided into two categories – they are either "flat" or "plain." The presence of a velarized consonant (*ṭ* or *ṣ*) in the ancestor form of a word is not the only possible factor inducing flatness. It can also be caused by an original pharyngeal **ʿ*. The examples *ămra* 'she says' and *⁺ămra* 'wool' cited above reflect Middle Aramaic *āmrā* and *ʿamrā* respectively. Similarly *ălpa* 'thousand' goes back to *alpā* but ⁺*ălma* 'people' comes from *ʿālmā*. Another source for flat words is borrowings from Turkish and Kurdish, e.g. in the Jewish dialects of Persian Azerbaijan (Garbell 1965: 34) *pul* 'fall!' (imperative) vs. ⁺*pul* 'stamp' (from Turkish *pul* 'stamp'). For the variety of Modern Assyrian which he describes, Tsereteli (1978: 36) states that the realization of *ṭ* is "abruptive," that is ejective.

Word Stress

Nouns are still stressed on the last syllable in Mlaḥsô and in the Jewish NENA dialects of Iran and eastern Iraq but in the majority of ENA languages stress has shifted to the penultimate (stress indicated by boldface): Mlaḥsô *gavro*, but Ṭuroyo *găwro* 'man'; Jewish Azerbaijan *goră*, but Christian Urmi *gora*, Neo-Mandaic *găvra* 'man'. The same is true for the original participles which now form the basis of verb inflection (see Verbs, p. 359): Mlaḥsô *ḥoze*, Jewish Azerbaijan *xaze*, but Ṭuroyo *ḥoze*, Hertevin *ḥaze*, Hassana *xaze*, Neo-Mandaic *hazi* 'he sees'; Mlaḥsô *ḥozyo*, Jewish Azerbaijan and Kerend *xăzyă* but Ṭuroyo *ḥŭzyo*, Hertevin *ḥăzya*, Hassana *xăzya*, Neo-Mandaic *hăzya* 'she sees'.

Penultimate stress (where it occurs) is the rule also when suffixes are added, e.g. Ṭuroyo *ṭuro*, Christian Aradhin *ṭura* 'mountain' but Ṭuroyo *ṭurone*, Christian Aradhin *ṭurane* 'mountains'. In verbal forms based on original participles stress cannot go beyond the original participle form, regardless of how many suffixes are added, e.g. Ṭuroyo *ḥozeno* 'I (m.) see', *ḥozenole* 'I (m.) see him', *ḥozewăynole* 'I (m.) used to see him'.

In most, if not all, NENA languages word stress has become phonemic on the morphological level, e.g. Ṭuroyo *malĭm* 'he collects' vs. *malĭm* 'collect!'; Jewish Azerbaijan *zdelu* 'they feared' vs. *zdelu* 'their fear'. In the Jewish dialect of Kerend (Iranian Kurdistan) we find, e.g., *twiră* 'broken (m.)' vs. *twiră* 'it (f.) got broken', *tori* 'my bull' vs. *tori* 'I broke', *zilex* 'we have gone' vs. *zilex* 'we went'.

In the present study, when the position of word stress deviates from the general rule, it is marked by ´ over the stressed vowel. However, in the verbal paradigms stress is marked here throughout in order to avoid ambiguity.

Stress Groups

In all NENA languages collocations of two, rarely three words which are closely bound syntactically can form stress groups (indicated here by = connecting the two words). In stress groups the second word loses its word stress, and the main stress of the collocation comes to be on the last syllable of the first word. Stress groups most frequently occur with numerals + counted nouns, e.g. Christian Aradhin *ṭillĭθ=năqle*, Ṭuroyo (Midən) *tloθo=năqlawoθe* 'three times', and with negations and a following verb or noun, e.g. Jewish Amedi *lă=xĭlle*, Ṭuroyo *lo=xile* 'he did not eat', Jewish Amedi *čŭ=mĭndi*, Ṭuroyo *tŭ=mede* 'nothing'.

Morphology

Pronouns

**Table 16.8   Independent personal pronouns,
Mlaḥsô, Ṭuroyo, Hertevin and Hassana**

		Mlaḥsô	Ṭuroyo (Midyat)	Hertevin	Hassana
Sg.	1c.	ono	ŭno	ana	ana
Pl.	1c.	elóna	äḥna	äḥnäḥ	äxni
Sg.	2c.	hat	hät	ahĕt	ahĭt
Pl.	2c.	hátun	hatu	äḥnitŏn	äxnütĭn
Sg.	3m.	híye	huwe	ahu	awa
	f.	híya	hiya	ahi	aya
Pl.	3c.	híyen	hĭnne	äḥni	ani

**Table 16.9   Independent personal pronouns,
Chr. Mangeš, Chr. Urmi, J. Azerbaijan, Neo-Mandaic**

		Chr. Mangeš	Chr. Urmi	J. Azerbaijan	Neo-Mandaic
Sg.	1c.	ana	ana	anä	ăn ~ ăna
Pl.	1c.	äxni	äxnän	äxnän	ăni
Sg.	2c.	m. ayĭt, f. ayät	ät	ät	ăt
Pl.	2c.	äxnutĭn	äxtün	ätxün	m. ättŏn, f. ättĕn
Sg.	3m.	awa	ăw	o	hax
Sg.	f.	aya	ăy	o	hax
Pl.	3c.	ani	aniy	oyne	hănni or
					m. hănnŏx,
					f. hănnĕx

Only a minority of languages (Mlaḥsô, Ṭuroyo and Hertevin) have preserved archaic 3rd person pronouns (cf. Middle Aramaic *hū, hī, hennōn/hennēn*). In the remaining languages their function has been taken over by the demonstrative pronouns (see p. 354). In Hertevin all the forms have initial *a-/ă-*. In Mlaḥsô the pronoun of the pl. 1 has been replaced by *elóna* 'to us'. For details see Jastrow 1990 and Hoberman 1990.

Demonstrative Pronouns

Mlaḥsô and Ṭuroyo in the west and Neo-Mandaic in the southeast have two sets of demonstrative pronouns to distinguish betweer: the categories of closeness ('this') and remoteness ('that'); most NENA languages have only a single set ('this/that').

In the NENA languages the most frequent forms of the demonstratives (close

Table 16.10   Demonstrative pronouns

		Mlaḥsô	Ṭuroyo	Kerend	Neo-Mandaic
'this'	Sg. m.	áno	hano	ăy ~ ăyă	a ~ aha ~ ahăyye ~ hăy
	f.	ózi	haθe		
	Pl. c.	áne	hani	ăy ~ ăyă	hănni ~ ănni ~ ăhni
'that'	Sg. m.	áwo	hawo	o ~ ăwă	hax ~ ax
	f.	áyo	hayo		
	Pl. c.	ánek	hanĭk	o ~ ăwă	hănnŏx ~ hănnĕx

and remote being the same) are: sg. m. *awa ~ ăw ~ o*, sg. f. *aya ~ ăy ~ e*, pl. c. *ani ~ ăn*. Kerend has reintroduced a distinction by assigning *ăy* to closeness and *o* to remoteness, dropping gender and number distinctions.

Interrogative Pronouns

	Mlaḥsô	Ṭuroyo	Hertevin	Chr. Urmi	Kerend	Neo-Mandaic
'who?'	*man*	*măn*	*măn*	*măn ~ maniy*	*mắni*	*măn*
'what'	*mun*	*mĭn*	*mahi ~ me*	*mu ~ mudiy*	*ma*	*ma ~ mo ~ mu*

Pronominal Suffixes
The pronominal suffixes are joined to nouns to express possession, to prepositions to express relation and to verb forms with copulative inflection to express a pronominal object. Before the suffixes the nominal ending *-o ~ -a* is dropped. (Examples: *emo* 'mother', *beta ~ beθa ~ bela* 'house', *baba* 'father'.)

Table 16.11   Pronominal suffixes, Mlaḥsô, Ṭuroyo, Hertevin and Hassana

		Mlaḥsô	Ṭuroyo	Hertevin	Hassana
Sg.	1c.	emi	emi	beti	beti
Pl.	1c.	eména	emăn	betăn	betăn
Sg.	2m.	emox	emŭx	betŏḥ	betŭx
	f.	emex	emăx	betăḥ	betăx
Pl.	2c.	emékun	emayxu	betehŏn	betoxŭn
Sg.	3m.	emav	eme	betĕw	betăḥ
Sg.	f.	ema	ema	beto	betăḥ
Pl.	3c.	emen	emayye	betehĕn	betehĭn

Relational Morpheme
The pronominal suffixes (see above) can be joined to a special morpheme expressing relation: *diδ-* in Ṭuroyo, *did-* in Hertevin and Jewish Azerbaijan, *diy-* in Hassana and Christian Urmi, *ald-* in Neo-Mandaic. Thus, in Ṭuroyo, *diδi* means 'mine, the one belonging to me': *băytŭx răb me diδi-yo* 'your (m.) house is larger

Table 16.12 Pronominal suffixes, Chr. Urmi, J. Azerbaijan, Kerend and Neo-Mandaic

	Chr. Urmi	J. Azerbaijani	Kerend	Neo-Mandaic
Sg. 1c.	betiy	beli	beli	beθe
Pl. 1c.	betăn	belăn	belăn(i)	beθăn
Sg. 2m.	betŭx	belŏx	belox	beθăx
f.	betăx	belăx	belăx	beθĕx
Pl. 2c.	betoxŭn	belxŭn	belăxun	m. beθxŏn, f. beθxĕn
Sg. 3m.	betu	belew	belef	beθi
Sg. f.	beto	belaw	belăf	beθa
Pl. 3c.	beté	belu	belu	beθu

than mine'. Foreign loans which have not been adapted to ENA morphology (i.e. lack the nominal ending -*o*, -*a*) usually do not take pronominal suffixes; these are instead suffixed to the relational morpheme, thus Hertevin *diwăn didĕw* 'his council', Ṭuroyo *wăxt diδi* 'my time'. In several dialects the relational morpheme + suffix produced a new, enlarged series of suffixes, which in turn can also be suffixed to nouns of the inherited stock, e.g. Ṭuroyo *u=wăxtăyδi* 'my time' (with definite article, see p. 357), Mlaḥsô *ṭaflézav* 'his child', Txuma *bábĕdye* 'his father', Neo-Mandaic *xĕzmădde* 'my service'.

Nouns

Nominal Endings
Original Aramaic nouns have the ending -*o* (Mlaḥsô, Ṭuroyo) or -*a* (remaining ENA languages) in the masculine, -*to* ~ -*θo* or -*ta* ~ -*θa* in the feminine. In the Jewish NENA dialects with final stress (see p. 353) the ending always has the lax vowel -*ă*. Examples:

Mlaḥsô	Ṭuroyo	Chr. Aradhin	J. Azerbaijan	Kerend	Neo-Mandaic	
tawro	*tăwro*	*tăwra*	*toră*	*toră*	*tora*	'ox'
turto	*tĭrto*	*tăwĭrta*	*tŏrtă*	*tortă*	*turta*	'cow'

Plural
The most common plural ending is -*e*, (Mangeš -*ĭ*, Christian Urmi -*i*) for the masculine, Ṭuroyo (Midyat) -*oθo*, Ṭuroyo (villages) -*oθe*, NENA -*aθa* ~ -*ata* ~ -*ale* for the feminine. Examples: Ṭuroyo *noše*, Hertevin *naše*, Jewish Azerbaijan *naše*, Christian Urmi *naši* 'men, people'; Ṭuroyo (Midyat) *tăwroθo*, Ṭuroyo (villages) *tăwroθe*, Christian Aradhin *tăwraθa*, Neo-Mandaic *taraθa* 'cows', Hertevin *băḥtata* 'women', Kerend *yomale* 'days', *ăxonăwale* 'brothers'.

Another frequent ending of the masculine plural is Ṭuroyo -*one*, NENA -*ane*, Neo-Mandaic, -*ana* ~ -*ani*. Examples:

Ṭuroyo	Hertevin	Chr. Aradhin	Chr. Urmi	Neo-Mandaic	
ṭuro	ṭura	ṭura	⁺ṭura	ṭura	'mountain'
ṭurone	ṭurane	ṭurane	⁺ṭurani	ṭurana	'mountains'

In Neo-Mandaic, *-ana ~ -ani* has been generalized as the masculine plural ending, e.g. *tărmida* 'Mandean priest', pl. *tărmidana ~ tărmidani*.

A feminine noun may have a masculine plural: Ṭuroyo *bĭḫto*, pl. *be͑e*, Hertevin *bĕ͗ta*, pl. *be͗e* 'egg'. There are also feminine nouns without an overt feminine ending in the singular; they usually have a feminine plural, e.g. Ṭuroyo *ṣăw͑o* (f.), pl. *ṣăw͑oθe*, Hertevin *ṣĕp͗a* (f.), pl. *ṣĕp͗ata*, Chr. Urmi *⁺sĭppa* (f.), pl. *⁺sĭppata* 'finger'. In all ENA dialects there is a small number of nouns with an irregular plural, e.g.:

Ṭuroyo	Hertevin	Chr. Aradhin	J. Azerbaijan	Neo-Mandaic	
ăbro	ĕbra	bruna	bronă	ĕbra	'son'
ăbne	ĕbne	brune ~ bnune	bronawe	ĕbrana	'sons'
šato	šeta	šeta	šată	šĕtta	'year'
ĭšne	šĕnne	šĭnne	šĭnne	ĕšna	'years'

Definiteness
Ṭuroyo has developed a full-fledged definite article with different forms for sg. m., sg. f. and pl. c. probably coming from shortened forms of the independent personal pronouns (see p. 354). It precedes the noun and forms a stress group (see p. 353): Ṭuroyo *u=tăwro* 'the ox', *i=tĭrto* 'the cow', *ăt=tăwre* 'the oxen', *ăt=tăwroθe* 'the cows'. Mlaḥsô has a similar system with *ə=* (sg. m. and f.) and *a=* (pl.). The Jewish dialects of Iranian Kurdistan, on the other hand, use a Kurdish suffix *-ăke*: Kerend *goră* 'man', *gorăke* 'the man'. In some ENA languages there is a tendency to use the demonstratives (see p. 354), often in their shortened forms *ăw ~ o, ăy ~ e, ăn*, also for definiteness, e.g. Hertevin *o zalama* 'that man' or 'the man', but this is not a full-fledged article. Most importantly, definiteness of a verbal object is expressed by adding a pronominal object suffix (see p. 370) to the inflected verb, e.g. Hertevin *ḥazĕn* 'I see', *ḥazĕn (ḥa) tora* 'I see an ox' but *ḥazĕnne tora* 'I see **the** ox' (literally 'I see him, ox'), – cf. Jastrow 1990: 97ff.

Indefiniteness is frequently expressed by means of the numeral 'one': Ṭuroyo *ḥa=găwro*, Mangeš *xa=gora* 'a man'. Kerend has unstressed *-e ~ -ek*, borrowed from Kurdish, in this function, e.g. *xă gorắ-e ~ xă gorắ-ek* 'a man'. Neo-Mandaic has borrowed the Persian indefinite marker *-i*: *găvra* 'man', *găvri* 'a man'.

Annexation (Genitive)
Annexation of nouns is based on a Middle Aramaic construction with the morpheme *d-* intervening between the two nouns, e.g. Syriac *bră d-malkă* 'the son of the king'. In most ENA languages the element *d-* is attached to the first noun instead, the final vowel of which may be raised, e.g. Hertevin *ĕbra* 'son' but *ĕbrĕd mălka*, Jewish Azerbaijan *bronă* 'son' but *bronit ⁺šultană* 'the son of the king'.

Voice assimilation of the final -*d* is widespread. Hertevin frequently applies total assimilation: *ĕbrĕm mălka*. In the Jewish dialects of Iranian Kurdistan the two nouns are simply juxtaposed: Kerend *bełă ăxoni* 'my brother's house'. Younger speakers generally use the Persian *ezāfe* morpheme -*e*, e.g. Kerend *bełắ-e ăxoni* (same meaning).

Loanwords

In all ENA languages some loanwords were completely assimilated. In Ṭuroyo the word *šuɣlo* 'work, affair' comes from Arabic *šuɣl* (same meaning) but is synchronically an Aramaic word since it has the masculine ending -*o* and forms an Aramaic plural *šuɣlone*. The majority of loanwords, however, were only partly adapted to Aramaic phonology and morphology. In Ṭuroyo as well as in most NENA dialects, partly adapted Kurdish feminine nouns receive a singular ending -*e* reflecting the Kurdish fem. oblique ending -*ē*. The plural has a suffix -*ăt* derived from the Arabic plural morpheme -*āt*. Thus the Kurdish feminine noun *čīrōk* 'story' is borrowed into Ṭuroyo as *čiroke*, pl. *čirokăt*. Masculine nouns are borrowed without such modifications, e.g. *sōz* 'promise' from Turkish *söz* 'word'.

Numerals

Table 16.13   Numerals 1–10

	Ṭuroyo (Midyat) m.	f.	Hertevin c.	Chr. Urmi c.	Neo-Mandaic c.
1	ḥa	ḥðo	ḥa	xa	hda
2	tre	tărte	te	tre	tre(n)
3	tloθo	tloθ	ṭlata	⁺ṭla	klaθa
4	ărbꜥo	ărbăꜥ	ărba	⁺arpa	ărba
5	ḥămšo	ḥămmĭš	ḥămša	xămša	hămša
6	ĭšto	šeθ	ĕšta	ĭšta	šĕtta
7	šăwꜥo	šwăꜥ	šoʾa	⁺šăva	šŏvva
8	tmĭnyo	tmone	tmănya	tmănya	tmănya
9	tĭšꜥo	čăꜥ	ĕčʾa	⁺ĭča	ĕčča
10	ꜥăṣro	ḥṣar	ĕṣra	⁺ĭsra	ăṣra

Some ENA languages have retained distinct masculine and feminine forms of the numerals for '1' to '10'. Thus in Ṭuroyo, there is *ḥămšo=yăwme* 'five days' from *yăwmo* (m.) 'day', but *ḥămmĭš=šabe* 'five weeks' from *šăbθo* (f.) 'week'. The Ṭuroyo dialect of Midən as well as many NENA dialects generalized the masculine forms. Only for '1' were distinct forms retained in some idioms, e.g. Midən *ḥa/ḥðo*, Mangeš *xa/xða*. When counting, the longer masculine forms are used in all languages; in this function the monosyllabic numerals for 1 and 2 are blown up to *xaʾa, treʾe* in some NENA dialects. Hertevin uses the forms *ḥda, tĕrte* in counting but otherwise *ḥa, te*.

Table 16.14 Numerals 11–19

	Ṭuroyo	Hertevin	Mangeš	Neo-Mandaic
11	ḥðäḥṣ̌ăr	ḥdi'ĕssăr	xadĭssăr	hdăssăr
12	trăḥṣ̌ăr	tre'ĕssăr	trĭssăr	trĕssăr
13	tloθäḥṣ̌ăr	ṭlata'ĕssăr	tĭltăssăr	klatăssăr
14	ărbäḥṣ̌ăr	ărba'ĕssăr	ărbăssăr	ărbăssăr
15	ḥämṣ̌aḥṣ̌ăr	ḥämša'ĕssăr	xămšăssăr	hămăssăr
16	ĭštäḥṣ̌ăr	ĕšta'ĕssăr	ĭštăssăr	šĕttăssăr
17	šwäḥṣ̌ăr	šo'ĕssăr	ĭšwăssăr	šŏvvăssăr
18	tmonäḥṣ̌ăr	tmana'ĕssăr	tmanĭssăr	tmanăssăr
19	čäḥṣ̌ăr	ĕčča'ĕssăr	tĭšassăr	ĕččăssăr

Note: There is no longer a gender distinction.

Multiples of Tens and Hundreds

	Ṭuroyo (Midyat)	Hertevin	Neo-Mandaic
20	ʿĭsri	ĕsri	ĕsrin
30	tleθi	ṭlati	klaθin
40	ărbʿi	ărbi	ărbin
50	ḥämši	ḥämši	hămšin
60	ĭšti	ĕšti	šĕttin
70	šăwʿi	šo'i	šŏvvin
80	tmoni	tmani	tmanin
90	tĭšʿi	ĕč'i	ĕččin
100	mo	ma	ĕmma
200	maθe	trema	tren ĕmma
300	tloθmo	ṭĕllădma	klaθa ĕmma
400	ărbăʿmo	ărbĕ'ma	ărba ĕmma
500	ḥämmĭšmo	ḥämmĕšma	hămša ĕmma
600	šeθmo	ĕššĕtma	šĕtta ĕmma
700	šwăʿmo	šăwwĕ'ma	šŏvva ĕmma
800	tmonemo	tmanĕ'ma	tmănya ĕmma
900	čăʿmo	ĕččĕ'ma	ĕčča ĕmma

Thousands and Compound Numbers
'1000' is ălfo in Ṭuroyo, ălpa in most NENA dialects, '2000' Ṭuroyo tre=ălfo, Hertevin tre=ălpa etc. Compound numbers start with the highest number, e.g. Mangeš ărba ĭmma w ărbi w ărba '444'.

Verbs

Generalities
Verbal roots consist of three, more rarely of four consonants. "Weak" roots contain one of the "weak" consonants ', w or y which don't always appear.

Of the six derivational classes or "stems" of Middle Aramaic only the three active stems (*pe'al*, *pa''el* and *af'el*) have survived in most ENA languages. Ṭuroyo and Mlaḥsô are unique in retaining also the three passive stems (*eθpe'el*, *eθpa''al* and *ettaf'al*), although the evidence for *ettaf'al* in Mlaḥsô is weak. Neo-Mandaic has preserved the *eθpe'el*, the evidence for an *eθpa''al* is weak. In the remaining languages passivity is expressed periphrastically. In a number of NENA dialects the reflexes of *pe'al* and *pa''el* have been merged.

There is only one element of the Middle Aramaic verb system which has been preserved in all ENA languages: the imperative. Neo-Mandaic has preserved the old Semitic perfect but not the imperfect. New tenses have been developed by means of the originally active and passive participles, in some NENA dialects also by means of the verbal noun (infinitive). All ENA languages have at least two basic tenses: present and preterite, some have in addition perfect and/or continuous present. The verbal systems increase in complexity as one moves from west to east. Whereas Ṭuroyo and the westernmost NENA dialects have only present and preterite, most NENA dialects have present, preterite and perfect; in Iranian Azerbaijan they also have a continuous present. Neo-Mandaic, however, has only present and preterite. From the basic tenses are formed secondary tenses/moods: subjunctive, future and imperfect from the present, continuous imperfect from the continuous present, remote preterite from the preterite, remote perfect from the perfect etc.

There are three different types of inflection which we shall call predicative, ergative and copulative.

1   In the predicative inflection the verbal base is derived from an old participle (either active or passive) in the *status absolutus*; the inflectional suffixes are shortened forms of the independent personal pronouns.
2   In the ergative inflection the verbal base is also derived from an old participle in the *status absolutus*; the participle is historically passive and indicates the **patient** of the action. The **agent** is expressed by inflectional suffixes which consist of the preposition *l-* 'to, by' + pronominal suffixes.
3   In the copulative inflection the verbal base is derived from an old passive participle or a verbal noun, in either case reflecting an old *status emphaticus*. The subject is expressed by the copula (see p. 372) which is either joined enclitically or precedes or follows the base as a free form. The verbal noun is preceded by the preposition *b-* 'in' which is, however, omitted in a number of dialects.

In the following description of the verb all examples use the root *grš* 'to pull' although this root does not occur in all ENA languages and even less so in all derivational classes (stems). All data from Middle Aramaic have been marked with an asterisk * in order to distinguish them from the modern data.

Verb Derivation

The symbols ^{P}, ^{E} and ^{C} following a base indicate the type of inflection (^{P} = predicative, ^{E} = ergative, ^{C} = copulative). The Neo-Mandaic preterite which is a continuation of the Middle Aramaic "perfect" is not included in this description – see Preterite, p. 366.

Stem I active reflects old *pe'al* and in the Jewish dialects of Azerbaijan and Iranian Kurdistan also to *pa''el* since there the two stems have been very largely merged. In general, the inflectional bases reflect the old active participle for the present, the old passive participle for the preterite, the old passive participle in the *status emphaticus* for the perfect and the old verbal nouns for the continuous present. However, in Mlaḥsô the bases of the perfect and in Ṭuroyo those of the intransitive preterite reflect an old verbal adjective. Both Kerend and Ṭuroyo have different preterite bases for transitive and intransitive verbs. In Kerend the preterite of intransitive verbs has *griš* with unshortened vowel and predicative inflection. In Ṭuroyo it has *gariš* (that is, the same basis, historically, which serves for the perfect in Mlaḥsô) with predicative inflection; in both Ṭuroyo and Kerend *griš* with shortended vowel and ergative inflection serves for the preterite of transitive verbs. The sg. m. bases are:

	Mlaḥsô	Ṭuroyo	Txuma	J. Azerbaijan	Kerend	Neo-Mandaic
Present:	$gore\check{s}^{P}$	$gori\check{s}^{P}$	$gari\check{s}^{P}$	$gari\check{s}^{P}$	$g\breve{a}ri\check{s}^{P}$	$gare\check{s}^{P}$

	Mlaḥsô	Ṭuroyo	Txuma	J. Azerbaijan	Kerend
Preterite:	$gri\check{s}^{E}$	$gari\check{s}^{P}/gri\check{s}^{E}$	$gri\check{s}^{E}$	$gri\check{s}^{E}$	$gri\check{s}/gri\check{s}^{E}$

	Mlaḥsô	Txuma	J. Azerbaijan	Kerend
Perfect:	$gari\check{s}^{P}$	$gri\check{s}a^{C}$	$gri\check{s}^{P}/gri\check{s}a^{C}$	$gri\check{s}a^{C}$

	Chr. Aradhin	Txuma	J. Azerbaijan
Cont. Pr.:	$gra\check{s}a^{C}$	$gra\check{s}a^{C}$	$garo\check{s}e^{C}$

Stem I passive reflects the old *eθpe'el* participle for the present (a formation that does not exist in the NENA dialects), the passive participle of *pe'al* for the preterite and the same participle in the *status emphaticus* for the perfect. Note the special case of Mlaḥsô which, for the preterite, employs the old *eθpe'el* participle with ergative inflection.

Stem I passive:

	Mlaḥsô	Ṭuroyo	Kerend	Neo-Mandaic
Present:	$megre\check{s}^{P}$	$m\hat{\imath}gri\check{s}^{P}$		$m\breve{e}gre\check{s}^{P}$
Preterite:	$megre\check{s}^{E}$	$gri\check{s}^{P}$	$gri\check{s}^{P}$	
Perfect:	$gri\check{s}^{P}$		$gri\check{s}\breve{a}^{C}$	

The actives of stems II and III reflect participles of old *pa''el* and *af'el*, respectively, while the corresponding passives (restricted to certain dialects) reflect old *eθpa''al* and *ettaf'al* participles. The inflectional bases of the present reflect the old active participles. The old passive participles have been collapsed with the active ones in Mlaḥsô and Ṭuroyo; thus, in Mlaḥsô and Ṭuroyo, the inflectional bases of the present and the preterite are identical, the only difference between the two tenses residing in the type of inflection. East of Ṭuroyo (that is, in NENA proper) the inflectional bases of the preterite have been distinguished from the present by changing the stem vowel *a* into *u*. The old formative *m-* of the participle has been shed in some dialects.

Stem II active:

	Mlaḥsô	Ṭuroyo	Mangeš	Chr. Urmi	Neo-Mandaic
Present:	*gareš*[P]	*mgariš*[P]	*mgariš*[P]	*gariš*[P]	*mgărrĕš*[P]
Preterite:	*gareš*[E]	*mgariš*[E]	*mguriš*[E]	*guriš*[E]	
Perfect:				*gŭrša*[C]	
Cont. Pr.:				*garoše*[C]	

Stem II passive:

	Mlaḥsô	Ṭuroyo	Mangesh	Neo-Mandaic
Present:	*mgareš*[P]	*migariš*[P]		*mgărraš*[P]
Preterite:	*mgareš*[E]	*mgariš*[P]	*mŭgriš*[P]	

Stem III active:

	Mlaḥsô	Ṭuroyo	Chr. Urmi	Kerend	Neo-Mandaic
Present:	*magreš*[P]	*măgriš*[P]	*măgriš*[P]	*măgriš*[P]	*măgreš*[P]
Preterite:	*magreš*[E]	*măgriš*[E]	*mŭgriš*[E]	*mĭgriš*[E]	
Perfect:			*mŭgriša*[C]		
Cont. Pr.:			*magroše*[C]		

Stem III passive:

	Ṭuroyo	Kerend
Present:	*mităgriš*[P]	
Preterite:	*mtăgriš*[P]	*mĭgriš*[P]

Verb Inflection

Predicative inflection will be exemplified by (1) the active inflection of the present of stem I in a number of dialects and (2) the passive inflection of the present of stem I in Ṭuroyo and the preterite of stem I in Ṭuroyo and Kerend. The inflectional bases are reflexes of old participles in the *status absolutus*, and the inflectional suffixes hark back to shortened forms of the independent personal pronouns. For the 3rd persons the inflectional suffixes are Ø. Stress is marked consistently in the whole paradigm.

Ergative inflection will be exemplified by the preterite of stem I. The inflectional bases are derived from old passive participles in the *status absolutus*, and the inflectional suffixes can be analyzed as consisting of the preposition *l-* 'for, by' + pronominal suffixes. The **patient** is expressed by the verbal base and the **agent** by the ergative suffixes, e.g.: **grīš lī* 'pulled is he by me' → 'I pulled (him)' etc. Stress is marked consistently in the whole paradigm.

Word stress never goes beyond the inflectional base, thus Christian Urmi *grĭšlŭx, grĭšloxŭn*. Ṭuroyo has a unique pl. 3c. suffix *-Ke* which doubles the base final consonant: *grišle* 'he pulled' but *grĭšše* 'they pulled'. By assimilating *l-* of

Table 16.15   Predicative inflection, active

	Mlaḥsô	Ṭuroyo	Hertevin	Kerend	Neo-Mandaic
Sg. 1m.	goréšno	gorášno	gắršĕn	gằríšnă	garéšna
Sg. 2m.	goršét	gúršĭt	gắršĕt	gắršét	gắršĕt
Sg. 3m.	goréš	górĭš	gáreš	gằrĭš	gáréš
Sg. 1f.	goréšno	gúršóno	gắršăn	gằršắn(a)	garéšna
Sg. 2f.	goršát	gúršăt	gắršăt	gắršăt	gắršĕt
Sg. 3f.	goršó	gúršo	gắrša	gằršắ	gắrša
Pl. 1c.	goršína	gúršína	gắršaḥ	gằršéx(in)	gằršénni
Pl. 2c.	goršítun	gúršútu	gắršítŏn	gằršétun	gằršéttŏn
Pl. 3c.	goršĭ́	gúrši	gắrši	gằršĭ́	gắršĕn

Table 16.16   Predicative inflection, passive

	Ṭuroyo	Ṭuroyo	Kerend
Sg. 1m.	mĭgrĭ́šno	grĭ́šno	grĭ́šnă
Sg. 2m.	mĭgróšĭt	grĭ́šĭt	grĭ́šet
Sg. 3m.	mĭ́grĭš	griš	griš
Sg. 1f.	mĭgrošóno	grišóno	grĭ́šăn(a)
Sg. 2f.	mĭgróšăt	grĭ́šăt	grĭ́šăt
Sg. 3f.	migróšo	grĭ́šo	grĭ́šă
Pl. 1c.	mĭgrošína	grišína	grĭ́šex(in)
Pl. 2c.	mĭgrošútu	grišútu	grĭ́šetun
Pl. 3c.	mĭgróši	grĭ́ši	grĭ́ši

Table 16.17   Ergative inflection

		Mlaḥsô	Ṭuroyo	Hertevin	Mangeš	Chr. Urmi	Kerend
Sg.	1c.	grĭ́šli	grĭ́šli	gréšli	grĭ́šli	grĭ́šliy	grĭ́šli
Pl.	1c.	grĭ́šlan	grĭ́šlăn	gréšlăn	grĭ́šlăn	grĭ́šlăn	grĭ́šlăn
Sg.	2m.	grĭ́šlox	grĭ́šlŭx	gréšlŏḥ	grĭ́šlŭx	grĭ́šlŭx	grĭ́šlox
	f.	grĭ́šlex	grĭ́šlăx	gréšlăḥ	grĭ́šlăx	grĭ́šlăx	grĭ́šlăx
Pl.	2c.	grĭ́šlekun	grĭ́šxu	gréšleḥŏn	grĭ́šloxĭn	grĭ́šloxŭn	grĭ́šlăxun
Sg.	3m.	grĭ́šle	grĭ́šle	gréšle	grĭ́šlĭ	grĭ́šli	grĭ́šle
Sg.	f.	grĭ́šla	grĭ́šla	gréšla	grĭ́šla	grĭ́šla	grĭ́šla
Pl.	3c.	grĭ́šlen	grĭ́šše	gréšle(hĕn)	grĭ́šle	grĭ́šlŭn	grĭ́šlu

the pl. 3c. suffix to the base final consonant the confusing of the sg. 3m. and pl. 3c. forms was prevented. In Hertevin these two forms are not distinguished consistently since *grĕ̆šle* is used along with *grĕ̆šlehĕn* for the pl. 3c. Cf., however, Christian Aradhin *grĭ̆šle* (sg. m.) vs. *grĭ̆šlɛ* (pl. c.).

Copulative inflection will be exemplified by the perfect of stem I. The inflectional bases are derived from old passive participles in the *status emphaticus*, while the inflectional morphemes derive from the copula (see p. 372). In many dialects they can either precede or follow the verbal bases as free forms or be suffixed to them.

Table 16.18   Copulative inflection

	Hassana	Txuma	J. Azerbaijan
Sg. 1m.	huwĭn griša ~ grĭšewĭn	iwĭn griša ~ grĭšawĭn	grišélen
Sg. 2m.	huwĭt griša ~ grĭšewĭt	iwĭθ griša ~ grĭšawĭθ	grišélet
Sg. 3m.	hule griša ~ grĭšele	ile griša ~ grĭšale	grišéle
Sg. 1f.	huwăn grĭšta ~ grĭštewăn	iwăn grĭšta ~ grĭštawăn	grĭštélän
Sg. 2f.	huwăt grĭšta ~ grĭštewăt	iwăθ grĭšta ~ grĭštawăθ	grĭštélät
Sg. 3f.	hula grĭšta ~ grĭštela	ila grĭšta ~ grĭštala	grĭštéla
Pl. 1c.	huwŭx griše ~ grĭšewŭx	iwăx griše ~ grĭšewăx	grišélex
Pl. 2c.	huwütĭn griše ~ grĭšewütĭn	iθŭn griše ~ grĭšeθŭn	grišéletun
Pl. 3c.	hune griše ~ grĭšene	ile griše ~ grĭšele	grišélu

Whereas in some dialects the perfect has become a straightforward active tense – 'he has pulled' – in other dialects it has preserved some ambiguity as to voice; thus, in Txuma, *grĭšale* can mean 'he has pulled' but also 'he has been pulled'.

The inflection of the imperative is exemplified by the imperative of stem I. The predominant Middle Aramaic vocalization with an *o* vowel has been preserved except for Mlaḥsô and Ṭuroyo where the less frequent *a* has been generalized. In Kerend the plural ending *-mun* has been generalized from IIIy verbs.

	Mlaḥsô	Ṭuroyo	Hertevin	Mangeš	Chr.Urmi	Kerend
Sg. c.	*graš*	*grăš*	*grŏš*	*grŏš*	*grŭš*	*grŭ̆š ~ gŭ̆rŭš*
Pl. c.	*grášun*	*grášu*	*grúšĕn*	*grúšu*	*grúšŭn*	*grúšmun ~ gŭ̆rŭšmŭn*

Neo-Mandaic is unique in preserving gender distinction both in the singular and the plural:

Sg. m.	*g'ṭŏl*	Pl. m.	*g'ṭŏlyon*
f.	*g'ṭul*	f.	*g'ṭĕlyĕn*

The imperatives of stems II and III are derived from the inflectional bases of the present tense, thus showing an initial *m-*. Some NENA dialects have imperatives without initial *m-* in stem II. It is likely that *m-* has dropped here. In Ṭuroyo, the imperative singular is always stressed on the last syllable.

Stem	Mlaḥsô	Ṭuroyo	Hertevin	Chr. Aradhin	Chr.Urmi	Kerend
II Sg. c.	*zabén*	*mzabăn*	*šadĕr*	*mbašĭl*	*⁺palĭṭ*	*zăbĭn*
Pl. c.	*zabénun*	*mzabénu*	*šădrŏn*	*mbăšlu*	*⁺pălṭŭn*	*zăbĭnmŭn*
III Sg. c.	*adméx*	*mănšăf*	*măḥlŏp*	*măplĭx*	*măptĭx*	*măsxĭn*
Pl. c.	*adméxun*	*mănšefu*	*măḥlupĕn*	*măp'lxu*	*măptĭxŭn*	*măsxĭnmŭn*

Neo-Mandaic has preserved gender distinction only in the plural. Since there is no *m-* prefix either in stem II or stem III, unlike the present stems II and III where Neo-Mandaic has *m-*, it is quite possible that the imperatives are derived directly from their Middle Aramaic ancestor forms, e.g.:

	stem II	stem III
Sg. c.	*bărĕx*	*ăhrĕv*
Pl. m.	*bărĕxyon*	*ăhrĕvyon*
Pl. f.	*bărĕxyĕn*	*ăhrĕvyĕn*

Formation and Function of the Tenses
A tense which is represented by a specific inflectional paradigm, will be called a primary tense. Secondary tenses are derived from primary tenses by means of tense markers. As pointed out on p. 359 the inventory of primary tenses varies a great deal from one language or dialect to the other. Thus a function which is expressed by a primary tense in one language may by expressed by a secondary tense in the other (or not at all). Here we shall divide all primary and secondary tenses into three groups: present/continuous present, preterite, and perfect.

Present and continuous present The morphological category of the present, based on the old active participle, is found in all ENA languages. In some archaic dialects such as Hertevin it can express actions performed generally or habitually (general present) as well as actions in progress (continuous present). Ṭuroyo and most of the NENA languages, however, developed a prefixed present marker, e.g. Ṭuroyo *ko-ḥoze*, Hassana *k-xaze*, Christian Aradhin *i-xaze* 'he sees'. This prefix originally served to specify a continuous present ("he is seeing" as distinguished from "he sees"); however, in most dialects, this function has weakened. The forms with present marker now simply denote indicative, as opposed to the subjunctive expressed by the unmarked form (see p. 365). Thus, in Ṭuroyo, *ko-ḥoze* indicates a general present indicative ('he sees'), whereas the actual present must be expressed by an additional inflected presentative *kalé* 'behold' (see Presentative, p. 374), e.g. *kalé ko-ḥoze* 'behold, he sees' → 'he is seeing'.

A number of dialects (e.g., the Jewish dialects of Azerbaijan and Iranian Kurdistan, but also Mlaḥsô) have lost the present tense marker in the strong verb and do not distinguish between general present (indicative) and subjunctive (see p. 365): Mlaḥsô *goréš*, Kerend *gărĭš* 'he pulls/may pull'. However, the difference is maintained in Iᵖ verbs, e.g. Kerend *hămĭr* 'he may say' but *kmĭr* 'he says', Mlaḥsô *omér* 'he may say' but *xomér* 'he says'.

A clearer distinction between (general) present and continuous present is found in those languages and dialects which have developed a special morphological category to express the continuous present, cf. Jewish Azerbaijan *găršen* 'I pull', *garóšlen* 'I am pulling'.

The present without a tense prefix is used as subjunctive in most ENA languages, e.g. Ṭuroyo *lazĭm d-gorĭš* 'it is necessary that he pull, he must pull'.

The present with a prefix *gŭd-*, *g-* (Ṭuroyo), *d-* (Mlaḥsô), *bĭd-*, *b-* (NENA) expresses the future: Ṭuroyo *mĭ=g-săymĭt*, Mlaḥsô *mun d-seymet?*, Hertevin *me b-ʾodĕt?* 'what will you do?' This feature is absent in the Jewish dialects of Iranian Kurdistan.

A past marker *-wa-/-wa* (in Ṭuroyo *-wăy-/-wa*) can be added to the above tenses to transpose them into the past. Thus the habitual present yields a habitual past, the continuous present a continuous past, the future a conditional. The past marker, always unstressed, is either suffixed to the inflected form or inserted between base and inflectional suffix. The rules vary from one language or dialect to the other.

Examples from Txuma:

habitual present → habitual past:
i-găršăx 'we (usually) pull' → *i-găršắxwa* 'we used to pull'
actual present → actual past:
bĭ-grášawīθ 'you (m.) are pulling' → *bĭ-grášawīθwa* 'you were pulling'
future → conditional:
bĭd-găršĭn 'I (m.) shall pull' → *bĭd-găršĭ́nwa* 'I (m.) would pull'

Examples from Ṭuroyo:

ko-gorăšno 'I (m.) pull, am pulling' → *ko-gorắšwăyno* 'I (m.) was pulling'
gorắšwăyno 'I (m.) pulled, used to pull'
g-gŭršo 'she will pull' → *g-gŭršowa* 'she would pull'

Preterite The morphological category of the preterite is used in all ENA languages to express past action (narrative past). Both Ṭuroyo and Kerend distinguish in the preterite of stem I between transitive verbs which have bases going back to the old passive participle **grīš* and are inflected ergatively, and intransitive verbs which are inflected predicatively. In Kerend the inflected bases are historically identical, the difference between transitive and intransitive verbs residing only in the type of inflection, whereas Ṭuroyo has bases harking back to an old deverbal adjective **garrīš*. Examples are *grĭ́šle* 'he pulled' (transitive) and *qăyĭm/qim* 'he stood up' (intransitive) in Ṭuroyo and Kerend.

In Neo-Mandaic the preterite continues the old "perfect" inflection of Middle Aramaic:

	Singular	Plural
3m.	*gʾṭăl*	*gʾṭălyŏn*
f.	*gĕṭlăt*	*gʾṭălyăn*
2m.	*gʾṭălt*	*gʾṭăltŏn*
f.	*gĕṭlit*	*gʾṭăltĕn*
1c.	*gĕṭlit*	*gʾṭălni*

Table 16.19 The preterite

| | | Transitive preterite | | Intransitive preterite | |
		Ţuroyo	Kerend	Ţuroyo	Kerend
Sg.	1c.	grĭšli	grĭšli	m. qayĭmno	qĭmna
				f. qayimóno	qĭmăn(a)
Pl.	1c.	grĭšlăn	grĭšlăn	qayimína	qĭmex(in)
Sg.	2m.	grĭšlŭx	grĭšlox	qayímĭt	qĭmĕt
	f.	grĭšlăx	grĭšlăx	qayímăt	qĭmăt
Pl.	2c.	grĭšxu	grĭšlăxun	qayimútu	qĭmetu
Sg.	3m.	grĭšle	grĭšle	qáyĭm	qim
Sg.	f.	grĭšla	grĭšlă	qayímo	qĭma
Pl.	3c.	grĭšše	grĭšlu	qayími	qĭmi

A past marker -wa-/-wa (in Ţuroyo -wăy-/-wa), as above, can be added to the preterite to yield a remote preterite, e.g. Ţuroyo grĭšwăyle, Txuma grĭšwale 'he had pulled', Ţuroyo qayimíwăyna 'we had stood up'.

Perfect The morphological category of the perfect expresses the resultative. This morphological category does not exist in all ENA languages. It is widely found in NENA but neither in Ţuroyo nor in Neo-Mandaic. Mlaḥsô, however, has a morphological perfect, utilizing the basis gariš which, in Ţuroyo, serves to express the preterite of intransitive verbs. Compare:

	Mlaḥsô	Ţuroyo	
Preterite	dmíxle	dámĭx	'he slept'
Perfect	damíx		'he has slept'
Preterite	grĭšle	grĭšle	'he pulled'
Perfect	gariš		'he has pulled'

The fact that Ţuroyo does not have a morphological perfect does not mean that Ţuroyo cannot express the resultative. This is done by using the tense marker ko-, thus kodámĭx 'he has slept', kogrĭšle 'he has pulled'. In other words, while Mlaḥsô damíx and Ţuroyo dámĭx correspond etymologically, the functional equivalent of Mlaḥsô damíx would be Ţuroyo kodámĭx.

This is the perfect inflection in Mlaḥsô, note the unusual pl. c. form ending in -a.

Sg. 1c. damíxno, pl. c. damixína
Sg. 2m. damixét, sg. f. damixat, pl. c. damixítun
Sg. 3m. damíx, sg. f. damixó, pl. c. damixá

A past marker -wa-/-wa, as on p. 367, can be added to the perfect to yield a pluperfect, e.g. Txuma grĭšeθŭn 'you (pl.) have pulled' → grĭšeθŭnwa 'you (pl.) had pulled'. This formation is not possible in the Jewish dialects of Iranian Kurdistan.

Weak and Irregular Verbs

Only three important types of weak verbs are considered: verbs with *y* or *w* as middle radical (root consonant) and verbs with *y* as last radical. Table 16.20, p. 369, shows the present, sg. 3m., sg. 3f. and pl. 3c. for each root type (*pyš/fyš* 'to stay', *qym* 'to stand up', *gwr* 'to get married', *ʾwd/ʾwl* 'to work, do', *ḥzy/xzy/hzy* 'to see').

IIy/w verbs usually preserve the middle radical in the sg. m. base: *payĕš* 'he stays, becomes', *gawĕr* 'he marries'. When the base is extended, as in the sg. f. and pl. c., the ensuing diphthong has mostly been monophthongized: **payĕš + -a > *păyša > peša* 'she stays', **gawĕr + -a > găwra* (= Chr. Aradhin) > *gora* 'she marries'. Some dialects have generalized the monophthongized base, yielding *peš* 'he stays', *hol/od* 'he does' (cf. Ṭuroyo *ʿowĭd* 'he works').

The pl. c. base of IIIy verbs has final *-n* in Ṭuroyo, Kerend and optionally in Jewish Azerbaijan, thus preserving the final consonant of the Middle Aramaic form (**ḥāzēn*), whereas *-n* has been dropped in strong verbs (**gāršīn* > Ṭuroyo *gŭrši*, Kerend *gărší*). In Neo-Mandaic, on the other hand, final *-n* of the plural base is also preserved in the strong verb (*gắṭlĕn*).

Verbs with *l, r* and *n* as last root consonant   The preterite inflection of III*l* verbs results in an *ll cluster: **qṭĭl-le* 'he killed'. In Ṭuroyo the *ll* cluster is reduced to single *l* and the lax vowel *ĭ* replaced by tense *i*: *qṭile* 'he killed'. In the plural, *ll* results from the doubling of the final root consonant and is not reduced (see p. 362). In Christian Urmi and Kerend *ll* is reduced throughout to *l* but there is no concomitant replacement of *ĭ* by *i*.

The cluster *rl which results in the preterite inflection of III*r* verbs is assimilated to *ḷḷ* in Ṭuroyo; the pl. 3c. suffix yields *ṛṛ*. In the remaining NENA dialects *rl is assimilated to *rr*. In Christian Urmi and Kerend *rr* is reduced to *r* without concomitant replacement of *ĭ* by *i*.

	Ṭuroyo	Mangeš	Chr. Urmi	Kerend	
III*l*	*qṭíle*	*qṭĭ́llĭ*	*qṭĭ́li*	*qṭíle*	'he killed'
	qṭĭ́lle	*qṭĭ́lle*	*qṭĭ́lŭn*	*qṭĭ́lu*	'they killed'
III*r*	*mĭ́ḷḷe*	*mĭ́rrĭ*	*mĭ́ri*	*bqĭ́re*	'he said (Kerend: asked)'
	mĭ́ṛṛe	*mĭ́rre*	*mĭ́rŭn*	*bqĭ́ru*	'they said (Kerend: asked)'

Similarly, the cluster *nl which results in the preterite inflection of III*n* verbs is assimilated to *ll* in Ṭuroyo (*mzabắlle* 'he sold'); the pl. 3c. suffix yields *nn* (*mzabắnne* 'they sold'). In the remaining NENA dialects *nl is assimilated to *nn*. In Christian Urmi and Kerend *nn* is reduced to *n* without replacement of *ĭ* by *i* (Kerend *zbĭ́ni* 'I sold').

In Kerend the reduction of the clusters *ll, rr, nn* without concomitant replacement of *ĭ* by *i* only takes place in verbs which are otherwise strong; in weak verbs, however, *ĭ* is replaced by *i*, thus, e.g. *qṭĭ́li* 'I killed' but *xíli* 'I ate', *bqĭ́ri* 'I asked' but *míri* 'I said'.

Table 16.20 Weak verbs, present

Root	Mlaḥsô	Ṭuroyo	Hertevin	Chr. Aradhin	Chr. Urmi	J.Azerbaijan	Kerend	Neo-Mandaic
Iʾy	peš	fóyiš	páyêš	páyiš	páyiš	peš	peš	qáyêm
	peyšó	fáyšo	péša	péša	péša	pešá	pešá	qíma
	peyší	fáyši	péši	péši	péšiy	peší	peší	qimên
Iʾw	govér	gówir	gáwêr	gáwir	gávir	od	hol	ávêd
	govró	gúro	góra	gáwra	góra	odá	holá	ấvda
	govrí	gúri	góri	gáwri	góriy	odí	holí	ấvdên
IIIʾy	hozé	ḥóze	ḥáze	xáze	xázi	xazé	xázé	házi
	hozyó	ḥízyo	ḥázya	xázya	xázya	xázyá	xázyá	házya
	hozí	ḥózin	ḥáze	xaze/i	xáziy	xazé(ni)	xazén(i)	házen

Verbs with Accusative Suffixes

There are various different ways of expressing the direct pronominal object (accusative object) of a verb, depending on the type of inflection (predicative, ergative or copulative) of a given verbal form.

The preterite of Neo-Mandaic, which is the only direct continuation, in all the ENA languages, of the older Aramaic "perfect" (see p. 366) stays outside the following discussion. It has inherited forms with added pronominal suffixes which still resemble the respective Middle Aramaic forms, e.g.

		+ suffix sg. 1	
g²ṭǎl	'he killed'	gǎṭle	'he killed me'
gěṭlǎt	'she killed'	g²ṭǎlte	'she killed me'
g²ṭǎlt	'you killed'	g²ṭǎlte	'you killed me'
g²ṭǎlyǎn	'they killed'	gǎṭlŏnne	'they killed me'
g²ṭǎltŏn	'you (pl.) killed'	g²ṭǎltŏnne	'you (pl.) killed me'
		+ suffix sg. 2m.	
g²ṭǎlni	'we killed'	g²ṭǎlnǎx	'we killed you (m.)'

In verb forms with copulative inflection (see p. 363) a set of pronominal object suffixes, identical with the possessives (see p. 355), is suffixed in certain dialects to the verbal base, e.g. Christian Urmi bǐptáxa ili ~ bǐptáxili 'he is opening', with added suffix sg. 3m. -u: bǐptáxu ili ~ bǐptáxuli (bǐ-ptax-u-li) 'he is opening him (it)', bǐgrášiva 'he was pulling', with added suffix sg. 3f. -o: bǐgrášova (bǐ-graš-o-va) 'he was pulling her'. The following examples from Txuma show the perfect form xziθa ila ~ xzīθala 'she has seen' with pronominal object suffixes:

Object suffix		
Sg. 1c.	xziθi ila	'she has seen me'
Pl. 1c.	xziθǎn ila	'she has seen us'
Sg. 2m.	xziθǔx ila	'she has seen you (m.)'
f.	xziθǎx ila	'she has seen you (f.)'
Pl. 2c.	xziθoxǔn ila	'she has seen you (pl.)'
Sg. 3m.	xziθe ila	'she has seen him'
f.	xziθa ila	'she has seen her'
Pl. 3c.	xziθé ila	'she has seen them'

Verb forms with predicative inflection take a set of object suffixes which consist of the pronominal suffixes (see p. 355) with the preposition l-. These object suffixes are identical with the suffixes of the ergative inflection (see p. 362). The l set suffixes are always suffixed to the inflected form, never to the verbal base. Table 16.21 shows Ṭuroyo ḥóze, Hertevin ḥáze, Kerend xǎzé 'he sees' with pronominal object suffixes.

Table 16.21 Pronominal suffixes

Ṭuroyo ḥóze	Hertevin ḥáze	Kerend xăzé	'he sees'
ḥozéle	ḥazéle	xăzéle	'he sees him'
ḥozéla	ḥazéla	xăzéla	'he sees her'
ḥozắlle	ḥazéle ~ ḥazélehĕn	xăzélu	'he sees them'
ḥozélŭx	ḥazélŏḥ	xăzélox	'he sees you (sg. m.)'
ḥozéläx	ḥazéläḥ	xăzéläx	'he sees you (sg. f.)'
ḥozắlxu	ḥazélehŏn	xăzéläxun	'he sees you (pl. c.)'
ḥozéli	ḥazéli	xăzéli	'he sees me'
ḥozélăn	ḥazélăn	xăzélăn(i)	'he sees us'

A specific feature of the *l* suffixes is the fact that they can express both direct (accusative) and indirect (dative) objects; thus Ṭuroyo *koḥozéli* can mean both 'he sees me' and 'he sees/finds for me'.

In verb forms with ergative inflection there are various concurring and partly overlapping ways of expressing a pronominal object.

1   The verbal base (inflectional base) of an ergatively inflected verb can take predicative inflectional suffixes to express the **patient** (logical object); to this inflected base are joined the ergative suffixes expressing the actor. Thus in Ṭuroyo *grišle* (← *griš* + *-le*) means 'he pulled him', literally, 'pulled is he by him'. By exchanging the inflectional base *griš-* (sg. 3m.) with *grišo-* (sg. 3f.) we get *grišole* 'he pulled her'. In some of the eastern dialects of NENA we find a paradigm fully inflected for the patient, e.g. Christian Urmi:

grīšli	'he pulled him'	
grišītli	'he pulled you (m.)'	
grišīnni	'he pulled me (m.)'	(← *grišīn* + *-li*)
grišáli	'he pulled her'	
grišătli	'he pulled you (f.)'	
grišănni	'he pulled me (f.)'	(← *grišăn* + *-li*)
grišéli	'he pulled them'	
grišétŭnli	'he pulled you (pl. c.)'	
grišăxli	'he pulled us'	

In Ṭuroyo and the westernmost dialects of NENA ergative verb forms can only be inflected for a 3rd person patient. Thus Ṭuroyo has *grišle* 'he pulled him', *grišole* 'he pulled her' and *grišile* 'he pulled them', but not *grišītle* 'he pulled you' etc.

2   In Ṭuroyo and some of the westernmost NENA dialects pronominal objects in ergatively inflected verb forms can be expressed by suffixing the *l* set of pronominal suffixes to the inflected verb form. However, since these suffixes are morphologically identical with the ergative inflectional suffixes, this implies that two identical sets of suffixes can follow one another in two subsequent morphological

slots. The inflectional suffix always comes before the object suffix, thus, e.g., Ṭuroyo ḥzélilŭx (ḥze-li-lŭx) 'I saw you (m.)' vs. ḥzélŭxli (ḥze-lŭx-li) 'you (m.) saw me'.

In Ṭuroyo and the westernmost NENA dialects the two morphological devices described under (1) and (2) above combine in the following way: a 3rd person direct pronominal object is expressed by the predicatively inflected verbal base whereas a 2nd or 1st person direct pronominal object is expressed by the l suffixes, thus, e.g., Ṭuroyo grišóli 'I pulled her' but gríšlilăx (not *grišắtli) 'I pulled you (f.)'. Consequently, a 3rd person object suffix of the l set always implies an indirect (dative) object (ḥzélile 'I saw/found for him') whereas a 2nd or 1st person suffix of the l set can imply both a direct or an indirect object (ḥzélilŭx 'I saw you (m.)' or 'I found for you (m.)').

3   A number of NENA dialects do not allow the l set of object suffixes with ergatively inflected verb forms at all. Instead they join the l suffixes to the corresponding forms of the general present which are then transposed into the preterite by prefixing a special past marker qăm, kĭm (< qdm), e.g.

Ṭuroyo vs.	Christian Aradhin	
ḥzéle	xzéle	'he saw'
	(ixazélŭx	'he sees you (m.)')
ḥzélelŭx	qămxazélŭx	'he saw you (m.)'

Ṭuroyo vs.	Mangeš	
šqíla	šqĭ́lla	'she took'
	(kšăqláli	'she takes me')
šqílali	kĭmšăqláli	'she took me'

In such dialects, as in Ṭuroyo, a 3rd person direct pronominal object is expressed by the predicatively inflected verbal base, the qăm/kĭm construction being used with 2nd or 1st person pronominal objects.

Copula and Possessive Expressions

Copula

Free and enclitic copula   All ENA languages possess an inflected copula which is used with non-verbal predicates. It harks back to the independent personal pronouns, partly supplemented with the particle *īθ which was already used as a copula in Middle Aramaic. In most ENA languages the copula has developed two sets of forms, one enclitic and one free.

Note that the free copula can follow or, more frequently, precede the predicate, whereas the bound copula is enclitical. Being a clitic and not a suffix – it has no influence on word stress, compare Ṭuroyo hắrke 'here', hắrke-no 'I am here' (clitic) vs. ḥóze 'he sees', ḥozéno 'I (m.) see' (suffix).

In most NENA dialects the initial i- of the enclitic copula coalesces with final

Table 16.22   Enclitic copula (allomorphs after a consonant)

		Ṭuroyo	Hertevin	Txuma	Chr. Urmi	Kerend	Neo-Mandaic
Sg.	1m.	-no	-ina	-iwĭn	-ivĭn	-yénă	-na(n)
	f.	-no	-ina	-iwăn	-ivăn	-yắn(ă)	-na(n)
Pl.	1c.	-na	-ĕḥnăḥ	-iwăx	-ivăx	-yéx(in)	-nin
Sg.	2m.	-hĭt	-ihăt	-iwĭθ	-ivĭt	-yet	-yăt
	f.	-hăt	-ihăt	-iwăθ	-ivăt	-yăt	-yăt
Pl.	2c.	-hatu	-ĕḥtŏn	-iθŭn	-itŭn	-yétun	?
Sg.	3m.	-yo	-ile	-ile	-ili	-ye	-ye
Sg.	f.	-yo	-ila	-ila	-ila	-yă	-ta ~ -ti
Pl.	3c.	-ne	-ini	-ilŭn ~ -ina	-ina	-yen(i)	-nŏn

Table 16.23   Free copula

		Ṭuroyo	Hertevin	Txuma	Chr. Urmi	Neo-Mandaic
Sg.	1m.	kĭtno	holĕn	iwĭn	ivĭn	ĕxte
	f.	kĭtno	holăn	iwăn	ivăn	ĕxte
Pl.	1c.	kĭtna	honăḥ	iwăx	ivăx	ĕxtăn
Sg.	2m.	kĭthĭt	holĕt	iwĭθ	ivĭt	ĕxtăx
	f.	kĭthăt	holăt	iwăθ	ivăt	ĕxtĕx
Pl.	2c.	kĭthatu	honitŏn	iθŭn	itŭn	m. ĕxtoxŏn
						f. ĕxtexĕn
Sg.	3m.	kĭtyo	hole	ile	ili	ĕxti
Sg.	f.	kĭtyo	hola	ila	ila	ĕxta
Pl.	3c.	kĭtne	honi	ilŭn ~ ina	ina	ĕxtu

-a of the predicate to yield *-e-*. In this case it is not possible to place a hyphen exactly at the morpheme boundary. A few examples of the enclitic copula in Ṭuroyo and Hertevin:

Ṭuroyo	Hertevin	
ṭắwwo-hĭt	*ṭáwehĕt*	'you (sg. m.) are good'
ṭắwto-hăt	*ṭótehăt*	'you (sg. f.) are good'
ṭắwwe-hatu	*ṭáwĕḥtŏn*	'you (pl. c.) are good'

The copula in negative sentences is always a free form. Examples in a few ENA languages are shown in Table 16.24.

There is also a past copula (free and enclitic forms) and a negative past copula (only free forms), e.g. Ṭuroyo *šafíro-wa ~ kĭtwa šafiro*, Hertevin *šăpiréwa* 'he was beautiful', Ṭuroyo *lắtwa šafiro*, Hertevin *lắwewa šăpira* 'he was not beautiful'.

Table 16.24   Negative copula

		Ṭuroyo	Hertevin	Txuma	Kerend	Neo-Mandaic
Sg.	1m.	lătno	lăwĕn	lewĭn	láyna	lĕxte
	f.	lătno	lăwăn	lewăn	láyăn(a)	lĕxte
Pl.	1c.	lătna	lăwăḥ	lewăx	láyx(in)	lĕxtăn
Sg.	2m.	lăthĭt	lăwĕt	lewĭθ	lăyt	lĕxtĕx
	f.	lăthăt	lăwăt	lewăθ	láyăt	lĕxtĕx
Pl.	2c.	láthatu	lăwĕḥtŏn	leθŭn	láytun	m. lĕxtoxŏn
						f. lĕxtexĕn
Sg.	3m.	lătyo	lăwe	lele	lăy	lĕxti
Sg.	f.	lătyo	lăwa	lela	láyă	lĕxta
Pl.	3c.	lătne	lăwe	lelŭn ~ lena	láyn(i)	lĕxtu

Presentative   Not all ENA languages have a presentative which means 'here he is' or 'here is', e.g. Ṭuroyo *kalé ~ kaléyo* 'here he is', *kalá kŭrfo* 'here is a snake'.

Possessive Expressions

'To have'   The widespread words for 'there is' and 'there is not', Ṭuroyo *kit* and *lăyt*, Christian Urmi *ĭt* and *lĭt*, Kerend *hit* and *lit*, are combined with the preposition *l-* + pronominal suffixes to express the notions of 'to have' and 'to have not'.

Table 16.25   To have

		Ṭuroyo	Hertevin	Chr. Urmi	Kerend	Neo-Mandaic
Sg.	1c.	kĭtli	ĕtli	ĭtliy	hĭti	ĕhle
Pl.	1c.	kĭtlăn	ĕtlăn	ĭtlăn	hĭtăn(i)	ĕhlăn
Sg.	2m.	kĭtlŭx	ĕtlŏḥ	ĭtlŭx	hĭtox	ĕhlăx
	f.	kĭtlăx	ĕtlăḥ	ĭtlăx	hĭtăx	ĕhlĕx
Pl.	2c.	kĭtxu	ĕtlehŏn	ĭtloxŭn	hĭtăxun	m. ĕhloxŏn
						f. ĕhlexĕn
Sg.	3m.	kĭtle	ĕtle	ĭtli	hĭte	ĕhli
Sg.	f.	kĭtla	ĕtla	ĭtla	hĭtă	ĕhla
Pl.	3c.	kĭtte	ĕtle ~ ĕtlehĕn	ĭtlŭn	hĭtu	ĕhlu

'To contain, to be able'   A similar construction with the preposition *b-* expresses the notions of 'to contain; to be able to' and their negatives: Ṭuroyo *kibe/lăybe*, Hertevin *ĕdbe/lĕdbe* etc. These constructions do not occur in the eastern part of the area.

Order of Elements
The preferred word order is SVO.

Table 16.26 To have not

		Ṭuroyo	Hertevin	Chr. Urmi	Kerend	Neo-Mandaic
Sg.	1c.	lắtli	lḗtli	lĭ́tliy	lĭti	lḗhle
Pl.	1c.	lắtlăn	lḗtlăn	lĭ́tlăn	lĭtăn(i)	lḗhlăn
Sg.	2m.	lắtlŭx	lḗtlŏḥ	lĭ́tlŭx	lĭtox	lḗhlăx
	f.	lắtlăx	lḗtlăḥ	lĭ́tlăx	lĭtăx	lḗhlĕx
Pl.	2c.	lắtxu	lḗtlehŏn	lĭ́tloxŭn	lĭtăxun	m. lḗhloxŏn
						f. lḗhlexĕn
Sg.	3m.	lắtle	lḗtle	lĭ́tli	lĭte	lḗhli
Sg.	f.	lắtla	lḗtla	lĭ́tla	lĭtă	lḗhla
Pl.	3c.	lắtte	lḗtle ~ lḗtlehĕn	lĭ́tlŭn	lĭtu	lḗhlu

Further Reading

Western Neo-Aramaic

Arnold, Werner. 1989–. *Das Neuwestaramäische.* 6 vols. (Semitica Viva 4, vols. 1–6). vol. 1, *Texte aus Baxʿa.* 1989. Vol. 2, *Texte aus Ǵubbʿadīn.* 1990. Vol. 3, *Volkskundliche Texte aus Maʿlūla.* 1991. vol. 4, *Orale Literatur aus Maʿlūla.* 1991. Vol. 5, *Grammatik.* 1990. Vol. 6, *Wörterbuch* (forthcoming). Wiesbaden: Harrassowitz.

—— 1989. *Lehrbuch des Neuwestaramäischen* (Semitica Viva, Series Didactica 1). Wiesbaden: Harrassowitz.

Correll, Christoph. 1978. *Untersuchungen zur Syntax der neuwestaramäischen Dialekte des Antilibanon* (Abhandlungen für die Kunde des Morgenlandes 44,4). Wiesbaden: Franz Steiner.

Spitaler, Anton. 1938. *Grammatik des neuaramäischen Dialekts von Maʿlūla (Antilibanon)* (Abhandlungen für die Kunde des Morgenlandes 23,1). Leipzig: DMG.

Eastern Neo-Aramaic

Avinery, Iddo. 1988. *The Aramaic Dialect of the Jews of Zākhō* (in Hebrew). Jerusalem: The Israel Academy of Sciences and Humanities.

Fox, Samuel Ethan. 1991–1992. "The Phonology and Morphology of the Jilu Dialect of Neo-Aramaic." *Journal of Afro-Asiatic Languages* 3: 35–57.

Friedrich, Johannes. 1959. "Neusyrisches in Lateinschrift aus der Sowjetunion." *Zeitschrift der deutschen morgenländischen Gesellschaft* 109: 50–81.

—— 1960. *Zwei russische Novellen in neusyrischer Übersetzung und Lateinschrift* (Abhandlungen für die Kunde des Morgenlandes 33,4). Wiesbaden: Franz Steiner (distributor).

Garbell, Irene. 1964. "Flat Words and Syllables in Jewish East New Aramaic of Persian Azerbaijan and the Contiguous Districts (A Problem in Multilingualism)." In *Studies in Egyptology and Linguistics in Honor of H. J. Polotsky,* ed. H. B. Rosen. Jerusalem: The Israel Exploration Society.

—— 1965. *The Jewish Neo-Aramaic Dialect of Persian Azerbaijan.* The Hague: Mouton.

Goldenberg, Gideon. 1992. "Aramaic Perfects." *Israel Oriental Studies* 12: 113–137.

Heinrichs, Wolfhart ed. 1990. *Studies in Neo-Aramaic* (Harvard Semitic Studies 36). Atlanta: Scholars Press.

Hetzron, Robert. 1969. "The Morphology of the Verb in Modern Syriac (Christian Colloquial of Urmi)." *Journal of the American Oriental Society* 89: 112–127.

Hoberman, Robert D. 1985. "The Phonology of Pharyngeals and Pharyngealization in Pre-Modern Aramaic." *Journal of the American Oriental Society* 104: 221–231.

—— 1988. "The History of the Modern Aramaic Pronouns and Pronominal Suffixes." *Journal of the American Oriental Society* 108: 557–575.

—— 1989. *The Syntax and Semantics of Verb Morphology in Modern Aramaic: A Jewish Dialect of Iraqi Kurdistan.* New Haven: American Oriental Society.

—— 1990. "Reconstructing Pre-Modern Aramaic Morphology: The Independent Pronouns. In *Studies in Neo-Aramaic* (Harvard Semitic Studies 36), ed. Wolfhart Heinrichs. Atlanta: Scholars Press. 79–88.

Hopkins, Simon. 1989. "Neo-Aramaic Dialects and the Formation of the Preterite." *Journal of Semitic Studies* 34: 413–432.

Jacobi, Heidi. 1973. *Grammatik des thumischen Neuaramäisch (Nordostsyrien)* (Abhandlungen für die Kunde des Morgenlandes 40,3). Wiesbaden: Franz Steiner (distributor).

Jastrow, Otto. 1993. *Laut- und Formenlehre des neuaramäischen Dialekts von Mīdin im Ṭūr ʿAbdīn.* (Semitica Viva 9). Wiesbaden: Harrassowitz.

—— 1988. *Der neuaramäische Dialekt von Hertevin (Provinz Siirt)* (Semitica Viva 3). Wiesbaden: Ḥarrassowitz.

—— 1990. "Personal and Demonstrative Pronouns in Central Neo-Aramaic." In *Studies in Neo-Aramaic* (Harvard Semitic Studies 36), ed. Wolfhart Heinrichs. Atlanta: Scholars Press. 89–103.

—— 1992. *Lehrbuch der Ṭuroyo-Sprache* (Semitica Viva, Series Didactica 2). Wiesbaden: Harrassowitz.

—— 1994. *Der neuaramäische Dialekt von Mlaḥsô* (Semitica Viva 14). Wiesbaden: Harrassowitz.

Krotkoff, Georg. 1982. *A Neo-Aramaic Dialect of Kurdistan: Texts, Grammar, and Vocabulary.* New Haven: American Oriental Society.

—— 1990. "An Annotated Bibliography of Neo-Aramaic." In *Studies in Neo-Aramaic* (Harvard Semitic Studies 36), ed. Wolfhart Heinrichs. Atlanta: Scholars Press. 3–26.

Maclean, Arthur John. 1895. *Grammar of the Dialects of Vernacular Syriac.* Cambridge: Cambridge University Press.

—— 1901. *Dictionary of the Dialects of Vernacular Syriac.* Oxford: Oxford University Press.

Macuch, Rudolf. 1965. *Handbook of Classical and Modern Mandaic.* Berlin: de Gruyter.

—— 1989. *Neumandäische Chrestomathie mit grammatischer Skizze, kommentierter Übersetzung und Glossar* (Porta Linguarum Orientalium, new series 18). Wiesbaden: Harrassowitz.

—— 1993. *Neumandäische Texte im Dialekt von Ahwāz* (Semitica Viva 10). Wiesbaden: Harrassowitz.

Marogulov, Q. I. 1976. *Grammaire néo-syriaque pour ecoles d'adultes (dialecte d'Urmiah),* trans. Olga Kapeliuk (Groupe Linguistique d'Études Chamito-Sémitiques Supplément 5). Paris: Librairie Orientaliste Paul Geuthner.

Nakano, Akiʾo. 1973. *Conversational Texts in Eastern Neo-Aramaic (Gzira Dialect)* (Study of Languages and Cultures of Asia and Africa A4). Tokyo: Institute for the Study of Languages and Cultures of Asia and Africa.

Nöldeke, Theodor. 1868. *Grammatik der neusyrischen Sprache am Urmia-See und in Kurdistan.* Leipzig: T. O. Weigel.

Odisho, Edward Y. 1988. *The Sound System of Modern Assyrian (Neo-Aramaic)* (Semitica Viva 2). Wiesbaden: Harrassowitz.

Pennacchietti, Fabrizio A. and Mauro Tosco. 1991. *Testi Neo-Aramaici dell'Unione Sovietica raccolti da Enrico Cerulli* (Istituto Universitario Orientale, Dipartimento di Studi Asiatici, series minor 35). Naples: Istituto Universitario Orientale.

Polotsky, H. J. 1961. "Studies in Modern Syriac." *Journal of Semitic Studies* 6: 1–13.

—— 1979. "Verbs with Two Objects in Modern Syriac (Urmi)." *Israel Oriental Studies* 9: 204–227.

—— 1986. "Neusyrische Konjugation." In *On the Dignity of Man: Oriental and Classical Studies in Honour of Frithiof Rundgren,* ed. Tryggve Kronholm and Eva Riad (Orientalia Suecana 33–35). Stockholm: Almqvist and Wiksell.

Ritter, Hellmut. 1967–1990. *Ṭūrōyo: Die Volkssprache der syrischen Christen des Ṭūr ʿAbdīn.* 5 vols. A, *Texte,* vols. 1–3. 1967–1971. Beirut: Franz Steiner (distributor). B, *Wörterbuch.* 1979. Beirut: Franz Steiner (distributor). C, *Grammatik.* 1990. Stuttgart: Franz Steiner.

Sachau, Eduard. 1895. *Skizze des Fellichi-Dialekts von Mosul.* Berlin: Verlag der Königlichen Akademie der Wissenschaften.

Sara, Solomon I. 1974. *A Description of Modern Chaldean.* The Hague: Mouton.

Tsereteli, Konstantin. 1978. *Grammatik der modernen assyrischen Sprache (Neuostaramäisch),* trans. Peter Nagel. Leipzig: VEB Verlag Enzyklopädie.

17 The Modern South Arabian Languages

Marie-Claude Simeone-Senelle

In the south of the Arabian Peninsula, in the Republic of Yemen and in the Sultanate of Oman, live some 200,000 Arabs whose maternal language is not Arabic but one of the so-called Modern South Arabian Languages (MSAL). This designation is very inconvenient because of the consequent ambiguity, but a more appropriate solution has not been found so far. Although there exists a very close relationship with other languages of the same Western South Semitic group, the MSAL are different enough from Arabic to make intercomprehension impossible between speakers of any of the MSAL and Arabic speakers. The MSAL also exhibit many common features with the Semitic languages of Ethiopia; their relationships with Epigraphic South Arabian (Sahaydic Languages, according to Beeston) remain a point of discussion.

There are six MSAL: Mehri (M), Ḥarsūsi (Ḥ), Baṭhari (B), Hobyōt (Hb.), Jibbāli (Jib.), also known as *Ehhkili, eḥkli, šhawri, šxawri, šheri, šḥeri, qarāwi* (cf. Johnstone 1981: xi), Soqoṭri (S.). (See p. 420 for other abbreviations used in this chapter.)

Mehri is the most widespread language, spoken by the Mahra tribes (about 100,000 speakers) and some Beyt Kathir, in the mountains of Dhofar in Oman, and in the Yemen, in the far eastern governorate, on the coast, between the border of Oman and the eastern bank of Wadi Masilah, and not in the Mukalla area, contrary to Johnstone's statement (1975: 94); in the north-west of the Yemen, Mehri is spoken as far as Thamud, on the border of the Rub' al-Khali.

The Yemenite Mehri speakers distinguish two groups among the Mehri dialects; they call the variety of Mehri spoken west of Ras Fartak [mehrīyət], and [mehriyōt] the Mehri of the *Sharqiya*, the eastern area (including the Mehri of Dhofar). Johnstone (1975: 94) quotes *məhrəyyət* as the name of the language in Dhofar.

The Mahra inhabitants of the desert steppe of the Yemen, as well as in the mountains of Dhofar in Oman, are semi-nomads who breed camels, cows and goats. Some bedouin in the Yemen are owners of four-wheel-drive cars which enable them to trade with other countries of the peninsula, providing supplies for numerous shops in the coastal towns and villages of the Mahra. In the area of Qishn, bedouin cultivate palm trees.

Ḥarsūsi [ḥərsíyət] is spoken by the Ḥarāsīs and the 'Ifār, in the area of Jiddat al-Ḥarāsīs (north-east of Dhofar). The number of speakers was put at no more than 600 by Johnstone (1977: x), but this reckoning was made during the period when many Ḥarāsīs had left their region to go and work in oil wells. Since then, many of them have returned.

Baṭḥari is the language of the Baṭāḥira who live on the southern coast of Oman, in the Jāzir area, between Hāsik and Ras Sharbithāt. Their number is put at about 300 (Morris 1983: 130); they are "pastoral cave-dwellers and fishermen" (Johnstone 1975: 94).

Ḥarsūsi and Baṭḥari are very closely related to Mehri; as for Hobyōt [həwbyốt], the very recent development of the research on this language (at least, Hobyōt spoken in the Yemen, discovered in 1985) relates it to the Mehri group, even though regular contacts with Jibbāli speakers have an effect upon this speech. The Hobyōt speakers, less than one hundred in number, claim to belong to the Mahra tribe. They breed camels, cows and goats in the mountains, on the border between Oman and the Yemen (in the area of Jadib and Hawf, and Haberut seems to be the northern boundary of their area). They spend the rainy season with their cattle in caves, up in the mountains, and then go down to their settlements of round houses covered with branches.

The Jibbāli language [gəblēt]/[śḥerēt] received many names in the scientific literature, the most common of which being Šḥauri, Eḥkili, Qarāwi, Šḥeri. Johnstone (1981: xi–xii) chose [Jibbāli] during fieldwork as the name that the speakers do not consider pejorative. It is spoken in Oman "by a number of communities of different social status and tribal origin, numbering together about 5,000" (Johnstone 1975: 94). Jibbāli speakers live in the mountains of Dhofar where they are semi-nomads, rearing camels and cows, and collecting frankincense; in the coastal villages of this area (Raysūt, Ṣalāla, Mirbaṭ, Sidḥ) they carry on various jobs. The Baṭāḥira, who breed cattle in the mountains of Wādi Ezdaḥ, east of the road to Thamrit, speak Jibbāli (Morris 1983: 143, n.1); the inhabitants of the Kūria Mūria Islands are fishermen who speak a specific variety of the Jibbāli language.

Like the Jibbāli speakers, the Soqoṭris have no particular word for their language; it is named Soqoṭri [skʌtri]. It is spoken in the Yemen, on the island of Soqoṭra and the neighbouring islets of 'Abd-al-Kūri and Samḥa. The inhabitants of Soqoṭra are put at 50,000, those of 'Abd-al-Kūri at about 250 (Naumkin 1988: 342, 359) and at ten or a dozen in Samḥa. On the coasts the inhabitants are fishermen and cultivate date palms; in the mountains cave dwellers. Bedouin rear camels, cows and goats; in hamlets people cultivate millet, and in the eastern area, they collect the gum of the dragon's blood tree. The inhabitants of 'Abd-al-Kūri and Samḥa live on fishing.

Dialectology and Sociolinguistic Situation
Mehri, Jibbāli and Soqoṭri have a very rich dialectology for which sociological and geographical parameters are relevant.

Map 4   Location of the MSAL region

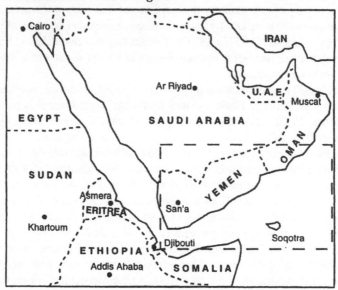

In the Mehri language, there is a very clear distinction between the variety spoken in Dhofar and in the far east of the Yemen and the western variety. Within one and the same dialectal area there are, in addition, differences between bedouin varieties and city or village dwellers' varieties. The dialect of Qishn, the former capital of the Mahra is very prestigious in the Yemen.

In Jibbāli, Johnstone (1981: xii) makes a distinction between the central, eastern and western dialects.

Regarding Soqoṭri, it is possible to distinguish four groups between the surveyed dialects: the dialects of the northern coastal villages (including the main one, Hadibo), those of the southern coast, the varieties spoken by the bedouin in the Hagher Mountains (in the center of the island), and the dialects of the area of Qalansiyah (far west). The dialect of ʿAbd-al-Kūri is apart, whereas that of Samḥa belongs to the western dialects of Soqoṭra (Naumkin 1988: 343, 344).

The languages spoken in Dhofar have a particular status because they are in contact with both Arabic (as the other MSAL) and the other MSAL of the region. Native speakers use their mother tongue for private purposes, in the family circle and with other speakers of the same language; many a speaker uses several MSAL, when these languages are closely related.

Intercomprehension between Soqoṭri or Jibbāli speakers and speakers of any other MSAL is impossible. When in contact with each other, they resort to Arabic, as with Arabic speakers. Both in Oman and in the Yemen, Arabic is the language used for official intercourse (administration, schools, the army). As for cultural activities, the texts collected since 1898 in Mehri, Jibbāli, Soqoṭri and Baṭhari prove that these languages possess a rich oral literature consisting mainly of tales and poetry.

Map 5   The Modern South Arabian languages

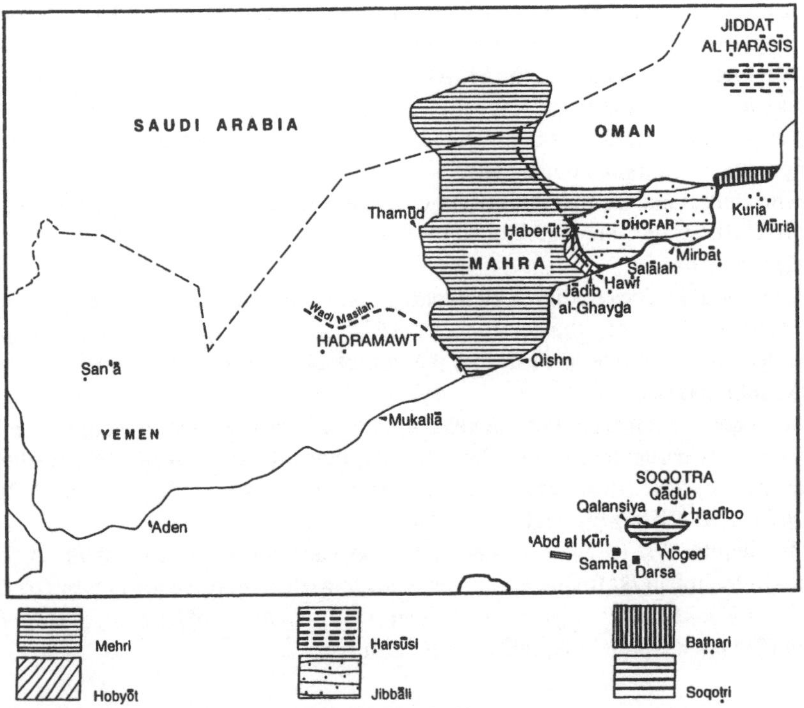

Source: Marie-Claude Simeone-Senelle, CNRS-LLACAN

Phonology and Phonetics

The Consonants

	plosive	fricative	ejective	nasal	liquid	rolled
labial	b	f		m		
interdental		θ ð	θ̣			
denti-alveolar	t d		ṭ	n	l	r
		s z	ṣ			
palato-alveolar		š	š̌			
lateral-alveolar		ś	ṣ́			
palatal	y					
velar	k g	x γ	ḳ			
labio-velar		w				
pharyngeal		ḥ ʿ				
laryngeal	ʾ	h				

The consonantal system of the MSAL is the closest, among the modern Semitic languages, to the reconstructed system of Proto-Semitic. They are the only ones with three alveolar fricatives. In addition, the MSAL also have a phoneme *ǧ*.

Another typical feature of the MSAL is the post-glottalized realization, as in the Ethiopian languages, of the emphatic consonants of the Semitic; it is of great interest because it questions the hypothesis of a Cushitic influence on the Semitic languages of Ethiopia in this matter.

The central dialect of Jibbāli (cJ) has a phoneme /ṣ̌/ (labialized *ṣ̌*) contrasting with /š/: JL *ebrítṣ̌* 'your (sg. f.) daughter', *ebrítš* 'his daughter', where the eastern dialect only has /š/.

Only Soqotri does not have interdentals. The merging of the interdentals with the dentals in some city dialects in western Mahra is a sociolinguistic phenomenon and does not lead one to infer that the consonantal system of Yemenite Mehri lacks interdentals.

In Soqotri, the merging of the velar fricatives /x/ and /γ/ with the pharyngeals /ḥ/ and /ʿ/ is particular to some dialects only, those studied before 1985; in other dialects the velar fricatives do occur, even in native words: SQa *xə́məh* (SQb *ḥímeh*) 'five'; SQa *γə́yǧ* (SHo *ʿéyǧ*) 'man'.

To Semitic */š/ (~ /s/ in Arabic and Ethiopian) corresponds /š/ or /h/ in the MSAL. In Jibbāli /š/ frequently corresponds to Mehri /h/, to Soqotri /h/ or /š/: JL *šő ʿ* (*b > Ø*), ML *hōba*, SQb *yhőbə ʿ* 'seven (m.)'; JL *-hum*, MQn *-həm*, SQa *-hən/ -šən* (3rd person plural masculine pronoun suffix).

The Laterals *ś* and *ṣ́*

These fricatives have an apico-alveolar articulation: the tongue tip is on the alveolar ridge and the lateral fricative sound is produced by the air flowing out of the passage opened by lowering the mid section of the tongue and retracting the corner of the mouth, generally at the right side. The glottalized *ṣ́* is often voiced (see below). This lateral articulation of *ḍ*, the Arabic reflex of *ṣ́*, was described in the eighth century by Sībawayhi.

The Ejective Consonants

The prevailing articulation of the 'emphatic' consonants is not, as in Arabic, a velarization, but a post-glottalization. For greater convenience, these consonants are written with a subscript dot, but the articulation is indeed ejective: [θ'], [t'], [s'], [š']/[š̃'], [ś'], [k']. The degree of this glottalization varies, depending on the position of the consonant in the word and on the dialects concerned: for instance, in some Soqotri dialects, the glottalization is weaker, and in the Mehri dialect of Qishn, the constriction of the glottis is not complete and provokes a laryngealization or creaky voice; under such conditions, some emphatics become voiced (for instance *θ* is often pronounced as [δ]). Johnstone (1975: 98) has shown that, in the languages of Dhofar, glottalized consonants are to be grouped with the voiced consonants from a morphological point of view: for instance, words with initial voiced or glottalized consonant take the prefix *a-/ɛ-*, which is the definite article in the nominal system and a morpheme of derivation in the verbal system, this morpheme being zero in front of voiceless consonants.

In the Mehri of Qishn, laryngealization may spread to the direct vicinity of the consonant or even to the entire word (Lonnet and Simeone-Senelle 1983: 191–193).

The Glottalized Palato-alveolar š́

This phoneme š́ ([ṣ̌] in central Jibbāli) occurs in all the MSAL. There are few occurrences of it and the phoneme never appears in the same words in the six MSAL: MQn *hašbá'*, ML *š́əbá'*, HHt *hīš́əbá'*, B (*ML*) *hašbáʕ*, ḤL *hašbá'*, J (*ML*) *'ɛšbáʕ*, but *JL 'išbáʕ*, HHf *'īš́əbáʕ*, SQb *'əsbaʕ* 'finger'.

š́ may be connected with some rules of phonetic evolution. This phonologized variant often comes from the palatalization of /ḳ/: J (*ML*) *šuyēt*, JL *š́uyēt*, ML *ḳáymət* 'judgment day'; SHr *š́édhər*, ML *ḳādər* 'pot'; J (*ML*) *məš́hayrér*, JL *məš́hérér*, ML *məḳhayrīr* 'shin bone'. It may be a very particular evolution of /ṣ/ or /š/: ML *š́əfdēt*, ḤL *š́əfdáyt* 'frog' (see Arabic *ḍufdaʕa*), but in a few occurrences, no explanation can be provided:

SQa *š́áʕš́aʕ* 'to take a little sip', *hǝ́nš́eh* '(name of) shellfish'
MQn *š́ənš́ə́n* 'snail (col.)'
MQn *š́áffī*, ML *š́əffáy*, HHt *š́ífe'*, B (*ML*) *š́əffáyh* 'elbow'
MDt *bəš́ī́n*, HHf *biš́ʕī́n* 'Tristram's grackle' (here, š́ may be a variant of š́ before ʕ)
JL *š́úrúm* 'to sulk'

The Pharyngeal ʕ

ʕ has a particular status in Ḥarsūsi and in some dialects of Mehri where it occurs very rarely (e.g., out of 403 words with a /ʕ/ in the root, [ʕ] occurs only in forty-four words, mainly borrowed words from Arabic). Generally, the pharyngeal is replaced by the laryngeal ', or is only but a virtual phoneme influencing the length and the timbre of the vowel in contact, sometimes inducing a diphthong. In Mehri, this phenomenon seems to be less common in the dialects of the Yemen (except those of the area of Qishn) than in the Mehri of Dhofar:

⟨ʕfr⟩: MDt, MJb *ʕ́ɔ́fər*, MQnB *ɔ́fər*, ML *'ɔ́fər*; ḤL *'áfər*; Hb. *ʕ́ɔ́fər*, B (*ML*) *ʕáfər*, JL *ʕ́ɔ́fər*; S (*ML*) *ʕáfər* 'red'

Often, where ʕ occurs, its status is unstable. The same speaker for the same word may or may not pronounce it: MDt *šáʕθayt* or *šáθayt* 'three', and its occurrence is not predictable: MDt, Hb. *fám* (sg.), *fáʕmtə* (pl.) 'foot, leg'; ML *rēʕi* 'herder' and *rō* 'to herd'.

The Laryngeal '

In Mehri, Hobyōt, Ḥarsūsi, the initial and non-etymological *h* and *h* may be the development of the laryngeal ': MQn, ML həbér, ḤL ḥəbyār 'female camels'; MQn, ML ḥáyb, Hb. ḥéb, 'father'. In a word such as MQn ḥəróh, ML ḥərōh, ḤL ḥərīh, (B (ML) ērīh) 'head', ḥ seems to be the trace of a lost article (absent in Mehri of the Yemen, Ḥarsūsi, Hobyōt but not in Mehri of Oman).

The So-called "Parasite h" in Soqoṭri

A typical feature of Soqoṭri, the occurrence of this non-etymological and non-morphological h (in nouns and very rarely in verbs) is related to the particular evolution of the long vowels and to the rules of stress in Soqoṭri: stress falls on the penultimate or antepenultimate syllable. The vowel (formerly long) of the syllable might be preserved by this h (more rarely by '): SQb ṣʌlə́lhɛn/ṣʌlélihɔn 'small valley, small stream'; SHo líbʰhɔn 'white'.

A particular articulation of the consonants, with the vocal cords apart at one end, occurs in Soqoṭri, and this phenomenon ([ʰ]), called murmur or breathy voice, may affect the neighbouring vowels and therefore contribute to the occurrence of the parasite h (Lonnet and Simeone-Senelle 1997).

Palatalization

The palatalization is common to all the MSAL (cf. the Semitic root ⟨kbd⟩ ~ ⟨šbd⟩ in MSAL) and a palatalized consonant may be phonologized (cf. /ṣ̌/).

Palatalized /g/, /k/ and /ḳ/ occur in all the MSAL, but to different degrees: /g/ > voiced pre-palatal [ž], [žʸ] in Soqoṭri, [ẓ̌] (labialized ẓ̌) in JL, voiced palato-alveolar [ğ] in Mehri and Hobyōt:

SQb [ɣáž-əh], SAK ['áẓ̌ʸəh] 'woman'
JL [ɣažét], HHt [ɣoğğít] 'big girl'
MQn [ɣağğến] 'boy'

In some Soqoṭri dialects, /k/ > [c], /ḳ/ > [ç], when in contact with /i/: SQa ikə̃́təb 'he writes', di-ḳáʿr 'of the house' and SQb icə̃́təb, dʲçaʿr.

The Retroflex Clusters

In the Mehri and the Hobyōt of the Yemen, /r/ plus a following denti-/lateral-alveolar consonant have both a retroflex articulation:

MQn [kíṭṣ̌], HHt [kéṭṣ̌] 'belly'
MMf [ḳáṛṇət] 'womb'
MQn ḵeśēr-l-śiǧártən [keśếṛḽṣ̌iǧáṛṭən] 'the barks of trees'
MJb harṣ̌ốm > [haṛẓ̌ốm] 'tops of the feet'

The Consonants /m/ and /b/

In Jibbāli, these two etymological consonants never occur in intervocalic position; this non-occurrence affects the length and timbre of the vowel; the long vowels and the nasalized ones are the phonetic results of this phenomenon: JL ɛrḥím, ɛrḥī́t/ɛrḥḗt 'beautiful'; ɣɔ̄r/yɣḗr/yɣbírə 'to meet'.

In Mehri, in the paradigm of a few verbs, /b/ does not occur in intervocalic position: MQn *ṭalōm* 'they requested' (*ṭalōb* 'he requested'); MQn *ṣɔ́ṭ/yəṣɔ́ṭ* ⟨ṣbṭ⟩ 'he took/he takes'.

The Processing of /l/

In Jibbāli, and in some Soqoṭri dialects, /l/ has a fricative variant *ź*: JL [gíźɔ́l] (*ML gīlɔ́l*) 'cooked/boiled (food)'; SQa [ṣáźəʕ] (SHo *ṣálʕ*) 'rib'.

In Eastern Mehri and sometimes in Ḥarsūsi, /l/ > *w*: ḤL [ḥəwḵāt] (MQn *ḥəlḵát*, *ML ḥewḵāt*) 'circle', with an analogical plural [ḥewēḵ] (*ML ḥelēḵ*).

In a stressed syllable *l* is reduced to zero and the length and timbre of the vowel change: *ML sēmək* 'I was safe' (/sɔ́lmək/).

Pausal Forms

In pausal forms, some final voiced consonants are often devoiced and realized as ejectives in Mehri of the Yemen. In some dialects of Soqoṭri, only final /ʕ/ is concerned:

MJb *dəmḗɣ* > [dəmḗx'] 'brain'
MQn *ǧíd* > [ǧít'] 'good'
SQb *ṭɔ́dəʕ* > [ṭɔ́dəḥ'] 'back'

The Vowels

Not all the vowels occur in all the MSAL. Systems vary according to each language. The quantity and timbre of the vowels are linked to stress rules and the consonantic environment (i.e. the occurrence or not of the glottalized, pharyngeals, velars).

Among the MSAL, Jibbāli and Soqoṭri are noticeable on account of the richness of the vocalic timbres. Diphthongs *ay*, *aw* frequently occur in Mehri, Ḥarsūsi and Hobyōt, but rarely in Soqoṭri and almost never in Jibbāli.

In Mehri the vowel system has two or three (according to the dialects) short vowels /a/, /ə/, (/ɛ/), six long vowels /ī/, /ē/, /ḗ/, /ā/, /ō/, /ū/. As Johnstone noted (1975: 103), it is difficult to distinguish phonetically *ō* from *ū* (even the same speaker may in the same sentence use *āmərút* or *āmərṓt* 'she said'), and *ī* from *ē*, even if rare minimal pairs do occur such as *ML kəbkīb* 'star' ≠ *kəbkéb* 'entry' and *ktōb* 'book' ≠ *ktūb* 'he wrote'.

In Jibbāli and Soqoṭri, the range of vowels is: *i, e, ɛ, ə, a, ɔ, o, u* (Johnstone 1981: xv). In these two MSAL, in which the range of vowels is larger, the contrast between long and short vowels is not always phonological. In Jibbāli, the long vowels result from the integration of the definite article (ε-/a-) or from the processing of b/w or of y:

JL ʾɛrní, def. ʾērni 'hare'
ʾɔb, def. ʾɔ̄b 'door'
šəgēb (š-gwb) 'to answer'
ōṣəf (wṣf) 'to describe'
ḳēl (ḳbl) 'to accept'
lūn (lbn) 'white (m.)'
gēr (gyr) 'to oppress'

In Jibbāli, nasal vowels are combinative variants resulting from the influence of m in intervocalic position: JL (xmr) xēr 'wine', oxɔ̄r 'to make drunk', axtīr 'to drink wine'; ylūʿ (lmʿ) 'it shines'.

In the Mehri of the Yemen, in Hobyōt and in Soqoṭri, vowels in contact with nasal consonants are frequently nasalized: MQn [amū̃ṣʌɣ] 'I chew'; HHf [tūmʰ] 'you (pl. m.)'; SQaB [ɣãs] (SQa ɣans), SNd [ʿãs] (SQb ʿans) 'elbow'.

Other Phenomena

Syllabic Structure and Stress
The most common syllabic structures are CV(C) or CV:. In initial position, we find (C)CV(C) or (C)CV:, and in final position: CV(C(C)) or CV:(C).

In Jibbāli, triconsonantal groups occur: JL śɔttf '(meat) to become dry', śśféf 'to be able to be dried', íkkbéb 'he stoops'.

The stress in Mehri, Hobyōt, Baṭhari, Ḥarsūsi is on the last long syllable or on the first syllable if there are only short syllables in the stress unit.

Jibbāli is particular in the sense that a word or a stress unit can have several stressed syllables: JL minšérɔ́t (ML mənkərét) 'middle finger'. When a word has only one stress, it is on the same syllable as the Mehri word: JL mišəndɔ́t (ML məkəndét) 'thumb'.

In Soqoṭri, the general trend is to have the stress toward the beginning of the word. This phenomenon has led to the dividing of the vowel, having lost stress and length, by the emergence of a so-called parasite h: SQa ḳáṭmehəm (ML ḳaṭmīm, JL ḳaṭmím) 'butter'; SQa ʾírhɛz (MQnB hayrēz, ML yərēz, JL ʾirɔ́z) 'rice'.

Gemination
Gemination occurs in all the MSAL to various degrees according to the language, very rare in Soqoṭri. It never has a morphological value (as in Arabic, for instance). Its origin may be lexical with roots C2 = C3, or C3 = C4, or C4 = C5:

MDt dəkk 'he sprung up', śxəwəllɔ́t 'she stayed'
ML ḳəṭəbbūt 'doll'
HHf mǧəllɔ́t 'type of house'
JL esəḥḥɔ́š 'he cured him' (aṣḥáḥ 'he cured')

The origin may also be phonetic or morpho-phonetic, due to the assimilation of some radical consonants in contact with *t* (derivational morpheme):

MDt *haδδūr* ⟨h-t-δr⟩ 'to take care'
MQn *'áṣṣʌd* ⟨'-t-ṣd⟩ 'to be anxious'
ML *ḱáššəl* ⟨ḱ-t-šl⟩ 'to be broken'
ḤL *háttəm* ⟨h-t-mm⟩ 'to be sad'
JL *múttəs* ⟨m-t-ss⟩ 'to be bitten'

In Jibbāli gemination occurs in the derived verbal themes (by vocalic prefix and vocalic modification): in the perfect, *eššóḱər* 'to squint' ⟨šḱr⟩, and/or in the imperfect: *yaššóḱərən, íffhɔ́š* 'he boils' (*efhéš*, causative of *fhɛš*).

The process of gemination in the MSAL is related to the syllabic structure. In the morphological variation of verbs and nouns, gemination does not affect the same consonant; a shifting of gemination may occur, and according to the forms of the paradigms, gemination affects either a consonant of the root or the derivational morpheme: MQnB *féttək* ⟨f-t-kk⟩ 'he got rid of' and sg. 3f. *ftəkkɔ́t, kʌṣṣáwr* ⟨ḱ-t-ṣr⟩ 'he shortened', and sg. 3f. *kʌṣarrūt; lšáḥḥaš* ⟨š-ḥšš⟩ 'he tracks (subj.)'; ḤL *kəṭṭəbōt* ⟨kṭbb⟩ (pl. *kaṭəbāb*) 'doll'; JL *dekk//yɔ́ddək* (subj.) 'to bump (against)'; *míxxəl*, active participle of *axlél* '(water) to penetrate'.

Morphology

Personal Pronouns

Table 17.1   Independent pronouns

		MY (*ML*)	HHf	ḤL	JL	SQa, SQb
Sg.	1c.	hoh (=)	hoh	hoh	hé	hɔh(hɔn), ho[h]
	2m.	hēt (=)	het	hēt	het	het
	f.	hēt (=)	hit	hēt	hit	hit
	3m.	heh (=)	heh	hah	šɛ	y[h]eh, heh
	f.	seh (=)	seh	sēh	sɛ	se[h]
Du.	1c.	tī (əkɔ́y)	tī	ətī	ti	ki[h]
	2c.	tī (ətáy)	tī	ətī	ti	ti[h]
	3c.	hī (hay)	hī	hī	ši	he[h]i, hi
Pl.	1c.	nḥa (ənḥa)	nḥa	ənḥā	nḥa, nḥan	ḥan(hɔn)
	2m.	tēm (ətēm)	tum [tūm[h]]	ətōm	tum	tan
	f.	tēn (ətēn)	ten [ten[h]]	ətēn	ten	tan
	3m.	hēm (=)	hum [hūm[h]]	hōm	šum	yhan
	f.	sēn (=)	sen [sen[h]]	sēn	sen	san

Independent Pronouns
The dual pronouns bear the marker of the nominal dual -*i*. In the Mehri language

Table 17.2 Pronouns with singular and plural nouns, verbs and prepositions

	MY = ML	HHf	ḤL	JL	SQb
Sg. 1c.	-i/-yɛ //-ī, əy	-i/-iyɔ //-ī	-i/-yɛ //-əni(yɛ)	-i/-i	-ɔyʰ, əʾ
2m.	-k/-kɛ //-ūk	-k/-kɛ //-ōk	-ək/-iyək //-ōk	-k/-ɛk	-k
f.	-š/-šɛ //-īš, ēš	-š/-šɛ //-īš	-əš/-iyəš //-əš	-š/-ɛš	-š
3m.	-h/-hɛ //-eh, īh	-h/-hɛ //-eh	-əh/-iyəh //-ɔ́h	-š/-ɛš	-h, -š
f.	-s/-sɛ //-īs	-s/-sɛ //-ēs	-əs/- iyəs //-īs	-s/-ɛs	-s
Du. 1c.	-ki/-iki //-īki, əki	-ki/-eki // [?]	-ki/-iki //-əki	-ši/-ɛši	-ki
2c.	-ki/-iki //-īki, əki	[?]	-ki/-iki //-əki	-ši/-ɛši	-ki
3c.	-hi /-īhi //-īhi, əhi	[?]	-hi /-ihi //-əhi	-ši/-ɛši	-hi
Pl. 1c.	-ən/-iən //-yən, īn	-ən/-yən //-ēn	-ən/-iyən //-ayn	-ən/-ɛn	-ən
2m.	-kəm/-ikəm //-īkəm	kum/-īkum //-ōkum	kən/-ikən //-ōkəm	-kun/-ɔkun	-kən
f.	kən/-ikən //-īkən	kən/-ikən //-ēkən	kən/-ikən //-īkən	-kən/-ɛkən	-kən
3m.	həm/- ihem //-ihem	hum/- īhum //-ōhum	həm/-iham //-ōhem	-hum/-ɔhum	-hən, -šɛn
f.	sən/-ısn/-īsən	sən/-īsən /-īsən	sən/-isən //-īssn	-sɛn/-sɛn	-sɛn

of Qishn and the surrounding area, there are no dual pronouns (pronominal and verbal duals are obsolete).

Independent pronouns generally stand for the subject of the sentence. It can be apposed to a noun with a suffix pronoun: MQn *beyt-i-hoh* 'it is my house'. With the connecting particle *ð-/d-*, it is used to express possession: MQn *sakkēr-k d-hēt* 'it is your sugar, (sugar) for you'. HHf *lhḗtə ð-hi* 'their (du.) cows', SQb *di-ḥan ḳaʿr* 'our house'. It can follow some prepositions: *JL lə-hés šɛ́* 'like him'.

Suffix Pronouns

In *ML, ḤL, JL*, the suffix pronouns can only be added to a definite noun (with an article): *ML a-γərōy-əh* 'his speech' (MQn *γərōyəh*), *ḤL a-mkō-kəm* 'their place', *JL ērúnɛ́š* 'his goats' (indef. form *ʾɛrún*).

In Mehri, Hobyōt, and Ḥarsūsi, the suffix pronoun is different after a noun and after a verb or a preposition. It also varies according to the number of the noun. In *JL*, pronouns only vary according to the number of the noun but have the same form after a singular noun, a verb or a preposition. In Soqoṭri, there is only one set of suffix pronouns. The 3m. has a *h* or *š* base.

When added to a verb or a noun, the suffix pronoun entails modifications of the basic pattern of the word, vocalic timbre and quantity, syllabic structure and stress:

MQn *γagēnṓt* > *γagēnáts* 'her girl', *γagēnū́tən* > *γagēnátsɛ* 'her girls'; *səbū́ṭ* > *səbṭáys* 'he beat her', *isū́bʌṭ* > *isəbṭɔ́s* 'he beats her'

HHf *γɔwɔ́tə* > *γwɔtîhum* 'their brothers'

ML nəxrīr > *anxráyri* 'my nose'

ḤL bəgōd > *bəgədáyn* 'he chased us'

JL réš > *érešésən* 'their heads', *kɔ́rɔ́š* > *kiršɔ́š* 'he thumped him'

At the sg. 1, after some prepositions, the suffix pronoun is *-ni*: MQn *hīni, ML háyni, ḤL háni, JL híni* 'for me'. In *ḤL, -ni* is used with numerous prepositions: *táni (ML tey, JL tɔ), báni (ML bī, JL bí), əm-bēnyéni wə bēnyū́k* 'between me and you'; and with most verbs: *ankʿəni* 'he came to me', *bəgədə́ni* 'he chased me', but *təxɔ́mi* 'you want me'. After many transitive verbs, the dependent pronoun is suffixed to the accusative marker *t-*: MQn *šink tēs* 'I saw her'.

Some prepositions in Mehri, HHf, *ḤL* and *JL* are followed by the same affixed pronouns as the plural nouns: MQn *nxālīhəm*, HHf, *JL lxinúhum* 'under them'.

In MDt, the suffix pronouns, after some prepositions, such as *ðār* 'on', *mən* 'from', are identical to those used with the singular nouns: *ðeyrək* 'on you' (but *būk* 'to you'), *mənk* 'from you', and *ðeyrki, mənki* (du. 2) (but *bīki*).

In Soqoṭri personal suffixes are very rarely suffixed directly to nouns or verbs (cf. Possession in Soqoṭri, p. 419).

After a verb, the pronoun is usually suffixed to the accusative marker *t-* or a prep. SQa, SQb *šínək teh* 'I saw him', SQa *bídə ʿayhən* 'he lied to them'.

Interrogative Pronouns

mōn (M, Ḥ), mūn (Hb.), mān (B), mun (Jib.), mon (S.) 'who?'
mun mən (Jib.) 'which of?'
hḗsən (M), īníh (Hb.), hínɛ (B), hā́sən, hášən (Ḥ), ʾíné (Jib.), ínɛm (S.)
   'what'?'

Nouns

Substantives have two genders (masculine and feminine), and three numbers (singular, dual and plural). Johnstone (1975: 112) claims that the dual is obsolete in the MSAL, except in Soqoṭri; yet, it seems that nominal dual is still alive in Mehri in the Yemen and Hobyōt.

Singular Nouns

The main patterns are: 'CVC(V)C, 'CV:C(V)C, C(V)'CVC, C(V)'CV:C, in Jibbāli 'CV'CVC, and for the quadriliterals CVCCV:C, or 'CVCCVC in Soqoṭri:

> ML *dabh*, HHf *dɛbh* 'honey', ḤL *dəbš* 'date-syrup', JL *dɛbš* 'honey'; SQb ʿans
>   'elbow'
> ML *ṣāhar*, MQnB *ṣáhar*, ḤL *ṣahr* 'back'; MQnB, HHf, SQa *šxɔf*, ML *šəxōf*, ḤL
>   *šxōf*, JL *núsub* 'milk'; ML *ɣəlḗṭ*, JL *ɣáléṭ* 'mistake' (with a diphthongization
>   in ḤL: *ɣəlawṭ*)
> MQnB, ML *ḳəṭmīm*, ḤL *ḳəṭmáym*, JL *ḳaṭmím*, SQa *ḳáṭmehəm* 'fresh butter'

The feminine marker is the ending -(V́)t in Mehri, Hobyōt, Baṭhari, Ḥarsūsi, Jibbāli, and -h in Soqoṭri (but -t occurs at the dual and plural). The vowel preceding the morpheme is /o/, /u/, /i/, /ə/ (long or short, according to the phonological system of the language):

> JL *ngɔst* 'pollution'
> MQn *ɣagēnṓt*, ML *ɣəgənōt*, JL *ɣɛbgɔ́t*, SML ʿəwgínoh 'girl'
> HHf *ɣɔgīt* 'big girl'
> MQn, ML *rḗsīt*, ḤL *rəšēt* 'snake'
> SQb *ɣáṣəh* (du. *ɣaṣéti*) 'woman'
> MQn *ḥarmēt*, JL *ḥarmɛ́t* 'woman'
> JL *ṣədfét* 'chance'
> MQn *kənəmít*, ML *kənəmūt*, BM *kənəmōt*, JL *šínít* 'louse'

In Soqoṭri there exists also a feminine form marked by a vocalic opposition: SQa *ṭáhrər* (m.), *ṭáhrer* (f.) 'wild goat', *šíbœb* (m.), *šíbib* (f.) 'old'.

In Mehri, Baṭhari, Ḥarsūsi and Jibbāli, some feminine nouns (borrowings from Arabic) have an -h ending:

> MQn *makīnah* 'motor', BM *ḥɛśmeh* (but B (ML) *həśmə́t*) 'honor', ḤL *kāməh*
> 'measure', ML *θáwrəh*, JL *θórəh* 'revolution'.

Dual

The dual marker for nouns is the suffix *-i*. In Mehri, Hobyōt, Ḥarsūsi and Jibbāli nouns are usually followed by the numeral 2. The speakers do not consider this *-i* as a nominal suffix, but as a numeral prefix; in MQn /ḥarmēti-trīt/ 'two women' is pronounced [ḥarmēt-itrīt]. In Soqoṭri, the numeral is usually omitted: SQb *fərḥáṣi d-bérki* '(the two) articulations of (the two) knees'. In Mehri, Hobyōt, Ḥarsūsi and Jibbāli some duals function as plurals (cf. Johnstone 1975: 113).

Plural

As in all the languages of the South Semitic group, the MSAL have internal and external plurals. A few plurals are suppletive plurals.

In all languages, one singular noun may have several plural forms: *ML* (sg. *ṣəffáy*) *ṣəfōf, ṣəfáwwət, ṣəfūtən* 'elbows'; HHf (sg. *ṣɛgerḗt*) *ṣigɔ́rtə, ṣəgēr* 'paths in a mountain'.

Internal Plurals

Johnstone (1975: 113) compares some of these plural patterns with Ethiopic rather than with Arabic.

The singular pattern is modified but does not have an affix. The most common patterns are ((sg.)/pl.):

* CCV:C (plural of many feminine singulars)

  ML (*nəḳṭāt*)/*nəḳāṭ, JL* (*nəḳṭɔ́t*)/*nḳɔṭ* 'dots'
  HHf (*nɔbɔ́t*)/*nbɛ́b, JL* (*nibbɔ́t*)/*nbéb* 'bees'

* CCV:CC, CCVCC (in Jibbāli CCⁱCVbCC), for quadriliterals (the long vowel may sometimes be diphthongized, or stressed (in Jibbāli only where *w > b*):

  MQnB (*mḳaṭä́r*)/*mḳáwṭər* 'caravans'
  ML, ḤL (*mənxāl, mə́nxəl*)/*mənōxəl*
  JL (*mənṣéf*)/*minébṣəf* 'mattresses'

A very common internal plural for quadriliterals is based on a vocalic opposition in the last syllable: *i/e*, or *ə* (S.), (sg.) > *o, ɔ/u* (pl.).

  MQn, *ML* (*ḥənīd*)/*ḥənōd, JL* (*nid*)/*nud* 'waterskins'
  MQn, *ML, ḤL* (*nxərīr*)/ *nxərōr, JL* (*naxrér*)/*naxrɔ́r, SQb* (*náḥrər*)/*náḥrur* 'noses'
  HHf (*iḳéybīn*)/*iḳéybūn* 'scorpions'

Some plural patterns correspond to Arabic plural of plural:

  ML (*xaf*)/*xəfáwf* 'hoofs' (Jib. *ɔxf ɔ́f*); *ḤL* (*mōtən*)/*mətə́wwən* 'flesh of backs' (cf. pl. *ML mətūn, JL motún*).

External Plurals

The singular pattern may or may not be modified, and the plural is marked by a suffixed and/or a prefixed morpheme.

- Suffixes -'V*t* and -(V)*tə*(*n*). Many feminine nouns, and some masculine nouns have this pattern:

  ML (*təmrīt*)/*təmártən* 'ear lobes'
  MQn (*hangəlūt*)/*hangáltən* 'jellyfish (p.)'
  HHf (*hɔ́rəm*)/*ḥayrɔ̄mte* 'roads'
  SQa (*réyʿeh*)/*reʿīhétən* 'female herders'

- Suffix -*t*, -*h*/-*t* in Soqoṭri:

  MQnB (*gəmmōl*)/*gəmmōlət* 'camel drivers'
  HHf (*ḱáṣ̌ər*)/*kʌṣ̌ɔ́rt* 'leopards'
  ḤL (*yərāb*)/*yə́rəbət* 'sacks'
  SQa (*ṣáhrəh*)/*ṣáhrət* 'sisters-in-law'

- Suffix -*īn* and -*íhɔn* (in Soqoṭri):

  MQn (*dənōb*)/*dənbīn* 'tails'
  ML (*kərɔ̄ṣ*)/*kərṣáyn* HHf (*ḱerɔ́ṣ*)/*ḱerṣīn* 'mosquitoes'
  JL (*gífún*)/ *gəfənín* 'tulchans'
  SQb (*ʿéyg*)/*ʿɔgéhən* 'men'
  SHr (*kɔʿöd*)/*kuʿdɛ́n* 'camel-calves'

- Plurals with an *m*- prefix, and those with ʾ-, with or without a suffix -*t*/-*h* (S.) masculine, and -*tən* feminine (cf. CA broken plurals *m*-CāCiC, ʾCCāC, ʾCCiCat):

  ML (*nīdéx*)/*mənádəx* 'smokes'
  JL (*kalbéṭ*)/*mḱálbəṭ* 'turnings (on a path)'
  HHt (*bīr*)/*hābyōr* 'wells'
  ḤL (*slēb*)/*həslōb* 'weapons', (*gawf*)/*həgwáft* 'chests'
  MQn (*bōb*)/*ḥābwēbət* 'doors'
  ML (*ḥirīt*)/*aḥyártən* 'female donkeys'
  JL (*ṣ́ɔ́b*)/*ɛṣ́bét* 'monitor lizards'
  SQa (*ḱódəher*)/*ʾaḱdɔ̄rəh* 'pots'

- In *JL* (cf. also Johnstone 1975: 113), some plurals with -*i* come from the dual. They are used (and felt) as plural:

  JL *lhóti* 'cows', *γagénəti* 'girls', *ḥérnəti* 'mountains (dim.)'

Adjectives

Like nouns, adjectives have two genders, but the plural of many adjectives is often of common gender. Except in Soqoṭri where there is a dual for adjectives, adjectives in the other MSAL have only two numbers.

Usually, feminine is marked by a -t/-h ending added to the masculine form, but, in Soqoṭri, it may also be marked by a vocalic opposition: SQa gɛ́ʿəlhal, gɛ́ʿəlhēl 'round', xɔbxɔ́b, xɔbxéb 'clumsy'. It is very scarce in Mehri: MJahn duwōl, diwōl 'worn out (pl.)'.

In all the MSAL, there are feminine adjectives without a feminine marker: MQn ḥanōb, ML nōb, BM nawb, JL um 'big'; it is often the case for adjectives concerning only females: SQa gáḥləl 'pregnant', íbši 'gravid'.

Many adjectival patterns are common with nouns. The C(V)Cī/íC (or CVCáyC) pattern is, like in Arabic, more common with adjectives than with nouns: MQn, ḤL dəwīl, ML dəwáyl 'old'; MQn səxīf, ML səxáyf, JL sxíf 'idiot'; SQa ḳaʿə́nhɛn 'curved'.

Although in Mehri and Ḥarsūsi, only the passive participle functions as an adjective, there are some adjective patterns Cā/ōC əC (cf. Arabic CāCiC): ML, ḤL ʾāgəz, JL ʿɔ́gəz 'lazy'.

In Jibbāli, the participle with -ún (f. -únt) suffix also has an adjectival (and sometimes adverbial) function: JL ṣəðrún, ṣəðrúnt 'stiff', rə́gfún 'timid' (and 'shivery'); there are also some examples in HHf.

Some examples of adjectives, sg. m., f./(du. m., f.)/pl. m., f. (or common):

HHf rekēk, rekēkət//rikɔ́k, rikɔ́ktɛ 'thin'; fə́rhun, fərhənt//fərhanīn, fərhanintə 'happy'; ʿɔ́fər, ʿafərɔ́t//ʿāfər
ML ʾɔ̄fər, ʾāfərōt//ʾāfər
B (ML) ʿāfər, ʿafərēt//ʿáfər
ḤL ʾáfər, ʾáfərōt//ʾáfər
JL ʿɔ́fər, ʿafirɔ́t//ʿafirétə
SQa ʿɛ̄fər, ʿɛ́féroh/ʿɛ̄fri, ʿɛ́fəróti/ʿɛ̄firíhin, ʿeferétən
SJms gives a common pl. ʿáfirétən, 'red'.

In Jibbāli, Ḥarsūsi and mainly in Soqoṭri, the phrase: ð-/di- + impf./pf., often has an adjectival function (cf. Relative Clauses, p. 417): ḤL ð-isdōd '(it is) sufficient'; JL də-míźɔ́t 'full (f.)'; SQa di-škər, di-škērøh/di-šəkərø, di-šəkə́rtø/di-škər 'kind.'

Deictics

In all the MSAL (except Soqoṭri for demonstratives), there are deictic forms with an -m or -n ending (cf. adverbs).

Deictics Referring to Time

'now': M ṣərōməh, Hb. nāṣʌnɔ, B nāṣərəh, Ḥ nōṣəh, nōṣərəh, Jib. naʿṣánu, náṣanu, S. náʿa

Table 17.3 Deictics referring to persons and things (demonstratives)

	Near, 'this' (m., f./pl.)	Far, 'that' (m., f./pl.)
MY	dōm, dīməh/lyōm	dēk(əm), dīk(əm)/lyēk(əm)
ML	ðōməh, ðīməh/əlyōməh	ðákmah, ðэ́kməh/əlyákməh
		ðēk, ðáyk/əlyēk
Hb.	ðɛn, ðin/lōn (HHf lénəh)	ðэ́hun, ðíhun/lэ́h(un)
B	ðánəməh, ðan, ðin/ílūn	
Ḥ	ðã, ðī; ðɔ̃n, ðénəh/lɔ̃ʰ	ðēk, ðīk/lək or
	ðánəməh, ðánəməh/lэ́ləməh (lэ́nəməh)	ðákəməh, э́kəməh/ʾэ́ləməh
Jib.	ðénu, ðínu/iźénu	ðэ́hun, ðúhun/iźɔhún (nearby)
		ðэ́kun, ðúkun/iźэ́k (further away)
S.	dəʰ, deʰ & dəš/dihi/lénha	dək, dəš/ diki/
	dэ́dha, dídha/э́lhaᵗ	dэ́dbok, dídbok/э́lbok§

Notes: † In some Soqoṭri dialects *ḥa* and not *ha*. *dэ́dha = də-d-h/ḥa* ⟨this-which/who-here⟩. One also seldom finds *dэ́dboʰ*. § *dэ́dbok = də-d-bok* ⟨this-which/who-there⟩.

Table 17.4 Deictics referring to space

	Near, 'here'	Far, 'there'
M	boh, būm, bōm, bawməh	ḥʌlōk, ḥʌlэ́kəməh
Hb.	boh, bōmə, būwə	ḥəloh, ḥɔlэ́k, ḥɔlэ́kəmə
Ḥ	būməh	ḥəlōk, ḥəlōkəməh
Jib.	bo, bun, b̠íun	lhõn, lэ́kun
S.	ha/ḥa, boʰ	bok

Note: In Soqoṭri *ha/ḥa* and *boʰ* are used in compounds: *lha/lḥa, lboʰ* 'here'; *diboh* /'id-boh/ 'to here'; as *boh* in MQn: *het lboh* 'bring here!'

'today': M *yemóh, yəmō*, Hb. *axэ́r*, B *ḥōr*, Ḥ *yəmōh*, Jib. *šẖɔr, šẖer*, S. *ḥer*
'tomorrow': M *géhməh, gēhəməh*, Hb. *gémə*, B *gēhəməh*, Ḥ *gēhəməh*, Jib. *ḳarérəh*, S. *ḳerīri, ḳerérəh*
'yesterday': M *yemšī, yəmšē*, Hb. *ʾmši*, Jib. *ʾəmšín*, S. *ʾəmšín*

Anteriority and posteriority may be expressed with prepositions: 'before-' (M *fənə-*, Jib. *fənɛ́-*, S. *féne-, fon-*) or 'after' (M *bād*, Jib., S. *baʿd*) plus temporal adverbs: M *fənəmš*, Jib. *fənémšín* 'before yesterday'; M *bād géhməh* 'after tomorrow'.

Numerals

The numerals in the MSAL have phonological, morphological and syntactical characteristics that distinguish them from Arabic and are of great interest for Semitic comparatism (cf. Johnstone 1983: 225).

Cardinals

Table 17.5 Cardinal numbers

	MSr (*ML*) HHf (m./f.)	*ḤL* (m./f.)	*JL* (m./f.)	SQb (SQa) (m./f.)
1	ṭāt/ṭīt (ṭāṭ/ṭáyṭ) ṭat/ṭéyt	ṭād/ṭət	ṭad/ṭit	ṭɔd/ṭéyʰ (ṭɔd/ṭah)
2	troh/trīt (θərō, θroh/θráyt, θrɛt) θro, θroh/θərīt	θərō/θərɔ́t	θroh/θrət	trøh/trih (trøh/treh)
3	šhalét/šyatīt (šhalīθ/šāθáyt) šhəlóθ/šhaθéyt	šəláyš/šāf(θ)áyt	šhəléθ/šɔθét	šéleh/šéʿtəh (šíleh/šɔ́ytəh)
4	hárba/ərbōt (árba/ərbōt) ʾɔ́rbaʿ/ʾərbʿáwt	ʾōrba/rəbōt	ʾórbaʿ/ʾərbaʿɔ́t	ʾórbɛʿ/ʾírbaʿ (ʾérbēʿ/ʾərbʌ́ʿah)
5	xáyməh/xmōh (xáyməh/xəmmōh) xāməh/xɔmmóh	xáyməh/xəmmōh	xīš/xōš	himeh/hóyməh (xɔ̄məh/xɔ̄məyʰ)
6	hett/yittīt (hət/yɔtīt) het/htet	háttəh/yətēt	šét/štət	yháʿt/hītəh (yɔ́ʿt/yētəh)
7	hōba/yibéyt (hōba/yəbáyt) hōba/hebíʿat	hōba/həbáyt	šōʿ/šəbʿɔ́t	yhōbəʿ/híbʿə (yēbəʿ/yēbəʿəh)
8	tmõni/təmənēt (θmōni/θəmənyēt) θemēni/θemēnit	θəmōni/θəmənēt	θõni/θīnɔ́t	témɔni/téməneh (təméni/təmɔ̄nəh)
9	sɛʾ/séyt (sē/sāt) sɔʿ/sáʿet	sē/sāʾáyt, səʿáyt	sɔʿ/saʿét	sɛʿ/séʿeh (saʿ/séʿəh)
10	ɔ́šər/ášərít (ʿɔ́šər/ʿášərīt) ʿɔ́šər/ʿašərīt	ʿɔ́šər/ʿašərēt	ʿɔ́šər/əšírét	ʿášər/ešéreh (ʿášər/ešīreh)

The numbers 1 and 2 are adjectives, and 2 follows the noun in the dual. For 3–10, masculine numerals count feminine nouns, and feminine numerals masculine nouns. They are usually followed by nouns in the plural form, and above 13 the noun is either plural or singular. After 12, 22, 32, etc., the noun may be in the dual: SQa *ʿešireh wᵘ - trøh šhéri* ⟨10 and-2 month (du.)⟩ 'twelve months'.

In all MSAL, numerals used after 10 are usually Arabic borrowings. But some old bedouin speakers still use the MSAL's number system above 10, especially for counting livestock. This system is as follows:

Number and noun agree in gender from 11 to 19. From 11 onwards the structure of numbers is: tens + "and" + units.

ML **11** *ʾáśərīt w- ṭāt* (HHf *ʿaśarīt w-ṭat*) (+ m.), *ʾōśər w-ṭáyt* (+ f.)
12 *ʾáśərīt w-θrōh* (HHf *ʿaśarīt w-θroh*), *ʾōśər w-θráyt*
13 *ʾáśərīt wə-šāθáyt* (HHf *ʿaśarīt w-šhaθéyt*), *ʾōśər wə-šhəlīθ*

The tens, when not borrowed from Arabic, are made by suffixation of *-ah*, *-oh*, *-øh*.

20 *ML* *ʿáśərəh*, SQa *ʿáśrøh*, but MQn *āšrīn*, and *JL* *ʿέśəri*
30 *JL* *šəlóh*, SQa *šελáh*, but *ML* *šəlāθáyn*

In Soqoṭri, from 30 onwards in some dialects and 40 in others, the multiples of 10 are constructed as follows: units + 10 (pl.):

30 *SL* *šēle ʿeśárhen* ⟨three tens⟩
SQaB **40** *ʾə́rbaʿ ʿaśā́rən*
50 *xέymʌ ʿaśā́rən*
60 *yáʿt ʿaśā́rən*
70 *yə́bʌʿ ʿaśā́rən*
80 *témenε ʿaśā́rən*
90 *sεʿ ʿaśā́rən*
100 MQn *miyēt*; *ML* *əmyīt*; HHf *míyut*, *JL* *mút*; SQa *mít*
1,000 MQn *ʾelf*; *ML* *ʾēf*; *JL* *ʾɔf*; SQb *ʾalf*

To count livestock, bedouin use specific items:

ML *ṭaḥōb* 'herd of about 100 camels'; *JL* *ṭɔ́ḥɔ́b* 'herd of 15 camels (and upwards)'; SQaB *méḥbər* '100 head of cattle'; *treh mεḥbéri* '200'.

In Mehri, Hobyōt, Jibbāli and partially in Ḥarsūsi (Johnstone 1975: 115–116), specific numerals are used for counting days above two. The noun 'day' (f.) is in the singular form:

	ML	HHf	JL
3 days	*šēləθ yūm*	*šhεlt yōm*	*śéləθ ēm*
4	*rība –*	*rībaʿ –*	*rīʿ –*
5	*xáyməh –*	*xām –*	*xīš –*
6	*šīdət –*	*hett –*	*šεt –*
7	*šība –*	*šēbaʿ –*	*šīʿ –*
8	*θīmən –*	*θēmən –*	*θīn –*
9	*tīsa –*	*tēsaʿ –*	*təsʿ –*
10	*ʾāyśər –*	*ʿέśər –*	*ʿáśər –*

Ordinals

The ordinals in *ML* and *ḤL* are formed on the pattern of the *nomen agentis*. Some ordinals are based on the ancient root of number; in SL, the ordinals, beyond *néšher* 'first', are formed by the numeral preceded by *di-*: *di-h(y)óbeh* ⟨which (is) seven⟩ 'seventh'. In *JL*, the data are not complete (cf. Johnstone 1975: 116).

Table 17.6   Ordinal numbers

	ML (m./f.)	*ḤL* (m./f.)	*JL* (m./f.)
1st	ḥāwīl/ḥāwəlīt	ḥāwīl/ḥāwəlēt	ʾénfí/ʾénfēt
2nd	məšēyər/məšəyərēt	məšə̄yər/məšəyərēt	mš/šáyər/ ⟨γyr⟩ 'other'
3rd	śōləθ/śəwθ̄īt	śēləś/śēlśət	
4th	rōbaʾ/rəbáyt	rēbaʾ/rēbat	
5th	xōməs/xəmhēt	xāməh/xāmhət	xīs/
6th	šōdəs/šəddēt	hētt/hēttət	
7th	sōbəʿ/səbáyt	hēbaʾ/hēbaʾt	
8th	θōmən/θəmənēt	θēmən/θēmnət	
9th	tōsaʾ/təsáyt	tēsaʾ/tēsaʾt	
10th	ʾáyśər/ʾáśərēt	ʾáśər/ʾáśərt	

Verbs

Root and Derived Themes

Like all Semitic languages, the MSAL have a verbal basic theme and derived themes. There is also a vocalic internal passive.

The Basic Theme

There are two different types of basic verbs, based on semantic and morphological criteria. The patterns of active verbs (Johnstone's type A) are: CəCō/ūC, CəCɔ́C, and that of middle verbs (state verbs, middle passive verbs, verbs whose subject is also the patient; Johnstone's type B) are: CīCəC, CéCəC. All MSAL have, with some verbs of type A, an internal vocalic passive, whose patterns are: CəCē/īC, Cí/éCəC, Ci/ī/CéC in MQn. This is a very dynamic passive formation in Soqoṭri.

The Derived Themes

As in all Semitic languages, the derived themes are characterized by internal vocalic modification, infixation (*t-*), and prefixation (*h-/ʾ-*, *š/ś-*, *n-*), but no derived theme is formed by gemination.

A prefixed vowel may occur in the theme with internal modification. For each verb, the prefixed morpheme *h-/ʾ-* cannot be found in all the forms of the conjugation.

In some cases, type A and B verbs have a different pattern for the same derived theme.

Table 17.7   Verbal themes (ō/ū in Mehri, é/í in JL and Soqoṭri)

	Mehri	ḤL	c/e J	S.
Simple verb				
A	CǝCóC	CǝCóC	Cɔ́Cɔ́C/CǝCɔ́C	Cɔ́CǝC
B	CěCǝC	CěCǝC	CéCǝC	CéCǝC
Passive	CǝCěC	CǝCěC	CǝCéC	CéCǝC
Derived themes				
Intern. modif.	(a)CóCǝC	(a)CéCǝC	(e)CóCǝC/Cɔ́CǝC	Cɔ́CǝC,CéCǝC
-t- infix (A)	Cǎ/átCǝC	CátCǝC	Cɔ́tCǝC/Cɔ́CCǝC	Cɔ́tCǝC
(B)	ǝCtǝCóC	ǝCtǝCóC	ǝCtǝCéC	
Prefix h/ʾ-	(hǝ)CCóC	(a)CCóC	(e)/(ɛ)CCéC	ɔ́CCǝC
Prefix š- (A)	šǝCCóC	šǝCCóC	š/šǝCCéC	šɔ́CCǝC
(B)	šǝCěCǝC	šǝCɔ́CǝC	š/šǝCéCǝC	šǝCéCǝC
Prefix n-	(ǝ)nCěCǝC	(ǝ)nCěCǝC	(ǝ)nCéCǝC	(ǝ)nCéCǝC
Quadriconsonantal	(ǝ)nCǝCCóC	(ǝ)nCǝCCóC	(ǝ)nCǝCéCéC	(ǝ)nCéCCǝ

- Theme with internal modification (and possibly vocalic preformant):

In the Mehri of Mahra, the derived theme does not have a prefix, and in the Mehri of Dhofar, in Ḥarsūsi and Jibbāli, it is often missing when C₁ is a voiceless consonant (ejective consonants are considered as voiced consonants).

In all languages, the imperfect has an augmentative -(ǝ)n (perf./imperf./subj. sg. 3m.):

ML, MQn	(a)CóCǝC/yǝCáCCǝn/yǝllCóCǝC (+ variants)
ḤL	(a)CéCǝC/yǝCěCǝCǝn/yǝCéCǝC
JL	(e/ɛ)Cɔ́CǝC/iCɔ́CCǝn/yCɔ́CǝC (ó or ɔ́) (+ variants)
S.	Cɔ́CǝC/iCɔ́Cǝn/liCɔ́CǝC (and CéCǝC/yǝCéCǝCǝn/ li-CéCǝC)

The classification of these verbs as 'intensive–conative' (Johnstone 1975, 1981) does not seem to hold when one considers the semantic value of the verbs in all languages. When the form is derived from a simple verbal form, it is always transitive and the meaning is usually factitive or causative. When no corresponding simple form exists, the derived verb can be transitive or intransitive; some are denominative:

MQnB rókǝb/irákbǝn/lǝrōkǝb = ML arōkǝb = ḤL arēkǝb = JL erókub 'to put (a pot) on the fire' (rěkǝb (type B, trans.) 'to ride')
MQnB wǔṭi/iwǎṭiyǝn = ḤL awēṭa = JL ōṭiʾ 'to bring down'
ML MQn ṣōli/iṣályǝn/lṣōli = ML aṣōli = ḤL aṣāl = JL eṣóli = SJMS ṣáli 'to pray'
JL egódǝl/gódǝlǝn/ygódǝl 'to tie, chain (a prisoner)'
SQa ḥōbi/iḥōbiǝn = ML ḥōbi '(baby) to crawl'
SJms zómil/yzómilǝn 'to saddle'

In Mehri, Jibbāli, Soqoṭri some verbs have a different pattern:

SQa *gēdaḥ/igīdhən/lígdaḥ* 'to come', *ḥīsab/iḥéʸsbən/liḥsáb* 'to count', *ší/tšīn* (sg. 2f.)/ *tšēi* (sg. 2f.) 'to listen'
ML *šēwər/yašáwrən/yašēwər* 'to consult'

In Jibbāli, verbs with C_2 = *h* and *x* "have both the *eCóCəC* and *eCCéC* pattern" (Johnstone 1981: xxi).
In all MSAL there are also some idiosyncratic verbs of both types (ibid.: xxv–xxvi).
• Theme with infix -*t*-:
In all languages, except Soqoṭri, there are two derived forms with -*t*-:

M, Ḥ   (*a, ə*)*CátCəC/yəCtəCū(ō)C/l/yəCtī(ē)CəC* (type A verbs)
        (*a, ə*)*CtəCú/ōC/yəCtəCī(ē)Cən/yəCtəCū(ō)C* (type B)
Jib.   *CɔtCəC/yəCtéCɔC/yəCtéCəC* (verbs type A) = Hb.
       əCtəCéC/yəCtəCíCən/yəCtəCɔC (type B). But in Jibbāli some verbs
       are irregular (cf. Johnstone 1981: xxiii–xxiv)
S.   *CɔtCəC/iCtɔCəC*

Let us remember here that in Mehri, Ḥarsūsi and Jibbāli, -*t*- induces gemination and gemination shifts within the word.
The suffix -*n* occurs in the imperfect of type B verbs.
This form with infix -*t*- (in reference to Arabic) was classified as causative and reflexive, but the value is more often that of a middle verb, not a causative. The derived verbs do not always correspond to a simple theme:

MQn *stəlūb/istəlībən/lstəlōb* 'to be armed, carry arms' = ML *əstəlūb*
ML *kətháwl* = ḤL *əktəhōl* = JL *ektḥél* 'to apply kohl'
B (*ML*) *yəmtēzḥan* 'he jokes'
HHf *iḥtámʕan* 'he listens'(*hēmaʕ* (type B) 'he hears')
ML *šētəm* (= HHf *šatɔ̃m* another pattern) = ḤL *šōtəm* = JL *šɔ́tέm* 'to buy' (*šɛ́m* 'to sell')
JL *fɔ́tgər/yəftégɔ́r/yəftégər* 'to burst; to be a great liar' (*fɔ́gɔ́r*, type A, 'to tell a lie'), *əftégér* 'to be proved to be a liar' (*efgér*, type B, 'to prove someone a liar')
S (*ML*) *ɔ́stəʔ* ⟨swy⟩ 'to be ready', SQa *šthédən* 'we got excited' (SL *šéheḍ* 'fear'), *kɔ́tnə* 'to eat' (*kānə* 'to feed')

Some of these derived verbs have a reciprocal value:

Hb. *əntáwḥɔm* = ML *əntáwḥəm* = JL *əntɔ̄ḥ* (pl. 3m.) = S (*ML*) *əntóḥo* (du. 3m.) 'they fought each other'
SQa *yiṣtáʕbø* 'they bit each other (du. 3m.)' (*šɔ́ʕəb* 'to bite')

- Theme with preformant h-/$^{\jmath}$:

ML, MQn	$h\partial CC\bar{u}(\bar{o})C/y\partial h\partial CC\bar{u}(\bar{o})C/y\partial /lh\acute{a}CC\partial C$
ḤL	$(a)CC\check{o}C/yaCC\check{o}C/y\partial h\acute{a}CC\partial C$
JL	$(e/\varepsilon)C_1C_2\acute{e}(\acute{\imath})C_3/\acute{\imath}C_1C_1\acute{e}(\acute{\imath})C_2\acute{\jmath}C_3/y\acute{\varepsilon}C_1C_2\partial C_3,\ y\acute{\varepsilon}C_1\partial C_2C_3$
S.	$\acute{\jmath}CC\partial C/y\partial C\acute{\varepsilon}C\jmath C(\partial n)/l\acute{\jmath}CC\partial C$

In Mehri (specially in the Mehri of the Yemen), the derivative morpheme h- is often missing at the suffix conjugation and indicative prefix conjugation but is always present in the subjunctive.

In Jibbāli, the conjugation may induce the gemination of one of the radical consonants (C_1 or C_2) at some persons of the imperfect and perfect.

In Soqoṭri, the imperfect may have the augmentative -n.

The most common meaning of this derived form is causative, or factitive:

MQn *frōḳ/yafrōḳ/ləháfrəḳ* 'to frighten' (*firəḳ*, type B, 'to be afraid')
ML *xlūf/yəxlōf/yəháxləf* 'to leave behind' (*xayləf*, type B, 'to succeed')
ḤL *akfōd/yakfōd/yəháḳfəd* 'to put down' (*ḳafōd* 'to descend') = M
JL *eshēḳ* 'to make someone grind fine' (*shaḳ* 'to grind fine'),
ebšél/yēššɔ́l/yébšəl 'to cook' (*béšəl*, type B, 'to be cooked') = ML *həb-hōl/yəhəbhōl/yəhábhəl* (*bəhēl*, passive) = ḤL *abhōl/yabhōl/yəhábhəl* (*bəhēl*) = SJms *'ə́bhəl*, passive *íbhal*

The value can also be middle, reflexive or middle passive:

MQnB = ML *hənṣūr* 'to have had enough sleep', ML *həṣráwb* = JL *eṣréb* 'to be ill' = ḤL *aṣráwb* '(woman) to feel labour pains'
SQa *'esēləmɔn* 'we greet each other' (du. 1, impf. with suffix -n)

- Theme with preformant $š$- ($\acute{s}$- in cJ):
As with the -t- derived form, in all languages, there is a different pattern for type A and B verbs.

M, Ḥ	$š\partial CC\bar{u}/\bar{o}C/l/ya\check{s}\partial CC\bar{u}/\bar{o}C/ya\check{s}\partial CC\acute{a}C$ (A)
M	$š\partial C\bar{e}C\partial C/ya\check{s}\partial CC\acute{a}C\partial n/ya\check{s}\partial C\bar{e}C\partial C$ (B)
Ḥ	$š\partial C\acute{\jmath}C\partial C/ya\check{s}\partial CC\acute{a}C\partial n/ya\check{s}\partial C\acute{\jmath}C\partial C$ (B)
Jib.	$š\partial CC\acute{e}C/ya\check{s}\partial C\acute{e}C\acute{\jmath}C/ya\check{s}\acute{\varepsilon}CC\partial C$ (A)
	$š\partial C\acute{e}C\partial C/ya\check{s}C\acute{e}C\partial C\partial n/ya\check{s}CC\acute{e}/\acute{e}C$ (B)
S.	$š\acute{\jmath}CC\partial C/ya\check{s}\acute{e}CC\jmath C/le\check{s}C\acute{e}C\partial C$
	$š\partial C\acute{a}C\partial C/ya\check{s}C\acute{e}C\partial C\partial n/le\check{s}CC\acute{e}C$ (B)

This form is considered as causative reflexive, but it also has other values, the most frequent being middle or passive. There are also some denominative verbs:

MQnB *šifkáwt* 'she got married' (*fūk̯* 'he gave in marriage') = ḤL *šəfáwk̯*

HHf *šxábər/išxabūr/yəšxábər* 'to inquire' = MQn *šəxbōr* = ML = JL *šxəbér* = S(ML) *šḥábər*

ML *šəxt̯ū* 'to be injured'= ḤL *šəxt̯ō* = eJ *šəxt̯e*, cJ *šxət̯e*

SQa *šət̯éyləm/yišt̯éyləmən/ləšt̯áləm* 'to dinner at night' (cf. Arabic ⟨δlm⟩ 'darkness')

MQnB *šənšūk̯* 'to take a snuff' (*ʾnšīk̯at* 'pinch of snuff')

• Theme with preformant -*n*:
All the verbs are intransitive. It mainly concerns quadri-consonantal verbs.
The patterns are MQn *naCiCūC*, JL *ənCéCəC* and *ənCéCéC*, S. *nCáCiC* for tri-consonantal verbs:

MQn *ʾmbéi/imbéin/ləmbéi* 'to bleat' (MJahn *bʿy* 'to bleat')

ḤL *ənk̯áyt̯a* 'to be thirsty; to be cut' (*k̯áwt̯a* ⟨k̯tʿ⟩ 'to be tired, to cut', *k̯et̯eyāt* 'thirst')

JL *ənḥérək* 'to move' (= *aḥtérék*); SL *nḥádid* 'to thunder'

and for quadri-consonantal verbs ML, ḤL *ənCəCCōC*; JL (*ə*)*nCəCCíC* and (*ə*)*nCəC*(*é*)*CéC*; S. *ənCáCəC*.
The meanings are middle, reflexive, reciprocal and sometimes intensive:

ML *ənḥat̯mūl* 'to be smashed' (= eJ (ML) *nḥat̯míl*) = ḤL *ənḥat̯əmōl/ yənḥat̯əmōl/yənḥat̯məl* (*ḥat̯əməl* 'to smash')

JL *əndaɣdáɣ* 'to be tickled, to tickle each other' (*edaɣdáɣ* 'to tickle')

SL *enk̯árk̯er* 'to be dusty' (*k̯árk̯ahar* 'dust')

In Jibbāli, the form is used for verbs of color: JL *ənkérkím* (*kerkúm* 'yellow dye') 'to become yellow' = SL *inkórkim*; *nʿífírér* 'to become red' (*ʿ5fər* 'red').

Conjugations

There is one suffix conjugation (perfect value) and two, sometimes three, prefix conjugations (indicative (imperfect value) and subjunctive; Jibbāli, the Mehri of Oman, and some verbs in Hobyōt have a particular conditional form).

The verb has three numbers: singular, plural and, except for the Mehri language of western Mahra, dual including the first person. In Jibbāli, Mehri of Mahra, and in Hobyōt, the dual is becoming obsolete. In Mahra, the young speakers of Mehri or Hobyōt use plural more frequently than dual.

The first two persons (sg., du.) and the 2nd pl. of the perfect have the suffix /k/.

The vocalic pattern of the subjunctive differs from the imperfect and has a prefix *l-* (for sg. 1c. du. 1c. in all the MSAL, and for sg. 3m., pl. 3m. in some languages).

Active verbs (type A), and middle verbs (type B) have a specific vocalic pattern in the basic theme.

There exists a vocalic passive for the basic theme of type A verbs and for some derived themes.

The imperfect of some derived verbs has an -*n* suffix.

The future, in the MSAL (except in Soqoṭri), has a special form that varies according to the language.

Table 17.8 Perfect suffixes

		M + Hb. + Ḥ	Jibbāli	Soqoṭri
Sg.	1c.	-k	-k	-k
	2m.	-k	-k	-k
	f.	-š	-š	-š
	3m.	—	—	—
	f.	-ōt/ūt/ēt	-ɔt	-oh
Du.	1c.	-ki	-ši	-ki
	2c.	-ki	-ši	-ki
	3m.	-ō/ē	-ó	-o
	f.	-tō/tē	-tó	-to
Pl.	1c.	-ən	-ən	-ən
	2m.	-kəm	-kum	-kən
	f.	-kən	-kən	-kən
	3m.	-əm/V	—	-V
	f.	—	—	—

Notes: Dialectal variants in brackets. V = internal vowel change.

Table 17.9 Imperfect affixes

		M + Hb. + Ḥ	Jibbāli	Soqoṭri
Sg.	1c.	ə/ɛ-	ə-	ə-
	2m.	t-	t-	t-
	f.	t- ... V/i	t- ... V	t- ... V
	3m.	yə/i-	yə-	i-
	f.	t-	t-	t-
Du.	1c.	ə- ... -o	ə- ... -o/-ɔ	ə- ... -o
	2c.	t- ... -o	t- ... -o/-ɔ	t- ... -o
	3m.	y-/i- ... -o	yə- ... -o/-ɔ	i- ... -o
	f.	t- ... -o	t- ... -o/-ɔ	t- ... -o
Pl.	1c.	n-	n-	n-
	2m.	t- ... V-əm	t-	t- ... V
	f.	t- ... -ən	t- ... -ən	t- ... -ən
	3m.	y-/i- ... V-əm	y-	i- ... V
	f.	t- ... -ən	t- ... -ən	t- ... -ən

Affixes of the -*n* suffix imperfect and conditional, for Mehri (Dhofar), and some verbs in Hobyōt, Jibbāli:

	Singular	Dual	Plural
1c.	ʾ-/l- ... -ən	ʾ-/l- ... -ay-ən	n- ... -ən
2m.	t- ... -ən	t- ... -ay-ən	t- ... -ən
f.	t- ... -ən	t- ... -ay-ən	t- ... -ən
3m.	y- ... -ən	y- ... -ay-ən	y- ... -ən
f.	t- ... -ən	t- ... -ay-ən	t- ... -ən

Subjunctive and Conditional

The subjunctive in all the MSAL (except for some derived verbs) differs from the imperfect. The conjugation of the conditional is derived from the subjunctive; the whole paradigm has an *n*- suffix.

In the subjunctive and conditional (except in Ḥarsūsi), an *l*- prefix is added to all vocalic prefixes: sg. 1c. and du. 1c., and in some Mehri dialects of the Mahra and in Soqoṭri sg. 3m., du. 3m. and pl. 3m (/y/ is realized as a vocalic [i]).

Non-occurrence of Prefixes

In Jibbāli and Soqoṭri, all the personal prefixes, or the *t*- prefix only, may be absent in the conjugation of some verbs: some derived verbs, simple quadriliteral verbs, simple hollow verbs and in the passive of simple and derived verbs. With these types of verbs, the prefix marker *l*- occurs in the whole paradigm of the subjunctive (and in the conditional, in Jibbāli).

Conjugations

Table 17.10   Simple verb (type A): active voice, perfect

		MQn (*ML*) 'to put something straight'	HHf 'to understand'	ḤL 'to write'	JL 'to be able'	SQb 'to understand'
Sg.	1c.	r(ə)kə́zk	ɣʌrébək	kətōbək	ḳə́dɔ́rk	ʿɔ́rɔbk
	2m.	r(ə)kə́zk	ɣʌrébək	kətōbək	ḳə́dɔ́rk	ʿɔ́rɔbk
	f.	r(ə)kézš	ɣʌrébəš	kətōbəš	ḳə́dɔ́rš/š̌	ʿɔ́rɔbš
	3m.	r(ə)kūz	ɣʌrōb	kətōb	ḳə́dɔ́r	ʿɔ́rɔb
	f.	r(ə)kəzūt	ɣʌrəbōt	kətəbōt	ḳə́dɔ́rɔ́t	ʿəréboh
Du.	1c.	(rəkə́zki)	ɣʌrōbki	kətōb(ə)ki	ḳə́dɔ́rš/š̌i	ʿərébki
	2c.	(rəkə́zki)	ɣʌrōbki	kətōb(ə)ki	ḳə́dɔ́rš/š̌i	ʿərébki
	3m.	(rəkəzō)	ɣʌrébo	kətəbō	ḳə́dɔ́rɔ́	ʿərébo
	f.	(rəkəztō)	ɣʌrébo	kətəbtō	ḳə́dɔ́rtɔ́	ʿərébəto
Pl.	1c.	r(ə)kūzən	ɣʌrɔ́bən	kətōbən	ḳə́dɔ́rən	ʿɔ́rɔ́bən
	2m.	r(ə)kə́zkəm	ɣʌrɔ́bkum	kətōbkəm	ḳə́dɔ́rkum	ʿɔ́rɔ́bkən
	f.	r(ə)kə́zkən	ɣʌrɔ́bkən	kətōbkən	ḳə́dɔ́rkən	ʿɔ́rɔ́bkən
	3m.	rkūzəm (rkáwz)	ɣʌrɔ́bum	kətōbəm	ḳə́dɔ́r	ʿɔ́rub
	f.	r(ə)kūz	ɣʌrōb	kətōb	ḳə́dɔ́r	ʿɔ́rɔb

Table 17.11 Simple verb (type A): active voice, imperfect

		MHf 'to break'	HHf 'to understand'	ḤL 'to strike'	JL 'to be able'	SQb 'to go down'
Sg.	1c.	εθōbər	εγɔ̄rəb	əlōbəd	əḳɔ́dər	əḳɔ́fəd
	2m.	təθōbər	tγɔ̄rəb	təlōbəd	tḳɔ́dər	təḳɔ́fəd
	f.	təθībər	tγɛ̄rəb	təlībəd	tḳídər	təḳɔ́fid
	3m.	yəθōbər	yiγɔ̄rəb	yəlōbəd	yḳɔ́dər	iḳɔ́fəd
	f.	təθōbər	tγɔ̄rəb	təlōbəd	tḳɔ́dər	təḳɔ́fəd
Du.	1c.	εθbərō	εγɔ̄rbo	əlbədō	əḳɔ́dɔ́rɔ́	əkáfədo
	2c.	təθbərō	tγɔ̄rbo	təlbədō	tḳədérɔ́	təkáfədo
	3m.	yəθbərō	yiγɔ̄rbo	yəlbədō	yḳɔ́dɔ́rɔ́	ikáfədo
	f.	təθbərō	tγɔ̄rbo	təlbədō	tḳɔ́dɔ́rɔ́	təkáfədo
Pl.	1c.	nəθōbər	nγɔ̄rəb	nəlōbəd	nəḳɔ́dər	nḳɔ́fəd
	2m.	təθábrəm	tγɔ̄rbum	təlōbədəm	təḳɔ́dər	təḳɔ́fəd
	f.	təθábrən	tγɔ̄rbən	təlōbədən	təḳɔ́dərən	təḳɔ́fədən
	3m.	yəθábrəm	yiγɔ̄rbum	yəlōbədəm	yḳɔ́dər	iḳɔ́fəd
	f.	təθábrən	tγɔ̄rbən	təlōbədən	təḳɔ́dərən	təḳɔ́fədən

Simple verb (type A): Active voice *Perfect* See Table 17.10, p. 403. In all MSAL (with very few exceptions in MQn) sg. 3m. = pl. 3f. and in Jibbāli sg. 3m. = pl. 3m. = pl. 3f.

In Soqoṭri, at sg. 3f., the same verb may have -vh, and -vt: SQa ḥelībǿh or ḥelībǿt 'it (sg. f.) is milked'.

In Mehri and Ḥarsūsi, the vowel of the suffix at sg. 3f. and du. 3 is ē for passives and some derived measures.

Imperfect See Table 17.11. The vowel change occurs for Soqoṭri at pl. 3m. In Mehri (Mahra and Dhofar), sg. 2f. may be t- ... V or t- ... V-i, depending on the type of verb, but many verbs have both conjugations. In HHf pl. 2,3m. are tə-, yə- ... -um. In all MSAL, pl. 2f. = pl. 3f.; in Jibbāli and Soqoṭri, pl. 2m. = sg. 2m = sg. 3f.

Subjunctive See Table 17.12, p. 405. In *JL* (Johnstone 1981: xvii), the subjunctive dual differs from the imperfect dual (indicative), in Jibbāli (Johnstone 1975: 109) the indicative and subjunctive duals are identical.

Imperative Except in Soqoṭri, the imperative form is identical to the subjunctive, without the prefix. In Mehri, sg. 2f. always has the suffix -i.

In Soqoṭri, command is expressed by the indicative imperfect and the prohibitive by the subjunctive form after a negative particle.

Conditional See Table 17.13, p. 405. The conditional does not occur in the Mehri of Mahra or in Soqoṭri. In Mehri (Dhofar), Jibbāli, it occurs rarely and it is limited to unreal hypothetical conditional sentences, the protasis of which is introduced by lu (*ML*), wili (HHf). In Ḥarsūsi and Hobyōt, it is limited, under the same conditions, to certain verbs.

The prefixes are those of the indicative imperfect, the suffix is, in the whole paradigm, -n.

Table 17.12   Subjunctive

		MQn (*ML*)	HHf	*ḤL*	*JL*	SQbH 'to know'
Sg.	1c.	lərkēz	lyʌrēb	əlbēd	lkɔ́dər	ləˤárəb
	2m.	tərkēz	tyʌrēb	təlbēd	tkɔ́dər	təˤárəb
	f.	tərkēz (tərkēzi)	tyʌrēb	təlbēd	tkídər	təˤárib
	3m.	lərkēz (yərkēz)	yiyʌrēb	yəlbēd	ykɔ́dər	ləˤárəb
	f.	tərkēz	tyʌrēb	təlbēd	tkɔ́dər	təˤáreb
Du.	1c.	(ərəkzō)	[?]	əlbədō	ləkɔ́drɔ́	ləˤrɔ́bo
	2c.	(tərəkzō)	[?]	təlbədō	təkdɔ́rɔ́	təˤrɔ́bo
	3m.	(yərəkzō)	[?]	yəlbədō	yəkdɔ́rɔ́	ləˤrɔ́bo
	f.	(tərəkzō)	[?]	təlbədō	təkdɔ́rɔ́	təˤrɔ́bo
Pl.	1c.	nərkēz	nyʌrēb	nəlbēd	nəkdér	nəˤáreb
	2m.	tərkēzəm	tyʌrēbum	təlbɔ́dəm	təkdɔ́r	təˤáreb
	f.	tərkēzən	tyʌrēbən	təlbɔ́dən	təkdérən	təˤárebən
	3m.	lərkēzəm	yiyʌrēbum	yəlbɔ́dəm	yəkdɔ́r	ləˤárib
	f.	tərkēzən	tyɔ̄rbən	təlbɔ́dən	təkdérən	təˤárebən

Table 17.13   Conditional

		ML (type A) 'to put something straight'	*ML* (type B) 'to get broken'	HHf 'to be, become'	Jibbāli 'to be able'
Sg.	1c.	lərkēzən	ləθbīrən	lkīnən	ləkdírən
	2m.	tərkēzən	təθbīrən	tkīnən	təkdírən
	f.	tərkēzən	təθbīrən	tkūnən	təkdírən
	3m.	yərkēzən	yəθbīrən	ykūnən	yəkdírən
	f.	tərkēzən	təθbīrən	tkīnən	təkdírən
Du.	1c.	lərkəzáyən	ləθbəráyən	[?]	nəkdɔ́rɔ́n
	2c.	tərkəzáyən	təθbəráyən	[?]	təkdɔ́rɔ́n
	3m.	yərkəzáyən	yəθbəráyən	[?]	yəkdɔ́rɔ́n
	f.	tərkəzáyən	təθbəráyən	[?]	təkdɔ́rɔ́n
Pl.	1c.	nərkəzáyən	nəθbīrən	nkūnən	nəkdérən
	2m.	tərkēzən	təθbīrən	tkīnən	təkdérən
	f.	tərkēzən	təθbīrən	tkūnən	təkdérən
	3m.	yərkēzən	yəθbīrən	ykīnən	yəkdɔ́rɔ́n
	f.	tərkēzən	təθbīrən	tkūnən	nəkdérən

The pattern of the simple verbs of type A, is like the subjunctive.

Simple verb (type B)   *Perfect*   See Table 17.14, p. 406. In Mehri sg. 3f. (type B) = sg. 3f. (type A). The conjugation of type B verbs in HHf (θēbər) and ḤL is the same as in Mehri. In *JL*, Johnstone gives *fɔ́ðər* as a variant, in the entire paradigm of the verb.

Imperfect   See Table 17.15, p. 406. In Mehri (*ML*), at pl. the conjugation of indicative type B is the same as the pl. passive voice (cf. Examples of the passive, p. 407).

Table 17.14   Simple verb (type B), perfect

		MHf (*ML*) 'to get broken'	JL 'to shiver with fear'	SQa 'to get broken'
Sg.	1c.	θɔ́brek (θɔ́brək)	féðərk	géšəlk
	2m.	θɔ́brek (θɔ́brək)	féðərk	géšəlk
	f.	θɔ́breš (θɔ́brəš)	féðərš/š̃	géšəlš
	3m.	θībər	féðər	géšəl
	f.	θəbrōt (θəbrūt)	fiðirɔ́t	géšələh
Du.	1c.	θɔ́brəki	féðərš/ši	géšəlki
	2c.	θɔ́brəki	féðərš/ši	géšəlki
	3m.	θbərō (θəbrō)	féðérɔ́	géšələ̷
	f.	(θəbərtō)	féðértɔ́	géšəltø̸
Pl.	1c.	θɔ́brən	féðərən	géšələn
	2m.	θɔ́brəkəm (-bər-)	féðərkum	géšəlkən
	f.	θɔ́brəkən (-bər-)	féðərkən	géšəlkən
	3m.	θɔ́brəm	féðər	géšel
	f.	θībər	féðər	géšəl

Table 17.15   Simple verb (type B), imperfect

		MHf (*ML*)	JL	(SJms) 'to remember'
Sg	1c.	εθbōr (ə-)	əféðɔ́r	ədékɔr
	2m.	təθbōr	təféðɔ́r	tdékɔr
	f.	təθbēr (θəbáyri)	tfíðír	tdékir
	3m.	yəθbōr	yféðɔ́r	ydékɔr
	f.	təθbōr	təféðɔ́r	tdékɔr
Du.	1c.	(əθbərō)	nfəðérɔ́	[?]
	2c.	(təθbərō)	tfəðérɔ́	[?]
	3m.	(yəθbərō)	yfəðérɔ́	[?]
	f.	(təθbərō)	tfəðérɔ́	[?]
Pl.	1c.	nəθbōr	nféðɔ́r	ndékɔr
	2m.	təθbīrəm (təθbīr)	tféðér	tdékɔr
	f.	təθbōrən	tféðɔ́rən	tdékɔrən
	3m.	yəθbīrəm (yəθbīr)	yféðér	ydékɔr
	f.	təθbōrən	tféðɔ́rən	tdékɔrən

Table 17.16   Subjunctive conjugation in Jibbāli (*JL*)

	Singular	Dual	Plural
1c.	ləfðɔ́r	nfəðərɔ́	nəfðɔ́r
2m.	təfðɔ́r	*tfəðərɔ́*	təðfér
f.	təfðír	tfəðərɔ́	təfðɔ́rən
3m.	yəfðɔ́r	yfəðərɔ́	yəðfér
f.	təfðɔ́r	tfəðərɔ́	təfðɔ́rən

Subjunctive See Table 17.16, p. 406. For type B, in Mehri, the subjunctive pattern is the same as the indicative with a *l*- prefix before some of the forms.

In Soqoṭri, it was not possible to elicit a full paradigm for the subjunctive forms of type B verbs.

The Passive
The vocalic passive form occurs in all MSAL. It is particularly frequent in Soqoṭri, which makes an important use of the impersonal passive.

The pattern of the passive of simple verbs is (pf./impf./subj.):

MQn   CīCéC/iCīCéC/l CīCéC
ML   CəCēC/yəCCōC/yəCCōC
JL   (ε)CCíC/i/éCCɔ́C/yəCCɔ́C
SQa   CīCe/əC/CūCəC/lCCɔ́C

Examples of the passive:

	active	::	passive	
MQn (*ML*)	xʌlū̧k	::	xīlḗk/ixīlḗk/ (xəlū̧k :: xəlḗk/yəxlōk/ –)	'to create'
	ləbū̧d	::	lībḗd (əwbūd :: derived form)	'to strike'
HHf	gelōd	::	gilēd/yagəlód/yə́gəlod	'to hit'
JL	lɔ̄d	::	līd ⟨lbd⟩	'to strike'
	šēm	::	ším ⟨š'm⟩	'to sell'
	erṣɔ́k	::	erṣík	'to bless'
SQa	ráḥaṣ/iróḥaṣ/lráḥaṣ	::	rīḥaṣ/rūḥaṣ/lerḥɔ́ṣ	'to wash, to cure'
	šḗdə	::	šídə	'to divide'

This vocalic pattern is valid for the passive of the simple verb and for some derived themes:

MQn	həḍkáwk (derived by *h*-)	::	hḍīkḗk		'to grind'
JL	oxōṭ	::	exíṭ ⟨xbṭ⟩ (derived by int. modif.)	'to load'
	effósx	::	efséx (derived by infixed -*t*-)	'to undress, to untie'
SJms	ʾə́nkaʿ	::	ʾínkaʿ (derived by pref.)	'to make go, to bring'

Generally, in Jibbāli and Soqoṭri, the personal prefixes do not occur in the passive form, therefore the prefix *l*- occurs in the whole paradigm of the subjunctive: SQa subj. pl. 2f.: *tšemaʿan* :: *ləšmáʿan* ('to make hear', derived by prefixed *š*, ⟨hmʿ⟩).

Verbal Tense and Modalities
Particles, preverbs and auxiliary verbs or periphrastic constructions are used to express tenses and modalities. The prefix conjugation has an imperfect value and the suffix conjugation a perfect one.

Main Aspectual–Temporal Markers
• δ-/d- (M, Hb., Ḥ), d-/ed-/id- (Jib.)

The prefix conjugation with this aspectual–temporal marker has a concomitant value. This marker does not occur before the *t-* prefix.

MQn *d-əhōriğ šīš mehrīyət* 'I am speaking Mehri to you'
ML *hoh δ-əšámələn təgərēt* 'I am dealing with merchants'
HHf *δ-iʿámər* 'he is saying'
ḤL *δ-aṣáwwər* 'I am stopping'
JL *d-igɔ́ləd* 'he is hitting' (*ygɔ́ləd* 'he (always) hits')

The suffix conjugation with this aspectual–temporal marker is a resultative perfective. It is a means to express the state resulting from an accomplished process:

MQn *ṣʌrɔ̄mʌh də-nfū̃s* 'now, he is gone'
ḤL *hoh δə-hēndək* 'I am sleepy'
JL *eṣəfərí ed-mízɔ̃t míh* 'the pan is full of water'

• *ber/bər/bɛr*
In Mehri, Hobyōt, Ḥarsūsi *ber* is an invariable preverb. In Jibbāli and Soqoṭri, *bər* is conjugated at the suffix conjugation. Its values and functioning are similar to CA *qad*.

With the prefix conjugation, examples are scarce; *bər* means 'now, already', and it often expresses that something has happened, as opposed to circumstances or another state/fact: MQn *bər isyūr lēken ihōrig láʾ* '[baby] already walks but he doesn't speak (yet)'.

In *JL*, after *ber*, the impf. is always with *d-*: *ber d-ikɔ́təb* 'he is already writing'; *nḥan bérən ed-nyéfəl ʿar šúylən* 'we've been neglecting our work'.

With the suffix conjugation, *ber* insists on the completion of the process, with a resultative value:

MQnB *wət myɔ̄rən bər kḗšā, iṭáwyəm teh* 'afterwards, when it is quite dried, they eat it'
HHf *hoh bɛr wtəlúmk* 'I am prepared'
ḤL *ḥádōtya nθ̣ēf, bər rəḥḗṣək tīsən* 'my hands are clean, I've just washed them'
JL *bérɔ́t ṣafḥɔ́t* 'she is past childbearing'
SQb *šarɪ̄ṭ bər mīleʾ* 'the tape is full (it has just stopped)'

With the future, it expresses imminence: MQn *bər ḥɔ́m əlté (u myɔ̄rən xʌdmō-na)* 'I am about to eat (and afterwards I'll work)'; *JL ber ḥa-yɔ́ktəb* 'he is about to write'.

Future
Soqoṭri is the only language that does not have a special future conjugation (the prefix conjugation is used). In Mehri, Ḥarsūsi, and Baṭḥari the future is expressed by means of a verbo-nominal form, the active participle, that only has a predica-

tive function. It varies in gender and number.

In the basic form, the participle has an -*a* suffix: C*ə*CC*ōn*-*a*, C*ə*C*ī*C*t*-*a*/ (C*ə*C-C*ōn*-*i*, C*ə*CC*áwt*-*i*)/C*ə*C*ēy*C-*a*, C*ə*CC*ūt*ə*n* (sg. m., f./(du. m., f.)/pl. m., f.). The active participle stem of the derived forms differs from the subjunctive pattern only by the addition of an *m*- prefix, and occasionally of an -*a* suffix. Gender opposition is neutralized at the plural of derived forms in MQnB and in *ML* (but not in MQn) and the common plural is identical to the nominal feminine plural: MQnB *məkaráwtən*, future (pl. c.) of *hakrawr* 'to go at midday'.

In these languages, the periphrasis: "want" + a subjunctive verb also has a future value.

In Hobyōt, the future consists of *méd*- + suffix pronoun + verb. The suffix pronoun refers to the subject; the verb is in the subjunctive (in some dialects, the particle is invariable): HHf *médiš-tətīk ḥmo* 'she will drink water', HHt *méd-yəntáwhɔm* 'they will fight one another'.

In Jibbāli, the subjunctive is preceded by the preverb *ha-/ḥ*-: JL *ha-yśóm* 'he'll buy', *ha-lɣád* 'I'll go', *ḥ-íḥí* 'he will look for'.

Adverbs, and Other Parts of Speech

Adverbs
Besides temporal deictics (cf. Deictics Referring to Time, p. 393), the common adverbs of time are:

> *sōbər* (M) *ṣēbər* (Ḥ) *sɔ́bər* (Jib.) *déhər* (S.) 'always'
> *ʾábdan* (M), *bdan* (Jib.) 'never, ever' (from Ar.)
> *mɣōrən* (M), *mɣɔ́rɛ* (Hb.), *məɣārə* (B), *mɣōrhən* (rare)/*mətəlē* (Ḥ), *mɣɔ́rɛ̄*
> (Jib.), *mser* ⟨mən + sar/ser⟩ (S.) 'afterwards, later on'
> *yəllílə* (M), *əlʿáyni/əlʿéni* (Jib.) 'tonight'
> *ɣasré* (Jib.) 'at night'

Some prepositions are used in constructions denoting time: *k*- in Mehri, Hobyōt, Ḥarsūsi, Jibbāli, and *l*- in Soqotri for periods of the day: *k-ṣōbaḥ* (M, Hb., Ḥ), *k-ḥáṣṣáf*/*k-ḥáṣaf* (Jib.), *lə-ṣabḥ* (S.) 'in the morning', and part of the year in MQn: *k-xáref* 'in autumn'.

Other Parts of Speech

Prepositions
The prepositions common to all MSAL are:

> *b*(ə)- 'in, with', *h*(ə)- 'to, for', *l*- 'against, on', *k* + N/š + suf. pro. 'with', *mən*
> 'from', *t*(ə)- accusative marker for personal pronoun
> *ðār* (M, Ḥ)/*ðér* (Jib.)/*ṭār* (MQn)/*ṭhar* (S.) 'on'
> *ənxāli* (M, Ḥ)/*nxín*, *lxín* (Jib.)/*nḥaṭ* (S.) 'under'

sār (M, Ḥ)/*ser* (Jib.)/*sar* (S.) 'behind'
fən, fənw- (M, B)/*fēn* (Hb.)/*fēn* (Ḥ)/*fénɛ ɛ, fən-έ-* (Jib.), (*di-*)*fónə, fénə* (S.)
   'before, in front of'

Some prepositions do not occur in all the MSAL:

bād/*baʿd* (M, Ḥ) (cf. Arabic) and *əm-bād*/*mən-bād* (M), *mən-ðér* (Jib.) 'after'
bərk/*brek* (M, Hb., B, Ḥ) 'in, inside, at'
tē/*tɛ*/*tā* (M, Ḥ, Jib.)/*ʾɛtēʾ* (Hb.) 'up to'
ʿan (Jib. 'from, than'/*ʿa(n)* (S.) 'from, to'
ken (Jib.)/*kən, kɛn* (S.) 'from'
ʾəd/*ʾid*/*d* (S.) 'in, to'/(*ʾe*)*d* (Jib.) 'to, up to', *ʾɛd* 'till' (Jib.)
yɔl (Jib.)/*diɔl* (*ʾəd* + ɔl) (S.) 'towards'
wdé- (M, Ḥ) 'towards'
ʿak/*ʿamk* (Jib.) 'in, at' (cf. *ʿamk* (M, Hb., Ḥ, S.) 'middle')

In Mehri, Hobyōt, Baṭhari, Ḥarsūsi and Jibbāli, *h-* 'to, for' is used in compound prepositions: *h-āl, h-al*/*h-ən* (M) 'to, at, with', *hné* + N (ML), *hné* + suf. pro. (MQn) 'at', *hel, helt-* (Ḥ) 'at', *her* (Jib.) 'to, up to, for', *hes* (Jib.) 'up to'.
Each language also has its own prepositions that do not occur in the others:

Ḥ: *wəl* 'towards', *əm-būn, mātōd* 'after'
Jib.: *tél* + N/*tɔ́l* + suf. pro. 'at, with', *mən- tél* 'from', *ʿémt* 'towards, to', *her* 'up to, to, for'
S.: *ʿaf*/*ʾaf* 'up to, until'

The same element can be either a preposition, a conjunction or an adverb:
hes 'up to' and 'then, when' (Jib.) and *hīs*/*his*/*hes* (M), *hīs*/*həs*/*əs* (Ḥ) 'when, since; like', *hes* 'like' (Hb.); *her* 'up to, to, for' and 'if, when' (Jib.).

Conjunctions
The main temporal conjunctions are:

teh/*teʾ*/*te*/*tē*/*tɛ*/*ta* (M, Hb., Ḥ), *tə-wət* (MQn), *ʾɛ*/*ɛl*/*ʾa* (Jib.) 'until, till, then when'
mət /*mayt*/*mit* (ML, Hb., Ḥ, Jib., S.), *wət*/*wet* (MQn), *her* (Jib.), *ḥákt ɛ-* 'when', *hes* (M, Hb., Ḥ, Jib.), *tœ*/*tə, ʿam* (S.) 'when, as'
lɔd/*lɔt, sɛ̄ʿ* (S.) 'when, while'
lol/*lɔ́l, ke, karámmə, kaném(m)ɔ* (S.) 'when, if'

The main causal conjunctions are: *ʾən*/*l-ən* (M), *yənn* (Ḥ), *l-ín*/*l-hin* (Jib.) 'because'.
The main final conjunctions are: *l-egirēh*/*l-agərē* (M) (but *l-ɛgeré* 'because, for' in Jibbāli), *hér* (Jib.), *ukɛn* (*'and'+'to be'*) and *kɛr* (S.) 'in order to, so that'.

Interrogative Particles

híne (Hb.), *híne*, *héni* (Jib.) 'why?'
kō, kóh (ML), *wəkō* (ML, MQn), *kɔ, wəkɔ́* (Hb.), *kɔh* (Jib.) and *hībáh* (ML),
   hībóh (MQn), *həbó* (Hb.), *hābō* (B), *həbō* (H), *'ɪ̃fo/'ɪ̃fɔl /fəl* (S.) 'how?
   why?'
mayt (M), *mit* (Jib.), *míh/mīh* (S.) 'when?'
ḥō (ML), *hō* (MQn), *hɔ́* (Hb.), *ḥān(ə)* (B), *ḥōnəh* (H), *hun, hútun* (Jib.),
   hɔn/ho/ho'o (S.) 'where?'
wəlē ⟨*w* + neg.⟩ (M), *flɔ, bé-flɔ́* ⟨*b* 'and' + *lɔ* neg.⟩ (Jib.) 'or else?'

Verbal Particles and Auxiliaries
Besides *ber*, and *d-/δ-*, other verbal particles and auxiliaries are used to express
durativity, iterativity, imminence, etc.:

ād-/'ād-/ād- + suf. pro. + perfect/imperfect, for the progressive (M, H)
'ād-/'ād-/ād- + suf. pro. + *'ar/'ar* (restrictive particle) + *mən* + suf. pro. + pf.
   'to have just ...' (M)
hal/xal + subj. (S.), *ləbōd* (aux.) (H), *'ɔd/'ad* (aux., pf.) + indicative (Jib., S.)
   'to keep on'
wīka/wēka (aux.) + subj. (M, H), *lá'af/lɔ́ɣəf* (aux.) + impf. 'to be used to'
'āzōm ⟨'zm⟩ (aux.) + subj. 'almost/very nearly' in the past (M, H)
ṣōr (aux.) + *d-/δ-* + imperf. (M) 'to begin to'

Syntax

Word Order
In the sentence, the order may be: subordinate clause + main clause or vice versa.
Topicalization and focusing are to be taken into account.

Clause Level
In nominal clauses, the order is subject + nominal predicate:

SQa *ṭáhin nāfə di-ɣagētən* '(to) grind (is) the work of women'
MQn *yimóh raḥmēt* 'today it rains' ⟨today rain⟩
BM *kéllas eká' lə bəṭáhrīt we hémahuw bit bəṭhār* 'all the earth (belonged) to
   the B. and their name (was) B.B.' ⟨all it (f.) earth to Bathari and name-them
   Bait Biṭhar⟩.

In verbal clauses, the order is VSO or SVO, but if the subject is an independent
pronoun it is always placed before the verb.

Phrase Level

Nominal Phrases

The definite article when it exists (in the Mehri of Oman, Ḥarsūsi, Jibbāli) is always prefixed to the definite item, noun or adjective whose first consonant is voiced or ejective/glottalized.

In a nominal phrase with two nouns, the word order is always *determinatum* + determiner; the same with adjectives: N + Adj.

In all languages, except Soqoṭri, the word order in possessive construction is: possessed + possessor (cf. Possession in Soqoṭri, p. 419).

The construct state is only found in some frozen constructions and special words (kinship nouns, parts of the body, and the item *baʿl* 'owner, possessor, he of …'). In the languages with a definite article, the two terms are usually definite, and if the determiner is a suffixed pronoun, the noun is definite, as opposed to Arabic syntax.

> MQn *bōli ḵā́sən* 'they of (the inhabitants) Qishn'
> ḤL *lēlt awkēb* 'the wedding night' ⟨night entry (def.)⟩
> JL *ēṭəb ōz* 'the teat of goat'
> SQa *bər ḵāḵa* 'nephew' ⟨son brother/sister⟩

This construction very rarely occurs in Hobyōt.

Usually a particle binds the *determinatum* to the determiner. This particle is *δ-/d-* after a singular noun, and *l-* (JL *íź*) after a plural noun. In Mehri, even with a plural noun the particle is often *δ-/d-*. In Jibbāli, *δ-* does not occur in a possessive phrase (the particle is *ɛ́*). In the languages with a definite article, both items of the phrase may be definite.

> MQn *hadūtən l-nūr* '(the) maternal aunts of Nur'
> MJb *kīs δ²-tōmər* 'sack of dates'
> HHf *šinót δə-ḵanyún* 'the sleep of babies'
> ḤL *əśnéwwət δə-ḥəyδōntən* 'jaw-joints' ⟨joints (def.) of ears⟩
> BM *nātuš le-ḥālīt* 'spots of rust'
> JL *mékék δə-ḵít* 'half a sack of food', *edaʿbéh iź-šxɔ́rtə* 'curses of the old women', *eṭb ɛ-ʾɛ́mɛ́š* 'the teat of its (f.) mother'
> SAK *ḵɔ́trəh d-dǿr* 'a drop of blood'

Verbal Phrases

The direct or indirect object follows the verb directly in verbal phrases. When the complement is pronominal, it is often (always in Soqoṭri) introduced by the accusative particle *t-*. Verbs with three valences have the pronominal complement preceding the nominal complement: V + (*t-*) suf. pro. + N. When both complements are pronominal, the order is the following: V + (*t*)-pr. suf. (beneficiary) + *t*-pr. suf. obj.

MJb *ṭəlōm tē-sən ḥmo* 'they ask them (f.) for water'
ML ṭəláwb-əh ṣalḥ 'they asked him for a truce'
HHf *wuzum t-ī te-h* 'he gave it to me'

Complex Sentences

In asyndetic constructions, the complement clause follows the main clause. In hypothetical conditional sentences, the protasis mainly precedes the apodosis. With causal, final and temporal clauses, the clause order varies.

Agreement Rules

Generally, the subject governs person, gender and number agreement in the verb. Personal and deictic pronouns, attributive and predicative adjectives agree in gender and number (including dual in Soqoṭri), also in definiteness for attributives, with the nouns they determine. Except in Soqoṭri, a dual noun often governs a plural agreement. With multiple subjects, agreement is always pl. m., even if one of the subjects is feminine.

Animate collective nouns govern a singular or plural (m. or f.) agreement: *ML həbɛ́r kálləs* 'all the camels' ⟨the-camels all-her⟩, *həbɛ́r əlyákəməh* 'those camels'; but the word for 'cow' in Jibbāli and HHf is f. in sg. and m. in pl. as regards concord: HHf *δɛ́nəh lɛ̄ˀ wuzúm tī tīs* 'this cow, he gave it (f.) to me', and in pl. *lɛ́nəh lhɛ̄tə, wuzúm tī tohum.*

Negations

The syntax of negation in all MSAL is different from that in Arabic. Each language has its own construction and in all of them (except in Jibbāli) perfect and imperfect conjugations have the same negation as well as declarative, interrogative (with an indicative verb) and prohibitive (with an imperfect and subjunctive verb) sentences in five of the six languages, the Soqoṭri of Soqoṭra being the exception.

In the Mehri of Oman, and some eastern dialects of the Mehri of the Yemen, in Hobyōt, in Jibbāli, the negative particle has two elements (ə)*l* ... *laˀ/ˀɔ(l)* ... *lɔˀ* enveloping the negated term:

ML ˀəl səbɛ̄b-i laˀ '(it's) not my fault', *əl awágəbkəm təsīrəm wə-tkalām aməláwtəy wəṭōməh laˀ* 'it is not fitting for you to go and leave the dead like that', *əl təhɛ̄ləz bɛy laˀ* 'don't nag me!'
HHt *l-šīn siyɛrɔ́t láˀ* 'we haven't ⟨with-us⟩ cars'
JL āxṭɛ́r ɔl ksɛ́ mίh hɛ́r yɔ́fhəṣ tίhum lɔ́ˀ 'the caravan did not find water to boil their meat', *embɛ́rɛ ōrói ɔ ytɛ́ ɛ yəśbáˤ lɔ́ˀ* 'the shy boy does not eat till he is satisfied', *ɔ tśɛ́rk δɔ́hun lɔ́ˀ* 'don't do that!', *ɔl ɛ́γbəδəš lɔ́ˀ* 'don't anger him!'

In Hobyōt, negation in declarative sentences may have only the postposed element, the construction being similar to what it is in the Mehri of the Yemen, Baṭhari and Ḥarsūsi. This variation can be observed within the use of individual speakers: HHf (*əl*) *ixóm yánṣoz šēhi lá᾽* 'he doesn't want to drink tea'. In prohibitive sentences, in Hobyōt, only the second element is present: HHf *tezēm lá᾽* 'don't give!'.

In the Mehri of Oman, in prohibitive sentences the negation is often marked by the postposed item alone, and in *JL*, optionally in prohibitive sentences the first item occurs alone, in a reduced form: *JL ᶜɔ tɔ́ktə́b* 'do not write!'

Sometimes, in *ML*, the first element occurs alone in interrogative sentences, and in Jibbāli, in complement clauses after verbs of fearing, hoping etc. (Johnstone 1981: 2).

In the Mehri of the Yemen, Baṭḥāri, and Ḥarsūsi, the negative particle is the morpheme *la᾽*. Always postposed to the negated term, it is often placed at the end of a clause:

> MQn *hēt hēs-t-ī hoh lá᾽* 'you are not like me' ⟨you like-prep.-me I neg.⟩,
> *kədūrən ngərē ́sxə́f də hāybī́t də bṓli gṓdəb lá᾽* 'we couldn't drink the milk
> of the camels of the inhabitants of Jadib', MQn *tgirā kahwēt lá᾽* 'don't drink
> coffee!'
> BM *rahak lā* '(it's) not far'
> ḤL *əkhṓl əyətér la᾽* 'I cannot speak', *təhémməh la᾽* 'don't bother about it!' (=
> ML *təhtə́mməh la᾽*)

In Soqoṭri, in declarative sentences, the particle of negation is *ɔl* (realized sometimes [ɔ́ź]) always preposed to the negated term or phrase: SQb *sɛ ɔl hówrəh* 'she (is) not black', *ɔl fśɛk* 'I didn't lunch'; SQaB *ɔl tənɔ́dək káləm dīye* 'you do not say anything good'.

In prohibitive sentences, the negative particle is *᾽al᾽a(n)/ha*, according to the dialect, followed by the subjunctive: SHr *᾽a tə́te* 'don't eat!', SQb *᾽a lə́zᶜam* 'don't sit down!' (subj. without pers. pref.), SQa *ha tígdehən* 'don't come (pl.)!'. But, in the dialect of the islet of 'Abd-al-Kūri, the particle is *ɔl* + subj.: *ɔl tšémtœl!* 'don't speak!'

Interrogation

Intonation alone is enough to express interrogation: MJb *təhṓrig məhriyṓt*? 'do you speak eastern Mehri?'

Some wh-words are always in head position: SQb *ho᾽o d-mésɛ kɔ̃n*? 'where has it rained?' ⟨where of-rain it-was⟩, *īnɛm d-haf de-ha w-ífol d-mey^h šɛm*? 'what is this place here, and what is its name?' ⟨and-how of-him name⟩; others always in final position: MQn *āmərk hībóh* 'what is it that you said? what did you say?', *hámməs mṓn*? 'what is her name?'; HHf *nkaᶜk men hɔ̃*? 'where do you come from?'

Among the latter, *wəlē* is always uttered after a pause: MQn *thɔ̃m hmo*? *wəlē᾽*? 'do you want water, or not?'

Interro-negative sentences are syntactically similar to negative sentences or interrogative ones: MQn *thɔ̃m kahwēt lá᾽*? 'don't you want coffee?'; S. *ɔl gə́ᶜərk*? 'aren't you ill?' (= 'how are you?').

Coordination (Phrasal and Clausal)

Coordination can be only mere juxtaposition, but most often the coordinating conjunction, is used: *wə* (*w*, *ū*, *u*) in Mehri, Hobyōt, Baṭḥari, Ḥarsūsi, Soqoṭri, and *b* in Jibbāli. This particle is affixed to the second term of the coordination: JL *hé b-hét* 'you and I'; SQb *b-ʿamḳ d-ḥadībo^h u-ḥáwləf* 'between Hadiboh and Hawlef'.

In narratives, *w/b* often indicates a new step in the relation of events. It means 'and thus, and suddenly': MJb *ɣaggēn u-ɣath kōsəm āgizón tūtóbən u-hem ṭáymən* 'a boy and his sister met women who were tanning and (thus) were thirsty'. *w* may also introduce a causative clause: SQaB *ɔl idīnɔt w-ɔl ṣ̌ə̄rət* 'she has not been found guilty because she did not do harm'.

When *w-* coordinates two negative clauses ('nor, or, neither ... nor'), it is immediately followed by the negative particle, even in the languages where this is at the end of the phrase: MQn *gehmōna-lá sḳóṭra u-la kūryamūrya u-la ābdəlkūri* 'I shall neither go to Soqotra nor Kurya Murya or ʿAbd-al-Kūri' (compare with: MQn *gehmōna sḳóṭra-lá, kūryamūrya-lá, ābdəlkūri-lá*, with the same meaning).

Conditionals

The apodosis is introduced by a particle.

Real Conditional

The verb in the protasis is in the suffix conjugation (perfect) or in the prefix conjugation (imperfect), the verb in the apodosis is in the indicative imperfect, future or subjunctive/imperative.

- M (*u-*)*lū*, *lē* '(even) if':
  MQn *ulū het ḳəhábk la' uzmēnəs* ⟨fut.⟩ *ha ērs* 'even if you don't come, I'll go to the wedding'
- M, Hb., Ḥ *'am*, *hām/ham*, *hɔm* 'if':
  MQn *ham xərāgək, tḵɔ́hk lá'* 'if I go out, you don't come' or 'if I am gone, you don't come'
  HHf *hɔm nɔkaʿ geḥme, médi-lʿamer heh* 'if he goes tomorrow, I'll tell him'
  ḤL *am bérək ś́éllək téni əlá'* 'if you can't give me a lift'
- MJb *hən*, MQn, Hb. *'en* 'if':
  MJb *hən thɔ́m tśənē imō', thakaṣɔ́wm* 'if you want to see what it is, you spend the afternoon (at home)' (*hɔ́m* occurs always in the imperfect as V₁ in an asyndetic construction)
  HJb *ṭād 'ɛn śɛ́nɔ xáṣməh, iḳərōb hənéh la* 'if someone sees his enemy, he doesn't go near to him'
- Jib. *her*, *hel* 'if, when':
  JL *hér siɛ́rɛh ɔl zḥōt híni lɔ', ḥa-l-əmtéḥɛk* 'if the car does not come to me, I'll get very annoyed'
- Hb. *haδ* ⟨ḥa + δ⟩ (for this construction, cf. Jib. *mit/miδ* + *āl/ē* 'when'):
  HHf *haδ siyūr ḥɔ́f, inōkaʿ bə-tōmər* 'if/when he goes to Hawf, he brings dates'

- S. *tœ, lɔd/t́ɔd* + subj.:

    SQa *tœ tigdə́ḥ* ⟨subj.⟩ *ḥan di-nəzɔ̄γɔn 'ɔk ə́kniyoh* 'if you go, we'll give you food' ⟨we who-give to-you (sg.) food⟩

    SQb *t́ɔd ligdaḥ* 'if he goes'

- S. *ke*:

    SQaB *kə rībən hes wu 'ɛsə tsɔ́kɔf* 'if we advise her, then maybe she'll calm down'

- MQn *əlḵā* (subj. sg. 3m. of *wīḵa'* 'to be, to happen') + subj., and future in the apodosis:

    MQn *əlḵā ḥáybi l-nkā ha-bārīs, āmələ́ya ḥáflɛh ḥanōbət* 'if my father goes to Paris, we'll give a big party'

Unreal Conditional

The verb in the apodosis is in the perfect or in a modal conjugation (subjunctive or conditional) and, for an unreal condition in the present, the verb in the protasis is in the perfect.

- MQn *əlḵā* (+ perfect in the protasis and the apodosis):

    MQn *əlḵá kəhə́b fəné ə́ilət yōm ksáynī bə-bēti* 'if he had come three days ago, he would have found me at home'

- *ML*, Ḥ *lū/lō*, Hb. *wili*. The conditional or the subjunctive occur in the apodosis:

    ML *lu ə́īnək tēk, l-əγrēbən* ⟨cond.⟩ *tēk əlá'* 'if I had seen you, I wouldn't have known you'

    HHf *wili nɔka' mə́in, hoh l-kīnən* ⟨cond.⟩ *fərḥənt* 'if he had come yesterday, I would have been happy'

- M *'ə́δə* (rare), Jib. *δ-kun* (⟨rel. + 'to be' pf. sg. 3m.⟩):

    JL *δ-kun 'áťi bun l-γédən* ⟨cond.⟩ *ə́əə̌ ɛ mskɛ́t* 'if 'Ali had been here, I would have gone with him to Muscat'

- S. *l'am, lémən*:

    SQa *l'am 'égib lēə̌ɔm tan* 'if he had wanted to kill us'

    SQa *lémən gə́daḥk, ə́īnək 'áli* 'if you had come, you would have seen 'Ali'

Subordination

Complement Clauses

Many verbs (motion, opinion, will) appear in an asyndetic construction with the verb of the complement clause, mainly when the subject is the same. The second verb is generally in the subjunctive:

MQnB *thɔ̄m tənḥāg* 'she wants to dance (subj.)'

HHf *ɛkhɔ́l lésbah* 'I know (how) to swim'

JL *'ágəb yhɛ́lbəs* 'he wanted to milk it (f.)'

SQaB *'égbən nəḥə́rə' mən məkéylhi* 'we wanted to look for a medicine-man'

Only SAK does not know asyndetic constructions whatever the V₁.

In Mehri, the quotative complement clause is introduced by the relator *d-/ð-*:
MQn *yāmərəm d-bōli yəntūf ḥaməlēya* ⟨fut.⟩ *kəbōbər* 'they say that the inhabitants of Yentuf are preparing torchlights'; MGa *ḥád yiʾōmər ðe tiwī ʾasəbāt shēləm toh ʾāynen* 'someone says that the flesh has been eaten up by the animals'.

In SAK the complement clause is always introduced by the conjunction *kɔ*: *egēboh kɔ tɔbɔš* 'she wants/wanted to cry'. In the other MSAL, the conjunction is often linked to the semantics of the V_1. Some of these elements are also prepositions or relators: *mən, l, d*, and the negative element *ɔ(l)* after verbs of dread and denial in Jibbāli (+ subj.):

> MQn *xzīw mən tāmḗrən* ⟨subj.⟩ *hīni əl-hɔ̄ wəzmītəna* ⟨fut.⟩ *-tēs* 'they refused (f.) to tell me where they would go'
> MQn *hēs hoh kannɔ̄n ɔkōbi d-genni ixárgɔ́m* 'when I was young, I thought that the jinns could appear'
> JL *ɣɔ́lɔ̄t ɔ tzɛm-š* ⟨subj.⟩ *fəndḗl* 'she refused to give him sweet potatoes'
> SHr *ḥaṣáyk ʾen seh təgódeḥən* ⟨imp.⟩ 'I know that she comes/is coming'

Relative Clauses

A relative clause can be placed directly next to the word it determines with an anaphoric independent pronoun, introduced by the conjunction of coordination *w*, but it is mostly introduced by a relative. The antecedent is determined by the article in the Mehri of Oman, Ḥarsūsi, Jibbāli. Relative particles are identical to the genitive particle/relator (cf. Nominal Phrases, p. 412–412). The relative clause also operates as an adjective (cf. Adjectives, p. 393), especially in Jibbāli and Soqotri: JL *etéθ-š ɛ-xerəgót* 'his woman who has died' (= his dead woman); SQa *fəréhəm di-škércæh* 'the girl who was good' (= the good girl), du. *ferīmi di-šəkœrtɔ*, pl. *fɔ́rhɔm di-škɔ́r*, or *nomen agentis*: *di-yhɔ́rək* 'who (m.) robs' (= robber).

Adverbial Clauses

Temporal Clauses
Time clauses are introduced by a subordinative conjunction, some of which are always followed by the subjunctive.

After *te* meaning 'until', the verb is in the subjunctive, but in the indicative when meaning 'when':

> MQn *aṣlōb ḥallīw te lɣalēk* ⟨subj.⟩ *ūrii* 'I am waiting for the night until I see the moon'
> ML *te gzōt ḥəyáwm* 'when the sun went down'
> MQnB *hes wəzūm tēs degēg, xʌzūt* 'when he brought the chicken to her, she refused (it)'
> HHf *hes isīyur ḥɔ̄f, inōkaʿ bə-tōmər* 'when he goes to Hawf, he brings dates'
> JL *ḥákt ēr* ⟨ɛ + ber⟩ *šéké ʾiyyέʾl ḥa-néhɛk hóhum* 'when they have watered the camels we'll call them'

SQa *lɔd* [*źɔd*] *itēbəl di-han ˀérəhɔn məḥādeb, ikēsə ṭáḥrer* 'when they come
    back from their field, they meet wild goats'
SAK *ho*ʰ *šink teš tə ntœf* 'he saw him when he felt'
SAK *ke ḳaṣɔ̄ˤəh izīdə wáyaˤ* ⟨Ar. *wagˤ*⟩ 'when/if she gets up, the pain increas-
    es'
SQa **kanémɔ**ʰ *ṭɔd géḥam lāxeym wukse ikōsə beyh ṣ̌ōdɔh* 'when/if someone
    catches a shark, it happens that he finds a fish in it'

Purpose Clauses
Purpose clauses are not always introduced by a conjunction, but the verb is always
in the subjunctive (except with *kɛr/ḳor, kor* in Soqoṭri).
• Without a conjunction:
    MQn *hēt lūni məɣráf d-ḥmo ləbrēd beh* 'you, bring me a tumbler of water in
       order/so that I freshen up (myself) with it'
• With a conjunction:
    MGa *siyērš mən fransa te būma* **legirēh** *təɣʌrīb mehrīyət* 'you came from
       France up to here, in order to speak Mehri'
    JL *embēré ḥɔ́gɔ́r tɔ* **hér** *l-əzɛ́mš* ⟨subj.⟩ *šé* 'the boy waited for me to give him
       something'
    SQaB *nˤámər* **ukɛn** *nɔ́rəbən* ⟨subj. pl. 1⟩ 'we (shall) act in order to deliberate'
    SQa *yəɣtēri gémhəl* **kɛr** *tigídhən* 'he calls his she-camels so that they come'

Copula, Existential and Possessive Expressions

Copula
The verbs 'to be', in all moods, or·an aspectual–temporal particle + a suffix pro-
noun referring to the subject, act as copulas.
• *kēn, kun, kɔn* 'to be' is only used as a copula of existence:
    MQnB *tkū̃nən bər bəhīl* 'they (f.) are already ready'
    HHf *ˤafərēt tkun his teθ* 'the demon (f.) is like a woman'
    JL *ˤínéθ təṭɔ́lén kərfɔ́fésən b-eṭúf b-ɔkkɔrkúm hér ətkénən lēnáti* 'women make
       up their faces with aloes and saffron to look (to be) white'
In Soqoṭri, like any verb, the copula can be preceded by the verb modifier *ber*:
SQa *berœh kɛ̄noh fḥam* 'it (f.) was already (completely reduced to) coal'.
• *wīḳa* ⟨wḳˤ⟩ 'to be, to become' can be used as a copula (Mehri, Ḥarsūsi) in
existential and possessive sentences:
    MQn *axɔ̄dəm l-gérēh lḳā ši drēhəm* 'I work to have money' ⟨I-work in-order-to
    I-should-be with-me money⟩.
• *ber* + suf. pro. referring to the subject is a copula in nominal clauses:
    MQn = MJb = HHf *bərs bə-ṣ̌áfōr* 'she is (now) in Dhofar'.
• *ˤād/ād/ˤɔd/ɔd* + suf. pro. referring to the subject (Mehri, Ḥarsūsi) or conjugated at the suffix conjugation (Jibbāli, Soqoṭri) is an existential copula 'to be, to
stay'. In Jibbāli *d-* occurs before the copula in positive clauses: *JL embéré d-ˀɔ́d
bún* 'the boy is still here'.

Existential and Possessive Expressions
Nominal sentences (without copula or particle) may express existence, attribution
or possession:

> MQn *ḥarmēt brek bēt* 'the woman (is) at home'
> HHf *ʿali ɣa ðə-fūl* 'Ali is Ful's brother'
> SQb *b-ʿamk d-ḥadībœ u-ḥáwləf, šek* 'between Hadibo and Hawlef, (there is)
>   Sheq'

Existential Particles
All the MSAL have the existential particle *ši* 'there is', that (in Mehri, Hobyōt,
Ḥarsūsi, Jibbāli) shares the same rules that any word in negative sentences: *ši
laʾ/ʾəl ši laʾ* 'there is not'. Soqoṭri has a second existential particle *íno* and a peculiar negative existential particle *bíši* 'there is not': MQn *ši raḥmēt* 'there is rain';
yillēləh ūrīt ši láʾ 'tonight there is no moon'; SQb *bíši rīho* 'there is no water'.

Existential Expressions
They are formed by a locative or attributive preposition + suf.pr.: *b-* 'in, at', *l-* 'to,
for', *š-* 'with':

> MQn *beh hādəbbīt ṭᴧr ləkəlīk d-ēyneh* 'he has a fly in the corner of his eye'
> MJd *ši ḥmo láʾ* 'I have no water'
> SQb *ši ho hǝri* 'I have a canoe' ⟨with-me I canoe⟩

Possession in Soqoṭri
Soqoṭri is different from the other MSAL in the way possession is constructed.
The pronoun referring to the possessor is either an independent pronoun, introduced by the relator *di-*, or a dependent pronoun introduced by the preposition
mə(n), the whole phrase precedes the possessed:

> SQa *di-het mʰer* 'your belly' ⟨of-you belly⟩
> *di-han maʿmáʿihɔn* 'our forefathers' ⟨of-we forefathers⟩
> *mɔ-s fénə* 'her face' ⟨from-her face⟩
> SHo *me-š šʰɛm saʿd* 'his name is Saʿad' ⟨from-him name S⟩

When the possessed is in a construct phrase or in a prepositional phrase, *di/mə*
+ pr. precedes the whole phrase:

> SQa *bīyəh di-hœ di-bēbeh* 'the mother of my father', *di-han mən-xalf* 'out of
>   their place' ⟨of-us from place⟩
> SQb *ɛzʿə́mk di-eyeh b-kaʿr* 'I lived in his house' ⟨I-lived of-him in-house⟩

Abbreviations Related to Language Names and Places

Language names are followed by the abbreviation of place names (for the data of my fieldwork*) or by the reference to the author.

B	Baṭḥari
BM	Baṭḥari from Morris 1983
Ḥ	Ḥarsūsi
ḤL	*Ḥarsūsi Lexicon*, Johnstone 1977
Hb.	Hobyōt
HHf	Hobyōt from Ḥawf
HHt	Hobyōt from the village of Hedemet (north of Ḥawf)
HJb	Hobyōt from Jādib
Jib.	Jibbāli
cJ	central dialect of Jibbāli
eJ	eastern dialect of Jibbāli
JL	*Jibbāli Lexicon*, Johnstone 1981
M	Mehri
MDt	Mehri from Damqawt
MGa	Mehri from al-Ghaydhah
MHf	Mehri from Ḥawf
MJahn	Mehri from Jahn
ML	*Mehri Lexicon*, Johnstone 1987
MO	Mehri of Oman
MQn	Mehri from Qishn
MQnB	Bedouin dialect in the area of Qishn
MY	Mehri of Yemen
S.	Soqoṭri
SAK	Soqoṭri from 'Abd-al-Kūri
SHo	Soqoṭri from Ḥadiboh
SHr	Soqoṭri from the Ḥagher Mountains
SJms	Soqoṭri from Johnstone's manuscript notes
SL	Soqoṭri from Leslau 1938, *Lexique soqoṭri*
SNd	Soqoṭri from Noged
SQa	Soqoṭri from Qalansiyah
SQaB	Bedouin dialect of the area of Qalansiyah
SQb	Soqoṭri from Qadhub

*All the fieldwork had financial support from the Ministère des Affaires Etrangères, the Centre National de la Recherche Scientifique, The University of Paris III, the University of Aden and the Centre Français d'Etudes Yéménites in San'ā. Fieldwork was done between 1983 and 1991 with the contribution of A. Lonnet, and by myself alone afterwards.

References

Johnstone, T. M. 1975. "The Modern South Arabian Languages." *Afro-Asiatic Linguistics* 1/5: 93–121.

—— 1977. *Ḥarsūsi Lexicon and English–Ḥarsūsi Word-List.* London: Oxford University Press.

Lonnet, A. and M.-Cl. Simeone-Senelle. 1983. "Observations phonétiques et phonologiques sur les consonnes d'un dialecte mehri." *Matériaux Arabes et Sudarabiques* 1: 187–218.

Morris, M. 1983. "Some Preliminary Remarks on a Collection of Poems and Songs of the Baṭāḥirah." *Journal of Oman Studies* 6/1: 129–44.

Naumkin, V. V. 1988. *Sokotrijtsy: Istoriko-etnograficeskij ocerk* [The Socotrans: A historical and ethnographical study]. Moscow: Nauka.

Further Reading

For a complete bibliography of Modern South Arabian Languages up to 1977 see:

Leslau, Wolf. 1946. "Modern South Arabic Languages: A Bibliography." *Bulletin of the New York Public Library* 50/8: 607–633.

Robin, Christian. 1977. *Bibliographie générale systématique (Corpus des Inscriptions et des Antiquités sud-arabes)*, Louvain: Peeters. 89–99.

Arnold, Werner. 1993. "Zur Position des Hobyot in den neusüdarabischen Sprachen." *Zeitschrift für Arabische Linguistik* 25: 17–24.

Bittner, M. 1913. *Charakteristik der Šḥauri-Sprache in den Bergen von Ḍofâr am persischen Meerbusen* (Kaiserliche Akademie der Wissenschaften, *Anz. Phil.-Hist. Kl.* Jahrg. 50). Vienna: Hölder.

—— 1909–1914. *Studien zur Laut- und Formenlehre der Mehri-Sprache in Südarabien* (Kaiserliche Akademie der Wissenschaften, *Sb. Phil.-Hist. Kl.* 162/5, 168/2, 172/5, 174/4). Vienna: Hölder.

—— 1913, 1918. *Vorstudien zur Grammatik und zum Wörterbuche der Soqoṭri-Sprache I, II, III* (Kaiserliche Akademie der Wissenschaften, *Sb. Phil.-Hist. Kl.* 173/4, 186/4, 5). Vienna: Hölder.

—— 1916–1917. *Studien zur Šḥauri-Sprache in den Bergen von Ḍofâr am persischen Meerbusen* (Kaiserliche Akademie der Wissenschaften, *Sb. Phil.-Hist. Kl.* 179/2, 4, 5, 183/5). Vienna: Hölder.

Jahn, A. 1902. *Mehri-sprache in Südarabien: Texte und Wörterbuch.* Vienna: Hölder.

—— 1905. *Grammatik der Mehri-Sprache in Südarabien* (Kaiserliche Akademie der Wissenschaften, *Sb. Phil.-Hist. Kl.* 150/6). Vienna: Hölder.

Johnstone, T. M. 1968. "The Non-occurrence of a t- Prefix in Certain Socotri Verbal Forms." *Bulletin of the School of Oriental and African Studies* 31/3: 515–525.

—— 1970a. "A Definite Article in the Modern South Arabian Languages." *Bulletin of the School of Oriental and African Studies* 33/2: 295–307.

—— 1970b. "Dual forms in Mehri and Ḥarsūsi." *Bulletin of the School of Oriental and African Studies* 33/3: 501–512.

—— 1980a. "Gemination in the Jibbāli language of Dhofar." *Zeitschrift für Arabische Linguistik* 4: 61–71.

—— 1980b. 'The Non-occurrence of a t-Prefix in Certain Jibbāli Verbal Forms." *Bulletin of the School of Oriental and African Studies* 43/3: 466–470.

—— 1981. *Jibbāli Lexicon.* London: Oxford University Press.

—— 1982. "The System of Enumeration in the South Arabian Languages." In *Arabian and Islamic Studies: Articles Presented to R. B. Serjeant*, ed. R. L. Bidwell and G. Rex

Smith. London and New York: Longman.
—— 1987. *Mehri Lexicon and English–Mehri Word-List, with Index of the English Definitions in the Jibbāli Lexicon*, compiled G. Rex Smith. London: SOAS.
Leslau, W. 1938. *Lexique soqoṭri (sudarabique moderne) avec comparaisons et explications étymologiques*. Paris: Klincksieck.
Lonnet, A. and M.-Cl. Simeone-Senelle. 1997. "La Phonologie des langues sudarabiques modernes." In *Phonologies of Asia and Africa*, ed. Alan S. Kaye. Winona Lake: Eisenbrauns, 337–372.
Müller, D.-H. 1902. *Die Mehri- und Soqoṭri Sprache*, volume 1: *Texte* (Südarabische Expedition 4). Vienna: Hölder.
—— 1905. Volume 2: *Soqoṭri-Texte* (Südarabische Expedition 6). Vienna: Hölder.
—— 1907. Volume 3: *Šḥauri-Texte* (Südarabische Expedition 7). Vienna: Hölder.
Naumkin, V. V. and V. Ya. Porxomovskij. 1981. *Ocerki po etnolingvistike sokotry* [Ethnolinguistic Studies of Soqotra]. Moscow: Nauka.
Simeone-Senelle, M.-Cl. 1991. "Récents développements des recherches sur les langues sudarabiques modernes." In *Proceedings of the Fifth International Hamito-Semitic Congress 1987*, volume 2, ed. H. G. Mukarovsky. Vienna: Beiträge zur Afrikanistik, 321–337.
—— 1991, 1992. "Notes sur le premier vocabulaire soqotri: Le Mémoire de Wellsted (1835)." *Matériaux Arabes et Sudarabiques* n.s. 3: 91–135, n.s. 4: 4–77.
—— 1993. "L'Expression du futur dans les langues sudarabiques modernes." *Matériaux Arabes et Sudarabiques* n.s. 5: 249–278.
—— 1994a. "Aloe and Dragon's Blood: Some Traditional Uses on the Island of Socotra." *New Arabian Studies* 2: 186–198.
—— 1994b. "La Négation dans les langues sudarabiques modernes." *Matériaux Arabes et Sudarabiques* n.s. 6: 187–211.
—— 1995a. "Magie et pratiques thérapeutiques dans l'île de Soqotra: Le médecin guérisseur." *Proceedings of the Seminar for Arabian Studies* 25: 117–126.
—— 1995b. "Incantations thérapeutiques dans la médecine traditionnelle des Mahra du Yémen." *Quaderni di Studi Arabi* 13: 131–157.
—— 1996. "The Soqoṭri Language: Situation and Presentation." *Proceedings of the 1st International Scientific Symposium on Socotra Island, Aden 26–30 March 1996*. University of Aden.
—— Forthcoming (a). "Soḳotri (langue)." *Encyclopédie de l'Islam*. Leiden: Brill.
—— Forthcoming (b). *La langue Mehri du Yémen: Présentation linguistique et textes*, Wiesbaden: Harrassowitz.
—— Forthcoming (c). "La Dérivation verbale dans les langues sudarabiques modernes." *Journal of Semitic Studies* 2 (1997).
Simeone-Senelle, M.-Cl. and A. Lonnet. 1985. "Lexique des noms des parties du corps dans les langues sudarabiques modernes. Première partie: La tête." *Matériaux Arabes et Sudarabiques* 3: 259–304.
—— 1988–1989. "Deuxième partie: Les membres." *Matériaux Arabes et Sudarabiques* n.s. 2: 191–255.
—— 1991. "Lexique soqoṭri: Les noms des parties du corps." *Semitic Studies in Honor of Wolf Leslau on the Occasion of his 85th Birthday, November 14th, 1991*, volume 2, ed. Alan S. Kaye. Wiesbaden: Harrassowitz. 1443–1487.
—— 1992. "Compléments à *Lexique soqoṭri*: Les noms des parties du corps." *Matériaux Arabes et Sudarabiques* n.s. 4: 85–108.
Simeone-Senelle, M.-Cl., A. Lonnet and S. Mohamed-Bakheit. 1984. "Histoire de Said, Saida, la méchante femme et l'ange: Un conte mehri suivi de commentaires linguistiques." *Matériaux Arabes et Sudarabiques* 2: 237–266.
Simeone-Senelle, M.-Cl. and M. Vanhove. 1995. "La Formation et l'évolution des auxili-

aires et particules verbales dans des langues sémitiques: Les langues sudarabiques modernes et le maltais." *Mémoires de la Société Linguistique de Paris (Journée
"Grammaticalisation", 20 janvier 1995* (forthcoming).

Testen, David D. 1992. "The Loss of the Person-Marker in Jibbali and Socotri."*Bulletin of
the School of Oriental and African Studies* 45: 445–450.

Thomas, B.. 1937. "Four Strange Tongues from South Arabia: The Hadara Group." *Proceedings of the British Academy*: 231–329.

Wagner, E.. 1953. *Syntax der Mehri-Sprache unter Berücksichtigung auch der anderen
neusüdarabischen Sprache*. Berlin: Deutsche Akademie der Wissenschaften.

—— 1959. "Der Dialekt von 'Abd-el-Kuri."*Anthropos* 44,2–3: 475–486.

18 Tigrinya

Leonid E. Kogan

Tigrinya is spoken as a native language by the overwhelming majority of the population in the Tigre province of Ethiopia and in the highland part of Eritrea (the provinces of Akkele Guzay, Serae and Hamasien, where the capital of the state, Asmara, is situated). Outside of this area Tigrinya is also spoken in the Tambien and Wolqayt historical districts (Ethiopia) and in the administrative districts of Massawa and Keren (Eritrea), these being respectively the southern and northern limits of its expansion. The number of speakers of Tigrinya has been estimated at 4,000,000 in 1995; 1,300,000 of them live in Eritrea (around 50 percent of the population of the country).

The name of the language, Tigrinya (*təgrəñña*), is the Amharic *nisbe* from the name of the Tigre province (in various European sources the spellings Tigrinya, Tigriña and Tigrigna may be found). The language has often been called Tigray (Tigrai) with the Tigrinya genitive suffix. Needless to say these names should not be confused with Tigré.

We know very little about the linguistic history of Tigrinya, since all written documents are of relatively recent date. With some rare exceptions, we possess no Tigrinya sources earlier than the beginning of the nineteenth century. It was at this time that more or less substantial Tigrinya word lists were recorded by European travelers. The Loggo Sarda code of traditional law (found in the church of Sarda, Ethiopia), which is probably the first production of Tigrinya written literature, also dates from the nineteenth century.

Today Tigrinya is, together with Arabic, the official language of Eritrea; it is a language of instruction, literature and media both in Eritrea and Ethiopia.

Phonology

Consonants
Tigrinya has the following consonantal phonemes:

p	t	č	k	kʷ			f	s	š	ḥ	h
ṗ	ṭ	č̣	ḳ	ḳʷ				ṣ			ʾ
b	d	ǰ	g	gʷ			v	z	ž	ʿ	
m	n	ñ			l	r	w		y		

Glottalized Consonants
The non-glottal element in the glottalized consonants (ṗ, ṭ, č̣, ḳ, ḳ*ʷ*, ṣ) is pro-nounced with more tension than in the respective simple consonants; both ele-ments are pronounced simultaneously (except for ṣ, where the glottal element follows the fricative).

Final Devoicing
b, *g*, and *d* are subject to word-final devoicing: *nab* [nap] 'to, towards', *ḥamäd* 'dust, soil' [ḥamät], *mäntäg* 'arrow' [mäntäk]. These forms are sometimes tran-scribed as [nab*ᵖ*], [ḥamäd*ᵗ*], etc.

Spirantization
The unvoiced velar stops *k*, *k*ʷ, ḳ, ḳ*ʷ* have uvular fricative allophones *x*, *x̣*, *x*ʷ, *x̣*ʷ (the first two sounds traditionally rendered here as k̲, k̲*ʷ*). The spirantization takes place when these stops are postvocalic and non-geminate. Compare, for example, the following realizations of the phoneme *k*:

kàfätä	'to open'	vs.	*täk̲äftä* 'to be opened'
ʾakkäḇä	'to collect'		*täräk̲bä* 'to be found'
ʾarkäḇä	'to reach'		*bärrik̲* 'high, elevated'

Postvocalic spirantization of *b* is a controversial point in Tigrinya phonetics. While special graphemes exist to denote spirantized allophones of the velars, this is not the case for *b*. According to the majority of studies, this phenomenon is lim-ited to the dialects of Tigre province (it has even been suggested that this feature has been borrowed from Amharic). However, in a recent study of Tigrinya acous-tic phonetics by Kiros Fre Woldu (1985), intervocalic spirantization of *b* was ob-served in the speech of five informants, all born in Asmara. Our informants always spirantized *b* in postvocalic position with the exception of word finally, where it is regularly devoiced (see p. 425): *näḇärä* 'to stay, live', *säḇḥe* 'to be fat', but *mädäp* (spelling *mädäb*) 'art, division, plan'.

Spirantization of *k* and *ḳ* occurs in word-initial position if the preceding word ends in a vowel and the two are pronounced without pause (external sandhi). Ex-amples: *səm ʾəta ḵaläyti dəma rut näḇärä* 'the name of the second was Ruth' (Ruth 1:4); *ʾəzi x̲əduy ḵəḇʾi* 'this precious ointment' (Mark 14:5). It is generally thought that spirantized *b* never occurs in word initial position, but it did observe such cases in the fast speech of our informants.

Labiovelars
The velar element of the labiovelars *k*ʷ, *g*ʷ and *ḳ*ʷ is identical with the non-labialized velars; the labial, pronounced simultaneously with the velar, is articu-lated as a bilabial sonorant *w*. Labiovelars are fairly stable only before *a* (*g*ʷ*al* 'young girl', *ḵ*ʷ*anḵ*ʷ*a* 'language'); before *ä* and *ə* they are rarely found. In this case, the labial element is transferred to the following vowel (*ä* > *o*, *ə*> *u*), e.g. *k*ʷ*ɔnnäna* (*konnäna*) 'to condemn', *k*ʷ*əḥli* (*kuḥli*) 'antimony'.

Laryngeals

The laryngeals ', *h*, *ḥ*, ' constitute a natural class because of their similar effects on vowels (see p. 428). ' is a glottal stop (Arabic hamzah), *ḥ* and ' are traditionally described as pharyngeal fricatives, voiceless and voiced respectively, but a more exact phonetic definition would be, perhaps, "emphatic laryngeals."

Gemination

Every consonant except a laryngeal can be geminated in Tigrinya. In glottalized consonants and labiovelars only the non-glottal (non-labial) element is geminated: *hakkänä* [hakk'änä] 'to try', *ḳʷɔṣṣal* [ḳʷɔṣṣ'al] 'green', *mäggʷɔtä* 'to discuss', *täkkʷɔsä* 'to burn'. Gemination in Tigrinya is phonemic and has an important distinctive role, as can be seen from the following minimal pairs:

> *hatäfä* 'to cross, to traverse (a desert etc.)' ≠ *hattäfä* 'to speak in one's sleep'
> *lägabi* 'contagious (a disease)' ≠ *läggabi* 'one who darns'
> *dəro* 'in former times, previously' ≠ *dərro* 'vigil preceding a feast'

Assimilation

Consonantal assimilation in Tigrinya is mostly regressive, and may be partial or complete. A case of partial regressive assimilation can be observed when a *n* shifts to *m* before a *b*: *'ambädbädä* 'to tremble' (< **'an-bädbädä*). This process, however, is fully lexicalized (cf. *'an-bäṭbäṭä* 'to pour out slowly') thus belonging to diachronic rather than synchronic phenomena. The third radical *g* and *ḳ* are always completely assimilated to the following *k-* in a number of the perfect forms of the Tigrinya verb: *hadägä* 'he left' ~ *hadäkka* 'you left'; *säräxä* 'he stole' ~ *säräkkum* 'you (pl.) stole'. In the jussive forms of reflexive stems *t* is completely assimilated to the first radical: *yəssäbär* (< **yət-säbär*) 'let him be broken', *yəḳḳäddäs* (< **yət-ḳäddäs*) 'let him be celebrated'.

Borrowed Phonemes

The phonemes *p* and *v* are rare and found in loanwords only: *politika* 'politics', *profäsor* 'professor', *räppäsä* 'to iron something well' (< Italian *ripassare*), *vagon*, *kravat*. The phoneme *ṗ* is also of limited occurrence, being attested mostly in borrowings from Ge'ez (which, in their turn, are also of foreign origin): *ṗaṗas* 'metropolitan', *'episḳoṗos* 'bishop', *ṗagume* (*ṗagʷəme*) 'the thirteenth month of the Ethiopian calendar'.

Palatals: *š, ž, č, ǰ, č̣, ñ*

Palatals in Tigrinya are considered by some scholars to be found only in loanwords from Amharic. The sounds *ǰ (ž)* and especially *č̣* and *š* are found, however, in words which obviously cannot be regarded as Amharic loanwords. Dozens of Tigrinya words containing palatals have no cognates in Amharic (e.g. *ǰärrämä* 'to be greedy, insatiable') or for phonetic reasons cannot be suspected to have been borrowed (*č̣əhmi* ~ Amharic *ṭim* 'beard on the chin and around the lips' or *ḥammuštä* 'five' ~ Amharic *amməst*). On the other hand, *č* and *ñ* do indeed occur mainly in borrowings from Amharic: *mäḵfäča* 'key', *mäč²e* 'to be suitable', *dañña* 'judge', *wädäränña* 'opponent'. The phonemic weight of *ž* seems to be light since it is of rare occurrence and often appears in free variation with *ǰ*: *žämmärä/ǰämmärä* 'to begin', *žəmmat/ǰəmmat* 'nerves, veins' etc.

Vowels
Tigrinya has seven basic vowels:

i	ə	u
e		o
ä		
	a	

Vocalic quantity is not phonemic.

Mid Front Vowels
The vowel *e* is almost always pronounced as a rising diphthong *ⁱe* (unless preceded by a laryngeal or a *w*). In fact, this can be described more accurately as a palatalization of the preceding consonant.

As to *ä*, it is a mid low front vowel: *nägädä* 'to trade', *zäḫän* 'time'. It has a back rounded allophone *ɔ* (see p. 428). In word-final position it is pronounced substantially closer: *däge* 'door'.

An interesting case exemplifying the relationship between *ä* and *e* is the following. The sg. 3m. perfect normally has an *ä* in the last syllable: *nägärä*; but when the last consonant is a laryngeal, this vowel is spelled as *e*: *sämˤe* 'to hear'. Since *ä* in this case did not, contrary to the Tigrinya phonetic laws, shift into *a* (which, if it follows a laryngeal, is often represented by the graphemes of the 1st order /-ä/), the best way to preserve its original character in spelling was to use graphemes of the 5th order (*-e*).

Shwa
ə is high central unrounded (in IPA transcription *i*). The phonemic status of *ə* seems to be certain and it cannot be regarded as an allophone of zero; see minimal pairs like *säḥafna* 'we wrote' versus *ṣäḥafəna* 'our writer'.

Vowel Harmony
The basic principle of vowel harmony in Tigrinya is the following: *ä* and *ə* in an open syllable preceding a syllable containing *o* or *u* shift to *o* and *u* respectively: *sälos* 'Tuesday' may be pronounced *solos*, etc. The best illustrative examples are adjectives and passive participles of the patterns *nəgur* and *nəggur*, which are very often pronounced as *nugur* and *nuggur* respectively: *ṣubbuḵ* 'good', *buzuḥ* 'much, numerous' etc.

Influence of Semivowels

ä in contact with *w* often becomes *ɔ* (or even *o*); *ə* shifts to *u* (*ŭ*). Examples: *yəmɔwwət* (*yəmɔwwut*) 'he dies', *wɔy* 'or, either', *muwrad* (instead of *məwrad*) 'to descend' (inf.), *yuwsäd* 'let him carry off!' (instead of *yəwsäd*). This process, however, is far from being universal (compare perfect forms of A and B types from roots with second radical *w*: *ṭäwɔyä* 'to twist' versus *sɔwwärä* 'to hide'). The same change occasionally occurs in contact with other labials: *kəfɔlṭu* 'in order that they know' (instead of *kəfälṭu*).

i in contact with *y* is often pronounced *ə*: *ḳäyyəḥ* 'red' versus *bälliḥ* 'sharp', *sälləyn* 'to praise' (3rd person singular gerund) versus *ʾabbidu* 'to calm' (same form).

Influence of Laryngeals

The following rules describe the influence of laryngeals on vowels in Tigrinya:

1 *ä* preceded or by a laryngeal becomes *a*: *ḥasämä* 'to be bad' versus *nägärä* 'to speak';
2 *ä* in a syllable closed by a laryngeal becomes *a*: *baḥri* 'sea' versus *kälbi* 'dog';
3 *ə* in an open syllable followed by a laryngeal with *a* (C*ə*H*a*-) shifts to *ä* or *a*: *täharrəs* or *taharrəs* 'you are plowing' versus *tənäggər*;
4 *ä* in an open syllable followed by a laryngeal with *ə, i, u* may shift to *a*: *yərəʾi* 'he sees' versus *yənäggər*.

Diphthongs

Combinations of vowel plus semivowel form diphthongs in Tigrinya, e.g. *läyti* 'night', *haymanot* 'faith, religion', *lɔwṭi* 'exchange', *ḥaw* 'brother', *ḥəywɔt* 'life', *yəfättəw* 'he loves'. All diphthongs are non-phonemic (i.e. can be divided into two phonemes: *sətäy* 'drink!' versus *səbär* 'break!'. *ä* is the thematic vowel of imperfect/imperative, *y* and *r* the third radicals of triconsonantal verbal roots *sty* and *sbr* respectively; *nägiromwo* (pl. 3m. gerund with sg. 3m. pronominal suffix) versus *nägiromwa* (same form with sg. 3f. pronominal suffix). Diphthongs are sometimes reduced to simple vowels: *mot* 'death' (< **mawt*), *bet* 'house' (< **bayt*); very often reduced and non-reduced forms are in free variation: *yəfättəw/yəfättuw/yəfättu* 'he loves', *yəftɔw/yəfto* 'let him love!', *ḳäyhe/ḳäḥe/ḳehe* 'to be red' etc.

Syllable Structure Restrictions

Only CV and CVC syllables are permitted in Tigrinya. Thus, no syllable or word can begin with a vowel, and no initial or final consonantal clusters occur. In rapid speech initial clusters are possible, however, especially if the second consonant is a sonorant. So, *təmali* 'yesterday' may also be pronounced *tmali*. Word-final clusters are dissolved by adding *-i* after the second consonant: *məkri* 'counsel, plan', *səmmi* 'poison', *säbäyti* 'woman, wife'. When a pronominal suffix is added, this

-*i* shifts into *ə*: *məkrəkum* 'your plan'.

Prosody

Stress in Tigrinya has no phonological value and easily shifts from one syllable to another. Dynamic stress is very weak and sometimes almost imperceptible. In many cases it falls on the last syllable, e.g. the euphonic -*i*: *rəʾəsì* 'head', *säbäytì* 'woman'. Pitch is an important element of the Tigrinya stress pattern, but it is also rather unstable. Dynamic stress and pitch may not coincide: *nä́bärà̀* 'to be' (´ – high pitch; `` ` `` – dynamic stress).

Sentence intonation is clearly predominant over the stress of an individual word. The relationship between these two features requires further investigation, but it is clear that rhythmical units very often do not coincide with single words.

Morphology

Pronouns

Personal Pronouns

Table 18.1   Personal pronouns

		Masculine	Common	Feminine
Sg.	1		ʾanä	
	2	nəssəka		nəssəki
	3	nəssu		nəssa
Pl.	1		nəḥna	
	2	nəssəkatkum		nəssəkatkən
	3	nəssatom		nəssatän

The old Semitic 2nd person pronouns (*ʾanta/ʾatta*, *ʾanti/ʾatti*, *ʾantum/ʾattum*, *ʾantən/ʾattən*) are used as vocatives: *ʾatta tämähari* 'O student!'. In polite address to somebody (singular) the forms *nəssəkum*, *nəssəkən* are employed.

Pronominal suffixes are used with nouns and prepositions (*ʿof* 'bird' exemplifies bases with consonantal ending; bases ending in vowels are exemplified with *ʿasa* 'fish') (Table 18.2).

There exist two series of pronominal suffixes used with a verb. The basic forms are given in Table 18.3.

The first series may be used to denote both the direct object and the indirect object: *kətmäkr-änni ṣäwwaʿku-ka* 'I called you in order that you give me a piece of advice'; *ḥadä däbtära ʾastämhari näbärä-nni* 'a däbtära was my teacher' (lit. 'was a teacher for me'). The second series (with -*l*-) can have the meaning 'for, for the sake of' but most often just denotes the indirect object: *zəgəbbär-ällu käbri* 'the burial which is made for him'; *nätu käläbet zəsärḥ-allu ṭäbbib* 'the smith who

Table 18.2   Pronominal suffixes

	Masculine	Common	Feminine
Sg. 1		ʿof-äy/ʿasa-y	
2	ʿof-ka/ʿasa-ḵa		ʿof-ki/ʿasa-ḵi
3	ʿof-u/ʿasa-ʾu		ʿof-a/ʿasa-ʾa
Pl. 1		ʿof-na/ʿasa-na	
2	ʿof-kum/ʿasa-ḵum		ʿof-kən/ʿasa-ḵən
3	ʿof-om/ʿasa-ʾom		ʿof-än/ʿasa-ʾen

Table 18.3   Pronominal suffixes with verb

	Masculine	Common	Feminine
Sg. 1		-ni/-läy	
2	-ka/-lka		-ki/-lki
3	-o/-lu		-a/-la
Pl. 1		-na/-lna	
2	-kum/-lkum		-kən/-lkən
3	-om/-lom		-än/-län

makes the ring for him'.

The relative particle in Tigrinya is zə (negative zäy). It is prefixed to the verb of the relative clause (see p. 443). If the verb is in the imperfect, several rules of juncture are observed:

1   the prefixes ʾə-, yə- fall: zənäggər 'one who says' or '(it is) myself who says';

2   before the prefixes nə- and tə- the relative particle may have the form ʾəy- (the same is true for the forms of the perfect of t- themes). In both cases the prefixes are geminated: ʾəttənäggər 'you who say', ʾəttänägrä 'what was said'.

The most common interrogative pronouns are: män 'who?', mən 'what?', ʾəntaway 'which?', ʾäyyänay 'which one?' (both referring to animate beings); ʾəntay, məntay 'which?' (both referring to inanimate beings).

Other modifiers: kull- (with pronominal suffixes) 'all, every', gälä 'some, certain', kaləʾ 'other'.

Nouns

Primary and Derived Nouns

Primary nouns are not derived from any consonantal root. No special meaning can be attached to their vocalic element(s), which form an integral part of the root. Derived nouns are produced from consonantal roots with the help of either special vocalic patterns or combinations of vocalic patterns with affixes. In most cases (of course, not always) we are able to establish for these patterns a more or less specific lexical or grammatical significance.

Some examples of primary nouns: *čäw* 'salt', *səm* 'name', *ṣäḇa* 'milk', *g"ənči* (*gunči*) 'cheek'; *fäläg* 'river', *ḥarmaz* 'elephant', *'ənḵ"aẖ"əho* 'egg', *šäfašəfti* 'eyebrows'.

Some examples of derived nouns: *kəfli* 'part, portion' (*käfälä* 'to divide'), *'anägagəra* 'manner of speaking' (*nägärä* 'to speak'; this is a very common pattern for "way, manner of action"), *mästä* 'drink' (*sätäyä* 'to drink'), *məwrädi* 'ladder, steps' (*wərädä* 'to descend'), *tə'əzaz* 'order, command' (*'azzäzä* 'to command'), *sənfəna* 'weakness' (*sänäfä* 'to be weak'), *'ərkənnät* 'friendship' (*'aräḵä* 'to be, become a friend').

Definiteness

An indefinite noun in Tigrinya needs no special marker. The numeral '1' (m. *ḥadä*, f. *ḥanti(t)*) is, however, very often used before an indeterminate noun, thus functionally approaching an indefinite article: *ḥadä mä'alti ḥadä däḇtära bə'agäməšät gəze 'ab ḥadä 'əmni täẖämmiṭu* ... 'one day a *däbtära* was sitting on a stone in the afternoon'.

Remote demonstratives (see p. 434) may function as definite articles. Examples: *'ətu₁ məšät₂ məs konä* ... 'when the₁ night₂ fell ...'; *'ətom₁ kahnat₂ 'ətom₃ däwäl₄ betäḵrəstyanat yədəwwəlu* 'the₁ priests₂ ring the₃ bells₄ of the churches'.

The definite article in Tigrinya is compatible with pronominal suffixes: *'ətu rə'əsu* 'his head' (lit. 'the-head-his'); the first element of a genitive construction (see p. 433) also may be preceded by the article: *'ətom wäläddi 'ətu ḵ"əl'a* 'the child's [the] parents'.

Gender

There are two genders in Tigrinya, masculine and feminine. Nouns denoting male and female animate beings exhibit agreement in gender: *'ətu wəddi* 'the boy'/*'əta g"al* 'the girl'; *'ətu 'anbäsa* (*'ambäsa* 'lion'/*'əta wa'ro* 'lioness' etc. A few nouns denoting inanimate entities have stable grammatical gender (thus, *ṣäḥay* 'sun' is masculine while *wərḥi* 'moon' is feminine), but most of them may agree as masculine or feminine indiscriminately even in the same sentence. For example, in *'əta ḵorbot 'əta säḇäyti* ... *təšəlləm-o* (lit. 'the leather, the woman ... adorns it') the article before *ḵorbot* is f., while the coreferential pronominal suffix *-o* of the verb is m.

Number

Singular nouns are unmarked. The plural may be expressed by suffixes (external plural) or by internal apophonic changes which may or may not be combined with affixation (internal or "broken" plural). The form of the plural is not determined by any features of the singular, and their relationship is purely lexical.

External Plural

The most frequent external plural marker is -at (-tat). If the noun ends in a consonant, -at is attached directly: nägär 'thing, affair': pl. nägärat; säb 'man': säḫat; maləkkət 'signal, sign': maləkkətat, etc. If a noun ends in a vowel, a -t- appears between this vowel and the plural suffix: ḥasäma 'pig': ḥasämatat; ʿasa 'fish': ʿasatat; ʾabbo 'father': ʾabbotat, etc. Less frequent external affixes of plural are -an and -ot (e.g. kəddus 'holy, saint' (noun and adjective): kəddusan; gʷɔyta 'lord': gʷɔytot; gʷasa 'shepherd': gʷasot).

Broken Plural

There are no exact rules of correspondence between a nominal pattern and types of broken plural; only some more or less frequent combinations may be listed:

nägri: ʾanagər, ʾangərti
      wɔrḥi 'month': ʾawarəḥ
      kʷɔṣli 'leaf': ʾaxʷṣəlti (ʾaxuṣəlti)
nəgri: ʾangar and ʾanagər
      bərki 'knee': ʾabrak
      nəhbi 'bee': ʾanahəb
nägär: ʾangar
      zämäd 'kinsman': ʾazmad

ʾangar is also the plural of biliterals resulting from the contration of -aw-/-ay-:

      bet 'house' (< *bayt): ʾabyat
      sor 'ox' (< *sawr): ʾaswar
nägra: nägaru
      säsḥa 'gazelle': säsaḥu
Quadriradicals:
      känfär 'lip': känafər, känäffər
      dəngəl 'virgin': dänagəl, dänäggəl
      bärmil 'barrel': bäramil, bärämmil
      ṭərmuz 'bottle': ṭäramuz, ṭärämmuz

Case Relations

Case relations are expressed mainly by prepositions. Since most of them are listed on p. 441, only direct/indirect object relations and the genitive construction will be analyzed here.

Direct/Indirect Object

The marker of both direct and indirect objects is nə- prefixed to the noun. In combination with the definite article it appears in the form nätu, näta etc. Examples: näta säḫäyti ʾaytənkəʾəwwa 'do not touch this woman!'; nätu sərnay yəkərkərəʾo 'they grind this wheat'; ʾətu dañña nə-nəgus bəkəlṭuf yəngär 'let the judge tell [it] quickly to the king'. For direct objects the use of *nə-* is optional (especially if the object is an inanimate being): *ḥadä dawit wɔyəm ḥadä mäṣḥaf kəddus käfitom* 'they open a psalter or a sacred book'; *'əta ḥarič ḥiza* 'she takes the flour'; more seldom with animate beings: *'ətu₁ säb₂ zə₃-xätälä₄ säb₅* 'the₁ man₅ who₃ killed₄ [another] man₂'.

Genitive Construction

The genitive relation may be expressed either by simple juxtaposition of two nouns or with the particle *nay* (*nota genitivi*).

In the first case the possessed usually precedes the possessor e.g. *gäza₁ wanna₂ 'ətä käbti₃* 'the house₁ of the owner₂ of the cattle₃' (cf., however, cases like *'ətu dorho₁ səga₂* 'the meat₂ of the chicken₁' or *kədan₁ 'attäḥaṣaṣəba₂* 'the manner₂ of washing clothes₁'). The possessed does not undergo any phonetic changes unless it ends in an *-i* (whether "euphonic" or "morphological"). This *-i* is often (but not always) dropped: *ḥəzb kätäma 'asmära* 'inhabitants of the city of Asmara' (in non-bound position *ḥəzbi*).

The genitive with *nay* may precede or follow the possessed without any difference of meaning, though examples of the first kind are considerably more numerous. Examples: *nay₁ ḥadä₂ däbtära₃ kʷɔlʿa₄* 'a child₄ of₁ a₂ däbtära₃'; *wɔrki nay gar* 'blood-money' (lit. the gold of recompensation').

Adjectives

Adjectival Patterns

The most widespread Tigrinya adjectives are formed from consonantal roots following several adjectival patterns:

näggir: *bälliḥ* 'sharp', *ʿammixʷ* 'deep'; note also *ʿabiy* (*ʿabəy*) 'big' (with gemination in the feminine *ʿabbay* only).
nəgur (originally passive participle): *ṣənuʿ* 'strong', *ṣəruy* 'pure, purified'.
nəggur: *ṣəbbux* 'good', *fəṣṣum* 'perfect'. In the last two patterns *ə* is most often pronounced as *u* (see p. 427).
nägar: *täṣay* 'opposed, contrary', *näxʷar* 'blind'.
näggar: *kʷɔṣṣal* 'green', *käddaʿ* 'rebellious, treacherous'.

The most common Tigrinya adjectival suffixes are the following:

-am(ma): *nɔwram* 'shameful' (< *nɔwri* 'shame'), *čäkam, čärkamma* 'ragged, poor'
-ay, -away, -awi: *taḥtay* 'low' (< *taḥti* 'low, inferior part'), *mədrawi* 'earthly' (< *mədri* 'earth')
-äyna, -añña, -əñña (these suffixes may have been borrowed from Amharic): *'unätäyna* (*'unätäñña*) 'true, real' (< *'unät* 'truth')
-an: *säkran* 'drunk'

Gender and Number of Adjectives
Grammatical gender can be formally expressed in the great majority of adjectives; the most remarkable exceptions being the type *näggar* and adjectives with the suffixes *-am, -äyna, -ähña*. Thus, e.g. *kärran* 'one with big horns', *habtam* 'rich', have one form for both genders; so does *ṣaʿda* 'white' (m./f.). The basic marker of the feminine is *-t*: *zämänawi* 'modern', f. *zämänawit*. It often causes phonetic changes in the base: *gərum* 'wonderful', f. *gərəmti*; *sǝbbux*, f. *sǝbbəxti* 'beautiful'.

Adjectives of the type *näggir* form the feminine apophonically. The form of the feminine is *näggar*, e.g. *ṣällim* 'black', f. *ṣällam*; *käyyəh* 'red', f. *käyyah*, etc.

While many adjectives form the external plural with the help of *-at* (e.g. *muluʾ* 'full', pl. *muluʾat*), there exist a number of adjectival patterns requiring broken plurals. The most remarkable one is the case of *näggir*, the plural of which is *näggärti*: *däkkix* 'small', pl. *däkkäxti*.

The same form of plural, whether external or broken, is used for both genders.

Gradation of Adjectives
The most frequently used device to form the comparative degree requires the use of the imperfect of a verb with the same root from which the adjective is derived and the preposition *ʾənkab* 'from, than'; *gäzay ʾənkab gäzaka yäʿabbi* 'my house is bigger than yours' (*ʿabəy* 'big').

Deictics
Tigrinya has two series of deictic pronouns making distinction between near ("this," also "the") and remote ("that") objects (variant forms are given in parentheses):

		Masculine	Feminine
Sg.	'this'	ʾəzu (ʾezuy)	əza (ʾəziʾa)
	'that'	ʾətu (ʾətuy)	ʾəta (ʾətiʾa)
Pl.	'these'	ʾəzom (ʾəziʾom, ʾəziʾatom)	ʾəzän (ʾəziʾen, ʾəziʾatän)
	'those'	ʾətom (ʾətiʾom, ʾətiʾatom)	ʾətän (ʾətiʾən, ʾətiʾatän)

(*ʾə-* may fall, especially in the middle of a sentence, so that *ʾəzu* becomes *zu* etc.)

Other deictics: e.g. *ʾabzuy* 'here', *ʾabʾu* 'there', *ʾənkabʾu* 'thence'.

Numerals

Cardinals

1	*hadä* (f. *hantit, hanti*)	6	*šədəštä* (*šudduštä*)
2	*kəlättä*	7	*šobʿattä* (*šoʿattä*)
3	*sälästä*	8	*šommontä* (*šommäntä*)
4	*ʾarbaʿtä*	9	*təšʿattä*
5	*hammuštä*	10	*ʿassärtä*

11 ʿassärtä ḥadä
12 ʿassärtä kələttä
20 ʿəsra
21 ʿəsra-n ḥadä-n (-n 'and' (see p. 442))

30	sälasa	70	säbʿa
40	ʾarbaʿa	80	sämanya
50	ḥamsa	90	täsʿa
60	səssa		

100 məʾti; 1,000 šəḥ; 10,000 ʾəlfi (ʿassärtä šəḥ is also used).

All the numerals except '1' have one form for both genders. The noun counted may appear in the singular or in the plural: ḥammuštä säḫäyti or ḥammuštä ʾanəsti 'five women'.

Ordinals

First: mäžämmärəya (also fälämay and ḳädamay, f. fälämäyti and ḳädämäyti); second: kalʾay, kələttäyna (f. kalʾayti).

Ordinals from third to tenth are formed from the consonantal roots of the respective cardinals according to the pattern nag(ə)ray: salsay 'third' (f. salsäyti) etc.

Verbs

Root and Derivation

Verbal roots are consonantal and may consist of two or more (in most cases three, sometimes four) radicals. These consonants usually remain unalterable throughout both the derivational and the inflectional paradigms and do not exert any influence on the adjacent non-radical morphemes. Verbs where one of the radicals is a laryngeal or a semivowel are denoted here as, e.g. 1w/y, 2H (H being any laryngeal) etc. These verbs present more difficulties as compared with the corresponding forms from "sound" verbs.

Derivational classes (called "themes" below) ideally express causation, passivity, reflexiveness etc., or combinations of these notions. Even though these semantic definitions do not always apply, the cases where they do are numerous enough to see that these formations are not completely lexicalized. The full range of the Tigrinya verbal themes is discussed in the following section; they are marked as I, II, III and IV.

Conjugations

A verb belonging to a certain theme is identified according to one of the four conjugational types (marked here as A, B, C, D). Traditionally the verbs are illustrated by the perfect (see p. 437). Type A is the unmarked one (nägärä); the B-type is characterized by the gemination of the second radical (näggärä), the C-type by the presence of an a after the first radical (nagärä) and the D-type by the repetition of the second consonant and an *a* between the repetitions (*nägagärä*). Accordingly, every verb may be classified as, e.g., IC (*nagärä*) or IIIB (*tänäggärä*) etc.

All the derived forms with their approximate semantic value are listed below.

I Forms without Prefixes

IA *nägärä*: *nägäsä* 'to reign', *gädäfä* 'to leave';
IB *näggärä*: *gäbbäṭä* 'to knead dough', *ḳärräṣä* 'to collect duty';
IC *nagärä*: *lašäwä* 'to be worn out', *zaräyä* 'to abate (of water)'.

These three forms are basic and the conjugation has no semantic correlation. Pairs like IB *ḳärräṣä* 'to collect duty' vs. IA *ḳäräṣä* 'to carve, to engrave' or IC *zaräyä* 'to abate' vs. IA *zäräyä* 'to defend somebody, to be partial (of a judge)' show that the respective root is used for two different verbs.

ID *nägagärä*: *ḥasasäḇä* 'to think again and again about something, to think out something' (*ḥasäḇä* 'to think'), *ḳätatälä* 'to kill many' (*ḳätälä* 'to kill'), *ḥararäsä* 'to plow a field partly, not thoroughly enough' (*ḥaräsä* 'to plow').

This form, usually called "frequentative," denotes a rather wide scope of notions with respect to IA, such as intensity (increasing or decreasing), attenuation, plurality of objects etc. Unlike IB and IC, it is fairly productive and only formally belongs to the "basic" themes, functioning more like the derived forms discussed below.

II Forms with *t-* Prefixed

IIA *tänägrä*: *täḳäftä* 'to be opened' (*ḳäfätä* 'to open'); a few verbs have an *ä* after the second radical: *täxäräḇä* 'to be presented' (*ḳäräḇä* 'to approach');
IIB *tänäggärä*: *täʾakkäḇä* 'to be assembled' (*ʾakkäḇä* 'to gather');
IIC *tänagärä*: *täfaxäyä* 'to be explored (a place)' (*faxäyä* 'to explore, to spy').

These forms are employed mostly to denote the passive of IA, IB and IC respectively.

IID *tänägagärä*: *täfädadäyä* 'to indemnify each other' (*fädäyä* 'to indemnify'), *täḥalaläxä* 'to defend each other' (*ḥalläxä* 'to defend oneself').

This form denotes reciprocity (IIC is also used for this purpose, e.g. *täfadäyä* alongside *täfädadäyä*).

III Forms with *ʾa-* Prefixed

IIIA   *ʾangärä: ʾaḵäyä* 'to make cry' (*bäḵäyä* 'to cry');
IIIB   *ʾanäggärä: ʾašäbbärä* 'to terrify' (*šäbbärä* 'to tremble');
IIIC   *ʾanagärä: ʾalaṣäyä* 'to make somebody shave the head' (*laṣäyä* 'to shave one's head'.

These forms are, in most cases, causatives for IA, IB and IC; the form IIID does not exist.

IV Forms with Prefixed *ʾa* and Gemination of the First Consonant
This prefix goes back to **ʾat-* with a complete assimilation of *t*, which appears when the first consonant is a laryngeal:

IVC   *ʾannagärä: ʾaffadäyä* 'to make two parties indemnify each other (e.g. of a judge)'; *ʾaffanäwä* 'to accompany somebody who leaves';
IVD   *ʾannägagärä: ʾabbäʾaʾasä* 'to make many people dispute one with the other'; *ʾattäḥaxʷaxʷɔfä* (*t* before *ḥ*) 'to make embrace one another'.

The meaning of both IVC and IVD themes is more or less the same: causative reciprocal ('to make somone do something together with someone else') and adjutative ('to help someone to do something'); IVD is perhaps associated with more intensive action.

Compound Verbs
There exists an important number of verbs which are combinations of the verb *bälä* 'to say' and a quasi-verbal element consisting of two or more radicals. The latter carries the semantic value of the construction and remains unaltered throughout the paradigm, while *bälä* (also used in other themes, especially in the causative, *ʾabbälä*) carries the inflection. A few examples of compound verbs: *ʿaw bälä* 'to cry' (*ʿaw ʾabbälä* 'to raise one's voice'); *təḵ bälä* 'to be straight' (*təḵ ʾabbälä* 'to put upright'); *bədəd bälä* 'to get up, to rise'.

Tenses
The Tigrinyan verbal system comprises three basic tenses, traditionally called perfect, imperfect and gerund. These relations may also be expressed by various combinations of these tenses with auxiliary verbs, special temporal prefixes etc.

Perfect
The perfect denotes past: *bəḥaṣe tädros gize kəlättä hadänti färänži nab ʾityoṗya hagär mäṣu* 'at the time of the Emperor Theodoros two French hunters came to Ethiopia'; *ʾab ʾasmära täwɔlädku* 'I was born in Asmara'. It may also be used to denote the present, usually in verbs with stative meaning: *məntay däläḵa* 'what do you want?'; *məntay gäbärka* 'what are you doing?' etc.

Table 18.4 IA perfect

	Masculine	Common	Feminine
Sg. 1		nägär-ku	
2	nägär-ka		nägär-ki
3	nägär-ä		nägär-ät
Pl. 1		nägär-na	
2	nägär-kum		nägär-kən
3	nägär-u		nägär-a

Imperfect

Table 18.5 IA imperfect

	Masculine	Common	Feminine
Sg. 1		ʾə-näggər	
2	tə-näggər		tə-nägr-i
3	yə-näggər		tə-näggər
Pl. 1		nə-näggər	
2	tə-nägr-u		tə-nägr-a
3	yə-nägr-u		yə-nägr-a

Derived Themes

	IIA yə-nəggär	IIIA yä-(ya-)nəggər	
IB yə-nəggər	IIB yə-nəggär	IIIB yä-(ya-)näggər	
IC yə-nagər	IIC yə-nnagär	IIIC yä-(ya-)nagər	IVC yä-(ya-)nnagər
ID yə-nägagər	IID yə-nnägagär		IVD yä-(ya-)nnägagər

The imperfect denotes an action in the present: *säḇat dəḳatat muḵʷankum ʾəfälləṭ* 'I know that you (pl.) are poor'; *ʾətu mäžämmärya ʿaynät nab kələttä yəḳəffäl* 'the first type is divided into two'; *ʾəta säḇäyti may täfälləḥ* 'the woman boils the water'.

Preceded by *kə-* and followed by another verb the imperfect expresses various modal and aspectual relations, such as possibility, wish, aim, beginning of an action etc. (Note that *ʾə-* and *yə-* prefixes fall when *kə-* is added.) Examples: *mannəm säb dayna kə-ḳowwən yəḳəʾəl* 'every one may become a judge'; *ḥadä nägär zäy-nə-fälläṭ nägär kə-däggəm žämmärä* 'he began reciting something that we did not know'; *ʾətu ʿədaga kə-trəʾi kädka* 'you went to see the market'. *kə* + the imperfect + *ʾayyu* expresses the future: *kə-ẖätlänna ʾəyyu* 'he will kill us', *gänzäḇu kə-həḇäkka ʾəyyä* 'I'll give you his money'. Composed with *ʾallo*, the imperfect denotes the immediate present *ʾəḥazo ʾalloḵu* 'now, I catch him'. In combination with *näbärä*, the imperfect denotes a durative action in the past: *ḥadä šəfta ʾab ḥadä ʿaḇiy bäräḵa yəẖəmmäṭ näḇärä* 'an insurgent was living in a large thicket'.

The Gerund

Table 18.6 IA gerund

		Masculine	Common	Feminine
Sg.	1		nägir-ä	
	2	nägir-ka		nägir-ki
	3	nägir-u		nägir-a
Pl.	1		nägir-na	
	2	nägir-kum		nägir-kən
	3	nägir-om		nägir-än

	IIA *tä-nägir-u*	IIIA *'angir-u*	
IB *näggir-u*	IIB *tänäggir-u*	IIIB *'anäggir-u*	
IC *nagir-u*	IIC *tänagir-u*	IIIC *'änagir-u*	IVC *'annagir-u*
ID *nägagir-u*	IID *tänägagir-u*		IVD *'annägagir-u*
	(*tänagagir-u*)		

Used independently, the gerund denotes the result of an action in the past (mostly from verbs with stative meaning): *məs män mäṣi'ki* 'with whom have you come?'; *ḥamimka-do? ḥamimä* 'are you ill? Yes, I am'. In most cases, however, the gerund is found followed by another verb in the perfect or the imperfect and denotes an action simultaneous or anterior to this one: *nabtu gäza tämälisa ... ṣubbuẖ 'əngera 'al'ila habätto* 'she went back to the house, took good bread and gave it to him' (lit. 'having gone ... and taken ... she gave ...'); *nabtu gäräb hadimu 'atəwä* 'trying to flee he entered the bush'; *näzi'atom ḳäṣṣilom 'ətom mäẖ"ɔnənti ḥadä käḫti täẖämmitu nəbäynu yəmäṣṣə'* 'following these, sitting on a beast the noble appears alone', *bäggi' 'aḅsilom bäli'om yəḳädu* 'having cooked the sheep and eaten they go'.

The gerund + *näḅärä* expresses the pluperfect (mostly in written language): *ḥaṣe tädros ḥadä märaḥ mägäddi yəkunkum bilom ḥadä säb hiḅomuwom näḅäru* 'the Emperor Theodoros (*pluralis majestatis*) had given them a person and then said: "Let him be a guide for you!"'. Composed with *yəkɔwwən*, the gerund denotes a possibility in the future: *ṣəḅaḥ bäzi sä'atzi tämälisä 'əkɔwwən* 'it is possible that I come back tomorrow'. In combination with *'allo*, the gerund serves to express the result of an action in the present: *säḅat ḥadä koynu räḳiḅnayyo 'allona* 'we have just found out that the men are similar'.

Moods: Jussive and Imperative
The jussive has the same prefixes as the imperfect; the fundamental difference consists in the vocalism of the base:

IA *yə-ngär* IIA *yə-nnägär* IIIA *yä-ngər (ya-ngər)*
IB *yə-näggər* IIB *yə-nnäggär* IIIB *yä-näggər (ya-näggər)*
IC *yə-nagər* IIC *yə-nnagər* IIIC *yä-nagər (ya-nagər)* IVC *yä-nnagər (ya-nnagər)*
                                                            IVD *yä-nnägagər (ya-nnägagər)*

All D-forms are the same as the corresponding forms of the imperfect.

The jussive is employed to express indirect commands (1st and 3rd persons): *yəngär* 'let him say!'; about its use to express negative commands see below.

The following is the paradıgm of the imperative:

	Singular	Plural
M.	nəgär	nəgär-u
F.	nəgär-i	nəgär-a

In derived forms the base of the imperative is in most cases identical to that of the jussive. The imperative is used to express positive commands only; negative commands are expressed by the jussive with the negative *ʾay*: *nəgär* 'say!' versus *ʾay-təngär* 'do not say!'.

Verbal Nouns and Particles

The pattern of the active participle in IA is *nägari* (f. *nägarit*, pl. *nägärti* or *nägaro*); the form of IB is *näggari*, derived forms *tänägari*, *ʾangari* etc. The form of the passive participle is *nəgur* (except for IB where it is *nəggur*: *gəttur* 'loaded' (a rifle) < *gättärä* 'to load'). An important number of active participles are substantivized, so that the term *nomen agentis* is also appropriate for this form.

The basic pattern of the infinitive is *məngar* (*mərkab* 'to find', *məngad* 'to trade' etc.; in B-forms the second radical is geminated (*mənəggar*): *məgəllal* 'to pour out'). This form may be employed for all the simple, passive and causative themes so that *mərkab* may mean 'to find', to make find, to be found' depending on the context. The infinitive is very often used with the preposition *nə-*: *nə-məngad* 'in order to trade'.

Verbs with "Weak" Radicals

In Tigrinya these present a great variety of forms, most of which, however, may be plausibly explained by the phonetic peculiarities of the "weak" consonants (see p. 428). Only the most common forms of IA are listed here. Quadriradical verbs also occupy an important place in the Tigrinya verbal system; the paradigm may be exemplified by *ṣmbr* 'to unite': *ṣämbärä, yəṣəmbər, ṣämbiru, yəṣämbər, ṣämbər*.

Verbs with Laryngeals

1*H* (*H* – any laryngeal; exemplified with *ʿṣd* 'to harvest'):
perfect *ṣaṣädä*, imperfect *yəʿaṣṣəd* (*yäʿaṣṣəd, yaʿaṣṣəd*), gerund *ʿaṣidu*, jussive *yəʿṣäd*, imperative *ʿəṣäd*;
2*H* (*mhr* 'to teach'):
mäharä (*məharä, maharä*), *yəməhər, məhiru, yəmhar, məhar*;
3*H* (*ṣlʾ* 'to hate'):
ṣälʾe (*ṣälaʾku*), *yəṣälləʾ, ṣäliʾu, yəṣlaʾ, ṣəlaʾ*.

Verbs with *w/y*

2*w/y* (*mwt* 'to die', *kyd* 'to go'):
mäwɔtä (*motä*)/*käyädä* (*kädä*), *yəkäyyəd*/*yəmɔwwət*, *käydu*/*mäwitu* (*moytu*),
    yəkyäd (*yəkid*)/*yəmwät* (*yəmut*), *kəyäd* (*kid*)/*məwät* (*mut*);
3*w/y* (*däläwä* 'to be strong'/*bäkäyä* 'to weep'):
däläwä (*dälo*, *dälä*)/*bäkäyä* (*bäkä*), *yədälläw* (*yədällu*)/*yəbäkkəy* (*yəbäkki*),
    däliwu (*dälyu*)/*bäkyu*, *yədlɔw* (*yədlo*)/*yəbkäy* (*yəbkä*), *dəlɔw* (*dəlo*)/
    sətäy (*sətä*). *w* in verbs 3*w* is often replaced by *y* (thus *däläwä* along-
    side *däläyä*).

Adverbs and Other Parts of Speech

Adverbs of time: *lomi* 'today', *ṣəbaḥ* 'tomorrow', *təmali* 'yesterday', *šəʿu* 'this
moment'; of place: *laʿli* 'above', *taḥti* 'below' (see also p. 434); interrogative:
ʾäḅäy 'where?', *mäʾas* 'when?', *kəndäy* 'how much?', *kämäy* 'how?'.

The most common prepositions are *nə-* 'to' (also direct and indirect object (see
p. 432)), *bə-* 'by, with the help of', *ʾab* 'in', *nab* 'towards', *kab* (*ʾənkab*) 'from,
than' (see p. 434), *məs* 'with, together with', *kəsaʿ* 'up to, until', *wəšti* 'in, in the
middle'. There exist compound prepositions, e.g. *ʾab laʿli* 'on, over'. A number
of prepositions is employed in combination with postpositions, e.g. *bə ... gəze* 'at'
(temporal): *bäḥase tädros gəze* 'at the time of the Emperor Theodoros'.

Interjections: *way*, *wɔyläy* 'woe is me!', *ʾakko* 'sure!', *ʾəlal*, *ḥoyä* 'long live!',
ʾəmbi 'no!, by no means!'.

Syntax

Word Order

The normal word order of the Tigrinya simple sentence is SOV: *ʾətu säḅʾay
gərawti yəḥarrəs* 'the man plows the fields'. Sometimes the object is placed at the
beginning: in this case the whole sentence, carrying a certain degree of emphasis,
is organized as a "relative complex" or "cleft construction" (see p. 443). Examples: *ʾəta dorho zə-hard-a wɔddi ʾəyyu* '(it is) the man (who) strangles the chick-
en' (lit. 'the chicken - this who strangles it - the man - it is'). The position of
adverbial modifiers is free, including the beginning of the sentence: *ʾətu fəre*[1]
dəhri nəʾaštoy gəze[2] *yəbässəl*[3] 'after a bit of time[2] the fruit[1] becomes ripe[3]'; *ʾabtu
laʿli ḥawwi*[1] *ṣällämti ʾaʾman*[2] *yəxämməṭu*[3] 'they put[3] black stones[2] on the fire[1]'.
Qualifiers (the article, adjectives, genitive with *nay*) are usually put before the
qualified nouns: *ḥadä bälliḥ kara* 'a sharp knife'; *nay ʾItiopya rəʾsä kätäma* 'the
capital of Ethiopia'. Likewise subordinate clauses usually come before the main
clauses.

Agreement Rules

Verbs, adjectives, personal and deictic pronouns and the article in Tigrinya usually agree with nouns in gender and number: *ʾətom kahnat ʾətu kəddaseʾom məs*

wɔddə'u ... naḫtu dägge-sälam yəmäṣu 'when the priests finish their service they go right to the door of the church'; *nəssatän kä'a dəmṣän ʿaw 'abbilän bäkäya* 'then they (women) raised their voices and wept'. However, the adjective agrees in gender in the singular only (see p. 434). Since the grammatical gender of most inanimate beings is highly unstable, the agreement may fluctuate even within one and the same text (see p. 431). Nouns denoting collectives (*ḥəzbi* 'people', *särawit* 'army' etc.) may agree with in singular or plural.

Assertions, Negations

The most common assertive adverb in Tigrinya is *'əwwä* 'yes'. The compound verbs *ḥərray bälä* and *'əšši bälä* are widely used as affirmatives: *däs 'əntäḫälo ḥərray yəḫəl ...* 'if he is pleased, he says "yes" ...'.

The most widespread verbal negative is the confix *'ay-...-n*: *nəḥna mənəm ḥadä nägär 'ay-gäḫärna-n* 'we did not do anything'; without *-n* in the jussive (*'ay-yəmut* 'let him not die!'. Another common negative is *'ayfal* (very often with pronominal suffixes): *'ayfal-kən däkkäy* 'no, my children!'. The verb *'əmbi bälä* means 'to say "no", to refuse'. To express 'there is no ...' *yällon* (conjugated as *'allo*) or *yälbon* (not conjugated) is employed; *naḫtu ḥagär ʿaḫäyti kätämatat yälbon* 'there are no big cities in this country'. The negative of the copula is *'ay-konän naytän 'anəsti təmhərti bəzuḫ 'aykonän* 'the women's education is not much'.

Questions

A general question is introduced by the postposed particle *-do* attached to that part of the sentence which is the main object of the question: *kənəwɔssəd-do* 'can we take [it]?'; *dəḥan-do 'allokum* 'are you well?'. The element *dəyyu* (*do* prefixed to *'əyyu*) serves to express 'is it ...?': *ḥakki dəyyu 'əttəḫəlänni zälla?* 'is it right what she says?'.

Pronominal questions are introduced by the interrogative pronouns (see p. 430) and interrogative adverbs (p. 441):

'əntaway 'ətu säb? 'who is that man?'
'əntay yədälli 'what does he want?'
mə'əntəməntay kämzuy təgäbbər? 'why do you act in this way?'
kämäy ḥadärkum? 'how have you spent the night?'
'əta säḫäyti kab 'aḫäy mäṣ'et? 'from where did this woman come?'

Coordination, Conditionals

The commonest coordinating conjunction in Tigrinya is *-n* suffixed to every one of the conjointed elements: *nay mäskäl mələkkət naḫtu gäṣu-n ləbbu-n käḫdu-n 'a'garu-n yəgäḫrällu* 'he makes the sign of the cross over his face, his heart, his belly and his feet'; *'əta kab kullän kätämatat 'erətra zə'aḫäyät-ən zəṣäḫäxät-ən kätäma 'asmära 'iyya* 'Asmara is the biggest and the most beautiful among the cities of Eritrea' etc. Two clauses are connected by *'əwwən* 'and' usually placed after the first phrase in the second clause: *nay ḥadä mähayyəm kʷɔlʕa bətəmhərtu bəzḥat däbtärä kəkɔwwən yəkəʾəl nay ḥadä däbtära kʷɔlʕa ʾəwwən mähayyəm kəkɔwwən yəkəʾəl* 'a child of an illiterate may become a *däbtära* if he studies much, and a child of a *däbtära* may be illiterate'. Alternative is expressed by *wɔy* (*wɔyəm*): *ḥadä kərši wɔyəm kəršən ʾaladən yəhəbə-wo* 'he gives him one thaler or one thaler and a half'. The commonest adversative conjunctions are *gən* (*nägär gən*) and *ʾəmbär*: *ḥadä ʕaynät ʾammäḥalal ʾəwwən ʾallo nägär gən ʾəzu mäḥalla nay ṣawɔta mäḥalla ʾəyyu* 'there is another kind of oath, but it is an oath for fun'; *gar däʾa yəkfäl ʾəmbär bəhənux ʾayyəmut* 'let him certainly pay the blood money, but he must not be strangled (must not die strangled)'. *ʾəmbär* is placed at the end of the positive element so that a translation 'and not, but not' is appropriate for it: *ʾab Mäxälä ʾəmbär ʾab ʾAddis ʾabäba täwɔlädku* 'I was born in Mäxälä and not in Addis Ababa'.

Conditional clauses are marked by *ʾəntä* 'if' followed by the perfect or the gerund: *ʾətu ʕədaga därahu kətrəʾi ʾəntä-kädka ... ʕassärtä bəxərši kəšəyyäṭa tərəʾi* 'if you go to see the chicken market, you will see that they are sold ten for a thaler'. They may also be marked by *ʾəntäkonä* (+ *zə-*) + verb (lit. 'if it is (that) ...'): *ʾətu xäraṣi bäməngəsti ʾəntäkonä zə-kəffäl ʾətu gäzaʾi dämozu yəhəbo* 'if the customer is paid by the government, it is the ruler who gives him his salary'. Clauses expressing an unreal condition are marked by *ʾəntä* (*ʾəntäzə-*) + imperfect; the verb of the apodosis (in the perfect) is preceded by *mə-* and may be followed by *näbärä* (in the gerund): *ʾətu ʾanbäsa ʾəntäzə-xättəl nabtu bäräka mə-täräfä näbiru* 'if he had not killed the lion, he would remain in the thicket'; *ʾAdam ḥaṭiʾat zäygäbärä ʾəntäzə-kowwən nəhna ḥəggusat mə-konna* 'if Adam had not sinned, we would be happy'.

Subordination

Complement clauses are marked by *kämzə-* 'that': *ʾəgziʾabḥer nəhəzbu kämzə-bäšhom ʾəngera kämzə-habom sämʕet* 'she heard that God visited his people and gave them bread'.

Temporal clauses are marked by *məs* preceding the verb in the perfect: *ʾəzuy məs gäbärä kämzuy balo ...* 'when he did it, he told him thus ...'; *kämzuy məs bälätto ḥafiru nab bäräkaʾu kädä* 'when she told him in this way, he went to his thicket, ashamed'. Other temporal conjunctions are *kəsaʕ zə́* 'until', *ʾənkab zə-* 'since' (*zə-* prefixed to the verb of the subordinate clause), e.g. *kəsaʕ ʾətu mäʕalti zəbäṣṣəh ʾatom wɔläddi ʾəngera zəbəllaʕ kässänadəwu yəṣänḥu* 'until this day comes, the parents spend the time preparing the bread that will be eaten'.

Relative clauses are introduced by *zə-* and, like all other qualifiers, precede the noun qualified: *ʾətu₁ ʾanbäsa₂ zə₃xätälä₄ säb₅ bəhakki zəfärrəh ʾaykonän* 'the₁ man₅ who₃ killed₄ a lion₂, indeed has no fear'. If the noun qualified is a direct object and, peculiarly, an adverbial modifier, a corresponding object suffix may be attached to the verb of the relative clause: *ḥadä ḥadä däbtära ḥadä ḥadä zäynəfält-o ʕaynät [ṣolot] dägimu* 'a *däbtära* reciting a kind [of prayer] that we do not know'; *nabtu bäräka ʾəzom ʾansəsatat zälläwə-wo yəkädu* 'they go to the thicket in which there are wild animals' (lit. 'to the thicket - wild animals - are in it (object suffix) - they go'). Relative clauses are very often combined with *ʾəyyu*: *ʾətu₁ säb₂ zə₃-xätälä₄ säb₅ zə₆-färd₇-og məngəsti₉ ʾəyyu₁₀* 'the man who killed another man is tried by the government' (lit. '[that] who₆ tries₇-him₈ the₁ man₅ who₃ killed₄ [another] man₂ is₁₀ [the] government₉').

Copular and Possessive Expressions

The copula and the *verbum substantivum* in Tigrinya are conjugated in the following way:

Table 18.7 Copula

	Masculine	Common	Feminine
Sg. 1		ʾəyyä/ʾalloku	
2	ʾika (ʾəka)/ʾalloka		ʾiki (ʾəki)/ʾalloki
3	ʾəyyu/ʾallo		ʾəyya/ʾalla
Pl. 1		ʾina/ʾallona	
2	ʾikum (ʾəkum)/ʾallokum		ʾikən (ʾəkən)/ʾallokən
3	ʾəyyom/ʾalläwu		ʾəyyän/ʾalläwa

The copula is used in sentences with nominal predicate in the present: *hawwɔy dəka ʾəyyu* 'my brother is poor'; *ʾabbuʾom ṭäbbib ʾəyyu* 'their father is a smith'; *zar səm färäs ʾəyyu* 'zar is the name of a horse'. The verbs *näbärä* and *konä* (in the future) replace the copula in the past and in the future: *kələttiʾom ʾawwən säräxti näbäru* 'both of them were thieves'; *ʿabiy säb kəkɔwwən ʾəyyu* 'he will be an important person'.

The verb *ʾallo* denotes existence and presence: *ʾab gäzay ʾalläwu* 'they are in my house'; *ʾabtu ṭäräf mägäggi naʾəštoy gäzawətti ʾallo* 'on the border of the road there are some houses'.

Existence in the past and in the future is expressed by *näbärä* and *konä*, respectively; in the last case the verb *hallɔwä* is also used.

The verb *ʾallo* with object suffixes is used to express possession. The first consonant of the suffix is geminated; the form of the verb depends upon the gender/number of the object possessed: *nab rəhux hagär kʷɔṣoro ʾallo-nni* 'I have a meeting in a remote country'; *ʾəta säbäyti hantit gʷal ʾallatta* 'this woman has one daughter'.

Acknowledgments

I wish to express deep gratitude to my informants Kasa Bälay and ʾArʾayä Gäbräʾəgziʾabher (both from Mäxälä) for their help in compiling the phonetic part of this chapter.

My most respectful thanks are to Professor Dr. I. M. Diakonoff who thoroughly read the manuscript and made a number of important suggestions and corrections.

Of special importance for me was the constant help of my comparative linguistics teacher, L. G. Hertzenberg, who devoted much time to discussing with me the most minute details of this contribution. I am deeply indebted to his vast knowledge and rich experience, which made his assistance truly invaluable.

Further Reading

da Bassano, Francesco. 1918. *Vocabolario tigray–italiano e repertorio italiano–tigray.* Rome: Casa Editrice Italiana di C. De Luigi.

Kiros Fre Woldu. 1985. *The Perception and Production of Tigrinya Stops.* Uppsala: Uppsala University, Department of Linguistics.

da Leonessa, Mauro. 1928. *Grammatica analitica della lingua tigray.* Rome: Casa Editrice Italiana di C. De Luigi.

Leslau, Wolf. 1941. *Documents tigrigna (éthiopien septentrional): Grammaire et textes.* Paris: Librairie C. Klincksieck.

Ullendorff, Edward. 1985. *A Tigrinya (Tǝgrǝñña) Chrestomathy.* Stuttgart: Franz Steiner Verlag Wiesbaden GMBH.

Voigt, Rainer M. 1987. *Das tigrinische Verbalsystem.* Berlin: Reimer.

19 Tigré

Shlomo Raz

Tigré is spoken mainly in Eritrea, and is the northernmost Ethiopian Semitic tongue. The majority of speakers are Muslims (above 60 percent); most of the rest are Christians. The number of speakers is put at between quarter and half a million (according to the Ministry of Education of Eritrea, February 1997, it is about 800,000). The Mansaʿ dialect is the only speech which has a corpus of written material, and as such may approach the concept of standard language. Written material consists of Bible translations, especially by members of the Swedish Evangelical mission, collections of texts in prose and verse and grammatical work by missionaries and European scholars. Two varieties of speech may be mentioned: first, that of the nomad tribe of Beni 'Amer who live close to the border with the Sudan. They are bilinguals, the other language they speak being the non-Semitic Beja, which is the substrate Cushitic language of Tigré as a whole. Their Tigré differs in many ways from that of Mansaʿ. Secondly, the Tigré language is used as a lingua franca along the Ethiopian coast of the Red Sea, notably in Massawa where it is is heavily influenced by spoken Arabic, which is another language medium in the same area.

Phonology

Consonants

The phonemic inventory of Tigré consonants consists of twenty-four phonemes, as shown on p. 447. The corresponding inventory of graphemes of traditional Ethiopic orthography by which most Tigré texts have been rendered includes also p/ṗ, č, and x, which appear in a small number of foreign words. All consonants except laryngeals (ʾ, ʿ, ḥ, ḫ) and semivowels (w, y) are subject to gemination. č, š, ǧ and ž may appear as the palatalized forms of t, s, d, and z (ž occurring only in this phonetic context). This palatalization takes place with dentals and alveolars, in final position, in forms to which the sg.1c. pronoun suffix is attached, e.g. masānit 'friends', masāničče 'my friends'; gazāz 'glass', gazāžže 'my glass' etc. The articulatory position of the variants of /q/ is post-velar, i.e. the same as that of /ʾ/ or /ʿ/; examples: [ʾaʿbər] 'tombs' (/ʾaqbər/), [maʾrəḥ] 'condition' (/maqrəḥ/). Followed by a laryngeal or by an ejective anywhere in the word, /ʾ/ and /ʿ/ may be in free variation with one another, as in [ʾarqay/ʿarqay] 'bed' (/ʿarqay/); [ʾalləṣ/ʿalləṣ] 'hawk' (/ʾalləṣ/).

b	d	g	ǧ	ʿ	
	t	k			
	ṭ	q			ʾ
			č̣		
f	z			ḥ	h
	s				
			ṣ		
	š		č		
m	n				
	l				
	r				
w		y			

Vowels

i			u
	e		o
		a	
		ā	

From the articulatory point of view each vowel is distinctive in regard to tongue height and tongue advancement, excluding the a/ā contrast which is in terms of vowel quantity, e.g. /gadəm/ 'now then, so, thus', /gādəm/ 'plain, country'; /man/ 'who?', /mān/ 'right (hand)'; /baʿal/ 'master, owner', /baʿāl/ 'holy day, holiday'. Exceptional is the case of words with a final CV-type syllable, when v is a low front vowel. In such a case no phonemic contrast of quality may occur and vowel duration is subject to stress and syllabic structure, e.g. [sábka] or [sabká] 'your people' (/sabka/); [sabká-tom] 'they are your people' (/sabka tom/); [ḥṓṣa] or [ḥoṣá] 'sand' (/ḥoṣa/). Instead of the a/ā contrast, Leslau (1945) and others prefer the use of the phonemic contrast ä/a which marks a difference of quality only between all vowels of Tigré. Such an approach facilitates the phonological description and also brings Tigré into line with some prominent Ethiopian Semitic languages, e.g. Amharic and Tigrinya, yet it ignores the existence of phonemic duration and its role in the syllabic structure and the accentual system (for a lengthier discussion of the problem see Raz 1983: 6–11).

Suprasegmental Features

The chain of speech stress in Tigré is non-distinctive and shifts easily from one syllable to the other. Even single words in isolation may be devoid of lexical stress, as in dáʾam or daʾám 'but'.

Morphology

Pronouns

The independent personal pronouns in Tigré are as follows:

Singular		Plural	
1c. *ʾana*		1c. *ḥəna*	
2m. *ʾənta*	2f. *ʾənti*	2m. *ʾəntum*	2f. *ʾəntən*
3m. *ḥətu*	3f. *ḥəta*	3m. *ḥətom*	3f. *ḥətan*

The forms used as pronominal suffixes are as follows (the order of forms is the same as in the previous table): sg.: *-ye, -ka, -ki, -u, -a*; pl.: *-na, -kum, kən, -om, -an*. In conjunction with verbs the pronominal suffixes have the following forms: sg.: *-ni/-nni, -ka/-kka, -ki/-kki, -o/-wo/-yo/-hu/-yu, -a/-wa/-ya/-ha*; pl.: *-na/-nna, -kum/-kkum, -kən/-kkən, -om/-wom/-yom/-hom, -an/-wan/-yan/-han*.

Reflexive, Reciprocal, Possessive, Interrogative and Relative Pronouns

For the reflexive pronoun the forms *nos* (*nafs* in the translation of the New Testament in Tigré), *raʾas* 'self' are used, e.g. *nosa təšannaqat* 'she hanged herself'; *raʾasu* 'he himself'. The reciprocal pronoun is expressed by means of *nosnos* or *ḥəd*, e.g. *ʾat ləblo nosnosom tahagāgaw* 'they conferred with one another saying …'. *ḥəd* is not conjugated and is usually used of two, e.g. *ḥəd ʾadməʿaw* 'they struck at each other'. The independent possessive pronoun consists of inflected *nāy*, e.g. *nāye* 'mine'. The interrogative pronouns are as follows: *mi* 'what?'; *man* 'who?, whose?, whom?'; *ʾayi* (inflected) 'which?'. The relative particle (= definite article, cf. Deictics and Definiteness, p. 450) is usually attached to the verb, immediately preceding it, e.g. … *dəgge wānin latətbahal* 'which is called "animal village"'.

Nouns

Gender

The gender of the singular noun is statable lexically, the plural form gender being subject to the state of animateness of the noun, e.g. masculine nouns: *kətāb* 'book', *gəndāy* 'log of wood', *fəluy* 'bull calf', *wad* 'son', *ʾənās* 'man'; feminine nouns: *gabay* 'road', *fəlit* 'female calf', *walat* 'daughter', *ʾəssit* 'woman' (note the *t* ending of the feminine animate form in the above examples).

Nouns Qualified by Numerals

A noun qualified by a numeral occurs in the singular form, e.g. *kəlʾe waʾat* 'two cows' (pl. *ʾaḥa* 'cows', *salas ḥāl* 'three maternal uncles' (pl. *ḥālotāt* 'maternal uncles').

The Basic Forms of Noun Formation

These are the collectives or the countable singulars. The collective nouns never occur with numerals, whereas the countable singulars may be modified by a numeral, e.g. *gabil* (coll.) 'people, tribes, nation', *gabilat* (countable sg.) '(one) tribe', *gabāyəl* (pl.) 'tribes, people'. *qaṭaf* 'leaves, foliage', *qaṭfat* 'leaf', *ʾaqaṭṭəf* 'leaves'. The concord typical of the collective is masculine singular, with one exception: animate nouns may have either singular or plural concord. The singulative is derived from the collective by means of suffixes. Either (1) *-at*, the gender of which is feminine, or less frequently, (2) the suffix *-āy*, the gender of which is masculine, is added, as in *rəšāš* 'lead', *rəšāšat* 'a bullet, a piece of lead', *bun* 'coffee', *bunat* 'a coffee bush/grain', *qadar* 'gnats', *qadrāy* 'a gnat'.

Plural Forms

These are suffixed plurals and broken plurals. Some suffixed plural forms are: *-āt*, *-otāt*, examples *gār* 'matter, thing', pl. *gārāt*; *ǧabhat* 'forehead', pl. *ǧabhotāt*. The broken plurals and the countable singulars are not predictable from each other's forms, though certain singular patterns correspond more often than not to certain plural patterns. Some types typical of the broken plural forms are as follows: *ʾaCaCCəC, CaCaCCəC, CaCaCCi(t), ʾaCCVC, ʾaCəCCat, CVCVC*. Some examples: *balasat* 'fig', pl. *ʾaballəs*; *kəffal* 'portion', pl. *kafaffəl*; *kadbet* 'floor', pl. *kadabbi(t)*.

Suffixed Derivatives

In addition to the formation of suffixed nouns dealt with hitherto, there are other noun plus suffix formations which form semantic classes of their own, as follows: diminutives ('a small'), e.g. *bāb* 'gate, door', *bebāy* 'small door, wicket', *mawrad* 'ring', *mawredat* 'little ring'; pejoratives ('a poor, bad'), e.g. *bet* 'house', *betāy* ruined house, house in poor condition', *ʾanās* 'man', *ʾanesat* 'worthless man'; augmentatives ('a big, large'), e.g. *baʿat* 'cave', *baʿāy* 'large cave'; paucatives ('a few'), e.g. *waʾat* 'cow', *waʿāt* 'a few cows'); paucative pejoratives ('some poor, bad'), e.g. *sab* 'men, people', *sabʾetām* 'a few people (paucative)', *sabʾetāt* 'some poor (= miserable) people'. Paucatives imply plural; the rest are singular and countable.

Participles

The active participle expresses the agent (the doer) and is also used in the formation of compound tenses (see p. 454), the passive one is mainly used as an adjective (see p. 450). All active participles excluding triradicals of type A (see p. 451) make use of the prefix *ma-* and the suffix *-ay*, and all passive participles have the ultimate vowel *-u-* (sg. m.) and *-ə-* (sg. f.).

Examples of active participles, type A: *qābəl* 'former', *qāblat* (f.), *qāblām* (pl. m.) *qāblāt* (pl. f.); Passive participle type A: *qərub* 'near, kin', *qərbət/qəreb* (f.), *qərubām* (pl. m.), *qərubāt* (pl. f.).

Patterns of type B, active participle: *maqatlāy, maqatlāyt* (f.), *maqatlat* (pl. m.

and f.). Examples: *ma'amrāy* 'scientist', *ma'amrāyt* (f.), *ma'amrat* (pl.); passive participle: *qəttul, qəttəl/qəttələt, qəttulām, qəttulāt.*

Type C, active participle: *maqātlāy, maqātlāyt* (f.), *maqātlat* (pl. m. and f.). Examples: *mawālmāy* 'slanderer', *mawālmāyt* (f.), *mawālmat* (pl.); passive participle: *qutul, qutlət* (f.), *qutulām* (pl. m.), *qutulāt* (pl. f.).

Infinitives
Type A verbs yield the forms *qatil, qətlat, qətlo, məqtāl, qətle, qatəl.* The form *qatil* seems to be the more frequent.

Nouns Denoting the Instrument, Place or Result
The name of the instrument has the prefix *ma-* and the suffix *-i* attached to the stem, the pattern being *maqtali*, e.g. *masawari* 'brush' (*sawara* 'to paint', type B, semivowels are not geminated). The pattern *məqtāl* is used in the expression of the name of the place, as in *məqwāl*, 'hiding place' (root *kwl*). The name of product or result (= resultative) is expressed by means of the pattern *qəttāl*, e.g. *hərrād* 'that which is/has been slaughtered', *həddāg* 'that which is/has been left'.

Suffixes -nna and -nnat
Abstract nouns having one of these suffixes are constructed from the stem CəCəC (triradicals), to which the suffix is added by means of the juncture feature *ə*, e.g. *bəṣṣəhənna/bəṣṣəhənnat* 'maturity'.

Prepositions
The most important ones are: *nāy* 'of', *'əl* 'to, for', *'əb* 'about (a topic), with (comitative), within', *'ət* 'in, on, to, against', *mən* 'from', *'əgəl* 'for, to', *kəm* 'like', *məsəl* 'with (comitative)', *'əgəl* 'as for'; compounds *mən la'al* 'above', *mən tahat* 'under', *'ət 'af* 'before' etc.

Adjectives
For the most part, the adjective precedes the noun which it qualifies, e.g. *bāb 'abi* 'big gate'. Adjectives may have suffixed plurals or broken plurals. The plural suffixes *-(y)ām* (m.) and *-(y)āt* (f.), are regularly used with participial adjectives (triradical, type A, see p. 449), e.g. *nāfə'* 'useful', *nāf'at* (sg. f.), *nāf'ām* (pl. m.), *nāf'āt* (pl. f.); *səbur* 'broken', *səbər/səbrat* (sg. f.), *səburām* (pl. m.), *səburāt* (pl. f.).

Deictics

Definiteness
The invariable particle *la-* serves as the definite article (cf. Pronouns, p. 448). The usual order encountered is article + qualifier + qualified, as in *lagendāb 'ənās* 'the old man'.

Demonstratives
The demonstrative forms for near objects are: *ʾəlli* (sg. m.), *ʾəlla* (sg. f.), *ʾəllom* (pl. m.), *ʾəllan* (pl. f.). For distant objects, the forms are (some variants occur) *lohay, loha, lohom, lohan*. The noun is preceded by the demonstrative adjective in the case of distant objects, e.g. *ʾəllan ʾamʿəlāt* 'these days', *ʾəb laʾawkād lohay* 'at that time'. The demonstrative adjective can both precede and follow the noun, as in *loha ʾakān loha* 'that place'.

Numerals
The cardinal numerals are as follows:

1	*worot/woro*	20	*ʿəsra*
	ḥatte (f.)	30	*salāsa*
2	*kəlʾot* (m.)	40	*ʾarbəʿa*
	kəlʾe (f.)	50	*ḥəmsa*
3	*salas*	60	*səssa*
4	*ʾarbaʿ*	70	*sabʿa*
5	*ḥaməs*	80	*samānya*
6	*səs*	90	*saʿa/tasʿa*
7	*sabuʿ*	100	*məʾət* (sg.)
8	*samān*		*ʾamʾāt* (pl.)
9	*səʿ*	1,000	*šəḥ* (sg.)
10	*ʿasər*		*ʾašḥāt* (pl.)

The Arabic loanword *ʾalf* '1,000', pl. *ʾālāf*, is occasionally used. To denote an unspecified large number the word *ʾəlf* (whose plural is also *ʾālāf*) may be used. *ʾəlf* is also used to denote '10,000'. The numbers 11 to 19 are expressed by placing the units numeral immediately after the invariable element *ʿasər* '10' while an optional *-wa* 'and' may connect both elements, e.g. *ʿasər (wa)ḥatte* 'eleven' (f.).

The ordinal number 'first' is expressed by *qadām* (m.), *qadāmit* (f.), *qadāmyām* (pl. m.), *qadāmyāt* (pl. f. [cf. Participles, pp. 449–50]). Ordinal numbers from second to eleventh are gender sensitive. The masculine has the patterns *CāCəC* and *CāCCāy*, and the feminine is *CāCCāyt*. For eleventh to nineteenth, invariable *ʿasər* is followed by the appropriate ordinal, with an optional *wa-* in between. *qadāmāy* (m.), *qadāmāyt* (f.) is used in the case of the numeral '11', e.g. *ʿasər waqadāmāy* 'eleventh'. The ending *-āy* forms ordinal numerals for round tens, hundreds and thousands.

Verbs

Types A, B, C and D
Type A is the basic stem in relation to which the form and meaning of the other types is considered. Type B has the medial radical geminated, e.g. *ʿallaba* 'to count'. Type C has a long *ā* after the first radical e.g. *dāgama* 'to tell'. Type D is

characterized by a repetition of the mid radical, with an *ā* in between, e.g. *balālasa* 'to answer repeatedly'.

Negation of the Verb

A verb is rendered negative by means of the prefixed article *ʾi-*, e.g. *ʾi-sarqa* 'he did not steal'.

Prefixed Derivatives of the Four Types of Verb

Verbs of each of the four types may occur with a preformative whose function and meaning is usually related to coexisting verbs of other types and derivatives. These are four preformatives: *tə-*, *ʾa-*, *ʾat-* and *ʾatta-*. In general terms *tə-* is used to express the passive form of type A and B verbs and reciprocity in type C and D verbs. The other three preformatives are used to express various aspects of the notion of causation.

Basic Morphological Categories of the Verb

Tigré has three morphological categories of the verb: perfect, imperfect and jussive.

Verb Inflection

Type A: *qanṣa* 'to get up':

Sg. 1	*qanaṣko*	Pl. 1	*qanaṣna*
Sg. 2m.	*qanaṣka*	Pl. 2m.	*qanaṣkum*
f.	*qanaṣki*	f.	*qanaṣkən*
Sg. 3m.	*qanṣa*	Pl. 3m.	*qanṣaw*
f.	*qanṣat*	f.	*qanṣaya*

Imperfect:

Sg. 1	*ʾəqannəṣ*	Pl. 1	*ʾənqannəṣ*
Sg. 2m.	*təqannəṣ*	Pl. 2m.	*təqanṣo*
f.	*təqanṣi*	f.	*təqanṣa*
Sg. 3m.	*ləqannəṣ*	Pl. 3m.	*ləqanṣo*
f.	*təqannəṣ*	f.	*ləqanṣa*

Jussive:

Sg. 1	*ʾəqnaṣ*	Pl. 1	*nəqnaṣ*
Sg. 2m.	*təqnaṣ*	Pl. 2m.	*təqnaṣo*
f.	*təqnaṣi*	f.	*təqnaṣa*
Sg. 3m.	*ləqnaṣ*	Pl. 3m.	*ləqnaṣo*
f.	*təqnaṣ*	f.	*ləqnaṣa*

Imperative (derived from the jussive): *qənaṣ, qənaṣi, qənaṣo, qənaṣa.*

Type B, perfect: *mazzana* 'to weigh'; imperfect/jussive: *ləmazzən* (sg. 3m.), *təmazni* (sg. 2f.); imperative: *mazzən, mazni,* etc.

Type C, perfect: *kātaba* 'to vaccinate'; imperfect/jussive *ləkātəb*; imperative: *kātəb.*

Type D, perfect: *balālasa* 'to answer repeatedly'; imperfect/jussive: *ləbalāləs*; imperative: *balāləs.*

Prefix *tə-.* After *tə-,* the distinction between A and B is neutralized. Perfect: *təqarrača* 'to be cut off'; imperfect /jussive: *lətqarrač*; imperative: *təqarrač. tə-*C: *təqābala* 'to meet'; imperfect/jussive: *lətqābal*; imperative: *təqābal. tə-*D: *tənabābara* 'to live a bit on agriculture and a bit on cattle herding'; imperfect/ jussive: *lətnabābar*; imperative: *tənabābar.*

*ʾa-*A: This is the sole instance of a triradical derivative where a formal distinction between the imperfect and the jussive morphological categories is maintained. Perfect: *ʾangafa* 'to save, to let escape'; imperfect: *lanaggəf*; jussive: *langəf*; imperative: *ʾangəf.*

*ʾa-*B: *ʾabaṭṭala* 'to stop, to bring to a standstill'; imperfect/jussive: *labaṭṭəl*; imperative: *ʾabaṭṭəl.*

*ʾa-*C, perfect: *ʾaṣābaṭa* 'to get hold of'; imperfect/jussive: *laṣābət*; imperative: *ʾaṣābət.*

There is no **ʾa-*D type. Its place in the system is taken by *ʾat-*D.

Prefix *ʾat-*: There is no **ʾat-*A (except with initial laryngeals). Its place in the system is taken by *ʾa-*A and *ʾatta-*A.

*ʾat-*B, perfect: *ʾatbaggasa* 'to cause to move off'; imperfect/jussive: *latbaggəs*; imperative: *ʾatbaggəs.*

*ʾat-*C, perfect: *ʾatrāsana* 'to heat'; imperfect/jussive: *latrāsən*; imperative: *ʾatrāsən.*

*ʾat-*D, perfect: *ʾatqabābala* 'to go to and fro'; imperfect/jussive: *latqabābəl*; imperative: *ʾatqabābəl.*

Prefix *ʾatta-* is functional only with type A verbs. *ʾatta-*A, perfect: *ʾattaqrača* 'to let cut off'; imperfect/jussive: *lattaqrəč.*

Quadriradical Verbs

The quadriradicals follow the order 1.2.3.4. as in *ʾambata* 'to begin', 1.2.1.2. as in *bačbača* 'to mix', and 1.2.3.3. as in *qarṭaṭa* 'to break into pieces'.

Compound Verbs

The first element in the compound may exist as a lexical entity or be dependent upon the occurrence of the compound. The second element of the compound is limited to three verbs: *bela* 'to say', *wada* 'to do, to make', and *gaʾa* 'to become'. Examples: *bəhal bela* 'to pardon, to excuse', *bəraf wada* 'to clear off', *hən gaʾa* 'to become speechless'.

Complex Expressions of Time Relations
More specific time relations than those mentioned on p. 452 can be expressed by means of a complex.

ʾəgəl + jussive + *tu* as the expression of futurity. This complex is regularly used in the expression of future tense, e.g. *fağər baṣəʿ ʾəgəl nigis tu* 'tomorrow we shall go to Massawa' (lit. 'tomorrow Massawa in order that we should go [it] is'). This complex is also used to express imminence.

Imperfect + auxiliary (*halla* or ʾ*alla*). The complex imperfect + *halla* (the verb of existence in the present) is essentially used to express an activity in progress at the time of speaking, or an actual state. This use resembles in meaning the English "present continuous" or "progressive," e.g. *ḥana hədāy nətfarrar hallena* 'we are going to the wedding'.

ʾ*əndo* + perfect + *ʿala (ṣanḥa)*. The notion expressed by this complex refers to (a result of) an event or a situation whose beginning (and end) is previous to another specified, or understood, point of time (approximating to the meaning of the past-perfect tense in English), e.g. *hətu ʾəgəl laʾəndo ḥawana laʿala ʾamlakot rabbi ḥaddasayu* 'he renewed the adoration of God which had been weakened'.

Perfect + *ka* + auxiliary. This complex consists of a verb in the perfect followed by the conjunction *ka-* (meaning 'and [then]') which is itself followed by an auxiliary verb. The auxiliary verb can be *halla*, *ʿala* or *ṣanḥa*. Perfect + *ka* + *halla* denotes the perfective past (approximating to the meaning of the present-perfect tense in English). Perfect + *ka* + *ʿala* expresses the past-perfect, whereas the verb *ṣanḥa* introduces the notion of 'already', e.g. *nafsu gesat kaṣanḥat* 'he had already died' (lit. 'his soul went and waited').

Participle + auxiliary. The complex participle + *halla* is mainly used to denote the present-perfect, e.g. *nəgus kabasa māṣəʾ halla* 'the king of Kabasa has arrived'. The complex participle + *ʿala/ṣanḥa* denotes the past-perfect.

Prepositions, Adverbs, Conjunctions, Interjections

Prepositions
Many adverbs and prepositions are similar in form. Distinction between such adverbs and prepositions is made here according to whether they lack or possess a complement (almost all prepositions may have pronominal suffixes), e.g. *məsəl nabraw* 'they lived together' (adverb); *məsəlka ʾəgayəs* 'I shall go with you' (preposition).

Adverbs
The linguistic stock from which adverbs are constructed comprises nouns, adjectives, infinitives, participles, particles, etc. Some words and particles function only as adverbs. The most frequent structure containing a noun or a verbal noun, is that of the nominal element preceded by the preposition ʾ*əb* 'with, by' (see Prepositions, above), e.g. ʾ*əb šafāg* 'quickly'.

Conjunctions

The main coordinating conjunctions are as follows: *wa-* 'and', *-ma* 'or', *wok* 'or', *ka-* 'and, and so, therefore' (corresponding to *fa-* in CA), *da'am* 'but', *da'ikon* 'on the contrary, rather'.

Interjections

These are (1) words used as interjections only and are morphologically unanalyzable, and (2) words otherwise belonging to other parts of speech, e.g. (1) *has/šət* 'be quiet!', *hə'/waha* 'ah!', *'ay/'ayo/yəwu* 'woe!', *gaddo'* 'oh wonder!'. (2) *hǝsse* 'excellent!' (*hǝsse*, pl. *hǝssetāt* 'honor, good deed' – a noun; √*hys*); *kǝn* 'away!' (*kǝn* 'there' – an adverb).

Syntax

Word Order in the Sentence

There are three main features of word arrangement typical of the Tigré sentence, as follows:

1   The main verb is regularly placed at the end of the sentence.
2   Complements and qualifiers precede the words they qualify.
3   The subject is usually placed at the beginning of the sentence, e.g. *worot 'ǝnās mǝsǝl nǝwāyu wǝṣewahu 'ǝt qišot 'ala* 'a man lived with his family and his cattle in a hamlet' (lit. 'one man with his cattle and his family in hamlet was').

A common phenomenon in speech is the word order in which a noun other than the subject heads the sentence. The word which occupies first place in the sentence is the topic, e.g. *'ǝssit hilata hawānit ta* 'the strength of a woman is her weakness' (lit. 'woman her-strength weakness [it] is').

Nominal Sentences

In sentences whose predicate is a nominal form, a copula pronoun must intervene. The paradigm of the independent copula consists of the following forms: singular: *tu* (m.), *ta* (f.); plural: *tom* (m.), *tan* (f.). In the first and second person, the forms encountered are those of the first and second person personal pronouns (see p. 448). Examples: *'ana mǝn gabil mansa' 'ana* 'I am from the tribe of Mansa''; *sab mansa' mǝn badirom kǝstān tom* 'the people of Mansa' are Christian from long ago'. In the negative *tu* is replaced by the suppletive fossilized form *'ikon*, as in: *higāye rǝtu' 'ikon* 'my speech is not correct'.

Expression of Existence and Possession

To express the notion of 'to be, to exist' (including the locative 'there is') in the present tense, the verb *halla* (type B, √*hlw*) is used. When this verb occurs in the perfect form, it has the meaning of present, e.g. *rabbi halla* 'God exists'. To denote past tense, the verb *ʿala* is used. These verbs are negated by means of the prefixed particle *ʾi-*, as in *ʾawtobus ʾiʿala. ʾəbbəlli sabab ʾəlli ʾagid ʾimaṣʾako* 'there was no bus. Because of this I have not come sooner'.

Possession is expressed by means of (1) the particle *bu* or *bədibu*, both forms being conjugated in all persons, e.g. *bəzuḥ ʾakətbat bədibye/bəye* 'I have many books', *lagaʾa ləgbaʾ wad ʾddām kəlʾe ʾade bədibu* 'every human being has two hands'; (2) the perfect forms of the verb *halla* conjugated in the 3rd person plus the particle *ʾəl-* (see Prepositions, p. 450), conjugated in all persons, e.g. *ʾana sanni masʾalit hallet ʾəlye* 'I have a good camera'.

Conditional Sentences

Sentences expressing real conditions have in the protasis either *mən* + perfect, or perfect + *mən gabbəʾ* (fossilized), and in the apodosis any construction excluding the perfect form, e.g. *kəlʾot mən lətbaʾaso lazayəd laməsməsa ʾat worot leṭa ʾikon* 'if two persons quarrel, usually the cause is not on one [of them] only'; *gale gaʾaw mən gabəʾ ləghu dibom* 'if anything happens to them, they are grieved about them'. Sentences which express unreal conditions have in the protasis either *mən* + imperfect or *wa* + perfect, and in the apodosis *wa* + perfect, e.g. *waʾəlli kəllu mən lətkattab kəlla laʾeddina-ma ʾəgəl lalətkattabo ʾakətbat waʾiʾaklattom* 'and if all of this were to be written, even the whole world would not suffice for the books to be written about it'; *rabbi waʾihabaya* 'had not God given it (i.e. the chieftainship) to her'.

The Modal Form **wa** + Perfect

The complex *wa* + perfect may serve as a special form for modal expressions denoting the unreality or uncertainty of the notion rendered by the predicate, e.g. *ʾəlla lataḥayəs bet mən ʾaya warakba* 'where could he find a house which would be better than this (one)?'; *lawəlādkum waṣaʿankum* 'you should have let your children ride [the donkeys]'.

References

Leslau, Wolf. 1945. "The Verb in Tigre (North-Ethiopic): Dialect of Mensa." *Journal of the American Oriental Society* 65: 1–26.

Raz, Shlomo. 1983. *Tigre Grammar and Texts* (Afroasiatic Dialects 4). Malibu: Undena Publications.

Further Reading

Hetzron, Robert. 1972. *Ethiopian Semitic: Studies in Classification* (*Journal of Semitic Studies* Monograph 2). Manchester: Manchester University Press.

Littmann, Enno. 1910–1915. *Publications of the Princeton Expedition to Abyssinia.* 4 vols. Leiden: Brill.

Littmann, Enno, and Maria Höfner. 1962. *Wörterbuch der Tigrē-Sprache: Tigrē–Deutsch–Englisch.* Wiesbaden: Franz Steiner Verlag.

20 Amharic and Argobba

Grover Hudson

Amharic has perhaps fifteen million speakers, in Africa probably fewer than only Arabic, Swahili, Hausa, and Oromo. Amharic is also the second most populous Semitic language, after just Arabic. It is the lingua franca and constitutionally recognized national language of Ethiopia, and the language of instruction of Ethiopian public education in the primary grades.

The traditional territory of the Amharas is the mountainous north-central part of Ethiopia consisting of the regions of Begemder (Gondar region), western Wello, Gojjam, and Menz. Today, however, perhaps the majority of town and city dwelling Ethiopians, except in largely Tigrinya-speaking Tigre province, are at least second-language speakers of Amharic. Except in the core Amhara areas of Shoa, Gojjam and Begemder, Amharic speakers are often bilingual, and probably most have another Ethiopian language as their native language.

Regional varieties or dialects of Amharic are recognized: of Shoa, Begemder, Gojjam and Menz–Wello. Differences are not major, and those which were mentioned by Bender et al. (1976: 90–8) are noted below. Addis Ababa is nowadays the focus of Ethiopian economic and social life, and Addis Ababa Amharic has become the prestige dialect.

Amharic manuscripts are known from the fourteenth century, and publication in Amharic has increased steadily since the turn of the century. Amharic publications today include writings of all sorts: poetry, newspapers, literary and news magazines, drama, novels, history, textbooks, etc. Amharic language magazines are published in the USA and Europe to serve the Ethiopian expatriate populations there. In 1972, a national language academy was established in Ethiopia, with the purpose largely to standardize the language and, especially, to guide the expansion of the Amharic vocabulary.

In recent and probably in ancient times, Amharic has had considerable geographic spread in territory earlier populated by speakers of other languages, first the southern Agaw language of north-central Ethiopia, and recently languages of the south such as Cushitic Sidamo and Omotic Kaffa. As a result, Amharic has considerable lexical and typological similarities with these other languages. Amharic also has borrowed from Ge'ez, a practice nowadays favored for the satisfaction of needs for technical, political, and other new vocabulary. Borrowing from Italian was common, especially during the Italian occupation of 1935–1941, but nowadays the principal source of borrowings is English.

Argobba, Amharic's sibling, is known in two separate areas: until recently west of the city of Harar, and at the eastern edge of Amhara territory about the Rift Valley escarpment towns of Ankober and Aliyu Amba in eastern Shoa. Probably most Argobba speakers are Muslims. All information reported below on the Argobba language is from Leslau 1959 and Leslau 1977.

Most sections of the survey of Amharic which follows conclude with pertinent comparative comments about Argobba, though, in some cases, information on Argobba is lacking. In some of the tables, Amharic and Argobba forms appear side by side.

Phonology

Consonants

Below are shown the thirty-one consonant phonemes of Amharic; vl = voiceless, vd = voiced, em = emphatic. The consonant phonemes have the phonetic values generally suggested by their symbolization, except as follows: the emphatic consonants are glottalic ejectives; *ň* is IPA *ɲ*, and, following common practice, the emphatic (voiceless) velar is here written *q* rather than *ḳ*.

vl	*p*	*t*		*k, k^w*	*ʾ*
vd	*b*	*d*		*g, g^w*	
em	*ṗ*	*ṭ*		*q, q^w*	
vl			*č*		
vd			*ǰ*		
em			*č̣*		
vl	*f*	*s*	*š*	*h, h^w*	
vd		*z*	*ž*		
em		*ṣ*			
	m	*n*	*ň*		
		l			
tap		*r*			
	w		*y*		

The labialized velars *k^w*, *g^w*, *q^w*, and *h^w* could be considered sequences of the consonant and *w*; however, their status as phonemes is suggested by the fact that the Amharic writing system provides unique characters for these in their occurrence before vowels other than *a* (before *a* there is a regular orthographic formation for labialization of all consonants).

The voiceless labial stops *p* and *ṗ* are rare, appearing only in loanwords, though some borrowings with *ṗ* are long established in the language, such as *ityoṗṗya* 'Ethiopia' (< Greek). The voiced labiodental fricative [v] occurs in some recent borrowings such as *volibol* 'volleyball'. The glottal stop, glottal fricative, and labialized velars do not occur at the end of syllables (or, thus, words), nor the alveopalatal nasal at the beginning of words. Otherwise, words begin and end with any of the consonants. In rural Amharic *ṣ* may be replaced by *ṭ* and *ž* and *ǰ* may be free variants. The glottal stop could be considered an allophonic effect of syllable-initial vowels, as in *[ˀ]ityoṗṗya* 'Ethiopia', *sä[ˀ]at* 'hour, clock/watch'.

As in Amharic, *p* and *ṗ* are lacking in Argobba except in borrowed words, and *ṣ* has been replaced by *ṭ*. Word-final *t > d*, usually, as in Argobba *bed* 'house' (Amharic *bet*), and *h* has survived where generally it has been lost in Amharic as in Argobba *hand* 'one' (Amharic *and*).

Consonant Allophones

The voiceless stops are slightly aspirated except when unreleased, and are released except before other stops and nasals within a phrase. The nongeminate voiced labial and velar stops *b* and *g* have fricative variants [β] and [ɣ] between vowels within words, e.g. *le[β]a* 'thief', *wa[ɣ]a* 'price'. For most speakers *qʷä >* *qo* and *qʷə > qu*, with resulting variants such as *qʷässälä/qossälä* 'he was wounded' and *qʷəṭər/quṭər* 'number', but for others the velar and labial stops are labialized before round vowels, e.g. *b[ʷ]ota* 'place', *q[ʷ]um* 'stop/stand!'. The glides *w*, *y* are extremely lax between vowels. In the northern dialects, except that of Gondar, there is palatal glide insertion after obstruents before the front vowels *i* and *e*, which may in this case be centralized: e.g. *bet > [bʸɛt]* 'house' and *hid > [hʸɨd]* 'go (sg. 2m.)!'. In Menz, the velar stops *k* and *q* are palatalized to *č* and *č̣*, respectively, before *i* and *e*.

Long Consonants

All the consonants except *h* may occur long (geminated) between vowels and occasionally word finally, with the approximate duration of a two-consonant sequence. Below, the long consonants are written as sequences of like consonants, except when lexically contrastive length must be distinguished from morphologically significant doubling, so e.g. *t:*, *s:*, are written. The retroflex phoneme *r*, singly a tap, is a trill when long.

Morphophonemic Palatalizations

When stem final and followed by the sg. 2f. suffix *-i*, the instrumental and agentive suffix *-i* and the conjunctive sg. 1 suffix *-e*, the alveolar consonants except *r* are replaced by the corresponding alveopalatals: *t > č, d > ǰ, ṭ > č̣, s > š, z > ž* (and optionally *ž > ǰ*), *ṣ > ṭ, n > ň*, and, except in the dialect of Menz, *l > y*. The suffix *-i* may be absent with these palatalizations. Note that these palatalizations do not occur before *i* and *e* otherwise (e.g. *set* 'woman'), not even in nouns suffixed by *-e* of the sg. 1 possessive (e.g. *bet-e* 'my house').

The same palatalizations occur with the cognate Argobba suffixes.

Vowels

The seven vowel phonemes of Amharic are shown below. The vowel phonemes have the phonetic values generally suggested by their symbolization, except as follows: *ə* is a high central vowel, IPA *ɨ*, and *ä* is a mid central vowel, IPA *ʌ*, according to some tending to low front [ɛ], especially after the alveopalatal consonants. The mid-front vowel *e* is lowered to [ɛ], after *h*, as in *h*[ɛ]*dä* 'he went'. Words begin and end in any of the vowels except that *ə* does not occur final in a phrase except with the question suffix *-nə* (see p. 481), nor *ä* word initially except in the interjection *ärä* 'really!'

i	ə	u
e	ä	o
	a	

Argobba has marginally, in addition to the seven vowel phonemes of Amharic, *a:* (long *a*) in Arabic loanwords. Leslau mentions round allophones of *ä* and *ə*, and long allophones of *i* and *o*. Argobba words begin but do not end in *ä*, having final *a* where Amharic cognates have *ä*.

Vowel Elision

Vowel sequences involving *ə* and *ä* are generally absent owing to the elision of these two by the other vowels; furthermore, *ə* is elided by *ä*: *bä-ərgəṭ* > *bärgəṭ* 'truly (lit. 'in truth')', *bä-anči* > *banči* 'by you (sg. 2f.)'. A sequence of like vowels is reduced to one: *asra-and* > *asrand* 'eleven', *yəbäla-al* > *yəbälal* 'he eats'.

Vowel Epenthesis

The high central vowel *ə* is epenthesized when disallowed consonant sequences arise in affixation, e.g. *y-nägr-h* > *yənägrəh* 'he tells you (sg. m.)'.

Vocalization

The sg. 3m. and pl. 3 verb-subject prefix *y-* is replaced by *i* between consonants: *s-y-hed* > *sihed* 'when he goes', *ənd-y-mäṭa* > *əndimäṭa* 'that he come(s)'.

Devocalization

The high vowels *i* and *u* (typically the suffixes *-i* and *-u* of the sg. 2f. and pl. 3 of verbs, respectively) are replaced by glides *y* and *w*, respectively, when followed by *a*: *tənägri-alləš* > *tənägryalləš* 'you (sg. f.) tell', *näggär-u-at* > *näggärwat* 'they told her'.

Stress

Stress is not prominent in Amharic, though main stress of words is typically audible on stems rather than affixes (though the plural suffix may be stressed), but more so on closed rather than open syllables. There is, however, little research on this topic.

Morphology

Pronouns

In Tables 20.1–20.3 (p. 462) are presented the independent pronouns and two sets of suffix pronouns. The Amharic object suffix pronouns are shown with the past tense verb *näggärä* 'he told', and the Amharic possessive suffix pronouns with the noun *bet* 'house'. As in Leslau 1959, the Argobba object suffix pronouns are shown with the past tense verb *gäddäla* 'he killed', and the Argobba possessive suffix pronouns with the noun *bed* 'house'.

Independent Pronouns

Amharic independent pronouns distinguish sg. 2pol., sg. 3pol. and pl. 3 forms, distinctions merged in verb paradigms. Sg. 2pol. *antu* is common only in Wello and Gondar. The four pronouns with *ass-* each have alternate forms with *ars-*, e.g. *ars-u* 'he', *ars-wo* 'you sg. pol.', which reflect the origin of these as reflexive–emphatics based on possessive forms (see p. 463) of **ars* 'head' or **kars* 'belly'. The pl. 2/3 forms reflect a plural morpheme *annä-* (as in *annä-täsfaye* 'those associated with Tesfaye') prefixed to the sg. 2/3m. forms, respectively. Since verbs agree with their subjects, the independent pronouns are redundant as subjects unless contrastive, in e.g. *ane näññ* 'it's me', *anta-m athedam* 'you (sg. 2m.) won't go either', and they appear rarely as subjects of verbs, as, for example, when contrastive.

Pronominal objects are ordinarily expressed as verb suffixes, so again the independent pronouns appear only rarely as objects, as when contrastive. When they do so appear, the independent pronouns like definite nouns are suffixed by the definite object suffix *-n* (see p. 465): *ane-n, antä-n*, etc., e.g. *asswa-n näggär-ku(-at)* 'I told her'.

As possessives, the independent pronouns have the possessive prefix *yä-*, e.g. *yä-ñña* 'our' (see p. 464). More commonly, pronoun possession is expressed by the possessive suffix pronouns (p. 463).

In Argobba the independent pronouns with the basis *kass-* perhaps derive from reflexive–emphatic pronouns consisting of the noun *kärs* 'belly' with the possessive suffixes. Argobba lacks the 2nd and 3rd person polite forms.

Object Suffixed Pronouns

Instead of sg. 3m. *-w* (*näggärä-w* 'he told him'), the form *-t* appears after round vowels, e.g. *näggär-u-t* 'they told him', *nägr-o-t* 'he, telling him'. After consonants other than alveopalatals the object suffixes of the sg. 1, sg. 3m. and pl. 1 have *ä*: *-äññ, -äw*, and *-än*, respectively, e.g. *näggär-k-äññ* 'you (sg. m.) told me', *wasäd-äw* '(you (sg. m.)) take him!' The initial part *-ačč* of the pl. 2 and pl. 3 suffixes probably reflects a plural suffix cognate with the noun plural suffix *-očč*.

There are prepositions *bä-* 'with, (up)on, against' and *lä-* 'for, in the interest of' which may be suffixed to verbs in the forms *-bb-, -ll-*, respectively, in which case they take the object suffix pronouns of the above set with the exception of sg. 3m.

Table 20.1   Independent pronouns

		Amharic	Argobba
Sg.	1	əne	äy
	2m.	antä	ank
	f.	anči	anč
	pol.	əsswo/antu	
	3m.	əssu	kəssu
	f.	əsswa	kəssa
	pol.	əssaččäw	
Pl.	1	əňňa	ənna
	2	ənnantä	ənnakum
	3	ənnässu	kəssäm

Table 20.2   Object suffix pronouns

		Amharic	Argobba
Sg.	1	näggärä-ňň	gäddäl-äň
	2m.	näggärä-h	gäddäl-ah
	f.	näggärä-š	gäddäl-ih
	pol.	näggärä-wo(t)	
	3m.	näggärä-w	gäddäl-e
	f.	näggär-at	gäddäl-ya
	pol.	(= pl. 3)	
Pl.	1	näggärä-n	gäddäl-änna
	2	näggär-aččəhu	gäddäl-əhu(m)
	3	näggär-aččäw	gäddäl-em

Table 20.3   Possessive suffix pronouns

		Amharic	Argobba
Sg.	1	bet-e	bed-ya/bed-e
	2m.	bet-əh	bed-ah
	f.	bet-əš	bed-ih
	pol.	bet-wo	
	3m.	bet-u	bed-u
	f.	bet-wa	bed-wa
	pol.	(= pl. 3)	
Pl.	1	bet-aččən	bed-enno
	2	bet-aččəhu	bed-əhu(m)
	3	bet-aččäw	bed-ämmu

-ät instead of *-äw*: *därräqä-bb-äññ* 'it dried up on me' (i.e., 'unfortunately for me'), *əndifärdə-ll-ät* 'that he judge in his favor'. When not suffixed to verbs, these prepositions accept the independent pronouns as their objects, e.g. *bäne* (< *bä-əne*) 'by/on me', *banči* (< *bä-anči*) 'by/on you (sg. f.)'.

Possessive Suffixed Pronouns
Instead of *-u*, the sg. 3m. form *-w* appears after round vowels, e.g. *bäqlo-w* 'his mule'. The vowel of the sg. 2m. and sg. 2f. suffixes is not epenthetic; *bet* + *š*, for example, would not require epenthesis. The initial part *-ačč* of the pl. 1/2/3 suffixes again probably reflects a cognate of the noun plural suffix *-očč*. The possessive suffix pronouns are mutually exclusive with the suffix of the definite article (see p. 464).

Reflexive–Emphatic Pronouns
These are expressed as possessives of the noun *ras* 'head', e.g. *ras-e* 'myself', *ras-aččən* 'ourselves', as in:

> *ras-u-n godda-w*
> self-his-Def. injured(he)-it
> 'He injured himself.'

Argobba reflexive pronouns are based on *näbs* 'soul' (*näbs-e* 'myself') or *dəmah* 'head'.

Interrogative Pronouns
These include *man* 'who' (*man-ən* 'whom'), *mən* 'what' (*məndər* in *məndər näw* (> *məndənnäw*) 'what is it?'), *mäče* 'when', and *yät* /*yet* 'where', which take the suffix *-m* (*-əm* with epenthesis) to provide negative indefinite pronouns, e.g. *man-əm almäṭṭam* 'nobody came', *yät-əm alhedəm* 'I won't go anywhere'. Other question words are *yätəññaw* 'which', *sənt* 'how much', *lämən* 'why' (lit. 'for what'), *əndä-mən* 'how' (*əndä* 'like'), and *əndet* 'how' (< *əndä-yät* 'like where').

Argobba interrogative pronouns include *ma(n)* 'who?', *mən* 'what?', *yedəññaw* (m.), *yeyeňňäwa* (f.) 'which?', *yed* and *če* 'where?', and *mäčče* 'when?' The suffix *-m* (*-əm* with epenthesis) forms negative indefinite pronouns, e.g. *mən-əm* 'anything'.

Nouns

Gender
Gender is mostly natural, but a few inanimate nouns are typically treated as grammatically feminine, including the sun and moon, names of countries, automobiles, and small animals such as mice, the latter reflecting a diminutive usage of feminine gender. Many feminine human nouns end in *t*, an archaic non-productive feminine ending, e.g. *ənnat* 'mother', *əhat* 'sister', *nəgəst* 'queen' (cf. *nəgus*

'king'), and there is a rare feminine suffix -*it*, as in *arogit* 'old woman' (*aroge* 'old'), *andit* 'a little one (f.)' (*and* 'one') (seen in the feminine definite article *it-u*, see Definiteness, below). The gender of a noun is apparent in its choice of pronoun, agreement with the verb, determiners, and the definite article suffix.

Argobba (as noted, p. 459), generally has *d* for Amharic word-final *t*, so thus in the archaic feminine suffix of e.g. *əhəd* 'sister'.

Definiteness

In masculine and common nouns, discourse-referential definiteness (= 'the above-mentioned') is expressed by the suffix -*u*/-*w* (-*w* after vowels). In feminine nouns, this is expressed by the suffixes -*wa* or -*it-u*: *wəša-w* 'the dog (m.)' (ambiguously 'his dog'), *dəmmät-wa* 'the cat (f.)' (ambiguously 'her cat') or *dəmmät-itu* 'the cat (f.)'. Definiteness is inherent in the possessive suffixes. The nouns *säw* 'man' and *set* 'woman' have special definite forms *säw-əyye-w* 'the man', *set-əyye-w* 'the woman' with a suffix -*əyye* perhaps indicating specificity (see below).

In Argobba the suffixes -*u*/-*w* (m.) and -*wa* (f.). indicate definiteness: *bed-u* 'the house (m.)', *aškär-wa* 'the (maid)servant (f.)'.

Indefinite Article

The numeral *and* 'one' functions as an indefinite specific article, especially on the introduction of human topics, as in *and säw(-əyye) mäṭṭa* 'a (certain) man came', where discourse continues about the man. Repetition of *and* expresses plural indefinite but inspecific 'some': *andand säw mäṭṭa* 'some (a few) people came'.

Argobba *hand* '1' does not so function (Leslau 1959: 254, 256).

Plurality

The regular suffix of plurality is -*(w/y)očč*: *bet-očč* 'houses', *zämäd-očč* 'relatives'. The *y* is transitional after *i/e*, but *w* may follow any vowel: *gäbäre-yočč*/ *gäbäre-wočč*. Alternatively, the vowel of the plural suffix may elide a preceding vowel: *mäkina-očč* > *mäkinočč* 'cars', *bäqlo-očč* > *bäqločč* 'mules'. There are some irregular plurals in *at* and *an*, including *qal-at* 'words', *qəddus-an* 'saints' (probably < Geʿez). With plural quantifiers, the plural suffix may be absent: *bəzu säw* 'many people', *hulät ləǰ* 'two children'. Adjectives may be pluralized (see p. 466) and, archaically, the relativized verb (see p. 482).

Argobba has the noun-plural suffix -*(a)č*, the vowel being absent following vowels: *bed-ač* 'houses', *bäqlo-č* 'mules'.

Genitive

The genitive of nouns is expressed by the prefix *yä*-: *yä-hanna ənnat* 'Hanna's mother', *yä-kenya ambasador* 'the Kenyan ambassador', *yä-səlk quṭər* 'telephone number'. This prefix is absent if another prefix precedes, as in *lä-hanna ənnat* 'for Hanna's mother'. The same prefix marks the verb of the adjective clause (see p. 482).

In Argobba the genitive prefix is *yä*: *yä-wädaǰ-əya* 'of my friend', which also is absent if another prefix is present: *bä-wädaǰ-əya färäs* 'on my friend's horse'.

Object Suffix
Definite objects of verbs, and sometimes indefinites in older writing, are suffixed by *-n*: *bet-u-n wäddädä* 'he liked the house', *abbat-e-n näggär-ku* 'I told my father'. A topicalized (raised as topic) definite accusative is marked as a "resumptive" object pronoun on the verb (cf. p. 480):

bet-u-n wäddäd-ä-w
house-the-Def. liked-he-it
'He liked the house.'

Argobba also suffixes *-n* to definite objects: *bäru-n atəkfäte* 'don't open the gate'.

Topicalizer
A suffix *-m* (*-əm* with epenthesis) marks nouns as topical, in the sense raised anew, returned to as topic, or contrastive with others; for example, in *ṭwat yohannəs-əm däwwälä-ňň* 'in the morning Yohannis called me', Yohannis is raised (anew or not) as a topic for further discussion, and in *yohannəs-əm yə-mäṭal* 'as for Yohannis, he will come/Yohannis will come too', Yohannis contrasts with others. In questions, an equivalent morpheme is *-ss*: *antä-ss?* 'what about you (sg. m.)?'.

Derived Nouns
The instrument or location of a verb is formed on the infinitive (see p. 475) with the suffix *-iya*: *mäṭräg-iya* 'broom' (*ṭ'ärrägä* 'he swept'), *awroplan maräf-iya* 'airport, runway' (*arräfä* 'he rested, it landed (of airplane)'). The agent of a verb is expressed by a special stem with *a* after the second consonant of triconsonantal and quadriconsonantal verbs, and the suffix *-i*: *sämi* 'hearer', *nägari* 'teller', *fällagi* 'seeker', *tärg^wami* 'translator'. In the agent of biconsonantal roots reconstructable as triconsonantals with medial *y* or *w*, the glide appears: *hiyǰ(i)* 'goer' (*hedä* 'he went'), *qäwami* 'stander' (*qomä* 'he stood').

A few other noun-deriving suffixes may be mentioned. An agent of a noun is formed with the suffix *-äňňa*: *qäld-äňňa* 'joker' (*qäld* 'joke'), *färäs-äňňa* 'horseman' (*färäs* 'horse'); this suffix also forms ordinal from cardinal numerals (see p. 467). Expressing characteristic association with the noun to which it is suffixed – nationality when suffixed to a country name – is *-awi*: *ingliz-awi* 'English(man)', *amät-awi* 'annually' (*amät* 'year'). An abstract noun of quality is derived with the suffix *-nnät*: *set-ənnät* 'womanhood' (*set* 'woman'), *dəha-nnät* 'poverty' (*dəha* 'poor').

In Argobba the instrument of a verb is also formed on the infinitive by the suffix *-iya*, as in *mäṭräg-iya* 'broom'. Other suffixes as in Amharic are *-nnät* (*läǰ-nnät* 'childhood') and -*äñña* (*bəlät-äñña* 'cleverness'), the latter also forming ordinal from cardinal numerals (see p. 467).

Adjectives

There are words which typically function as adjectives, that is, attributive to nouns, such as *təlləq* 'big', *aroge* 'old (of non-human things)'. However, these have some of the morphological characteristics of nouns, for example functioning non-attributively and taking the definite article and plural suffixes: *təlləq-u* 'the big one', *təlləq-očč* 'big ones', *qonǰo-wa* 'the pretty one', *qonǰo-wočč* 'pretty ones'. The definite suffix attaches to the adjective, but a possessive suffix attaches to the noun: *təlləq-u bet* 'the big house' vs. *təlləq bet-u* 'his big house'. The definite object suffix -*n* appears also on the adjective: *qonǰo-wa-n mäkina šäṭä* 'he sold the pretty car.' The plural suffix attaches to the noun: *qonǰo mäkina-wočč* 'the pretty cars'. Unlike other noun modifiers, *hullu* 'all' may follow its noun: *säw hullu* 'all the people'.

Some adjectives form a plural implicating 'variousness', by reduplicating their middle consonant: *tələlləq ləǰočč* 'various big children' (*təlləq* 'big'), *räǰaǰǰəm wattaddäročč* 'various tall soldiers' (*räǰǰəm* 'tall'). These may still be pluralized when predicative: *tələlləqočč naččäw* 'they are big (ones)'.

The suffix -*am* derives from a noun an adjective meaning 'having particularly or excessively a quality associated with the noun': *hod-am* 'greedy, gluttonous' (*hod* 'stomach'), *mälk-am* 'attractive, nice' (*mälk* 'appearance'). The suffix -*amma* derives an adjective of similar but somewhat intensified meaning: *fərey-amma* 'fruitful' (*fəre* 'fruit'), *ṭen-amma* 'healthy' (*ṭena* 'health').

The predicative comparative of adjectives is expressed by a prepositional phrase with *kä-* or *tä-* 'from', e.g. *kä-yonas əne dəha näññ* 'I am poorer than Yonas' (lit. 'from Yonas I am poor'). A predicative superlative is a comparative in relation to 'all': *kä-hullu əne dəha näññ* 'I am poorer than all' (= 'poorest'). (Adjectives, however, often have cognate verbs with which comparisons may also be expressed, e.g. *kä-ne əssu räǰǰəm näw* or *kä-ne əssu yəräzzəmal* 'he is taller than me'.) Comparisons are often reinforced by one of the fixed form (lacking subject agreement) simple nonpast verbs *yələq* (*läqqa* 'he/it surpassed'), or *yəbälṭ* (*bälläṭä* 'he/it exceeded'), as in:

Haylu k-antä yəbälṭ bäṭam qäččən nä-w
Haylu from-you (sg. 2m.) more very thin is-he
'Haylu is much thinner than you.'

Concerning comparison clauses, see p. 484.

Argobba has adjectives, including *hačir* 'short' (Amharic *ačər*), *rəhuq* 'far' (Amharic *ruq*). As in Amharic, the quantifier expressing 'all', *diyyu(m)*, may follow its noun: *mäsob-ač diyyu(m)* 'all baskets'.

Demonstratives

		Amharic	Argobba
Near	Sg. m.	*yəh*	*hud*
	f.	*yə(hə)čč(i)*	*huy*
Far	Sg. m.	*ya*	[o:]*d*
	f.	*yačč(i)*	[o:]*y*
Near	Pl.	*ənnäzzih*	*h*[u:]*lläm*
Far	Pl.	*ənnäzzya*	*(w)*[o:]*lläm*

The demonstratives distinguish singular and plural, and near (proximal) and far (distal). The Amharic plural forms reflect the plural prefix *ənnä-* with locatives *əzzih* 'here' and *əzzya* 'there'. The demonstratives function attributively (*yəh bet* 'this house') and pronominally (*ya näw* 'that's it').

Argobba plural forms appear to be cognate with Amharic *hullu* 'all', and the final *-m* of these apparently cognate with Amharic *-m* (see p. 465). The long vowels of the plurals are as given by Leslau. 'Here' and 'there' are *bä-hud* (lit. 'at-here') and *b-o:d* ('at-there'). Apparent cognates of Amharic *yəh* 'this' and *ya* 'that' are *yih/yah* 'here, take'.

Numerals
The cardinal numerals are shown below:

	Amharic	Argobba		Amharic	Argobba
1	*and*	*and*	12	*asra-hulät*	*assər ket*
2	*hulät*	*ket*	20	*haya*	*kiya*
3	*sost*	*sost*	30	*sälasa*	*sasa*
4	*arat*	*arbit*	40	*arba*	*harba*
5	*amməst*	*amməst*	50	*hamsa*	*hamsa*
6	*səddəst*	*səddəst*	60	*səlsa*	*səlsa*
7	*säbat*	*sa'int*	70	*säba*	*säba*
8	*səmmənt*	*səmmənt*	80	*sämanya*	*sämanya*
9	*zäṭäñ*	*žähṭʷäñ*	90	*zäṭäna*	*zäṭäna*
10	*assər*	*assər*	100	*mäto*	*mäto*
11	*asr-and*	*assər-hand*	1000	*ši*	*ši*

In Amharic, calendar years are expressed e.g. *ši zäṭäñ mäto səlsa sost* (thousand nine hundred sixty three) '1963'. Ordinal numerals are formed with the suffix *-äñña* (which also forms noun agents: see p. 465): and *-äñña* 'first', *assər-äñña* 'tenth'. There is an apparent dissimilation in 'ninth': *zäṭäñ-äñña* > *zäṭänäñña*. In royal titles 'first' is expressed by *qädam-awi* (*qdm* 'precede') and 'second' by *dagm-awi* (*dgm* 'repeat'), e.g. *qädamawi haylä səllasi* 'Haile Sellasie I', *dagmawi mənilək* 'Menelik II'.

Argobba cardinal numerals from 50 are identical to those of Amharic, which probably influenced them, or from which they are borrowed. Argobba ordinal numerals as in Amharic have the suffix -äñña, e.g. hand-äñña 'first', ket-äñña 'second'.

Verbs
Verbs consist of a stem and affixes.

Stems
Stems consist of a number of (root) consonants (typically three), a pattern of vowels, and, in the conjunctive and infinitive, for some verbs the stem-forming suffix *t* which replaces an otherwise lost stem-final consonant. In Table 20.4 (below) are presented the five stems – past, nonpast, imperative/jussive, conjunctive, and infinitive – of representative Amharic verbs of the twelve most common types. Consonant length (gemination) is shown by ":".

Table 20.4   Amharic verb stems

	Past	Nonpast	Imp.	Conjunct.	Inf.	Gloss
A	käf:äl-	-käfl	kəfäl	käfl-	mä-kfäl	'pay'
B	fäl:äg-	-fäl:əg	fäl:əg	fäl:əg-	mä-fäl:äg	'want'
A	qär:ä	-qär	qər	qär-t-	mä-qrä-t	'remain'
B	läy:ä	-läy:	läy:	läy:-ət-	mä-läy:ä-t	'separate'
A	bäl:a	-bäla	bəla	bäl-t-	mä-bla-t	'eat'
B	läk:a	-läk:a	läk:a	läk:-ət-	mä-läk:a-t	'measure'
	qom-	-qom	qum	qum-	mä-qom	'stand'
	hed-	-hed	hid	hid-	mä-hed	'go'
	sam-	-səm	sam	səm-	mä-sam	'kiss'
	bar:äk	-bar:k	barək	bark-	mä-baräk	'bless'
	mäsäk:är	-mäsäk:ər	mäskər	mäskər-	mä-mäskär	'testify'
	fänäd:a	-fänäd:a	fända	fänd-ət-	mä-fända-t	'burst'

The first three pairs of stems in Table 20.4 illustrate verb types which contrast by length of the second consonant, usually termed types A (short consonant) and B (long consonant). None of the twelve types are differentiated by meaning, but at somewhat greater than chance probability A-type verbs are intransitive and B-types transitive. The type of *bar:äk* (tenth row), with *a* after the first consonant, is often termed "C-type." The type of *käf:äl* (first row) is the most numerous.

The typical dictionary entry or citation form of Amharic verbs is the past stem with the sg. 3m. suffix -*ä*, even though, as the table shows, types A and B are nondistinct in this stem. In Shoan or Addis Ababa Amharic, the conjunctive stem of biconsonantal verbs with a back round vowel characteristic (*qum* in the table) is *qom*, and of those with a front vowel characteristic (*hid* in the table) *hed*.

Biconsonantal verbs (rows 3–9) can typically on comparative evidence be seen to derive from verbs of three consonants, one of which was lost with reflex as a vowel characteristic in some environments. Similarly, the type of *fänäd:a* represents a four-consonant root which lost the fourth. Verbs which lost the last consonant are those whose conjunctive and infinitive stems are suffixed by *t*. Biconsonantals with a medial vowel characteristic, the types of *qom*, *hed*, and *sam*, lost the medial consonant with the vowel as reflex.

Stems with Initial *a*
Some stems have initial *a*, the historical reflex of a lost pharyngeal or laryngeal stem-initial consonant. In Table 20.5 are compared the stems of *a*-initial verbs corresponding to verbs of rows 1–4 and 11 of Table 20.4.

Table 20.5   Amharic stems of verbs with initial *a*

Past	Nonpast	Imp.	Conjunct.	Inf.	Gloss
al:äf	alf	əläf	alf	m-aläf	'pass'
ad:än	ad:ən	ad:ən	ad:ən	m-ad:än	'hunt'
ay:	ay	əy	ay-t	m-ayä-t	'see'
am:a	ama	əma	am-t	m-ama-t	'slander'
anäk:äs	anäk:əs	ankəs	ankəs	m-ankäs	'limp'

Doubled Verbs
So-called "doubled verbs" have repetition of a consonant. In Table 20.6 are shown stems of doubled verbs corresponding to the types of rows 1, 2, 3, 6 and 11 of Table 20.4. The doubled verb characteristic is shown in the table as the repetition of a consonant, whereas long consonants which characterize conjugations (columns) are shown with ":".

Table 20.6   Amharic stems of doubled verbs

Past	Nonpast	Imp.	Conjunct.	Inf.	Gloss
bär:är	bärr	bərär	bärr	mä-brär	'fly'
däl:äl	däl:əl	däl:əl	däl:əl	mä-däl:äl	'cajole'
šäš:ä	šäš	šəš	šäš-t	mä-ššä-t	'flee'
ṭäṭ:a	ṭäṭ:a	ṭäṭ:a	ṭäṭ:-ət	mä-ṭäṭ:a-t	'drink'
dänäg:äg	dänäg:əg	dängəg	dängəg	mä-dängäg	'decree'

In Table 20.7 are presented the five stems of representative Argobba verbs of ten types corresponding to the Amharic types of Table 20.4 less B-types *läy:ä* and *läk:a*. Medial *h* is not entirely lost in Argobba as in Amharic, and survives, for example, in the type of *sähaq*. Argobba B-type verbs are characterized by the vowel *e* after the first consonant in past and nonpast stems, as well as by consonant length. There is a gap in the data for the conjunctive stem of the *gäb:a* type, presumably *gäb-d*. The appearance of *t* rather than expected *d* in the infinitive of this

Table 20.7 Argobba verb stems

Past	Nonpast	Imp.	Conjunct.	Inf.	Gloss
sädäb	sädb	sədäb	sädbə-d	mä-sdäb	'insult'
bed:äl	bed:əl	bäd:əl	bäd:əl-d	mä-bäd:äl	'wrong'
mäš:	mäš	məši	mäš-d	mä-mši-d	'be evening'
gäb:a	gäb	gəbi		mä-gbi-t	'enter'
qom	qom	qum	qom-d	mä-qom	'stand (v.i.)'
hed	hed	hid	hed-d	mä-hed	'go'
sahaq	si:q/sähq	saq/sähaq	siq-d/sähaq-d	mä-saq	'laugh'
mar:äk	mar:ək	mar:ək	mar:ək-d	mä-mar:äk	'capture'
dänäg:äṭ	dänägṭ	dängəṭ	dängəṭ-d	mä-dängäṭ	'startle (v.i.)'
bärät:a	bärät:	bärt	bärtə-d	mä-bärti-d	'be strong'

type (also in that of the verb 'say', see p. 480), could reflect sporadic Amharic influence.

The stems of a representative Argobba non-geminating A-type verb with initial *a* are as follows: past *arräf* (= *ar:äf*), nonpast *arf*, imperative *əräf*, and conjunctive *arfə-d*. The infinitive of this type, theoretically *aräf*, is missing in the data. Argobba cognates of Amharic stems with initial *a* often have initial *h*.

The Four Basic Verb Conjugations

The four basic verb conjugations past, nonpast, imperative (jussive), and conjunctive are characterized by the stems of Tables 20.4–20.7 plus subject prefixes and/or suffixes.

Past

The subject suffixes of the past conjugation are seen in Table 20.8; the gloss of the Amharic verb is 'tell' and of the Argobba verb 'insult'.

The sg. 1 and sg. 2m. suffixes *-ku/-k* have alternates *-hu/-h*, respectively, after vowel-final stems: *qärrä-hu* 'I remain', *bälla-hu* 'I ate'. Sg. 1 *-hu* may also appear after stem-final consonants: *käffäl-hu* 'I paid'. The vowel of the Amharic sg. 1 suf-

Table 20.8 Past

		Amharic	Argobba
sg.	1	näggär-ku	säddäb-ku
	2m.	näggär-k	säddäb-k
	f.	näggär-š	säddäb-č(-i)
	pol.	(= pl. 3)	
	3m.	näggär-ä	säddäb-a
	f.	näggär-äčč	säddäb-äd̯
	pol.	(= pl. 3)	
pl.	1	näggär-(ə)n	säddäb-ən
	2	näggär-aččəhu	säddäb-kum
	3	näggär-u	säddäb-u

fix -ku/-hu is voiceless when word final (voiced in e.g. näggär-ku-t 'I told him'). The pl. 2 suffix -aččəhu probably reflects -ačč 'plural' plus -hu cognate with -ku of the Argobba suffix. The suffix -u of pl. 3 suppletes the stem-final vowel a: bäll-u 'they ate', but, otherwise, the elisions mentioned on p. 460 apply when suffix vowels follow stem vowels: qärrä-ä > qärrä 'he remained', läkka-ä > läkka 'he measured'.

The main verb negative past is formed by prefixing al- and suffixing -m: al-näggär-ku-m 'I didn't tell', al-näggär-nə-m 'we didn't tell'. Subordinate verbs lack the suffix: ənd-al-mäṭṭa 'that he didn't come'. Object suffix pronouns follow the subject suffix and precede negative -m: näggär-äčč-əh 'she told you (sg. m.)', al-näggär-ku-t-əm 'I didn't tell him'.

In Argobba, the sg. 3m. form has final a vs. ä of Amharic. The raised t of the sg. 3f. ending is a voiceless release, as reported by Leslau. The negative past has the prefix al- and the suffixes -m in the pl. 3 form (al-säddäbu-m), -aw in the pl. 1 and pl. 2 forms (al-säddäbn-aw and al-säddäbkum-aw, respectively, and -u/-w otherwise (-w after vowels, e.g. al-säddäb-k-u 'you (sg. 2m.) didn't insult', al-säddäba-w 'he didn't insult').

Nonpast

The subject prefixes and suffixes of the nonpast are shown in Table 20.9, where again the gloss of the Amharic verb is 'tell' and of the Argobba verb 'insult'. The table shows forms which as affirmative main verbs combine with an auxiliary, for which see Table 20.10.

Nonpast verbs in subordinate clauses typically have an adverbial clause prefix such as s- 'when' (see p. 484), with which there is epenthesis before the subject prefix t, which may be geminated (s-t-nägr-i > sət(tə)nägri 'when you (sg. f.) tell'), and vocalization of the subject prefix y as i (s-y-hed > sihed 'when he goes'). When followed by the sg. 2f. suffix, stem-final alveolar consonants except r are replaced by their alveopalatal alternates (see p. 459) in which case the vowel i of this suffix may be absent, as in tə-käfč(-i) 'you (sg. f.) open' < tə-käft-i.

Table 20.9 Nonpast

		Amharic	Argobba
Sg.	1	ə-nägr	ə-sädb
	2m.	tə-nägr	tə-sädb
	f.	tə-nägr-i	tə-sädb-i
	pol.	(= pl. 3)	
	3m.	yə-nägr	yə-sädb
	f.	tə-nägr	tə-sädb
	pol.	(= pl. 3)	
Pl.	1	ən(nə)-nägr	əl-sädb-ən
	2	tə-nägr-u	tə-sädb-u
	3	yə-nägr-u	yə-sädb-u

The negative of the nonpast is formed by prefixing *a-* and, in main verbs, suffixing *-m*: *a-y-nägr-əm* 'he won't tell', *b-a-y-nägər* 'if he doesn't tell'. The sg. 1 prefix of the negative nonpast is *l-* instead of *ə-* of the affirmative: *a-l-hed-əm* 'I won't go', and the subject prefix *t-* is usually lengthened after the negative prefix: *a-ttə-nägər* 'she doesn't tell'.

As an affirmative main verb and except when part of a compound verb (see p. 477), the nonpast is suffixed by an auxiliary verb historically derived from forms of the verb of presence (p. 476). The subject prefixes and suffixes of this conjugation are shown in Table 20.10, where again the gloss of verbs of the Amharic examples is 'tell' and of the Argobba examples, 'insult'. The final vowel of the sg. 1 auxiliary *-allähu* is voiceless when word final. The pl. 2/3 suffix *-u* of the simple nonpast (Table 20.9) is absent with the suffixation of the plural auxiliary verb unless an object suffix cooccurs with a pl. 3 subject as in *yə-nägr-u-t-al* 'they tell him'.

Table 20.10   Compound nonpast

		Amharic	Argobba
Sg.	1	ə-nägr-allähu	ə-sädb-älluh
	2m.	tə-nägr-alläh	tə-sädb-ällah
	f.	tə-nägr-i-alläš	tə-sädb-ällih
	pol.	(= pl. 3)	
	3m.	yə-nägr-al	yə-sädb-äl
	f.	tə-nägr-alläčč	tə-sädb-ällädʼ
	pol.	(= pl. 3)	
Pl.	1	ən(nə)-nägr-allän	əl-sädb-ällən/ə-sädb-ənänən
	2	tə-nägr-allaččəhu	tə-sädb-älləhum
	3	yə-nägr-allu	yə-sädb-ällu

Object suffix pronouns follow the stem and precede the suffixed auxiliary: *yə-nägr-aččäw-al* 'he tells them/him (pol.)', *ə-nägr-əh-allähu* 'I tell you (sg. m.)'.

Argobba nonpasts have the pl. 1 prefix *əl-*. Argobba negative nonpasts are prefixed by *a-*, but *a-l-*, as in Amharic, in the negative sg. 1 form. Negative singular forms are also suffixed by *-u* (e.g. sg. 3m. *a-y-sädb-u*), negative 2nd and 3rd plural forms by *-m* (e.g. pl. 2 *a-t-sädb-u-m*), and the negative pl. 1 by *-aw* (*a-l-sädb-ən-aw*) (Leslau: 262). The suffixed negatives are presumably, as in Amharic, main-verb forms.

Imperative/jussive

The imperative has only 2nd person forms: sg. m., sg. f., and pl., respectively *nəgär*, *nəgär-i*, *nəgär-u*. Stem-final alveolar consonants of sg. 2f. imperatives have the usual palatalizations (see p. 459, e.g. *wəsäǰ(i)* 'take (sg. f.)! vs. *wəsäd*, sg. m.). The negative imperative is expressed by the 2nd person negative jussives.

The jussive consists of the imperative stem plus prefixes and suffixes, as seen in Table 20.11, in which again the gloss of verbs of the Amharic examples is 'tell'

Table 20.11   Jussive

		Amharic	Argobba
Sg.	1	lə-ngär	lə-sdäb
	2m.	tə-ngär	tə-sdäb
	f.	tə-ngär-i	tə-sdäb-i
	pol.	(= pl. 3)	
	3m.	yə-ngär	yə-sdäb
	f.	tə-ngär	tə-sdäb
	pol.	(= pl. 3)	
Pl.	1	ən(nə)-ngär	lə-sdäb-ən
	2	tə-ngär-u	tə-sdäb-u
	3	yə-ngär-u	yə-sdäb-u

and of the Argobba examples 'insult'. Instead of *ə-* of the nonpast and as in the negative nonpast, the sg. 1 subject prefix is *l-*.

The jussive expresses 'may (it be so that) V', or 'would that V', e.g. *yə-ngär-əh* 'may (it be so that) he tell you (sg. m.)', although 1st and 3rd person jussives are typically understood in the meaning 'let V', e.g. *yə-hid* 'let him go', *ənnə-hid* 'let us go'. The jussive is not employed in subordinate clauses. Negatives of the jussive, like negative nonpasts, are prefixed with *a-* and, as in the negative nonpast, negatives of the 2nd person jussives may have lengthening of a subject prefix consonant: *a-t(tə)-hid-u* 'don't go! (pl. 2)'.

Imperatives in Argobba are sg. 2m. *sədäb*, sg. 2f. *sədäb-i*, and pl. 2 *sədäb-u*, with the usual palatalizations, as in Amharic, of stem-final alveolars in sg. 2f. forms. The jussive pl. 1 as well as sg. 1 prefix is *l*. Negative jussives are prefixed by *a-* (Leslau gives only 2nd person negative forms), and the subject prefix *t-* of the 2nd person forms is lengthened: *attəsdäbu* 'don't insult!' (pl. 2).

Conjunctive
This conjugation, sometimes termed 'gerundive' or 'converb', consists of a stem and subject suffixes. Its simple form, except in Gojjam Amharic, functions only

Table 20.12   Conjunctive

		Amharic	Argobba
Sg.	1	nägər-:e	sädb-əč
	2m.	nägr-äh	sädb-əd-ah
	f.	nägr-äš	sädb-əd-ih
	pol.	(= pl. 3)	
	3m.	nägr-o	sädb-əd-o
	f.	nägr-a	sädb-əd-a
	pol.	(= pl. 3)	
Pl.	1	nägr-än	sädb-əd-än
	2	nägr-aččəhu	sädb-əd-əhum
	3	nägr-äw	sädb-əd-äm

Table 20.13 Compound conjunctive

		Amharic	Argobba
Sg.	1	nägər-:e-alləhu	sädb-əč-älluh
	2m.	nägr-äh-al	sädb-əd-ähal
	f.	nägr-äš-al	sädb-əd-ihäl
	pol.	(= pl. 3)	
	3m.	nägr-o-al	sädb-əd-ul
	f.	nägr-alläčč	sädb-əd-alläd
	pol.	(= pl. 3)	
Pl.	1	nägr-än-al	sädb-əd-änäl/sädb-əd-änällən
	2	nägr-aččəhu-al	sädb-əd-əhumäl
	3	nägr-äw-al	sädb-əd-ämäl

as a subordinate verb. In Table 20.12 are shown simple conjunctive forms of Amharic 'tell' and of Argobba 'insult'. The conjunctive and the nonpast stems are alike in the verb type of these examples, but not in others, as seen in Table 20.4. In sg. 1 forms the stem-final consonant is lengthened, resulting in epenthesis before the long consonant, e.g. *nägərre-w wäṭṭahu* 'I told him and left', which if alveolar other than *r*, has the usual palatalizations, e.g. *wäsəǰǰe* 'I taking' (*wsd* 'take').

The simple conjunctive may be used to express all but the last of a sequence of states or events, the last, main, verb being of any form: *därs-äw bällu* 'they arrived and ate'/'having arrived, they ate', *käfl-än ənnəhedallän* 'we will pay and go/ 'having paid, we will go'. The subjects of the conjunctive and main verb need not be the same: *särq-o assäru-t* 'he having robbed, they imprisoned him'. Followed by an invariable auxiliary *näbbär*, it expresses an event in the past prior to another, at which latter time the significance of the previous event was still effective or significant (like an English "past perfect"): *əne sə-mäṭa hed-o näbbär* 'when I came, he had gone', *bält-än näbbär* 'we had eaten'. In the Gojjam dialect the simple (main verb) conjunctive has a negative form, like the past with prefix *al-* and suffix *-m*.

The alveolar stop which appears in Amharic conjunctive stems of verbs which lost the final consonant appears with all Argobba conjunctive verbs as *d* (with epenthetic *ə*) instead of *t* of Amharic, but as *č*, *t* palatalized, in the sg. 1 form. The Argobba compound conjunctive has no negative forms.

The conjunctive, like the nonpast, combines with an auxiliary verb suffix based on the verb of presence (see p. 476), and the resulting compound conjunctive expresses a past event with still present effects, like an English "present perfect." Table 20.13 (above) presents forms of the compound conjunctive, again with the Amharic verb 'tell' and the Argobba verb 'insult'.

In neither Amharic nor Argobba does the compound conjunctive have negative forms.

Infinitive
The Amharic infinitive consists of a stem prefixed by *mä-*, e.g. *mä-ngär* 'to tell': *mängär gədd näw* 'to tell is a necessity', *mä-hed yəwäddal* 'he likes going'. Where purpose is expressed, the infinitive is prefixed by *lä-*: *lä-mä-hed yəfälləgal* 'he wants to go'. In *a*-initial stems, *ä* of the prefix is elided: *m-adär* 'to spend the night', *m-ayät* 'to see'. The negative infinitive has the prefix *alä-*: *alä-mä-ngär* 'not to tell'. The infinitive may take the possessive pronoun suffixes (Table 20.3) as subject: *mä-ngär-wa* 'her telling', *mä-hed-aččən* 'our going'.

In Argobba also the infinitive has the prefix *mä-* and a special stem for some verb types: *mä-sdäb* 'to insult', *mä-näggäd* 'to trade' (B-type verb). Instead of expected *d*, in the infinitive *mä-gbi-t*, *t* appears (see Table 20.7).

Copula
There is a copula, a verb of 'being' conjugated irregularly. The Amharic copula has only nonpast forms, seen in Tables 20.14 and 20.15. Except for the sg. 3f. form *näčč*, with a subject suffix as in the past tense, the Amharic copula is analyzable as a stem *nä-* with the object suffix pronouns. Of the two sg. 3f. forms, *näčč* is more common nowadays. In the copula, as in the pronouns but not in the verb conjugations, there is a sg. 2pol. form distinct from the pl. 3 form.

Table 20.14   Affirmative copula

		Amharic	Argobba
Sg.	1	näňň	näň
	2m.	näh	nah
	f.	näš	nih
	pol.	näwot	
	3m.	näw	ne
	f.	näčč/nat	näd
	pol.	(= pl. 3)	
Pl.	1	nän	nänna
	2	naččəhu	nəhum
	3	naččäw	nem

The negative nonpast copula is formed on a stem different from that of the affirmative, *dällä* (*dollä* in Gojjam), and has the suffixes of the regular past. In the past, the verb of being or existence is expressed by regular past forms of the stem *näbbär* 'be': *näbbär-ku* 'I was', *näbbär-k* 'you (sg. m.) were' etc., with regular negatives, e.g. *al-näbbär-ku-m* 'I was not'. In the future, this is expressed by regular nonpast forms of the stem *hon* 'be/become', e.g. *yə-hon-al* 'he will be(come)'.

Except for sg. 3f. *näd*, with a suffix of the past conjugation (cf. Amharic *näčč*), the Argobba present affirmative copula is analyzable as a stem *n-* with the object suffix pronouns. The Argobba present negative copula has the negative prefix *a-* and the stem *hun* with, except for sg. 3m., pl. 1, and pl. 3 forms apparently influ-

Table 20.15   Negative copula

		Amharic	Argobba
Sg.	1	ay-dällä-hu-m	a-hun-ku
	2m.	ay-dällä-h-əm	a-hun-k-u
	f.	ay-dällä-š-əm	a-hun-ču
	pol.	(= pl. 3)	
	3m.	ay-dällä-m	a-hun-e-yu
	f.	ay-dällä-čč-əm	a-hun-äd-u
	pol.	(= pl. 3)	
Pl.	1	ay-dällä-n-əm	a-hun-änna-w
	2	ay-däll-aččəhu-m	a-hun-kuma-w
	3	ay-däll-u-m	a-hun-em-u

enced by the affirmative copula, subject suffixes of the regular past plus the negative suffix *u*. The Argobba verb of existence in the past is expressed by regular past forms of the stem *əmbär* 'be' (cognate with Amharic *näbbär*), and existence in the future by nonpast forms of the stem *hon* 'be(come)'.

Verb of Presence

The verb of presence in the nonpast, of locative sentences and presentatives such as 'there is a …', is shown in Table 20.16. The stem is *allä*, which appears only in this conjugation. Though it expresses a nonpast, this verb, a *qärrä*-type of Table 20.4, has the form and subject suffixes of the past. The negative nonpast verb of presence, as a main verb, is the stem *yällä* with subject suffixes of the past plus the suffix -*m* of the negative past: e.g. *yällä-hu-m* 'I am not present'. With locative adverbs the copula may replace the verb of presence: *əzzih näw/əzzih allä* 'he is here/here it is'.

The verb of presence in the past and also the verb of existence is a regular past formation of the root *nbr*: *näbbär-ku* 'I was (present)', *näbbär-k* 'you (sg. m.) were (present)'. Presence in the future employs the stem *nor* (< *näbr*): *yə-nor-al* 'he/it will be' (which in the past means 'reside, live': *əzzya nor-äčč* 'she lived there'). With locatives, presence in the future may also be expressed with the regular nonpast stem *hon* 'be/become', e.g. *yəhonal* 'he will be (present)'.

In Argobba the verb of presence in the nonpast has the form, including subject suffixes of the past, presumably of the type of *qälla* (Table 20.7). The negative verb of presence in the nonpast has its own stem *yellä/ellä* with the suffixes of the negative past. Presence in the past, like existence in the past, is expressed as a regular past formation of the stem *əmbär*, and presence in the future as a regular nonpast formation of the stem *hon* 'be(come)'.

Possession

Possession is expressed by the verb of presence with the object suffixes, the verb stem ordinarily agreeing in gender and number with the thing(s) possessed: *mäkina allä-ňň* 'I have a car' (car is(-to-)me), *əhəte bəzu ləjočč allu-at* 'my sister has

Table 20.16   Verbs of presence

		Amharic	Argobba
Sg.	1	allä-hu	hall-uh
	2m.	allä-h	hall-ah
	f.	allä-š	hall-ih
	pol.	(= pl. 3)	
	3m.	allä	hall-a
	f.	allä-čč	hall-äd
	pol.	(= pl. 3)	
Pl.	1	allä-n	hall-ən
	2	all-aččəhu	hall-əhu(m)
	3	all-u	hall-u

many children', *əhət alläčč-əw* 'he has a sister'. For possession in the past the stem is *näbbär*: *bäqi gänzäb näbbär-at* 'she had enough money'. Amharic has other such "impersonal" verbs, which take as their object the subject of their usual translation equivalent, including verbs for being hungry and being thirsty: *rabä-ññ* 'I am hungry' (hungers-it-me), *ṭämm-aččäw* 'they are thirsty' (thirsts(-it)-them).

In Argobba, possession is expressed as in Amharic, with the verb of presence and the object suffixes, e.g. *hall-e* 'he has' ('it is to him'), *hallə-ya* 'she has' ('it is to her').

Other Compound Verb Formations
Amharic progressive and other modal verbs are expressed with various of the above simple conjugations plus auxiliary verbs. Obligation is expressed by infinitives with the verb of presence and the suffixed prepositional phrase *bb* + object suffix (see p. 461), e.g. *mäblat allä-bb-əññ* 'I have to eat', *mähed yällä-bb-əš-əm* 'you (sg. f.) don't have to go'. Habitual or conditional past is expressed by the simple nonpast and *näbbär*: *yə-nägər näbbär* 'he used to tell'/'he would have told'. Progressive aspect is expressed by the past prefixed by *əyyä-* plus the copula in the nonpast and forms of *näbbär* in the past: *əyyä-fällägä-w näw* 'he is looking for it', *əzziya əyyä-särračč näbbäräčč* 'she was working there'. "To intend to" or "be about to" is expressed by the simple nonpast prefixed by *l-* and the invariable sg. 3m. forms *näw* in the nonpast and *näbbär* in the past: *l-i-hedu* (< *l-y-hedu*) *näw* 'they intend to go', *l-ən(nə)-ṭäyyəq näbbär* 'we intended to ask'. For other adverbial clauses and their verbs, see p. 484.

Derived Verbs
There are three quite productive types of derived verb, two causatives and a passive, plus some less productive patterns of stem change for deriving verbs.

Causatives of intransitive verbs are typically formed with the prefix *a-*, for example *a-fälla* 'he boiled (caused to boil)' (*fälla* 'it boiled'); *y-a-säkər* 'he/it intoxicates, causes to get drunk' (*yəsäkral* 'he gets drunk'). Some transitive verbs whose meanings involve benefit to the self, e.g. 'eat', and 'dress', also form causatives with *a-*: *a-bälla* 'he caused to eat', *y-a-läbs-allu* 'they cause to put on (clothing)/they dress (others)'. A verb in initial *a*, intransitive or not, forms its causative with *as-*, e.g. *as-ammänä* 'he causes to believe'. Conjunctive and imperative/jussive stems of *a*-causatives of triconsonantal verbs differ from the basic stem: *a-skər* 'cause to get drunk! (sg. m.)' vs. basic *səkär*, *a-skər-o* 'he, causing to get drunk' vs. basic *säkr-o*. Imperative/jussive stems of *a*-causatives of biconsonantal verbs with medial *a* also differ from the basic stem: *a-səm* 'cause to kiss (sg. m.)!', with epenthetic *ə*, absent in the presence of a suffix vowel: *a-sm-i* 'cause to kiss (sg. f.)!' vs. basic *sam* 'kiss (sg. m.)!'.

Causatives, or factitives, of transitive verbs are formed with the prefix *as-*, for example *as-gäddälä* 'he caused to kill', *y-as-fälləg-al* 'it is necessary' (lit. 'it causes to want/seek'). The *as*-causative of an intransitive is an 'indirect' causative with potential for two agents, e.g. *as-mäṭṭa* 'he caused someone to bring' (cf. *mäṭṭa* 'he came', *a-mäṭṭa* 'he brought (caused to come)', 'import' (v.t.)). Both objects of the causative verb, if definite, are suffixed by the definite object suffix *n* (see p. 465). *As*-causatives of verb types that distinguish non-geminating and geminating (B-type) stems are formed as B-types; thus the *as*-causative parallel to *yə-säbr-al* 'he breaks' is *y-as-säbbər-al*. The imperative/jussive stem of an *as*-causative of a biconsonantal verb with medial *a* differs from a basic stem: *as-lək-u* 'cause to send (pl.)!' vs. basic *lak-u* 'send (pl.)!'.

Passives are formed with the prefix *t(ä)-* and/or stem changes, e.g. *tä-bälla* 'it is eaten'. Some of these derivatives express a reflexive, e.g. *t-aṭṭäbä* 'he washed himself' (*aṭṭäbä* 'he washed'), or an intransitive of a transitive, e.g. *tä-mälläsä* 'he returned (v.i.)' (*mälläsä* 'he returned (v.t.)'). Past and conjunctive passive stems of verb types which distinguish A and B-type are identical to B-type basic stems, plus *tä-*. Passive stems of the nonpast, imperative/jussive and infinitive, some different from basic stems, are shown in Table 20.17. These have lengthening of the stem-initial consonant as the result of assimilation of the passive prefix *t*. With a nonpast, jussive or infinitive stem with initial *a*, the prefix *t* is lengthened, e.g. *yə-tt-amän* 'it is believed', *mä-tt-aläf* 'to be passed'.

A derived verb expressing reciprocity is formed by prefixing *t(ä)-* and providing the vowel *a* after the first consonant of the stem: *tä-naggäru* 'they conversed (told to each other)' (*näggärä* 'he told'), *tä-mattu* 'they hit each other' (*mätta* 'he hit'). This formation may express a habitual as in *täballä* 'he habitually ate' (*bälla* 'he ate'). Causatives of verbs of this formation are formed by prefixing *a* and, as the result of assimilation of *t-*, lengthening the stem-initial consonant: *annaggärä* 'he caused to converse'. This formation may express an 'adjutative', meaning 'help to V', as in *affal(l)ägä* 'he helped to seek' (*fällägä* 'he sought, wanted'), *awwallädäčč* 'she acted as midwife, helped to give birth' (*wällädäčč* 'she gave birth').

For a few verbs with *a*-initial basic stems, the compound prefix *as-t-* forms a causative of a passive: *as-t-awwäqä* 'he notified, announced' (*awwäqä* 'he knew'), *as-t-arräqä* 'he reconciled' (*t-arräqu* 'they were reconciled').

Table 20.17   Amharic passive stems

Nonpast	Imp.	Inf.	Gloss
k:äf:ät	tä-käfät	mä-k:äfät	'be opened'
f:äl:äg	tä-fäläg	mä-f:äläg	'be sought'
f:äj:	tä-fäj	mä-f:äjä-t	'be consumed
l:äy:	tä-läy	mä-l:äyä-t	'be separated'
b:äl:a	tä-bäla	mä-b:äla-t	'be eaten'
l:äk:a	tä-läka	mä-l:äka-t	'be measured'
s:am	tä-sam	mä-s:am	'be kissed'
š:om	tä-šom	mä-š:om	'be appointed'
g:et	tä-get	mä-g:et	'be adorned'
b:ar:äk	tä-baräk	mä-b:aräk	'be blessed'
m:äzäg:äb	tä-mäzgäb	mä-m:äzgäb	'be recorded'
z:äräg:a	tä-zärga	mä-z:ärga-t	'be stretched'

There are "defective" verbs, some very frequent, which lack basic stems and only occur in one of the derivational patterns mentioned above, such as *a-därrägä* 'he did', *tä-därrägä* 'it was done', *as-qämmäṭä* 'he put, placed', *tä-qämmäṭä* 'he was seated, seated himself'.

An archaic prefix *n-* appears isolated in a number of such defective verbs, always preceded by one or both of the prefixes *a-* or *t-*, especially quadriconsonantal and reduplicative verbs, including *tä-n-bäräkkäkä* 'he knelt', *a-n-ṣäbarräqä* 'it glittered', *tä-n-ṭäläṭṭälä* 'it hung, was suspended'.

A derived verb expressing repetition, sometimes with attenuation of action, is formed by reduplicating the historical next-to-last consonant with the preceding stem-vowel *a*: *sasamä* 'he kissed repeatedly/a little' (*samä* 'he kissed'), *näkakka* 'he repeatedly/barely touched' (*näkka* 'he touched'), *läqaqqämä* 'he picked repeatedly/here and there' (*läqqämä* 'he picked'). There are two somewhat productive derivations expressing attenuative and intensive meanings and employing the verb 'say', for which see p. 480.

Causatives in Argobba are formed with the prefix *a*, and geminating-type causatives with *as-*; *a*-initial stems take only *as-*. Passives are derived with *t(ä)-*, and again *tä*-passives are treated as geminating types. The Argobba *tä*-stem in the past is formed with initial *ə* and assimilated *t*: *ənnekkäsa* (< *ət-nekkäsa*) 'he was bitten' (cf. *näkkäsa* 'he bit'). There is a derived reciprocal formed as in Amharic with assimilated *t* and the stem-vowel *a*: *ənnakkäsu* 'they bit one another'. Argobba has defective (never unprefixed) verbs with causatives prefixed by *as-t(ä)-*, and a number of verbs with a non-productive prefix *n* which, unlike in Amharic, may be unaccompanied by *a-* or *t-*: past *ən-ṭäläṭṭäla* 'hang (v.i.)' with *a*-causative *a-n-ṭäläṭṭäla*.

Denominal Verbs
Verbs may be derived from nouns by abstracting the consonants of the noun and assigning the resulting root to a verb type. Typically such denominal verbs are geminating (B-) types: e.g. from *märz* 'poison' (n.), *mä-märräz* 'to poison'.

Compound verbs with "say" and "do"
Many Amharic intransitive verbs are expressed as idioms consisting of a word with a final long consonant followed by the verb "say," including *bəqq alä* 'he appeared' and *qučč alä* 'he sat down'. Transitive verbs employ "do" instead of "say": *bəqq adärrägä* 'he caused to appear'. There are two somewhat productive derivations of word stems for compounding with "say," one expressing an attenuative meaning as in *wäddäqq alä* 'he fell a little' and the other an intensive as in *wədəqq alä* 'he fell hard' (*wäddäqä* 'he fell').

The verb "say," it should be noted, has irregular imperative and conjunctive stems: *tolo bäl* 'be quick (sg. m.)!', *bəlo* 'he, saying', which preserve etymological stem-initial *b*; past and nonpast sg. 3m. and infinitive forms are *alä* 'he said', *yəl-al* 'he says' and *m-alät* 'to say'.

Argobba also has compound verbs with "say," including *qäs ala* 'he was slow', and *bəq ala* 'he appeared', and compound transitives with *mäñña* 'do'. The verb "say" has imperative and conjunctive stems with etymological *b*: *bäl* 'say! (sg. m.)', *bədo* 'he, saying' (infinitive *malät*).

Syntax
Regarding Argobba syntax, Leslau (1959: 271–273) gives some information on syntactic morphology, which is reported below along with the Amharic data.

Main Constituent Order
With few exceptions (e.g. some cleft sentences, p. 483), the verb is final in Amharic main clauses, as in:

tämari-w təyyaqe ṭ*äyyäq-ä*
student-Def. question asked-he
'The student asked a question.'

The verb is also final in subordinate clauses, as seen in examples below. Typically, the subject is first in the sentence, as in the above example. However, with the combination of a topicalized (definite, backgrounded) object and a focused subject (new or foregrounded information), the object precedes the subject, and a "resumptive" object pronoun is suffixed to the verb, as in:

yəh-ən wämbär yohannəs särra-w
this-Obj. chair Yohannes made-he-it
'Yohannes made this chair.'

Pre-subject instrumental prepositional phrases are similarly expressed as resumptive suffixes on the verb.

bä-mäṭrägiya-w setəyye-w bet-u-n ṭärräg-äčč-əbb-ät
with-broom-the woman-the house-Def.-Obj. swept-she-with-it
'The woman swept the house with a broom.'

Interrogative pronouns are preverbal; they are not fronted: *Yohannəs mən fällägä* 'what did Yohannis want?', *säwoččʼu yet hedu* 'where did the people go?'

Question Particles

Yes–no questions may be marked by rising intonation, sentence-final question words *ənde* 'really?' or *wäy*, or the literary/archaic verb suffix *-nə*; for example, *Aster təhedaläčč way/ənde* 'will Aster go?' *Aster təhedaläčč-ənə*. A one-word "reprise" question may be marked by a suffix *-ss*: *təhedalləh (wäy) – awon. ančiss* 'will you (sg. 2m.) go? – Yes. And you (sg. 2f.)?'.

Noun Phrase Order

The head noun is final in the noun phrase: *ṭəru mäls* 'a good answer', *yä-ṗeṭros addis mäkina* 'Petros's new car'. In a few noun phrases borrowed from Geʽez or modeled on Geʽez, this order is reversed, and *ä* is suffixed to the attributive head noun: *bet-ä mäṣahəft* 'library' (lit. 'house-of books'), *ṣär-ä abəyot* 'counter-revolutionary' (lit. 'enemy-of revolution').

Prepositions and Postpositions

Some typical prepositions are *bä-* and *ə-* 'at, in', *lä-* 'for', *kä-* 'from' (*tä-* in northern dialects), *səlä-* 'about' and *əndä-* 'like' (the latter two may be written as separate words). Some positional relations, however, are expressed with postpositions, and some with circumpositions, including *(ə-) ... lay* 'on, upon', *(bä-) ... wəsṭ* 'in(to), inside', *kä-... bä-fit* 'before, in front of', *kä-... bä-hʷala* 'after, behind': e.g. *betu wəsṭ gäbba* 'he went into the house'. The four postpositions *lay* 'top', *wəsṭ* 'interior', *fit* 'front', and *hʷala* 'back' are nouns.

Clause Coordination

Noun phrases are coordinated by suffixing *-nna* to the next-to-last noun: *bal-ənna mist* 'husband and wife'. Clauses may also be coordinated with *-nna* if the verb to which the conjunction is suffixed is a past, simple nonpast, or imperative: *tänässu-nna wäṭṭu* 'they got up and left', *yəmäṭa-nna yayal* 'he will come and he will see' (*yəmäṭa* is simple nonpast, lacking the main verb auxiliary suffix *-al*), *hid-ənna əyʽ* '(you (sg. 2m.)) go and see'. Alternatives are coordinated with *wäy-m* or *wäy-s* after the first noun phrase or clause, the latter for questions (cf. the question particle *wäy*, p. 481). The role of coordinated clauses is often fulfilled by clauses of simple conjunctive verbs (see p. 473), which need no conjunction. "Exception" or "but"-clauses are coordinated with *(nägär/daru) gən* 'but', first in the clause.

The suffix expressing "and" in Argobba is *-nna*, "but" is *(nägär) gən*, and words expressing "or" are *we-m* and *we-s*, the latter for questions.

Adjective (Relative) Clauses

These are formed by prefixing *yä-* (also the prefix of possession, see p. 464) to the verb in the past and *yä-mm-* to the verb in the nonpast. The dialect of Gojjam has simply *m-* as the prefix for nonpast verbs, and the dialects of Menz and Wello *əmm-*, the latter also known in older Amharic literature.

> *kä-gurage yä-tä-gäññä hawlt*
> in-Gurage Rel.-Pas.-found(-it) statue
> 'a statue which was found in Gurage'

> *səlä-tarik yämm-i-nägər mäṣəhaf*
> about-history Rel.-it-tell book
> 'a book which tells about history'

The head noun of the adjective clause may be object of a preposition, which appears as a suffix of the relativized verb:

> *ya yä-tä-wälläd-ku-bb-ät bet näw*
> that Rel.-Pas.-born-I-in-it house is
> 'That's the house I was born in.'

If the verb has another prefix, such as *bä-*, *yä-* is absent: *səlä-tarik bä-mm-i-nägər mäṣəhaf* 'in a book which tells about history'. In the dialect of Gojjam and in the older Amharic literature, the plural verb of an adjective clause may take the plural suffix of nouns *-očč*, e.g. *yä-mäṭṭ-očč säw-očč* 'the people who came'.

The relative verb form appears in a cleft sentence, for which see p. 483.

In Argobba the past tense verb of an adjective clause is prefixed by *yä-*: *ähe-yän yä-näkkäs-e wəšša* 'the dog which bit my brother' (*yä-näkkäs-e* 'which bit him'). The nonpast verb of an adjective clause is prefixed by *yämm-* or *əmm-*: *yämm-isädəb su* 'a man who insults', *əmm-isädbu suč* 'men who offend'. If the verb is preceded by another prefix, *yä* is absent: *tä-wäddäqa bet* 'from a house which fell'.

Noun Clauses

A noun clause can be formed with the prefix *l-* and the nonpast, where the subject of the resulting noun clause and main clause are ordinarily the same:

> *l-ə-wäsd-aččäw a-l-fälläg-əm*
> that-I-take-them Neg.-I-want-Neg.
> 'I don't want to take them.'

The same meaning may be expressed with an infinitive verb as follows: *ənnässu-n lä-mäwsäd a-l-fälləg-əm* (lit. 'them-Obj. for-to take Neg.-I-want-Neg.') 'I don't want to take them'.

Another noun clause expressing purpose, whose subject need not be that of the main clause, employs the prefix *ənd-*:

əndə-n-mäṭa yəfälləg-allu
that-we-come want-they
'They want us to come.'

A somewhat literary noun clause similar in meaning is expressed with the simple nonpast verb followed by the word *zänd*: *yə-mäṭa zänd ənnə-fälləg-allän* 'we want him to come'.

As adjectives may function as nouns, so adjective clauses may function as noun clauses; for example:

yä-tä-gäññä-w gurage wəsṭ nä-w
Rel.-Pass.-found(-it)-Def. Gurage in is-it
'What was found is in Gurage(land).'

yämm-i-nägr-əš wəšät nä-w
Rel.-he-tell-you (sg. f.) false is-it
'What he tells you (sg. f.) is false.'

As definite objects of the verb, such clauses are suffixed by the definite object suffix *-n*:

yä-ṣaf-k-äw-n anäbbäb-ku
Rel.-wrote-you (sg. m.)-it-Def. read-I
'I read what you wrote.'

Very frequent in Amharic are "cleft" sentences expressing presupposed propositions and employing the nominalized relative clause. The following sentences presuppose that 'someone ordered it'.

y-azzäz-u-t əssaččäw n-aččäw
Rel.-ordered-he (pol.)-it he (pol.) is-he (pol.)
'It is he (pol.) who ordered it.'

y-azzäz-u-t man n-aččäw
Rel.-ordered-he (pol.)-it who is-he (pol.)
'Who is it who ordered it?'

The latter may be more common than the simpler question *man azzäzut* 'who ordered it?'. In such sentences an exception to verb-final order is common, the copular verb being in medial position and the noun clause last: *əssaččäw naččäw y-azzäz-u-t* 'it is he who ordered it'.

Adverbial Clauses

These are marked by a complementizing/subordinating prefix on the clause-final past or nonpast verb. A common time clause is expressed with the prefix *s-* 'when' (*t-* in northern dialects other than Gondar) and a common conditional clause with the prefix *b-* 'if', both with the nonpast verb. An example of the former is:

> *tämari ṭəyyaqe s-i-ṭäyyəq astämari-w a-y-mälləs-əm*
> student question when-he-ask teacher-Def. Neg.-he-answer-Neg.
> 'When a student asks a question, the teacher doesn't answer.'

Direct speech in a time clause with *s-* and the verb "say" expresses imminent intent: *əwäṭalləhu s-i-l* 'when he was about to go out' (lit. 'when he said "I will go out"') (the stem of 'say' in this form is simply *-əl-*, the vowel of which is elided by the subject prefix *i- < y-*).

Some adverbial clauses are expressed by prepositional prefixes plus the past form of the verb, or with circumpositions (with a preposition and a postposition; cf. p. 481), for example: *kä-* 'if', *əyyä-* 'while', *kä-... ǰämmər-o* 'since' (*ǰämmər-o* 'he,'beginning'; or with appropriate conjunctive subject suffix), *bä-... gize* 'when', *kä-... bäh^wala* 'after' (*bä-h^wala* lit. 'at back'), *kä-... bäfit* 'after' (*bä-fit* lit. 'at front'). An example of the latter is:

> *kä-zännäb-ä bäfit bet gäbba-n*
> from-rained-it before house entered-we
> 'Before it rained, we entered the house.'

Adverbial clauses are also expressed by three prepositional prefixes which occur only with the past form of verbs or with the nonpast prefixed by *mm-*; these are *əndä-* 'like, as', *səlä-* 'because', and *əskä-* 'until'. Some examples are *əssu əndä-ṣafä* 'like he wrote', *əssu səlä-mm-i-ṣəf* 'because he writes', *əskä-mm-i-mäṭa* 'until he comes'. The 'until' clause, however, may employ *əsk-* plus the simple imperfect: *əsk-i-mäṭa* 'until he comes'.

Comparative clauses may be expressed by relative and causative conjunctive forms of stative verbs, such as *yä-bälläṭä* 'which exceeds', *y-annäsä* 'which is less, and *a-bälṭ-o* 'he/it making it greater'.

> *kä-ňňa yə-bälläṭä ənnässu särr-u*
> from-we (which) it-exceeded they worked-they
> 'They did more than us.'

> *kä-ňňa əsswa a-bälṭ-a taṭänalläčč*
> from-us she Causative-exceeding-she studies
> 'She studies more than us.'

Time clauses in Argobba are expressed with *s-* 'when' with the simple nonpast and *bä-... gize* 'when' (lit. 'at ... time') with the past. "After" clauses employ *tä-* with the past followed by *čugga* or *bäjed*, and "since" clauses *tä-* with the past followed by *čoga* or *čugga*. Conditional clauses are expressed with the prefix *b-* 'if' and the nonpast verb, and an "in order that" clause with *l-* and the simple nonpast. 'Because' is *sälä-* plus the verb in the past.

References

Bender, M. Lionel, J. D. Bowen, R. L. Cooper and Charles H. Ferguson. 1976. *Language in Ethiopia*. London: Oxford University Press.

Leslau, Wolf. 1959. "A Preliminary Description of Argobba." *Annales d'Éthiopie* 3: 251–273.

—— 1977. "Argobba Vocabulary." *Rassegna di Studi Etiopici* 26: 21–43.

Further Reading

Dawkins, C. H. 1969. *The Fundamentals of Amharic*. Addis Ababa: Sudan Interior Mission.

Kane, Thomas L. 1990. *Amharic–English Dictionary*, 2 vols. Wiesbaden: Harrassowitz.

Leslau, Wolf. 1967. *Amharic Textbook*. Wiesbaden: Harrassowitz.

—— 1973. *English–Amharic Context Dictionary*. Wiesbaden: Harassowitz.

—— 1995. *Reference Grammar of Amharic*. Wiesbaden: Harrassowitz.

Ullendorff, Edward. 1965. *An Amharic Chrestomathy*. London: Oxford University Press.

21 Harari

Ewald Wagner

Harari is the language spoken by the people living inside the walls of the city of Harar in southeastern Ethiopia. The urban area outside the walls is occupied by the Amharic-speaking administrators, teachers, soldiers etc., while the country-side is populated by several Oromo-speaking tribes and the Argobba, who nowa-days speak Oromo, too. The frontier of the Somali-speaking area is some fifty to a hundred kilometers from the city.

Formerly, the population inside the walled city was estimated to be circa 30,000 individuals. After the 1974 revolution, however, the Rural Property Act of 1975 and the Urban Property Act of the same year destroyed much of the Hararis' means of existence, which led to a large-scale emigration to other parts of Ethi-opia, specially to Addis Ababa, and to foreign countries (Saudi Arabia, Canada etc.). The number of Harari speakers inside the walls was reduced to about 8,000 as members of other ethnic groups, especially Christian Amharas, flocked in. As a result, considerable diaspora colonies of Hararis developed outside the city, that of Addis Ababa numbering more than 20,000.

The names Harar and Harari are used by native speakers only when writing. In spoken language, they use *ge:y* 'town' for Harar and *ge:y sina:n* 'language of the town' for Harari. The Amhara call the language *adarəñña*, that is, the Oromo name *adare* with an Amharic ending.

While Harari now is a speech island, in the time before the sixteenth-century Oromo invasion there might have been a coherent Semitic-speaking area up to the Eastern Gurage languages which, together with Harari, according to Hetzron's classification, form the Eastern group of "Transversal South Ethiopic" (Hetzron 1972: 42–44, 119). In the region of Bissidimo is a village named Koromni in which the women speak Harari while the men speak Oromo. This may be a rem-nant of a former larger extension of Harari, but it may also be due to a military colony of the Emirs of Harar or to trade relations.

We know Harari in two chronologically different forms. Ancient Harari is writ-ten in Arabic letters because the Harari are Muslims. Ancient Harari literature is mostly religious. The author of at least one text is known and can be dated in the middle of the eighteenth century. It is not impossible, however, that some texts are even older. In written texts the ancient form of the language was used until the sec-ond half of the nineteenth century. Modern Harari might have developed during

486

the nineteenth century. It differs from Ancient Harari in vocabulary, morphology and syntax. The most important differences will be mentioned in the following paragraphs.

Harar was the center of Islam in southeast Ethiopia and this had its effects on the language. There are many Arabic loanwords in Ancient as well as Modern Harari. The vocabulary of Modern Harari is also much influenced by Oromo. The impact of Somali is less. It may be that Arabic and Oromo had also their influence on the Harari phonological system (see below).

Phonology

Consonants

The consonant phonemes of Harari are:

	labials	labio-dentals	apicals	palatals	velars	pharyn-geals	glottals
plosives	b		d, t, ṭ		g, k, q		ʾ
affricates				ǧ, č, č̣			
fricatives		f	z, s	š	(γ), x	ḥ	
nasals	m		n	ñ			
laterals			l				
vibrants			r				
half-vowels	w			y			

As in the other Ethio-Semitic languages the emphatic consonants ṭ, č̣, and q are glottalized and not velarized. γ occurs only in Arabic loanwords.

The main changes in comparison with Geʿez are: Geʿez ṣ, ḍ became ṭ: Geʿez ṣarḥa 'to shout' > Har. ṭaraḥa 'to name'; Geʿez ḍərs 'molar tooth' > Har. ṭirsi. Geʿez š became s: Geʿez karš 'belly' > Har. karsi. Geʿez h, x became ḥ: Geʿez hal-lo: 'to be'> Har. ḥal 'there is'; Geʿez xadara 'to stay' > Har. ḥadara 'to spend the night'. Geʿez ʿ became ʾ: Geʿez samʿa 'to hear' > Har. samaʿa. Sporadic changes are: Geʿez k may become x: Geʿez ko:na 'to be' > Har. xa:na, but Geʿez karš 'bel-ly' > Har. karsi. Geʿez ʾ and ʿ (via ʾ) may become zero. So the verbs IIʾ/ʿ mostly have two or three forms: laʾaxa and la:xa (Geʿez laʾaka) 'to send'; ṭaʾana, ṭa:na and ṭe:na (Geʿez ṣaʿana and ṣəʾəna) 'to load'.

d, t, ṭ, s, n, and l can be palatalized, becoming ǧ, č, č̣, š, ñ, and y. The palataliza-tion is regularly caused by the final -i of the sg. 2f. of the nonpast (see p. 497). Some examples are: iǧi (Geʿez əd) 'hand'; če:xa (Geʿez takala 'to plant') 'to build'; č̣a:ya (Geʿez ṣala:lo:t) 'shadow'; ša:ra (Geʿez saʿara) 'to abolish'; iñña (Geʿez nəḥna) 'we'; ixi:y (Geʿez əkəl 'food') 'cereal'.

Harari has given up the gemination of consonants in verbal morphology, but there exist lengthened consonants as archaic relics in nouns and – also in verbs – in consequence of assimilation, at the junction of morphemes and by other reasons.

Vowels

The vowel system of Harari gives some problems. Normally Harari is considered as one of the few Ethio-Semitic languages in which vowel length is phonemic. This is due to the fact that on the phonetic level long vowels can easily be perceived in Harari speech and that these long vowels are not free variants and not conditioned by the position of the word in the sentence. The long vowels are lexically or morphologically fixed. There are, however, some reasons which speak against the phonemic value of vowel length. First, it is almost impossible to find minimal pairs with the opposition between short and long vowels. Second, if one considers the variant *ä* of *a* and the variant *ə* of *i* as the intended vowels, it is possible to construct a vowel system in which all vowels differ in quality so that the quantity may be neglected: *ä, a:, e:, ə, i:, o:, u:*. Third, the orthography of Ancient Harari does not make use of the ability of the Arabic script to express vowel length: plene and defective writing is mixed up without any rule.

A possible remedy to the problem may be that the phonemicity was revived in Harari by outside influence. Through Islamization, a lot of Arabic words overflowed the language and after the Oromo invasion a new wave of loans intruded into Harari. In both donor languages vowel quantity is very relevant. By this the Hararis won back their sensitivity to the importance of vowel quantity. That might have affected autochthon words in which length and shortness originally were realized only due to position, but then became stabilized according to the most frequent use, so that length and shortness became lexically fixed. This may explain that there are no minimal pairs. Since the long and the short form of each vowel originated from a single phoneme, oppositions can only emerge from neologisms.

Tentatively, we may establish the following vowel system for Harari:

> *a* (with the allophones: *ä* inside the word beside other consonants than ', *ḥ*, and
> palatals; *e* beside palatals; *å* after w)
> *a:*
> *i* (with a free variant *ə*)
> *i:*
> *u* (with a free variant *ə*)
> *e* (seldom)
> *e:*
> *o* (seldom)
> *o:*

This vowel system is very similar to that established by Ernst-August Gutt for Silte, which is the nearest relative to Harari (Gutt 1983: 37–73): see p. 510.

Peculiar Phenomena

Neither stress nor tones are phonemic in Harari.

Morphology

Pronouns

Independent Personal Pronouns
The independent personal pronouns are:

Sg.	1c.	*a:n*	Pl.	1c.	*iñña, iñña:č*
	2m.	*axa:ax*		2c.	*axa:xa:č*
	f.	*axa:š*			
	3m.	*azzo*		3c.	*azziya:č*
	f.	*azze*			

There exist polite forms for sg. 2 *axa:xu* and sg. 3 *azziyu* which seem to be the original forms of the plural while the forms in *-a:č* are secondarily formed with the nominal plural suffix (see p. 492). The elements *-x, -š, -zo, -ze, -xu, -ziyu* are taken over from the possessive suffixes (see below). The origin of *ax-* and *az-* is not clear.

The independent personal pronouns need not be used in verbal sentences because the verb expresses the persons sufficiently.

In Ancient Harari the independant personal pronouns are often combined with the genitive marker *z(i)-* to form independent possessive pronouns: *ya: rabbana: zixa:xin tana za'an balana* 'O our lord, we are yours. Call us: mine'; *zi-iñña ḥa:ǧa:t* 'our needs'. In Modern Harari this construction no longer exists because the genitive marker became obsolete (see p. 492).

Personal Suffixes

Possessive Suffixes
The possessive suffixes attached to substantives are:

Sg.	1c.	*-e, - e'e, - eye*	Pl.	1c.	*-zina*
	2m.	*-xa*		2c.	*-xo*
	f.	*-xaš*			
	3m.	*-zo*		3c.	*-ziyu*
	f.	*-ze*			

The sg. 2f. is a combination of the sg. 2m. and the original element for the sg. 2f. *-š* (< *-ki*), which is still found as object suffix attached to verbs (see above). The forms with *z-* are composed of the genitive marker *z(i)-* and the original suffixes: •*zi-o* > *-zo* (*-o* still existed in Ancient Harari: *sumo* 'his name'); **zi-ha:* > *-ze*; **zi-hum* > *-ziyu*. Perhaps it would be more logical to analyze these forms as a combination of *zi-* and the independent pronouns: **zi-huwa* > *-zo*; **zi-hiya* > *-ze*; **zi-nəḥna* > *-zina*; **zi-hum* > *-ziyu*, but the Ancient Harari *-o* 'his' speaks against this.

Another solution would be to suppose a lost prepositional element: *zi-lahu >
*zilo > *ziyo > *zo; *zi-laha: > *zila: > ziya > -ze; *zi-lana > *zi-lna > *zinna >
-zina; *zi-lahum > *zilhu(m) > *zillu > -ziyu. These, however, are all speculations.

In Ancient Harari forms with z- existed also for the 2nd person since the independent possessive pronouns formed by a combination of z(i)- with the independent personal pronoun (see p. 489) could be used as suffixes, too: fadli-zixa:x
'your excellence'.

Since Modern Harari normally uses postpositions instead of prepositions there
are no special forms for the combination preposition + suffix except inside verbal
constructions (see Object Suffixes, below). The postpositions are placed behind
the independent personal pronoun: a:n-be 'with me'. In Ancient Harari prepositions also, could be used with the independent personal pronouns: imal-axa:x
'without you'; t-axa:x massa 'like you'.

Object Suffixes

The object suffixes are attached to the verb either directly (for the accusative) or
together with the prepositions -b- ('in, by, with, from, to the detriment of') or -l-
('for, to the benefit of'). The suffixes are (acc. behind a verbal form ending in a
consonant):

Sg. 1c.	-añ	Pl. 1c.	-ana
2m.	-ax	2c.	-axu
f.	-aš		
3m.	-a	3c.	-ayu
f.	-e		

The following examples show the changes and contractions that take place if
the verb ends in a vowel. Examples are also given for preposition + suffix.

Table 21.1   Object suffixes: verbs ending in a vowel

		Past sg. 3m. sabara 'he broke'	Past pl. 3c. sabaru 'they broke'	Simple nonpast sg. 3m. yisabri 'he breaks'
Sg.	1c.	sabare:ñ	sabaruñ	yisabrañ
	2m.	sabare:x	sabarux	yisabrax
	f.	sabare:š	sabaruš	yisabraš
	3m.	sabare:w	sabaro	yisabra
	f.	sabare	sabare	yisabre
Pl.	1c.	sabare:na	sabaruna	yisabrana
	2c.	sabare:xu	sabaruxu	yisabraxu
	3c.	sabare:yu	sabaruyu	yisabrayu

The suffix -a of the sg. 3m. in yisabra 'he breaks him' is hard to explain. While
the -w in sabare:w 'he broke him' seems to be the old *-hu, the form sabaro 'they

Table 21.2 Preposition and suffix

		Jussive pl. 3c. + -b- yake:bu + -b- 'may they testify against'	Imperative sg. 2f. + -b- ke:bi + -b- 'testify (f.) against!'
Sg.	1c.	yake:b(u)buñ	ke:b(i)biñ
	2m.	yake:b(u)bux	
	f.	yake:b(u)buš	
	3m.	yake:b(u)bo	ke:b(i)ba
	f.	yake:b(u)be	ke:b(i)be
Pl.	1c.	yake:b(u)buna	ke:b(i)bina
	2c.	yake:b(u)buxu	
	3c.	yake:b(u)buyu	ke:b(i)biyu

broke him' again can be analyzed more easily as *sabaru-a* than as *sabaru-hu*. The suffix -*e* of the sg. 3f. might have been taken over from the possessive suffix -*ze*. In the prefix conjugations the final -*u* of the plural and the final -*i* of the sg. 2f. may be preserved or elided before the preposition -*b*-. In the case of elision the plural or the feminine can be recognized only through the assimilated vowel of the suffix: *yake:buba > yake:bubo > yake:bbo* 'they may testify against him' against *yake:bba* 'he may testify against him'; *ke:bibañ > ke:bibiñ > ke:bbiñ* 'testify (f.) against me!' against *ke:bbañ* 'testify (m.) against me!'. Another explanation could be that the vowels of the forms with preposition follow the analogy of the forms with accusative objects, for instance: *yake:ba* : *yake:bo* = *yake:bba* : x; x = *yake:bbo*.

Demonstrative Pronouns
The demonstrative pronouns for the near are:

Sg. m. *yi* 'this' Pl. c. *yiya:č, ḥiya:č*
  f. *yitta, itta, ḥiya, ḥi:ya*

The demonstrtive pronouns for the remote are:

Sg. m. *ya', azzo* Pl. c. *azziya:č*
  f. *yatta, azze*

The demonstrative pronouns with the element *y* can be used independently and as attributes. In the latter case they precede the substantive. The other demonstrative pronouns which originate from Harari or Arabic personal pronouns seem to be used independently only. The whole system seems to be incomplete.

Interrogative Pronouns
The interrogative pronouns are: *ma:n* 'who'; *min* 'what'; *a:y* 'which'. They can be combined with postpositions to form interrogative adverbs, for instance: *min-*

le, mille 'why'; *a:y-kut* 'how'.

Reflexive Pronouns

The reflexive is either expressed by the reflexive forms of the verb or by *aṭṭi*, for instance *aṭṭi-zo* 'he himself'. Wolf Leslau derives it from *a:ṭ* 'bone' (< *ʿaṣəm*). *aṭṭi baṭṭi* means 'one another'.

Nouns

Definiteness

The noun can be made definite by adding the possessive suffix of sg. 3m. *-zo* (see p. 489): *ga:r-zo* 'his house' and 'the house'. This, however, is not obligatory. In most cases definiteness can only be deduced from the context.

Gender

Harari does not distinguish between the genders through a form element. An inherited *t*-element at the end of the word no longer means that a noun is feminine. Some nouns are feminine by nature, for instance female persons and localities: *a:y* 'mother'; *ge:y* 'land, town'.

Number

The plural morpheme is *-a:č*: *ga:r* 'house', *ga:ra:č* 'houses'. This suffix need not be placed if the plurality is clear from the context or if it is not emphasized. After cardinal numbers the counted noun stands in the singular or in the plural. An adjective belonging to a plural has no *-a:č*.

A dual does not exist.

Case System

The nominative (subject case) has no special form.

In Modern Harari the genitive is only indicated by its position before the reigning substantive: *liǧ ga:r* 'the house of the boy'. In Ancient Harari the relative element *zi-* normally functioned as a genitive marker: *zi-da:na ṭa:ya* 'the shadow of the cloud', although the modern construction was possible, too: *zar mi:y* 'the water of the river'. The opposite sequence of words was rare. It seems to have been an Arabic influence: *di:nat ge:y* 'the wealth of the land'.

The accusative can be indicated by the suffix *-w*. In older transcriptions (Cerulli, Leslau) this *-w* occurs only after vowels while after consonants the accusative suffix is written *-u*. It should be, however, *-uw*, the *-u* being only a helping vowel. The *-w* could have been taken over from the verbal object suffix (*sabare:w* 'he broke him', cf. p. 490).

The placing of the accusative suffix is not obligatory. Definiteness, obviously, does not play a part in it.

Other relations between the verb and its objects must be expressed by postpositions, e.g. the dative *-le* (< *la-*), the locative instrumental *-be* (< *ba-*).

Adjectives

On the whole, Harari is not very rich in adjectives. They are often substituted by relative clauses. Many of the existing adjectives are formed according to the patterns *sabi:r*, *sibi:r*, *saba:r*, *siba:r*. There are, however, also other patterns.

As attributes, the adjectives are placed before the qualified substantive: *gidi:r maga:la* 'the big market'. As predicatives, they stand before the copula: *ga:r gidi:rin ta* 'the house is big'.

There are no special patterns for gradation. 'Than' with the comparative is expressed by the postposition *-be*. The superlative must be paraphrased by a genitive or postpositional construction.

In Ancient Harari there existed a pattern *asbir* which could be formed only from Arabic roots. Together with the verb *a:ña* 'to make' it formed phraseological verbs: *afriḥ a:ña* 'to give pleasure' (Ar. *frḥ*); *akrim a:ña* 'to be generous' (Ar. *krm*); *asliḥ a:ña* 'to make happy' (Ar. *ṣlḥ*).

Numerals

The numerals are:

	Cardinals	Ordinals
1	*aḥad*	*aḥatta:n*
2	*koʾot, ko:t*	*koʾotta:ñ*
3	*šiʾišti, ši:šti*	*šiʾišta:ñ*
4	*ḥarat*	*ḥaratta:ñ*
5	*ḥammisti*	*ḥammista:ñ*
6	*siddisti*	*siddista:ñ*
7	*sa:tti*	*sa:tta:ñ*
8	*su:t*	*su:tta:ñ*
9	*ziḥṭañ*	*ziḥṭañta:ñ*
10	*assir*	*assirta:ñ*
11	*asra:ḥad*	
12	*asra:ko:t*	
13	*asra:ši:šti*	
20	*kuya*	
30	*sa:sa*	
40	*ḥaratassir, arbaʾi:n(a), arbi:n(a)*	
50	*ḥammistassir, xamsi:n(a)*	
60	*siddistassir, sitti:n(a)*	
70	*sa:ttassir, sabʾi:n(a)*	
80	*su:tassir, tama:ni:n(a)*	
90	*ziḥtana, tisʾi:n(a)*	
100	*baqla*	
1000	*kum, alfi, alfa*	
1935	*alfa ziḥtañ baqla sa:sa ḥammisti*	

The suffix for forming the ordinal numbers is now -*ta:ñ*, but originally it could have been -*a:ñ* (cf. Amharic -*äñña*) to which the *t* was added by wrong separation in those cases in which the cardinal number ended in *t*.

Verbs

Roots
The Harari verbal roots normally have three radicals. Verbs with four radicals also occur. Biradical roots may be interpreted as triradical with one weak radical.

Types
The triradical verb has four types which are differentiated by the vowel behind the first radical:

Type A: *sabara*
Type B: *se:bara*
Type C: *sa:bara*
Type D: *so:bara*

The quadriradical verb has two types:

Type A: *gilabaṭa*
Type C: *liqa:laqa*

Normally the difference between the types is only formal and no longer semantic. It is only in combination with some derivational classes that a former semantic value is preserved, so the reflexive *ta-* (see below) + type C expresses reciprocity: *taga:dala* 'to quarrel with each other' from *gadala* 'to kill'. An adjutative is formed by the combination of the *at*-causative and the type C: *atha:rasa* 'to help to plow' from *harasa* 'to plow'.

Derivational Classes
The derivational classes are formed by the reduplication of the second radical or by prefixes or by the combination of both. The simple reduplication forms the frequentative which expresses repeated or intensive action:

Type A, B, C: *siba:bara*
Type D: *suba:bara*

ta-Reflexive

Type A: *tasabara*
Type B: *tase:bara*
Type C: *tasa:bara*
Type D: *taso:bara*

The meaning of the *ta*-reflexive is reflexive, passive or merely intransitive. The *ta*-form of type C expresses reciprocity (see p. 494). The same is true for the *ta*-form of the frequentative: *tasba:bara*.

a-Causative

> Type A: *asabara*
> Type B: *ase:bara*
> Type C: *asa:bara*
> Type D: *aso:bara*

The *a*-causative is formed from intransitive verbs to make them transitive.

at-Causative

> Type A, B, C: *atbe:rada*
> Type C: *atba:rada*
> Type D: *atbo:rada*

Verbs of the type A and B form their *at*-causative according to type B; those of the type C either according to the type B or C. The type C of the *at*-causative also forms causatives of the reciprocal and adjutatives (see p. 494). The causative of the reciprocal is formed by the *at*-form of the frequentative, too:

> Type A, B, C: *atbira:rada*
> Type D: *atbura:rada*

Note: The paradigm verb is changed from *sabara* to *barada* here because in case of *sabara* the *t* of *at*- has to be assimilated: *assabara* etc.
The prefix *an*- and its reflexive *tan*- are no longer productive.

Tenses and Moods
Harari has two main tenses and two moods. The tenses are the past, formed in the type A by the stem *sabar*- + suffixes, and the nonpast, formed by the stem -*sabr*- + prefixes and suffixes. The moods are the jussive, formed by the stem -*sbar*- + prefixes and suffixes, and the imperative formed by the same stem + suffixes. The forms (sg. 3m.; imperative sg. 2m.) are:

Ground stem:	A	B	C	D
Past	*sabara*	*se:bara*	*sa:bara*	*so:bara*
Nonpast	*yisabri*	*yisi:bri*	*yisa:bri*	*yi/usu:bri*
Jussive	*yasbar*	*yase:bri*	*yasa:bri*	*yaso:bri*
Imperative	*sibar*	*se:bri*	*sa:bri*	*so:bri*

Frequentative:	A, B, C			D
Past	*siba:bara*			*suba:bara*
Nonpast	*yisba:bri*			*yusba:bri*
Jussive	*yasba:bri*			*yasuba:bri*
Imperative	*siba:bri*			*suba:bri*

ta-Reflexive:	A	B	C	D
Past	*tabarada*	*tabe:rada*	*taba:rada*	*tabo:rada*
Nonpast	*yitbarad*	*yitbe:rad*	*yitba:rad*	*yitbo:rad*
Jussive	*yatbarad*	*yatbe:rad*	*yatba:rad*	*yatbo:rad*
Imperative	*tabarad*	*tabe:rad*	*taba:rad*	*tabo:rad*

ta-Reflexive of the frequentative = reciprocal stem:

Past	*tabra:rada*
Nonpast	*yitbira:rad*
Jussive	*yatbira:rad*
Imperative	*tabra:rad*

a-Causative:	A	B	C	D
Past	*asabara*	*ase:bara*	*asa:bara*	*aso:bara*
Nonpast	*yasabri*	*yasi:bri*	*yasa:bri*	*yasu:bri*
Jussive	*yasbir*	*yase:bri*	*yasa:bri*	*yaso:bri*
Imperative	*asbir*	*ase:bri*	*asa:bri*	*aso:bri*

at-Causative:	A, B, C	C = causative of the reciprocal		D
Past	*atbe:rada*	*atba:rada*		*atbo:rada*
Nonpast	*yatbi:rdi*	*yatba:rdi*		*yatbu:rdi*
Jussive	*yatbe:rdi*	*yatba:rdi*		*yatbo:rdi*
Imperative	*atbe:rdi*	*atba:rdi*		*atbo:rdi*

Causative of the reciprocal = adjutative:

	A, B, C	D
Past	*atbira:rada*	*atbura:rada*
Nonpast	*yatbira:rdi*	*yatbura:rdi*
Jussive	*yatbira:rdi*	*yatbura:rdi*
Imperative	*atbira:rdi*	*atbura:rdi*

The nonpast was the normal form for present and future in main clauses in Ancient Harari. In Modern Harari it is restricted to some subordinate clauses. In main clauses it is superseded by the compound nonpast which is built by combining the simple nonpast and the auxiliary *ḥal* 'to exist' (see p. 507): *yisabri* + *ḥal* = *yisabra:l*. Also for the past two new compound tenses developed, both formed with the auxiliary *na:ra* 'was': *sabara na:r(a)* forms a pluperfect while by *yisabri na:r(a)* a habitual action in the past is expressed.

Conjugations

Table 21.3   Conjugated forms

		Past	Nonpast	Compound nonpast	Jussive	Imperative
Sg.	1c.	sabarxu	isabri	isabra:x	nasbar	
	2m.	sabarxi	tisabri	tisabra:x	atsibar (neg.)	sibar
	f.	sabarši	tisabri	tisabra:š	atsibari (neg.)	sibari
	3m.	sabara	yisabri	yisabra:l	yasbar	
	f.	sabarti	tisabri	tisabra:t	tasbar	
Pl.	1c.	sabarna	nisabri	nisabra:na	nasbar	
	2c.	sabarxu	tisabru	tisabra:xu	atsibaru (neg.)	sibaru
	3c.	sabaru	yisabru	yisabra:lu	yasbaru	

In the forms *sabarxi* (sg. 2m.), *sabarti* (sg. 3f.), *isabri* (sg. 1c.), *tisabri* (sg. 2m.; sg. 3f.), *yisabri* (sg. 3m.), and *nisabri* (pl. 1c.) the final *-i* is euphonic and is deleted if an object suffix is added: *sabarxañ, sabartañ, isabrax, tisabrañ, yisabrañ, nisabrax*. Contrary to that, the *-i* of *sabarši* (sg. 2f.) and *tisabri* (sg. 2f.) is original and not deleted: *sabaršiñ, tisabriñ*.

The *-i* of the sg. 2f. of the nonpast causes the palatalization of the final epicals *d, t, ṭ, s, n, l* (> *ǧ, č, č̣, š, ñ, y*): *tilamǧi* from *lamada* 'to learn', *tilabši* from *labasa* 'to dress', *tinadyi* from *nadala* 'to make a hole'. The palatalization can also affect the first and second radical and even the prefix: *tikačbi* from *kataba* 'to write', *tisagǧi* and *tišagǧi* from *sagada* 'to prostrate', *čiki:bi* from *ke:ba* 'to testify'.

In the compound nonpast the object suffixes are inserted between the main verb and the auxiliary: *tisabraḥat* 'she breaks him', *t/cišabriyuḥuš* 'you (f.) break them', but *yisabruxa:l* 'they break you (m.)' with the *-u* of the plural on the main verb, not on the auxiliary.

In the jussive the sg. 1c. has the prefix *na-* (like the pl. 1c.) and not *a-*. This *n* originates from a conjunctional *l-* as some forms preserved in Ancient Harari show: *l-ilmad* 'I may learn' (variant reading: *lalmad*, already with *a* in analogy to the other persons).

Passive Voice and Impersonal Verbs
Harari has two different ways to express the passive voice. One is the *ta*-reflexive; the other works by making the subject of the active sentence object of a verb in pl. 3c.: *agaduñ* 'I was tied', literally 'they tied me'. This construction is also possible with intransitive verbs, corresponding to the French *on* or German *man*.

There exist some impersonal verbs in Harari. The verb stands in the sg. m. to which the actor is added as accusative suffix: *ṭararañ* 'I am thirsty', cf. German *mich dürstet*.

Verbal Nouns and Participles
In Ancient Harari the infinitive was formed by the pattern *siba:ro:t*: *liba:so:t*

'dressing' from *labasa* 'to dress'. In Modern Harari this form is extinguished with a few exceptions, for instance *niba:ro:t* 'life' from *nabara* 'to live'. The modern infinitive is formed through the prefix *ma-*: *maktab* 'writing' from *kataba* 'to write'.

In Harari no active participles exist. They are replaced by relative clauses. The passive participle is formed as in North Ethiopic languages by the pattern *subur*: *šumuq* 'hidden' from *še:maqa* 'to hide'. For emphasis the second radical may be lengthened: *subbur*.

Verbs with Weak Radicals
Verbs with *ʾ*, *w*, *y*, *ḥ* as one of their radicals and some verbs with *b* as the first radical differ in their forms from the normal triradical verbs.

Iʾ-Verbs
The Iʾ-verbs have no type C and no *a*-causative. The causative is formed with *at-*. In the forms of the Iʾ-verbs *ʾ* is partly preserved, partly lost, and partly assimilated, for instance:

	Basic stem A	Basic stem B
Past	*agada* 'to tie'	*e:mada* 'to tell'
Compound nonpast	*yaʾagda:l* or *ya:gda:l*	*yi:mda:l*
Jussive	*yagad*	*ye:mdi*

	ta-Reflexive B
Past	*taʾe:mara* or *te:mara* 'to obey'
Compound nonpast	*yitte:mara:l* (< *yitʾe:mara:l*) from *taʾe:mara* or *yite:mara:l* from *te:mara*
Jussive	*yatte:mar* or *yate:mar*

IIʾ-Verbs
The IIʾ-verbs may have two or three forms in the past and in the imperative:

Past	*taʾana*, *ta:na* (cf. Geʿez *ṣaʿana*), *ṭe:na* (cf. Geʿez *ṣaʾəna*) 'to load'
Compound nonpast	*yiṭi:na:l*
Jussive	*yaṭe:n*
Imperative	*taʾan*, *ta:n*, *ṭe:n*

The conjugation of *ṭe:na* became identical with that of the IIy-verbs (see p. 500) and the type B of the III inf.-verbs (see p. 500).

In the type B the *ʾ* may be assimilated to the third radical:

Past	*se:ʾada* 'to distribute'
Compound nonpast	*yisi:ʾda:l* or *yisi:dda:l*
Jussive	*yase:ʾdi* or *yase:ddi*

In the IIʼ-class the types C and D do not exist. In the frequentative either the second or the third radical is reduplicated: *siʼa:ʼada*, but *lixa:xa* from *laʼaxa* or *la:xa* 'to send'.

IIIʼ-Verbs
In the IIIʼ-class the ʼ is preserved in the past of all types and in the jussive and imperative of type A. If the ʼ gets lost, the class becomes identical with the III inf.- class:

	A	B	C	D
Past	*nasaʼa*	*he:maʼa*	*qa:baʼa*	*go:raʼa*
	'to take'	'to calumniate'	'to anoint'	'to slaughter'
Compound nonpast	*yinasa:l*	*yihi:ma:l*	*yiqa:ba:l*	*yigu:ra:l*
Jussive	*yansaʼ*	*yahe:m*	*yaqa:b*	*yago:r*
Imperative	*nisaʼ*	*he:m*	*qa:b*	*go:r*

Verbs with ḥ
The verbs with ḥ do not differ much from the strong verbs. In some forms an *i* before ḥ becomes *a*, for instance *yaḥadga:l* for **yiḥagda:l* 'he abandons' or *laḥas!* for **liḥas!* 'lick!'.

Iw-Verbs
Most forms of the Iw-class are regular. In the nonpast there is a contracted form *yu:qta:l* besides *yiwaqta:l* from *waqaṭa* 'to crash'. The verb *waṭaʼa* 'to go out' has an irregular palatalization in the nonpast:

Past	*waṭaʼa*
Compound nonpast	*yu:ča:l*
Jussive	*yawṭaʼ*
Imperative	*wiṭaʼ*

While some causatives build regular forms, in others *awa* becomes *a:*, for instance *warada* 'to go down', *a:rada* 'to put down'; *waṭaʼa* 'to go out', *a:ča* 'to bring out, to take off':

Past	*a:rada*	*a:ča*
Compound nonpast	*ya:rda:l*	*ya:ča:l*
Jussive	*yu:rd*	*yu:č*
Imperative	*u:rdi*	*u:č*

From this causative a second one with *at-* can be formed:

Past	*ate:rada*
Compound nonpast	*yati:rda:l*
Jussive	*yate:rdi*
Imperative	*ate:rdi*

Iy-verbs do not exist.

IIw- and IIy-Verbs

The IIw-class is characterized in the past by an *o:* between the first and the last radical and the IIy-class by an *e:* in this position. These vowels undergo the same ablaut as the vowels of the types D and B. By this the IIw-class becomes identical with the type D of the IIIinf.-class and the IIy-class with the type B of the IIIinf.-class (and at the same time with the *ṭe:na*-form of the IIᴾ-class and in the nonpast, jussive and imperative with the type B of the IIIᴾ-class). There does not exist any type difference inside the IIw- and IIy-classes.

Some IIw-verbs have an *a:* between the first and the last radical. They are mostly irregular. The most important are: *xa:na* 'to be', *ḥa:ra* 'to go' (conjugated like *xa:na*), *a:ša* 'to make', *a:qa* 'to know'. *ba:ya* 'to say' is originally not IIw, but has the etymology *bhl*.

Past	*xa:na*	*a:ša*	*a:qa*	*ba:ya*
Compound nonpast	*yuxu:na:l*	*ya:ša:l*	*yu:qa:l*	*yila:l*
Jussive	*yaxni*	*yu:š*	*yu:q*	*yal*
Imperative	*xu:n*	*u:š*	*u:q*	*bal*

The irregular verb *di:ǧa* 'to come' has an *i:* in the nonpast (*yidi:ǧa:l*) and an *e:* in the jussive (*yade:ǧ*).

Verbs with a Weak Third Radical (IIIinf.)

In the IIIw- and IIIy-classes the third radical got totally lost so that there is no difference between the two anymore. The verbs form the same types and derivation classes as the strong triradical verb. It is possible to derive the forms of the verbs with a weak third radical from the *sbr*-patterns of the strong verb by the elision of *ar* if the last radical was preceded by an *a* and by the elision of *r* if the last radical was not preceded by an *a*. It only has to be noted that the euphonic *i* after a consonant cluster has to be placed anew and that the infinitive ends in *-a*. Some examples: type A *baka* 'to cry', type D *qo:ča* 'to cut', *ta*-reflexive of type B *tame:ča* 'to be suitable', *a*-causative of type A *agaña* 'to find', *a*-causative of the frequentative *afra:ra* 'to threaten':

Past	*sab(ar)a*	*baka*	*so:b(ar)a*	*qo:ča*
Compound nonpast	*yisab(r)a:l*	*yibaka:l*	*yusu:b(r)a:l*	*yuqu:ča:l*
Jussive	*yasb(ar)*	*yabki*	*yaso:b(r)i*	*yaqoč*
Imperative	*sib(ar)*	*bik*	*so:b(r)i*	*qo:č*
Infinitive	*masb(ar)*	*mabka*	*maso:b(ar)*	*maqo:ča*

Past	*tase:b(ar)a*	*tame:ča*	*asab(ar)a*	*agaña*
Compound nonpast	*yitse:b(ar)a:l*	*yitme:ča:l*	*yasaña:l*	*yagab(r)a:l*
Jussive	*yatse:b(ar)*	*yatme:č*	*yasbi(r)*	*yagñi*
Imperative	*tase:b(ar)*	*tame:č*	*asbi(r)*	*agñi*
Infinitive			*masb(ar)*	*magña*

Past	asba:b(ar)a	afra:ra
Compound nonpast	yasba:b(r)a:l	yafra:ra:l
Jussive	yasba:b(r)i	yafra:r
Imperative	asba:b(r)i	afra:r
Infinitive	masba:b(ar)	mafra:ra

The verb *ri'a* 'to see', which is at the same time II' and IIIinf., and its *a*-causative *a:ra'a* 'to show' have irregular forms:

Past	ri'a	a:ra'a
Compound nonpast	yira:l	ya:ra:l
Jussive	yar	yu:r
Imperative	ri	u:r
Infinitive	mara	mo:ra'

The paradigm shows that the causative follows the patterns of *a:ša* 'to make' (see p. 500) in the nonpast, jussive, and imperative.

Ib- and IIb-Verbs

The verbs *bala'a* 'to eat' and *baqa* 'to be enough' lose their first radical in the nonpast, *-iba-* becoming *-o:-* via *-iwa-*: *yo:la:l* 'he eats' and *yo:qa:l* 'it is enough'. The other Ib-verbs are regular. An initial *b* also disappears in some forms of the verb *ba:ya* 'to say' (see p. 500).

The root *nbr* 'to live, stay, be' loses the *b* in the past: *na:ra*. The other forms are regular: *yinabra:l* 'he lives'.

Quadriradical Verbs

The basic forms of the quadriradical verbs are:

Past	gilabaṭa	'to invert'
Compound nonpast	yiglabṭa:l	
Jussive	yaglabṭi	
Imperative	gilabṭi	

There exists also a type C and a frequentative. The usual derivational classes with the prefixes *ta-*, *a-*, and *at-* can be formed, too.

Adverbs

The adverbs are formed by placing the postposition *-be* behind the adjective: *ama:n* 'good', *ama:n-be* 'well'.

Syntax

Word Order
The normal order is subject–object–predicate. The placement of adverbial expressions is quite free, but not behind the verb. The qualifier precedes the qualified: adjectives, genitives and relative clauses stand before the substantive. Inside a sentence subordinate clauses precede the main clause.

Agreement Rules
Female beings and localities are feminine and govern the feminine in verbs, if subjects, and pronouns. Adjectives express no gender. A plural noun marked as such governs the plural agreement, *ad formam*, not *ad sensum*.

Negations
In Ancient Harari a sentence was negated by placing *al-* before the past and the infinitive and *a-* before the nonpast and the jussive: *albo:xu* 'I did not enter', *alḫuro:t* 'not going', *aybaqli* 'it does not grow', *anatte:ša* 'may we not act'. *a-* developed from *al-* by assimilation and later reduction of the lengthened consonant. This is shown by the sg. 1c. in which the *l* was preserved: *alqabṭi* 'I do not miss'.

The imperative cannot be negated. It is replaced by the second person of the negated jussive.

In Modern Harari a negative main clause has always to comprise the element *-m*. In the past it is normally placed at the end of the verb: *alsabara-m*. The final *-m* can also be attached to another part of the sentence: *gi:š alzalama gir-um* (*-u-* stands to avoid a consonant cluster at the end of the word) 'if it does not rain tomorrow'.

In the nonpast the simple forms are replaced by the compound forms which consist of a combination of the simple nonpast and the auxiliary verb *ḥal* (see p. 496). The negative of *ḥal* is *e:l(-um)* (see p. 507). The *-m* is normally inserted between the main and the auxiliary verb:

Sg.	1c.	*isabrume:x*	Pl.	1c.	*nisabrume:na*
	2m.	*tisabrume:x*		2c.	*tisabrume:xu*
	f.	*tisabrume:š*			
	3m.	*yisabrume:l*		3c.	*yisabrume:lu*
	f.	*tisabrume:t*			

The *-u-* again, has the function of avoiding a cluster of three consonants. It is missing where it is not needed: *yiki:bbe:me:l* 'he does not testify against her'. As in the past, it seldom occurs that the *-m* is separated from the verb: *yi:m mullu' waqti:m yitlamade:l* 'this is not taught whole day'.

In subordinate clauses the negative jussive is used for the negative nonpast:

Sg.	1c.	*ansibar*	Pl.	1c.	*ansibar*
	2m.	*atsibar*		2c.	*atsibaru*
	f.	*atsibari*			
	3m.	*aysibar*		3c.	*aysibaru*
	f.	*atsibar*			

The paradigm shows that there is no -*m* in subordinate clauses in the nonpast. The same is true for the past: *zalsabara* 'who did not break'.

Questions

There is a special interrogative form of the nonpast in Harari. It is formed by inserting an -*i:n* between the main and the auxiliary verb: *yidi:ǧi:nal?* 'does he come?', *tidi:ǧi:naxu?* 'do you (pl.) come?' In the negative an -*i:* is placed behind the auxiliary verb: *yisabrume:li:?* 'does he not break?'. The negative shows that the interrogative morpheme is the -*i:* only while the -*n*- seems to be the same morpheme which can be found in positive copular sentences (see p. 507) and which is substituted by -*m* in negative copular sentences.

Subordination

Relative Clauses

While Ancient Harari was quite poor in methods of subordination there are many possibilities to subordinate a clause in Modern Harari. Most of these developed from relative clauses, so it is advisable to first have a look at these.

In Harari the relative clause normally precedes the qualified substantive (see p. 502). As in other Semitic languages the relationship between the relative clause and the qualified substantive has to be expressed by a pronominal suffix (or infix) attached to the relative verb (Ar. *a:ʾid*): *qabi:la:č yinabribo:za:l to:ya* 'regions in which tribes live'.

In Ancient Harari the relative element *zi*- was placed before the verb only in the past: *zisabara* 'who broke', *zalsabara* 'who did not break', while in the nonpast no relative element was placed. The relative relationship was only expressed by the position of the simple nonpast before the qualified substantive: *yima:ǧ gafi-zo* 'his servant who is better'. Only negative relative clauses in the nonpast were characterized by a prefixed *z*-: *zaybarsi naga:ši* 'the king who will not be abolished'.

In Modern Harari nothing has changed for the past. In the positive nonpast the relative element is inserted between the main and the auxiliary verb: *yisabriza:l wi:ǧ* 'the boy who breaks', *tisabriza:t qaḥat* 'the woman who breaks'. For the negative relative clause the *z*- is placed before the negative jussive: *zaysibar* 'who does not break'.

The Harari relative clause is to a high degree nominalized. It can be determined by the article: *zigadara-zo xizi:r abo:ñ masgidin ta* 'the one which is the biggest is the Xazi:r Abo:ñ Mosque'. It can stand in the accusative form: *yizarfi:w xitarbañ!* 'keep away from me what is worst!'. The nominal plural morpheme -*a:č* can be added. This suffix may pluralize the subject or the object of the relative clause: *zimaḥaṭuña:č* 'those who beat (past) me', *t/čimaḥṭiyuza:ša:č* 'those whom you (f.) beat (present)', *kabi:rnat yibazḥibeyuza:la:č* 'those in whom the piety is much'.

In Modern Harari the relative clause is often used to form cleft sentences, a construction which did not exist in Ancient Harari. Contrary to Amharic, the Harari cleft sentence always needs a pseudo-object suffix pronoun. This pronoun is added also to a passive verb and is always a sg. 3m., independent from the subject of the sentence: *mačin ta liği zitmaḥaṭe:w?* 'when was it that the boy was beaten = when was the boy beaten?', *mačin ta zitmaḥlaṭša?* 'when were you (f.) beaten?'.

The relative clause can be placed in a circumstantial accusative (Ar. *ḥa:l*) expressing a circumstantial clause (English 'while'): *yisakza:l di:ǧa* 'he came while running', lit. 'as a running one'.

Conjunctional Clauses

Normally Harari indicates subordination by a conjunction. Most conjunctions follow the verb of the subordinate clause, some precede it. The conjunctions placed behind the verb often developed from nouns with a preceding relative clause.

saʾa

saʾa (or as enclitic -*sa*) is an Arabic loanword originally meaning 'hour' (Ar. *sa:ʿa*). Preceded by the relative past, it forms temporal and conditional clauses: *ǧa:miʾa zitqo:fala saʾa laǧna atḥe:baruñ* 'when the university was closed the board asked me', *bari ǧugal ziqo:rarxi-sa me:taqxa-dale koʾot gidi:r ga:ra:č ḥalu* 'if you approach the wall of the gates, there are two big buildings, one on either side of you'. This construction did not exist in Ancient Harari.

kut(a)

-*kut(a)* preceded by a relative clause forms comparative clauses. Though -*kut* is a derivation of the comparative element -*ku*, it must have functioned as a noun on its way to becoming a conjunction, because it can be followed by an article or can be placed in an accusative: *arafa yidgadarbaza:l-kutaw ḥe:ǧna gira* 'if we consider how ʾArafa is celebrated', literally 'the manner in which ʾArafa is celebrated'.

-*kut* also forms final or 'that'-clauses. In this case it is preceded by the simple nonpast: *waldi yibazḥile:-kut tixašat* 'she wants that the children become more to her advantage'. This simple nonpast must be interpreted as a relative clause, too, being a relic of Ancient Harari where relative clauses in the nonpast lack the relative element. The correctness of this interpretation is shown by negative clauses in which the *z*- already occurred in Ancient Harari (see p. 503) *koʾot muǧtamaʾa:č aḥadnat-ziyu zayṭibaq-kuta xa:na* 'it happened that the unity of the two societies did not become strong'.

qe:ssi

qe:ssi is a noun meaning 'quantity'. Preceded by a simple nonpast, which again must be interpreted as an ancient relative clause, it forms temporal clauses, meaning 'as long as', 'until': *i:d yu:č qe:ssi yinabra:lu* 'they remain till the celebration is finished'.

-be

Preceded by a relative clause, the postposition *-be* forms different subordinate clauses corresponding to the different meanings of the postposition: *zina:re:w-be ma:ǧe:wi:?* 'is he better than he was before?', *ziqaraʾe:w-be ḥafaze:w* 'because he read it, he knows it by heart', *zalzalama-be ga:r igaba:x* 'I go home before it rains'.

   -be preceded by the simple nonpast and followed by the verb of existence *ḥal* forms an aspect ('just doing, doing right now'): *sina:n-zo:w yabaslo:-be ḥalu* 'they are just inquiring about the matter'.

-le

-le is identical with the postposition *-le*. In Harari it forms causal ('because, since') and final clauses ('to'). If it is causal it is preceded by a relative clause: *zanasa qi:ma-le zatwa:xabeyu-le garab yiṣṭoḥol* 'they give him a share because he helped them to buy at a lower price'. The final *-le* is preceded by the simple nonpast: *yifatḥo:-le waṭṭu* 'they went out to unload it'. The simple past again, may be interpreted as an old relative clause. The final *-le* clause already existed in Ancient Harari and was taken over into modern times unchanged. The causal *-le*-clause came into existence only in Modern Harari. So the relative clause was constructed the modern way.

gir

gir forms conditional clauses ('if'). Originally, it was a Cushitic loanword meaning 'time'. There might have happened a similar development to that of the more modern *saʾa* (see p. 504), forming temporal clauses first and then conditional clauses (cf. German *wenn*). In Modern Harari *gir* is preceded by the past, while in Ancient Harari there occurred also the simple nonpast: *qa:t tixaš gir wari:qa bala!* 'if you want *qa:t* call Wari:qa!'. This again can be interpreted as a relative clause. Whether or not this is also true for the modern past, is not clear. Here a *zi-* should be expected which does not occur: *qala če:xala gir zingo:-be yixadnaḥal* 'if he builds an upper floor he covers it with corrugated iron'.

-ma:m

-ma:m is preceded by the jussive and forms concessive clauses ('though'). It cannot be interpreted as a relative clause. Perhaps, *-ma:m* is a combination of *-ma* (see p. 506) and the adversative *-m*: 'I go out though it rains', lit. 'I go out and may it but rain'. An example for a *-ma:m*-clause is: *ḥilqi-zo yazbaḥ-ma:m yi masgida:č fiz-be ṭiṭṭi:tin ta* 'though their number is large these mosques are very small'.

im-

im- followed by the negative simple nonpast forms a temporal clause with the meaning 'before': *hara:s imatwiṭaʾ u:ga tu:čume:t* 'before she is not out of her period as a woman in childbed she will not go into the street'. The underlying preposition *im-* (etymologically = Ge'ez *əm(na)*) was still very common in Ancient Harari, but has been lost in Modern Harari. Also, the conjunctional function seems to be extinguished in Modern Harari now. The most recent examples I know originate from the early 1960s.

is-

is- followed by the past, forms temporal clauses of different meanings like 'while', 'as long as', 'after', 'since': *maki:na safi ta:gir maki:na-zo la:y-be isa:l yalqa:lqa:l* 'but the tailor chews *qa:t* while he is at his sewing machine'. In older Modern Harari (first half of this century) the *(i)s* could also be inserted between the main and the auxiliary verb of the compound nonpast: *yilsa:l* 'while he says'. This construction, however, is now totally replaced by the synonym *-za:l* (see p. 503).

kil-

kil- followed by the past forms temporal clauses, too: *dukka:n-le dukka:n kil-wa:lala sadaqa yisa:mta:l* 'while he goes from shop to shop he collects alms'. The connection with the Ancient Harari preposition *kal-* 'like' and the Modern Harari preposition *kil-* 'toward' is not clear.

-ma

In Harari the suffix *-ma* is used to express almost the same meanings as the gerund in the other languages, so *-ma* has to be located between coordination and subordination: *a:y tidalgi-ma walda:č-ze:w tali:qat* 'while working, the mother brought up her children', *inči sabaru-ma ila ga:r adi:ğo* 'after he had split the wood, he brought it to the house', *yidge:b-ma a:w-zo:-bah aħada koʾot yilume:l* 'he sits down and does not agree with his father'. There are special rules of agreement between the main verb and the preceding *-ma*-verb. As the first example shows, for instance, the auxiliary verb of the compound nonpast is not repeated before *-ma*.

Infinitive

The infinitive can be used to replace several kinds of subordinate clauses, corresponding either to the case in which the infinitive stands or to the postposition which follows: *ziña:t šaħan ga:r gambari saṭra:w mabo:ʾa-ze:w yanqu:rriza:l* 'while he waits that the beams of dawn enter the cracks at the door of the house', *maga:la ba:yti-le nitna:faʾbaħana* 'we use it in order to say "market"', *ge:y usuʾ isla:m muxna-zo:-be arabi-be baği:ħ kilma:č warasa* 'because the Harari are Muslims they inherited many words from Arabic'.

-nat

The suffix *-nat* formed abstracts in Ancient Harari: *nabi* 'prophet', *nabinat* 'prophethood'. In Modern Harari *-nat* got a second function. It can be added to a relative clause: *aḥmad kiz yi:dza:lnatuw a:mnume:x* 'I do not believe that Aḥmad tells a lie', literally 'I do not believe in Aḥmad's one-who-tells-a-lie-ness'.

Copular and Possessive Expressions

ta

The Harari copular verb is *ta*. It is conjugated by adding the object suffixes (see p. 490):

Sg. 1c.	*tañ*	Pl. 1c.	*tana*
2m.	*tax*	2c.	*taxu*
f.	*taš*		
3m.	*ta*	3c.	*tayu*
f.	*te*		

In the positive main clause the copular sentence includes the suffix *-n*. Theoretically it may be placed behind every word of the sentence, but normally it is attached to the predicative expression which as a rule, precedes the copular verb: *titxita:tala:za:t indo:čin te* 'those who supervise it are the women' (*-i-* is inserted if the word before *-n* ends in a consonant), *yitta:waqa:za:l ga:r ḥawa:z sum-be:n ta* 'it is by the family names that they know each other'.

In subordinate clauses the *-n* is missing: *tumtu zitayu qabi:la:č* 'tribes which are blacksmiths'.

The copular verb is negated by *al-*. Instead of *-n* the sentence contains a *-m* (see p. 502) *zar'i baği:hum alta* 'the grain is not much'. Like the *-n* the *-m* is missing in subordinate clauses.

In the past *ta* is substituted by *na:ra*, also preceded by *-n* in positive main clause: *imtiḥa:n liḥimin na:ra* 'the examination was easy'. The negative of the past is *anna:ra* (< *alna:ra*) accompanied by *-m*: *yi:-kutum anna:ra* 'it was not so'. In subordinate clauses *-n* and *-m* again are missing.

ḥal

The verb of existence is *ḥal* 'there is'. It is conjugated like a past though the meaning is that of the nonpast. The past is expressed by *na:ra*, which, when substituting *ḥal*, has no *-n* in the sentence: *gidi:r katamaya:č yida:bliza:lu u:ga:č ḥalu* 'there are roads which connect the big towns', *baği:ḥ ge:ya:č na:ru* 'there were many (places named) ge:y'.

The negative of *ḥal* is *e:l* 'there is not': *zalḥa:re:w bandar e:lum* 'there is no town which he did not visit' (in this sentence the *-m* is attached to *e:l* and not to the predicate noun). *e:l* can be a combination of *i:-* (the Ge'ez negation) and *ḥal*.

By adding the object suffixes *ḥal* becomes the possessive expression ('to have'): *a:n gidi:r sandu:q ḥalañ* 'I have a big box', *awwal-be zina:re:w-kut-be* 'as he had it in former times', *e:lañum* 'I have not'.

The object suffixes can also be attached together with the preposition *-b-*. In this case *ḥalba* has three meanings: 'there is in him', 'it is with him = he has', 'it is to his disadvantage = he has to, he must'.

References

Gutt, Ernst-August. 1983. "Studies in the Phonology of Silte." *Journal of Ethiopian Studies* 16: 37–73.

Hetzron, Robert. 1972. *Ethiopian Semitic: Studies in Classification.* Manchester: Manchester University Press.

Further Reading

Cerulli, E. 1936. *Studi etiopici*, volume 1: *La lingua e la storia di Harar.* Rome: Istituto per l'Oriente.

Goldenberg, Gideon. 1968. "New Texts in Harari." Review article of Wolf Leslau, *Ethiopians Speak: Studies in Cultural Background*, volume 1: *Harari. Lěšonénu* 32: 247–263 (in Hebrew).

—— 1983. "Nominalization in Amharic and Harari: Adjectivization." In *Ethiopian Studies Dedicated to Wolf Leslau*, ed. S. Segert and J. E. Bodrogligeti. Wiesbaden: Harrassowitz. 170–193.

Leslau, Wolf. 1958. *The Verb in Harari (South Ethiopic).* Berkeley and Los Angeles: University of California Press.

—— 1963. *Etymological Dictionary of Harari.* Berkeley and Los Angeles: University of California Press.

—— 1965a. "Gleanings in Harari Grammar, 1." *Journal of the American Oriental Society* 85: 153–159.

—— 1965b. *Ethiopians Speak: Studies in Cultural Background*, volume 1: *Harari.* Berkeley and Los Angeles: University of California Press.

—— 1970. "The *ma*-Clause in Harari." In *Mélanges Marcel Cohen*, ed. D. Cohen. The Hague: Mouton. 263–273.

Wagner, Ewald. 1983. *Harari-Texte in arabischer Schrift.* Wiesbaden: Steiner.

—— 1994. "The Harari Expression of 'While'." In *New Trends in Ethiopian Studies: Papers of the 12th International Conference of Ethiopian Studies*, volume 1. East Lansing: Michigan State University. 1323–1329.

22 The Silte Group (East Gurage)

Ernst-August Gutt

The Silte group comprises the following major varieties: Silte, Inneqor (Azarnat), Wolane forming a dialect cluster and the more divergent Zway. Most of the data here are from Silte, the few data for Zway, added by the editor, come from Leslau 1992.

According to the 1984 census, about 500,000 people usually speak Silte in their homes. Silte and Inneqor are adjacent, situated on the Rift Valley escarpment in Ethiopia. Wolane and Zway are geographically separated from the rest and from each other (Wolane to the north-west, Zway to the east of the other two).

Most of the East Gurage people are Muslims, with noticeable elements of an animistic religion. There are also enclaves of Ethiopian Orthodox Christians. A division between highland and lowland population is economically relevant: the highlanders' main crop is ensete, the false banana plant (*ensete edulis*); in the lowlands: grain and cattle raising. A significant number of Siltes are traders, spread around the towns of Ethiopia. The important cash crops are red pepper and qat, a plant the leaves of which contain a stimulant.

Dialectal variation is mostly phonological, involving the occurrence of the glides *h*, *'*, *y*, *w*, mostly in word-initial position, though there is also some morphological variation. In the southern areas of the Silte group there is a tendency toward various kinds of glottalization, probably under the influence of neighboring Hadiya. Thus *p̣* occurs in place of *b* in geminate consonants or clusters: *hap̣p̣i* 'then' for *abbi*, and *harp̣añño* 'hare' for *arbañño*. Geminates may be glottalized: *ha'na* 'that (acc.)' corresponding to *anna*, *bal'la* 'much' corresponding to *balla*. In Wolane, *'* and *q* appear to be interchangeable. Zway appears to show more substantial differences from the other dialects. A remarkable feature in the Silte group (except apparently for Wolane) is the contrastive vowel length.

Phonology

Consonants
Most varieties of the Silte group have basically twenty-five consonants *p̣, t, č, k, b, d, j, g, ṭ, č̣, q, f, s, š, z, ž, m, n, ñ, l, r, w, y, h, ʾ*. All of these, except *h* and *ʾ*, can occur geminated. Wolane is reported to have a labialized set of velar stops plus *h^w*. The change *q > ʾ* is attested in some dialects.

Minimal pairs based on gemination:

bala	'he ate'	*balla*	'much'
gawo	'forest'	*gawwa*	'foolish'
daama	'bronze colored cattle'	*daamma*	'wild honey'

Vowels
With the apparent exception of Wolane, the Silte group vowel system falls into two sets of five short and five long vowels: *i, e, a, o, u* and *ii, ee, aa, oo, uu*. While there can also be a quality difference between *i* (which can be centralized [ə]) and *ii* as well as between *a* (which can be raised to [ä]) and *aa*, the length distinction affects all five vowel pairs, and hence seems to be the relevant contrast.

Examples for contrastive vowel length:

sir	'root'	*siir*	'tough leather'
keša	'container for red pepper	*beesa*	'kind of coin'
bala	'he ate'	*baala*	'he said'
goro	'season'	*gooro*	'hunger'
mut	'death'	*muut*	'thing(s)'

All short vowels may appear optionally voiceless before pause. After the bilabial glide *w* the contrast between *i* and *u* and between *a* and *o* is neutralized.

Assimilation
Alveolar stops and affricates totally assimilate to a following coronal obstruent. With the paucal suffix *-ča* added to nouns and with the passive prefix *t-* or the sg. 3f. suffix *-t* added to verbs note: *abot* 'father' *abočča* 'fathers'; *baad* 'country', *baačča* 'countries'; *čaala* 'know', *yaččaala* 'that which was known'; *aytisačaan* 'that which will not be drunk' (= undrinkable); *heeda* 'he went', *heett* 'she went'.

Partial regressive assimilation can optionally occur when a glottalized and a non-glottalized consonant are juxtaposed: *iṭqeebalaan* 'he will receive' (from *i-t-qeebalaan*); *ruuq* 'far', *ruukča*.

Morphology

Pronouns

Independent pronouns (Zway, when divergent, in braces):

Sg. 1	*ihe* {äya} 'I'	Pl. 1	*iña* {əñña}	'we'
2m.	*ata* 'you (m.)'	2	*atum*	'you (pl.)'
f.	*aš* {ači} 'you (f.)'			
3m.	*uha* {ut} 'he'	3	*uhnu* {ənom}	'they'
f.	*iša* {it} 'she'			

Complement pronoun suffixes:

Sg. 1	*-ñ*	Pl. 1	*-na*
2m.	*-ka* after C, *-ha* elsewhere	2	*-kum* after C, *-mmu* elsewhere
f.	*-š*		
3m.	*-ii* after C, *-y* elsewhere	3	*-iimmu* after C, or *i*
f.	*-eet*		*-ymu* after V other than *i*

Possessive pronoun suffixes:

Sg. 1	*-ee*	Pl. 1	*-na*
2m.	*-aa/aaha*	2	*-aammu*
f.	*-aaš*		
3m.	*-ka*	3	*-niimmu*
f.	*-ša*		

Benefactive and detrimental pronoun suffixes (see p. 525):

	Benefactive	Detrimental
Sg. 1	*-ññ*	*-biñ*
2m.	*-nka*	*-biha*
f.	*-nš*	*-biš*
3m.	*-nnii*	*-bii*
f.	*-nneet*	*-beet*
Pl. 1	*-nna*	*-bina*
2	*-nkum*	*-bimmu*
3	*-nniimmu*	*-biim*

bi- has the allomorphs: *-bu* following *u*; *-b* before vowel, and *-bi* elsewhere.

The suffix *-nn* has the following allomorphs: *-ñ* before *ñ*, *n* before other consonants, and *-nn* elsewhere.

Nouns

Morphologically, nouns have the following general structure:

(Prefix) (Distributive) STEM (Acc. or Vocative) (Particle) (Copula) (Possessive Suffix) (Article)

The initial position can be taken by any preposition (*ba-*, *la-*, *ta-* see p. 514) or the genitive marker *ya-*. The latter is elided when there is a preposition: *yasaalo gaar* 'Salo's house', *basaalo gaar* 'in Salo's house'. The distributive marker: *-sa-* 'each' may occur, preceded by the genitive marker (or a preposition). With a distributive marker, the noun must also have a possessive suffix: *sab ya-sa-gee-ka heeda* 'the people went each one to their home'.

Following the stem, either the accusative or vocative suffix can occur: *waaj* 'elder brother', *waaj-o* '(hey-m.), elder brother'; *gaar-a gaba* 'he entered the house (acc.)'.

The next position can optionally be filled by either of the pragmatic particles *-w* 'how about, as to' or *-m* 'also': *raanji-w* 'as to a thief'; *raanjim* 'a thief also', or a copula *raanji-n* 'he is a thief'.

The copula can be followed by a possessive suffix: *čuuloo-n-ša* 'it is her child' [child-is-hers]. The possessive suffix can, of course, occur without the copula: *čuuloša* 'her child'.

In the final position the definite article *-ii* for masculine or *-te* for feminine can be found: *inṭ* 'tree', *inṭii* 'the tree'; *garajja* 'girl', *garajjate* 'the girl'. If a noun has the copula plus a possessive and/or a definite article, the copula always precedes these suffixes. Here are examples of combinations of several of these suffixes:

aaddee-na-w-ka 'as to his mother (acc.)' [mother-acc.-as-to-his]
likki-n-ee 'It is my measure/size' [measure-copula-my]

Definiteness, Number and Gender

These three categories are interrelated in the Silte group. For example, the suffix *-te* can mark definiteness with feminine gender and singular number.

Gender

Gender is mostly determined naturally, not grammatically. Thus humans and animals are given the gender according to their sex. A comparatively small number of inanimate nouns are specified for gender; thus *wari* 'moon' is usually given masculine gender and *ayr* 'sun' feminine, hence *warii* 'the moon', *ayrite* 'the sun'. Similarly, trees are usually treated as feminine.

Number

Semantically, a three-way distinction exists between singular, paucal, and plural. However, morphologically only the paucal is marked – the other two categories are unmarked. Thus, while *uunča* refers to a small number of stones (paucal), *uun* may refer either to one or a large number of stones. The context disambiguates such unmarked expressions.

There are two basic morphological types of paucal formation for adjectives and nouns: (1) suffixation of -ča (-čča after a consonant cluster or a geminate); word-final short vowels are elided before the suffix:

Suffixation of -ča:
çaaf   'leaf'   çaafča
bolaale   'long trousers'   bolaalča

or (2), for many nouns mostly ending in a short vowel, reduplication of the last consonant with insertion of the vowel aa and replacement of the original final vowel by o: alaga 'stranger', alagaago; amoole 'salt bar', amoolaalo. When the last consonant is geminate, only the degeminated, single consonant is repeated: burre 'big tin/can', burraaro.

Most words with reduplicated paucal allow further suffixation as well: bala 'calamity' balaalča; bošo 'young ensete plant' bošaašča.

Definiteness
Definite articles mark gender, -ii (-y after vowel) for masculine, and -te for feminine. However, these two articles can fulfill further functions. The masculine -ii can signal a large number or collective of items, regardless of their gender, while the feminine -te can refer to one item (singulative) and/or to a small specimen.

For example, in addition to denoting definiteness, the expression gaarte 'the (f.) house' implies a single house considered to be small. By contrast, the expression gaarii 'the (m.) house' is neutral as to size, and it may refer, as an alternative to its singular meaning, to a collective or large number of houses. The collective use overrides natural gender: indaaččii maṭa 'the women have come (sg. m.)'.

There is no indefinite article. However, the indefinite pronoun add (pl. addadd) is often used to introduce entities not assumed to be contextually known.

The definite article is not used for the generic statements: baqlo allaha sadabeetaane, daraqtaat dalša 'Allah cursed the mule and its womb has become barren'. Here baqlo 'mule', with no article, refers not to a particular mule, but to the species.

Case
Silte uses four prepositions and two suffixes to mark case relations on nominal phrases. The form of nominals that occurs in subject position (nominative) is morphologically unmarked. The following table gives some indication of typical correlations between these markers, case and semantic roles. (The question of whether the prefixes are prepositional or case markers is beyond the scope of this description.)

Prepositions

Marker	Gloss	"Typical" semantic role
ya-	'of'	genitive: possessor
la-	'to'	dative: experiencer, goal, location, benefactive, theme (see p. 526)
ba-	'in, with'	instrument, source, location, detrimental
ta-	'with, than'	comitative, point of comparison (origin)

Suffixes

	Function
-a	accusative theme, range
-o ~ -(a)w/-(a)y (m./f.)	vocative addressee (special vocative pronouns: *kool tee* 'hey, you (m./f. singular or plural)'

The **genitive** modifies a noun; it can indicate possession, substance of which something is made (*ya-saar gaar* 'a thatch roofed [= of-grass] house'), or some other relation (*ya-taačeena marka* 'yesterday's matter').

The **accusative** is used for definite objects, indefinite objects have no overt case marker, though some dialects use the accusative marker even here. It has the following allophones: *-n(a)* after proper names, pronouns and with nouns with possessing suffixes that begin with a long vowel (*išaana* 'her (acc.)'), *-e* after palatal consonants, Ø after vowel, *-a* elsewhere. It may further be used adverbially, usually indicating a range of time or location or some more abstract relation. See p. 525.

Benefactive is for the beneficiary, also with inanimate nouns: *la-gaar-ii qurat wagga yaabeezu-nniy-aan* ('to-house-the roof spikes they-make-for-him-aux.') 'one prepares spikes for the roof of the house'. **Detrimental** (= instrumental) has the opposite meaning: *gaar-a-y oonṭu-buy* 'house-acc.-the they-closed-to-his-detriment'.

Morphological Properties and Processes with Nouns
Common morphophonemic changes with suffixes are the following. Word-final vowels are dropped directly before a plural suffix. Word-final vowels are lengthened immediately preceding the accusative suffix *-na*: *maaṭa, maaṭaana* 'younger brother$_{acc.}$'); or the pragmatic markers *-m* and *-w*: *addeñña, adeññaam* 'first, first also'; or the masculine definite article: *bučo, bučooy* 'dog, the dog'.

Adjectives
Basic adjectives: *fayya* 'good', *booz* 'bad', *yaroore* 'big', *qall* 'small'. Derived adjectives: (none of the derivations is productive; they are all lexically determined).

Denominal adjectives in *-añña*:

gutt	'middle'	*guttañña*	'average'

Denominal adjectives in *-atañña*:

kasb	'work'	*kasbatañña*	'industrious'

Denominal adjectives in *-aančo*:

bitar	'marriage'	*bitaraanco*	'newly-wed

Denominal adjectives in *-a(a)m(a)*:

maniija	'pride'	*maniijaam*	'proud'

Denominal adjectives in *-a(a)taam* (denoting ampleness):

ayb	'milk'	*aybaataam*	'giving much milk'

The noun of agent of verbs (see below) has often an adjectival sense: *qoommara* 'be strong', *qoommaari* 'strong'; *qañe* 'to envy', *qañiilo* 'envious'.

There are no special adjectival forms for comparison; if the point of comparison is explicit, it is marked by *ta-* plus the suffix *-ko* 'like':

uha ta-ihee-ko maniijaam
'He is prouder than I.'
ittate laam taattitate-ko aybaataamint
'This cow gives more milk than that one.'

Stative verbs with *ta-* often express comparison:

yahe gaar ta-atay ifeettaan
'My house is bigger than yours.'
feeq ta-laam yaansaan
'A goat is smaller than a cow.'

Deictics

Basic forms: *itta* 'this' and *atta* 'that' to which the definite article (m. or f.) is added: *ittaay, ittate* 'this'; *attaay, attate* 'that'. So far no meaning difference has been noted.

	'This'	(def.)	(def. f.)	'That'	(def.)	(def. f.)
Nom.	*itta*	*ittaay*	*ittate*	*atta*	*attaay*	*attate*
Gen.	*yiitta*	*yiittaay*	*yiittate*	*yaatta*	*yaattaay*	*yaattate*
Dat.	*illii*	*illitaay*	*illitate*	*allii*	*allitaay*	*allitate*
Acc.	*inna*	*innay*	*innate*	*anna*	*annay*	*annate*
Abl.	*ittii*	*ittitaay*	*ittitate*	*attii*	*attitaay*	*attitate*
Instr.	*ibbii*	*ibbitaay*	*ibbitate*	*abbii*	*abbitaay*	*abbitate*

There are parallel variants with *iyii* and *ayii*. Sometimes prepositions are added to the inflected forms, e.g. *biibbi* for **ba-ibbi*; **la-alli* becomes *laalli*; **ta-itti* becomes *tiittii*.

Plurals (paucals) are formed by adding *sur*: *ii sur*, *ittaay sur* 'these'; *ayii sur*, *attaay sur* 'those' etc.

Numerals

Cardinal Numbers

1	*add*	10	*assir*	40	*arba*
2	*oošt*	11	*asradd*	50	*amsa*
3	*šeešt*	12	*asroošt*	60	*sidsa*
4	*araatt*	13	*asrašeešt*	70	*siba*
5	*ammist*	17	*asrasaabt*	80	*sumna*
6	*siddist*	20	*kuya*	90	*ziṭana*
7	*saabt*	21	*kuya add*	100	*baqqil*
8	*summut*	25	*kuya ammist*	200	*oošt baqqil*
9	*ziiṭaññe*	30	*saasa*	1,000	*kim*

Ordinal Numbers

These are formed from cardinal numbers by adding the suffix *-lañña*: *addilañña* 'first', *ooštilañña* 'second', etc.

Verbs

Root Structure and Stem Formation

Overall, the description of verb roots requires reference to the following parameters:

- number of root consonants
- gemination pattern of root consonants
- nature of thematic (root) vowel
- nature of root final radical
- presence of a special nasal element

Roots can differ according to whether the penultimate root consonant is geminated or not:

biconsonantal verbs:	*gaba*	'enter'
	bada	'take'
triconsonantal verbs:	*harata*	'take a mouthful'
	rawwaṭa	'run'
quadriconsonantal verbs:	*dinabaṭa*	'be surprised'
	sinaṭṭala	'develop oneself, be trained'

However, for a significant number of verbs one root vowel, the "thematic vowel," needs to be specified as well. Thematic vowels can be *ee*, *aa*, *oo*, and *o*:

biconsonantal verbs with thematic vowel:	*qeera* 'watch, wait'
	goora 'slaughter'
triconsonantal verbs with thematic vowel:	*maagada* 'kindle'
	eewada 'tell'
	ţoollaba 'beg'

The final radical can be of four kinds: (1) ending in a consonant only; (2) ending in consonant followed by *a*; (3) ending in a non-palatal consonant with following *a* palatalized to *e*; (4) ending in a palatal consonant with following *a* palatalized to *e*. The nature of the final radical can best be seen in the imperative sg. m.; palatal consonants are depalatalized preceding back vowels, so the underlying non-palatal consonant appears, for example, preceding the infinitival ending *-oot*:

	consonant only:	*waaba*	*waab*	'give!'
4	consonant plus *a*:	*qeera*	*qiira*	'watch!'
5	non-palatal consonant plus *e*:	*noze*	*nuz*	'be angry!'
6	palatal consonant plus *e*:	*sače*	*sič sikoot*	'drink!'

The nasal element appears in bi- and triradical verbs: *anže* 'see', *eenza* 'hold', *oonţe* 'close', *andara* 'spend the night', *eenqafa* 'embrace'. All but one of these verbs begin with a vowel. The one verb that begins with a consonant is: *soonče* 'smell good'. The nasal does not count as a radical consonant. Thus *anže* 'see' inflects like a biconsonantal verb, and *andara* 'spend the night' like a triconsonantal one.

Derivation Classes
Derived stems are primarily viewed from a morphological point of view, since the semantic characteristics tend to overlap and are unpredictable at times. The derivational processes attested as below:

1   Prefixation of *at-* plus change of the first vowel *a* to *ee*; this most often has a **causative** meaning.

faqa	'hit'	*atfeeqa*	'cause to hit'
jammara	'begin'	*ajjeemmara*	'cause to begin'
dinabaţa	'be frightened'	*addineebaţa*	'make frightened'
foge	'inflate'	*atfooge*	'cause to inflate'
zaače	'herd'	*azzaače*	'cause to herd'
eeffe	'cover'	*ateeffe*	'cause to cover'

This is the only derivation process that can be applied to virtually any verb, basic or derived itself.

2 Prefixation of *a-* to intransitive verbs; this tends to result in a **transitive** meaning, but in many cases the outcome is not predictable:

raaje	'be old'	*araaje*	'make old'
wakaba	'buy'	*awakaba*	'sell'
gaba	'enter'	*agaba*	'place inside; marry'

3 Prefixation of *ta-*; in most cases this **passivizes** underived transitive verbs:

čeeñe	'give birth'	*tačeeñe*	'be born'
waaba	'give'	*taaba*	'be given'
eewada	'tell'	*teewada*	'be told'

4 **Lengthening** of thematic *a* to *aa*; this is usually accompanied by the prefixation of *ta-*. Semantically it often indicates a reciprocal, iterative or very intensive process. With the prefix replaced by *at-*, a causative meaning obtains:

faje	'finish'	*rawwaṭa*	'run'
tafaaje	'destroy each other'	*taraawaṭa*	'to run here and there'
atfaaje	'cause people to destroy each other'	*atraawaṭa*	'make run here and there'

5 There are at least two distinct kinds of **reduplicative** formations: type 1 involves the first root consonant, type 2 the second root consonant (only the simple consonant is reduplicated, not a geminate). Semantically, reduplication often indicates multiple actions: either doing something repeatedly or doing something to many objects, people, etc. For a number of verbs it indicates that the activity is done "a little," not completely or properly.

Type 1 reduplication ($C_1VC_2(V) \rightarrow C_1aaC_1VC_2(V)$) (only biconsonantal):

laaha	'send'	*laalaaha*	'send many people, or something to many places'
qeera	'wait'	*qaaqeera*	'watch repeatedly, many times'
čeeñe	'give birth'	*čaačeeñe*	'give birth many times'

Type 2 reduplication ((C_1)$VC_2(V) \rightarrow (C_1)iC_2aaC_2(V)$):

faje	'finish'	*fijaaje*	'finish many things'
aje	'hit'	*ijaaje*	'hit many times, in many places, many people'
eema	'slander'	*imaama*	'slander many times'
eenza	'hold'	*tiinzaaza*	'hold each other'
qatala	'kill'	*qitaatala*	'kill many animals, people'
jammara 'begin'		*jimaammara*	'to start a little bit'

Some verbs employ both types of reduplication, with different meanings: *foge* 'inflate'; type 1 reduplication: *atfaafooge* 'cause to be swollen in many places'; type 2 reduplication: *fugaage* (*fogaage*) 'inflate many times'.

With both types the original thematic vowel may also be lengthened: *kinabala* 'return (v.t.)'; *kinaanaabala* 'turn again and again, turn over many times'; *foge* 'inflate' *atfaafooge* 'cause to be swollen in many places'.

The reduplicated verb stems can have one or more of the derivations that a basic verb can have: causative in *at-*, passive in *ta-*, and, much more rarely, transitive with *a-*:

soonče 'smell'

Reduplicated	Transitive	Causative
saasoonče	*asaasoonče*	*assaasoonče*
'many things give a smell, something gives a smell many times'	'smell different things'	'cause each other to smell something'

jammara 'begin'

Reduplicated	Causative	Passive
jimaammara	*ajjimaammara*	*tajmaammara*
'start a little bit'	'cause to be started a little bit'	'be started a little bit'

Silte has many **compound verbs** consisting of an uninflected morpheme and an inflected helping verb like *baala* 'say', *mañe* 'build' (mainly intransitive), *aše/ añe* 'do, make' (mainly transitive), e.g. *buube baala* 'flee in fright', *buube aše* 'cause to flee in fright'.

Aspect and Tense

Aspect is indicated by the internal inflection of the verb stem; tense is marked by the conjugational affixes used and/or by auxiliaries. Each verb has three stem forms: perfective, imperfective and a third one not marked for aspect, the non-aspectual stem. The perfective stem is used to form simple past, present perfect and past perfect tenses, the imperfective stem for the formation of the present/ future and past-imperfective tenses; the non-aspectual stem serves for the infinitive and imperative.

Perfective stem *masak-*

Simple past	*masaka*	'he guided'
Present perfect	*masakaan*	'he has guided'
Pluperfect	*masaka naar*	'he had guided'

Imperfective stem *mask-*

Present/future	*i-maskaan*	'he guides/will guide'
Continuous past	*i-mask naar*	'he was guiding'

Non-aspectual stem *m(i)sak-*

Imperative/jussive	*misak*	'guide! (sg. 2m.)'
	yamsak	'let him guide!'
Infinitive	*misakoot*	'to guide'

The stem formation makes use of two distinct morphological means: changes in the consonant–vowel pattern of the root and raising of the thematic vowel. Thus the verbs can be divided into two broad classes:

Class 1: All verbs with thematic *a*; taking the perfective stem as basic, the other two are derived by omitting the first and second vowel respectively:

Perfective	Imperfective	Non-aspectual
(C)CVC(VC)	(C)CVC(C)	CC(VC)
		CCC(C)
sač-e 'drink'	*i-sač-aan*	*sič*
bataka 'pull out'	*i-batk-aan*	*bitak*
sinabata 'stay some days'	*i-snabt-aan*	*sinbit*
(Note the epenthetical *i*.)		

Class 2: All verbs with a thematic vowel other than *a*. Thematic *e* is raised to *i*, *o* to *u* in the non-aspectual stem:

jeeje 'reach'	*i-jeej-aan*	*jiij*
noze 'be angry'	*i-noz-aan*	*nuz*

Raising verbs with thematic *aa* are exceptional in that the *aa* is raised to *ii* in the imperfective aspect (not all such verbs undergo raising, e.g. *raaje* 'be old' *i-raaj-aan*):

čaama 'taste good'	*i-čiim-aan*	*čaam*
laaha 'send'	*i-liih-aan*	*laah*

Class 2 verbs with more than two radicals omit the vowel of the last radical in both the imperfective and non-aspectual stem forms:

šeebala 'dance'	*i-šeebl-aan*	*šiibl*
ţooqasa 'beg'	*i-ţooks-aan*	*ţuuks*

Conjugation

The inflectional structure of verbs in the Silte group is as follows:

(Negative) (Person) STEM (Person) (Ben./Detr.) (CPS) (Aux.)

In forms based on the imperfective and non-aspectual stems, both prefixes and suffixes mark the person.

As elsewhere in Ethio-Semitic, sentence constituents other than the subject may be marked in the morphology of the verb: benefactive (ben.), detrimental/instrumental (detr.) and complement person suffix (cps), see above. The complement person suffixes can occur without either the benefactive or detrimental/instrumental markers, but these last two categories require the presence of the person markers.

The present tense auxiliary (*-na* in Zway):

Sg. 1	*-aahu/-aaw*	Pl. 1	*-aan*
2m.	*-aaha*	2	*-aammu*
f.	*-aaš*		
3m.	*-aan*	3	*-aan*
f.	*-aat*	Impers.	*-aan*

The past auxiliary is *naar-* (past tense form of verb of existence).

The category "impersonal" is used to indicate what some unspecified group of individuals or people in general do. It may be glossed as 'people', 'one', 'they'.

Perfective Stem Conjugations
Added to the perfective stem these mark the subject in the simple past:

Sg. 1	*-ku* after C, *-hu/w* elsewhere	Pl. 1	*-na*
2m.	*-ka* after C, *-ha/aa* elsewhere	2	*-kumu* after C,
f.	*-š* word finally, *-ši* elsewhere		*-mmu* elsewhere
3m.	*-e* in palatal verbs, *-a* elsewhere	3	*-u*
f.	*-ta* preceding an object suffix, *-t* elsewhere	Impers.	*-i*

Simple past
Simple past of a C-verb 'I guided', etc.:

	Masculine	Feminine	Plural	Impersonal ('People/one guided')
1	*masakku*		*masakna*	
2	*masakka*	*masakš*	*masakkumu*	
3	*masaka*	*masakt*	*masaku*	*masaki*

Simple past of palatal verbs 'I wanted', etc.:

1	*kašeehu/w*		*kašeena*	
2	*kašeeha*	*kašeeš*	*kašeemmu*	
3	*kaše*	*kašeet*	*kasu*	*kasi*

Simple past of Ca-verbs:

1		*balaahu/w*	*balaana*	
2	*balaaha*	*balaaš*	*balaammu*	
3	*bala*	*balaat*	*balu*	*bali*

Present perfect: The perfective stem plus the present tense auxiliary (with *-nu* or *-mma* in Zway).
'I have guided', etc.

1		*masakkoo*	*masaknaan*	
2	*masakkaa*	*masakšeeš*	*masakkumoommu*	
3	*masakaan*	*masaktaat*	*masakoon*	*masakeen*

These forms involve the following vowel contraction processes: $u + aa \rightarrow oo$, $a + aa \rightarrow aa$, $i + aa \rightarrow ee$.

For palatal and Ca-verbs the present perfect is formed analogously, except that the following additional contraction rule is required for the 3rd person masculine of palatal verbs: $e + aa \rightarrow aa$ *kašaan* 'he has wanted'.

Pluperfect: The simple past tense forms plus the auxiliary *naar* uninflected except in sg. 1c.
'I had guided', etc.

1		*masakku naarku*	
2	*masakka naar*	*masakš naar*	
3	*masaka naar* etc.		

Negative forms based on the perfective stem are formed with the prefix *al-*: *almasaka* 'he did not guide', *almasakaan* 'he has not guided', *almasaka naar* 'he had not guided'.

Imperfective Stem Conjugations
Some of the person markers used with imperfective stem involve both prefixes and suffixes. The prefixes are as follows:

(y)i-	/__C	*y-* /__V	sg. 1, sg. 3m., pl. 1, pl. 3, impersonal
ti-	/__C	*t-* /__V	sg. 2m., sg. 2f., sg. 3f., pl. 2.

The suffixes are *-i* sg. 2f., pl.1 *-na*, pl. 2/3 *-u*, impersonal *-i*. The second person feminine suffix palatalizes the last consonant of the stem: $d \rightarrow j$; $t \rightarrow č$; $t \rightarrow \check{c}$, $s \rightarrow š$, $z \rightarrow ž$, $n \rightarrow ñ$, $l \rightarrow y$.

Continuous past: The conjugated imperfective stem followed by the past tense auxiliary.
'I was guiding', etc.

1		*imask naarku*		*imaskina naar*	
2	*timask naar*	*timaski naar*	*timasku naar*		
3	*imask naar*	*timask naar*	*imasku naar*	*imaski naar*	

Present/future: The present tense auxiliary is added to the imperfective with its person affixes, with the necessary vowel contractions.
'I guide', etc.

1		*imaskaahu*		*imaskinaan*	
2	*timaskaaha*	*timaskeeš*	*timaskoommu*		
3	*imaskaan*	*timaskaat*	*imaskoon*	*imaskeen*	

Negative

Negative present/future (prefix set 1):
'I will not guide', etc.

1		*ilawmask*		*ilawmaskina*	
2	*ittimask*	*ittimaski*	*ittimasku*		
3	*ilamask*	*ittimask*	*ilamasku*	*ilamaski*	

Zway has *ti-* in main clauses and *a-* in subordination.
Negative continuous past (prefix set 2)
'I was not guiding', etc.

1		*almask naar*		*almaskina naar*	
2	*atmask naar*	*atmaski naar*	*atmasku naar*		
3	*aymask naar*	*atmask naar*	*aymasku naar*	*aymaski naar*	

Non-aspectual Stem Conjugations

The infinitive is formed by suffixing *-oot* (prefixing *wä-* in Zway) to the non-aspectual stem: *misakoot* 'to guide'; *kisoot* 'to want'.

The jussive also combines prefixes and suffixes, **the imperative** uses only suffixes. The suffixes are the same as those used with the imperfective stem. The prefixes are (the *a* is elided preceding another vowel):

l(a)-   sg. 1, pl. 1 (*ya-* is also used for pl.1)
t(a)-   sg. 3f.
y(a)-   sg. 3m., pl. 3, impers.

lamsak	'let me guide'	*lamsakna/yamsakna*	'let us guide'
misak	'guide! (m.)'	*misaku*	'guide! (pl.)'
misaki	'guide! (f.)'		
yamsak	'let him guide'	*yamsaku*	'let them guide'
tamsak	'let her guide'	*yamsaki*	'let one guide'
yiima	'let him gossip!'	*tuunt*	'let her close!'

The negative infinitive is formed by prefixing *al-* to the affirmative: *almisakoot* 'to not guide'.

The suffix set for the negative imperative/jussive is the same as for the affirmative, but the prefixes are those found in the negative prefix set 2 (see p. 523). Examples: *almisak* 'let me not guide'; *atmisak* 'don't guide (m.)'; *aymisak* 'let him not guide'; *aymisaki* 'let people not guide'.

Derived Forms
The passive is formed by prefixing *ta-* (*-t-* after another prefix). The vocalic pattern of the active perfective stem is maintained here. Thematic *ee* and *oo* are raised here too, but not *aa*.

Table 22.1   Active vs. passive stem forms

	Perfective		Imperfective		Non-aspectual	
	Active	Passive	Active	Passive	Active	Passive
'eat'	bala-	ta-bala-	i-bala-	i-t-bala	bila-	ta-bala-
'guide'	masak-	ta-masak-	i-mask-	i-t-masak-	misak-	ta-masak-
'beg'	ţooqas	ta-ţooqas	i-ţooqs-	i-t-ţooqs-	ţuuqs-	ta-ţuuqas-
'mix'	liqaalaq-	ta-lqaalaq-	i-liqaalq-	i-t-liqaalaq-	liqaalq-	ta-liqaalaq-

Agent Nouns
There is no instrument noun. Agent nouns can be formed in two ways.

1   Verbs ending in a palatal radical add the suffix *-iilo* to the perfective stem:

amoge	'work reluctantly and badly'	*amogiilo*	'reluctant worker'
zaače	'watch, look after'	*zaaqiilo*	'watchman'
bače	'weep, cry'	*bačiilo/bakiilo*	'crybaby'

The suffix may be added to the palatalized or non-palatalized form of the verb stem.
2   Non-palatal verbs add the suffix *-i* to the last root consonant of the perfective stem, palatalizing that consonant where possible; the last, non-thematic vowel is lengthened to *aa*: *qoommara* 'be strong'; *qoommaari* 'strong'; *amasala* 'pretend' *amasaay* 'pretending'.

Adverbs and Other Parts of Speech
Some adverbs are formed from adjectives by suffixing *-ko* 'like' (*-ako* after consonant): *fayya* 'good', *fayyako* 'well'; *booz* 'bad', *boozako* 'badly'.

Syntax

Word order

Sentence Level

The word order is essentially of the SOV type. The order of the constituents other than the almost strictly final verb (cf. p. 526, subject or complement NP in post-verbal position) is comparatively flexible, though the preferred order is the subject before complements. Adverbial constituents are free to occur anywhere preceding the verb.

yoolay kreetii akku inna jiingo jeejaan
[see! ditch-the now this-obj. until it-has-reached]
'See, the ditch has lasted until now.'

ittaay hullam gina iseečče-waa ayba ya-ṭaafe injeera ibalaan
[this all time butter-and cheese of-teff pancake he-eats]
'This one eats all the time butter, cheese and teff pancakes.'
(Teff is a kind of grain (*Eragrostis tef*) grown in Ethiopia.)

ba-saasaa-m ayaam saasaa-m biṭṭe tigaagraat
[in-thirty-and day thirty-also bread she-bakes]
'And in thirty days she also bakes thirty loaves of bread.'

Objects and some other complements may be marked by pronominal suffixes after the verb (see p. 511).

muuta-y   ba-ingir-kaa-y   ragaṭay
[thing-the by-foot-his-the he-kicked-it]
'He kicked the thing with his foot.'

la-miiš-ii add faranka la-sijaara yoobuyaan
[to-man-the one 10-cent-coin for-cigarette they-give-him-AUX]
'They give the man 10 cents for a cigarette.'

Adverbs may be represented on the verb by the suffixes -*bi* or -*nn* (see p. 511). -*bi* expresses a locative, instrumental or detrimentative meaning: *masakkubuy* 'I guided against him'; *masakšibeet* 'you (sg. f.) guided against her'; *ikašnabihaan* 'we will want against you (m. sg.)'. -*nn* has a benefactive meaning: *masakkaññ* 'you (sg. m.) guided for me'; *masakanna* 'he guided for us'; *masakkumunniimmu* 'you (pl.) guided for them'. These examples can be full sentences.

balaahu-ym-aahu [I-ate-them-Pres. Pf.]   'I have eaten them.'
oonṭeet-bi-iimmu [she-closed-DETR-pl. 3]   'She locked them in.'
(or 'she locked (the door) to their detriment')

Some verbs can take up to three noun phrases in the accusative case:

ihe safiyyaa-n dum-a-ša iseečče qabaahu
[I Safiyya-acc. hair-acc.-her butter I-smeared]
'I smeared Safiyya's hair with butter.'

Impersonal verbs cannot take an overt subject NP. When a verb complement or adverbial constituent is to be marked inflectionally in an impersonal verb, its form changes to the 3rd person plural subject, but it still does not take an overt subject NP:

la-gaar-ii makkazo wagga yaanu-nniy-aan
[for-house-the main-pole spikes they/one-make-BEN-sg. 3m.-AUX]
'One prepares spikes for the main pole of the house.'

Topicalized NPs are placed in sentence initial position:

la-ihe inna-y faranka la-sijaara waabu-ñ
[For-I this-obj.-the 10-cent-coin for-cigarette they-gave-sg. 1]
'As for me, they gave me these 10 cents for a cigarette.'

Sometimes a subject or complement NP occurs in post-verbal position:

waabši-ñ-aaš way weej?
[have-you (f.)-given-sg. 1 interr. children]
'Have you given me children?'

This seems to happen most often at the end of a (longer) speech quotation, perhaps to remind the audience of who the speaker is:

biitbileet gina "aay, yeeš bay; yahun. allaha yaabaš. nibari" baataane taqeebalteetaat ufrite
[when-she-says-sg. 3f. time "oh here say; let-it-be. Allah may-he-give-sg. 2f. live (2f.)!"] she-said-and she-received-her mouse-the]
'When she said this, the mouse said, "Oh, here you are! OK! Thank you! May you live!" and received (the milk) from her.'

Phrase Level

Noun Phrase
The linear sequence of constituents in the NP is as follows:

(Det) (Quant) (Modifier) (Source Gen.) HEAD (*hull*)

The positions of DETERMINER, SOURCE, GENITIVE and HEAD seem to be fixed. Determiners usually take the initial position, the head of the NP is at the end. A genitive of source (see example below) immediately precedes the HEAD. Nothing may be inserted between the source genitive NP and the head of the NP. Only *hull* 'all' may occur after the NP head.

> *yasab diinet* 'people's possession'
> *inna-y adda fayya ya-saar gaar*
> [this(obj.)-the one good of-grass house]
> 'this one good thatched house' (genitive of **source**)
> (but not: **ya-saar fayya gaar*)

> *weejee-nee hulla-m-kaa-y*
> [children-obj.-sg. 1 all-obj.-PART.-sg. 3m.-the]
> 'all of my children'

The relative ordering of quantifier and modifier is variable:

> *oošt fayya qirṭ dačč*
> [two good acres land]
> 'some two good acres of land' (i.e. the size of the acres is good)

> *fayya oošt qirṭ dačč*
> 'some good two acres of land' (again the measure is good, not the land)

Determiners Demonstratives and the indefinite pronoun *add* 'one' (pl. *addadd* 'some') function as determiners.

> *add nagda kitaabañña*
> [one visitor [Islamic] scholar]
> 'a visiting scholar'

> *ittaa-y ya-saalo fayya gaar*
> [this$_{subj}$-the Salo's good house]
> 'this good house of Salo's'

Quantifiers The quantifier slot can be filled by definite or indefinite numerals, or an NP with a numeral: *summut sabča* 'eight people'; *addadd sab* 'some people'; *oošt qirṭ fayya dačč* 'two acres of good land'.

The numeral itself can be modified by *add* 'one' when the amount is deemed insufficient:

> *add oošt qirṭ dacc taabayaan* [one two ...]
> 'He was given just two acres of land.'

Modifiers The modifiers may be adjectives, genitive phrases (other than genitive of source), and relative clauses. Several of these categories can cooccur in sequence: *ṭeem qalam* 'black color', *yaadde lij* 'mother's son'. Furthermore:

wado-kaa-y ya-jeeje-bii čuulo
[turn-his-the REL.-it-arrived-DETR.-sg. 3m. child]
'the child whose turn had come'

y-iišaa-na aynat gana laam
[of-her-obj. kind another cow]
'another cow like her'

fayya-te bareeda y-oonti-te garajja
[good-the pretty REL.-she-is-the girl]
'the good girl who is pretty'

The order of constituents within the modifier slot is variable:

yaabbona fatt dačč or *fatt yaabbona dačč*
[of-father-our wide land] [wide of-father-our land]
'our ancestor's wide land'

NP head The head is usually a noun, but pronouns or adjectives of various kinds may also fill this slot.

Position of the definite article The definite article, *-ii* for masculine (*-y* after vowel) and *-te* for feminine are suffixed to the first constituent of the NP.

ya-lawṭa-y wakt	[of-change-obj.-the time]	'the time of the change'
itta-te ya-saalo laam	[this-the of-Salo cow]	'this cow of Salo's'

In this last example the definite article is suffixed to the demonstrative pronoun. It can also be added to words that already have a possessive suffix: *dumka* 'his head' ~ *dumkaa-y* 'his head'.

Position of case marking in NPs There seems to be some freedom in where the case marking occurs. It tends to mark the first constituent of the NP, but it may appear elsewhere as well:

Accusative case: *šeešt-a zamaan* 'three years', *asroošt-a birr-a* 'twelve Birr (Ethiopian currency), *add-a ruuq-a baad* '(to a) far away country', *šeešt birr-a* 'three Birr'.

Dative case: *la-baad-naa-y sab* 'to the people of our country', *la-allitaa-y la-add lij* 'to that one son'.

Circumpositions   The preposition-portions are the same as the case marking prefixes *ba-*, *la-*, and *ta-* already described. They may be combined with various postpositions: *ba-... baldaale* 'except', *ba-... alqare* 'besides, except, but' (sometimes also *balqare*), *la-/ba-... darr* 'above', *ya-... eet* 'at, to someone'. *...-a fare* 'without', *...-a fono* 'to, toward', *ba-... gina* 'at ... time', *ta-... gina* 'together with', *ya-... gina* 'in the case of', *la-/ba-... qada* 'in front of', *la-/ba-... sir* 'under' etc.

Agreement Rules

Verbs agree with the subject in person, number, and gender. Pronouns, whether independent or suffixed, agree with their referents in person, number and gender.

Converbs (see below) need not have the same subject as the verb with which they are syntactically associated, hence need not show agreement with that verb:

miišii maṭaane mištikaay heett. 'The man came$_{converb}$ and his wife went.'

In noun phrases, the article agrees in gender with the head; there may or may not be number agreement between adjectives and the head:

oošt yaroore karaabča   or   *oošt yarooraaro karaabča*
[two big oxen]   [two big pl. oxen]
'two big oxen'

Assertion and Negation

This distinction is generally marked in the inflection of the verb. With copular expressions there is the option to use an independent negation particle *inko* (also *unko*) together with the affirmative form of the copula.

Questions

Sentence questions can be marked by a rise in intonation at the end of the sentence, and/or by the interrogative particle *way*. The pragmatic particle *-w* 'how about ...?' can also be used to mark questions: *ata-w* 'how about you?'

Pronominal questions make use of the interrogative words *maa* 'who?', *min* 'what?', *ayne* 'where?', *mače* 'when?', *aynako* 'how?', *laayiš* 'from where?', *aytaay* 'which?', *lamin* 'why?', and others.

Complex Sentences

Converbial Construction

The most common way of forming complex sentences is by using converbs. These are non-final verb forms, specified for person, number, gender, and aspect, but not for tense, which is determined by the verb on which they depend. There are two variant forms: a short and a long converb, with no apparent semantic difference. The long converb is formed by suffixing *-aane* (*-m* in Zway), the short

one by suffixing -*a* to any one of the three stems. The familiar vowel contractions
u+a(a) → *o(o)*; *i+a(a)* → *e(e)*; *a+a(a)* → *a(a)* apply: *heedaane* (long), *heeda*
(short) 'he having gone'; *heedeene* (long), *heede* (short) '(people) having gone';
heedoone (long), *heedo* (short) 'they having gone'.

The following sentence exemplifies both the long and the short form of of the converb (CVB):

> *wadaroom baalabii eet ikaš-a čimm yaañ-aane gaaray imañbiyaan eet*
> *laṭibañña yeed-aane issaalaan*
> [fiber-and where-it-is place he-seeks-CVB he-gathers-CVB house-obj.-the
>   (REL.)he-builds-LOC.-sg. 3m. place to-soothsayer he-goes-CVB he-asks]
> 'He seeks a place where there is fiber, he gathers it and goes to a soothsayer and
>   asks where he should build the house.'

Converbs cannot occur in a sentence without a main verb. They may be grammatically dependent on either main or subordinate verbs:

> *išaam waratt-aane lakolo azar hoont-aane may tiisačim add waraaba ladar*
> *azar hoon-aane may isač naar*
> [and-she she-went-down-CVB downwards she-was-CBV water when-she-
>   drank a hyena upwards he-was-CVB water he-was-drinking]
> 'When she went down to the river and was drinking water downstream, a hyena
>   was drinking water upstream.'

Converbs express a variety of semantic relations to the governing verb, sentence
coordination, adverbial modification, etc.

Coordination
The suffixed conjunction -*waa* is used mainly for coordinating nominals.

> *baadd eet miiš-waa mišt naaru*
> [in-one place man-and wife they-were]
> 'A man and a woman lived in a certain place.'

> *lasabii qaawwa-waa saafra yoobuyaan*
> [to-people-the coffee-and snack they-give-them]
> 'They give coffee and a snack to the people.'

> *summutt-waa ziiṭṭaññe saat*
> [eight-and nine hour]
> 'eight and nine o'clock'

It is also used to coordinate subordinate clauses of the same category:

> *tiyaawakb-waa tiyookb* ... [when-he-sells-and when-he-buys]

-*waa* is not used to coordinate sentences. Converbial structures (see p. 529) fulfill the role of coordination between sentences, among other tasks.

Conditionals

Real Conditions
'If' is *ba-* added to a perfective stem: *b-eewatkañ yeedaahu* 'if you tell me, I will go'; negative *b-aleewatkañ ilawweed* 'if you don't tell me, I won't go'. With the discourse suffix -*m*, the meaning is 'even if/though': *ba-ṭooqasa-m ataruy* 'even though he begged, they refused'; *b-aleewatkañi-m yeedahu* 'even if you don't tell me, I'll go'. Prefixed *la-* before a perfective means 'just in case': *jamaal lamaṭa, iiwday* 'if Jamal happens to come, tell him!'.

Hypothetical (Counterfactual) Conditionals
'If' is *bi(i)-* attached to the imperfective stem: *bi-tooddeeta mannam giza taašinneet naar* 'if you loved her, you would have done anything for her'; negative *ba-*: *ba-toodeeta mannam giza lalaašeehanneet* 'if you did not love her, you would not have done anything for her'.

Quotative Constructions
Direct speech quotations always require the verb *baala* 'say', even if there is another speech act verb in the sentence. *baala* (or one of its inflected forms) always comes after the direct speech; all other constituents of the embedding sentence precede the direct quotation:

> *mištite "ayne heeda?" baata tasaaltay*
> [wife-the where he-went? she-said-CVB she-asked-him]
> 'The wife asked him, "Where did he go?".'

Indirect speech quotations are formed with a relative clause and the suffix -*ko* 'as, like': *mištite ayne yeeda-ko tasaaltay* 'The wife asked him where he had gone.'

Subordination

Relative Clause
Relative clauses are marked by the relative form of the verb. In the past tense, they have the prefix *ya-*: *ya-moota karaab* 'an ox which died'. Imperfective relative verbs are unmarked in the affirmative and keep their auxiliary: *imaçaan* 'he will come'; *imaçaan sab* 'people who will come'. The relative uses the negative prefix set 2 (see p. 523). Example: *sab ila-sač* 'people don't drink' vs. *ay-sačaan sab* 'people who don't drink'.

Complement Clause
Purpose clauses have inflected imperfective stems, prefixed by *li-* 'to':

gaaraka liiheed kaše
[house-obj.-his to-he-go he-wanted]
'He wanted to go home.'

Relative verbs with the suffix *-ko* 'as, like' are used in complement clauses.

yeeda-ko išlaaw.
'I know that he went.'

Other Subordinate Clauses
The verb in temporal clauses is the inflected imperfective stem + the prefix *tii-:*

gaara tii-tgaba boozako dinabatt
'When she entered the house, she got a bad fright.'

Circumpositions + perfective provide special meanings: *ba-... zoof* 'after', *ta-... ko* 'as soon as':

lijaša ba-rakabteet zoof taknabalt
'After she had found her child, she returned.'

baarreka ta-bala-ko timirta gaara heeda
'As soon as he had eaten his lunch, he went to school.'

Copular, Existential and Possessive Expressions

Copular Sentences
The copula is irregular. It has three tenses. In the present tense it takes a suffix; for the future the imperfective forms of the verb *hoona* 'become' are used. In the past the copula suffix cooccurs with the verb *naara* 'was'.

The Present Tense Copula

Sg. 1	*-nku*	Pl. 1	*-nna*
2m.	*-nk*	2c.	*-nkumu*
f.	*-nš*		
3m.	*-n*	3c.	*-niimu*
f.	*-nt*		

Examples:

zeegaa-nna
[poor-COP. (pl. 1)]
'We are poor.'

attaay miiš duureešša yoonaan
[that-the man rich he-will-be/become]
'That man will be/become rich.'

mištite bilṭint naart
[wife-and-the clever-COP. (sg. 3f.) she-was]
'The wife was clever.'

If the complement consists of a phrase, the copula is suffixed to its first constituent:

addaddii zeegaa-n sab
[some-the poor-COP. (sg. 3m.) people]
'Some are poor people.'

If the word to which the copula is suffixed has a possessive suffix, the copula precedes the possessive (or determiner), cf. p. 512:

mutoot-in-kaay
[to-die(= infinitive)-COP. (sg. 3m.)-his-the]
'He is going to die.' (= it is his dying)

With personal pronouns and proper names the copula has the uninflectible form *-t*:

yañaam baalagaara waanna ataa-t
[of-us-and enemy main you-COP.]
'And you are our main enemy.'

karaabčaay ya-uhnu-t
[oxen-the theirs-COP.]
'The oxen are theirs.'

yamaṭaatte faaṭmaa-t
[REL.-she-came-the Fatima-COP.]
'It is Fatima who came.'

Existential Expressions

The verb of existence is *ala* 'there is' (neg. *eela*), past tense *naara* (*alnaarku* 'I was not (present))'. Both are inflected like simple past tense verbs: *alahu* 'I am (present)' (*eelahu* 'I am not (present))', *naarku* 'I was (present)', etc.

Possessive Expressions

Possession is expressed by the verb of existence with object suffixes. The subject suffix refers to the thing possessed, the object suffix to the possessor. *kitaab ala-ñ/eela-ñ* 'I have/don't have a book', *feeqča alu-y/eelu-y* 'He has some/hasn't any goats', *waašt naart-eet/alnaart-eet* 'she had/didn't have an older sister'.

Reference

Leslau, Wolf. 1992. "Sketches in Ethiopian Classification, 3. The Position of Zway." In *Gurage Studies: Collected Articles.* Wiesbaden: Harrassowitz. 554–558.

Further Reading

Gutt, Eeva H. M. and Hussein Mohammed. 1996. *Trilingual Dictionary Silt'e–Amharic–English* (shorter version). Addis Ababa: Summer Institute of Linguistics.
Gutt, Ernst-August. 1983."Studies in the Phonology of Silt'i." *Journal of Ethiopian Studies* 16: 37–73.
—— 1986. "On the Conjugation of the Silte Verb." *Journal of Ethiopian Studies* 19: 91–112.
—— Forthcoming. "A Concise Grammar of Silt'e." In *Trilingual Dictionary Silt'e–Amharic–English* (longer version), E. H. M. Gutt and H. Mohammed. Addis Ababa: Addis Ababa University Press.
Leslau, Wolf. 1979. *Etymological Dictionary of Gurage*, volumes 1–3. Wiesbaden: Harrassowitz.

23 *Outer South Ethiopic*

Robert Hetzron

Outer South Ethiopic (OSE) languages are spoken in the area west and south of Addis Ababa. Gafat has recently become extinct and was spoken in the Goddjam Governorate General, in Western Ethiopia. The rest, the Gunnän-Gurage tongues, are spoken in the so-called Gurage region, a Semitic enclave surrounded by Rift Valley (Highland East) Cushitic languages, about 100 km south of Addis Ababa, along with East Gurage (see "Silte," Chapter 22 in this volume) which belongs to the other major branch of South Ethiopic. Even though the area of GG is separate from the one recently vacated by Gafat by hundreds of kilometers, it is reasonable to posit that once there was a continuous OSE territory enclosing the ones mentioned and what is between them. Whether the map of Africa by the Dutch geographer Abraham Ortelius (1527–1598), which shows Gafat and Gurage to be contiguous, is to be taken as a proof remains to be seen.

Gurage is known to be the scene of the ensete-culture, where much of the economy is based on the false banana plant (*ensete edulis*) which is used as food and as raw material for clothing and utensils by the population.

The history of the people who speak these languages is limited to recent times. Catholic missionaries were active in Chaha, leaving there a minor cultural heritage, churches and citrus plantations. The Soddo are usually Coptic Christians; among the Chaha and others one finds Roman Catholics, and, along with some Muslims, there is survival of the native religion as well.

Gafat has the oldest document within this group, a translation (from Amharic, itself from Ge'ez) of the Songs of Solomon, commissioned by the Scottish traveler James Bruce in the 1870s. Elicited by Wolf Leslau, Chaha has become the only GG language with a literary product: *Shinega's Village* by Sahle Sellasie, a vivid description of life in Chaha country. Otherwise, texts are available in linguistic publications.

After pioneering research by Marcel Cohen, H. J. Polotsky and others, it was Wolf Leslau who put Gurage (with East Gurage included) on the map, through numerous publications. Since then, G. Goldenberg has given details of Soddo, Carolyn M. Ford of Chaha, J. F. Prunet of Inor.

Genetically speaking, OSE divided into an ***n*-group** (Gafat, Soddo (Kistaninnya, Aymellel) and Goggot (Dobbi)) and a ***tt*-group** (Muher, and the other branch, Western Gurage (**WG**), consisting of Masqan and a major branch **CP-**

535

WG, subdivided into Central Western Gurage (**CWG:** Ezha, Chaha, Gumer, Gura) and Peripheral Western Gurage (**PWG:** Gyeto, Inor (earlier called Ennemor), Endegen, Ener). This is based on an isogloss in the main verb markers (p. 544) . Typologically, Soddo, Goggot and Muher form an *a posteriori* unit ("Northern Gurage," **NG**), relatively archaic, the only languages to have preserved full use of the main verb markers (the other languages exhibit traces only). Other typological features and vocabulary items, but not genetic criteria, connect the Gunnän-Gurage (**GG**) languages, i.e. OSE without Gafat, with East Gurage. The above abbreviations will be used in the text.

The surrounding Cushitic languages, of the Sidamo type, left a very deep mark on GG, throughout the structure of language. Inevitably, the official language Amharic, widely spoken in the area, has also left a noticeable imprint.

The "dialect vs. separate language" division works above the level of the CWG and PWG clusters. For the latter two groups, dialectal boundaries are not clear and the resemblance level of the constituent units is so great that it is better to consider both as dialect clusters and not separate languages. However, though grammar makes them separate, all the GG languages are quite similar, passage from one of them to the other is easy. Some mixed idiolects, Chaha–Ezha, Chaha–Muher, have also been found, especially in children of mixed marriages.

The following is a selective comparative statements showing phenomena shared by all the languages involved, as well as phenomena characterizing only some of them.

Phonology

Phonologically, the most conservative language is Soddo, and the most innovative: Inor. Parentheses indicate that the phoneme in question does not occur in all the languages.

Consonants

The Inventory
The noncoronal consonants (those where the closure is not done with the tongue) have labialized counterparts. The velars have palatalized counterparts as well.

b	b^w	(β)	d	ǧ z	ž g	g^w	g^y
(p)	(p^w)	f f^w	t	č s	š k	k^w	k^y
			ṭ	č̣	q	q^w	q^y
m	m^w		n	(ñ)			
(w̃)	$(\tilde{\beta})$	(r̃)					
w			r, l		h, (ʾ)	h^w, $(ʾ^w)$	h^y

Distribution
Nasalized consonants occur in PWG only, as a result of lenition (see p. 537). Con-

sonantal gemination exists in Gafat, Soddo, Goggot, Muher, Masqan and Ezha, which have no p/p^w ($< *bb$), and [β] (which nowhere occurs word initially) is not phonemic. Elsewhere, except Ener, gemination is but sporadic. In these languages, geminate consonants (as in *säbbära* 'he broke') were first devoiced (Ener *säppärä*, then degeminated (Chaha–Inor *säpärä*). CWG has no *ñ*. /l/ is rare, and is often geminated in Chaha and Inor. Soddo, Goggot, Muher, Inor, Ener and Endegen have /ʾ/ coming from *q*, but in the latter three, it may also be the trace of an older *ʿ or *ʾ, forming a cluster with a voiced consonant that has no voiceless counterpart (β, w, w̃, m, β̃, n, r, r̃, l, y): Inor *säm a* 'he heard' ($< *sam^ʿa$, elsewhere *säm(m)a*).

Lenition
These are consonantal alternations governed by position and morphophonemic criteria. The former start out as subphonemic, articulatory changes, e.g. initial *b-* → intervocalic *-β-* after a prefix, but when intervocalic *b* arises, the *b*/β alternation becomes phonemic.

In the CPWG languages, the following changes take place when a word-initial consonant receives a prefix:

b- → *-β-* (Chaha, Gyeto, Inor) *-w-* (Endegen, Ener)
n- → *-r̃-* (Inor)/*-r-* (CWG, Gyeto)
m- → *-β̃-* (PWG, sometimes *-w-* in Ener)
m^w- → *-w̃-* (Inor, Ener)/*-w-* (Endegen)

Two basic verb classes are distinguished throughout Ethiopian according to whether the mid radical is geminate or not in the past. In the nonpast, these are always geminate. This is descriptively still true of Gafat, Soddo (except for *-nn-* < *-ll-*), Goggot, but Muher, Masqan and Ezha exhibit also qualitative change for three instances: as against geminate/nongeminate, they have *nn/r, kk/h, kk^y/h^y*. The rest have altogether dropped gemination and added voiceless ~ voiced alternations: Gafat: *bällä/yəbälä*, Soddo: *bänna-/yəbäya-*, Masqan/Ezha: *bänna(-)* ~ *yəbära*, Chaha-Inor: *bäna/yəβära* 'he ate/eats' (see further p. 538).

Third radicals may only have the second term of these alternations.

Liquids
The phoneme /l/ is the "weak point" of the phonemic system throughout the area, *l* → *n* is common. But the most systematic changes took place in CWG and PWG. Leaving details aside, /l/, /r/ and /n/ merged in the following way: always *n-/-n(n)-* in initial position or in original gemination; *-r-* intervocalically, though *-r̃-* in Inor when it comes from *n*, *r* elsewhere. When a prefix is added, initial *n-* becomes *-r-* (*-r̃-* in Inor, but remains *-n-* in Endegen and Ener). A new /ll/ (always geminated) was later added to these languages.

Internal Labialization (IL)
As a result of the absorption of an original final **u:*, the *tt*-languages labialize the
relatively last noncoronal consonant in some morphological context: the impersonal, pl. 3m. and the infinitive in PWG except Gyeto, and before light sg. 3m.
object suffixes in Masqan, CWG and Gyeto: Masqan: *yagd* 'he ties' + *-nn* 'him/it'
→ *yag^{w}d-ənn*.

End Palatalization (EP)
In PWG other than Gyeto, in the morphological contexts of impersonal, pl. 3m.
and infinitive, end palatalization accompanies internal labialization; it occurs by
itself in pl. 3f. in the same languages and in the Muher impersonal. It involves the
dental consonants: *d* → *ğ*, *t* → *č*, *ṭ* →*č̣*, *z* → *ž*, *s* → *š*. In addition, in the sg. 2f. form
of the prefix conjugations, the tt-languages have end palatalization also involving
the velars and postvelars, and *r* → *y*. This phenomenon, in both of its manifesta-
tions, affects the **last** consonant of the verbal word, e.g. *wəṭäq/wəṭäq^y* 'fall!' (sg.
m./f.).

Vowels

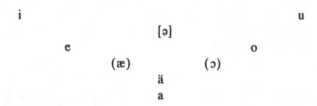

The vowel *ɔ* occurs in Chaha and Muher, *æ* in Goggot, Muher, Chaha, Gumer and
Inor. Both come from diphthongs. [ə] is not a phoneme, but an epenthetic vowel
meant to dissolve undesirable consonant clusters. The labial vowels *o/u* are indistinguishable from *ä/ə* after a labialized consonant.

Relevant vocalic length exists only in PWG, which has double vowels (new
formations), consisting of two moræ: Inor *moodä* 'he died' (cf. Chaha *m^{w}ätä-*),
and also word-final diphthongs *-ua/-oa*, alternating with *-u-/-oo-* before a further
suffix.

Long Nasalization
This is clearly attested in Inor only, though traces in the other PWG languages
(minus Gyeto) suggest that it used to be more widespread.

In Proto-PWG, in a non-initial, non-geminate position, the following changes
took place: *m* → *β̃*, *n* → *r̃*, *m^w* → *w̃*; root-final *β* → *m^w*. The creation of this set of
nasal fricatives had consequences: nasality spread to the neighboring phonemes
chainwise, through direct contact in both directions, in the following manner: all
vowels are affected, *r* → *r̃*, *β* → *β̃*, *w* → *w̃*. Though themselves not perceptibly nasalized, ' and *y* let the nasalizing chain pass through them. When the nasalizing

chain encounters any other phoneme, nasalization stops, and, unless word final, the end of the nasal chain produces an imperfectly closed *n*. Examples: *näpärä* 'he was, lived, there was' has Chaha *yəräßər* in the present, but in Inor the corresponding **yəräßər* becomes [yə̃rä̃ß ə̃r̃]; for Chaha *yəmäsər*, Inor has [yə̃ßä̃ⁿsər]; for Chaha *ayß* 'cottage cheese', Inor has [äyə̃ß] 'milk'.

Stress

In most languages stress, a slight raise of the pitch, is not relevant. Only PWG has a system that is meaningful even for grammar. The following presentation refers to Inor, where these phenomena were investigated in detail.

The basic stress rule is: a final closed syllable is stressed; when the final syllable is open, the stress is penultimate: *ä-säp'ärä* 'he broke$_{rel.}$', *yəsäß'ər* 'he breaks'. Final *-e*, *-i* are always stressed: *yəsäwər-'i* 'one breaks/they break it$_m$.' (a synchronic interpretation of these as **/äy/* and **/əy/* does not work for other reasons). Long vowels and diphthongs behave like a sequence of two vowels: *bi'd* 'house', *ga'ara* 'loin'. What complicates the system is that these languages possess a multi-functional suffix *-m* which produces a final closed syllable, attracting stress, and in PWG it disappeared, at a period when the old vocalic length was still relevant, after final short vowels, leaving the expression of its function to the surviving, now functionally distinctive stress. Thus, Proto-PWG (still so in Chaha) *säpär'äm* 'he broke' (≠ subordinate *-säp'ärä*) became PWG **säpär'ä* (≠ subordinate *-säp'ärä*). But one more step was added by the introduction of an accentual harmony rule. A short vowel in a penultimate open syllable is also stressed when followed by a final stressed syllable with a vowel other than *-e/-i*: *säp'ä'rä* 'he broke'. This creates a sequence of two stressed syllables, with the acoustic effect of a sequence of two high tones, with two peaks. Another accentual harmony occurs in a sequence *-CC'e/i-'i* where the final stress is a substitute for *-m*: *säpärš'i'i* 'you$_{sg. f.}$ broke it$_m$.'. Finally, some suffixes have their own stress and do not alter the stress of their host: one more source of dual stress: *yəsäß'ər-k^w'e* 'he will break' (definite future).

Morphology

Pronouns

Verbal subject affixes are not included here.

Gafat has no gender distinction in the plural. Soddo pl. 2/3m. has *-u-* before a suffix. In GG 2nd person pronouns original oblique pronoun person markers took over.

The GG possessive pronouns come from suffixed independent pronouns, the occasional connective *-ä-* harks back to the genitive prefix *-yä*.

Table 23.1   Independent pronouns

		Gafat	Soddo	Muher	Ezha	Inor
Sg.	1	anät(ti)	ädi	anä	əyya	əya
	2m.	ant(ä)	dähä	ahä	ahä	ahä
	f.	anči	däš	ahʸ	ahʸ	ašä
	3m.	wət	kʷa	hʷa	hʷət	huda
	f.	yət	kʸa	hʸa	hʸət	hida
Pl.	1	ənni	əñña	əñña	yəna	ina
	2m.	ənnant{ä/tum}	dähəm(u-)	ahəmʷ	ahu	ahua
	f.		dähma	ahma	ahma	ahaa
	3m.	ə(nnä)llämʷ	kənnäm(u-)	hənnämʷ	həno	hunoa
	f.		kənnäma	hənnäma	hənäma	hənaa

Table 23.2   Possessive pronouns

		Gafat	Soddo	Muher	Ezha	Inor
Sg.	1	-(ə)ǧǧä	-äddi	-äñña	-äna	-ña
	2m.	-(ə)ha	-dä	-ahä	-ahä	-ahä
	f.	-(a)š	-däš	-ahʸ	-ahʸ	-aš
	3m.	-(ə)ho	-kʷan/-(ä)w	-uhta	-ota	-hʷa
	f.	-(ə)hä	-ki	-əhʸta	-eta	-ša
Pl.	1	-(ə)nnä	-ñña	-ənna	-ändra	-nəra
	2m.	-(ä)hamʷ	-dähəm(u-)	-ahəmʷ	-ahu	-ahua
	f.		-dähma	-ahma	-ahma	-ahaa
	3m.	-(ə)llämʷ	-hənnäm(u-)	-hənnämʷ	-ohna	-hunoa
	f.		-hənnäma	-hənnäma	-ähnäma	-hənaa

Complement Pronoun Suffixes
These comprise three sets:

O: basically the object pronouns also for the recipient;
B: used for 'in, with (instr.), to the detriment of';
L: for 'for, in favor of'.

In addition, GG has two major allomorph classes: heavy, after sg. 2f. and plural subjects which used to end in a long vowel, and light elsewhere, except for mixed use after sg. 1 of the past. Light O suffixes have two subsets, one after the past and one after the other forms. Further complications do not fit into the framework of this survey. In the following, I am only giving the system of one language, Muher. Gafat has the pl. 2/3 endings *-hum ~ -kkəml-(nnä)mʷ*. The allomorphs are light and heavy as in GG (though sg. 2f. is light). In PWG and Gafat, the plural ending *-ual-mʷ* disappears before pronoun suffixes.

Table 23.3   Complement pronoun suffixes: O, L, B

Person of complement	O Light Past	Nonpast	Heavy	L Light	Heavy	B Light	Heavy
Sg. 1c.	-e	-e	-ññ	-nni	-nni	-bbi	-bbi
2m.	-nnaxä	-xä	-kkä	-nxä	-nnəkkä	-bxä	-bbəkä
f.	-nnahʸ	-hʸ	-y	-nhʸ	-nnəkʸ	-bhʸ	-bbəkkʸ
3m.	-nn/-u	-ʷ/ʸː	-ya	-no	-nno	-wä	-bbʷä
f.	-nna/-wa	-ːa		-na	-nna	-ba	-bba
Pl. 1c.	-nä	-änä	-nnä	-nnənä	-nnənä	-bbənä	-bbənä
2m.	-nnaxmʷ	-xəmʷ	-kkəmʷ	-nxəmʷ	-nnəkkəmʷ	-bxəmʷ	-bbəkkemʷ
f.	-nnaxma	-xma	-kkəma	-nxəma	-nnəkkəma	-bxəma	-bbəkkəma
3m.	-nnämʷ	-ːämʷ	-yämʷ	-nämʷ	-nnämʷ	-bämʷ	-bbämʷ
f.	-nnäma	-ːäma	-yäma	-näma	-nnäma	-bäma	-bbäma

Nouns

Gender and Number

Except for a few residual -t endings (məs/məšt 'man/woman'), nouns have no feminine endings. For plural-marking, Gafat has -ač, Soddo and Goggot have -očč, but for some nouns Soddo has a reduplicative ending -aCä (C = repetition of the last consonant): gurz/gurzazä 'old man/men'. Soddo also has cases of broken plural, on Cushitic borrowings: gäräd/gərid 'girl/girls' (also gəridadä for 'girls'). The tt-languages usually do not mark the gender and the number on the noun; these are indicated only by agreement: on definitizers, coreferential pronouns and, if subject, on the verb: Inor: bariq huda/hida/hunoa/hənaa 'old + person he/she/they_m./they_f.' for 'the ~ that old man/old woman/old men ~ people/old women'. Yet a handful of nouns have suppletive plurals: Inor äč/deengʸa 'boy/boys', and one broken plural, Inor gäräd/gərʿed 'girl/girls'.

Definiteness

The definite article is placed after the first component of the noun phrase, thus after the qualifier if there is one. It is -š in Gafat: wäy-əš gäǧǧä 'the new house' (lit. 'new-the house), feminine also -it. It precedes the object ending -n. In GG its use is restricted to a "discourse-referential" function: "the above-mentioned." Soddo, Goggot, Masqan and Inor have the ending -i (Soddo has an optional feminine article -iti), Muher and Ezha have -we, the rest (often Inor as well) use postposed 3rd person independent pronouns (see Gender and Number, above).

For newly introduced items, there is an indefinite article, the same as the numeral 'one' in Soddo and Goggot, and the original form of this numeral (a)at ≠ əmma(a)t 'one' the present form.

Case Marking

As in Amharic, as against three sets of adverbal pronoun suffixes a longer list of adnominal case markers are used.

Adnominal Prefixes, Suffixes and Circumfixes/-Positions

The subject, most objects and cognate instrumentals (for compounds as in English *spoon-feed*) have zero marking.

Prefixes: *-(y)ä-* for the dative, optionally for definite objects and for the genitive 'of'; locative *bä-* 'in/at' and ablative from'; comitative *tä-* '(along) with', *bä-/tä-* 'than' (for comparative constructions), Gafat *(əm)mä-* 'in/at, from, than'.

Suffixes: Gafat only: optional *-än* for an object; Soddo *-yy(än)*, Goggot–Muher *-t*, PWG *-i*, Gafat postposition *fänna*, elsewhere *-e* for 'toward'; *-sən*, Gafat *sälä* 'till, as far as'. There is an optional vocative in *-o*.

Samples of circumfixes/-positions: *(y)ä-* ... *hä(ma)*/Gafat *əndä* 'like'; *bä-* ... *f"är*/Gafat *laǧǧä* 'on'; Gafat *tä-* ... *biǧǧä/dibä* 'with (comitative)', etc. In genitival construction, the initial *(y)ä-* of the possessor drops if there is a further preposition: Inor *ä-məs biid* 'the man's house', but *bä-məs biid* 'in the man's 'house'.

Adjectives

Adjectives exhibit no gender or number, except for some sporadic cases of middle reduplication Soddo *gəddər/gədəddər* 'big/big, every one of them'. They are understood to be comparative adjectives if a basis of comparison is present with the prefix *bä-* or *tä-* optionally followed by a form of verb 'exceed' or 'be better', e.g. Inor *bä-/tä-hunoa (yāřää⁽ nämädä-n-ə* ['than-them (he + exceeds) he + loved-himending'] 'he liked him more than them'.

Demonstratives

The basic pattern is *zəh/za* for 'this ~ these/that ~ those' with no distinction of gender and number. In CWG and PWG *hə/ha* is also attested, with no discernable difference in meaning. PWG has *waa/haa* for 'this/that' (or pl.) before nouns, but *waada/haada* 'this/that one' by itself. Inor has presentative pronouns of the *voici* type: *yähä/yäš/yähua/yähaa* 'here is for you (sg. m./sg. f./pl. m./pl. f.)' with object pronouns. Gafat has *əññə/aññə* 'this/that', optionally combined with the definite article, presentative *ənnäho*.

Numerals

The basic cardinal numbers in Soddo and Inor are:

	Soddo	Inor		Soddo	Inor
1	*quna (att)*	*əmmaat (aat)*	8	*səmmənt*	*süüt*
2	*kitt*	*wər'et*	9	*zäṭäñ*	*žïʾä̃*
3	*sost*	*so'ost*	10	*assər*	*assər*
4	*aratt*	*arβ'ät*	20	*kuya*	*huya*
5	*amməst*	*am'əst*	30	*sassa*	*bä'ər*
6	*səddəst*	*sədəst*	100	*mäto*	*hü*
7	*säbatt*	*säβ'at*	1000	*ši*	

The parenthesized *att/aat* are used as an indefinite article, or in counting: "1, 2, 3 ..." but not as numerals with nouns. "Teens" and "tens + digits" are formed by adding digits to the tens (which end in *-a*).

Ordinal numbers get a suffix: *-əläññä* in Masqan, *-änä* in Chaha; in Inor, final *-t* is replaced by *-čä*.

Numerals may be followed by possessive endings; if a suffix *-m(ä)-* is inserted, totality is implied: Inor *soʾost-nərä* 'we three', but *so osčä-mä-nərä* 'all three of us'.

The expression for 'all': Soddo *kulləm*, Chaha *ənnəm* are the only modifiers that follow the noun modified.

Note also the system used, beyond "yesterday/tomorrow" for a full week before and after: Inor *saβʾätərä* 'six days ago' *saβʾätä* 'six days from now' (containing the archaic ordinal form of 'six').

Verbs

Root Classes

Verbs with only consonantal radicals (which may be subject to morphophonemic alternations, cf. p. 537) are **sound**, and those with one or two vocalic radicals are **weak**. The latter may have some features of their own in the conjugations. Most verbs have three radicals, a good number have four (many of them have the repetitious 1-2-1-2 pattern: *ǧəfäǧäfä* 'germinate'), and very few have two (Chaha *šä-* 'want').

Vocalic **first** radicals result from the disappearance of initial **ḥ* or **x*. In PWG, the initial vowel is lengthened after a prefix. Another source is the disappearance of initial **ʾ* and **ʿ*. In PWG, after prefix, the ʾ reappears (representing ʿ as well). In the other languages, all of these merge and no changes take place: Inor *anäβä/yāāřə̄β* 'he milked/milks' **√ḥlb*) vs. *akädä/yaʾagəd* 'he tied/ties' (**√ʾgd*), but Chaha *anäbä/yarəb* and *akädä/yagəd*.

Vocalic **mid** radicals may be *a ~ ä, e ~ i, o ~ u* representing old gutturals or semivowels, but original **h* produces *a ~ ə/Ø*, Soddo *daqo/yədäqu* 'he laughed/laughs' (**√ḏhq*), but *šalo/yəšlu* 'he knew/knows' (**√khl*). PWG may have ʾ as a mid radical for old **ʾ/ʿ*; for **h* it has short vowels: *harä/yəhər* 'he knew/knows' (*√*khl*), but long ones for the rest: *daaʾä/yədää ʾ* 'he laughed/laughs' (*√*ḏhq*).

Final *a-* is the vocalic **last** radical when resulting from the disappearance of a guttural. As above, PWG distinguishes between verbs that originally had **ḥ* or **x*, – the *-a* is lengthened before a suffix, and verbs with original **ʾ* or ʿ: the vowel remains short, and, if compatible (see p. 536), a glottal stop appears before the *-a*: *yəfäda* 'he unties' – *yəfädaa-ku* 'he unties it (/him)' (*√*ftḥ*), but *yəgäfa/yəgäfaku* 'he pushes /him' (*√*gfʾ*) and *yəβʾära/yəβʾära-ku* 'he eats /it'. Verbs coming from roots with final **-y* have an alternation *-ä/Ø*. Unlike in sound verbs, the *-ä* is stable throughout the past tense conjugation (see p. 544), and there is Ø ending in the other forms though, if palatalizable, the second radical will be palatalized in most of its conjugation in other than PWG, except in pl. 3m. and in the impersonal: Chaha *bäkʸä/bäkʸähu/bäkäbo/yəβähʸ* 'he/I/they cried/he cries'.

OSE makes use of **compound descriptive** verbs consisting of an uninflected interjection, onomotopoeia or a word derived from a nominal or verbal root, plus a conjugated verb 'say' for intransitive use or a verb 'make' for transitive acceptations: Gafat *čəq balä* 'be quiet', Inor *akəya barä* 'agree' ('say alright'), *gawgaw barä* 'be insane' (cf. *gawa* 'stupid', *gawgawt* 'madness'), Masqan *daqq barä* 'laugh' (cf. the verb *daqä* 'laugh').

Derivation Classes

There are three lexically determined base forms: **Type A** with a vowel *-ä-* between the first two radicals in the indicative, with the penultimate consonant geminated or devoiced (in non-geminating languages) in the past, **Type B** with a palatal vowel (*e/i*) or palatalized first radical in the same position and gemination/devoicing in all tenses, and **Type C** with *-a-* with gemination/devoicing in the indicative. Finally, a **reduplicative** (frequentative, iterative) may be derived from root through repetition of the mid radical with an *ä* or *a* in between. The first occurrence of the radical has the weak degree and the second the strong one (see p. 537), e.g. Ezha *səbäbbärä-* 'smash' (cf. *säbbärä* 'break').

The above forms may have further prefix extensions, labeled according to their productive use, even though they are often lexically determined: *tä-* **passive reflexive** and, with Type C or the reduplicative: **reciprocal**. The prefix *a-* is a **causative**; *at-* is a more productive **causative** or **coercive**. Quadriradical verbs, including the reduplicative, may have intransitive *ən-/tän-* and transitive *an-* for **gradual**.

Tenses and Moods

The basic tense/mood forms are the suffix-conjugated **past**, the prefix-conjugated **nonpast** and **jussive**, the latter supplemented with suffixes in sg. 2f. and in the plural (pl. 1c. not in Soddo and Gafat).

The following categories refer to **main clauses** only.

The past form alone expresses the **past** tense. In an affirmative main clause, they are followed by a **"main verb marker"** in Soddo, Goggot and Muher (simplistically put: *-n* (Soddo/Goggot) or *-tt* (Muher) after original long vowels (sg. 2f., pl. 2/3m.f.) and *-u* elsewhere (after original short vowels or consonants). Gafat requires no special ending and the rest have *-m* or equivalent (final stress often in PWG) in the main position. The ending *-m* forms a **present perfect** in Soddo, Goggot and Muher. **Past perfect** is expressed by adding an invariable "was" to the past tense form. See further p. 546, Coordination. In negation, marked by *al-/an-* (and a suffix *-ka/-ta/-da* in PWG), there is no present perfect.

The nonpast form is a **present** in CWG/PWG, a **present–future** elsewhere. In Soddo, Goggot and Muher main verb markers are used in main clauses. CWG/PWG have two **future** tenses, a nonpast-based **definite** one when the future action or happening is deemed certain, and a jussive-based **indefinite** one for uncertainty, wishful thinking, fear of what may happen, etc. (see more below). A **durative–habitual** past obtains when the nonpast form is followed by an invariable "was": Soddo *yəbəl näbbär* 'he kept saying'. In negation, marked by *t-* in Soddo main clauses and *a-* (+ gemination where it exists) elsewhere, with a further suffix *-kal-tal-da* in PWG main clauses, there is only a present–future everywhere and a negated durative–habitual based on *b-* + negative nonpast.

Conjugations

Gafat makes a gender distinction in sg. 2/3, GG has gender in all non-1st-persons and has, in addition, an impersonal (from an old pl. 3m.) corresponding in function to a general agent "one" or to an agentless passive (for IL + EP see p. 538).

Person marking is summed up in Table 23.4, below.

Table 23.4   Person marking

	Past Singular	Plural	Present/Jussive Singular	Plural
1c.	-hu/hʷ	-nä	*Pr.* ä-/-n-/*Juss.* nə-	nə- ... -nä
2m.	-hä	-həmu/-hu(a)	tə-	tə- ... -ämu
f.	-hʸ/š	-həma/-haa	tə- ... -i/ EP, etc.	tə- ... -äma
3m.	-ä	-mu/-o/-ua	*Pr.* yə-/*Juss.* (y)ä-	yə- ... -ämu
f.	-äčč/-ätt	-äma/-aa	tə-	yə- ... -äma
Impersonal		IL + EP		yə- ... IL + EP

In the past, some languages have *k* instead of *h*. In the present sg. 1c. *-n-* is used after a subordinating prefix. In pl. 1 Gafat and Soddo have no suffixal element. See p. 540.

The definite future is formed by attaching a suffix *-te* to the present in CWG, but in PWG only to those persons of the present that have a suffix, the rest have *-kʷe*. The indefinite future is the jussive form (but with *ä-* in sg. 1c.) plus *-šäl-se* (< 'want'). The *t*-converb (see p. 547) consists of a root form with a palatal vowel toward the end + *-t(t)ä-* + the past tense endings.

In Type A, the thematic vowel of the stem is lexically determined in GG, e.g. Chaha *yəsβər* 'let him break!', but *yərkäβ* 'let him find!'. In the affirmative 2nd persons, i.e. in the imperative, there is no prefix: *səβər* 'break!', but there is one in prohibitions: *atəsβər* 'don't break!'. The imperative of 'come' is suppletive sg. 2m. *nähä* 'come!' for the verb *mäṭṭa/čänä*, etc.

Verbal Nouns and Participles

There are two types of infinitives based on the jussive stem, with a prefix *wä-* (the only type in Gafat, Soddo, Goggot and Muher) or with a suffix *-ot*, or developments thereof. There are no productive participles, only some scattered relics survive.

Syntax

Word Order

The typical word order is "Sentence–Adverb (Time, the type 'therefore', 'afterwards')–Subject–Complement(s)–Verb" with very few exceptions. Qualifiers (adjectives, demonstratives, numerals, possessors, with the exception of definite articles which are placed after the first word of the noun phrase: Soddo *yä-č̣ạkk-i awreočč* 'the [-*i*] animals of the forest', Inor *a β̃ǝs huda*ᵢ *adood* 'the*ᵢ* man's mother') and quantifiers (except for postposed 'all') precede the element qualified, subordinate clauses stand before the governing clause.

Agreement rules

The verb expresses person, number and gender. As the CPWG noun itself rarely marks number and gender (see p. 541), the agreement is based on meaning: Ezha *siṭar*ᵢ *wässädä*/Inor *siṭaar*ᵢ *wäsädäč* 'the devil*ᵢ* took', where the Ezha devil (Satan) is masculine, the Inor one feminine, as revealed by the verb. Demonstratives and adjectives have no agreement, but in PWG definite articles ≅ distant demonstratives do, again with the meaning: e.g. Inor: *äsäm huda*$_{sg. m.}$/*hida*$_{sg. f.}$/*hunoa*$_{pl. m.}$/*hǝnaa*$_{pl. f.}$ 'the brother/sister/brothers ~ siblings/sisters'.

A definite case-marked nominal complement may be referred to by a complement pronoun suffix after the verb of the same clause for emphasis; in CPWG, gender and number may only be explicit in the suffix, Ezha *tǝkäna*ⱼš *b*ʷ*änan-n*ᵢ-*ǝm* 'he ate [him*ᵢ*], my son*ⱼ*'.

Questions

Sentence-questions may have an optional sentence-final particle -*we*. Interrogative pronouns are placed directly before the verb, so will the answer word. Some of these: 'who' is *m*ʷ*a(n)* (a composite representation), is *mǝn/r* 'what, which' (may be followed by a noun), *mǝqar* (*qar* 'thing') is 'what' (self-standing), 'where' has *aay, eti* and the like, 'why' is "for + what," Inor *a β̃ə̄f̃*. For "when," Chaha has at least two forms, one for the nonpast, one for the past: *mäčä yǝtänšä* 'when will he come?', but *mäčrä čä꞉ɪäm* 'when did he come?' (-*rä* is the remnant of a word meaning 'day').

Coordination

Phrasal coordination

In Soddo/Masqan/Gafat, the particle -*nna*/-*nna* ~ -*wa*/-*mma* is placed after all non-final constituents of the conjoining: Gafat *wǝt-ǝmma abo-ho-mma alǝ-ho* 'he-and father-his-and brother-his', Masqan *säb-wa awre* 'people and animals'. For a closer connection, -*m* (or equivalent) may be placed after all the constituents: Ezha *at mǝst-ǝm mǝs-ǝm* 'a woman and a man' (preceded by 'one ~ a').

Conditionals in Chaha

	If-clause	Then-clause
Real	*bä-* + Past or	Regular main verb
	b-/t- + Nonpast	
Unreal	*tä-* + Past	CPWG (archaic) jussive, elsewhere
		Nonpast + *ba(nä)* 'was'

Examples:

Real: *bä-šä/b-išä äčänšä* 'if he wants it, I (may) come'
Unreal: *tä-šä ätän ba* 'if he (had) wanted, I would (have) come'.

Converbs

Converbs (also called "gerunds") are a category overlapping what coordination and subordination are meant to achieve. They are marked by an ending *-m* (or, partly, final stress in PWG, see p. 539), which may be attached to one of the basic tense forms: past, nonpast, jussive in agreement with a governing tense/mood-marking verb: Masqan *bänna-m wärä* 'he ate and left' *yǝbära-m yar* 'he eats and leaves/he will eat and leave', *yäbra-m yar* 'let him eat and leave!', but in subordination marking no tense *-m* combines with the past: Masqan *bänna-m tǝyar* 'when he had/will have eaten and left/will leave' (see p. 548). Thus, the nonfinal coordinate clause will have the *m*-converb form which only marks tense/mood, and the person of the subject (most often, but not necessarily the same as the subject of the governing verb: Inor *ä-wǝrʾ ečä-m-äh*ᵂ*noa-y adood gänäžaa-m-ta ä-gäräd adood tä-gäräd-ša tǝ̄rǟ β̄r̄β̄-ä-gäräd-ša äw̄äQMō-yä* 'the mothers of both became old and one took the girl's mother to live with her daughter', lit. 'of-both-Topic-their_sg. m.-the mother became + old_pl. f.pl.-Converb-*ta*[see below] of-girl-mother with-daughter-her lives_sg. f.-in + order + to to-daughter-her-the one+ brought-her-M[main past ending]).

In addition, the converb may be an adverbial modifier, in which case it is always in the past, e.g. Masqan *täzäbbärä-m yar* 'he is going back', lit 'he returned-*m* he + goes'.

The *t*-converb in the CPWG languages (see p. 545) occurs before negative verbs, and, in alternation with the *m*-converb, before forms other than the past: Inor *täzäpetä yaark*ᵂ*e/ayaarka* 'he will/will not go back'.

An element *-ta, tannä* etc. may follow the converb to optionally mark a bigger break between the clauses.

Subordination

Subordination is marked on the clause-final verb.

Tense-marking Subordinations

Complement Clauses

For quoting what has been said, **direct speech** (see p. 549) is used, but verbs like
"think, see, know" also combine with a **quotative** form that consists of the past or
nonpast of the verb with the case marker 'like', e.g. Gafat *ənd(ä)*, Soddo *yä-bän-
na-hom/yəbäya-hom äšlu* 'I know that he ate/is eating'. **Purposive** clauses governed volitive verbs have nonpast + 'like': *yəbäya-hom äšo* 'I want him to [that
he] eat'.

Relative Clauses

These are marked by *yä-* before the past and zero with the nonpast or by a suffix
-ka/-ta/-da in Ennemor; they precede the noun qualified: Chaha/Ennemor
yəsäβər/yəsäβər-(ka) məs 'the man who breaks'. With complement relatives pronoun suffixes after the verb will mark the case relation: Gumer y-aba-na $ær æ^{\flat} b_i$-
$iwär$-$wä_j$ $mädär$ 'to$_i$ the place in$_j$ which my father tends his cattle' lit. 'of-father-
my cattle in/to$_i$-he + tends-in$_j$ + it place'.

Temporal Clauses, etc.

The rest of the subordinate forms indicate no tense. They combine with past or
nonpast forms, independently of the time reference. The most important ones are:
with the nonpast: *t-* ... (*-ka/-ta/-da* in PWG) or *b-* 'when, while [the latter with no
suffix in PWG]' *t-* ... *sən* 'until'; with the past: Chaha *bä-/tä-* ... *gam^{w}ä* ["time"]/
yəfte/anq^{y}ä for 'when'/before/after', *yä-* ... *-e* 'because of', etc.

Copular and Possessive Expressions

The copula and the locative-existential verb ("there is") have a suppletive system.
The main present tense of the copula (present also in those languages that have
present-future elsewhere) is based on an *-n*-containing element + past tense endings (but see below for sg. 3m.), with the verb *härä*, etc. for subordination; the
locative main verb on CWG *närä*, PWG *anä-* Gafat, Soddo, Goggot *yən(ä)-*, etc.
The main past tense of both is *ba(a)nä/näb(b)ärä* or an invariable *ba*; the future
and all the subordinate forms are based on *h^{w}ärä-* 'to be'. A further main present
copula, often combined with the other one *-t(t)-* is used next to pronouns, often in
cleft constructions: Inor *waa zänga iiya-t-(ən)-a ar* 'this thing is mine' (lit. this
thing mine-is-(is)-thing'). The negative forms are also suppletive in the present.

The formal predicate is always a verb (including the copula). When the semantic predicate is an adjective, the following constructions have been observed
in the present tense:

Goggot/Masqan	*zi məss fäyya-n/-w*	'... good-is'
Chaha	*zə məs wähe qar-u*	'... good thing-is'
Inor	*waa məs wähe-n-a ar*	'... good-is-thing'
	'This man is good'	

As illustrated, in PWG the present tense affirmative copula is word final only if there is no suffix. If there is one, it precedes the suffix: Inor *waa məs äsäm-ənä-ña* 'this man is my brother' (lit. '... brother-is-my'), see below.

Possession is expressed by affixing object suffixes to *əzz-* (in the present only) in Gafat, elsewhere to the existential locative verb. The 3rd person possessor stands in the beginning of the sentence, as a topic, with no case mark: Gyeto *aat məs hoyt išta baanäßa-y-tä* 'a man had two wives' ('... was-him-Suffix').

Particles

In GG, clitic particles appear right after the verb or noun, preceding all other suffixes, though one finds some fluctuation when it cooccurs with the definite article. The most important one is *-m(-)*, a multifunctional particle (converb, past tense, conjoining) which, after the first phrasal element may stand for a contrastive topic 'as for', and some other kind of emphasis. The interrogative counterpart is *-š-*.

Examples: Masqan *näggade-mm-i/näggade-yi-m* 'and (as for) the merchant' (Topic-Article/Article-Topic), Inor *bər'äm-nä-ša* 'it is her **odor**' (lit. odor-Emph.-is-her).

Special features

While all these languages have a word for "yes," there is no "no" word – a negative verb must be used.

There is a predilection for using direct speech, even when no actual speaking takes place. Verbs of asking, answering, thinking, etc. are connected with the preceding direct speech by means of a converb of the verb 'say' (*bal/rä*), Inor *"waga oorskʷe" təyaaçämṭ* 'when he thought saying(!) "I will inherit money"', Soddo *sanqi-m "täkkäfät" yəbəl näbbär* 'the door wouldn't open' ('kept saying "I won't open"').

Further Reading

Ford, C. M. 1991. "Notes on the Phonology and Grammar of Chaha Gurage." *Journal of Afroasiatic Languages* 2(3): 231–296.

Goldenberg, G. 1968. "Kəstanəñña, Studies in a Northern Gurage Language of Christians." *Orientalia Suecana* 17: 61–102.

Hetzron, R. 1977. *The Gunnän–Gurage Languages.* Naples: Istituto Orientali di Napoli.

Leslau W. 1956. *Étude descriptive et comparative du Gafat (Éthiopien Méridional).* Paris: Klincksieck.

—— 1992. *Gurage Studies: Collected Articles.* Wiesbaden: Harrassowitz.

Index

Abbott, N. 44
Abboud, P. 298
abjads 16
  accents 30
  consonants 27
  description 27–35
  development 19–22
  letter names 33–5
  letter order 30–3
  origin 18–19
  vowels 30
  writing materials 41–2
ablaut 138
absolute state
  Akkadian 76, 80–1
  Aramaic 123
  Sayhadic 226
abugida 16, 17
  description 38
  history 23–4
accents 30
accusative
  adverbial 216
  Akkadian 79, 89
  Aramaic 123
  Classical Arabic 214–15, 216
  Eastern Neo-Aramaic 370
  Ge'ez 248–9
  Harari 492
  paronomastic (cognate; internal) 88
  Silte 514
  Ugaritic 135
active voice

  Arabic dialects 305
  Silte 524
  Ugaritic 138
adjectives
  Akkadian 81–2, 87–8
  Amharic 466
  Arabic dialects 284–5
  Aramaic 124
  Argobba 466
  Canaanite 180
  Classical Arabic 192, 194
  Eblaite 110
  Ge'ez 249
  Harari 493
  Hebrew 152–3, 164
  Modern Hebrew 319–20, 322–3
  Modern South Arabian Languages 393
  Outer South Ethiopic 542
  Phoenician 180
  Sayhadic 230
  Silte 514–15
  Syriac 124
  Syro-Aramaic 110
  Tigré 450
  Tigrinya 433–4
  Ugaritic 134, 135–6
adjuncts, synthetic 88–9
adverbial clauses
  Amharic 484–5
  Argobba 484–5
  Classical Arabic 217
  Modern Hebrew 328–9
  Modern South Arabian Languages 417–18

adverbs
  Aramaic 127
  Canaanite 184
  Ge'ez 255
  Harari 501
  Hebrew 155
  Modern South Arabian Languages 409
  Phoenician 184
  Sayhadic 237
  Silte 524
  Tigré 454
  Tigrinya 441
  Ugaritic 140–1
affirmation 167
afformatives, denominal
  Akkadian 75, 76–7
  Canaanite 179
  Phoenician 179
Afghan Arabic 263, 265
Agmon-Fruchtman, M. 325
agreement (concord) rules
  Arabic dialects 301–2
  Aramaic 128
  Canaanite 185
  Ge'ez 256–7
  Harari 502
  Hebrew 166–7
  Modern Hebrew 326–7
  Modern South Arabian Languages 413
  Outer South Ethiopic 546
  Phoenician 185
  Sayhadic 238
  Silte 529
  Tigrinya 441–2
  Ugaritic 142–3
agreement/disagreement particles 203
Akkadian 69–98
  decipherment 43
  external inflection 75–84
  internal inflection 70–5
  logographic writing 18
  morphophonemics 85–7
  Old Akkadian 7, 69
  phonemics 69–70
  script 17, 18, 25–7
  subgrouping 7, 8
  syntax 87–98
  texts 69

transcription 25
transliteration 25
Algerian Arabic 265
allative (ventive) 83
alphabets 16–17
  description 36–8
  history 22–3
Altaic script 21
alternation, morphophonemic
  Akkadian 85–7
  Hebrew 151–2
Amharic 457–85
  borrowings 457–8
  dialects 457
  Gurage region 536
  morphology 461–80
  phonology 458–60
  printing 42
  script 38
  syntax 480–5
  texts 457
Ammonite 174–86
  texts 175
  see also Canaanite; Phoenician
Amorite 100
  linguistic imperialism 3
  morphology 103–4
  phonology 101, 102–3
  script 17, 20, 101–2
  syntax 104
  texts 102
Anaiza Arabic (Najdi) 271, 273
Ancient Harari 486
Ancient Hebrew see Hebrew
Andalusian (Spanish) Arabic 263, 265, 270
apocopate 217–18
apodoses
  Akkadian 95
  Canaanite 185
  Hebrew 169
  Modern South Arabian Languages 416
  Phoenician 185
  Sayhadic 239
  Tigré 456
Arabic
  Afghan 263, 265
  Algerian 265
  Andalusian (Spanish) 263, 265, 270

Basran school 48–9
bedouin dialects *see* bedouin Arabic
Christian dialects 266–7
Classical *see* Classical Arabic
communal dialects 266–7
comparative Semitics 55–6
creoles 263
dialects 263–309
  emphatics 275–7
  interdentals 275
  jiim 274–5
  kaaf 273
  labials 275
  laryngeals 277
  lexicon 308
  morphology 281–98
  phonotactics 279–80
  syntax 298–308
diglossia 188, 267
Eastern dialects 265
gender-based differences 267
grammatical theory 50–5
grammatical tradition 46–57
Greek influence 48
Hijaaz 266
Jewish dialects 266–7
Juba 263, 280
Jugari 263, 265, 270, 271
Kufan school 48–9
Kuwaiti 265, 271, 273
letter names 35
lexicons 49–50, 55–6
Libyan 265
markedness 54–5
Mauritanian 265
Modern Standard 188–9, 267
Moroccan 265
morphology 52–5
morphophonology 53–4
Muslim dialects 266–7
Nigerian 277, 279, 280, 281
numerals 40
paleography 44
pharyngealization 8
phonetics 54
pidgins 263
printing 42
roots 52–3

script 21
stems 52–3
subgrouping 7, 8, 9, 10, 12–13
syntax 51–2
Tamiim 266
Tunisian 265
Uzbeki 263, 265, 270, 271
vowel letters 22
vowel points 23
Western dialects 265
Yemenite 273, 275
word division 25
Aramaic 114–30
  Classical *see* Classical Aramaic
  epigraphy 44
  Imperial (Official) *see* Imperial Aramaic
  Late Jewish Literary 118
  Middle 116–17, 122
  Modern *see* Modern Aramaic
  morphology 121–7
  Old *see* Old Aramaic
  paleography 44
  periods 114–19
  phonology 119–21
  script 20–2
  Standard Literary 115, 116
  subgrouping 7, 10
  syntax 127–30
  texts 114–19
  vowel letters 22
Archi, A. 101
Argobba 457–85
  morphology 461–80
  phonology 458–60
  syntax 480–5
Arnold, W. 334
Ashkenazi script 21
aspect
  Arabic dialects 304–5
  Aramaic 126
  Hebrew 156–8
  Silte 519–20
  Ugaritic 137–8
assertions
  Aramaic 128
  Sayhadic 238–9
  Silte 529
  Tigrinya 442

Ugaritic 143
assimilation
  Silte 510
  Tigrinya 426
Assyrian
  Middle Assyrian 69
  Old Assyrian 69
  script 21
  Soviet Union 36–8
al-Astarabadhi, Radi l-Din 50, 52, 55
asyndesis 171
attributes, nominal 213
attributive clauses 200–1, 213–14
attributive modifiers 165
Aymellel 535
Azarnat 509
  see also Silte
Azeri 348

Baalbaki, R. 49
Babylonian 118
  Classical 69
  imperfective formatives 126
  Late 69
  Middle 69
  Old 69
  phonology 120
  Standard 69
  vowel points 23
  vowels 121
Bakalla, M. 263
Barth's Law 103
Barthélemy, J.-J. 43, 44
Barth-Ginsberg law 138
Bathari 378–420
Bauer, H. 43
Bax'a 334–47
bedouin Arabic 266
  ghawa syndrome 281
  qaaf 270
Beeston, A.F.L. 13
Bendavid, A. 313
Bender, M. 457
benefactive 514
Bergsträsser, G. 5
Berman, R.A. 313, 315, 318, 322, 325, 326
bilinguals 43
binyanim

Hebrew xvi, 158–61
  Modern Hebrew 320–22
Birnbaum, S.R. 44
Blanc, H. 266, 276, 313
Blau, J. 9, 12, 188, 312
Bohas, G. 50, 54
Bolozky, S. 318
Bordreuil, P. 33
boustrophedon script 24
Brahmi script 21
Brockelmann, C. 5
Bruce, J. 535
Buckley, J. 44

Cagni, L. 101
Cairene 265, 276, 280
  qaaf 270
Canaanite 174–86
  lexicon 186
  morphology 176–85
  script 20
  subgrouping 4, 7, 10, 174
  texts 174
  see also Ammonite; El-Amarna;
    Hebrew; Moabite; Phoenician
Canaanite Shift 176
cantillation mark 30
Caplice, R. 7
Carter, M. 47, 48, 51
case
  Akkadian 77–82
  Arabic dialects 284
  Aramaic 123
  Canaanite 180
  Classical Arabic 195–6
  Eblaite 108–9
  Ge'ez 248–9
  Harari 492
  Hebrew 153
  Imperial Aramaic 123
  Outer South Ethiopic 541–2
  Phoenician 180
  Samalian 123
  Sayhadic 230
  Silte 513–14
  Standard Old Aramaic 123
  Tigrinya 432–3
  Ugaritic 135

Caspari, K.P. 46
Catford, J.C. 277
causative verbs 477–9
Central Semitic 7, 8–11
Cerulli, E. 492
Chaarmuuch 270
Chaha 535, 536
Christian dialects
    Arabic 266–7
    Palestinian Aramaic 117
circumpositions 529, 532
circumstantial clauses
    Arabic dialects 307–8
    Classical Arabic 216–17
    Hebrew 169
Classic Babylonian 69
Classical Arabic 187–218
    dialects 187
    grammar standard 188
    letter order 32–3
    morphology 191–211
    phonology 189–91
    post-Islam 187–8
    pre-Islamic 187
    script 27
    syntax 211–18
    texts 187–8
Classical Aramaic 117–18
    phonology 120
    vowels 121
clause division 24–5
clause types
    Arabic dialects 306–8
    Modern South Arabian Languages 411
cleft sentences 306
Code of Hammurapi 69, 100
Cohen, D. 9
Cohen, M. xvi, 244, 247, 535
comparative clauses
    Canaanite 186
    Phoenician 186
complement clauses
    Akkadian 87–8
    Canaanite 186
    Hebrew 169–70
    Modern South Arabian Languages 416–17
    Outer South Ethiopic 548
    Phoenician 186

Silte 531–2
Tigrinya 443
complement deletion 97
complement pronouns
    Outer South Ethiopic 540
    Silte 511
complex sentences 529–32
compound verbs
    Amharic 477
    Silte 519
    Tigré 453
    Tigrinya 437
concord see agreement rules
conditional
    Arabic dialects 308
    Canaanite 185
    Ge'ez 258
    Hebrew 169
    Modern Hebrew 329
    Modern South Arabian Languages 403,
        404
    Phoenician 185
conditional sentences
    Classical Arabic 217–18
    Tigré 456
conditionals
    Aramaic 129
    Modern South Arabian Languages 415–16
    Old Aramaic 129
    Outer South Ethiopic 547
    Sayhadic 239
    Silte 531
    Tigrinya 442–3
    Ugaritic 143
conjugations
    Akkadian 86
    Amharic 470–74
    Amorite 103–4
    Arabic dialects 292–3
    Argobba 470–74
    Harari 497
    Modern Hebrew 320–22
    Modern South Arabian Languages 401–7
    Outer South Ethiopic 545
    Sayhadic 234–5
    Silte 520–24
    Tigrinya 435–7
conjunctional clauses 504–6

conjunctions
  Akkadian 94–6
  Canaanite 184
  Harari 504–6
  Hebrew 155, 168–72
  Modern South Arabian Languages 410
  Phoenician 184
  Tigré 455
  Ugaritic 141
conjunctive
  Amharic 473–4
  Argobba 473–4
connective particles 203
consonants
  abjads 27
  Akkadian 70
  Amharic 458–9
  Amorite 102–3
  Arabic dialects 270
  Aramaic 119–20
  Argobba 459
  Canaanite 175
  Classical Arabic 27, 189–90, 270
  Eastern Neo-Aramaic 348–50
  emphatic *see* emphatics
  Ge'ez 38, 243, 244–5
  Harari 487–8
  Hebrew 27, 147–9
  Imperial Aramaic 119–20
  Middle Aramaic 335, 348–9
  Modern Hebrew 314–15
  Modern South Arabian Languages 381–5
  Modern Standard Arabic 270
  Old Arabic 270, 271
  Old Aramaic 119
  Outer South Ethiopic 536–8
  pharyngealization 8
  Phoenician 175
  Punic 175
  Sayhadic 222–3
  Silte 510
  Syriac 27
  Tigré 446
  Tigrinya 424–7
  Ugaritic 27, 132–3
  Western Neo-Aramaic 334–5
construct state
  Akkadian 76, 79

  Aramaic 123
  Canaanite 179
  Classical Arabic 195, 214
  Eblaite 108
  Hebrew 153
  Modern Hebrew 319, 330–31
  Modern South Arabian Languages 412
  Old Aramaic 129
  Phoenician 179
  Sayhadic 226, 228
continuous past 522–3
converbs
  Ethiopian Semitic xvi, 11
  Outer South Ethiopic 547
  Silte 529–30
Cooper, R.L. 312
coordination
  Amharic 481
  Aramaic 128–9
  Argobba 481
  Canaanite 185
  Ge'ez 258
  Hebrew 168–9
  Imperial Aramaic 129
  Modern South Arabian Languages 415–16
  Old Aramaic 129
  Outer South Ethiopic 546
  Phoenician 185
  Sayhadic 239
  Silte 530–1
  Tigrinya 442–3
  Ugaritic 143
copula
  Amharic 475–6
  Arabic dialects 303
  Argobba 475–6
  Eastern Neo-Aramaic 360, 363–4, 370, 372–4
  enclitic *see* enclitic
  Ge'ez 260
  Harari 507
  Modern Hebrew 329–30
  Modern South Arabian Languages 418
  Outer South Ethiopic 548–9
  Sayhadic 240–1
  Silte 532–3
  Tigrinya 444
creoles 263

Cross, F.M. 44
cryptic writings 106–7
cuneiform script 18, 25–7
    wedges 18, 41
    word division 25
    writing materials/techniques 41
Cushitic 242, 536
Cyprus dialect 174–86
    see also Canaanite; Phoenician

Damascene *qaaf* 270
definite article
    Canaanite 178
    Modern South Arabian 11
    Phoenician 178
    Silte 528
definiteness
    Amharic 464
    Arabic dialects 298–9
    Argobba 464
    Classical Arabic 195
    Eastern Neo-Aramaic 357
    Harari 492
    Hebrew 152–3
    Modern Hebrew 325, 326–7
    Outer South Ethiopic 541
    Sayhadic 226, 228
    Silte 513
    Tigrinya 431
    Western Neo-Aramaic 339
deictics
    Arabic dialects 300
    Canaanite 177–8
    Ge'ez 250
    Modern South Arabian Languages 393–4
    Phoenician 177–8
    Sayhadic 230–1
    Silte 515–16
    Tigré 450–51
    Tigrinya 434
    Ugaritic 136
Deir Alla 114–15, 125
deletion 96–8
demonstrative pronouns
    Akkadian 84
    Amharic 467
    Arabic dialects 287
    Aramaic 122

Argobba 467
Canaanite 177
Classical Arabic 200–1
Eastern Neo-Aramaic 354–5
Harari 491
Jewish Palestinian Aramaic 122
Middle Aramaic 122
Modern Hebrew 325
Outer South Ethiopic 542
Phoenician 177–8
Sayhadic 230–1
Silte 527
Syriac 122
Tigré 451
Ugaritic 134, 136, 143
Western Neo-Aramaic 338
Demotic Egyptian 40
denominal verbs
    Amharic 479–80
    Argobba 479–80
    Hebrew 161
derivational class xvi
desiderative 83
determined state *see* emphatic state
determinative pronouns 18
    Akkadian 84
    Aramaic 129
    Canaanite 178
    Phoenician 178
    transliteration 25
determiners 325–6
detrimental (instrumental) 514
Dhorme, E. 43
diacritic points 23
Diakonoff, I.M. 101
Diem, W. 12, 188
diglossia 188, 267
Dillmann, A. 255, 256, 257
diminutives 284
diphthongs
    Arabic dialects 279
    Aramaic 121
    Classical Arabic 279
    Eastern Neo-Aramaic 352
    Eblaite 106
    Old Byblian 176
    Phoenicina 176
    Tigrinya 428

direct speech 549
Ditters, E. 47
Djidjelli 270
Dobbi (Goggot) 535, 536
Dolgopolsky, A. 8
Donner, H. 44
Druze dialects 276–7
al-Du'ali, Abu Aswad 47, 48
dual markers
  Akkadian 78
  Arabic dialects 283
  Canaanite 179
  Classical Arabic 194, 202
  Eblaite 108–9
  Hebrew 152
  Modern South Arabian Languages 391,
    401
  Phoenician 179
  Sayhadic 228, 234

East Semitic 7
East Syriac
  script 21
  vowel points 23
Eastern Canaanite languages see Canaanite
Eastern Neo-Aramaic 347–75
  morphology 354–75
  phonology 348–53
Eblaite 100–1
  cryptic writings 106–7
  phonology 101, 104–6
  script 17, 101–2
  subgrouping 6, 7
  Sumerian borrowings 112
  syntax 111–12
  texts 100–1, 102
  vocabulary 109
Edessan script 21
Edomite 174–86
  see also Canaanite; Phoenician
Egyptian demotic 40
ejective emphatics
  Akkadian 8
  Modern South Arabian Languages 382–3
elatives 197–8
Elymaic script 21
emphatic (determined) state
  Aramaic 123

Sayhadic 228
emphatics xvi
  Arabic dialects 275–7
  ejective 8, 382–3
  Modern Standard Arabic 277
  pharyngealized 8
enclitic
  Eastern Neo-Aramaic 372–3
  Sayhadic 237
  Ugaritic 133–4
Endegen 536
Ener 536
Ennemor 535, 536
epenthesis
  Amharic 460
  Hebrew 152
Epigraphic South Arabian see Sayhadic
epigraphy 44
ergative 360, 362–3, 371–2
Estrangelo script 21, 23
Ethiopian Semitic see Ethiopic
Ethiopic
  converbs xvi, 11
  letter names 35
  numerals 40
  paleography 44
  pharyngealization 8
  printing 42
  script 24
  script direction 24
  subgrouping 7, 8, 11, 12
  vowel notation 24
  see also Ge'ez
existential constructions (be)
  Amharic 476
  Argobba 476
  Eastern Neo-Aramaic 374
  Ge'ez 260
  Harari 507–8
  Modern Hebrew 329–30
  Modern South Arabian Languages 419
  Silte 533
  Tigré 455–6
  Tigrinya 444
Ezha 536

Faber, A. 8, 9
Fakhariyah 114, 125, 127

al-Farra', Abu Zakariya 47, 48, 49, 50
featural script 16, 17
Fellman, J. 312
Ferguson, C.A. 188, 267
Fischer, W. 299
Fisherman, H. 313
Fleisch, H. 13, 48
Ford, C.M. 535
formulas 306
fractions
    Arabic dialects 286
    Aramaic 125
    Sayhadic 232–3
Friedrich, J. 36–7, 43
Fück, J. 188
future
    Modern South Arabian Languages 402,
        408–9
    Silte 523

Gafat 535
Galilean 117
    phonology 120
Garbini, G. 3
Ge'ez 242–60
    abugida 24, 38
    and Arabic 13
    Cushitic loan words 242
    morphology 246–55
    phonology 243–6
    pronunciation 243–4
    subgrouping 7, 12
    syntax 255–60
    texts 242–3
Geers, F.W. 8
Gelb, I.J. 7, 100
gematria 33
gemination
    Amharic 469–70
    Modern South Arabian Languages 386–7
    Tigrinya 426
gender
    Akkadian 77–82
    Amharic 463–4
    Arabic dialects 282
    Argobba 464
    Canaanite 179
    Classical Arabic 193–4

Ge'ez 247
Harari 492
Hebrew 152–3
    Modern Hebrew 318
    Modern South Arabian Languages 390
    Outer South Ethiopic 541
    Phoenician 179
    Sayhadic 225–6
    Silte 512
    Tigré 448
    Tigrinya 431, 434
    Ugaritic 135
genitive
    Akkadian 79, 93–4
    Amharic 464
    Argobba 464–5
    Classical Arabic 214
    Eastern Neo-Aramaic 357–8
    Harari 492
    Hebrew 161–4
    Modern Hebrew 330–1
    Silte 514
    Tigrinya 433
    Ugaritic 135, 136
    Western Neo-Aramaic 339–40
gerunds
    Modern Hebrew 331
    Tigrinya 439
Gesenius, W. 43, 44
Gibson, J.C.L. 44
Gilgamesh 69
Glinert, L. 325
glottalization xvi
Goetze, A. 5, 10–11
Goggot (Dobbi) 535, 536
Goldenberg, G. 7, 9, 13, 535
Gordon, A. 318
Gordon, C.H. 101
government 87–9
Greek
    alphabet 32
    influence on Arabic 48
    letter names 35
    numerals 40
    script 22
    script direction 24
    vowel points 22–3
Greenberg, J.H. 4

Grohmann, A. 44
Grotefend, G.F. 43
Gubb'adin 334–47
Guillaume, J.-P. 50, 54
Gumer 536
Gura 536
Gurage
  Central Western 536
  Gunnän-Gurage 535, 536
  Northern 536
  Peripheral Western 536
  Silte *see* Silte
  Western 535
Gutt, E.-A. xvi, 488
Gyeto 536

Hadramitic 220–21
  see also Sayhadic
Haile, G. 44
Haldar, A. 100
Harari 486–508
  Ancient 486
  Ge'ez loanwords 487
  morphology 489–501
  phonology 487–8
  syntax 502–8
Harris, Z.S. 5, 10
Harshav, B. 312
Harsusi 378–420
Hatran 116
  script 21
Haywood, J. 55
Hebrew 145–73
  Biblical 59, 62–3, 145–6
  binyan xvi, 158–61
  grammatical tradition 59–64
  Late Biblical 146
  letter names 35
  Masoretic 59, 148–9, 172
  Middle (Mishnaic) 146
  Modern *see* Modern Hebrew
  morphology 152–61
  numerals 40, 154
  orthography 147–52
  paleography 44
  pharyngealization 8
  phonology 147–52
  printing 42

Qara'ites 59
Rabbanites 59
regional dialects 146–7
script 20, 21–2
square Hebrew script 20, 21
Standard Biblical 146
subgrouping 8, 9, 10
syntax 161–72
tannaitic (early Rabbinic) literature 145–6
texts 145–6
Tiberian system 59
triradicalism 62
valence 160–1
vowel points 23
word division 25
Hessels, J.H. 42
Hetzron, R. 4–9, 11–12, 13, 486
Hijaaz Arabic 266
Himyaritic
  decipherment 43
  letter order 33
Hincks, E. 43
Hittite 19
Hoberman, R.D. 347, 354
Hobyot 378–420
Hoenigswald, H.M. 4, 145
Holes, C. 273
holophrases 306
Hopkins, S. 348
Howell, M. 46
Hudson, G. xvi
Huehnergard, J. 6–10, 13
Huffmon, H.H. 100
Hurrian script 19

Ibn al-Anbari, Abu Barakat 49
Ibn Jinni, Abu l-Fath 50
Ibn Manzur, Ibn Mukarram 55
Ibn Mujahid, Abu Bakr 46
Ibn al-Sarraj, Abu Bakr 48, 50, 51, 54
Ibn Sida 55
imperative
  Akkadian 82, 83
  Amharic 472–3
  Argobba 472–3
  Classical Arabic 209
  Eastern Neo-Aramaic 360, 364–5
  Modern Hebrew 318

Modern South Arabian Languages 404
Sayhadic 235–6
Silte 523
Tigrinya 440
Western Neo-Aramaic 344
imperfect
  Akkadian 9
  Arabic 9
  Arabic dialects 265, 292
  Aramaic 9
  Canaanite 183
  Central Semitic 8–9
  Classical Arabic 206–9
  Eblaite 110–11
  Hebrew 9
  Modern South Arabian Languages
    401–3, 404, 405, 407–8
  Phoenician 183
  Sayhadic 234–5
  Tigré 452–3
  Tigrinya 438
  Ugaritic 9
imperfective formatives (preformatives)
  126
Imperial Aramaic (Official Aramaic) 115–16
  consonants 119–20
  morphosyntactic change 125
  nasalization 120
  vowels 120
impersonal pronouns 122–3
impersonal verbs
  Harari 497
  Silte 526
indefinite adjectives 134
indefinite article
  Amharic 464
  Argobba 464
indefinite pronouns
  Aramaic 122–3
  Canaanite 178
  Imperial Aramaic 122
  Phoenician 178
  Sayhadic 225
  Ugaritic 134
independent personal pronouns
  Amharic 461
  Arabic dialects 287
  Argobba 461

Eastern Neo-Aramaic 354
Harari 489
Modern South Arabian Languages 387–9
Outer South Ethiopic 540
Sayhadic 224–5
Silte 511
Tigré 448
Western Neo-Aramaic 337
indicative 82
infinitive
  Amharic 475
  Argobba 475
  Canaanite 183
  Harari 506–7
  Jewish Literary Aramaic 127
  Modern Hebrew 318
  Outer South Ethiopic 545
  Phoenician 183
  Sayhadic 236
  Silte 523
  Tigré 450
  Tigrinya 440
  Ugaritic 138
inflections
  Akkadian 75–87
  Classical Arabic 206–11
  Modern Hebrew 318–20
Ingham, B. 299
ink 41
Inneqor (Azarnat) 509
  see also Silte
innovations
  morphological/phonological 4
  shared 6–7
Inor (Ennemor) 535, 536
instrumental 514
interjections
  Canaanite 185
  Classical Arabic 203
  Phoenician 185
  Tigré 455
internal object 215–16
interrogative pronouns
  Akkadian 84
  Amharic 463
  Arabic dialects 291
  Aramaic 122, 128
  Argobba 463

Canaanite 178
Classical Arabic 201–2
Eastern Neo-Aramaic 355
Eblaite 108
Ge'ez 257–8
Harari 491–2
Hebrew 167
Modern Hebrew 327
Modern South Arabian Languages 390,
    411, 414
Phoenician 178
Tigré 448
Tigrinya 430
Ugaritic 134, 143
Western Neo-Aramaic 338
see also questions
Iranian script 21
Ishaq, Yusuf 38

Jacobite (Serto) script 21
Jakobson, R. 276
Jastrow, O. 38, 299, 354, 357
Jewish
    Arabic 266–7
    Babylonian 118
    Late Jewish Literary Aramaic 118
    Yiddish 22
Jibbaali (Sheri) 263, 378–420
Johnstone, T.M. 13, 378–80, 382, 385, 390,
    394, 396, 397–9, 404–5, 414
Juba Arabic 263, 280
Jugari Arabic (Uzbekistan) 263, 265, 270,
    271
Jurjani, 'Abd al-Qahir 50, 55
jussive
    Amharic 472–3
    Aramaic 126
    Argobba 472–3
    Classical Arabic 208
    Hebrew 158
    Mesopotamian 126
    Outer South Ethiopic 544
    Samalian 126
    Sayhadic 235
    Silte 523
    Tigré 452–3
    Tigrinya 439–40

Kerend 348
Kharoshthi script 21
Kienast, B. 192
Kimhi, J. 172
Ki-Nubi 263, 280
Kiros Fre Woldu 425
Kisa'i 48
Klugkist, A.C. 20
Knudson, E.E. 8
Kopp, U.F. 44
Kormakiti 265
Kouloughli 50
Krumbacher, K. 267
Kurdish 348, 358
Kuwaiti Arabic 265, 271, 273

Ladefoged, P. 277
Lambdin, T. 254
Langhade, J. 55
Larcher, P. 55
Late (Classical) Aramaic *see* Classical
    Aramaic
Late Babylonian 69
Late Jewish Literary Aramaic 118
Late Punic (Neo-Punic) *see* Punic
Lehn, W. 276
length xvi
    Hebrew 149–51
lenition xvi
    Outer South Ethiopic 537
Leslau, W. xv, 244, 447, 458, 460, 464,
    467, 472, 480, 492, 509, 535
letter names 33–5
letter order
    abjads 30–3
    Ugaritic 132
lexical deletion 97–8
lexicostatistics 5
Libyan Arabic 265
Lidzbarski, M. 44
limitative genitive (genitive of relation) 94
locative 78
logographic writing 16, 18
logosyllabary
    description 25–7
    history 17–18
Lonnet, A. 384

Ma'lula.334–47
Maddieson, I. 277
Madhabic (Minean) 220–1
  see also Sayhadic
Makonnen, A. 244, 247
Maltese 263–309
  alphabet 36
Mandaic 118, 347–75
  alphabet 36
  paleography 44
  print 42
  script 21
  vowel letters 22
Mansa' dialect 446
Marçais, W. 267
Masoretic 59, 148–9, 172
Masqan 535
matres lectionis 22, 23
Mauritanian Arabic 265
Mehri 378–420
Mesopotamia
  mathematics 38
  writing materials 41
Mesopotamian 114
  Amorite texts 101
  decipherment 43
  Eblaite texts 101
Middle Aramaic 116–17, 122
  demonstrative pronouns 122
Middle Assyrian 69
Middle Babylonian 69
middle voice 138
Minean (Madhabic) 220–1
  see also Sayhadic
Mishnaic 146
Mittwoch, E. 244
Mlahsô 347–75
Moabite 174–86
  see also Canaanite; Phoenician
Modern Aramaic
  alphabet 36–8
  script 21
Modern Hebrew 312–32
  binyanim 320–2
  language variation 331–2
  morphology 317–23
  morphophonology 315–16
  orthography 315

phonology 313–17
script 22
syntax 323–31
vowel points 23
Modern South Arabian Languages 378–420
  definite article 11
  geographical location 379–80
  morphology 387–419
  pharyngealization 8
  phonology 381–7
  subgrouping 8, 11
Modern Standard Arabic 188–9, 267
modifiers 528
mood
  Akkadian 74, 82–3
  Arabic dialects 304–5
  Canaanite 181
  Harari 495–6
  Hebrew 158
  Outer South Ethiopic 544–5
  Phoenician 181
  Sayhadic 235–6
  Tigrinya 439–40
  Ugaritic 139
Morag, S. 312
Moritz, B. 44
Moroccan Arabic 265
morphophonemics
  Akkadian 85–7
  Classical Arabic 191
  Hebrew 151–2
  Silte 514
  Ugaritic 142
morphophonology
  Arabic 53–4
  Modern Hebrew 315–16
Morris, M. 379
Moscati, S. 5
Msirda 270
Mubarrad, Ibn Yazid 48, 49
Muher 535, 536
Muslim dialects
  Arabic 266–7
  Baghdadi 267, 270, 273

Nabatean 116
  script 20
Najdi 271, 273

nasalization 120
Naumkin, V.V. 379, 380
negation
  Akkadian 96
  Arabic dialects 302
  Aramaic 128
  Babylonian 128
  Canaanite 184
  Central Semitic 9
  Classical Arabic 215
  Eastern Neo-Aramaic 373–4
  Ethiopian Semitic 11
  Ge'ez 257
  Harari 502–3
  Hebrew 167–8
  Middle Aramaic 128
  Modern Hebrew 327–8
  Modern South Arabian Languages 413–14
  Outer South Ethiopic 549
  Phoenician 184
  prohibitive negative markers 8
  Sayhadic 238–9
  Silte 522, 523, 524, 529
  South Semitic 11
  Tigré 452
  Tigrinya 442
  Ugaritic 143
Neo-Aramaic languages 334–75
  Eastern see Eastern Neo-Aramaic
  Northeastern 347–75
  pharyngealization 8
  subgrouping 8
  Western see Western Neo-Aramaic
Neo-Assyrian 69
  cuneiform syllabary 26
  printing 42
Neo-Babylonian 69
Neo-Punic see Punic
Nestorian see East Syriac
Nigerian Arabic 277, 279, 280, 281
Nöldeke, T. 188
nominal attributes 161–2
nominal patterns 71–3
nominal predicates 87
nominal sentences
  Classical Arabic 211–13
  Tigré 455
nominalization

Akkadian 92–4
  Modern Hebrew 331
nominative
Akkadian 79
  Aramaic 123
  Sayhadic 230
  Ugaritic 133, 135
nonpast
  Amharic 471–2
  Argobba 471–2
  Harari 495–6
  Outer South Ethiopic 544
non-verbal expressions 129–30
normal state 76, 77–8
North Ethiopic 7, 12
  see also Ge'ez; Tigré; Tigrinya
Northeastern Neo-Aramaic 347–75
Northwest Semitic
  abjads 27
  and Arabic 12–13
  letter order 32
  numerical order 33
  subgrouping 7, 9–10
noun clauses
  Amharic 482–3
  Argobba 482–3
noun phrases
  Akkadian 98
  Amharic 481
  Arabic dialects 299–300
  Argobba 481
  Classical Arabic 213–15
  Hebrew 165
  Modern South Arabian 412
  Silte 526–7
  Ugaritic 142
noun states
  Akkadian 76, 80–1
  Aramaic 123
  Hatran 123
  Palmyrene 123
nouns
  Akkadian 75–82
  Amharic 463–6
  Amorite 103
  Arabic dialects 281–4
  Aramaic 123
  Argobba 463–6

Canaanite 178–80
Classical Arabic 191–8
diptotic 195–6
Eastern Neo-Aramaic 356–8
Eblaite 105, 109
Ge'ez 247–9
Harari 492
Hebrew 152–3
Modern Hebrew 318–19, 322–3
Modern South Arabian Languages 390–2
Old Babylonian 77–8
Outer South Ethiopic 541–2
Phoenician 178–80
Sabean 13
Sayhadic 225–30
Silte 512–13
Tigré 448–50
Tigrinya 430–3
triptotic 196
Ugaritic 134–5
Western Neo-Aramaic 338–40
number
Akkadian 77–82
Arabic dialects 283–4
Canaanite 179–80
Classical Arabic 194–5
Ge'ez 247–8
Harari 492
Hebrew 152–3
Modern Hebrew 318
Modern South Arabian Languages 401
Outer South Ethiopic 541
Phoenician 179–80
Sayhadic 228–30
Silte 512–13
Tigrinya 431–2, 434
Ugaritic 135
numerals 38–40
Amharic 467
Arabic 40
Arabic dialects 285–6
Aramaic 124–5, 130
Argobba 468
Canaanite 180–1
Classical Arabic 198–9
Demotic Egyptian 40
Eastern Neo-Aramaic 358–9
Ge'ez 250–1

Greek 40
Harari 493–4
Hebrew 40, 154
Modern South Arabian Languages 394–7
Outer South Ethiopic 542–3
Phoenician 180–81
Sayhadic 231–3
Silte 516
Syriac 40, 124
Tigré 448, 451
Tigrinya 434–5
Ugaritic 136–7
Western Neo-Aramaic 340

object clauses
Akkadian 88
Arabic dialects 307
object deletion 97–8
object suffixes
Amharic 461–3, 465
Argobba 461–3, 465
Harari 490–1
objective genitive 93
Obrecht, D. 276
Official Aramaic see Imperial Aramaic
Old Akkadian 7, 69
Old Aramaic 114–15
consonants 119
vowels 120
word division 25
Old Assyrian 69
Old Babylonian 69
Old Byblian 174–86
see also Canaanite; Phoenician
Old Persian 117
Oromo 486–7
Ortelius, A. 535
ostraca 41
Outer South Ethiopic 535–49
morphology 538–45
phonology 536–8
syntax 546–9
Owens, J. 49–53

palatalization 384
paleography 44
Paleo-Hebrew script 20
Palestinian 23, 117

Palmyrene 116
  decipherment 43
  script 21
paper 42
papyrus paper 41–2
parchment 42
Pardee, P. 33
participles
  Canaanite 183–4
  Classical Arabic 210
  Ge'ez 249–50
  Harari 497–8
  Outer South Ethiopic 545
  Phoenician 183–4
  Sayhadic 236
  Tigré 449–50
  Ugaritic 138
particles
  Eblaite 111
  Outer South Ethiopic 549
passive
  Amharic 478
  Arabic dialects 287–8, 305
  Aramaic 125
  Classical Arabic 209–10
  Harari 497
  Middle Aramaic 125
  Modern South Arabian Languages 402, 407
  Samalian 125
  Sayhadic 233–4
  Silte 524
  Ugaritic 138
passive participles 322
past tense
  Amharic 470–1
  Argobba 470–1
  Eastern Neo-Aramaic 366–7
  Harari 495–6
  Outer South Ethiopic 544
  Silte 521–2
  suffix conjugation *see* perfect
pausal forms
  Classical Arabic 191
  Modern South Arabian Languages 385
perfect 8
  Akkadian 8
  Arabic dialects 292

Canaanite 182–3
Classical Arabic 206–8
Eastern Neo-Aramaic 367
Eblaite 110
Modern South Arabian Languages 401, 404, 405, 408
Phoenician 182–3
Sayhadic 234–5
South Semitic 11
Tigré 452–3
Tigrinya 437–8
West Semitic 8
Western Neo-Aramaic 343
permansive (stative) 87
personal names
  Amorite 104
  Eblaite 106, 108, 110
personal pronouns
  Akkadian 84
  Arabic dialects 287
  Aramaic 121–2
  Canaanite 176–7
  Classical Arabic 202–3
  Eblaite 107
  independent *see* independent personal pronouns
  Modern Hebrew 317
  Modern South Arabian Languages 387–9
  Phoenician 176–7
  Sayhadic 224–5
  Syriac 121–2
  Tigrinya 429–30
  Ugaritic 142–3
Pettinato, G. 7, 101
pharyngealization 8, 277
Philippi's Law 107
Phoenician 174–86
  epigraphy 44
  lexicon 186
  morphology 176–85
  script 19, 20
  word division 25
phonemes
  Akkadian 69–70
  Classical Arabic 189–90
pidgins 263
pluperfect 522

plural
  Amharic 464
  Arabic 10
  Arabic dialects 283–4
  Argobba 464
  Canaanite 180
  Classical Arabic 194–5
  Eastern Neo-Aramaic 356–7
  Eblaite 109
  Ge'ez 247–8
  Hebrew 10, 152
  Modern South Arabian Languages 391–2, 401
  Phoenician 180
  Sayhadic 228–30, 234
  Sumerian 109
  Tigré 449
  Tigrinya 431–2
  Ugaritic 10
  Western Neo-Aramaic 338
Polotsky, H.J. 535
possessive expressions (have)
  Amharic 476–7
  Arabic dialects 303–4
  Argobba 476–7
  Eastern Neo-Aramaic 374
  Ge'ez 260
  Modern Hebrew 329–30
  Modern South Arabian Languages 419
  Outer South Ethiopic 549
  Sayhadic 240–1
  Silte 533
  Soqotri 419
  Tigré 455–6
  Tigrinya 444
possessive pronouns
  Akkadian 84
  Aramaic 130
  Hebrew 163–4
  Outer South Ethiopic 540
  Silte 511
  Tigré 448
possessive suffixes
  Amharic 463
  Harari 489–90
postpositions
  Amharic 481
  Argobba 481

Hebrew 155
predicate deletion 97–8
predicative
  Akkadian 76, 81–2
  Classical Arabic 216–17
  Eastern Neo-Aramaic 360, 362, 370
prefix conjugation see imperfect
prepositions
  Akkadian 88–9
  Amharic 481
  Aramaic 124
  Argobba 481
  Canaanite 184
  Classical Arabic 199
  Eblaite 111
  Ge'ez 255
  Hebrew 155
  Jewish Palestinian Aramaic 124
  Modern South Arabian Languages 409–10
  Phoenician 184
  Sayhadic 237
  Silte 514
  Tigré 450, 454
  Tigrinya 441
  Ugaritic 141
presence, verb of
  Amharic 476
  Argobba 476
present tense
  Eastern Neo-Aramaic 365–6
  Silte 523
  Western Neo-Aramaic 343
present perfect 522
printing 42
proclitic pronouns 133–4
prohibitive negative marker 8
pronominal suffixes
  Akkadian 81–2
  Aramaic 130
  Canaanite 177
  Classical Arabic 202–3
  Eastern Neo-Aramaic 355–6, 370–2
  Eblaite 107–8
  Hebrew 163–4
  Modern South Arabian 389
  Phoenician 177
  Tigré 448
  Tigrinya 429–30

Western Neo-Aramaic 337
pronouns
  Akkadian 83–4
  Amharic 461–3
  Ammonite 175–8
  Amorite 103
  Arabic dialects 287–91
  Aramaic 121–3
  Argobba 461–3
  Canaanite 176–8
  Classical Arabic 200–3
  Cyprus dialect 177
  Eastern Neo-Aramaic 354–6
  Eblaite 107–10
  Edomite 176–8
  Ge'ez 246–7
  Harari 489–92
  Hebrew 153–4
  Moabite 176–8
  Modern Hebrew 317
  Modern South Arabian Languages
    387–90
  Old Byblian 176–8
  Outer South Ethiopic 539–40
  Phoenician 176–8
  Punic 176–8
  Sayhadic 224–5
  Silte 511
  Tigré 448
  Tigrinya 429–30
  Ugaritic 133–4
  Western Neo-Aramaic 337–8
prosody 429
protasis
  Akkadian 95–6
  Canaanite 185
  Classical Arabic 217–18
  Modern South Arabian Languages 416
  Phoenician 185
  Tigré 456
Proto-Canaanite
  script 19
  word division 25
Proto-Ethiopian 12
Proto-Sinaitic
  letter names 33–5
  script 19
Prunet, J.F. 535

punctuation 25
Punic 174–86
  script 20
  see also Canaanite; Phoenician
purpose clauses 418

Qatabanian 220–1
  see also Sayhadic
quadriradical roots
  Akkadian 75
  Arabic dialects 296
  Tigré 453
quantifiers
  Classical Arabic 197–9
  Hebrew 154
  Modern Hebrew 325–6
  Silte 527
questions
  Amharic 481
  Arabic dialects 302–3
  Aramaic 128
  Argobba 481
  Canaanite 185
  Classical Arabic 213
  Ge'ez 257–8
  Harari 503
  Outer South Ethiopic 546
  Phoenician 185
  Silte 529
  Tigrinya 442
  Ugaritic 143
  see also interrogative pronouns
quotative constructions 531
Qur'an 46–7, 50, 187–8, 267

Rabin, C. xvi, 5, 56
Rashi script 22
Ravid, D. 313, 315, 326
Rawlinson, H.C. 43
Raz, S. 447
reciprocal pronouns 448
reflexive pronouns
  Amharic 463
  Argobba 463
  Harari 492
  Sayhadic 233
  Tigré 448
relatedness, models 3–5

relative clauses
  Akkadian 92–3
  Amharic 482
  Arabic dialects 307
  Aramaic 129
  Argobba 482
  Canaanite 186
  Classical Arabic 200–1
  Ge'ez 259
  Harari 503–4
  Hebrew 171–2
  Modern Hebrew 328
  Modern South Arabian Languages 417
  Outer South Ethiopic 548
  Phoenician 186
  Sayhadic 225, 227, 240
  Silte 531
  Tigrinya 443–4
  Ugaritic 143
relative particles
  Arabic dialects 287
  Sayhadic 225
  Tigrinya 430
relative pronouns
  Akkadian 84
  Aramaic 122
  Canaanite 178
  Eblaite 108
  Phoenician 178
  Tigré 448
  Ugaritic 134, 143
resumptive pronouns 171–2
Rodgers, J. 6, 7, 11
Rödiger, E. 43
Röllig, W. 44
Roman alphabet 36
roots
  Arabic 52–3
  Arabic dialects 273–4
  triradical see triradical roots
roots, nominal
  Canaanite 178–9
  Classical Arabic 191
  Phoenician 178–9
  Tigrinya 430–1
roots, verbal
  Akkadian 70–5, 85–6
  Aramaic 125

Canaanite 181
Classical Arabic 203–6
Eastern Neo-Aramaic 360–2 , 368
Eblaite 111
Harari 494
Hebrew 155–6
Modern Hebrew 320–2
Modern South Arabian Languages 397
Outer South Ethiopic 543–4
Phoenician 181
Sayhadic 233
Silte 516–17
Tigrinya 435
Ugaritic 140
Rosenhouse, J. 266
Rubinstein, E. 313
Rundgren, F. 48

Sabean 220–2
  abugida 23–4
  script direction 24
  texts 220, 221
  see also Sayhadic
de Sacy, S. 44
Sakkaki, Mohammad 50
Samalian 114
Samaritan 118
  phonology 120
  printing 42
Sayhadic (Epigraphic South Arabian) 220–41
  morphology 224–37
  phonology 222–4
  syntax 237–41
  texts 220, 221
  see also Hadramitic; Minean;
    Qatabanian; Sabean
schwa
  Hebrew (shewa) 149–51
  Tigrinya 427
  Western Neo-Aramaic 336
Schwarzwald, O. 313, 315
scripts 16–44
  cuneiform see cuneiform scripts
  decipherment 42–3
  direction 24
  word/clause division 24–5
  writing materials/techniques 41–2

Segert, S. xv, 139
Sellasie, S. 535
Semitic *a* xvi
sentences
   Arabic dialects 306
   Classical Arabic 211–13
   complex 529–32
   conditional *see* conditional sentences
   nominal *see* nominal sentences
   Silte 529–32
   verbless 237–8
Sephardic script 21
Serto script 21
Sheri 263, 378–420
Sibawayhi, Ibn 'Uthman 47, 48, 49, 50, 51,
   54, 188
Siculo Arabic 265
Sidamo 536
signs 17–18, 25–7
   designation 25
   reading 25
   transcription 25
   transliterations 25
Silte 509–34
   morphology 511–24
   phonology 510
   syntax 525–33
Simeone-Senelle, M.-Cl. 384
Sinaitic script 21
Sobelman, H. 263
Soddo 535, 536
Soqotri 263, 378–420
South Arabian
   Epigraphic *see* Sayhadic
   Modern *see* Modern South Arabian
      Languages
   script 19
   script direction 24
   word division 25
South Ethiopic 7, 12
   Outer *see* Outer South Ethiopic
South Semitic 7, 11–12
   Eastern *see* Modern South Arabian
      Languages
   Western 11–12
   see also Ethiopian Semitic; Old South
      Arabian
Southeast Semitic 7

Southwest Semitic 33
spirantization 425
Standard Babylonian 69
Standard Literary Aramaic 115, 116
Standard Syrian (Western Old Aramaic)
   114
Steiner, R. xv
stems xvi
   Amharic 468–9
   Arabic 52–3
   Classical Arabic 205–6
   Eastern Neo-Aramaic 360–2
   Ugaritic 137
   Western Neo-Aramaic 340
stress
   Amharic 460
   Arabic dialects 280–1
   Classical Arabic 190
   Eastern Neo-Aramaic 353
   Ge'ez 246
   Hebrew 149–51
   Modern Hebrew 316–17
   Modern South Arabian Languages 386
   Outer South Ethiopic 539
   Tigré 447
   Tigrinya 429
   Western Neo-Aramaic 336
subgrouping, genetic 3–13
   cultural/geographical 5–6
   language relatedness models 3–5
   major divisions 7–12
   shared innovations model 6–7
   traditional 5–6
subject deletion 96–7
subjunctive
   Akkadian 82–3
   Aramaic 129
   Classical Arabic 207
   Modern South Arabian Languages 401,
      403, 404, 406
   Western Neo-Aramaic 342–3
subordination
   Akkadian 88–9
   Aramaic 129
   Canaanite 186
   Classical Arabic 217–18
   Ge'ez 259–60
   Harari 503–7

Hebrew 169–72
Modern Hebrew 328–9
Modern South Arabian Languages 416–18
Outer South Ethiopic 547–8
Phoenician 186
Sayhadic 239–40
Silte 531–2
Tigrinya 443–4
Ugaritic 143
suffix conjugation *see* perfect
suffix pronouns *see* pronomial suffixes
Sumerian
in Eblaite 112
logographic writing 18
plural nouns 109
script 17–18
Sumerograms 101
Sweden, Turoyo 38
syllabic structure
Classical Arabic 190
Modern South Arabian Languages 386
Tigrinya 428–9
syllabic writing 16
synharmonism 352–3
Syriac
East *see* East Syriac
Estrangelo 21, 23
imperfect formatives 126
letter names 35
numerals 40, 124
paleography 44
phonology 120
printing 42
script 21, 23
script direction 24
texts 118
vowel points 22–3
vowels 30, 121
Syro-Aramaic 110
Syro-Palestine
borrowings from 112
writing materials/techniques 41–2

Talmon, R. 49
Tamiim Arabic 266
Targumic 117
Taylor, A. 16
temporal clauses

Outer South Ethiopic 548
Tigré 454
Tigrinya 443
tense
Akkadian 73–4
Arabic dialects 304–5
Aramaic 126
Eastern Neo-Aramaic 365
Eblaite 110–11
Harari 495–6
Hebrew 156–8
Modern South Arabian Languages 407–9
Outer South Ethiopic 544–5
Sayhadic 234–5
Silte 519–20
Tigrinya 437–9
Ugaritic 137–8
Western Neo-Aramaic 340–3
tense vs. aspect controversy xv–xvi
terminative 78
Tesnière, L. 52
Tetragrammaton 20
Tiberian
Hebrew 59
vowel points 23
Tigré 446–56
morphology 448–55
phonology 446–7
subgrouping 7, 12
syntax 455–6
texts 446
Tigrinya 424–45
morphology 429–44
phonology 424–9
subgrouping 7, 12
texts 424
topicality
Amharic 465
Arabic dialects 306
triradical roots
Akkadian 74–5
Hebrew 62
Tunisian Arabic 265
Turoyo 347–75
Sweden 38

Ugaritic 131–44
abjad 27

alphabet 132
  decipherment 43
  letter order 32
  lexicon 144
  morphology 133–41
  phonology 132–3
  script 19–20, 131
  script direction 24
  subgrouping 5, 9, 10–11
  syntax 142–3
  texts 131
  word division 25
  writing materials/techniques 41–2
  writing system 133
Ullendorff, E. 5
umlaut 336
Uzbeki Arabic 263, 265, 270, 271

ventive 83
verbal clauses
  Hebrew 166
  Modern South Arabian Languages 411
verbal nouns
  Arabic dialects 282
  Aramaic 127
  Babylonian 127
  Classical Arabic 211
  Fakhariyah 127
  Harari 497–8
  Hebrew 164
  Outer South Ethiopic 545
  Syriac 127
  Syrian Old Aramaic 127
  Tigrinya 440
verbal particles 411
verbal phrases
  Arabic dialects 304–5
  Classical Arabic 215–17
  Modern South Arabian Languages 412–13
  Ugaritic 142
verbal predicates 87
verbal sentences
  Classical Arabic 211–13
  Sayhadic 238
verbless clauses 165–6
verbless sentences 237–8
verbs
  Akkadian 71–3, 82–3, 87, 91–2

Amharic 468–80
  Arabic dialects 291–8
  Aramaic 125–7
  Argobba 468–80
  Canaanite 181–4
  Classical Arabic 203–11
  compound see compound verbs
  Eastern Neo-Aramaic 359–75
  Eblaite 110–11
  Ge'ez 251–5
  Harari 494–501
  Hebrew 155–61
  impersonal see impersonal verbs
  Modern South Arabian Languages 397–
    409, 411
  Outer South Ethiopic 543–5
  Phoenician 181–4
  Sayhadic 233–7
  Silte 516–24
  Tigré 451–4
  Tigrinya 435–41
  Ugaritic 11, 137–40
  Western Neo-Aramaic 340–7
Versteegh, C. 48, 49, 263
Virolleaud, C. 43
vocative
  Akkadian 79
  Ugaritic 135
Vogüé, le Comte de 44
voice
  Sayhadic 234
  Ugaritic 138
Voigt, R.M. 7, 9
volitive mood
  Canaanite 183
  Hebrew 158
  Phoenician 183
Vollers, K. 188
von Soden, W. 7, 10
Vööbus, A. 44
vowel deletion
  Arabic dialects 280
  Modern Standard Arabic 280
vowel letters 22
vowel points 22–3
vowels
  abjads 30
  Akkadian 70

Amharic 459–60
Ammonite 176
Arabic dialects 270, 278–80
Aramaic 120–21
Argobba 460
Babylonian 121
Classical Arabic 30, 190, 270, 278–9
Classical Aramaic 121
Eastern Neo-Aramaic 350–1
Eblaite 106
Geʻez 245–6
Harari 488
Hebrew 30, 147–9
Imperial Aramaic 120
Mandaic 22
Moabite 176
Modern Hebrew 314
Modern South Arabian Languages 385–6
Modern Standard Arabic 270
Outer South Ethiopic 538–9
Phoenician 175
Punic 175–6
reduced/assimilated 176
Sayhadic 223
Silte 510
Syriac 30, 121
Tigré 447
Tigrinya 427–8
Ugaritic 132, 133
Western Neo-Aramaic 335–6
Western Syriac 121

Wagner, E. xvi
wedges 18, 41
Wehr, H. 188
Weil, G. 48, 49
Weiss, B. 50
West Semitic
  numerals 40
  subgrouping 8
Western Gurage 535
Western Neo-Aramaic 334–47
  morphology 337–47
  phonology 334–6
Western Old Aramaic 114
Western South Semitic 11–12

Western Syriac 121
Wexler, P. 313
Wild, S. 55
Wolane 509
  see also Silte
word division 24–5
word order
  Akkadian 89–91
  Amharic 480–1
  Arabic dialects 300–1
  Aramaic 127–8
  Argobba 480–1
  Canaanite 185
  Eastern Neo-Aramaic 374
  Eblaite 111–12
  Geʻez 255–6
  Harari 502
  Hebrew 165–6
  Mesopotamiam 127
  Modern Hebrew 323–5
  Modern South Arabian Languages 411–13
  Old Aramaic 127
  Outer South Ethiopic 546
  Phoenician 185
  Sayhadic 237–8
  Silte 525–9
  Standard Literary Aramaic 128
  Tigré 455
  Tigrinya 441
  Ugaritic 142
Wright, W. 46
writing 16
  materials 41–2

Xalil 48, 49

Yemenite Arabic 273, 275
Yiddish 22

al-Zabiydi, M. 55
Zabiid 277
Zaborski, A. 9
Zadok, R. 100
Zway 509
  see also Silte
Zwiep, I.E. 64